IMMIGRATION CANADA

EVOLVING REALITIES
AND EMERGING CHALLENGES IN
A POSTNATIONAL WORLD

immigration canada

AUGIE FLERAS

UBCPress

VANCOUVER & TORONTO

22 21 20 19 18 17 16 15   5 4 3 2 1

Printed in Canada on FSC-certified ancient-forest-free paper
(100% post-consumer recycled) that is processed chlorine- and acid-free.

Library and Archives Canada Cataloguing in Publication

Fleras, Augie, 1947-, author
Immigration Canada: evolving realities and emerging challenges
in a postnational world / Augie Fleras.

Includes bibliographical references and index.
Issued in print and electronic formats.
ISBN 978-0-7748-2679-2 (bound). – ISBN 978-0-7748-2681-5 (pdf). –
ISBN 978-0-7748-2682-2 (epub)

1. Canada – Emigration and immigration – History – 21st century. 2. Canada
– Emigration and immigration – Government policy. I. Title.

JV7225.2.F54 2015   325.7109′051   C2014-906578-7
                                                         C2014-906579-5

Selections of Chapters 3, 5, 7, 8, 9, and 10 appeared previously
in Augie Fleras, *Unequal Relations: An Introduction to Race, Ethnic, and
Aboriginal Dynamics in Canada,* now in its 7th edition, and are reprinted
here with permission by Pearson Canada Inc.

Canadä

UBC Press gratefully acknowledges the financial support for our publishing
program of the Government of Canada (through the Canada Book Fund),
the Canada Council for the Arts, and the British Columbia Arts Council.

This book has been published with the help of a grant from the Canadian
Federation for the Humanities and Social Sciences, through the
Awards to Scholarly Publications Program, using funds provided by
the Social Sciences and Humanities Research Council of Canada.

UBC Press
The University of British Columbia
2029 West Mall
Vancouver, BC V6T 1Z2
www.ubcpress.ca

contents

PREFACE

CANADIANS AND AMERICANS have historically associated immigration and immigrants with powerful images. On the American side are glowing references to the "tired," the "poor," "the wretched" and "huddled masses yearning to breathe free" – the paean from Emma Lazarus's poem "The New Colossus," which is affixed to the pedestal supporting the Statue of Liberty. Never mind that historians now dispute whether those who disembarked on Ellis Island were either tired or poor. Most were of working age, healthy enough to survive the trans-Atlantic crossing, full of energy and optimism, and sufficiently solvent to pay for their passage (Gabaccia 2006). The "huddled masses" myth also glosses over the exclusion of the unwanted – such as racialized minorities, homosexuals, the poor, slum dwellers, individuals with physical and mental disabilities, political dissidents, and criminals (Johnson 2003).

On the Canadian side of the border is another myth-making machine. References to Pier 21 in Halifax – the "Gateway to Canada" – portray Canada as a welcoming land of immigrants. Just as New York's Ellis Island served as a portal for immigrants from 1892 to 1954, Pier 21 was a primary entry point from 1928 to 1971 for over one million immigrants, refugees, and displaced persons (including myself and my family). It also doubled as a departure point for nearly 500,000 military personnel during the Second World War. But like that of Ellis Island, the symbolism of Pier 21 conceals as much as it reveals. The huddled masses imagery commemorates the pluck of newcomers who fled war-ravaged Europe in hopes of striking it rich. The fact that the huddled masses concept largely excluded racialized minorities speaks volumes. A pattern of selectivity, comparable to that of the United States, prevailed here and was consistent with a long-standing brand of Canada as a white man's country.

Implicit within the huddled masses myths are a number of popular and persistent (mis)perceptions (Gogia and Slade 2011). First, many assumed that the huddled masses were anxious to abandon their home countries for the opportunities and freedoms of their destination. Immigrants uncomplainingly endured "minor" inconveniences such as petty prejudice and overt discrimination, and rarely flinched from menial labour in forestry, farming, and mining, if only to bolster their prospects of acceptance and success. Second, it was tacitly assumed that they would abandon their ancestral roots in transitioning from "there" to "here." Dual loyalties were suspect; accordingly, newcomers were obliged to demonstrate their exclusive commitment to Canada. Third, expectations of achievement were unquestioned. The huddled masses may have been tired and poor, but the land of opportunity beckoned with promises of abundance for those who were willing to work hard, play by the rules, and unconditionally embrace Canada. A litmus test of rags-to-riches stories underscored the heroics of risk taking.

However compelling these perceptions, reality at present is decidedly different (Sears 2008). Instead of a huddled masses motif, Canada more accurately displays a bimodal pattern of immigration (Johnson 2003). Highly skilled and sought-after designer immigrants who are selected for potential success and permanent residence are offset by the less fortunate (from refugees to unskilled temporary foreign workers) who occupy the bottom of the priority list because of their "provisional" status, "peripheral" skills, and "precarious" prospects (Fleras 2010; Goldring, Berinstein, and Bernhard 2007; Jason Foster 2012). Patterns and flows are no less disjointed. Orthodox notions about immigrants and integration are unravelling in a world where people can take advantage of instantaneous communication, relatively cheap international travel, and sophisticated smuggling rings (Guy Arnold 2011). A transnational orientation has emerged that challenges models of international migration as a linearity of fixed points between finalized locations, with migrants as people who permanently abandon their homeland for life-long residence in another country (Crush et al. 2013). Emerging instead is a model of immigration as processes and discourses involving many actors, at different levels, and across numerous domains (Simmons 2010). Immigrants themselves are eschewing a fixed and straight line trajectory from "there" to "here" for one that zig-zags back and forth. Their integration no longer reflects the inevitability of a passive absorption into Canada. The marvels of technology and communication enable them to reaffirm their homeland linkages and cultural connections, in the process bending the rules of belonging and identity along transnational and diasporic lines. Clearly, then, contemporary migration neither matches the huddled masses myth nor reflects conventional models of immigration and immigrants. Not surprisingly, both government policy and public perceptions are conflicted and confused by the demands of this changing reality.

The globalization of trade, capital, and talent has also transformed the concept of immigration governance as related to settlement, integration, and citizenship. Transnational flows of goods, investments, and people have increasingly routinized mobility, resulting in migration patterns that intersect and overlap in multiple and sometimes conflicting ways (Nieswand 2011). Even notions of society and statehood are under attack by the border-bending forces of global migration. Nation-states are increasingly experiencing a disruptive shift in their relationship to immigration and immigrants. Their once-uncontested status as a place of physical sovereignty and controlled borders is increasingly yielding ground to societies as a network of postnational nodes of multiple attachments and hybridic identities (Simmons 2010; Freeland 2011). This raises a profoundly unsettling question for society building: In a globalizing world of transmigration and diasporas, does it still make sense to talk about immigration and immigrants within the framework of place-based governance models, from citizenship to multiculturalism, especially when migrant notions of identity and belonging are no longer territorially anchored in national space (Carruthers 2013)? In a so-called borderless world of migrant mobility, how do we explain the proliferation of security walls and the militarization of border controls (Brown 2014; Hansen and Papademetriou 2014)? What is a societal governance to do when immigrants are no longer boxed into a fixed trajectory from starting point to final destination? What is society for when more flexible arrangements encourage immigrants to remain emotionally connected to their homeland? Who benefits when people are neither really here nor there but, more accurately, citizens of everywhere yet nowhere? Confusion and uncertainty of such magnitude have proven unsettling: Governments and national policies are put in the awkward position of struggling to understand and contain what is largely beyond their control and comprehension (Freeland 2011).

The politics of immigration remains the issue that rarely speaks its name for fear of unsettling national myths or angering the immigration lobby (from lawyers and consultants to special interest groups) (Francis 2009; Gibson 2009). The range of acceptable discourse on immigration is remarkably narrow; for example, when the environmental activist David Suzuki suggested in a Paris-based publication that Canada was "full" and that its immigration policy was "disgusting," the immigration minister Jason Kenney criticized his comments as "anti-immigration," "xenophobic," and "toxic and irresponsible" (Abma 2013; McCullough 2013). But, however valid or invalid Suzuki's critique, there is a price to pay for any crippling silence that ensues. Immigration may be one of Canada's most complicated challenges in reshaping its political and socio-economic landscapes (Geislerova 2007). Nevertheless, public debate on the subject is surprisingly muted. For the most part, Canadians see it as a low-priority item, unlike health or the economy, which have a more immediate impact on their lives. They might be reluctant to broach the topic for fear of exposing their ignorance. Or perhaps they are muzzled by political correctness, the anxiety of being condemned as racist for speaking out on inconvenient truths that masquerade as polite fictions.

Insofar as it exists, the immigration debate focuses on four core issues: (a) *how many* (is the current annual total of about 250,000 newcomers appropriate?); (b) *which kind* (what is the right balance of admissions based on family, economic, or humanitarian class?); (c) *where from* (about 80 percent of immigrants come from non-English-, non-French-speaking sources); and (d) *what for* (on what grounds should immigration be justified?). Doing what is rational, realistic, and right strikes at the heart of these debates (Glennie et al. 2014). Policy makers confront a series of complex migration management imperatives – from attracting the highly skilled to securing borders while separating out unauthorized migrants from those in need of humanitarian protection (Collett 2013). Sorting through these issues boils down to politics and difficult tradeoffs among different priorities and diverse agendas, including national interests and public opinion (Boyd 2013; Mulley 2013). Paradoxically, debates over immigration and asylum are not only about legal status, tradeoffs, or economic impacts but also about membership in a community of value and values (Bridget Anderson 2013).

A number of topical questions must be addressed, preferably as part of a national debate on Canada's immigration policy and program (Siddiqui 2013a; also Rodríguez-García 2010). Is the current immigration model working? Is it the best one for Canada and Canadians? Should the immigration program reflect Canadian values or advance national (and vested) interests (Kelley and Trebilcock 2010)? Does Canada's immigration model need to be revamped in light of twenty-first-century realities? Or can it be put back on track with a bit of tweaking or a dash of additional resources? If immigration is about society building, where do temporary foreign workers fit into the picture? How relevant is Canada's multiculturalism as immigrant governance in a transmigratory world (Mawani 2008; Jedwab 2014)? To what extent does a globalizing world unsettle references to immigration as Canada building (Fleras 2011a)? Should citizenship be based on a one-size-fits-all model? Or should it be customized (differentiated) to render citizenship more palatable for all migrants regardless of status (Bauder 2011)? Answers to these questions are tricky and elusive. Yet they must be actively courted, as they are in this book, if Canada is to retain its lofty position as an immigration society.

Even more perplexing is a seeming reluctance to grapple with the crisis in Canada's refugee determination process (Showler 2006). The numbers are certainly impressive enough. An annual entry of between thirty and forty thousand asylum seekers as refugee claimants was not uncommon, though the totals dropped to about ten thousand in 2013, in addition to some twelve thousand refugees who are sponsored annually by private and government interests. Such numbers provoke a backlash. Critics of the system assert that anyone who makes it to Canada can claim refugee status, no matter how flimsy the claim or how safe their country of origin. How else to explain the following anomaly? Neither the United States nor Canada has required visas for Hungarian tourists, yet only 32 Hungarians applied for refugee status in the United States during 2010, whereas Canada processed 3,200 applicants in 2011, or 14 percent of its overall total (Selley 2011, 2013). Clearly, Canadians should be primed to debate the hot-button topics of (a) who is a refugee, (b) how we find out, (c) whether the current system works, (d) whether it's fair, and (e) what the alternatives are for processing persons who need protection. But a massive indifference dominates instead. Apart from think-tanks such as the Fraser Institute and refugee lobby groups such as the Canadian Council for Refugees, the silences are deafening. Much of what passes for public input into Canada's immigration agenda consists of a small coterie of drivers: (a) immigrants and their relatives and friends in Canada, (b) the so-called immigration industry, consisting of the lawyers and consultants whose livelihood depends on immigrants, and (c) business sectors in search of relatively cheap and disposable labour (Gibson 2009, 219). Yet the "silences within" cannot persist for much longer, because of the following glitches: (a) the substantial backlog of refugees/asylum seekers, about forty thousand in early 2012, a drop from sixty thousand in mid-2009 (CIC 2012b; Centre for Israel and Jewish Affairs 2013), (b) a spate of seemingly frivolous claims that clog the pipeline for "bona fide" refugees, (c) a reluctance to deport failed claimants that hardly inspires confidence in enforcement, and (d) an understaffed Immigration and Refugee Board, whose sometimes risible rulings prompt incredulity or contempt (Rehaag 2009). Even recent government moves to tighten up the refugee system without much public input into rationale and objectives have drawn criticism for heavy-handedness (Siddiqui 2013b; Beiser and Bauder 2014).

The paradox is inescapable: Immigrants and immigration are embraced as a positive solution to the challenges of Canada building (Clarkson 2011; Collier 2013). They helped to create Canada, continue to contribute today in growing the economy, and will undoubtedly do so in the future. However, according to Grubel and Grady (2012) and others (Canadian Centre for Immigration Policy Reform 2010), immigration and immigrants impose a profoundly negative political, economic, social, and cultural impact on Canada. Seemingly unbridgeable stances over migration are known to generate fissions and exacerbate fissures that are at odds with national unity and social cohesion (Markus and Semyonov 2011). Of particular relevance is the governance challenge of securing a cohesive and inclusive Canada at a time when migrants increasingly embrace the transnational loyalties that transcend national/local boundaries (also Castles, Hugo, and Vasta 2013; Carruthers 2013 for Australian context). However critical the need for discussion and debate, politicians have historically shied away from immigration issues because of the complexities involved, the emotional nature of the issues, breaches to those "comforting fictions" that paper over awkward truths, and fear of political fallout from being smeared as anti-immigration (Gibson 2009).

The exception to the political mute button is former immigration minister Jason Kenney. In a relatively short time, the minister (also known as the "Minister of Curry in a Hurry" for aggressively courting the ethnic vote) streamlined Canada's immigration program along neo-liberal lines, consistent with labour market realities (Editorial, *Globe and Mail* 2012). He introduced a range of often controversial initiatives for firming up the immigration program, which toughened laws on human smuggling; reduced interim health services for failed refugee applicants and safe country rejections; curbed applications from parents and grandparents to reunite permanently with their children; reduced a backlog of immigrants who were already in the pipeline; shifted admission to needed skills while imposing a moratorium on skilled worker applicants who lacked arranged employment; expanded the number of temporary foreign workers to about 340,000 by the end of 2012; cracked down on "crooked" immigrant consultants; facilitated the eviction of non-citizen foreign criminals while restricting appeals access for those who offended in Canada; tightened language requirements; redesigned admission to focus on individuals with needed skills; and revamped the citizenship path to better reflect selective aspects of Canadian history and mainstream values (McPartland 2012). These reforms may be impressive and overdue, but criticism invariably accompanied changes that were related to content (the emphasis on short-term labour market needs, a dearth of evidence-based policies, a less welcoming environment for newcomers) and process (the increase in ministerial powers and the use of omnibus legislation to ram home programs [Alboim and Cohl 2012; Yalnizyan 2012]). Ratna Omidvar (2012a, A17), president of the Maytree Foundation, explains how changes to the immigration program may be reshaping Canada's social landscape, albeit in often unintended ways:

> The changes are coming at a furious pace on an almost daily basis. By seeking to eliminate the backlog by expunging those waiting in the queue, we choose efficiency over fairness. By moving to "super visas" and away from permanent residence for our immigrants' parents and grandparents, we choose transience over inclusion. When employers select workers who will become future citizens with little guidance, we choose head-hunting

over nation-building. When we raise the bar on language, we choose homogeneity over diversity. By streamlining the refugee adjudication process, we may be choosing efficiency over human rights. Finally, when we say to employers, "Pay temporary foreign workers less than you might pay Canadians," we choose exploitation over fairness.

Reaction in the midst of this upheaval is mixed. For some, Canada's immigration program is out of control and requires a wholesale overhaul (Sears 2008); for others, it's under control, albeit in need of additional fine-tuning; and for still others, a degree of trepidation prevails not only in sorting out the positives (benefits) from the negatives (costs), but also in figuring out what's going on. Questions revolve around the nature of Canada as a society of immigrants, its national identity and terms of belonging, and who should be accepted or not (see also Spoonley and Bedford 2012). Consequences and effects are no less politically slanted (Goldin, Cameron, and Balarajan 2011). They range in scope from concerns about national security and terrorist profiling to domestic issues over education and health care. Then there are those who suggest that the system's apparent dysfunction is actually a massive government ruse to justify reforming immigration along neoliberal lines (Broadbent 2012). To the extent that dialogue exists, its cacophony is generating more heat than light. Debates over immigration invariably elicit intense and irrational emotions when they (a) challenge conventional notions of state sovereignty, (b) entail complex decisions and tradeoffs, (c) impose unacceptable costs or inconvenience on society members, and (d) expose hypocrisies of governance or commitment (Papademetriou 2003; Harell and Stolle 2010).

This "conspiracy of silence" (Gibson 2009, 213) may strike many as counterintuitive. Sociologically speaking, Canada is one of the few countries whose normative status as an "immigration" society puts it in select company (alongside New Zealand, Australia, the United States, and several others). Unlike countries that are largely ad hoc destinations for asylum seekers or guest workers, Canada has a managed migration model that is constructed along principled lines, geared toward acceptance of immigrants, enriched by their contribution, and defined by their presence (Boyd and Alboim 2012). As a prototype of a normative immigration society (as well as a society of immigrants, used in the descriptive sense), Canada incorporates immigration as central to its national imaginary. It also has a proactive framework in place to (a) regulate the intake of immigrants, (b) assist their settlement and integration, (c) ensure that they have the same rights as all Canadians, including an expectation of permanent residence and citizenship, and (d) acknowledge their status as Canada-building assets (also Reitz 2012b). Not surprisingly, with a total immigrant intake of nearly 5 million between 1990 and 2010, Canada's annual immigration rate on a per capita basis ranks among the world's highest (Grubel 2009). Nor should anyone be surprised to learn that, with nearly 21 percent of its population as foreign-born, Canada is second only to Australia in the proportion of immigrants to the population (CIC 2013b).

It is within a context of concern and criticism, of progress and stalemate, of conviction and confusion, that this book addresses the politics of rethinking immigration and reframing immigrants through the prism of evolving realities, emerging challenges, and shifting discourses. Mindful of the politics at play over current patterns, contemporary debates, and future trends, *Immigration Canada* provides readers with insights into the rationale and logic behind these transformational challenges and contested changes. The book describes, analyzes, and reassesses immigration in a Canada that is rapidly changing, increasingly diverse, more uncertain, and globally connected. Widely circulating misconceptions about immigration and immigrants are debunked by (a) analyzing debates from multiple perspectives, (b) using playful inversions to expose shibboleths that conceal more than they reveal, (c) problematizing all "comforting fictions" as grounds for critically informed reflections rather than definitive conclusions, and (d) acknowledging the evolving and contested nature of debates over immigration and immigrants. In particular, it addresses how the interplay of transmigration and transnationalism is transforming immigration from a thing (noun) to a process (verb). Finally, though the book generally focuses on Canada, it also contextualizes immigration within the broader framework of global capitalism in (re)aligning flexible labour with surplus capital along neoliberal lines (Wood 2009; Simmons 2010; Bauder 2011).

This endeavour cannot come too soon. Pressure is mounting to rethink both immigration and immigrants (Satzewich and Wong 2006; Geislerova 2007; Karim 2007; Mawani 2008; Simmons 2010). As Goldin, Cameron, and Balarajan (2011, 1) point out in *Exceptional*

People, "We live in a dynamic age of global integration, where the re-connection and mixture of the world's people is challenging dominant norms and practices in many countries. Disintegration and integration are simultaneous and interwoven. Cultural codes adapt. New economies emerge. Innovation prospers. Social institutions struggle to adapt." To take advantage of this "exceptionality," Canada's immigration policies and priorities are undergoing unprecedented levels of adjustment and reform. The scope of announcements and press releases from the Office of the Minister of Citizenship and Immigration has proven dizzying for anyone who wishes to make sense of what is going on, and why. The number and range of changes, both real and proposed, make it doubly important to launch a robust debate into the role of immigration and immigrants in crafting the kind of Canada we want (Alboim 2009; Campana 2012). It's my hope that reframing the topic of immigration and immigrants against the backdrop of evolving realities, emergent challenges, and shifting discourses will stimulate informed insights, both critical and constructive as well as aspirational and inspirational.

PART 1

reappraising migration

TO SAY THAT we live in provocative and perplexing times is (to steal a phrase) an understatement of colossal proportions. Nowhere is this more succinctly expressed than by the politics of immigration in Canada and abroad. References to immigration and immigrants no longer mean what they once did. Whether managed or unregulated, immigration rarely conforms to conventional models, historical trends, or contemporary expectations. It frequently entails a series of moves within and across borders, with far-reaching consequences for sending and receiving countries (Spoonley and Bedford 2012). Immigrants themselves differ in terms of how, why, where, and when. Their reasons for leaving, returning, or circulating have yet to be fully fathomed, although presumably they range from the social to the personal. Not surprisingly, the concepts, theories, and assumptions informing the study of immigration and immigrants have struggled mightily to cope with these facts.

Part 1 of this book reappraises both theoretical and substantive issues related to immigration and immigrants. The first chapter maps out the conceptual terrain by introducing the debates and controversies regarding the topic in Canada and abroad. Immigrants and immigration unsettle conventional notions of unity, identity, and community (Lawlor 2012). They also pose a progressive dilemma (Banting 2010), a tension between respecting differences while integrating minorities as equals, without foreclosing a commitment to the collective and the shared. Chapter 1 unravels core questions with respect to what is going on, how, why, and with what consequences. How are migrants changing the world? Conversely, how are global changes transforming both migrants and migration patterns (Jacobs 2010)? In light of contemporary politics and contested dynamics, how appropriate is Canada's immigration model? What ambiguities inform its immigration program, public attitudes toward immigrants, and immigrant experiences? Responses to these questions are framed around three major themes – topics, perspectives, and discourses – that secure both a distinctive content and an organizational framework.

Chapter 2 reconceptualizes global migration. It acknowledges that the obvious is not always self-evident; as a result, explanatory frameworks are proposed that problematize the movement of people across borders. The chapter begins with an overview of international migration, defines the key terms of reference, briefly surveys theoretical frameworks to explain how and why people migrate, and concludes by acknowledging the value of both neo-push-pull models and global/transnational models of global migration. It also demonstrates how shifting explanatory frameworks reflect changes in analyzing immigrants and immigration. Of particular note are those discursive frames in rethinking immigration, not as a fixed field of location (a thing), but as a networked and vigorous dynamic of multiple flows and cross-border linkages (a process) across the broader contexts of time and space (Simmons 2010).

1

twenty-first-century migration

CANADA IN THE NEW GLOBAL REALITY

THE POLITICS OF CANADIAN IMMIGRATION

DESPITE THE PERVASIVENESS of obstacles, costs, and danger, migration is a recurrent component of the human condition (Segal, Mayadas, and Elliott 2006; Castles and Miller 2009; Scheffer 2010). With nearly 215 million people living outside their birthplace, humans appear to be a species on the move in a constant quest to improve lives and life-chances or to escape confining environments, natural disasters, and social turbulence. In the language of conventional push-pull theories, people are "pushed out" from their homeland because of political oppression, ethnic conflicts, demographic pressure, environmental despoliation, and economic stagnation. They are also "pulled into" another country to take advantage of opportunities, freedom, security, and excitement. Some migrate voluntarily in search of fulfillment or challenges; others are compelled to leave because of circumstances beyond their control; and still others go because they can. Lastly, migrants may select a final destination for the long haul, or they may circulate frequently to capitalize on opportunities farther afield.

Admittedly, a different spin is possible. The 215 million individuals who reside outside their homeland account for a minuscule portion of the world's 7 billion people. That over 97 percent of the world's inhabitants remain in their country of birth points to humans as a relatively sedentary lot. Understandably so, since cross-border movements often entail a high level of risk; possession of ample resources, connections, and motivation; and the appropriate qualifications for entry into a new country (Simmons 2010). Whatever the reasons for migration, the movement of people is neither an anomaly to curb nor a problem to control. It represents a normal and routine process because of broader social transformations related to this globalizing era (Pécoud and de Guchteneire 2005; Castles and Miller 2009). The failure of countries to make the most of this potential benefit or to dampen its more costly disruptions is not without consequences (Bitran and Tan 2013). A disservice is done in not rethinking immigration and reframing immigrants at a time of evolving realities, emergent challenges, and shifting discourses. Benefits are also squandered by mishandling the interests of both newcomers and sending/receiving countries.

Virtually every developed country has experienced a dramatic increase in immigration, albeit with numerous ups and downs (Castles and Miller 2009; Segal, Elliott, and Mayadas 2009; OECD 2013, 2014). Popular catchment countries such as Canada and Australia have long endorsed immigration as principle and practice (Jacobs 2010). The collective inclination of immigration societies is geared toward integrating and transforming newcomers into productive citizens (Reitz 2011a), even if the numbers of people who cross borders with or without documentation can prove aggravating at times (Martiniello and Rath 2010). For Europe, the challenge is much different (Lawlor 2012; Triadafilopoulos 2012). European nation-states were rarely defined as immigration countries (Fleras 2009a). They saw themselves as predominantly "complete civilizations" whose primary business as emigrant countries lay in exporting people. Yes, migrants (most of whom consisted of guest workers) could be economically useful. Yet they were never seen as an integral component of national identity or as major contributors to society building. More often than not, they were associated with social problems and security risks, ranging from crime and terrorism to public health issues. Relations between the foreign- and native-born were grounded in tension, mistrust, and fears of invasion by cohorts of the poor or uncultivated. Not surprisingly, as Martiniello and Rath (2010) note, the politics of immigration generated passionate debates and polarizing controversies in both the public domain (including the media) and the political sector. Concern over the porosity of borders because of globalization and the politics of securitizing society in the post-9/11 era have also exerted pressure for staunching the flow of irregular migrants (van Munster 2010).

The paradoxes, patterns, and politics of immigration are no strangers to Canada. Immigrants have long proven pivotal in building the country, even if Canadians are sometimes indifferent to this accomplishment (Li 2003; Knowles 2007; Kelley and Trebilcock 2011). On the whole, Canada has become a more vibrant society because of immigrants (Ibbitson 2005; Michael Adams 2007; Bitran and Tan 2013). Patterns of immigration to Canada corresponded with the changing requirements of its economy. A pre–First World War concentration on agricultural development and domestication of the West gradually segued into a post–Second World War demand for unskilled labour to extract resources or stimulate industrial growth. More recently, emphasis has shifted toward a reliance on highly skilled immigrants as part of a master plan in transitioning toward a global/knowledge economy (Reitz 2003; Simmons 2010). Furthermore, immigrants continue to drive the Canada-building process (Hiebert and Ley 2003). They provide a possible solution to the problems of (a) an ageing population, (b) shrinking birth rate, (c) diminishing tax base, and (d) the skills shortage in an information-based economy. No less critical is their contribution in re-energizing Canada's economy, thanks to consumer spending habits, optimistic outlook, entrepreneurial spirit, and international connections. In short, a fundamental inversion is at play: intense competition for the brightest and the best creates a new global migration reality, one in which Canada needs immigrants more than they need Canada.

Canadians for the most part have embraced immigration with the kind of civility and open-mindedness that many envy or expect (Michael Adams 2007). Countries from the Netherlands to Australia may have rethought their commitment to immigration in light of post-9/11 security concerns, but Canada retains historically high levels of support for immigration without any sign of an anti-immigrant backlash at political or grassroots levels (Hiebert 2006). According to a major study/survey by Transatlantic Trends (2010), it continues to punch above its weight, having accepted more immigrants in proportion to its population size than any other country during the past 20 years.

For example, Canada admitted nearly 281,000 newcomers in 2010, its highest total in 57 years, at a time when most countries were cutting admission rates.

Canada's pioneering efforts are internationally applauded. Its point system for rationalizing newcomer entry along more open and transparent lines is emulated by countries such as Australia, the United Kingdom, and New Zealand. Relatively straightforward access to citizenship status has culminated in high naturalization rates, resulting in more spirited levels of newcomer participation in political and social life (Bloemraad 2006). A raft of government-funded services and benefits facilitates active integration and settlement of immigrants into an accommodating host population. Newcomer satisfaction with general settlement services puts Canada at the forefront of countries in successfully integrating newcomers (UNDP 2009; OCASI 2012; Vineberg 2012). Compared to many Europeans and Americans, Canadians appear favourably disposed toward immigrants as a resource and benefit instead of a problem or cost (Transatlantic Trends 2010). National attitudes remain positive because of a proactive immigration program that is both publicly supported and widely (if sometimes begrudgingly) admired. Predictably, perhaps, no political party dares to challenge the status or legitimacy of Canada's immigration program for fear of self-detonating an electoral backlash.

Still, this cheerful picture has a darker side. Canada may be a land of immigrants, yet Canadians remain sharply conflicted over the pros and cons of immigration. Support for immigration comes with strings attached; for example, diversity is seen as good, but newcomers are expected to integrate through immersion in mainstream values (Environics Research Group 2011). Canada's immigration policy is criticized as out of control and out of step, with a corresponding negative impact on society (Bissett 2008). Those on the political right complain that too many of the wrong kind are being admitted (Grubel 2009, 2013); those on the left protest that not enough of the right kind are accepted; and those in the middle may be confused over who or how much or what kind. Particularly vitriolic are attacks on Canada's refugee status determination program. It is perceived as broken beyond repair, as the Achilles heel of the immigration program in general (Collacott 2010b). Admittedly, Canadians are not alone in criticizing immigration and immigrants. People around the world are concerned over the impact of immigrants on the environment, national identity, social cohesiveness, and core cultural values (Spoonley and Tolley 2012). But Canada's glowing international reputation as one of the world's most welcoming immigration countries (Economist 2010b) puts the program in the crosshairs of criticism. The list of reproaches includes the following:

> Immigration rules are outdated and increasingly inappropriate in twenty-first-century Canada. The interplay of transmigration and diaspora networks is changing the concept of immigration, along with the mental maps to understand immigrant realities (Mendelsohn 2013).
> Rules are manipulated to advance crass political considerations rather than national interests. For example, the government persists in admitting large numbers of newcomers, despite an iffy economic situation for both them and Canadian-born workers (Picot and Sweetman 2012). An alternative criticism contends that immigrants no longer serve Canada's interests, but expect Canada to cater to their agendas (Jonas 2011).
> Newcomers continue to be duped by unscrupulous immigration consultants and opportunistic lawyers, thus jeopardizing the legitimacy of the entire program (Rankin 2007).
> The system is overburdened and bureaucratically inept (Ibbitson 2005; Thompson 2010). Proof of this is revealed by the backlog of applicants for entry into Canada, which peaked at just under one million, resulting in delays of up to six years just to *begin* the application process (compared to perhaps six months for an applicant to Australia) (Hawthorne 2008).
> Aspects of the immigration program are sexist and racially discriminatory, not necessarily deliberately, but because their seemingly neutral rules negatively affect the most vulnerable.
> The process of determining the status of refugees under the Immigration and Refugee Board (IRB) is too strict or too lenient or too inept. The system's credibility is further decimated by its subjectivity. For example, one IRB member ("DM") rejected all 169 asylum cases between 2007 and 2010, seven other members had a success rate of less than 10 percent, and yet another enjoyed a 100 percent success rate (Keung 2011e; Yang 2011; also Rehaag 2009, 2012).

To put it bluntly, Canadians remain "reluctant hosts" (Avery 1995). They can appear welcoming but can also be obstructionist or even obfuscatory. Their ambivalence (or antipathy) toward newcomers is camouflaged by a folksy veneer of mealy-mouthed platitudes. Evidence suggests that Canadians are accepting of immigrant differences, provided they are relatively minor and as long as costs and inconvenience are kept to a minimum. But anxieties mount over the ethno-religious immigrants who seem unable to tame their differences or are unwilling to integrate in a specified way (Cramme and Motte 2010). Canadians have also proven to be "confused" hosts, prompting critics to accost Canada for wanting the benefits of a robust immigration program without the attendant costs of immigrant settlement. This ambivalence ("immigration yes, immigrants no") is compounded by a growing unease over forces and flows beyond the country's immediate control (see Satzewich and Wong 2006; Castles and Miller 2009; Simmons 2010). Canadians are befuddled by the emergence of transnational immigrants who prefer repeated moves and strong homeland linkages instead of a straight-line trajectory culminating in permanent residency and singular citizenship (also Spoonley 2009). These transmigratory dynamics upset conventional models for studying immigration. They also question whether multiculturalism and citizenship as place-based governance models can do the job of integrating immigrants (Fleras 2011a, 2011b). Not surprisingly, many are frustrated by the absence of constructive dialogue regarding the following points:

> The displacement of a taps-off, taps-on approach by a sustained economy model of immigration. Congruent with this shift is the selection of skilled immigrants on the basis of a human capital model instead of a labour market needs model. Recent government moves toward a hybrid model acknowledge the value of balancing human capital with labour markets by customizing the selection of immigrants to advance economic interests (CIC 2012a).
> The welter of new admission paths for immigrants (there are up to 60 entry points at present). Devolutionary moves by the federal government bestow powers of selection on the provinces, employers, and even universities. Despite benefits, many see this decentralization of decision making as fraught with perils (Broadbent and Omidvar 2008).
> A dramatic spike in the number of temporary foreign workers. At the end of 2012, approximately 338,000 temporary foreign workers resided in Canada, triple the number of a decade ago. This surge poses a dilemma in defining an appropriate model for selecting newcomers:

Should migrants be selected as citizens in the making or as guest workers on the run? A short-term focus caters to immediate labour market needs despite the potential for long-term repercussions. An emphasis on longer-term economic priorities, citizenship frameworks, and Canada-building futures could yield larger returns, even if the payoff is indirect or delayed (Reitz 2011a).

> An emergent bifurcated and polarized labour market, with well-qualified immigrants offset by unskilled migrants in low-wage employment (Wood 2009). Unlike asylum seekers, irregular migrants, and those under family reunification, highly skilled immigrants are framed as wanted and welcome. Yet they continue to experience deteriorating economic conditions related to employment and earnings (Triadafilopoulos 2013).

> What about unauthorized migrants who enter Canada without documentation, overstay tourist visas, or disappear into the underground of an informal work economy if permanent residency or refugee status is rejected (Keung 2013c)?

> Canada may persist in selecting the brightest and the best as an immigration priority. Yet the continued discounting or underutilization of immigrant experiences, skills, and credentials for employment purposes is proving a major embarrassment and an unacceptable waste of talent.

> Concern over Canada's refugee status determination process is tempered by a general reluctance to debate, for fear of offending refugee-friendly groups, ruffling comforting fictions that paper over awkward facts, or disturbing a national consensus.

> The seeming dysfunctionality of the refugee determination system under the IRB is upping the ante for constructing a model that is workable and fair.

A number of paradoxes notwithstanding, issues related to immigrant numbers or immigration rarely evoke public discourse, despite or because of their centrality to Canada (Black and Hicks 2008; Wente 2010; but see *Globe and Mail* 2012). Much of this reticence reflects the paralyzing effects of (a) political correctness, (b) the lucrative immigration industry, (c) an electoral system that rewards immigration-pumping politicians, (d) a politically neutral language that disguises dislike or concern, and (e) fear of poking a political hornet's nest (Grubel 2009). In short, immigration represents a hot-button issue with a potency to inflame passions and expose deep fissures. Not un-expectedly, central authorities historically tended to recoil from any comprehensive and principled policy reform, preferring hastily con-structed homilies in response to periodic crises (Mamann 2010). But no more, as recent government moves to strengthen and streamline the program by making it fast, flexible, and focused have catapulted immigration to the top of the national agenda.

Failure to constructively debate immigration does a disservice to Canada. But newcomers are no less penalized by the "tyranny of silence," especially as Canada's immigration program undergoes unprecedented challenges owing to their numbers, patterns, and demands. For immi-grants, getting in is one thing. The liberalization of admission categories along market lines is offset by the securitization of Canadian borders along stricter criteria in defining who enters. Settling down, fitting in, and moving up have proven equally challenging. Immigrants and refugees flock to Canada with the best of intentions for making a posi-tive contribution. But Canada has not always proven the utopia that many had expected. True, both immigrants and refugees possess the rights of citizenship and the multicultural right to inclusiveness. Nevertheless, the de jure does not always match the de facto; after all, immigrant success depends on achieving attainment in a socially constructed system that neither reflects their lived experiences nor advances their interests. Many newcomers continue to encounter ob-stacles that not only besmirch Canada's reputation as an immigrant-friendly country, but also intensify their levels frustration, up to and including violence turned inward (suicide) or outward (domestic abuse) (Biles and Burstein 2003; Scheffer 2010). Formidable barriers flourish in a society whose welcome mat may be yanked out at the slightest provocation. Moreover, Canada's much-vaunted tolerance has been put to the test in the long-simmering aftermath of 9/11 amid fears that loose immigration regulations and lax enforcement foster a haven for terrorists (Bell 2013b). Growing concerns over securitiza-tion have spawned an antipathy toward new Canadians that some-times borders on the xenophobic, with calls for rigorous screening procedures including DNA testing, immigrant and citizenship tests, and energetic deportation mandates.

Various government commitments and programs facilitate the inte-gration of newcomers (Wayland 2006), including the $600 million allocated by Ottawa to improve their settlement and the entrenchment of official multiculturalism as a collective platform for articulating relevant issues (Fleras 2009b). But dangers lurk in excluding both the foreign- and Canadian-born from national dialogue over the why, who, what, and how of immigration in a country whose diversity agenda encompasses Aboriginal politics and Québécois nationalism. Dramatic changes in the immigration environment (both inside and outside the country) exert pressure on reviewing Canada's immigration program (CIC 2011b). Proposed in any review are issues related to goals and objectives, overall numerical targets and selection criteria for admission, as well as those involving adjustment processes to facilitate the settlement, acceptance, and integration of immigrants (Beach, Green, and Reitz 2003). Consider the following blocks of questions pertaining to the politics of getting in, formulating immigrant governance, and assessing immigration.

Getting in:
> Why should Canada accept immigrants? How many, where from, what kind?
> What immigration model should prevail – human capital or labour market?
> How can Canada control its immigration program in a globalizing world?
> What is the relationship between differing conceptions of Canadian nationhood and immigration patterns (Samers 2010; Simmons 2010; Bauder 2011)?
> What can be done to improve Canada's refugee status determination system?

Formulating immigrant governance:
> How much and what kind of diversity can immigrants bring with them without corrupting Canada?
> What is the best way of integrating immigrants – by respecting their differences or emphasizing our commonalities?
> How relevant is multiculturalism as a governance model for facilitating the settlement and integration of immigrants, especially when their notions of settlement and integration are increasingly decoupled from a singular space (Fleras 2011b), while relatively static concepts such as immigrant communities are eroded by more fluid notions of global networks (Bitran and Tan 2013)?

> Does national citizenship still make sense in a world of constant movement, rootless identities, and splintered loyalties (Carruthers 2013)?

Assessing immigration:
> Is there a disconnect between public attitudes toward immigration and those of politicians and policy makers?
> How has the threat of terror, both imported and homegrown, altered both people's perceptions of immigrants and government handling of the immigration portfolio?
> Can assessment of immigration and immigrants be framed along the lines of costs or/and benefits?
> How do immigrants contribute to or detract from Canada building?

These questions cannot be left unanswered if a mutually beneficial immigration agenda is to be pursued. Yet responses (if they are forthcoming) elicit intense emotions that often defy rational discussion or crystallize into rigid polarities. The topic can generate hysteria, even hostility, especially when cherished notions of Canada and Canadianness are contested. Nevertheless, a level of deliberation is required that transcends political slogans or ideological posturing (see also Swain 2007). Constructive debate over immigration is more relevant than ever (Alboim 2009; Grubel 2013). Conventional notions of immigration are increasingly out of step with actual behaviour and practical commitments (also Spoonley 2009). National narratives about the subject have shifted as well in response to controversies sparked by each successive wave of immigrants, government moves to modify its policies and programs, and media preoccupation with immigrants as problem people. The conclusion is inescapable: Now is the time for a balanced, critically informed, and multi-perspectival debate over immigration issues.

Problem or solution? Cost or benefit? Good, bad, or in between (see Chomsky 2007; Swain 2007)? A sense of balance is critical in assessing immigration as a solution to twenty-first-century challenges, resulting in tradeoffs that entail compromise and accommodation. The economic, social, and demographic benefits of immigrants are unmistakable, but so too are costs and downsides. Those who obsess over the negative are no less ideologically myopic than those who rhapsodize about the positives (Castles and Miller 2009). Nor should the assessment be based entirely on utilitarian terms of liability or asset

(Alboim and Cohl 2012). The importance of immigration to Canada goes beyond demography or economy. Issues of Canada building are involved as well (Ibbitson 2005). As former immigration minister Sergio Marchi (1994, iii) once commented in connecting immigration with national identity, "Immigration is fundamentally· about nation-building – about deciding who we are as Canadians and who we want to become. We need a clear and practical vision of the kind of nation we want to build."

Immigration has transformed the very concept of Canada. It has reconfigured the demographic contours of Canada's once monocultural landscape and historical dualities into a cosmopolitan kaleidoscope of cultures, colours, and connections, with striking implications for national unity and societal identity. In announcing the establishment of a National Museum of Immigration in the March 2010 Throne Speech, the Harper government confirmed the reciprocal link between immigration and Canada building: "Our identities are bound up in the stories of ancestors from hundreds of lands" (*Toronto Star* 2010; also Madokoro 2010). Brave words indeed, but a different narrative voices concern over the immigration program's ability to deliver the goods. Are current levels of immigration appropriate in light of relatively high unemployment (approximately 7.5 percent) (Siddiqui 2013a)? Is Canada taking advantage of the talents associated with highly skilled and educated newcomers (Bitran and Tan 2013)? Is decentralizing admissions to provinces a good idea? Is the booming influx of temporary foreign workers a short-term gain with long-term costs? Of particular concern is a leaky refugee status determination process that critics believe relegates Canada to a global patsy and international laughingstock. It is within the context of celebration and criticism, of progress and stalemate, of conviction and confusion, that an incursion into the politics of recent immigration reform is justified.

RECASTING THE STUDY OF IMMIGRANTS AND IMMIGRATION: THE BOOK

Few political challenges are as pressing as immigration and immigrants. But debates on the topic tend to be narrow in scope, including a domestic-only focus on entry, policy, or outcomes. Issues related to the broader context are glossed over, from global economics to pre-migration preparation and post-migration transnationality. Both the media and conservative think-tanks routinely associate immigrants

1 OBSERVATION

Remaking Canada: The Jason Kenney Revolution

POLITICAL LEGACIES COME and go. But it's quite possible that in years to come, the Conservative government's lasting legacy may well be the changes made by Immigration Minister Jason Kenney. Approve or disapprove, like him or loathe him, there is little question of Kenney's formidable status as one of the more influential ministers in modern Canadian public life (Editorial, *National Post* 2013). Canada under Kenney experienced more unprecedented changes in transforming immigration and citizenship than at any other time in its history, according to an expert panel (including Naomi Alboim and Monica Boyd) at the 15th annual National Metropolis Conference (Radia 2012; Zilio 2013; also Suhasini 2012). His tough-love measures to remake the country by remaking immigration expose him as a target for both criticism and praise (Selley 2013). Yet the initiatives and changes to immigration and the refugee system are unparalleled in a portfolio that is better known for playing it safe, mouthing platitudes, and decision making by lobby-capture.

Both Kenney and Stephen Harper have made it clear that the purpose of immigration reform is to transform a passive, rigid, and non-responsive system to one that is proactive, fast, flexible, and focused on driving the Canadian economy. Chris Alexander, the successor to Jason Kenney as citizenship and immigration minister, put it aptly: "The Government of Canada's number one priority remains economic growth and job creation. Immigration plays a key role in Canada's long-term prosperity and we are committed to seeing newcomers succeed across the country" (Canada News Centre 2014, 3). Consistent with this commitment are moves to (a) actively recruit economic migrants for Canada's labour market needs; (b) protect the integrity of its borders by rooting out abuses, either by dissuading migrants from entering the country or by removing those who are here "illegally" (jumping the queue or overstaying); and (c) replace existing programs at odds with public confidence with new initiatives resulting in quicker processing times and mutually beneficial economic prosperity (Radia 2012). In 2012 alone, Ottawa proposed or passed the following initiatives with respect to immigration, refugee determination, and citizenship (Black and Keung 2012).

Immigration and immigrants:
> The government proposed a new program, titled An Expression of Interest System, in which employers would choose candidates from a new pool of pre-screened skilled workers.
> The point system would be adjusted accordingly to emphasize language skills and younger migrants, and steps were taken to improve the vetting of professional credentials to ensure their Canadian equivalency.
> A new direction in the Federal Skilled Worker Program was announced, involving the promise of permanent residency to skilled trade workers (from pipefitters to heavy-equipment operators), to relieve labour shortages in the construction and gas/oil exploration business. Immigrants under the program will have their education abroad assessed against a Canadian educational standard.
> Bill C-43 (still before Parliament) provides the government with sweeping powers to bar entry for "public policy considerations." The detention of "irregular arrivals" will be at the discretion of the minister of public safety. As well, Ottawa proposes to deport permanent residents who are sentenced to six months or more for committing a crime.
> The tightening of rules regarding spousal sponsorship hoped to plug loopholes and abuses. Foreigners who are sponsored as spouses must remain in a relationship for two years before being granted permanent residency. Otherwise, they are deported. This rule does not apply to those who find themselves in situations of abuse or neglect.
> Proposals to pay temporary foreign workers between 5 and 15 percent less than the prevailing local wage did not sit well with various stakeholders and were subsequently rescinded.
> Immigration consultants must register with the government to ensure that their services meet standards of disclosure and accounting (Grubel 2013).

> For foreign migrant workers under the Seasonal Agricultural Worker Program, Ottawa eliminated the special parental benefit (from sick or parental leave to benefits for newborn or sick children).
> The immigration backlog will be reduced by 40 percent, from more than a million to about 616,000 (Canadian Press 2013a).

Refugees:
> The government compiled a list of 29 safe countries (now 37 countries capable of providing state protection for citizens), on the basis of combined rates of rejection, withdrawal, and abandonment (75 percent; only a 60 percent threshold was required for abandoned or withdrawn cases). Claimants from safe countries will be processed more quickly, unable to appeal their decision except to the Federal Court on matters of law, and deported from Canada within a year. Other claimants will have their cases heard within 60 days of referral to the Immigration and Refugee Board (Bissett 2013).
> In response to the highly publicized arrival of Tamil asylum seekers on the BC coast in 2009 and 2010, certain groups of refugees were designated as "irregular arrivals." The law equips the state with powers of mandatory arrest and detention for up to one year, while banning even successful asylum seekers from applying for permanent residence, family reunification, or a travel document for five years.
> Initiatives were introduced in which fairness for asylum seekers whose claims were plausible was balanced with strictness for those whose claims were plausibly false. To ensure quick and credible results, Kenney introduced new divisions in the refugee category (Simpson 2013): (a) sponsored abroad as individuals in vulnerable situations, (b) landed in Canada as refugee claimants, (c) those from designated (safe) countries of origin, and (d) massed (irregular) arrivals.
> Ottawa announced that it would cut supplementary health benefits (vision, dental, medical) for failed refugee claimants and claimants from safe countries unless they posed an emergency or a health risk to Canadians.
> Under the Protecting Canada's Immigration System Act, biometric measures (fingerprints and photos) were introduced for applicants

from 29 countries. These data will be used to cross-check those who were previously deported or have criminal records.

Citizenship:
> Prospective Canadian citizens between the ages of 18 and 54 must provide proof of proficiency in either French or English.
> Citizenship was revoked for more than three thousand people who falsified their admission/application forms or had failed to reside in Canada for three of the four years prior to applying for citizenship.

Changes carried over into the first half of 2013. According to Citizenship and Immigration Canada, they include (a) a drastic decline in the number of asylum claims with the introduction of stricter refugee assessments, (b) an increase in the number of international students to over 100,000 as proof of Canada's success in attracting the brightest and the best, (c) an additional nine thousand highly skilled workers under the Canadian Experience Class (Editorial, *National Post* 2013), and (d) tightening up the Temporary Foreign Worker Program (to remove the 15 percent wage disparity, increase application fees, confer authority to revoke work permits, and improve the Labour Market Opinion strategy [Deveau 2013]). Reforms to this program aim to solidify its use as originally intended: that is, to fill acute skills shortages on a temporary basis rather than by supplying cheap and pliant labour at the expense of jobs or training for Canadians (Gross 2014; Grant, Curry, and Chase 2013).

The conclusion is difficult to avoid. As "Jason Kenney's Canada" (Editorial, *National Post* 2013) remarked, even if Kenney were to quit tomorrow (in fact, he was shuffled off to the Employment and Social Development portfolio in mid-July 2013 but remained as minister of multiculturalism), his legacy in remaking Canada by remaking immigration was all but assured. This whirlwind of changes is bound to have a direct impact on Canadians and what Canada will look like in the future (Suhasini 2012; Zilio 2013). Reaction to this assessment depends on where one stands on the political spectrum. For some, Kenney did a disservice to Canada's humanitarian tradition (see Dauvergne 2013), in part by manipulating anxieties over security or fraud as a smokescreen to promote draconian change (see Radia 2012). Haroon Siddiqui (2013b) challenged Kenney's reforms as unpopular, needlessly ideological, unworkable, unhelpful to both the economy and newcomers, and an attack on Canadian values. For others, his initiatives bode well for Canada building by addressing a key twenty-first-century challenge: finding jobs for workers, and workers for jobs, in an era of chronic labour shortages and high unemployment (Ibbitson 2013). The fact that UN Watch, a Geneva-based human rights group, presented Kenney with its Moral Courage Award in 2014 for speaking up for the victims of tyranny around the world will surely add to his lustre (Clarke 2014b). One thing is certain, however (Suhasini 2012): Kenney has left an indelible imprint in remaking Canada's immigration program, while remaking Canada in the process.

with illegality, security risks, and social problems, thereby skewering any balanced understanding (Fryberg et al. 2012). Narratives that go beyond a simplistic reference to bad/good, costs/benefit, problem/solution, and wrong/right are often excluded (Fleras 2011b). In hopes of contesting conventional narratives, this book is committed to the goal of rethinking Canadian immigration and reframing immigrants within a globalizing context of developing realities, nascent challenges, and fluid discourses.

Both emergent dynamics and contested realities make it clear that though Canada may well qualify as a quintessential immigration society, it cannot be divorced from global developments that complicate a business-as-usual mindset (Ehrkamp and Leitner 2006; Malloch-Brown 2011). There is a pressing need to rethink the conceptual frameworks for understanding contemporary immigration (including policies, assumptions, and programs) and the relational status of immigrants/refugees (from settlement to citizenship). A globalizing world marked by acceleration, differentiation, and integration provides a brand new optic for analyzing international migration (Bitran and Tan 2013). The focus is on hybridity, mobility, and fluidity instead of a relatively static either/or framework. The challenge lies in synthesizing these factors by recasting them along new lines in hopes of coaxing fresh interpretations from outdated narratives. Three tropes are of relevance here: topics, perspectives, and discourses (Noble 2011).

Topics

Rethinking immigration and immigrants builds upon, yet goes beyond, conventional *topics*. There may be much to commend in addressing traditional topics related to the history of Canadian immigration, analysis of current programs, immigrant economic misadventures, benefits/costs of immigration through mutually reinforcing impacts and implications, and the dysfunctionality of the refugee determination system. Canada yields a motherload of literature on immigration and immigrants, although this richness comes with strings attached. Most tends toward the historical (Knowles 2007); focuses on a single issue (economics, Picot and Sweetman 2012; or law, Dauvergne 2005); is highly polemical, either critical (Grady 2009; Grubel 2009; Gogia and Slade 2011; Grubel and Grady 2012) or ideological (Kymlicka 2005; Bloemraad 2007); is ruthlessly empirical in its assessment at the expense of non-measurable contributions (Grubel 2013); is prone to outdatedness (Elliott and Fleras 1991); or fixates on Canada as a relatively self-contained entity outside of global dynamics (Li 2003; but see Simmons 2010 as an exception).

This book does not shy away from these issues, though it addresses them along non-conventional lines. For example, the history of immigration and Canada is important, not in its own right, but in terms of demonstrating its continuities into the present. This book incorporates a balanced dialogue – critical and informed yet constructive and hopeful – in uncovering the complexities, challenges, changes, and contradictions associated with immigration and immigrants. It focuses on the contemporary without ignoring history; embraces comprehensiveness without loss of specificity over the politics, demographics, and economics of immigration; deconstructs the debate over Canada's refugee determination system without falling into the trap of polemics; promotes a multi-dimensional exploration of controversial issues without sacrificing an overarching vision; situates immigration in a national framework without sacrificing a global dimension; addresses the paradigmatic impact of these changes without abandoning lip service to the slogan "the more things change ..."; and explores the implications of these shifts in reconfiguring Canada as a twenty-first-century immigration society without ignoring continuities from the past.

This book also grapples with topics and themes that elude orthodox debates and analyses. That much can be expected of a field of astonishing changes in policy and programs, including (a) a revised selection system for federal skilled workers, (b) an expanding Temporary Foreign Worker Program, (c) new paths of permanent admission for qualified foreign workers and international students, (d) increased provincial control over immigration, (e) restrictions on family reunification, (f) the fast-tracking of refugee claimants from so-called safe countries, and (g) enhanced border security through Smart Border agreements and safe third-country arrangements. No less important is engagement with issues of gendered immigration; a tilt toward designer immigrants; the promises and perils of the Temporary Foreign Worker Program; media coverage of immigrants; the politics of immigration in a context of growing securitization; the immigration crisis in America in general, Arizona in particular, and its implications for Canada; transmigration as immigrant process; transnationality as paradigm shift in rethinking migration, citizenship, and integration; the relevance of official multiculturalism; and a reformulation of citizenship models along more multi-dimensional lines.

Perspectives

A commitment to new *perspectives* is pivotal in reframing narratives of immigration and immigrants. If framing is defined as a process for organizing information to promote a particular perspective, reframing entails a reorganization of information through selection, emphasis, and exclusion in hopes of drawing attention to some hitherto unknown aspects of reality, thus encouraging a preferred reading or interpretation (Fleras 2011a). The interplay of globalization with the global movement of (trans)migrants puts pressure on newer perspectives that often invert conventional approaches yet may coax fresh insights from tired topics, including:

> *Migration as norm.* Too often immigration is pictured as a departure from the norm of staying put (see Bakewell 2007). Or it is perceived as a problem to be fixed by policies that address root causes. But reframing it as a normal component in a transformational world reinforces its status as an inescapable feature of global societies (Castles and Miller 2009). Exploring the idea that mobility rather than stability is a natural order of affairs – migrants are known to live with a "permanent sense of the temporary" and a "temporary sense of the permanent" (Hennebry 2012) – also has the effect of repriming immigration discourses along vibrant lines (Samers 2010).

> *Unproblematizing migrants.* A perception that immigration and immigrants are problematic is common enough. But the emergence of transmigrants and their transnational links should bolster the reframing of migrants as assets and opportunities in a globalizing world (Goldin, Cameron, and Balarajan 2011; Bitran and Tan 2013). Diasporas too have emerged as significant global players, with many countries regarding them as vital economic assets or developmental partners (Vertovec 2005; Geislerova 2007; Crush et al. 2013). Although almost 3 million Canadians live abroad, Canada does not have a coordinated diaspora strategy. Canadians, in turn, harbour an unflattering mindset toward what they perceive as Canadians of "convenience" (Kenny Zhang 2007).

> *Engendered immigration.* Many migration perspectives often reflect a male bias as the norm (Boyd 2006). The lack of a gender lens and gender-specific experiences glosses over an awareness of gender as a key explanatory variable (a difference that makes a difference). References to the feminization of migration (Caritas Internationalis 2010) include (a) the conditions under which women migrate, (b) their predominance in certain migration flows (such as trafficking and smuggling), (c) circumstances that encourage them to become transnational migrants, and (d) the perils (and promises) in making the transition from there to here (Boyd and Grieco 2003; Castles and Miller 2009; Piper and French 2011).

> *Multiculturalism as immigrant governance.* Multiculturalism is sometimes criticized as a policy framework that encourages transmigrant cultural practices and transnational social identities (Mansur 2011). A

multicultural agenda may thwart Canadian unity by compromising mainstream values, segregating newcomers into isolated communities, devaluing citizenship, precluding people's integration into society, and compromising allegiance to the country. Others contend that multiculturalism is a crucial component, not only in helping immigrants to settle down, fit in, and move up, but also in constructing a cohesive and integrated society (Reitz 2011a). Still others point to a dilemma: To what extent is Canada's multicultural governance model outdated (Mawani 2008; Shome 2012)? How relevant is a place-based multiculturalism as governance for integrating migrants, when newcomer ideas of identity and belonging are increasingly uncoupled from a sense of place (Carruthers 2013)? In a transnational world of transmigrants, is there any point in even talking about immigration and immigrants within the context of territorially grounded frameworks of integration and citizenship? That dilemma alone makes it doubly important to rethink the relevance of multiculturalism as an inclusive immigrant governance against the backdrop of (a) a globalizing world of transmigration, (b) a Canada of superdiverse individuals, (c) a commitment to accommodating different ways of accommodating differences, and (d) a changing and contested postnational Canada (Fleras 2014b).

> *Negotiating citizenship.* New perspectives on citizenship are clearly in ascendancy. Just as immigrant communities are no longer framed as identifiable bodies of people who interact on the basis of common language and culture, so too is the singular conception of citizenship sharply contested. A new conceptual toolkit is required as immigrant consciousness and identities are reconfigured along transmigratory lines and transnational networks (Blommaert and Rampton 2011). Awareness is also growing for the need to customize notions of citizenship by acknowledging how people differ in their relationship to the state (Lloyd L. Wong 2007-08). Admittedly, critics of dual citizenship (or transmigration) often see identity and belonging along win-lose lines wherein one invariably detracts from the other. Others disagree: They suggest that second-generation immigrants may express a stronger sense of belonging to Canada than the first generation or the general population (Jedwab 2007-08), even in a globalizing world where notions of identity and belonging are increasingly detached from a spatial mooring (Fleras 2011b).

> *Securing borders in a world on the move?* The movement of people is inescapable in a globalizing world of free markets, with a corresponding realignment of investment and finances, goods and services. Yet this global diaspora clashes with government struggles to "discipline differences" by securing borders, securitizing admission, militarizing enforcement protocols, and consolidating bureaucratic obstacles to permanent residency and citizenship (Martinez 2009; Fleras 2011b; Rodríguez-García 2012). The politics of securitization complicates the prospect of fluidity and cross-border movement in the twenty-first century: mobility for the highly skilled but restrictions for the unwanted or unskilled (Esses et al. 2008; Castles 2013).

> *Benefits and costs.* Current debates over benefits and costs must be reframed in ways that bypass binary oppositions such as voluntary versus involuntary, temporary versus permanent, international versus internal, legal versus irregular, and good versus bad (King, Skeldon, and Vullnetari 2008). Attention should focus on a "both/and" framework instead of a rhetorically charged "either/or" frame that tends to polarize issues along zero-sum lines (Jedwab 2007-08; Hugo 2013). Or, alternatively, a SWOT framework (strengths, weaknesses, opportunities, and threats) should be employed to achieve a more nuanced analysis (Kenny Zhang 2007). For example, the contested porosity of borders, due to technology advances and shifting political environments, makes it increasingly awkward to dichotomize "host" society from diasporic/ immigrant communities (Berns-McGown 2007-08).

Discourses

Lastly, consider the emergence of new *discourses*. Over 15 years ago, Massey et al. (1998) criticized the study of international migration as mired in the modernist/industrial past, with a concomitant set of economic arrangements, social institutions, political agendas, and cognitive outlooks. For Massey and his colleagues, it was time to reassess the idea that international migration is a linear and permanent displacement of people from one nation-state to another (also Castles 2010). In keeping with the spirit of a call to intellectual arms, this book proposes an alternative model for thinking about immigration and immigrants. Immigration must be reconceptualized as a multi-field of flows that connect, contest, and complicate (Simmons 2010). A focus on fluidity, circularity, interconnectedness, and temporality calls for a new discursive framework that is more contextual in outlook, dynamic in orientation, and global in scope. The implications of this rethinking – one that reconceptualizes this domain as a verb/process, not a noun/thing – are particularly evident in discourses that situate immigrants and immigration within the broader context of globalization, as both host countries and newcomers grapple with issues of belonging and identity. Three discursive frames play a role in recalibrating the discourse: rethinking immigration, reframing immigrants, and repositioning the narrative.

Rethinking Immigration: From Noun (Thing) to Verb (Process)

Immigration was historically perceived as primarily a domestic policy issue. Taps were turned on when Canada required more immigrants for demographic or economic purposes and turned off when they were considered an unacceptable cost. This model reinforced the state's centrality for controlling its borders and advancing national interests. But a focus on the local, fixed, and self-contained is no longer appropriate. Instead of being framed as a *thing,* immigration is increasingly perceived as a *process* that involves flow, connectedness, globalization, and transnationality.

A paradigm shift is emerging that re-envisions immigration as a process involving the evolving realities of a globalized world. No longer seen as a movement between fixed points, immigration is now situated as occurring across ever-broadening contexts, from the local to the national and global (Simmons 2010). Both sending and receiving countries become increasingly co-dependent on migration, making it difficult to stop, and migrant moves assume an impetus of their own (Castles and Vezzoli 2009). Nicholas Van Hear (2010, 1531) writes to this effect:

> The starting point ... is to view migration as a process which is an integral part of broader social transformations, but which also has its own internal dynamics and which shapes social transformation in its own right. Migration is linked in complex ways to class, gender, generation, ethnicity, and other social cleavages which are embedded in hierarchies of power and social status, in positions in home and host countries, and in work and domestic

relationships, all of which may be transformed in the course of the migratory process.

For immigrants, the transition from there to here is no less dynamic and contextual (Broadbent 2009b). Immigration in the past was usually seen as a highly individualized activity. A person or a family decided to emigrate in reaction to push-pull factors, without much input from relatives or community fanfare. Immigrants would sever ties with their homeland as the price for citizenship, belonging, and involvement in their new country.

In reality, however, the migration process entails a series of situational developments, from the move itself (means of migration and choice of destination), to conditions experienced by migrants (entry conditions and integration into receiving countries), to migrant outcomes and opportunities and their impacts on development in originating countries (such as transfers and remittances to the home country) (Chappell and Glennie 2009). Labour migrants are not isolated individuals who seek to improve their lot. They are also family members who are sent abroad to support those left behind or to provide a buffer against sudden declines in economic productivity, in part by diversifying their portfolio of risks (Segal, Mayadas, and Elliott 2006). Family and community members continue to play a key role in sending people overseas, in hopes of securing future sponsorships or steady remittances (which for some countries are now as important as foreign aid and direct investment [Chappell and Mulley 2010]). In other words, immigration as discourse and practice may be as much about those who stay behind as those who leave (Levitt 2007).

Reframing Immigrant Experiences: From the National to the Transnational

Traditionally, immigration was believed to encompass a permanent move to a new country. In addition, governments and host communities expected that immigrants would identify with and be loyal to a single national community with a common culture and set of core values (Ehrkamp and Leitner 2006). Splintered allegiances and divided attachments were discouraged or dismissed; after all, multiple loyalties were thought to generate unnecessary tensions, threaten national unity and identity, or complicate patterns of governance (Baron 2009).

Attainment of citizenship was proof that newcomers had permanently transferred their allegiance to the new country (Spoonley 2009). In short, society building was predicated on a continuous process of including some into the national community, while excluding others, in large part by twinning national belonging and spatial location (Landolt 2007).

But conventional notions of migrant identity, attachment, and belonging are uprooted by the combination of low-cost travel and digital communication technologies with the aggressive recruitment of skilled professionals (Spoonley and Bedford 2012). Circular/repeat/temporary movements and transnational linkages have emerged as plausible options because of globalization (a process of expanding, deepening, and accelerating all forms of worldwide interconnectedness), with its corresponding collapsing of place/space linkages that conflates the local and national in fostering social formations along geographically discontinuous sites (Landolt 2007). Rethinking immigration draws attention to the logic and dynamics of migration, which occurs in a globalizing world but is nonetheless intensely local with respect to settlement and integration, and is mediated by a national agenda of politics and policies. However inadvertently, even host countries often facilitate a move toward transnational identities and attachments by (a) providing access to dual or multiple citizenship, (b) creating a pool of permanent residents with near citizenship rights, and (c) easing restrictions in defining a model citizen (in part because of growing uncertainties in defining the values of Canadian citizenship). Multilocal social spaces are created when newcomers demonstrate a belonging to Canada without abandoning an identification with their homeland (Levitt 2007). Some see this criss-crossing of borders both physical and psychological as a revolutionary shift to embrace; others perceive it as a dangerous precedent at odds with society building; and still others view it as a reality that must be addressed without forfeiting its benefits.

Immigrant identity is no longer what many thought it was. Such a shift is consistent with poststructural views of the world, not as a solid perma-structure but as a fluid network of changing flows, or what Zygmunt Bauman (2000) calls "liquid modernity." A new type of immigrant and immigrant experience is emerging, one that neither severs ties with the home country nor passively assimilates into the host country. The relevance of the transnational paradigm as an explanatory framework should not be underestimated (Inglis 2007). Unlike the old paradigm, which framed immigration as a static field of location, transnationality offers a new conceptual lens for understanding the complex and contested world of immigrants in an age of globalization, diasporic politics, and rapid communication and transportation (Satzewich and Wong 2006; Satzewich and Liodakis 2013). Settlement into a new homeland does not dissuade immigrants from constructing diasporic communities that offer solidarity, support, information, and identity (Brinkerhoff 2009; Crush et al. 2013). Clearly, immigrants are embedded in, identify with, and participate in multiple communities without necessarily dissolving or even weakening identification with the host country (Kenny Zhang 2007).

Perhaps a sense of perspective is helpful. Domestic affairs cannot be divorced from global contexts beyond the nation-state; for example, transnationalism reflects both a logical extension of multiculturalism as governance and a challenge to conventional immigrant governance, especially when governments increasingly tighten both admission and residency by securitizing society and militarizing borders (Satzewich and Wong 2006; Inglis 2007; Mawani 2008). Similarly, the concept of citizenship is contested in a transmigration era of fluidity and flux. An expanded notion is emerging that elevates citizenship beyond a legal status with a singular and similar bundle of rights and responsibilities. The concept of a nationally bounded citizenship is now outflanked by a postnational model that proposes citizenship rights in both the host and home county alongside a broader human rights discourse (Ehrkamp and Leitner 2006). Their co-existence in two worlds enables transnational migrants to organize their lives across borders without necessarily experiencing confusion or contradiction. In turn, migrant-receiving countries create frameworks that simultaneously encourage transmigrant linkages yet discourage cross-border movement (Landolt 2007). The end results are twofold. First, immigrants participate simultaneously across differing spheres of co-existence in both host and home countries, while connecting with multiple identities that transcend national boundaries. Second, this liberalization of movement and citizenship is offset by government measures to restrict patterns of belonging, identity, and cross-border movements. The contradiction is palpable: Never before has the potential for migration been greater, and never before has government control over who belongs been more stringent.

Repositioning the Narrative: Challenging the Binaries (from Either/Or to Both/And)

Canada's immigration program is widely regarded as a model to emulate. It offers a principled and transparent approach for attracting so-called useful migrants while barring the unwanted and unwashed. A utopian (good) immigration program is based on a win-win formula for all stakeholders. As a wealthy post-industrial society, Canada requires both skilled and unskilled workers to sustain its prosperity, while securing a tax base to offset the costs of an ageing population and plummeting birth rate. Consider the possibilities: Workers from developing countries find good jobs that facilitate their settlement and integration into the country; Canadians benefit from exposure to their diversities, connections, energy, and creativity; and source countries prosper from overseas remittances (Simmons 2010). For some, then, benefits prevail. Immigration is endorsed as the solution to Canada's problems with respect to a shortage of skilled labour, declining birth rate, and need for international competitiveness. For others, immigration entails unacceptable costs. Immigration and immigrants are defined as a potential recipe for disaster (Cramme and Motte 2010), as a threat to national cultures, cohesion, and identity because of cultural differences that conflict with mainstream values (such as gender and sexual equality); an unwillingness to integrate or assimilate to the host society while making unacceptable demands for accommodation; and a tendency to embrace a plethora of social ills, from crime to welfare dependency (Ehrkamp and Leitner 2006).

Discourses about immigrants are no less hotly disputed. So-called bad immigrants who negatively affect Canada stand in sharp contrast to good ones, who are framed as pivotal in addressing Canada's needs, identity, and imagined future. Good immigrants espouse liberal attitudes, are legally here, and are assets to society and the economy. To ensure their status as model immigrants, they must demonstrate their gratefulness for Canada's generosity, remember their place as invited guests and defer accordingly, and vigorously exhibit a singular commitment to Canada as their permanent home (Simmons 2010). A distinction between good and bad refugees is also upheld. Good refugees, who conform to preconceived notions of acceptability, are persecuted individuals who need Canada's protection from blatantly repressive regimes. They observe conventional protocols for entry and placement. Bad refugees arrive unannounced and jump the queue, self-select for entry on the basis of their needs rather than those of Canadians, and rely on human smuggling rings to finagle their way into the country.

These oppositional frames make it clear – migration theories and immigrant discourses in Canada tend to be driven by simple categorizations and binary oppositions (King, Skeldon, and Vullnetari 2008). But the binary oppositions are misleading (International Migration Institute 2006). Distinctions between sending and receiving countries are increasingly blurred as many developing countries (particularly middle-income ones) evolve into transit(ional) zones (Newland 2011). People's reasons for migrating are rarely so straightforward that they fit snugly into a push-pull framework. Nor should transmigrants be framed along binaries such as local versus global or homeland versus host country. They must be understood instead through their multiple social, economic, political, and cultural relationships, as they navigate their identities and allegiances from country of origin to host country (Inglis 2007). Less tenable than ever are those popular discourses that dichotomize immigrants into polarities of good (benefits) or bad (costs).[1] The impact of immigrants is much more complex and nuanced, not so much a case of either benefits or costs depending on context, criteria, or consequences. More accurately, it's about both benefits and costs that function concurrently. If the debate is to be propelled forward, the narrative must shift toward a cost and benefit discourse that captures the multi-dimensionality of global migration.

The repositioning of the immigrant narrative puts a unique spin on who needs whom. Do immigrants need Canada, or does Canada need immigrants? A long-standing binary assumed that immigrants need Canada and that Canadians play gracious hosts. The backlog of nearly one million people who wished to enter Canada served as proof. Not surprisingly, public perceptions and political debates display a strong host society bias in prioritizing national interests related to security, prosperity, and identity, while paying little attention to migrants' experiences and struggles (Ehrkamp and Leitner 2006). Moreover, there remains a tendency to see immigration as a problem, with immigrants as troublesome constituents who must be controlled (Castles and Miller 2009). Yet in a world of intense competition for the brightest and best, a playful inversion is apropos. It is Canada who needs immigrants rather than the other way around, if only to capture their enthusiasm, energy, and entrepreneurship, while offsetting the demographic crunch and labour shortage issues, in addition to enhancing its own overseas trade and investment linkages (Globe and Mail 2012).[2] Clearly, then, a new lens for rethinking immigration and immigrants is required that reimagines Canada's twenty-first-century prospects in the art of managing people movement by doing what is workable, necessary, and fair (see also Jurado and Bruzzone 2008).

2

global migration, international migrants

PATTERNS, PERSPECTIVES, PARADOXES

RETHINKING THE ISSUES, REFRAMING THE DEBATES
ON 6 JUNE 2006, UN secretary general Kofi Annan proclaimed to the General Assembly, "We are in a new migration era" (quoted in Bloemraad 2007). How did he arrive at this assessment? Four factors jump out: First, international migration has boomed, with respect to number, sources, and types (Rygiel 2010). The combination of economic migrants who come to work and asylum seekers who seek refuge embodies a core dynamic in driving the globalization-era revolution, in the process reshaping the economic, political, and social contours of societies around the world (Collier 2013; Glick Schiller, Basch, and Blanc-Szanton 1992; Grugel and Piper 2007; Papademetriou 2012). To be sure, the free movement of people under globalization applies primarily to the highly skilled of the First World (Tendoh 2009), resulting in a two-tiered pattern that is likely to persist into the foreseeable future (Castles and Miller 2009; Scheffer 2010). The consequences of this global ferment are far-reaching: The cross-border movement of people in search of opportunity, excitement, or escape is challenging notions of border security and state sovereignty. The concept of people on the move also raises questions about the politics of managing migration (Geiger and Pécoud 2011; Nieuwenhuysen, Duncan, and Neerup 2012). Immigrants are increasingly perceived as security risks and/or economic

threats, precisely because of their globe-trotting status (Guild 2009). Accordingly, as Stephen Castles (2007, 352) argues, migration research in the globalization era of transmigration and diaspora will require a fresh set of theoretical tools and analytic frameworks.

The promise of international migration is unmistakable, especially for countries in the global South. It represents one way of (a) alleviating pressures and minimizing dangers; (b) maximizing opportunities in a world of growing economic and social inequities; (c) easing spiralling population growth, especially among the poor in developing countries; (d) averting rampant starvation and disease, sectarian violence and civil wars, state oppression and military unrest; and (e) responding to environmental catastrophes associated with the depletion of valued resources, from water to fuel. Even developed countries are being reshaped by international migration. What were once emigrant societies, such as those in Europe, are now societies of immigrants, with a corresponding affront to national identity, institutional inclusion, and newcomer integration (see Anton and Pilipp 2010). But a paradox underpins this transformation: Rich economies depend on migrant workers. The end result is a proliferation of precarious jobs and informal labour markets involving cheap unskilled labour (Castles and Vezzoli 2009). Yet many European jurisdictions possess neither explicit policies nor formal programs to regulate immigrant intake or facilitate their settlement. Nor do they envision the arrival of all newcomers as normative or desirable (Massey 2003). Yes, newcomers may enrich or enlighten, yet they are not taken seriously in defining the national imaginary. This toxic brew of structural gaps, security issues, cultural differences, and ideological indifference bodes poorly for the future, as pointed out in the foreword to ENAR Report (2012, 1):

> A growing number of voices are speaking up against migrants and minorities. These voices are not just those of the usual extremists, but also voices of mainstream decision-makers. Regrettably, these voices disparage contemporary migration as a "threat" to society and denigrate integration in ways that introduce fears in the hearts of people and often with negative clichés. They repeatedly talk about "floods of migrants and refugees" and relate migration and migrants to increased crime, the bringing in of diseases, the building of parallel societies, and the lowering of

school standards ... society having to cover the cost of immigrants. We hear these largely uninformed voices espouse such populist sentiments as "immigrants are taking away jobs from EU citizens," "immigrants are driving down wages," and "migrants are abusing the welfare state."

Second, just as international migration is undergoing change, so too have migrants. They are more numerous than ever, more diverse in their country of origin and destination, more willing to take risks, and more politicized in their demands for recognition of rights (Esses et al. 2010; Vertovec 2010; Fleras 2012b, 2012d). European emigration has slowed to a crawl since the 1960s, unlike that of Africa, Asia, and Latin America. The variety of destination countries has changed as well. In addition to immigrant-receiving countries in the Antipodes, South America, and North America, both Western Europe and Middle Eastern countries continue to attract hefty numbers (Massey 2003). More recently, suggests Madeleine Sumption (in Grant 2011), policy analyst at the Washington-based Migration Policy Institute, migrants are seeking out the booming economies of Brazil, Russia, India, China, Indonesia, and Turkey. They, too, are responding to a structural demand for labour that is commensurate with the logic of post-industrial economies. A segmented labour market prevails, one that offers good jobs for the privileged few, but for many only precarious work (dirty, dangerous, difficult, and dull) that nationals shun even during a recession, prompting employers to rely on migrants as an economic lifeline. As William Robinson (2007) concludes in pinpointing the global-capitalism-migration nexus,

> The transnational circulation of capital and the disruption and deprivation it causes, in turn generates the transnational circulation of labor. In other words, global capitalism creates immigrant workers ... In a sense, this must be seen as a coerced or forced migration since global capitalism exerts a structural violence over whole populations and makes it impossible for them to survive in their homelands.

In short, international migration does not necessarily arise from a dearth of economic growth in underdeveloped countries: Development itself is a catalyst in moving people about. Migration is most active in developing countries, where economies are experiencing rapid growth, uneven development and structural adjustments create inequality and displacement, and fertility rates are plunging because of consumerist lifestyles. Any society that is transitioning toward a nascent market economy confronts a massive displacement of people from traditional occupations. Many of the dispossessed drift into nearby cities, whereas the presumably lucky few migrate abroad in search of opportunity or safety (Massey 2003; Jayapal 2011; Otero 2011). Douglas Massey (2009, 26-27, emphasis added) writes to this effect:

> International migration originates in the social, economic, and political transformations that accompany the expansion of capitalist markets into nonmarket or premarket societies (as hypothesized under world systems theory). In the context of a globalizing economy, the entry of markets and capital intensive production methods into peripheral nonmarket and premarket economies disrupts existing social and economic arrangements and brings about the widespread displacement of people from customary livelihoods, creating a mobile population of wage-laborers who actively search for new ways of achieving economic sustenance. Studies consistently show that international migrants do not come from poor, isolated places that are disconnected from world markets, but from regions and nations that are undergoing rapid change as a result of their incorporation into global trade, information, and production networks. In the short run, international migration does not stem from a lack of economic development, but from development itself.

Third, a global/transnational frame of reference is displacing a national framework, both as an empirical reality and an explanatory framework. Migration is the most tangible evidence of globalization and concrete expression of global interconnectedness, which in turn generates additional cross-border movements (Cramme and Motte 2010). The economic, political, and social upheaval induced by globalization enhances the incentive to migrate in ways hitherto unnoticed or unexplained. But the globalization of migration is not necessarily recognized at international levels. Migration policies continue to be formulated at the national level, generally favouring the admission of the better educated at the expense of low-skilled workers who may be rotated in and out of the country as seen fit (Fleras 2010). No global body exists to oversee the movement of people, in contrast to the international institutions that facilitate market-based policies around trade and finance (Goldin, Cameron, and Balarajan 2011). With few exceptions, nation-states have been reluctant to regulate international migration around multilaterally binding norms or international bodies (Kunz, Lavenex, and Panizzon 2011). Yet the very magnitude and benefits of international migration presume some degree of international cooperation and shared responsibility. As Goldin, Cameron, and Balarajan (2011, 217) point out in making a case for establishing global institutions to regulate migration, "Migratory flows are the orphan of the international system, with powerful countries arguing against a global migration organization and a rule-based system. Fair rules protect the weakest against the strongest players, and the absence of such rules means that the richest and most powerful nations are able to make up their own rules regarding migration." An international perspective is long overdue – one that frames migration issues from a global perspective without diminishing the salience of the nation-state in constructing a reciprocal governance framework (Robinson 1998) (see the final section of this chapter).

Fourth, global movements of people are normal. International migration can no longer be seen as an anomalous, random, or isolated feature of the human condition, as it once was due to the long-standing sedentary bias that informed migration debates (Bakewell 2007). To the contrary, the exodus of migrants reflects the natural consequences of broader processes across borders, involving complex sets of interactions, relationships, networks, and population movements (Castles and Miller 2009). Mobility is vital to human development; movement itself is the natural expression of the wish to choose where to live and how to pursue life chances; and relocation is a must because of human and natural disasters (Sheller and Urry 2006; Caritas Internationalis 2010). No less counterproductive are references to migration as a problem to solve, either by strengthening border control or reducing poverty in origin countries (Newland 2011). International migration is a normal social activity in a world of change, complexity, and diversity (International Migration Institute 2006; Castles 2013).

The conclusion seems obvious enough. The twenty-first century may well be defined by the movement of people from one country to another, from one continent to another, from one hemisphere to another (Guterres 2007; OECD 2013). With up to 215 million people on the move outside of their homeland – resulting in an aggregate population poised just behind that of Indonesia as the world's fifth-most populous country – relatively few countries are untouched by international migration (Papademetriou 2003). All industrial and developed countries are now societies of immigrants (although not necessarily immigration societies), whether or not they recognize this reality through official policies or cultural norms. The challenges associated with the new migration are twofold: first, pressures on the sovereign state for controlling the movement of people (especially irregular migrants) across potentially porous borders; second, the emergence of transnational connections that transcend national sovereignty. The concurrency of transmigrant (or diasporic) relations across two or more countries is thought to undermine the unalloyed loyalty once seen as critical to the governance of sovereign nation-states (Carruthers 2013). Not surprisingly, international migration management requires a rethinking of policies and programs to establish a global governance with teeth (Geiger and Pécoud 2011).

These and other developments are proving controversial, especially for countries in search of legal/political mechanisms to regulate movement and facilitate integration (Massey 2009). Migration may well constitute the defining challenge of the twenty-first century, not so much in terms of whether to approve it, but in managing it more effectively (Rodriguez-Garcia 2012). Yet migration mismanagement has proven the rule rather than the exception, since many countries have neither articulated policies to regulate entry nor implemented programs to maximize the positives (Esses et al. 2010). Debates about appropriate responses and workable solutions are further complicated by political and social uncertainties that frame international migration as an extremely fraught domain in the post-9/11 era (Inglis 2007). Shifting socio-historical circumstances require a new explanatory framework (Glick Schiller, Basch, and Blanc-Szanton 1992) that acknowledges the multi-dimensionality of international migration (Castles and Miller 2009; Simmons 2010). Of particular noteworthiness is the emergence of transmigrant models of migration. Pierrette Hondagneu-Sotelo (2003, 16) extols the value and validity of a new transnational lens as explanatory framework:

Transnationalism, which emphasizes the ongoing attachments that immigrants maintain with people and institutions in their places of origin, has seriously challenged conventional ideas about immigrants and immigration. Rather than viewing immigration as a linear one-way process that requires immigrants to sever all connections with the old country, scholars inspired by transnational approaches examine how people stay connected and often form a cohesive community across nation-state borders.

Certainly, a general theory of international migration is neither possible nor desirable. Any proposed conceptual framework must grapple with the broader dimensions of contemporary society within a global context; incorporate complexity, contextuality, and diversity; and recognize both structural and systemic aspects without losing a sense of agency or history. Endorsed as well is the concept of international migration as a holistic totality involving complex social interactions across a wide span of institutional structures and informal networks between and within both sending and receiving countries.

Deconstructing the challenges and complexities of (re)conceptualizing the politics and dynamics of international migration is more important than ever. This is particularly true for Canada, where immigration has transformed a society of immigrants into an immigration society with a principled commitment to managing migration and integrating newcomers (Hiebert and Ley 2003; Waters 2003; Kelley and Trebilcock 2010). First, however, Box 2 gives an overview of terms to deconstruct and describe the various types of migrants.

GLOBAL ESTIMATES, PATTERNS, AND TRENDS

According to Douglas Massey (2003), the history of modern (Western) international migration can be divided into four stages. The mercantile period, from 1500 to 1800, saw world migration dominated by European outflows due to colonization and economic expansion across vast areas of the world. The industrial period of migration, from about 1800 to the late 1920s, reflected factory development in Europe, a corresponding displacement of farmers from traditional livelihoods, and the spread of capitalism to former colonies in the New World. Large-scale emigration was rooted in structural transformations that overtook European countries as they became incorporated into a global network of massive flows of capital, raw materials, and goods. Canada,

2 OVERVIEW

Deconstructing Migrants and Migration

Migrants

The generic term *migrants* applies to any kind of movement – leaving (emigrant) or arriving (immigrant) – from one place to another, usually for purposes of settlement across borders. It can also refer to temporary rather than permanent settlement. Types of migrants reflect patterns of migration, including intercontinental, intracontinental (between countries), interregional (within a country), and rural-urban (Castles and Miller 2009).

Irregular migrants

This umbrella term covers those who illegally cross borders, legal entrants who overstay their entry visas or work without permission, family members of migrant workers who enter illegally, and asylum seekers who fail to qualify as refugees. Irregular migrants are also known as undocumented or unauthorized migrants.

Illegal migrants

This term is widely yet incorrectly applied to people who enter or stay without proper authorization – who self-select to enter a country. Many argue that the term is misleading and inaccurate, because (according to international law) self-proclaiming as an asylum seeker who asks for refugee status is never illegal. However, those who overstay their work and tourist visas, or those whose refugee claims have failed and who go underground, may be loosely labelled "illegal" (but see arguments of the No One Is Illegal movement [Goodman 2012; Abji 2013; Bauder 2013; Keung 2013c]).

Immigrants*

Immigrants are incoming newcomers who are born elsewhere, voluntarily arrive, and are entitled to permanent status on the basis of two grounds: to be reunited with their families or because of promised economic benefits as workers or entrepreneurs. Countries have differing definitions of who is an immigrant, based on criteria such as voluntary or forced (asylum) or permanent or temporary resident status. Thus, tourists or temporary foreign workers are usually not included in this category. In some cases, naturalization (citizenship) erases a person's status (or stigma) as immigrant; in other cases, a foreign-born person will always be counted as an immigrant, at least for statistical purposes (Somerville 2009; Blinder 2013).

Permanent residents

Permanent residents are authorized to live and work in Canada without citizenship status, provided they meet residency requirements and do not forfeit their status because of serious criminality or security violations (CIC 2012a). Also known as landed immigrants.

Foreign-born

Those who were not born in their country of residence regardless of length of stay in the receiving country.

Foreign nationals

Immigrants and children of immigrants who are not recognized as citizens by the host country.

Emigrants

Persons who leave a country to reside in another.

Refugees

Refugees are forced to flee from their home country and cannot return because of a well-founded fear of persecution or death based on race or ethnicity etc. (convention refugees). They are entitled to permanent status because they need protection, with a legitimate (Geneva Convention) claim to asylum.

Protected persons
  This made-in-Canada term acknowledges refugee-like status for those who need protection from environmental catastrophes or undemocratic states that appear indifferent to their plight. Because of safety concerns rather than persecution per se, they cannot return home or be returned.

Asylum seekers
  Persons who seek sanctuary (refuge) in another country by declaring refugee status.

Internally displaced persons
  Internally displaced persons are forced to flee their home but continue to reside inside their home country.

Stateless persons
  Status-less persons who are not considered nationals (or citizens) by any state.

Undocumented persons
  Individuals who reside in a country but lack official status (illegally). Reasons include visa overstays or lapsed temporary worker permits (see also irregular migrants).

Evacuees
  People who are temporarily evacuated from a crisis zone but are expected to return once hostilities subside.

Guest workers/temporary workers
  Individuals who enter on a temporary basis and must leave upon completion of their job or expiry of their permit.

Professional transients
  Highly skilled but contractually based temporary workers who migrate from one country to another to take advantage of opportunities.

Diaspora†

A contested signifier, "diaspora" historically referred to violent ruptures of peoples or nations, from forced expulsion to persecution, culminating in exile and a yearning to return. More commonly, it refers to transmigrant communities that have settled outside their ancestral homeland for a variety of reasons (Zine 2012). It also applies to those transmigratory/transnational practices that link individuals in their host country to relatives and friends in the sending country (Vertovec 2005). This diaspora network emphasizes the linkages maintained by people who remain connected by a shared sense of identity (Bitran and Tan 2013).

Transmigrants

Transmigrants move to another country without necessarily disconnecting ties, both physical and psychological, with their homeland (a phenomenon called transnationalism).

Sojourners

Subject to a labour flow in which temporality defines migration, sojourners are constantly on the move in search of opportunity and are perceived as such by the host country.

Chain migration

A series of international moves that link family members or a closely related group.

---

* The term "immigrant" might imply a coherent and agreed-upon object toward which individuals can express an opinion. In reality, public perceptions of immigrants ("imagined immigrants") tend to diverge from the set of people defined as immigrants by government statistics or public policy (Blinder 2013).

† Diaspora is too often applied to ever-broadening types of population movement, thus stretching the category to an awkward point (Brubaker 2005). Criteria traditionally focused on (a) dispersion, either forced or voluntary; (b) orientation to homeland as a source of value, identity, and loyalty, and (c) maintenance of a distinctive identity vis-à-vis the host country. For our purposes, "diaspora" refers to an interactive space of multiple connections and narratives (from an imagined place of origin to adoptive home) that influences a person's sense of self and citizenship in a world of increasing connections and intersections (Berns-McGown 2013).

Australia, New Zealand, the United States, and Argentina were the main migrant-receiving countries at the turn of the twentieth century (Massey et al. 1998; Castles and Miller 2009; Wanner 2011).

Migration from Europe shrank with the outbreak of the First World War, resulting in a four-decade period of stagnation. The 1920s were characterized by an economic nationalism in which restrictions were imposed on the movement of goods, capital, and labour. Migration came to a virtual standstill during the Great Depression and the Second World War. An annual average of 621,000 newcomers may have entered the United States from 1900 to 1930, but the figure free-fell to about 53,000 per year during the 1930s and 1940s (Massey 2003). After the Second World War, this decline reversed as substantial numbers of Europeans once again emigrated to traditional receiving countries, thus paving the way for the post-industrial period in which migration became truly global in scope. The 1960s increased the number of sending and receiving countries, as well as the number of migrants from the less-developed states. Migrants were often temporary foreign workers from the Middle East who went to European countries such as Germany, as well as workers imported from former colonies in the case of Britain and France. European reliance on this group for less-skilled jobs eventually created problems of integration when the economy faltered and public support dwindled (OECD 2012).

Another shift was grounded in geopolitical disruptions (Wanner 2011). Globalization reached its nadir with the collapse of the communist regime and the demise of the Cold War in the early 1990s (Massey 2003). With globalization, European countries that historically embraced large-scale emigration, including Spain and Italy, emerged as net receivers of migrants. The return of extensive cross-national flows of capital, goods, and information reinforced the status of countries such as Hungary and Poland as both receiving and sending regimes. The globalization of international migration in the 1990s and early 2000s also fortified Middle East countries and East/Southeast Asia as migrant-receiving destinations, albeit by relying on temporary workers to fill gaps in the domestic labour market. International student mobility attracted increased attention during this period, and asylum seeking emerged as a major factor and an awkward preoccupation for policy makers, particularly after the events of 9/11 (OECD 2012). These trends will probably persist in the future: The numbers of international migrants are unlikely to drop significantly, concedes the OECD (ibid.), given emigration pressures in the poorer countries, the continued globalization of the world economy, and the growing reliance of developed countries on migrants.

Currently, the world is poised for yet another migration boom. The proportion of immigrants in most industrialized countries of the North continues to grow vis-à-vis the general population. Immigrants now account for over 20 percent of the population in Australia, New Zealand, and Canada, 14 percent in Spain, 13 percent in the United States and Germany, and about 11 percent in France, Britain, and the Netherlands (Perucca 2010). The most striking feature of this global transformation is a globalization-inspired explosion of cross-border flows of investment, trade, ideas, and (to a lesser extent) people (Castles and Miller 2009). The sheer magnitude of international migration is demonstrated in Box 3.

The numbers say it all: International migration is reshaping our world (International Migration Institute 2006; Castles 2013). It plays a central role in reflecting yet advancing global transformations related to social, political, cultural, and economic change (OECD 2014a). Its centrality to domestic and international politics is well documented (and pursued in this text), and the socio-economic consequences of global migrants have proven both a source of prosperity and a cause for concern (Grugel and Piper 2007). The concomitant social dynamics and ideological shifts are encompassed in a series of practical challenges for the twenty-first century, as outlined below (also Stalker 2009; International Organization for Migration 2013).

The globalization of immigration:
> The combination of new transport technologies and economic adjustments along with political (colonial) upheavals has unleashed a worldwide movement of people. The globalization of migration means that more countries are being affected by migratory movements, both coming and going, though the fiscal impact (costs or benefits) of immigration in the host country might be negligible (OECD 2013; Jolly 2013). As a result, the dichotomy between migrant-sending and migrant-receiving countries is dissolving as most countries experience both emigration and immigration.
> International migration patterns are increasingly more complex and more diverse in connecting people and societies over ever-larger distances (International Migration Institute 2006). Once established,

3

International Migration

Estimated number of international migrants worldwide in 2010	215 million
Percentage of world's population who are migrants, 2010	3.1% (up from 2.9% in 2000)
Top five destination countries by numbers	
United States	42.8 million
Russian Federation	12.7 million
Germany	10.8 million
Saudi Arabia	7.3 million
Canada	7.2 million
Top five countries with the highest share of international migrants (including temporary foreign workers) per total population*	
Qatar	86.0%
United Arab Emirates	70.0%
Kuwait	68.8%
Jordan	45.9%
Singapore	40.7%
Bottom five countries with the lowest share of international migrants per total population	
Indonesia	0.1%
India	0.4 %
Romania	0.6 %
Nigeria	0.7%
Japan	1.7%
Permanent foreign-born population as percentage of the total population, 2009*	
Australia	31%
New Zealand	27%
Israel	25%
Canada	24%
United States	13%

If settled into one country, migrants would constitute
the world's fifth-largest country

China	1.3 billion
India	1.2 billion
United States	300 million
Indonesia	240 million
Immigrant-land	215 million

Top source countries for immigrants

Mexico	10.0 million
India	9.0 million
Bangladesh	6.5 million

Percentage of global migrants who are women	49%

Countries with the largest share of women as a percentage
of international migrants

Nepal	68%
Mauritius	63%
Barbados	61%
Montenegro	61%
Estonia	60%

Countries with the smallest share of women as a percentage
of international migrants

United Arab Emirates	27%
Qatar	26%
Oman	21%
Bhutan	18%
Bangladesh	14%

Estimated remittances sent by migrants, 2010	$440 billion
Internally displaced persons in the world, 2010	27.5 million
Number of world refuges, 2010	15.4 million

---

* But see Kobayashi, Li, and Teixeira (2012) for a slightly different set of figures.

Sources: Facts and Figures, 2011, International Migration Statistics, http://www.migration
policy.org; MPI Data Hub, Migration Facts, Stats, and Maps; Migration Policy Institute, 2011,
http://www.migrationpolicy.org.

these links are sustained and reproduced through an expanding web of social networks involving the globalization of labour, commodities, and financial markets. They are difficult to abort since the flow of immigrants takes on a life of its own as newcomers follow a pipeline of familiar destinations (Ben-David 2009).

> The uneven effects of globalization have spawned a glut of people in search of employment. Foreign-born workers in industrialized countries now comprise a growing percentage of the total labour force. Nevertheless, the search for employment is but one of many motives for international migration, although migrants generally respond to the persistent demand for labour in post-industrial economies (Massey 2003; Newland 2011).

> Staunching the flow of unwanted migrants remains a key priority for many countries. Contrary to popular belief, boosting economic development in sending countries rarely curbs their emigration (Newland 2011). Nor have large investments by foreign governments or companies meaningfully reduced out-migration pressures in developing countries. If anything, the resulting improvements may intensify decisions to leave.

> For reasons that range from opportunity to security, migrants are moving over larger distances and across a diverse array of countries (International Migration Institute 2006). Rising incidences of temporary, intermittent, return, and circular migration put the onus on a more transnational approach to integration and citizenship. The changing and complex ways in which immigrants are embedded in regional and global contexts also exert pressure on rethinking the notion of belonging and identity (ibid.).

> In a 24/7 online world of interconnectedness, migrants do not always make a clean break from home. They may nurture multiple links as "citizens of everywhere," with an inclination to move where opportunity beckons (Bitran and Tan 2013). But notions of citizenship remain anchored in the primacy of a sedentary population, with a corresponding singular (one size fits all) citizenship. The global competition for talent makes it clear that citizenship laws must address the reality of migrants as a mobile demographic situated within a global network of countries that are increasingly viewed as nodes of convenience rather than as sites of physical space (Freeland 2011).

> Framing migration at the national level is no longer appropriate (Georgi and Schatral 2011). Proposed instead is a global framework

that acknowledges the magnitude of the challenge (Arshad-Ayaz 2011). To date, moves toward global frameworks include the establishment in 1951 of the International Organization for Migration, whose primary goal as an international agency working with governments and civic society is to assist migrants and states to respond to migration in ways that benefit everyone (Georgi and Schatral 2011).

Immigration and global capitalism:

> International migration originates in the social, economic, and political transformations that accompany the expansion of capitalist markets into pre-market societies. The relatively unfettered flow of capital in a globalizing world is accompanied by a flood of dispossessed and uprooted transnational workers. The entry of markets and capital-intensive production disrupts existing economic and social arrangements. This displacement of people from customary livelihoods results in a mobile population actively searching for new ways of achieving economic security in the midst of market failures (Massey 2003). In other words, international migration stems from development itself rather than its dearth. It also reflects a real-world reaction to injustice, oppression, and inequality (Zapata-Barrero and Pécoud 2012).

> The globalization of immigration is crucial in reflecting, reinforcing, and advancing the geopolitics of global capitalism (Webb 2010). Demographic changes in immigration societies create a demand for immigrant labour, yet political interests and public concern recoil at the prospect of losing control or incurring costs. Various measures are introduced to deter migrants (especially unwanted ones) without shutting off the intake valve, while bolstering social cohesion through integration contracts and citizenship tests (Castles and Miller 2009).

> Immigrants are responding to a global demand for menial labour. Employers turn to them because of structural changes to post-industrial economies – a segmented labour market of good jobs for the labour elite versus precarious jobs that are shunned by the native-born. But even economic migrants do not base their decision to move primarily on economic considerations. Nor do migrants arbitrarily select a destination. The many hazards that accompany migration put a premium on selecting places of familiarity and connections (Poros 2011). The presence of existing social networks is a powerful inducement in minimizing the risks (Stalker 2009).

> Low-skilled and irregular migrants remain the elephant in the room. Most countries want the highly skilled, with corresponding provisions in place to attract this lucrative demographic (Esses et al. 2010). Yet they rely heavily on low-skilled workers while searching for politically acceptable ways of sourcing them without antagonizing organized labour (Collett 2010). Developed countries will continue to restrict migration from the developing world, in effect deterring so-called illegal migrants from arriving or staying, even as they lower barriers to admit those who have wealth or skills (Massey 2003).

Global migration trends:
> International migration is generally framed as following a South-North flow, but there is growing recognition that it is divided roughly equally along South-North, South-South, and North-North lines (Poros 2011). A much smaller volume follows a North to South trajectory (Newland 2011). In 2012, the United States remained the world's number one destination for permanent migration, with just over one million new settlers, followed by Germany (400,000), the United Kingdom (283,000), and Canada (258,000) (OECD 2014a).
> The movement of people is not necessarily between countries. The overwhelming majority of migrants move within their own countries. It is estimated that 740 million people are internal migrants, or nearly four times the number who migrate internationally. Even more significant is the increased cultural diversity concentrated in booming global cities, where up to 40 percent of the population may consist of culturally different migrants (International Migration Institute 2006; also Sandercock 2006).
> The world is teeming with millions of desperately poor people who want to improve their lot by migrating to developed nations. But the poorest of the poor rarely do so because migration is an expensive proposition that is beyond their reach (Stalker 2009).
> Immigrants who enter a developed country for the first time may not intend to settle permanently. They are not necessarily motivated by a desire to maximize their earnings overseas as much as to overcome economic problems at home. Temporarily working abroad helps to generate earnings of value to diversify risks, accumulate cash, and finance local production and consumption. The accumulation of foreign experiences and the exposure to new lifestyles result in a motivational

shift toward additional trips of longer duration, with the eventual likelihood of permanent settlement.

> Climate and environmental changes have a clear effect on international migration. Environmental impacts will simply increase as populations expand and natural hazards such as droughts or flooding proliferate, as competition intensifies for scarce resources, and as certain areas become uninhabitable because of rising sea levels (Susan Martin 2013). Paradoxically, however, uprooted people with few resources and fewer options will often gravitate *toward* vulnerable areas such as congested urban regions (Glennie 2011). Catastrophic environmental changes may also obliterate the very capital that people need for migrating, thus trapping them in environmentally toxic zones (ibid.).

The multi-dimensionality of international migration:

> Irregular migration is a growing global phenomenon. By 2004, up to 30 million (or 10 to 15 percent) of the world's migrants were in irregular situations – that is, without legal status in their country of residence (Bloch and Chimienti 2011). Majorities in all countries surveyed by Transatlantic Trends (2009) express concern over their presence.

> Migration is no longer about young men in search of employment. Women account for a growing cohort of international migrants (49 percent globally, Caritas Internationalis 2010), including 52 percent in Canada in 2010 (CIC 2011c), where they work as primary income earners in domestic labour, the entertainment field, factories, nursing, and teaching. Recognition is growing that migration corresponds with various stages of the life cycle, such as migration at retirement or family relocation for improved access to health care (International Migration Institute 2006).

> Family reunification represents the largest stream of legal migrants for many receiving countries. Such is the case in the United States, although Canada is an exception. And yet many of these countries, including Canada, are cracking down on the eligibility of family migrants despite evidence that points to family ties as a precondition for successful settlement and integration (Newland 2011).

> Those who emigrate abroad because of economic upheavals do not randomly disperse. They often choose destinations that are already linked to their home countries, whether through trade, treaties, or colonial links or through social ties – from student exchange programs to tourism to family.

> It's widely assumed that the exodus of skilled migrants has a negative impact on their countries of origin. (It is estimated that 29 percent of migrants to OECD countries in 2010 possessed a university degree, up from 24 percent in 2000 [Clemens 2013].) Yet there are positives for their home countries, even if they never return, including the promotion of trade and investment, the transfer of money, skills, technology, and ideas (such as democracy), the creation of businesses/entrepreneurship, and the encouragement of economic development (ibid.; Newland and Plaza 2013; Ratha 2013).

EXPLAINING GLOBAL MIGRATION: THEORIES AND PERSPECTIVES

The question of why people migrate continues to intrigue (Jeffrey Cohen 2011; Spoonley and Bedford 2012). What are the reasons behind the international migration phenomenon? For some, it stems from a combination of factors that push people out or pull them in. For others, it is a response to the spatially uneven effects of global capitalism and the worldwide penetration of direct foreign investment into developing countries (Castles and Miller 2009). For still others, neoliberal globalization is a key catalyst (Castles 2013).[1] The scale, scope, and complexity of cross-border flows have increased substantially in response to the interplay of economic restructuring and neoliberal adjustment programs and new economies of labour migration, with a corresponding reduction in government spending and downsizing of job creation (Grugel and Piper 2007; also Massey 2003, 2009). Climate change and natural disasters have also unsettled human existence, prompting many to pull up roots for fortunes elsewhere, despite border-crossing risks or host country wrath (Guterres 2007). In short, the drivers of global migration are numerous. They range from growing inequality/security gaps between the global North and global South to uneven economic development, rapid demographic shifts, technological innovations in communication and transportation, and the influence of the migration industry (Castles 2013).

In 1973, the United Nations concluded that any theorizing of migration confronted a conundrum. No one could realistically expect all hypothetically relevant factors and their relationship to be organized into a single coherent theoretical framework in an empirically testable form to guide future research (Bodvarsson and Van den Berg 2009; Bauder 2012; Kobayashi, Li, and Teixeira 2012). Forty years later, there is still no single model of immigration. According to Bodvarsson and Van den Berg (2009), sociologists, economists, political theorists, and politicians advance differing reasons for why people migrate, with the result that explanations offered in one field rarely resonate in another. Moreover, no unified theory can possibly account for the complex interplay that animates global movement (Folson 2005; Castles and Miller 2009; Newland 2011). After all, how can a single framework possibly incorporate the entirety of reasons that range from forced displacement (including desperation and persecution) and opportunity (from study to work) to cultural values (Jeffrey Cohen 2011) and adventure such as lifestyle changes (Benson and O'Reilly 2009)? In some cases, people are fleeing persecution, human rights abuses, and armed conflicts; others are escaping hardship and uncertainties in developing countries with weak economies and unstable governance; and for still others, the lure of opportunity and excitement is too much to resist (Castles and Miller 2009). This diversity of factors is rendered even more complex by non-linear circuits of return and repetition (Rygiel 2010). Many migrants, as transmigrant actors in transitioning from there to here, are not abandoning their homeland identities, sense of belonging, or social connections. Preferred instead is a sense of "being here" without necessarily abandoning an "over there."

Clearly, the politics of international migration and the dynamics of global migrants are proving a governance challenge of significant proportions. Such an assessment puts the onus on explanatory frameworks that address international migration as interdisciplinary and multi-dimensional, and generally beyond the purview of a single theory (Samers 2010; Bauder 2012). Each discipline and perspective imparts a distinctive look at different aspects behind the what, why, and how: (a) What structural factors in developing countries encourage emigration? (b) What economic forces in developed countries create a demand for migrant services? (c) What motivates migrants to move internationally in response to macro-level forces? (d) What social and economic forces account for the global movements of people, and how do they reflect, reinforce, and advance the migratory process? and (e) How do government policies respond to international movements of people (Massey 2003)? Three paradigms are relevant in responding to these questions – economic models, rational choice/push-pull/neopush-pull models, and globalization/transnational models.

Economic Models

Economic models have proven popular in explaining the flow of people from one country to another (Jennissen 2007). Marxist thought established that migration and the expansion of global capitalism are intertwined in a complex and exploitative relationship in mines, fields, and factories, culminating in trajectories of underdevelopment and dependency (Barber and Lem 2012). Neoclassic economic models argue that wage differentials between countries prime the migration pump, with labour flowing from low-wage areas to higher-wage regions. Relative deprivation models concur with this interpretation; that is, the perception of income differences prompts migration. But a new economy of labour migration model disagrees with the exclusive focus on individual workers and economic incentives. Wider social entities come into play as well, including households that, by pooling their resources, bank on remittances to justify their "overseas" investment. A dual labour market model, which reflects the pull of needed labour into more developed countries, consists of two segments: the highly skilled and the low-skilled. The latter do the jobs that the native-born spurn because of poor wages or precarious working conditions. Finally, world systems models explore migration from a global perspective. Uneven economic development because of colonialism or capitalist penetration may create imbalances that are conducive to movement across borders. These models have attracted criticism, but each possesses explanatory value, albeit as part of a more comprehensive model.

Rational Choice/Push-Pull/Neopush-Pull Models

The once popular push-pull model is straightforward enough. It links unfavourable conditions (push) in the sending country with the perceived opportunities (pull) of the host country. Emigrants are pushed out because of poor living standards, lack of economic opportunities, and political repression. They continue to be pushed out because of (a) persistent cross-country disparities, (b) economic growth in developing-world countries, (c) rural displacement and urbanization, (d) rising educational standards across the globe, (e) the expanding working-age population in developing countries, and (f) environmental stresses (Goldin, Cameron, and Balarajan 2011). They are pulled into receiving countries by economic prospects, the availability of work and opportunity because of growing labour and demographic gaps, adventure and lifestyle preferences, and political freedoms. Migrants are assumed to make a cost-benefit calculation that weighs the projected costs of moving against the expected benefits of staying (Massey 2003). According to this "rational-choice" model, people move as individuals in hopes of maximizing their opportunities, are largely unaffected by time and space constraints, and rely solely on their own resources unrelated to family and community circumstances. Not surprisingly, the single unattached migrant (usually male) dominates this model (International Migration Institute 2006).

The popular push-pull model has been criticized as ahistorical, excessively individualistic, essentialistic, deterministic, blinded by the principle of rational choice, and too market-oriented (Higgins 2013). Nor does it fit well with the transmigrant/transnational approach. In framing immigration as a linear, calculated (rational), and mechanical movement of people from there to here, this static conceptual framework is currently challenged by models that emphasize immigration as a field of flows and linkages entailing high levels of complexity, diversity, mobility, and contextuality (Simmons 2010). Or as a lead article in *The Economist* (2011) put it, "In contrast to a flat world of maps where sharp lines demonstrate the end of one country and the beginning of another, the real world is more fluid since people do not have borders in the way that parcels of land do, but wander and migrate from place to place." The robust rationality at the heart of the push-pull model is also thought to gloss over the non-economic dimensions of the migration experience. People are known to make irrational or impulsive decisions based on insufficient information or resources, and decision making may occur in contexts that are largely beyond personal control.

As noted earlier, the concept of migration is increasingly framed as a verb/process rather than a noun/thing. This shift tends to undermine the legitimacy of the push-pull model. Reality is more complicated than that conveyed by "economic man" models, as Massey (2003) argues, although policy makers continue to base their decisions on a host of false assumptions. A push-pull model can be expanded by folding its rationality into a more dynamic, complex, and contextual framework (Sirojudin 2009). A neopush-pull model acknowledges an interplay of agency and structure (people make choices, albeit within contexts that may be beyond their control) (also Bakewell, de Haas, and Kubal 2011). This model marries the idea of migrants as free and rational agents in pursuit of pragmatic gain with that of wider forces largely beyond their control, ranging from the socio-economic relations between countries to the centrality of family and friends in facilitating movement and ongoing transmigrant linkages (O'Reilly 2012). A more holistic push-pull model addresses the following interplay of contextual dynamics that puts significant weight on the effects of historical relations between the economic interests of wealthy states and global economic institutions in propelling the global movement of people: (a) rational-choice individuals, households, and communities who calculate options involving cost/benefit considerations, (b) market-driven supply and demand, (c) world systems theories that see immigration as a response to capitalist penetration in uprooting members of developing societies whose livelihood becomes linked to commodity (rather than subsistence) production, and (d) the centrality of networks and relations in supporting the decision to move (Massey 2003; Higgins 2013). But even this revamped push-pull model may prove no explanatory match for various globalization models and transnational paradigms (Faist 2010).

Globalization/Transnational Models

References to immigration as a global phenomenon are not new (Inglis 2007; also Kivisto 2001). Variations in dependency/underdevelopment theories and world systems theories embraced earlier versions of global migration. Dependency theories challenged modernization theories by arguing that contact with the West created more underdevelopment. World systems theories put the emphasis on distortions of power, privilege, and wealth among world regions (Freitas, Levatino, and Pécoud 2012). According to this "world-system" mode of thinking, a global division of labour enriches wealthy (metropolitan) countries and fosters an underdeveloped dependency in poorer (periphery) countries. Migration reflected this structural inequality as the dispossessed and the desperate scoured the world in search of work and survival.

Newer versions go one step farther because of changing circumstances. A globalization perspective emphasizes the unequal distribution of global economic and political power as a principal driver of international migration.[2] The global economy unleashes strong forces and the systemic conditions that incite larger and more diverse flows of migrants from developing countries (Pulitano 2013). A reliance on cheap labour in capital-rich economies generates an unofficial demand for low-skilled migrant workers in contrast to an openly articulated plea for skilled workers. Migrant flows are intensified by the combination of structural adjustment with neoliberal governance philosophies and the growing reliance on commodity export for wealth creation. Structural adjustment policies implemented by the World Bank or International Monetary Fund exert additional pressure on the world's poor to troll the world for opportunities abroad. The establishment of regional trade agreements provides a catalyst and a framework in prompting people's movements despite efforts to bolster border controls against a rush of "unwanted" migrants (Castles and Miller 2009; Skeldon 2010; Bloch and Chimienti 2011). The consequences can prove catastrophic, as demonstrated in Box 4.

Transnationalism as a paradigm acknowledges the centrality of globalization as the context for global migration (de Wenden 2011). Globalization is transformative in establishing a global system of analysis, with the border-spanning movement of labour representing one of these flows accompanying the reconfiguration of societies and national economies along cross-border lines (Hiebert and Ley 2003). References to globalization as a theoretical lens reinforce the importance of shifting from a nation-state-centred analysis to the global system as the primary unit of explanation. Consider the contrast to conventional explanatory frameworks. So-called nationalist paradigms associated with push-pull and rational-choice theories defined nation-states as the primary units of analysis, assumed that migrants made a definitive break with their homelands, and posited unidirectional migration that culminated in permanent displacement (Brubaker 2005; Dunn 2005). Migrants were depicted as relatively isolated individuals who abandoned their home country, discarded traditional social ties and cultural values, and struggled to cope in the new country because they had no other choice. Christine Inglis (2007, 95) sums it up:

> Throughout the twentieth century the focus of much mainstream social science research on migratory movements was on the New World countries of immigration such as Australia, Canada, and the United States, which were committed to national development based on extensive immigration. The focus of theorising was on patterns of settlement and incorporation ... The dominant theoretical model ... was that of assimilation which anticipated a

process whereby incorporation involved the total "disappearance" of the newcomers and minorities into the larger society.

A transnational model signals the onset of a new paradigm for the study of global migration (Faist 2010). Migrant transnationalism also challenges the governance of modern nation-states (Halm 2012). Just as contemporary globalization differs in logic and scope from the worldwide movements of people and goods during the nineteenth century, no less different is the current model of transnationalism. A global frame of reference rejects the validity of assuming that people will live their lives in one place, according to one set of national or cultural norms, in countries with impermeable borders (Levitt 2004). Rather, they are likely to work, pray, socialize, and express political interests in several cross-cutting contexts. The notion of migration as a single journey is rejected as well in explaining newcomer movements, identities, and communities (Robinson 1998; but see Kivisto 2001). A broader conceptual framework is proposed, involving a sensitivity to the multiple realities in which migrants operate. Flows and counter-flows of people, information, goods, and services are set against the cross-national connections that absorb individuals into networks of families and communities (Castles and Miller 2009). Cheap communication and travel secure the basis for more flexible and circular movements of people who preserve their links with home (Waters 2003; Collett 2010). A transnational model also examines both poles of the migration flow, especially where movement is driven by the presence of prior links between countries because of colonization, trade, investment, military activities, political influence, and cultural ties (Folson 2005). Shifting the focus of immigration as a noun (thing) to a verb (process) reinforces the worth of a transnational model, as is conveyed by Glick Schiller, Basch, and Blanc-Szanton (1992, 1), early pioneers in this field:

> Our earlier conceptions of immigrants and migrants no longer suffice. The word *immigrant* evokes images of permanent rupture, of the uprooted, the abandonment of old patterns, and the painful learning of a new language and culture. Now, a new kind of migrating population is emerging, composed of those whose networks, activities, and patterns of life encompass both their host

4 OBSERVATION

Crisis in Food Self-Sufficiency: Structural Causes of Mexican Labour Migration

*Extralegal activities burgeon whenever the legal system
imposes rules that thwart the expectation of those it excludes.*
— HERNANDO DE SOTO (2000)

AMERICANS ARE TORN regarding the 11 to 12 million undocumented migrants who live in the United States. Should they abide by the rule of law, demonstrate compassion for migrants, respect human rights, or acknowledge economic necessity (Pickus and Skerry 2006; Meissner et al. 2013)? Those who want more enforcement and deportation disagree with those who wish to expand the temporary worker program and to legitimize a path toward legalization for the undocumented (Sumption and Bergeron 2013; also see Chapter 6).

Too often ignored in these debates is the wider structural context that propels the unauthorized movement of Mexican migrant workers (see Castles 2013). It can be traced to contradictions in the structure of the NAFTA (North American Free Trade Agreement) economy. The very nature of free trade agreements such as NAFTA demonstrates the ability of the economically powerful to hammer home an advantage, with potentially devastating consequences for the weaker partner and local economies. NAFTA may have opened America to trade and investment, but it slammed shut the door to Mexican labour, despite its centrality to the American economy (Jayapal 2011). NAFTA also maximized American access to Mexican resources, markets, and agricultural and manufacturing sectors, even as it restricted Mexican access to US transportation, agricultural, and textile sectors. Worse still, Mexicans were unable to maintain their agricultural subsidies and manufacturing tariffs (although the United States maintained most of its own). As a result, increasingly impoverished Mexican farmers had to compete with subsidized industrialized farming in the United States. American corn flooded the Mexican market at prices below the cost of local production. Nearly 1.3 million Mexican farmers were driven out of business, and incomes plummeted for the remaining self-employed farmers, from about 2,000 pesos per month in 1991 to 228 pesos in 2003 (ibid.). Pramila Jayapal (ibid.), executive director of OneAmerica, captures the despair and dearth of options open to Mexican farmers due to the loss of food self-sufficiency and the impossibility of a living wage:

> What would you do if you could no longer feed your family? What would you do if your country's economy has just been destroyed by a neighboring country to the north and now their economy was booming and there were jobs there that needed more and more agricultural workers because their own workers were moving away from that kind of labour in the fields? What would you do if your wife was sick, or your children could not get an education where you were anymore?

In short, this exercise in the US-Mexico regional integration process known as NAFTA broadened the asymmetries between the two countries. Without the benefit of free labour mobility, Mexico's asymmetrical integration into the North American economy negatively affected its food self-sufficiency and labour sovereignty, resulting in substantial out-migration rates of up to 500,000 undocumented Mexicans each year to the United States, primarily as a cheap source of unskilled labour (Otero 2011). The cheap labour/export-led model created a stagnant economy owing to the declining manufacturing sector (the assembly plants of the maquiladora industry – foreign-owned factories in which imported parts are assembled into products for export). It also hastened Mexico's incorporation into and dependency upon the orbit of the American economic system (Delgado-Wise and Guarnizo 2007).

and home societies. Their lives cut across national boundaries and bring two societies into a single social field.

In short, a transnational paradigm offers new possibilities for understanding international immigration along contemporary lines. The interplay of globalizing and transnational processes and "technologies of deterritorialization" (Sun et al. 2011, 515), alongside the mobility of global migrants, sets the stage for changing how we think and talk about migration. This paradigm in the making offers new assumptions, posing new questions and new theories and methodologies that transcend the concept of states as containers of society. A sociology beyond society defines reality not as fixed places (noun) but as implicated within complex networks, relations, connections, and processes – not spaces of places but spaces of flows (Urry 2000). A transnational model challenges an exclusively nationalistic framework by locating migrants within global social fields (Levitt 2004; Mawani 2008; Castles and Miller 2009). This model eschews static paradigms with their sedentary bias, stable structures, fixed territories, and linear models. Proposed instead are mobility-based perspectives involving social entities within systems of fluidity and movement, or what Bauman (2000) calls liquid modernity, with complex networks of social relations as transmigrants construct multiple and deterritorialized homes, belongings, and identities (Sheller and Urry 2006). Prominence is also attached to human agency in formulating migration flows (Mainwaring 2013). Migrants are not passive victims of structural forces but actors who seek to improve livelihoods and, in the process, change the world they live in through their actions and interactions (Freitas, Levatino, and Pécoud 2012).

The discursive shift has proven invaluable in reconceptualizing immigrants and immigration with respect to their impact on sending and receiving countries. A transnational model embraces the principles that (a) migration cannot be understood within the context of a single state (either sending or receiving); (b) migratory movements are not unidirectional but rather complex, fluid, and ongoing; (c) migration and settlement (or incorporation) must be viewed as dynamic and interrelated; (d) differing magnitudes of scale are involved, from the personal to the community, from the national to the international (Inglis 2007); and (e) national models of society building are compromised by the transmigrant identities and belonging that transcend national boundaries (Fleras 2012c; Carruthers 2013). In other words, a distinction is critical. Transnationalism as a process may prove an exaggeration in the real world. After all, migrants may prefer a definitive break from their homeland rather than diasporic ties (Levitt 2004). But transnationalism as a paradigm shift is proving transformative as an explanatory framework that captures the realities and dilemmas of global migration.

A drift away from a methodological nationalism of the past is consequential in other ways. Attention is drawn to those who do not migrate yet stay connected through diasporic networks. It also emphasizes both local-to-local connections as they are integrated into vertical and horizontal connections across borders; questions common sense categories such as integration and settlement; and reinforces how multiple belongings are not mutually exclusive but involve a simultaneity of experiences and connections across fields. Peggy Levitt (ibid., 3) speaks glowingly of a transnational lens and the implication of a social fields paradigm for analyzing the once improbable – that migrants increasingly construct a constellation of strategies at different stages of their lives within the context of a host country's integration commitments:

> A transnational lens, then, is both a perspective and a variable. It departs from a different set of assumptions about social organization than those usually employed by social scientists and policy makers. It locates migrants within social fields that combine several national territories rather than expecting them to move back and forth between two impermeable nation-states and exchange one national identity for another.

A transnational model is also proving gender sensitive. It acknowledges the differing experiences of women and men in both the sending and receiving countries, including how gender relations are transformed by movements across borders (Caritas Internationalis 2010; Piper and French 2011). This approach draws attention to the placement of both male and female workers within the specific segmented labour market to which they migrate. It also situates their aims and strategies within a local/national/international nexus. A transmigrant perspective on the gendered experiences of refugees and immigrants links places of origin, processes of migration and flight, and places of new settlement. For example, consider the gendered dimensions of so-called astronaut families and satellite kids. Male parents may return to their country of origin to maximize financial opportunities, whereas the women and children remain in the host country for the purposes of education or naturalization (Waters 2003). The implications are promising. The varying experiences of both women and men at home and abroad are rendered more visible when gendered migration is situated transnationally. As well, a transnational focus situates gendered migration processes within a global political economic context. For example, intensification of export-led production in the developing world differently implicates male and female workers because of the contested and changing roles of women in both the receiving and sending countries (Strategic Workshop 2002; Boyd 2006).

Putting Transnationality under a Critical Lens

There is much to commend in endorsing a transnational model of migration. Migration is no longer perceived as a social problem, as it once was because of the sedentary bias that informed migration studies. A transmigration paradigm re-embeds migration within a general understanding of society and social/global change. The end result is liberating in coaxing fresh perspectives from the complexities of contemporary migratory processes (Castles 2010, 2013). Admittedly, one should be skeptical about grand claims involving a distinction between national and transnational models. Simplistic assumptions that challenge unidirectionality, permanence and finality, and assimilationism may satisfy model building without necessarily reflecting reality (Brubaker 2005). Excessive emphasis on transmigration and transnationality as radical breaks and epochal shifts may be equally misplaced. Research to date concentrates on case studies of those who are engaged in transnational activities, thus giving the impression that transmigration is perhaps more widespread than reality permits (Levitt 2004). In brief, transnationalism is not a new phenomenon. It has a long history, particularly in the Asia Pacific region where the "home" state seeks to maintain contact with former citizens, and the receiving country capitalizes on their links for economic or diplomatic reasons (Kivisto 2001; Inglis 2007). Moreover, not all migrants maintain transnational connections, opting instead for a clean break. Instead of continuously partaking of transnational practices (Levitt

2004), most migrants may prove to be occasional transmigrant activists, sometimes identifying with their homeland or engaging in actual relations and practices, but also focusing on activities in their country of settlement.

Too often the concept of transnationality implies a world of collapsing nation-states. But it may be premature to bury the salience of the nation-state as a difference-maker. A globalized world of transmigrant movements across seemingly porous borders does not necessarily undermine the relevance of the nation-state in defining who gets in, why, and how. Nevertheless, there is sharp debate over the relevance and relation of the nation-state against the backdrop of global markets, multilateralism, and regional integration (Castles and Miller 2009).

For some, a global order anchored in the Westphalian doctrine of the sovereign nation-state is dissolving into a more fluid and contested concept of living together. The term "translocality" conveys the idea that nation-states are increasingly displaced as the exclusive mediator of connectivity, communication, and commitment between and across political and migrant communities (Lyons and Mandaville 2008). Even reference to the nation-state is being whittled away as the technology revolution renders the idea of physical space less relevant for a socially networked global society (Freeland 2011). Lastly, migration processes are becoming so entrenched yet resistant to government control, as Castles and Miller (2009) argue, that new political forms may emerge, with a corresponding realignment of patterns related to interdependence, transnational organizations, and bilateral and regional cooperation.

Others are skeptical of any transformative change. The proliferation of transnational networks with nodes of control in multiple locations may be one thing. But despite announcements of its demise, the nation-state is unlikely to disappear because of migratory movements. It remains firmly in control as the fundamental unit of organization in the international order; it continues to command the loyalties and passions of most humans; it increasingly defines itself as a community of values rather than a disparate collection of migrants, and its boundaries remain as tightly controlled as ever, albeit with varying degrees of success (Bridget Anderson 2013). Moreover, in fostering the smooth accumulation of capital, capitalism and globalization have paradoxically affirmed the enduring import of the nation-state. Even reference to the free movement of people in a borderless world is an exaggeration.

More accurately, mobility is relatively free for the skilled from the First World but not for the unskilled from the periphery (Tendoh 2009). What prevails is a case of continuity in change, since newer patterns of international migration (from transmigration to circular migration) are not nearly as new as pundits and polls would have us believe (Kivisto 2001).

For still others, it's not a case of either/or. Nation-states may no longer be the only game in town, but they are hardly irrelevant, at least, judging by how secessionist movements strive to secure the legitimacy and power associated with formal nationhood. Nation-states determine who gets in (Earnest 2008), and they also confer formal citizenship and corresponding entitlements. In other words, a sense of perspective is helpful: The nation-state continues to play a role in global affairs, though not exclusively. It constitutes one of many (f)actors that affect people's lives, options, or constraints (Barcham 2005). In that sense, a transnational model provides a useful corrective in situating immigration as something that happens within a social field, involving interlocking networks of social relations across borders and between communities, linking those who stay and those who move.

PARADOXES IN GLOBAL MIGRATION: OPEN MIGRATION, CLOSED BORDERS

The centrality of international migration to contemporary existence has proven paradoxical. On the one hand is a positive spin – that immigrants are a quick-fix solution to complex problems related to labour shortages. On the other hand is a dark side – involuntary or forced migration due to capitalist expansion and corporate inroads, ranging from slavery and indentured labour in the colonies to guest/temporary foreign workers in industrialized economies (Grugel and Piper 2007; ILO 2014). Or consider the paradox: Immigrants are seen as beneficial to society building because they bring demographic and economic value, but they are also seen as troublesome constituents who create problems involving costs or inconvenience (Bloch and Chimienti 2011). The politics of global migration is dilemma inducing for politicians and policy makers. Those who are vocally in favour of yet more international migration include special interest groups such as employers, ethnic lobbies, immigration lawyers and consultants, and humanitarian groups. Opposed are nativist politicians, labour unions, and environmentalists who demand greater government control even if restrictions may trample on human rights protocols.

The politicization of global migration has proven double-edged in other ways. Politicians and policy makers confront mounting public pressure to control migration. But the root causes of international movements may be beyond their control. Moreover, few societies (but especially the settler societies of New Zealand, Australia, Canada, and the United States) have the stomach to openly confront the challenges of migration for fear of disrupting national identities, exposing their weaknesses in governance and security, and eroding their capacity to enforce unpopular laws. In the hope of giving the impression of control without appearing heavy-handed, they turn to symbolic policy instruments such as enhanced border protection, get-tough disincentives that criminalize asylum seekers (see Chapter 6), and immigrant detention tools (Massey 2003; Hall 2012). The internationalization of human rights generates yet more challenges (Abji 2013). Moves to ratify international legal instruments for protecting the rights of migrant workers have faltered over fears of imperilling national interests (Ruhs 2012). Guaranteeing protection for all migrants regardless of legal status may compromise a country's right to political and economic sovereignty vis-à-vis the rights of non-citizens (Bauder 2011; Lamey 2011b). Not surprisingly, migrants who are in search of jobs or safety tend to be framed as problems, rather than as victims of corporate-driven global capitalism.

Migration constitutes a defining feature of the current era, a world defined by globalization, open borders, and countries that are structurally dependent on migrants for economic and social reasons (Hollifield 2012; Bridget Anderson 2013). References to a new borderless world sprang into life with the fall of the Berlin Wall and the onset of the post–Cold War paradigm, which is constructed around a belief in the unfettered movement of capital and goods (Carr 2012a). But a migration without borders (much less a borderless world) has proven more elusive. The Universal Declaration of Human Rights may have stipulated the right to leave a country, but there is no corresponding right to enter another one, a contradiction that nullifies the right to exit (Pécoud and de Guchteneire 2009). Rather than eliminating barriers to migrant movements, governments around the world have introduced exclusionary border enforcement strategies – from detention to removal (Goldring and Landolt 2012, 9) – to deter would-be migrants from work or asylum (Steiner 2009; Christopher Anderson 2013). But conventional forms of border control are losing their effectiveness.

New measures have been introduced to regulate entry of unauthorized/ unwanted migrants (Christopher Anderson 2013), including mandatory indefinite detention, use of offshore processing (as in Australia's Pacific Solution of transferring asylum seekers to Nauru or Manus Island [Young 2013]), extensive naval interdiction programs, and punitive smuggling penalties (Grewcock 2013).

Clearly, then, a global migration crisis looms (Hollifield 2012; Khory 2012; Christopher Anderson 2013). This crisis is reflected in complex and ongoing debates over national security, state sovereignty, territorial integrity, citizenship, and unity and identity within the broader context of global politics and intersecting processes related to economic crisis, border security, regulation programs, human rights, immigration settlement and integration, and climate change. Much of the controversy springs from the historically high levels of international migration, together with a movement of people across porous yet fortified borders. But whereas mobility may be promoted and celebrated, at least in theory, international migration is feared and repressed by territorially bounded and security-conscious countries (de Wenden 2011). Even skilled migrants are subject to fundamental dilemmas and numerous tradeoffs ranging from conflicting rights to opposing political principles (Freitas, Levatino, and Pécoud 2012). Not surprisingly, discourses pertaining to national security and border control inform and shape contemporary debates and analytical frameworks (Khory 2012). The scope and impact of managed migration responses are pervasive and punishing, including militarized border zones, outsourcing migration controls to countries with weak traditions of refugee protection, third-country agreements, pushbacks of migrants' boats from territorial waters, detention centres pending deportation, stringent visa requirements for refugee-producing countries, bureaucratic obstacles that allow countries to evade their legal obligations to process asylum appeals, and satellite technologies to monitor, intercept, and deter.

A fundamental paradox is at play in curbing the international migration flows championed by global economic dynamics (Massey 2003; McGovern 2012). Migration prior to 1914 may have been relatively open (at least for Europeans who emigrated to settler colonies), but current flows are increasingly constrained by policies that bar the permanent import of the poor and unskilled from developing countries (Brubaker 2005; Grugel and Piper 2007). The permeability of borders in the face of determined asylum seekers and undocumented migrants has unleashed powerful forces that create larger and diverse flows of migrants, yet also promotes conditions in developed countries for more restrictive controls (Massey 2009). To be sure, social elites can move around at will because they live in a world anxious for their skills or wealth. But the vast majority of the world's population endures an opposite experience – increasingly stringent border control (Scheffer 2010). And yet governments are unable to curb the migration-generating forces that are largely beyond their control, and the constitutional order of liberal-democratic societies exerts additional pressure to respect universal human rights protocols pertaining to migrants (Ruhs 2012).

The conclusion seems inescapable: A global apartheid has emerged in which the rich industrialized countries collude to create a worldwide system of migration controls that serves the interest of markets and global elites while excluding the impoverished from admission. To the extent that a borderless world exists, Ghassan Hage (2014) writes, it remains the reserve of the economic and cultural elite (artists, academics), in effect reinforcing how class intersects with race and often gender to create sites of spatial openness alongside a proliferation of protective walls (Brown 2014). The limiting of people's freedom of movement occurs just as the need to migrate is greater than ever because of free market ideologies, resource wars, environmental despoliation, and the rise of authoritarian states that work in cahoots with transnational corporations (Fekete 2012a). A vast military-industrial complex has evolved to police unwanted migrants, despite the contradiction of fortifying national frontiers in an era of footloose capitalism, blatant inequities between countries, and growing demand for migrant labour (Harding 2012). A human cost is unavoidable when the world's richest countries concede the centrality of migration to offset their skill shortages and ageing/declining population but then turn around and revoke the entry of migrants from the poorest countries who are in search of a fairer share (Carr 2012b; Fekete 2012b). The creation of militarized borders within a system of managed global migration plays into the politics of deterrence. It also criminalizes asylum seekers and excludes migrant workers from entitlements and access to the welfare state. Ironically, the creation of the fortress mentality for defining who gets in may ramp up (however inadvertently) the flow of so-called illegal migrants that this model of border enforcement purports to abolish (Carr 2012b).

Obviously, the age of migration is riddled with paradoxes. To one side are endless references to transmigration and transnationalism in a globalized world of international migration flows and pathways that are increasingly fluid, diverse, and unconventional (Benton 2013). To the other side is the looming presence of national security, the securitization of migration, and border control in shaping contemporary debates over migration and immigration policies (Mountz 2010; Khory 2012). As Reece Jones (2013) from the North American Congress on Latin America points out in analyzing the aftermath of the 1989 Berlin Wall collapse, the age of migration is not what it appears to be, especially when the rich countries of the global North flex their muscles in deciding how to open the pipeline. Immigration appears to have become an instrument over which to exercise control in a time of great uncertainty, change, and fear (Papademetriou 2012; Bridget Anderson 2013). The construction of 27 new walls and fences on political borders by both democracies and totalitarian regimes – ostensibly for security purposes but also for internal reasons, from preserving sovereignty to protecting cultures – makes a mockery of the new mobility (and cosmopolitanism) as a human right.[3] The interplay of increasing border restrictions and escalating anti-immigrant tirades (Rodríguez-García 2012), combined with the complexity and scale of international migration, intensifies the need for fresh approaches to conceptualizing migration. New models, theories, and practices to address and accommodate these flows (Joppke and Siedle 2012) must complement a rethinking of migration in terms of its impact on both sending and receiving countries.

In sum, optimism and pessimism jostle at the confluence of international migration. The political and economic contours of an emerging new order remain largely unclear: The conventional and the old refuse to relinquish ground, whereas the new struggles to capture a critical mass of support to advance its agenda. Proposed as a response to the paradox is a compromise that bridges the extremes between open borders and the fortress mentality (Massey 2003). Rather than a problem to solve, international migration should be framed and managed as a reciprocal exchange involving the overlapping interests of both sending and receiving countries (Newland 2011). Policy makers should acknowledge global migration as a natural part of economic globalization in need of international cooperation for effective management. Just as flows of capital and commodities are managed by multilateral agreements and institutions (such as NAFTA and the World Trade Organization) for the benefit of trading partners, so too should international migration come under the aegis of multilateral frameworks. Multilateral moves to maximize benefits and minimize costs for migrants and migration countries could prove a win-win development for everyone involved, even if the benefits are not necessarily apparent at the outset.

PART 2

immigration canada

CANADA'S IMMIGRATION PROGRAM possesses an enviable reputation as a principled framework for stipulating who gets in (Biles, Burstein, and Frideres 2008; Reitz 2012a). There is much to admire in a system that is grounded on colour-blind principles, transparent in process, universalistic in application, and equitable in outcomes. However valid such accolades, a less flattering narrative looms as well. Canada's approach to managed migration may offer an edge in the governance sweepstakes (Harell and Stolle 2010). Nevertheless, its immigration program is not immune to criticism in light of hidden agendas, underlying premises, designs, structure, and consequences both intended and unintended (Bissett 2013). Nor should its exalted status exempt it from exploring immigration packages from elsewhere for "best practices." Comparisons to the United States and Australia throw the strengths and weaknesses of Canada's immigration program into sharper relief. Criticisms of the program are varied and selective as well as constructive yet negative. They focus primarily on the quantity and quality of newcomers, including criticisms of the refugee status determination system, which many see as in desperate need of a major makeover.

Recent changes to the immigration program have proven no less controversial in responding to shifting Canadian realities and current government agendas. Under the Conservative government, Canada is overhauling its immigration program by cutting backlogs and excising abuses as well as introducing new programs and fine-tuning existing ones (Boyd 2013). 2013 was no exception in forging a fast, flexible, and focused system that Immigration Minister Chris Alexander proclaims will be without compare by global standards (Wingrove 2014b). Yet these neoliberal initiatives in advancing a demand- rather than supply-based immigration agenda also reflect a downside: namely, increased vulnerabilities for immigrants and refugees largely because of a slanted emphasis on economic priorities over family reunification and refugee protection (CCR 2014). They include a package of moves toward heightened securitization of Canadian borders; proposed tightening of citizenship requirements, making it more difficult to acquire but easier to lose; stricter criteria for families to reunite on a permanent basis; tighter restrictions on asylum seekers to access protection on humanitarian grounds; and increased provincial/employer roles in the selection of economic migrants. These game-changing developments raise a number of difficult questions that cannot be left unanswered without imperilling Canada's long-term interests. Do Canadians want a ruthlessly pragmatic shift in immigration policy to override ethical concerns and principles of justice (Siddiqui 2013b)? What level of importance should be attached to economic considerations such as labour recruitment in making decisions about immigrants? Should the immigration program be transformed into a platform that treats immigrants as just-in-time labour commodities for employers rather than as citizens-in-waiting for Canadian communities? Why should decisions about immigration management and admissions be monopolized by the executive branch of the federal government (including the minister of immigration) instead of shared with public servants, parliamentary scrutiny, and consultation with the general public (Boyd 2013)?

In short, radical changes to Canada's immigration program are making it more difficult to enter and stay but easier to detain and remove. The creation of a two-tier migration program is complicated by the prospect of second-class citizenship for some new Canadians if the proposed Citizenship Act is enacted (Adams, Macklin, and Omidvar 2014). The charge that Canada is losing its status as a global pacesetter in migration management puts the onus on an open national debate about "who gets in, how, and why" rather than on the current system, in which seemingly innocuous changes are surreptitiously folded into marginally related omnibus bills (Beiser and Bauder 2014). Now more than ever, in other words, Canadians need to pay more attention to what is going on with regard to federal immigration management if they want to build a Canada that everybody – both newcomers and Canadian-born – can be proud of.

Part 2 of this book begins by exploring the principles, politics, and practices of Canada's current immigration model. Chapter 3 is primarily concerned with analyzing admission categories with regard to who got/gets in, how, and why. The chapter acknowledges that Canada is an outlier among immigrant societies in actively soliciting immigrants (E.G. Austin 2011). Unlike European countries that have only recently emerged as destinations for mass migration, Canada was forged by immigrants, and it has a long history of managing immigration for nation-building purposes (Boyd and

Alboim 2012). The chapter pays homage to this centrality by providing a historical overview of immigration as an ongoing dynamic of patterns and practices, in the process suggesting both continuities and changes. It continues by deconstructing the immigration program at the level of family and economic class admissions (the refugee class is discussed in Chapter 5). Canada's immigration program has undergone significant changes to tighten the criteria for admission; to improve the economic outcomes of newcomers whose labour market performance has deteriorated in recent years; to better respond to short-term regional labour shortages associated with commodity booms; to redistribute new Canadians beyond the three largest cities; and to limit abuses to the admission process (Ferrer, Picot, and Riddell 2012). The chapter concludes by dissecting current debates over Canada's immigration program.

Chapter 4 examines recent moves to recalibrate Canada's immigration program along neoliberal lines (Fleras 2010). Like other countries, Canada is increasingly selective in attracting the right kind of immigrant (namely, those who are relatively young, with strong language proficiency, recognizable education credentials, and a job offer or in-demand skills) (Levinson 2013). It also discourages the entry of unwanted migrants (from asylum seekers to the low-skilled) through a combination of regulations, restrictions, and interdiction (also Jurado, Brochmann, and Dolvik 2013). The politics of admission is played out in differing ways. To one side are moves to fast-track designer immigrants (low-cost, high-yield individuals) as permanent residents; to the other side is a focus on demand-side temporary foreign workers (TFW), whose precarious employment status resonates with "guest worker" overtones. In between are designated migrants whose provisional status secures a possible entry point for admission. The creation of this new three-tiered track – designer, demand, or designated – reinforces a reliance on (im)migrants as commodified labour instead of Canada-building citizens. The chapter analyzes how Canada's commitment to customize immigration labour market lines is proving double-edged, as is the case with the Temporary Foreign Worker Program. A welcome yet worrying departure is in place that arguably strives to balance Canada's short-term labour market needs with long-term society-building goals (Segal, Elliott, and Mayadas 2009; Haimin Zhang 2012).

The global refugee crisis strikes at the heart of international relations, contemporary developments, and current debates (Betts and Loescher 2011; Bull 2011). Debates focus on causes, consequences, and responses to human displacement, especially as the concept of "who is a refugee" expands and border controls stiffen. Millions of people around the world appear to be circumventing normal immigration channels in search of safety and/or work, thus making it more important than ever to solidify a system for distinguishing the genuine from the bogus (Collacott 2010b). Not surprisingly, one of the more controversial domains in Canada's immigration program is refugee status determination – that is, which asylum seekers are entitled to refuge and protection. The Refugee Protection Division of the Immigration and Refugee Board (IRB) is entrusted with this mandate, for better or worse, and Chapter 5 examines whether the IRB is capable of addressing the questions of "who is a refugee?" "how do we find out?" "is the system working?" and "is it fair?" Controversial efforts to correct the flaws in the refugee program have done little to dampen disagreements or forge a consensus. The chapter concludes by asking what must be the obvious question: Is it possible to construct a better refugee status determination system for those who need protection from persecution or disasters without trampling on the rights of those with unverified claims?

In an effort to sharpen our understanding of Canada's immigration program, Chapter 6 examines America's immigration program along historical lines and contemporary debates. The chapter demonstrates that, despite sharing a common border, Canada and the United States endorse fundamentally different logics for determining who gets in. America's emphasis on family-based immigration stands in stark opposition to Canada's focus on economic immigrants within the context of labour market needs. The fact that the US-Mexico border is somewhat porous creates a political crisis that threatens to derail, divide, and diminish. The chapter also demonstrates the need for a mindset shift to address the crisis of undocumented migrants. As explained by Howard Zinn, author of *A People's History of the United States,* in praising Guskin and Wilson's *Politics of Immigration* (2007), "We desperately need to put aside false information about immigrants, to see them as we see ourselves, with honesty and compassion."

3

who got in? who gets in?

CONTINUITY AND CHANGE
IN CANADA'S IMMIGRATION PROGRAM

MANAGING IMMIGRATION, IMAGINING MIGRANTS

A PROACTIVE AND principled program of immigrant admission underpins the basis of an immigration society. Canada is no exception to this society-building rule (also Reitz 2012b). Numerous formal guidelines are in place for defining who is accepted (Boyd and Alboim 2012). A series of protocols regulate the intake of new Canadians in an effort to (a) buffer Canada from excessive numbers and unwanted admissions if open borders were to prevail, (b) ensure sufficient resources for the settlement and integration of those who enter conventionally (including $600 million allocated for 2011-12) (CIC 2011b), and (c) exercise Canada's sovereign right to define membership (who belongs). Certainly, a principled approach to immigration and immigrant admission invariably entails a complex set of regulations. These rules also attract criticism as intrusive or excessive when they ensnarl immigrants in red tape and bureaucratic delays. Nevertheless, there is much to commend in an immigration program that takes a fair approach to annual numbers, source countries, and proportions accepted under each admission category.

The imperative to regulate who gets in is not without justification. It is estimated that about 13 percent of the world's population, if given a chance, would resettle in another country (Anderssen 2012). Contrary to popular belief, however, Canada isn't the first choice for aspirants;

the United States is first, the United Kingdom second, and Canada third. Another survey by the OECD (2014a) ranked Canada fourth in the total number of permanent residents who landed in 2012, behind the United States, Germany, and the United Kingdom. Recent changes to the immigration program may make Canada a less attractive destination (Black and Keung 2012; Keung 2013a). Under former immigration minister Jason Kenney (2012a), Ottawa implemented the following restrictions: a prioritization of English- and French-language skills; a proactive linking of Canadian employers with prospective overseas immigrants; a reliance on just-in-time or ready-for-work immigrants; a focus on labour market needs rather than human capital models; a rejection of skilled worker applicants whose credentials fall off the labour grid; a two-year moratorium on parental sponsorships and federal skilled workers who lack job guarantees; suspension of the entrepreneur class; and an annual cap of seven hundred for the investor category (now scrapped) (Bellissimo 2012). Additional changes include a steep rise in temporary worker visas without any public discussion over merits or costs; entitling corporations to deduct up to 15 percent of high-end temporary workers' wages (since rescinded); and eliminating access to special health benefits for unskilled migrant workers during the off season (Keung 2012b). Somewhat less controversial are significant increases in the number of provincial nominees under a patchwork quilt of admissions and an expanded number of entry portals instead of a single gateway (Alboim 2009; Fleras 2010; Kelley and Trebilcock 2010). Finally, the processing of refugee claimants on a case-by-case basis is being superseded by an approach grounded on country of origin (safe versus non-safe) and method of arrival (massed versus individual) – a heavy-handed response that penalizes all asylum seekers regardless of circumstances (Hussan, Dill, and Majeed 2012).

Criticism aside, Canada's admission program elicits admiration, both at home and abroad (Biles, Burstein, and Frideres 2008; Transatlantic Trends 2010; Reitz 2011a). Indeed, Australia, New Zealand, and the United Kingdom have incorporated aspects of Canada's system in hopes of regulating their inward flow (Chappell and Mulley 2010). But emulation is one thing, reality another. Glitches in the Canadian system have drawn scrutiny and criticism, in part because controversies over immigration invariably tap into deeper conflicts (Kelley and Trebilcock 2010; Canadian Centre for Immigration Policy Reform

2011; TD Economics 2012). According to Jason Kenney (2012c), the current system is "slow, rigid, and passive," and largely unresponsive to Canada's needs. It has also been accused of misreading Canada's economic requirements by emphasizing the wrong qualifications for entry. It has come under fire for realigning the focus of immigration, from one of Canada building and citizenship to that of just-in-time economic expansion by hired hands (see Fleras 2010). Last but certainly not least, the refugee status determination system has drawn scathing opprobrium for its ineptitude (real and perceived) in processing asylum seekers.

CANADA: AN IMMIGRATION SOCIETY

Canada can be described as a society of immigrants. Immigrants constitute just over 20 percent of its population, thanks to a lively immigration program, and this figure is expected to rise as Canadian birth rates continue to decline. Canada is also one of the few countries that qualify as *immigration societies*. According to Martin and Zurcher (2008), only five countries plan for the arrival of immigrants – Canada, the United States, Australia, New Zealand, and Israel (though Israel accepts only those of Jewish ancestry as permanent residents). These countries endorse the idea that economies thrive on a continuous source of newcomers as valued permanent residents rather than as rotated temporary workers (Weinstock 2008). Each country has its own criteria (policy and programs) for admission either by choice or displacement to settle permanently or work temporarily (Gogia and Slade 2011). Membership by the foreign-born is based on a commitment to (a) principles rather than ancestry, (b) an inclusive pluralism that respects differences and removes discriminatory barriers, (c) a fluid and accommodative national identity, and (d) a relatively easy path to naturalization, including the right to multiple citizenships (Jacobs 2010; Jupp 2011; Nussbaum 2012). Conversely, as Weinstock (2008) concludes, non-immigration societies tend toward opposite choices since immigration and immigrants are framed as a necessity to be tolerated instead of assets to be treasured.

The small number of immigration societies may seem odd, especially with about 215 million migrants on the move. But few societies have acknowledged the reality and importance of immigration for fear of (a) disrupting national identities, (b) exposing weaknesses in national governance and security, (c) undermining state capacity for enforcing unpopular laws, and (d) blowing the cover off a carefully constructed yet politically fragile elite consensus (comforting fictions). Migrants are despised and demonized as problems rather than seen as the victims of failed societies, structural readjustments, or aborted development (Fleras 2009b). A distinction between a society of immigrants and an immigration society – between the empirical and the normative – is critical. Many societies may qualify as the former if defined along descriptive lines; the few that can legitimately claim to be immigration societies must

> employ a principled framework to regulate admission;
> generate programs to facilitate the integration and settlement of immigrants;
> entitle migrants to all rights, including the right to permanent residency and citizenship; and
> see immigration and immigrants as society-building assets and as central to national identity (see also Ucarer 1997; Reitz 2012a).

Canada clearly subscribes to each of these attributes, at least in theory if not always in practice. As an immigration/settler society, it consists primarily of immigrants and their descendants whose presence is deeply ingrained in the national consciousness as a cornerstone of history and a resource for the future. A selective immigration strategy that increasingly targets specific and regional labour markets is employed, aimed at minimizing immigrant reliance on state support. Newcomers to Canada are entitled to a broad and generous set of settlement and integration progams in addition to immediate and undifferentiated access to social benefits that do not require long residency, as is the case in many European countries (Koning and Banting 2011). Their value to Canada building is gleefully acknowledged, as a comment from Prime Minister Stephen Harper reveals: "Canada's diversity, properly nurtured, is our greatest strength. Our tolerant and welcoming immigration policy represents Canada's great competitive advantage over most of the rest of the world" (quoted in Mickleburgh 2006). A fair and democratic immigration policy provides a framework that is both transparent and colour-blind (see also Cavanagh and Mulley 2013). Programs to integrate newcomers are taken for granted and rarely elicit resentment or disapproval (Bauder 2011). Canada can also be described as an immigration society whose status is reinforced by immigration as (a) an empirical fact, (b) a set of ideological norms, (c) official policies and programs, (d) practices pertaining to settlement and integration, and (e) a social contract in which newcomers promise to play by Canada's rules, while Canada promises to protect their interests.

Some countries, such as Germany, have historically denied the need for or existence of immigrants, thereby rejecting any normative status as immigration societies (Schmid-Druner 2006; Triadafilopoulos 2012). If anything, Germans defined themselves as a "complete society" (Castles and Miller 2009) whose nationhood rested on ethnically based and blood-related criteria, including (a) a shared sense of history, culture, and destiny; (b) an elitist concept of citizenship that excluded outsiders; and (c) a belief in the need to export surplus population (Zick, Pettigrew, and Wagner 2008; Nussbaum 2012). Immigration was perceived as an anomaly or a regrettable necessity, entailing a high cost, a potential loss of social control, and an erosion of national culture, identity, and unity (Rodríguez-García 2010). Or, alternatively, immigrants were couched in positive economic terms, although this perception did not make them crucial as contributors to national identity or society building. The consequences of a "needed but not wanted" mentality have proven migrant-unfriendly. The main goal of Germany's immigration policy was to prevent immigration (*Der Spiegel* Staff 2013). Policies were devised to stabilize inflows, limit long-term stays, discourage permanent residence, reject foreign qualifications, restrict participation and involvement, label newcomers as guest workers, and withhold citizenship and attendant rights to ensure the purity of the nation (Pécoud and de Guchteneire 2005). As one scholar put it,

> Europe, in general, has tended to hold onto the 1950s-1970s conception of immigration as a temporary phenomenon. For the most part, immigrants have been considered to be temporarily invited workers (guest workers) who must cost the country as little as possible because these immigrants' contribution is valued as nothing more than the circumstantial contribution of labor; in this way, they are not perceived as imminent citizens, who will form permanent attachments to the host society, and become part of the political process and social fabric. (Rodríguez-García 2010, 265)

Not surprisingly, much of what passed for immigration in Germany embodied a guest worker scheme *(gastarbeiter)*. Like most European countries, Germany opted to employ temporary migrant workers on a casual basis (Goodman 2012). Expected to return home upon completion of their contract, guest workers were not eligible for full citizenship and democratic rights. Public resentment eventually grew when they remained in Germany, often forming parallel communities, in part because of a misguided accommodation program (Fleras 2009a) that resulted in their exclusion from mainstream society (Triadafilopoulos 2012). The subtext was unmistakable: Germany was white, Christian, and Western, so that everybody else had to remain at the periphery or outside its borders (*Der Spiegel* Staff 2013).

This anti-immigration antipathy is under increased pressure across Europe. Former sending countries now have little option but to embrace immigration as a means to offset the effects of an ageing population and a falling birth rate, to defray the expense of costly welfare programs, cope with the shortage of skilled professional workers, and comply with obligations under EU membership (Munz and Ohliger 2005). For example, since 2000, restrictions on German citizenship no longer apply to children born of lawfully resident foreign parents. The Sussmuth Commission, also created in 2000, proposed a new immigration paradigm modelled after a Canadian-style point system (Jacoby 2011). Immigrants would be selected on the basis of their potential contribution as skilled workers for a knowledge-based economy in the hopes of aligning long-term demographic projections with short-term labour market needs (Bauder 2009). Admittedly, most of the commission's recommendations were rejected or watered down, including both a point system and a provision for the permanent immigration of skilled and unskilled workers who lacked EU resident status. Nevertheless, passage of the 2005 Immigration Act (also referred to as the Residence Act) established a single statutory framework for managing immigration into Germany, incorporating provisions on the entry of foreigners into Germany, their residence in the country, various residence purposes (e.g., a new employment-based visa for highly qualified professionals [Jacoby 2011]), the termination of residence, and asylum protocals (Schmid-Druner 2006). However well intentioned such accommodation, any significant transformation toward an immigration society will encounter obstacles (Economist 2010a). Immigrants may account for nearly 13 percent of Germany's population (almost

20 percent if their children are included [*Der Spiegel* Staff 2013]), including one million migrants in 2012, nearly half of whom left during the calendar year (Hawley and Wilder 2013). Immigration to Germany is no longer about cheap menial labourers and guest workers, but about highly educated and skilled individuals from the European Union who are in demand and willing to move on in search of opportunity (*Der Spiegel* Staff 2013). In short, both mindsets and institutions in a new Germany must rethink the paradox of needing immigration but not wanting immigrants (Böhmer 2010). Or as Bauder (2011, 4) writes in framing the challenge,

> For much of its modern history, Germany has been described as an ethnic nation. The German name for "Germany" illustrates this identity. Deutschland refers to the "land" of the people who are "deutsch" (i.e., German). In this way, the match between national territory and ethnic identity is explicit in the country's name; immigration does not occupy an important role in the manner in which the nation is defined. Recently, however, the fact that millions of non-Germans now live in the country has challenged Germany's historical identity as an ethnic nation.

The scenario is fundamentally different in Canada. Support for immigration and immigrants remains robust, with few if any signs of declining political or public support (Transatlantic Trends 2010; Environics Research Group 2011; Reitz 2012a). Yet, despite this general consensus (*Globe and Mail* 2012), the politics of immigration continues to attract criticism and concern (Canadian Centre for Immigration Policy Reform 2010). This is hardly surprising; after all, (a) Canadians subscribe to an idealistic image of immigrants and immigration at some variance with realities on the ground, (b) news media coverage is driven by comforting fictions that expose discrepancies between immigration ideals and immigrant realities, and (c) government programs and initiatives reflect a commitment to advancing this ideal, albeit in a context of political tradeoffs, often with uneven results. Immigrants themselves are changing with respect to origins, expectations, experiences, and outcomes. They are also struggling with issues of belonging and identity in an effort to link their past with the present, in transitioning toward the future. For example, though "immigrant" normally implies a departure from one country and permanent residence in another, the politics get tricky when immigrants refuse to relinquish ties with the home country, thereby forfeiting their consent to undivided loyalty and singular identity (Caldwell 2009).

CANADIAN IMMIGRATION HISTORY: WHO GOT IN?

Following Confederation, immigration policy quickly evolved into a cornerstone of Canadian society building (Kelley and Trebilcock 2010). Canada's survival as independent and prosperous depended on immigrant-generated economic expansion of settlers, producers, and consumers. Immigration initiatives were designed to increase the population, produce economies of scale, and domesticate the sparsely populated West (Grubel 2013). Initial immigration legislation was largely skeletal in nature, thus conferring vast swathes of discretionary power to authorities to administer and micro-manage. But immigration into Canada posed relatively few obstacles for those with the right national origins and ethnocultural backgrounds (Loewan and Friesen 2009). Of course, barriers existed in light of government policies and priorities that focused on population growth and Western settlement. Yet they were largely informal and discretionary, generally lacking in transparency, focused on exclusion rather than admittance, and reflective of Canada's exalted status as a "white man's country" (Thobani 2007; Baldwin, Cameron, and Kobayashi 2011). Initial admission policies were essentially racist in orientation, assimilationist in objective, nativist in content (i.e., with an intense dislike of anything foreign), and exclusionary in outcome (Abu-Laban 1999; Wallis and Fleras 2008). Nativism fused with racism to create xenophobic attitudes that deprived racialized minorities of rights while securing the basis of white Anglo-Canada (Peter Ward 1990). Immigration regulations distinguished between preferred and non-preferred "races" (Thobani 2007). A preference for more assimilable whites, those from Britain and Northern Europe (Bissett 2013), contrasted with the dismissal of inferior "races" as incompatible with Canada's bracing climate or its British heritage (Simmons 2010). Exclusions based on prevailing notions of race and ethnicity were institutionalized around conventional notions of national identity and homogeneity (Triadafilopoulos 2012).

Early immigration laws were discriminatory in both intent and consequences (Zaman 2012). The 1869 Immigration Act and subsequent amendments such as the 1910 Immigration Act upheld a white Canada policy by excluding undesirables, such as criminals, the destitute, the morally disreputable, the "deranged and mentally unfit," the diseased, nationalities who were unlikely to assimilate, labour-leftists, and city dwellers. Passage of the 1910 Immigration Act empowered authorities to exclude any persons belonging to a race that was thought unsuited to the climate or Canadian requirements. Strict limitations were imposed on racialized minorities such as Japanese, Chinese, and African Americans, through restrictions of citizenship rights under contract labour schemes (Hari, McGrath, Preston 2013) and through head taxes or regulations such as the Continuous Journey Rule, which required a non-stop ticket to Canada purchased in the home country. The fact that ocean-plying steamships required refuelling at some point before arriving at Vancouver or Halifax ensured a de facto exclusion behind a facade of seeming neutrality.

A "racial pecking order" of preferences prevailed (Walker 1998). Dominant perceptions of Canada as a white man's country bolstered the entry of immigrants from the so-called superior stock of Western Europe (Zaman 2012). This category was virtually exempt from entry restrictions except for certain formalities (Abella and Troper 1983). At the bottom of this racialized heap were blacks and Asians, whom many pitied as inherently inferior and ultimately unassimilable. The Irish, too, were deemed culturally and economically dangerous – a poor, ignorant, and knavish people prone to crime, joblessness, drunken lasciviousness, and "papist" religious convictions contrary to English Canada's Protestantism. Between these two poles were the non-preferred classes, consisting of immigrants from Eastern and Middle Europe and Russia. Admired for their brawn and industry but suspect because of their political affiliations or economic beliefs, they were defined as "dangerous," particularly the Bolsheviks who dared to challenge the principles of free enterprise (Avery 1995). Such ambivalence paved the way for the First World War incarceration of nearly nine thousand persons of enemy alien birth, such as Ukrainians and Germans. A special "restricted" permit class controlled the entry of equally undesirable groups such as Jews and Mediterranean folk.

Initial moves for governing the admission of foreign individuals were driven by a combination of ideological considerations, political expediency, international obligations, and the market requirements of a colonial economy (Fleras 2012e). Outcomes were also decided by an interplay of factors and pressure groups, including racism and ethnocentrism (Fleras 2014a); the agricultural bias of Canada's early immigration policies; the pivotal role of private and business interests in recruiting immigrants for national economic development; recognition of Canada's Commonwealth commitments; and debates over aborting high levels of out-migration to the United States (Avery 1979). A conflict of interest prevailed: namely, how to preserve Canada's whiteness without embracing an overtly racist immigration program while securing an adequate supply of cheap migrant labour (Thobani 2000, 2007). In response, immigration policy and practice evolved into a kind of contested site, with competing blocs jockeying to impose agendas or advance vested interests (Avery 1995).

Immigration remained a source of controversy for an expanding array of interests (Kelley and Trebilcock 2010). Employers applauded the government for its aggressive recruitment of newcomers (more than 3 million between 1896 and 1914). By contrast, trade unions resented migrant workers as a threat to white workers, and nationalists argued for a more selective admissions program to preserve the racial purity of the anglo race. Political parties also engaged in endless polemics over who was desirable or assimilable, preferred or non-preferred (Thobani 2000). But all agreed regarding one overriding orthodoxy: The country's long-term interests depended on excluding those who were (a) unsuited to its conditions, (b) incapable of assimilating, (c) or a threat to Canadian stability, interests, values, and institutions (Avery 1979). Non-preferred immigrants were tolerated as long as they quietly toiled away in remote regions, at tasks deemed too demeaning and demanding for white Canadians (typically in labour-intensive extractive industries such as mines and lumber camps, in addition to railway and domestic work). This ambivalence was especially striking in the (mis)treatment of Chinese "guest workers," or "sojourners," whose status as "fodder" to foster Canadian capitalist expansion superseded their potential as citizens-in-waiting (see Box 5).

Historically, Canada's immigration program responded to labour demands or settlement needs. Settlement of the Prairies required large numbers, with immigration totals peaking at 400,870 in 1913. Wars and the Depression substantially lowered the figures, which bottomed out at 7,576 in 1942. In response to a 1920s labour shortage and growing demands for a more liberal immigration program to import continental Europeans, the Canadian government formalized an agreement in September 1925 with the CPR and CNR. The railway companies were allowed to control the recruitment of European agriculturalists

5 CASE STUDY

From "Yellow Peril" to Model Minority: Chinese Immigrants in a Xenophobic Canada

CANADA IS FREQUENTLY described as an immigration society. With the possible exception of Aboriginal people, all Canadians are immigrants or descendants of immigrants. Immigration has played a pivotal role in Canada's national development and will continue to do so in the future. The need for immigrants to offset the costs of an ageing population and a dipping birth rate, while ensuring a supply of skilled labour for domestic growth and international competitiveness, will ensure that.

But Canadians seem curiously ambivalent about immigration and immigrants. They have long relied on immigrant labour as a catalyst for nation building and capitalist expansion (Bolaria and Li 1988; Kelley and Trebilcock 2010). However much they are committed to immigration in principle, Canadians display an aversion to immigrants in general. Or, to put it facetiously, yes to immigration, no to immigrants. This ambivalence was sharply evident in the past, when newcomers entered a country that differed markedly from that of today (Avery 1979; Boyd and Vickers 2000; Knowles 2007). Canadians may be upset to learn that racism was openly and ruthlessly directed at the racialized others who were deemed inferior and inadmissible. Both the courts and the legal system were institutionally implicated in Canada's racist treatment of immigrants prior to entry and upon settlement (see Backhouse 1999). For example, a court ruling that prevented Chinese men from hiring white women to work in laundries was not considered discriminatory, because it applied to all Chinese males (Walker 1998). Even more dismaying in a country that claims to hug the high moral ground is an awareness that institutionalized racism underpinned Canada building and capitalist expansion.

Few groups endured as much racism and discrimination as the Chinese (Abrams and Moio 2009; Zaman 2012; Coloma 2013; Tchen and Yeats 2014). Canada's treatment of Chinese immigrants is an embarrassment that many Canadians would prefer to gloss over (Baureiss

1985; Li 1998). The earliest Chinese migrants came to Canada in 1858 as sojourners (transient workers) to take advantage of the gold rush. The second cohort arrived as virtually indentured labour to assist in building the Canadian Pacific Railway. Chinese migrants were seen as cheap and exploitable workhorses for the most hazardous sections of the railway, yet expendable once the task was complete. A split labour market model prevailed: Chinese workers earned $1.00 a day (only 80 cents if they did not buy provisions from the company store), compared to $2.00 a day for Canadian workers or $3.50 for American workers (Lee 1997).

Public antipathy was palpable. With nearly seventeen thousand arrivals from mainland China between 1882 and 1885 (the total population in British Columbia was fifty-three thousand in 1891) (Xiao-Feng and Norcliffe 1996), federal plans to import an additional five thousand Chinese labourers for the construction of the Grand Trunk Railway elicited a sharp editorial rebuke in the September 1906 issue of *Saturday Night:* "We don't want Chinamen in Canada. This is a white man's country and white men will keep it so. The slant-eyed Asiatic with his yellow skin, his unmanly humility, his cheap wants, would destroy the whole equilibrium of industry ... We cannot assimilate them. They are an honest, industrious, but hopelessly inferior race" (quoted in Fraser 1989, 12). Upon completion of the railway, many Chinese workers capitalized on their savings to return to China. Others, less fortunate, found themselves stranded in Canada because of insufficient funds for return passage, with few options except as unskilled employment in laundries and landscaping. Those who stayed behind were subject to caricature by media elites, the calculated indifference of politicians, and abusive treatment by the general public. In the same year the railroad was completed, the BC government passed the 1884 Chinese Regulation Act, arguing that the Chinese were incapable of obeying laws, did not respond well to emergencies, and were inclined to vandalize cemeteries. The demonization of the Chinese knew no limits. They were frequently subjected to racial invectives by organized labour, which pilloried them as strike-breaking scabs. Others vilified them as a kind of "yellow peril" at odds with the purity and integrity of a white man's country (see Kil 2012; Coloma 2013;

Tchen and Yeats 2014). The exploitation of the Chinese as a political football or as electoral scapegoats played into the hands of white xenophobes. Paradoxically, even the withdrawal of the Chinese into their own communities rarely secured protection; to the contrary, it had the perverse effect of inflaming public hostility by reinforcing suspicion and inciting violence (Donaldson 2013).

Provincial legislation sought to destroy the community bonds of early Chinese residents, restrict political activity, and inhibit healthy social growth (Vasil and Yoon 1996; Yu 2009). According to Xiao-Feng and Norcliffe (1996), virtually every industry in British Columbia relied on Chinese labour. Nevertheless, the Chinese were targets of prejudice and discrimination, exploited as cheap labour, and manipulated as strike-breakers in defiance of labour union regulations. They were denied the right to vote, eventually prohibited from working on government projects or in coal mines, excluded from holding hand-loggers' licences, prevented from settling on Crown land, barred from the professions of law or pharmacy, and banned from hiring white women to work in Prairie restaurants or laundries. Numerous tactics were deployed for restricting their entry in a "White Canada Forever" (a popular barroom song and political rallying cry [Yu 2009, 1015]). Nonetheless, these stalling tactics proved ineffective because of the demand for cheap labour during the railway construction period (Bolaria and Li 1988; Satzewich 2000).

The lack of political voice or electoral representation rendered Chinese Canadians vulnerable to victimization (Roy 1989; Coloma 2013). This is not to say that they passively accepted these injustices. Protests, strikes, and lawsuits were often employed in reaction to negative government legislation and discriminatory practices (see Ip 1998). But resistance proved somewhat futile. Under public pressure, successive governments imposed financial disincentives to deter entry. The first federal Chinese Exclusion Act, in 1885, imposed a head tax of $50 on Chinese immigrants. This amount was increased by increments until it peaked at $500 in 1903 – a sum equivalent to two years' wages or the cost of a new home in Vancouver. An additional $200 was required in 1910 as landing tax for all Asian immigrants. Between 1886 and 1923, more than $22 million was collected in head tax payments. Admittedly, the first Immigration Act of 1869 had imposed a duty tax of $1.00 to $1.50 per person for all entrants, and a 1914 landing fee of $250 was universally applied. But only the Chinese were singled out for special taxation.

The head tax may have temporarily derailed the flow of Chinese migrants, but it did not curb it (Xiao-Feng and Norcliffe 1996). The federal government curtailed Chinese immigration in 1923, with passage of the Chinese Immigration Act. The Chinese became the only demographic to be specifically prohibited by race from entry to Canada. This exclusionary injunction forced the separation of Chinese men from their wives and partners, in effect terminating any population growth. Only 44 Chinese individuals were granted permission to enter Canada between 1923 and 1946 (ibid.). This racist ban was lifted in 1947, with repeal of the Chinese Immigration Act and passage of Canada's first Citizenship Act, although, until 1962, only spouses and unmarried children of Chinese people in Canada could enter. By contrast, immigration from Europe and the United States was relatively unrestricted. The introduction of the point system in 1967 facilitated ease of entry for Chinese immigrants, either from Hong Kong or Taiwan, but none from the communist mainland.

The status of Chinese Canadians has improved in recent years. Successive generations have moved from a marginalized position to more active involvement in securing their status as Canadian citizens. Chinese Canadians are increasingly seen as model minorities because of their work ethic. But old habits die hard, and racist attacks persist because of these citizens' lofty achievements (Gilmour et al. 2012). Their paradoxical status as model minorities puts Asian Canadians in an awkward position: they are needed yet rejected, desired yet undesirable. For example, Asian Canadians might be admired as immigrants and workers when they benefit Canada but are disavowed as the "other within" when they challenge or disrupt the status quo (Coloma 2013; also Zaman 2012). Instead of being labelled inferior or unassimilable, they are criticized for ostensibly un-Canadian cultural practices (Heer 2012). They are chided for creating a host of social problems, from monopolizing spaces in medical schools to driving up real estate prices in Vancouver, from establishing ethnic enclaves in the Greater Toronto area to taking up too much university space, raising the competitive bar of success for non-Asian students, and throwing a damper on a party-hearty university scene (see Findlay and Kohler 2010; also Gilmour et al. 2012). These attacks are less direct than in the past. Nevertheless, the undercurrent of thinly veiled dislike for the so-called yellow peril is no less disconcerting, suggesting that racism in racialized societies never disappears. Rather, it assumes a different set of disguises, expressions, and codes to better blend with changing environments. Plus ça change, plus c'est la même chose.

and domestic servants through occupational certificates previously denied to those from non-preferred countries (mostly Baltic and Slavic countries) (CMIP 21 2013). The federal government's role was primarily restricted to medical checks and issuing visas. More than 185,000 Central Europeans arrived under the terms of this controversial agreement, but the agreement was cancelled in 1930, in part because of massive unemployment during the Depression and disagreement over policy goals. In 1931, entry was restricted to British subjects, American citizens, dependants of permanent residents in Canada, and agriculturalists from Northern and Western Europe. Migrants from Southern and Eastern Europe were discouraged, whereas most Asians were prohibited from entry between 1923 and 1947 (Castles and Miller 2009). Injustices in the immigration program included the exclusion of Jewish émigrés, even in the face of a pending persecution of Jews in Germany (Kelley and Trebilcock 2010). In contrast to Argentina, which admitted sixty-three thousand Jewish refugees during the 1930s, Canada accepted only five thousand, in part because its lack of a refugee policy condoned a discretionary decision-making climate, both unfair and lacking transparency (Abella and Troper 1983).

The Second World War and its aftermath proved a wake-up call. Humanitarian concerns emerged once Canadians became aware of their country's complicity in dooming Jewish refugees. Shifts in the acceptability of racial discrimination put Canada on the alert, without necessarily dislodging concerns over mass migration, especially from the Far East, for fear of tampering with the fundamental character and composition of the Canadian population (King 1947, 2544-46). The Immigration Act of 1952 conferred on the governor-in-council sweeping discretionary powers in defining admission based on nationality, peculiarity of customs, suitability or lack thereof, and probability of assimilation into Canada (Haque 2012; Whitaker 1987). The need to take advantage of the post-war economic boom resulted in an immigration policy that emphasized population growth, short-term skilled labour needs, and economic development. A 1947 policy expanded the range of admissions to include (a) British subjects and American citizens who met standards of health and character, (b) those who were qualified to work in labour-starved primary industries, (c) sponsored relatives from European countries such as Greece or Italy who had strong family connections, and (d) refugees and displaced persons under international supervision. Quotas still applied for most non-Europeans, in effect reinforcing a "white-only" immigration policy (Bissett 2013), despite a growing demand for skilled and unskilled labour (Lorne Foster 1998).

In 1962, Canadian immigration laws underwent a radical change in defining who got in. Political reasons prevailed in shifting to a universal skills-based selection criterion. Global developments, from decolonization movements to the advent of human rights culture and the stigma of racial discrimination, and Canada's projected image as a progressive society, established a different normative context that emphasized economic considerations rather than preserving Canada's character (Haque 2012; Triadafilopoulos 2013). Dwindling admissions from Europe, combined with blunt charges of a racist immigration program (Jakubowski 1997; Triadafilopoulos 2012), prompted Canada to endorse a difference-blind approach in which any qualified person would be eligible for entry, based primarily on personal merit and societal contribution. The selection process was deracialized (made colour-blind) by shifting the selection criteria from national origin and racialized ethnicity to skills, education, and experience (Hawkins 1974; Eva Mackey 1998). Further reforms in 1967 stipulated the entry of four major immigrant classes: family, assisted relatives, independents, and refugees. A point system of evaluation was introduced to ensure transparency in the selection process. Both independent and assisted-relative applicants were numerically graded and assessed with respect to occupation, education, and language expertise (50 points out of 100 to qualify). Still, the system was not entirely free of systemic bias. The point system continued to favour male applicants who had educational credentials or work skills in the countries that housed Canadian embassies for processing applicants (visa offices were almost exclusively located in Britain, Europe, and the United States [Bissett 2013]) (Abu-Laban 1999). Furthermore, interviewing officers had the discretionary power to refuse or accept an applicant regardless of the points achieved (Bissett 2013).

Passage of the Immigration Act in 1976 formalized a framework of legal authority and transparency to what historically was accomplished behind closed doors and by regulatory change alone (Bissett 2013). The act codified rules for admission and articulated a principled framework to balance the goals of (a) family reunification, (b) protection of legitimate refugees, (c) enhancement of Canada's prosperity and global competitiveness, and (d) preservation of its integrity. Immigration policy and programs focused on protecting national interests, ensuring sufficient immigrants for economic growth, reuniting families, and providing a safe haven for those in need of protection. The federal government retained primary responsibility for the selection of immigrants and policy setting (e.g., the act obligated the government to table in Parliament its proposed level of immigration for the coming year [Bissett 2013]) without altogether abdicating a degree of consultation/negotiation with the provinces over policy agenda, immigration levels, and settlement measures. A historical commitment to a labour market/taps-on, taps-off approach was increasingly balanced by a human capital model, with its focus on multi-talented immigrants as integral to sustainable economic growth. Immigrants did not just serve the needs of labour, according to this line of thinking; they also represented consumers and investors whose global connections underpinned Canada's economic performance.

A further realignment followed passage of the 2002 Immigration and Refugee Protection Act (IRPA). Canada's first major change to its immigration program since 1976, the act sought to shore up the program by (a) imposing additional restrictions on entry, (b) recruiting immigrants who easily integrated into the workplace and society, (c) emphasizing flexible and transferable skills as income-generating potential, (d) strengthening language and educational requirements as a precondition for entry (Picot and Sweetman 2012), and (e) firming up sponsorship rules to share the burden of costs in resettlement.

Denis Coderre, who was then immigration minister, defended the rationale behind the new law: "Our strategy is designed to strike a balance between attracting workers with flexible skills, reuniting families and being tough on those who pose a threat to Canadian security, all the while maintaining Canada's humanitarian tradition of providing a safe haven to people in need of protection" (CIC 2003, 5). The current immigration program continues to manage the multiple objectives under the IRPA (CIC 2011b). To be sure, the act lacked detail, despite its status as a legal federal framework for immigrant and refugee protection, with specifics left to executive discretion (Kelley and Trebilcock 2010). The act also attracted criticism for transforming immigration into what James Bissett (2013, 4) terms a "mass visa factory" based largely on "paper qualifications." He writes disapprovingly:

> The new legislation came into effect in 2002 and proved to be a disaster. Almost immediately, a backlog of successful applicants began to build up in embassies abroad. Either by design or accident, the new act stipulated that anyone who met the newly designed selection criteria "shall" be accepted. In addition, the new selection criteria heavily weighted the points allotted for years of education and dropped the "occupational demand" factor, thus removing from the system any mechanism for regulating numbers. The act also broadened the family class to include parents and grandparents of any age ... Soon there was a backlog of 600,000 applicants waiting for their visas, later to grow to more than a million.

Still, the act purports to balance immediate short-term labour needs with the realities of a skilled workforce and citizens for the future. It also fosters the development of a prosperous economy whose benefits are shared nation-wide and works to reunite families, construct viable communities, and fulfill Canada's international obligations through settlement of refugees and assistance for asylum seekers.

Clearly, the dynamics of and rationale behind immigration into Canada have evolved over time (Knowles 2007; Siemiatycki 2012). The current program differs from that of the past in terms of focus, rationale, underlying assumptions, and anticipated outcomes. Its emphasis is on whom to let in and how many. The nature of immigrants, with respect to origins, requisite skills, and expectations, has shifted as well with the introduction of colour-blind criteria for entry. Changes in immigration patterns are no less evident, both more transient and complex than in the past, with periods of sojourning increasingly more common in a world of circular/repeat migration, dual citizenship, and transnational communities (Willis and Yeoh 2000).

This historical overview draws attention to recurrent themes that persist into the present. First, immigration represented a response to Canada's society-building demands related to the economy and population (see Li 2003). The prime objectives have rarely wavered – to grow the Canadian economy – adjusted for labour market needs specific to various stages of economic development (Reitz 2013). The developmental trajectory included (a) a labour pool for agriculture and settlement, (b) skilled labour for post-war industrialization, and (c) professional and skilled tradespeople to capitalize on a globalized and post-industrial economy (Sears 2008). Second, immigration decisions reflected a host of differing values and interests. Canada initially perceived itself as a staples-based and grain-exporting British-European society, with immigration and immigrants aligned accordingly (Simmons 2010). This extractive model was followed in the mid-twentieth century by perceptions of Canada as a European-based manufacturing society, with immigrant labour producing goods for national consumption and export trade. By the 1990s, the preferred image was of Canada as a sophisticated multicultural niche player in the global market. The customizing of immigrants focused on advancing its post-industrial knowledge economy and securing its competitiveness in international trade (ibid.). Historically, then, the following three models have linked Canada building and immigration (Siemiatycki 2012; also Simmons 2010):

> From the 1860s to the 1960s, the focus was on building a white British Protestant Canada. A racist and exclusionary orientation prevented or limited the migration of blacks, Asians, and Jews who were deemed unfit for farming.
> From the 1960s to the 2000s, the intent was to build a multicultural Canada with the aid of global human capital. The introduction of the point system transformed immigration because immigrants were chosen from around the world on the basis of their potential contribution to manufacturing and resource extraction rather than their identity or nationality.

> Currently, the emphasis is on building a super-diverse and globally competitive country, incorporating a fast and flexible workforce that is consistent with the market-oriented principles of neoliberal globalization (Department of Finance 2006). The adoption of increased security measures is no less important, following 9/11 and the 7/7 attacks in London (see Keung 2013a for an overview).

Third, the immigration program proved a balancing act for the Canadian government. As a member of the Commonwealth, Canada had to tread carefully in disallowing the entry of non-preferred Commonwealth members (from India, for example). Then, as now, it confronts the challenge of attracting the right kind of immigrants with the appropriate skills. Yet it must also deter unwanted migrants, ensure the reunification of families, and comply with UN human rights protocols. Fourth, in terms of recruitment, selection, and control, the immigration program has long proven a contested site of competitive interests and ideologies. For example, business/land developers and transportation/shipping companies supported immigration as a steady source of wealth creation. Opposed were organized labour and the general public, which typically favoured a restriction of the immigrants who depressed wages, increased job insecurity, and threatened to diminish Canada's living standards (Stoffman 2002). In between were the politicians, who wanted votes and who bent with the winds of expediency. Consider how the government justified its decision in the 1990s to maintain the annual immigration total at about 250,000 despite economic downturns, on the ground that higher levels would enable the ruling party to construct stronger ties (and votes) with ethnic communities (Bissett 2013). Police, bureaucrats, and health officials expressed varying levels of trepidation for reasons both real and imagined (Satzewich and Liodakis 2010). The government found itself sandwiched between competing interests, sometimes aligning with one side, then with the other, depending on the political climate. Sometimes it capitulated to private (business) interests or to public agitation as the circumstances dictated, and sometimes it took the high road, guided by a commitment to Canadian values and national interests (Kelley and Trebilcock 2010).

WHO GETS IN? CANADA'S IMMIGRATION PROGRAM

Canada embraces a diverse tapestry of immigrants and refugees from many parts of the world. Its robust immigration program creates a staunchly heterogeneous country, whose reputation as a multicultural mosaic needs little prompting. Canada's ethnocultural composition has undergone a radical transformation since the passage of the British North America (Constitution) Act of 1867, when only 8 percent of its population was of neither British nor French descent (Harney and Troper 1975). Between 1896 and 1914, the demographics shifted, with the arrival of 3 million immigrants from Central and Eastern Europe to domesticate the West. Immigration increased substantially prior to and just after the First World War. The post–Second World War period resulted in yet another immigrant boom of newcomers and refugees from the war-devastated countries of Europe. Sources of immigration began to change during the 1980s, and the refugee program became plagued with abuses, both of which rekindled controversy over who got in, why, and how. But before we look at the issue of who gets in, the following overview examines Canadian immigration and ethnocultural diversity between 2006 and 2011, based on data from Statistics Canada (2013).

Immigrant and ethnocultural diversity in Canada, 2006-11:

> A total of 1,163,000 newcomers arrived between 2006 and 2011, boosting Canada's foreign-born population to 6,776,000. Canada possesses one of the highest proportions of foreign-born (20.6 percent of its population), followed by Germany and the United States at about 13 percent. Nearly 24 percent of Australia's population in 2010 was foreign-born, putting this country near the head of the newcomer class.

> Of all newcomers, about 58 percent came from Asia, including the Middle East. The Philippines was the leading country of newcomers to Canada, accounting for 13 percent of arrivals, followed by China and India at about 10.5 percent each. The overall share from Africa, the Caribbean, and South and Central America increased slightly, from 10 percent in 2006 to 12.5 percent in 2011.

> Forty-three percent of newcomers chose to settle in Ontario, followed by Quebec at 19 percent, British Columbia at 16 percent, and Alberta at 12.4 percent. Overall, 95 percent of Canada's foreign-born lived in these four provinces, with Ontario at 53 percent, British Columbia at 18 percent, Quebec at 14.5 percent, and Alberta at 9.5 percent.

> Ninety-one percent of foreign-born lived in one of 33 Census Metropolitan Areas (CMAs), with about 63 percent of both recent arrivals

and the immigration population settling in the "MTV" cities of Montreal, Toronto, and Vancouver.

> Toronto remained the destination of choice. It housed 37.5 percent of all foreign-born in Canada, who constituted about 46 percent of its own population and about 70 percent of all the foreign-born in Ontario. Between 2006 and 2011, about 33 percent of immigrants settled in Toronto, followed by Montreal at 16 percent and Vancouver at 13 percent.

> Mid-size cities also experienced significant growth. Calgary took in 6 percent of newcomers, whereas Edmonton and Winnipeg received about 4 percent of the total.

> Recent immigrants are relatively young, with a median age of just under 32 (the median age for the total immigrant population is 47.4). Nearly 59 percent of newcomers between 2006 and 2011 were in the core working age of 25 to 54, whereas 4.4 percent fell into the older working-age bracket of 55 to 64, and 14.5 percent were drawn from the younger working-age bracket of 15 to 24.

> Between 2006 and 2011, 47.5 percent of immigrants identified as Christians, 17.4 percent as Muslims, and 4.8 percent as Sikhs (19.5 percent identified as no religion).

> More than 200 ethnic origins were reported, 13 of which contained in excess of 1 million self-identified members. Just over 10.5 million gave "Canadian" as their ethnic origin (both single and multiple origins), followed by English (6,500,000), French (5,000,000), Scottish (4,700,000), Irish (4,500,000), and German (3,200,000). Rounding off the top ten were Italian, Chinese, First Nations, Ukrainian, and South Asian.

> Racialized minorities comprised 6.3 million persons, or 19.1 percent of Canada's population, up from 16.2 percent in 2006. Sixty-five percent were born outside Canada.

> The largest racialized minority groups were South Asians (25 percent of the total), Chinese (21 percent), and blacks (15 percent).

> Ninety-five percent of racialized minorities lived in Ontario, Quebec, Alberta, and British Columbia, with Ontario home to just over half (52 percent) of the national total.

> Ninety-six percent of racialized minorities lived in cities, including 2,600,000 in Toronto and 1,000,000 in Vancouver. Racialized minorities accounted for 47 percent of Toronto's population (Vancouver was close behind at just over 45 percent). In the Ontario cities of

Markham and Brampton, they accounted for 72 and 66 percent, respectively.

Much of this ethnocultural diversity can be attributed to Canada's balanced and principled immigration program (Picot and Sweetman 2012). Canada differs from the many countries that take an ad hoc approach toward admission: Citizenship and Immigration Canada maintains a tightly controlled selection program that responds to labour market needs without sacrificing the health, safety, and security of Canadians, while fostering family reunification and honouring Canada's humanitarian commitments and tradition. Admission is based on non-discriminatory ethics: Foreign nationals are assessed without regard to race, nationality, ethnic origin, colour, religion, or gender. The year 2012 was a typical one for immigration, with respect to admission categories and patterns of selection, as demonstrated by the figures in Box 6.

CATEGORIES OF ADMISSION

Canada's immigration policy is informed by three broad objectives: to reunite families, fulfill Canada's humanitarian obligations for those who need protection, and promote a vibrant economy. These objectives are implemented through three main admission categories for permanent entry: Family class immigrants are sponsored by their family members. Individuals in the refugee class, who fear returning to their homeland, find sanctuary in Canada. They may be assisted by government or privately sponsored, and may already have landed in Canada or are refugee claimants. Members of the economic class are selected for their skills and contribution (CIC 2011c). In 2008, highly skilled temporary foreign workers (TFW) became eligible to apply for permanent resident status, as did international students with Canadian degrees and some postgraduate work experience. Most TFW, however, do not have the necessary skills to apply. The number of non-permanent entrants (temporary foreign workers) has shown strong growth (nearly 340,000 TFW by the end of 2012), in the hope of off-setting labour shortages across the country.

Family Class

The family class recognizes the need for reuniting families to facilitate the integration of newcomers into Canada. It comprises foreign

6

Immigrants by Landing Class and Totals, 2012 and 1997

Class	2012	1997
Family class (25.27%)	64,901	59,538
Spouses and partners	39,471	
Parents/grandparents	21,778	
Others	3,652	
Economic class (including dependants) (62.4%)*	160,617	127,613
Federal skilled workers	38,577	
Federal skilled workers + spouses and dependants	52,790	
Business immigrants (includes entrepreneurs, self-employed, investors + spouses and dependants)	10,069	
Provincial/territorial nominees + spouses and dependants	40,829	
Canadian Experience Class + spouses and dependants	9,353	
Live-in caregivers + spouses and dependants	8,999	
Refugees/Protected persons (9%)	23,056	23,863
Government assisted	5,412	
Privately sponsored	4,212	
Inland protected persons/refugees landed in Canada	8,578	
Refugee dependants	4,854	
Other immigrants (3.5%)	8,936	
Subtotal	257,510[†]	
Number of temporary foreign workers and foreign students (2012)[‡]		
Temporary foreign workers	213,573	
International students	104,810	
TOTAL	575,893	

* This includes Quebec-selected skilled workers and business applicants.

† In 2012, 257,515 immigrants came to Canada, with slight increases in both the family and economic classes but a decrease in the number of refugees (CIC 2013c). The number of temporary foreign workers and foreign students increased as well to 318,383 (CIC 2013b). In 2012, males comprised 126,457 of the admissions and females 131,430. By province, 38.4 percent of immigrants settled in Ontario, followed by 21.5 percent in Quebec, and British Columbia and Alberta with about 14 percent.

‡ Excludes visitors who came to Canada for personal or business reasons.

Source: CIC (2013b, c).

nationals who are sponsored by their own family members (CIC 2013b). One family member migrates first (either voluntarily or involuntarily as an asylum seeker) and sends for (sponsors) the remaining members once he or she has gained citizenship or permanent residency. A chain migration strategy permits the entry of immediate family members, including a spouse (or fiancé), parents, grandparents, dependent and unmarried children under 19 years of age, and orphaned brothers, sisters, nieces, nephews, and grandchildren, provided, of course, they do not impose excessive demands on health or social services (recent immigration law waived this criteria for spouses and children [Liston and Carens 2008]), they pass security checks, and do not have a criminal record. In 2013, the government introduced more stringent criteria for sponsoring parents and grandparents (Fitzpatrick 2013). Those who want to sponsor a family member must prove that they can financially support him or her for up to three years (only Revenue Canada Agency notices of assessment will be accepted as proof), with the minimum base income level increased by 30 percent to ensure compliance. The sponsorship commitment period was extended from 10 years to 20 years, although sponsored persons (except for the elderly) must also sign an agreement to strive for self-sufficiency (Satzewich and Liodakis 2013). Non-immediate members of a family, such as aunts or uncles, must secure additional points for entry.

Processing times for family class sponsorship can vary: 50 percent of cases involving spouses/partners and dependent children are finalized within 6 months, 75 percent within 12 months (CIC 2011d). In contrast, it may take 30 months or more to finalize 50 percent of admissions involving parents or grandparents (Wayland 2006). To ensure the authenticity of family relationships, individuals from Africa, the Caribbean, India, and Pakistan may be asked to undergo DNA testing. It should be noted that the federal government continues to whittle away at family reunification as a priority (Jabir 2014). For example, in 2011, Ottawa imposed a two-year moratorium on parental sponsorship to deal with the unmanageability of a seven-year backlog for sponsoring parents and grandparents. A multi-entry super visa, valid for 10 years, was introduced (and is now permanently established), allowing multiple entries of two years' duration as long as parents possess private health insurance and are financially solvent (Editorial, *Globe and Mail* 2011c). Applications for sponsorship will be resumed in 2014 but limited to five thousand per year to offset a backlog of eighty thousand applicants. Stricter conditions such as higher financial requirements will be imposed to reduce the number of older immigrants, who are thought to impose a burden on health care services (Jabir 2014; Fitzpatrick 2013).

Economic Class

Immigration has always sought to fulfill multiple short-term and long-term economic goals (Picot and Sweetman 2012). Not surprisingly, a major source of landing for immigrants is the economic class, which includes federal skilled workers, business people, provincial nominees, and live-in caregivers, all of whom possess the skills to make a contribution to the economy (CIC 2013b). Between 1980 and 1995, most immigrants entered by way of family relations, but this has changed. According to both 2011 and 2012 data, just under 63 percent of newcomers were in the economic class, a figure that is likely to persist (or increase) in the future, especially since economic immigration was featured prominently in Canada's Economic Action Plan 2012 (Canada 2012).[1] The Jobs, Growth, and Long-Term Prosperity Act, which became law in late June 2012, emphasized the need for a fast, flexible, and responsive system in selecting the best applicants (not necessarily the first-come, first-served applicants, as in the past). Immigration Minister Jason Kenney pinpointed his government's economic focus, with immigration playing a key role: "The Government's No. 1 priority remains the economy. We recognize the importance of immigration to our labour market and we value the contributions of skilled immigrants who add to our international competitiveness" (quoted in Kleiss 2011; also CIC 2011d). Stephen Harper confirmed this commitment with a similar announcement: "We will ensure that, while we respect our humanitarian and family reunification objectives, we make our economic and labour force needs the central goal of our immigration efforts in the future" (quoted in Friesen and Curry 2012).

Most economic class entrants are federal skilled workers, a trend that is likely to continue as long as Canada covets skilled immigrants whose training and education costs are defrayed elsewhere. These individuals have the skills to enter the labour market and establish themselves in Canada (CIC 2013b). Admission under the economic class is largely point-based (see Box 7). The principal applicant is assessed on the numerical grounds of job-related skills, age, official-language knowledge, and education. He or she may also undergo an interview/assessment for adaptability. The number of points necessary for entry varies, with 67 points required for skilled workers and the self-employed. Applicants from the business class (both investor and entrepreneur) can earn up to 35 points for their commercial experiences and connections. Assisted relatives also receive credit as nominated immigrants (5 points) but require additional top-up points to qualify. Everyone in this category must pass the usual health and security clearances. Each adult applicant must also pay a $550 application fee ($150 for those under 22 years of age and not a spouse or common-law partner) and a $490 right-of-landing fee to a maximum of four members per family. The landing fee for refugees was waived in 2000.

In recent years, the government has attempted to reduce the backlog of applications under the Federal Skilled Worker Program while

7

The Federal Skilled Worker Point System

Maximum points allowed	Criteria for points
Education: 25 points	25 points for education (maximum for PhD or MA, 5 points for high-school diploma)
Language skills: 28 points (24)*	28 points for language proficiency (up to 20 points for first official language – reading, writing, speaking, understanding; up to 8 points for the second official language)
Work experience: 15 points (21) *	15 points for work experience (top points for 4 years of experience in a highly skilled occupation)
Employment status: 10 points	10 points for arranged employment in Canada
Age: 12 points (10)*	12 points for age (maximum points for those between 18 and 35; 0 points if over age 46)
Adaptability: 10 points	10 points for adaptability (5 points for full-time job experience in Canada; 5 points for full-time study in Canada; 5 points for having a close relative in Canada; 5 points for a spouse with a university degree)

* Note recent changes to the point calculus, with point allocations prior to 2013 in parentheses.

capping the number of new applicants based on Canada's economic needs and processing capacity (CIC 2011d, 2012a). In 2008, Ottawa's Action Plan sought to eliminate the backlog of immigrants by introducing new regulations that meant Citizenship and Immigration Canada was no longer obligated to process every application that it received. Nor was it obliged to offer permanent residency to every successful applicant (thus creating the backlog). Admissions were restricted to those who met specific criteria such as having a firm employment offer or in-demand job skills (CIC 2009b). Passage of Bill C-50 in June 2008 empowered the immigration minister to prioritize applicants in the Federal Skilled Worker Program in response to labour shortages. To match newcomers with real jobs, entry of skilled workers was limited to those with a firm employment offer or those whose skills matched 1 of 29 (originally 38) priority jobs. In June 2011, the annual quota for new federal skilled worker applications was capped at ten thousand overall (those with firm job offers in Canada were exempted from this total), with five hundred per eligible occupation (CIC 2011b). Effective 1 May 2014, the federal government announced a final cap of 25,000 applications under the Federal Skilled Worker Program (again, no cap for those with qualifying job offers), with one thousand applications maximum per priority occupation. These will be the last applicants under the current system before introduction of the Express Entry Program in 2015.

The Federal Skilled Worker Program was temporarily suspended in June 2012 pending changes to the point grid (those who had a qualifying job offer or were applying under the PhD stream were exempted [Reitz 2012b; Suhasini 2012]). A new selection system took effect on 4 May 2013, at which time the program was reopened, and a fixed number of applications were allocated to those who are most likely to succeed in Canada – younger individuals with Canadian experience and proficiency in French or English (CIC 2012c; Tobi Cohen 2012b). Applicants must pass a minimum official language threshold, and their credentials would be assessed beforehand to determine compatibility and value to Canada, with points allocated accordingly (CIC 2012c; Levitz 2012b). By contrast, the points allowed for overseas work experience were revised downward to put more emphasis on indicators of immigrant success. In early 2013, the new Federal Skilled Trades Program began fast-tracking up to three thousand foreign skilled tradespersons, including electricians, welders, and heavy duty equipment mechanics for the construction, transporation, and manufacturing sectors (Keung 2013b). To qualify, applicants must have a job offer in one of 43 in-demand occupations or be job-ready upon arrival, with a certificate of qualification and two years of work experience in the same skilled trade as the job offer (Boyd 2013). Basic language proficiency is necessary (Chase 2012). As well, the Start-Up Visa Program was introduced in April 2013 (initially, 2,750 visas annually), which awards permanent residency to entrepreneurs who have funding, qualify for admission, and are approved by venture capital investors (Bradbury 2013; Riddell 2013).

The economic class embraces the business subcategory, encompassing a broad range of admissions, including investors, entrepreneurs, and the self-employed. The Self-Employed Persons Program seeks applicants with (a) the intention or ability to become self-employed in Canada, (b) relevant experience to contribute to its cultural or athletic success, and (c) experience in farm management or a willingness to purchase and manage a Canadian farm. Both the investor and entrepreneur subcategories entail a transfer of funds as a precondition for entry. The "entrepreneurial" program selects immigrants with a demonstrated ability to establish or to buy and manage a business that will create at least two full-time jobs for non-family members. The amount of investment to qualify varies across Canada, but an entrepreneur must possess a minimum net worth of $300,000, legally obtained, with taxes paid. Under the "investor" program, applicants must meet the usual immigration criteria, with proven business experience and a demonstrated net worth of $1.6 million legally obtained. A business applicant receives permanent resident status in exchange for signing a declaration to invest $800,000 in a Canadian fund for five years under the management of Citizenship and Immigration Canada (CIC 2011d). The investment is subsequently returned without accrued interest.

However enticing the program, reality has proven less kind. The program has prompted criticism and charges of fraudulent abuse (O'Neil 2013), cumbersome delays (up to five years to process applicant files), and gross mismanagement that undermines potential benefits. As of June 2011, the government imposed a temporary moratorium on entrepreneur class applicants, and it capped investor applications at 700 per year (CIC 2011b); the quota was filled in 30 minutes, resulting in a pipeline of about 25,000 investor applicants (Keung 2012a). In mid-2012, Ottawa suspended applications for the

8 OBSERVATION

Rethinking the Point System

FOR MANY CANADIANS, the popularity and support of Canada's immigration program is synonymous with its much-touted point system for admission. Under the point system, immigrants are admitted on the basis of a sufficient number of qualifications and experiences, such as language or education levels (Papademetriou and Sumption 2011). A point system is easy to like: it's transparent, flexible, and easily adjusted to reflect changing economic conditions. It doesn't openly discriminate, although its emphasis on education, language, and skills represents a barrier to many groups, including women who lack equal access to these criteria in their homeland (Agnew 2009). On the downside, this kind of entry system excludes employers from the selection process, thus compromising their input into decision making of immediate relevance to the economy. By contrast, an employer-driven system such as in the United States (see Chapter 6) allows employers to select immigrant workers, subject to government regulations. This arrangement maximizes the use of immigrants for employment purposes, although the system can be manipulated to access cheaper labour or exploit dependent workers. Compare the following selection grids:

POINT ALLOCATION BY SELECTION CRITERIA AND IMMIGRATION SYSTEM

Criteria	Canada	Australia	New Zealand
Education	25%	30%	25%
Language	28%	13%	Mandatory
Work experience	15%	7%	23%
Age	12%	15%	12%
Arranged employment	10%	10%	23%
Adaptability	10%	27%	19%
Maximum points	100	200	265
Pass mark	67	120	140

Source: TD Economics (2012, 8).

There is another option. Papademetriou and Sumption (2011) argue that a hybrid system combines the advantages of both – namely, job flexibility and freedom of movement with the promise of future employment. The creation of a searchable database under a compromise arrangement entitles employers to review resumés of workers, make a job offer, and expedite the transfer process (Broadbent and Omidvar 2008). Such an immigrant-selection system often relies on a temporary-to-permanent visa pathway that admits workers on a temporary basis without necessarily obstructing a path to permanent residency for those with good integration prospects. The introduction of both the Canadian Experience Class and the Provincial Nominee Program constitute moves toward a hybrid selection system.

Another hybrid system reflects how Canada might rethink its selection of newcomers. In a talk titled "Immigration Sickness," Dr. Kwame McKenzie (cited in Goar 2013) attended to the following points in advocating for an evidence-based selection program that predicts successful immigration. Two strong predictors of immigrant success and adaptability prevail: (a) resiliency (the ability to bounce back) and (b) "emotional IQ" (a blend of skills for making the best of any situation). Both predictors are measurable, judging by the actions of corporate headhunters who rely on them in their search for talent. To be sure, McKenzie argues, there is much to commend in the government's desire to build a fast, flexible, and focused system to address Canada's labour market needs. Its decision to introduce an Expression of Interest pipeline in early 2015 to better match employers with skilled immigrants might offset some of the weaknesses of a scattershot approach to selection (Boyd 2013; CIC 2013d). But such an agenda can prove short-sighted since the economy and the labour market are changing rapidly. Moreover, whereas workers grow the economy, adaptable people build a country in which immigrants can thrive and contribute (Beiser and Bauder 2014; Jabir 2014).

investor programs (ibid.). It has promised to launch a new pilot program in mid-2013, aimed at luring start-up companies and entrepreneurs to Canada (Canadian Press 2013a). The Immigration Investment Program was terminated in early 2014, despite its popularity in more than 20 countries that copied and adopted this model (Marchi 2014).

Quebec's Immigration Program

Quebec has a relatively autonomous and distinctive immigration program for skilled workers and professionals (CIC 2011b). It determines the volume and composition of its own permanent immigration (currently allows 25,300 admissions annually), uses the program to attract capital to fund Quebec's businesses and increase employment, targets francophones to maintain French language and culture, and controls the creation and implementation of federally funded social and linguistic integration programs (Jedwab 2012; Rodríguez-García 2012; Fernando and Leahy 2014). Its selection criteria for skilled workers and professionals differ from those used elsewhere in Canada. Any applicant can qualify under any occupation listed in the Quebec skilled worker category, with or without a job offer from a Canadian employer. A two-step process is involved: The first step requires the issuing of a Quebec selection certificate, which entitles the bearer to a Canadian permanent resident (immigrant) visa. To qualify for the certificate, an unmarried applicant must score at least 49 points, based on the criteria in Box 9, whereas an applicant with a partner or spouse must score at least 57 points. An additional 6 points may be awarded for adaptability upon an interview. A single person then requires at least 55 (49 + 6) points to obtain a certificate, whereas a married person or an individual in a common-law relationship requires 63 (57 + 6) points. Processing fees amount to $406 for the principal applicant and $156 for the spouse (de facto or otherwise) and each dependent child. The selection factors are summarized in Box 9, to 20 March 2012.

The second step entails federal approval: Individuals whose applications have been vetted must complete medical and security/criminal examinations under the authority of the Canadian government before they receive a permanent resident (immigrant) visa. It should be noted that Quebec also possesses a Quebec Experience Class, consisting of two categories. One encompasses foreign graduate students who have studied for two years in Quebec and have taken an intermediate-level French course, and the other comprises skilled temporary foreign

9

Quebec's Point Grid for Skilled Workers

Training and education	Up to 28 points (cut-off score is 8 points)
Validated employment offer	Up to 10 points
Work experience	Up to 8 points
Age	Up to 16 points
Language proficiency	Up to 22 points
Stay and family in Quebec	Up to 8 points
Spouse's characteristics	Up to 16 points
Children	Up to 8 points
Financial self-sufficiency	1 point

workers with at least 12 months of work experience in Quebec and placement in an intermediate-level French-language course.

DEBATING CANADA'S IMMIGRATION MODEL: WHAT FOR, HOW, WHERE, WHAT KIND?

Canada's immigration program is subject to constant scrutiny and endless criticism (Canadian Centre for Immigration Policy Reform 2010; Bissett 2013; see also Chapter 7). A general pro-immigration consensus may prevail (Reitz 2011a), but debates persist over competing visions and divergent goals in terms of what for, how many, where from, what kind, and where to. The key questions are fairly straightforward: "What kind of immigration model do Canadians want?" "Is the current model working?" That is, can it cope with the volume and kinds of applicants who qualify under Canada's rules? What type of immigrants do Canadians favour? Before we discuss these questions, a look at Canada's immigration model is in order. In Box 10, the column at the left pinpoints the core provisions of the model, and the right-hand column expands on the provision in question.

10 OVERVIEW

Canada's Immigration Model

Core provisions	Attendant features
Centrality of immigration to Canadian identity/imaginary and to Canada building	> Canada is an immigration society > Immigrants are a solution to problems
Rules/protocols to regulate admissions	> Managed immigration framework for immigrant admission > Principled and proactive > Transparent/objective/accountable/non-discriminatory > Balance of family, economic, and humanitarian classes (self-interest and humanitarianism) > Balance short-term labour needs with long-term Canada-building citizens > Until recently, based on principle that those who qualify are on a first-come, first-served basis > Increasingly a shared jurisdiction (Ottawa, provinces, private interests) > Protect health, security, and safety of Canadians
Immigrants are society-building assets	> Crucial to sustained economic growth > Labour market and human capital models > International linkages as key to global economy > Cultural enrichment
Immigrants are permanent residents with rights and rights to citizenship	> Settlement model of immigration (not just market correction/contract labour) > Relatively easy path to citizenship, based on commitment to principles/ideals > Social contract between migrants and state > A thin national identity that makes it more accommodative
Programs for settlement/integration	> Multiculturalism, employment equity > Immigration settlement services such as ESL programs, Welcoming Communities Initiative such as TRIEC > Respect for differences, removal of discriminatory barriers > Inclusive principle – no one is excluded

There is much to commend in this immigration model for advancing Canada's normative status as an immigration society. Nonetheless, the model is subject to criticism. For some, it is not discerning enough in accepting and rejecting applicants (CIC 2013b), a fact that facilitates the entry of the undeserving and the unproductive. Even successful admissions may encounter additional difficulties in having their credentials recognized. According to Jason Kenney (cited in Radia 2011), work is under way with the provinces and more than four hundred professional licensing bodies to streamline the process of credential recognition for foreign-trained professionals. Yet the process is condemned as too little and too slow, prompting calls to rationalize the patchwork of settlement services or transfer responsibility and funding to the provinces, who are in a better position to know what's best (TD Economics 2012).

In that Canada's current immigration policies are being criticized for fraying at the edges, a dialogue cannot come too soon. Four key questions must be addressed: What for? (why does Canada need immigrants?) How many? Where from? What kind? (Hiebert 2006; Knowles 2007; see also Chomsky 2007; and Swain 2007 for the United States). The answers may strike at the heart of the immigration debate, yet agreement is notoriously elusive (for example, see Picot and Sweetman 2012). The debate remains as polarized as ever, in large part because ethnically neutral language and culturally freighted criteria often mask racism (Sakamoto et al. 2013). Debate is further intensified/splintered by recent developments in the immigration portfolio (Boyd and Alboim 2012), including (a) increasing ministerial discretion powers to allow flexibility in decision making, (b) decentralizing and devolving the selection and admission process, (c) significantly increasing temporary foreign workers to address short-term labour needs, and (d) creating a protocol to process residency applications from within.

What For? Does Canada Need Immigrants?

Why does Canada continue to accept immigrants and refugees? It may want more immigrants because of tradition, openness, obligation, or compassion for the less fortunate. But does it need them (Canadian Centre for Immigration Policy Reform 2010)? Some say yes. Immigrants and society building are strongly linked, of proven economic and demographic benefit, and indispensable in advancing national interests. Others say maybe, or it depends. Immigration may be necessary; however, costs and benefits must be accurately assessed and impartially articulated to ensure informed decision making. For example, despite government moves to tighten up the selection process, recent immigrants may be imposing a "fiscal burden" on Canada of up to $20 billion per year, in large part because their earnings and taxes are not high enough to offset the benefits and services they receive from government (Grubel 2013). Yet this fiscal burden may reflect the workings of an economy (rather than immigrant shortcomings) that underemploys newcomers and diminishes payroll taxes by refusing to recognize credentials, educational attainments, and overseas work experience.

Still others say no: Canada's immigration agenda policy is highly politicized (ibid.). Canadian politicians spar for immigrant votes, with each party doing its best to play the "immigration card" for securing an electoral edge in major cities (Lang 2011; Bissett 2013). Immigration decisions appear to be driven by the well-intentioned but possibly mistaken belief that perpetual growth is required in making Canada better (Grubel 2009; Weld 2009). Critics counter accordingly: If a shortage of labour is the problem, why not utilize largely untapped Aboriginal labour (or underemployed permanent residents) instead of turning to overseas recruits? Is there really a skilled labour shortage that cannot be addressed by locals, as employers assert? Or do employers simply prefer to use cheap and uncomplaining migrants with a strong work ethic, thereby avoiding the costs of improving working conditions or paying a fair wage (Ruhs and Anderson 2010)? Unless the program is used in a timely, temporary, and targeted sense, it also diminishes any incentive for training Canadians to do these jobs (McKenna 2012).

How Many? Does Canada Accept Too Many Immigrants?

Immigration totals, of approximately 250,000 per year, have remained steady for nearly two decades. Annual numbers are set by the immigration minister and routinely receive parliamentary approval without much public input into rationale and consequences (Grubel 2013). Critics accuse Canada of stretching its "absorptive capacity" by accepting too many immigrants and refugees at a time when many young Canadians are unemployed or underemployed (Grady 2009). Supporters disagree and propose higher totals to counterbalance the effects of skills shortages and population decline (Saunders 2012b). Some suggest that numbers be increased to about 350,000 (or approximately 1 percent of Canada's population, a figure the Liberal Party continues to endorse). Others insist on 150,000 as the preferred annual total that brings Canada in line with worldwide proportions and post-war averages. Still others suggest that Canada should accept an unlimited number of newcomers; after all, immigration controls are racist, inefficient, costly, and morally unjustified in an overpopulated world. Still others recommend that the numbers should be adjusted, based on the health of the economy (Abbott and Beach 2011; Picot and Sweetman 2012).

Which answer is acceptable? What is too much or not enough, and how can we determine a suitable figure? On what grounds? For example, a survey conducted by Forum Research for Postmedia (*National Post*) in March 2013 found that 70 percent of 1,755 Canadian adults polled supported limits on immigrant numbers, including 58 percent of those born in another country (Ligaya 2013). When is the absorptive capacity stretched to the limit? Is there a principled way to justify any proposed levels? (It should be noted that since 2008, Ottawa has capped the processing of immigrant applications in an effort to eliminate backlogs and expedite matters [CIC 2011c].) What is the right balance between permanent residents as potential nation builders and temporary foreign workers who serve short-term labour needs (although concerns are mounting that they are permanently temporary) (CIC 2011b; Maloney 2013)?

Where From? Does Canada Accept Too Many Immigrants from Non-Traditional Sources?

Since the 1980s, most immigrants to Canada have come from so-called non-convention countries, including about 60 percent from Asia and the Middle East. In 2010, the top five source countries for permanent residents were the Philippines (13 percent), India (10.8 percent), the People's Republic of China (10.8 percent), the United Kingdom (3.4 percent), and the United States (3.3 percent) (CIC 2011c). That kind of distribution invariably prompts a reaction, even from the well intentioned. As others have noted, references to source countries are not simply about geography or birthplace. Rather, they serve as proxy (or code or subtext) in rejecting the unacceptable religious and cultural attributes that are thought to be at loggerheads with Canadian values (also Bridget Anderson 2013). Should Canada seek more Euro-American immigrants, or is that pipeline largely closed? Should we focus on immigrants who are most likely to succeed in Canada, including those who have language skills, are relatively young, and come from countries with a reputation for hard work (Scoffield 2011; Levinson 2013; Solomon 2014)? What is the proper proportion? Can any ratio be justified or attained, keeping in mind that Canada no longer has the luxury of cherry picking whom it wants from where? It must compete with other industrialized countries for the brightest and best, and immigration is also increasingly influenced by global forces beyond its control (Simmons 2010). The federal government is taking greater control over which refugees can be accepted into Canada, in part by limiting the number of applications from Canadian sponsors such as church groups and by moving toward an approach that selects refugees from specific countries such as Iraq and Turkey (Keung 2013f).

What Kind? Does Canada Recruit the Wrong Class of Immigrants?

Admission rates in the family, economic, and refugee classes are uneven. Canada also possesses a bimodal immigration program that attracts both the highly skilled and those who lack the skills to make a direct and immediate contribution. For example, 43 percent of permanent residents who were admitted into Canada in 2008 possessed a university degree (BA, MA, PhD), but 32.9 percent had less than 12 years of schooling (Alboim 2009). In theory, Canada wants to attract the brightest stars, but does it actually need highly educated newcomers who will compete with their Canadian-born counterparts? Should it be seeking immigrants who are fluent in one or both official languages? For example, in 2008 nearly 72 percent of the permanent residents admitted into Canada said they had a knowledge of French, English, or both (CIC 2009b). Additional research indicates that about 10 percent of economic class entrants lack English/French capabilities, as do about 33 percent in the family class or dependants in the economic class and about 50 percent in the humanitarian category (Boyd 2009). Yet research clearly demonstrates that low levels of language competence are parlayed into unfavourable labour market outcomes and delayed integration into society (CIC 2012c).

Reaction is predictable. Some argue that the employment needs of the private sector should drive the selection of immigrants and that those whose social and economic skills contribute directly to Canada should be chosen (Grubel 2013). Jason Kenney made economic growth and prosperity (i.e., growing the Canadian economy [Jabir 2014]) a clear priority: "We need more newcomers working and paying taxes and contributing to our health-care system. That is the focus of our immigration program" (quoted in Alarcon and Law 2011; also Radia 2011). Not surprisingly, the Federal Skilled Worker Program is positioned as the cornerstone of Canada's immigration program, since it alone selects future citizens on their potential economic contribution, ability to successfully integrate, and commitment to Canada as their permanent home (Broadbent and Omidvar 2008). Moves to expedite immigrant integration into the labour market are contingent on changes to the selection criteria. Applicants who tend to fare better economically will be rewarded if they speak English or French, are relatively young, and have job offers, Canadian work experience, or postgraduate degrees from Canada (Friesen and Curry 2012). But can Canada justify skimming off the cream of the developing world, to its detriment and cost, without cautioning immigrants about the obstacles in finding employment? Should the point system be overhauled to attach more importance to skilled tradespeople who could make a significant contribution (Vineberg 2012)? Perhaps the focus should be on bringing in less-skilled immigrants (as the Provincial Nominee Program is doing) who will take on the precarious work – dirty, dull, dangerous, and difficult – shunned by the Canadian-born.

Even the rationale for economic admissions generates controversy. Until recently, the immigration program subscribed to a human capital model as the basis for admission. Under this model, general competences are sought, with the flexible and transferable skills to (re)adapt to the rapidly changing labour market scene. All credentials for immigration purposes are treated equally (no distinction is made between a PhD in fine arts from a recently accredited university and one in combinatorial mathematics from the University of Waterloo). Both language competencies and claimed expertise are self-reported, with a corresponding potential for deceit or discrepancies. The net result is admission with limited host-language competence, unrecognizable credentials and qualifications, and unwanted expertise in the labour market (Hawthorne 2008). Finally, unlike in the past, when Ottawa played the principal role in admissions, today's applicants can choose from up to 50 streams operated by the provinces, employers, and educational institutions. Complications, fragmentation, and confusion inevitably result (Omidvar 2012a).

11 OBSERVATION

Doing It Better Down Under: Can Canada Learn from Australia?

CANADA'S ECONOMIC CLASS as an admission category is hardly exempt from criticism. For some, the problem lies in the selection process. Applicants may be chosen on the basis of their human capital (the human capital model encourages the admission of highly educated migrants with language competency, even without a job offer or specific work skills [Ruhs and Anderson 2010]). But these applicants are not necessarily a good fit for the labour market in an economy that needs truck drivers and bricklayers instead of nuclear physicists or music teachers. For others, the lengthy delays in application are problematic, not only in bulky backlogs but also in the loss of qualified applicants to other destinations. As of 2008, 620,000 skilled worker applicants were in the entry pipeline, with average processing times at about 63 months. Although this figure was reduced somewhat to just over 463,000 applicants by 2012 (Keung 2012a), the end result is a frustrating and dangerous queue because of insufficient resources for processing applicants, who bounce in and out of an overburdened system.

Countries in the Antipodes have explored ways for improving a real jobs-based admission program (Shane 2012). In New Zealand, for example, the backlog of skilled workers was eliminated with the introduction of an expression-of-interest system in which skilled immigrants were plucked from a pool of prospective applicants (Shane 2012). Or consider Australia's adoption of a more robust labour market model for immigrants to overcome flaws in a human capital model. Planned mass migration since 1947 was a key feature in transforming Australia from an insular white British society to a cosmopolitan multicultural one in which more than a quarter of the population is foreign-born (Castles, Hugo, and Vasta 2013). Reforms were introduced in 1999 to consolidate a match between skilled immigrants and employment. They focused on employability (Hawthorne 2007), including (a) more stringent pre-migration English testing (candidates must achieve vocational-level scores or higher on an independently administered International English Language Testing System or its equivalent), (b) mandatory pre-migration credential screening prior to arrival by the relevant national or state licensing body, and (c) modifications to the point system by concentrating on the core employable factors of skills, age, and English-language competence, especially for in-demand occupations (including 20 bonus points for applicants who were qualified in in-demand fields). Top priority was assigned to international students who completed post-secondary education in Australia, together with those who had a genuine job offer or previous work experience. In other words, Australia's immigration program has moved from the principle of prospective employability (human capital) as a selection criterion to that of actual employment as grounds for admission (labour market ready).

Initial results have proven promising. Outcomes have vastly improved for principal applicants from racialized minority groups and other disadvantaged groups, including women and older immigrants. Immigrants are now employed in fields for which they were trained, have access to professional and managerial status, and earn more as a group than the Australian-born. During the two years after the human capital model was abandoned, 81 percent of economic migrants (a figure that rose to 83 percent in 2006) had secured work within six months of their arrival (compared to 60 percent in Canada) (Hawthorne 2007).

Not everyone accepts this rosy assessment, however. Critics find no evidence that Australia's immigration policy facilitated immigrant integration into the labour market. Chinese immigrants did no better than their Canadian counterparts in earnings or employment levels, whereas earnings for South Asian immigrants have deteriorated since the 1980s (Clarke and Skuterud 2012). According to Clarke and Skuterud (ibid.), overall performance advantage is driven by differences in who gets in rather than differences owing to labour market conditions. Changes in source country composition might help to explain why the average Australian immigrant outperforms the average Canadian immigrant. The introduction of rules that favour English-language speakers not only ensures relatively fewer Asian immigrants, compared to Canada, but invites proportionately more British immigrants (20 percent versus 5 percent). British immigrants in both countries rapidly assimilate into the local labour market, with earning and employment levels similar to those of the native-born. In short, immigrants in Australia do better than those in Canada, not because of an enlightened admissions program but because of a shift toward demographics that are most likely to succeed and integrate (Woolley 2012).

Resistance to family class immigrants is mixed. Some believe in refusing family class immigrants, whose earnings rarely match costly health and social services (Collacott 2006; Bissett 2009a). The subtext is clear: Parents and grandparents impose a fiscal burden by over-utilizing social services and crowding health care space (Grubel 2013; Thompson 2011b). A similar line of reasoning and criticism is directed at refugee claimants. Others believe that upping the family reunification category is critical since family separation represents a costly consequence. Reuniting new Canadians with their extended families may facilitate the settlement and integration process, especially in the context of lengthy labour market integration (Busby and Corak 2014; Wayland 2006). Nor should the social and indirect contributions of family reunification as public good be ignored (Dench 2006; Solberg 2006; Vanderplaat 2006). Lastly, the promise of family reunification may prove the inducement to entice the brightest and the best to come and stay.

Responses to these four questions rarely agree. Even more intriguing is how these questions embed additional issues pertaining to (a) deterioration in economic outcomes of new immigrants, (b) occupational and labour shortages, (c) immigration levels and business cycles, (d) regional distribution of newcomers, (e) application backlog, and (f) mix of short-term and long-term migrants (see Picot and Sweetman 2012). Yet challenges posed by immigrants to liberal democracies such as Canada go deeper than concerns and debates over cohesion, employment, or admission categories. As Bridget Anderson

(2013) points out, they strike at the heart of liberal principles of equality, rights, and membership in addition to societal assumptions about social relations and sovereignty. For, in the final analysis, modern societies define themselves not as arbitrary collections of individuals bound by common legal status; rather, they see themselves as communities of value and values, made up of people who share common ideals (about what is acceptable, desirable, and normal) and exemplary patterns of behaviour (from hard working to law abiding). Clearly, then, some degree of dialogue and consensus is necessary if Canada's immigration program is to remain relevant, publicly supported, and of mutual benefit to both Canadians and newcomers. Tradeoffs will be necessary in light of emergent trends unsettling the immigration program. The shift from long-term nation-building needs – including restrictions to the federal skilled worker class, the expansion of the Provincial Nominee and Temporary Foreign Worker Programs, and the creation of the Canadian Experience Class – to a focus on short-term labour needs promises to be a game-changer (Alboim 2009).

4

recalibrating canada's immigration program

CUSTOMIZING IMMIGRANTS, COMMODIFYING MIGRANT LABOUR

FRAMING THE NEW IMMIGRATION

THE *NATIONAL POST* (Gallagher 2008a) recently ran a contest in which readers were asked to describe Canada in six words or fewer. The winning entry put it convincingly: "Canada – a Home for the World." Much can be gleaned from this homily, thanks to the arrival of some 10 million immigrants of diverse origins since the Second World War, including nearly 5 million between 1991 and 2011, many from the so-called non-traditional sources of China, India, Pakistan, and the Philippines. Numbers confirm the obvious: Canada is a society of immigrants and its commitment to proactively select and settle newcomers reinforces its normative status as an immigration society. And despite a modest uptick in Canadian concerns over immigration numbers and politics, nothing in the conceivable future suggests a departure from this business-as-usual agenda (Nanos 2010).

Not everyone accepts this sanguine assessment. For some, the adherence to a so-called mass immigration model is problematic (Collacott 2009; Bissett 2009a, 2013; Stoffman 2009b; Canadian Centre for Immigration Policy Reform 2010).[1] Reference to "mass" as "many" and "undifferentiated" builds on a popular (politically correct?) perception of immigration as (a) a normal aspect of the human condition, (b) resistant to centralized control, (c) of overall benefit to society, and (d) a right, such that admission cannot be denied (Browne 2003). For critics, this kind of orthodoxy is unjustified and counterproductive (Gibson 2009). Canada's immigration program is criticized for lacking coherence and rationale except for presenting the country as little more than a global hostel for a mélange of foreign passports (Gallagher 2008a). A mass immigration program is thought to have challenged the very notion of "what Canada is for," compromised living standards, eroded national identity, shredded the socio-cultural fabric, and exposed Canadians to the dangers of extremism (Grubel 2009). Of course, Canada is not the only country with immigration issues, mass or otherwise. It's neither immune to global migration dynamics nor an exception to economies that depend on migrant labour. Nevertheless, it might well be one of the few where a robust immigration program is entrenched as an article of faith, a structural necessity, a policy norm, and a sacred cow. Anyone who dares to question its lofty status as a litmus test of Canadianness is doomed to political suicide or, worse still, social ostracism (Gallagher 2008a; McCullough 2013).

For others, however, a muscular immigration program reinforces Canada's imposing perch as a society of immigrants. Canada's immigration program reflects a long-term nation-building strategy, with a focus on integrating newcomers into an inclusive society and a healthy labour market (Reitz 2013). This managed program has garnered widespread popularity and public support, including worldwide recognition as a "best practice" (Reitz 2010b). On the whole, Canada constitutes a more vibrant society because of immigrants and their optimistic outlook, global linkages, entrepreneurial spirit, and investment capital. Their role as producers and consumers contributed and continues to boost economic productivity and national prosperity. They also offer a solution to the multi-pronged challenges of an ageing population, shrinking birth rate, diminishing tax base, and looming skills shortage (see Miner 2010). Not surprisingly, Jeffrey Reitz (2010b, 16) cautions the Canadians who would tamper with success: "Canada would be wise to go slow in changing what has been regarded, both internationally and by most Canadians, as a highly successful immigration program."

Disagreements aside, both critics and supporters concur over one truism: Immigration policies historically operated on the principle of stimulating economic activity and developmental growth by facilitating entry of the wanted while blocking the unwanted (Bauder 2008a; Basok and Bastable 2009). Since the 1990s, the immigration program has reflected, reinforced, and advanced a neoliberal agenda for making the country more economically competitive in a global market economy. The words of former immigration minister Jason Kenney (2012d) underscore what many already suspected: "The government's number one priority remains jobs, economic growth, and long-term prosperity." In seeking to grow the economy, Citizenship and Immigration recalibrated the admission process to focus on newcomers who are ready to fit into Canada through their education, language, culture, and age (Levinson 2013). Again, in the words of Jason Kenney (2012d), "We are embarking on a program of transformational change to move from a slow, rigid, and passive, really a supply-driven immigration system, to a fast, flexible, and pro-active, demand-driven immigration system." A commitment to market principles has also revised Ottawa's role in admitting newcomers. Nowhere is this more evident than in federal moves to off-load responsibility for immigrant selection to provinces, employers, and universities. This off-loading comes with costs. Multiple entry portals are created that may be difficult to coordinate, monitor, or regulate. An increased reliance on demand-driven temporary foreign workers (or migrant workers) also reinforces a commodifying of labour along more precarious lines.[2] The implications of this shift from immigrants as nation builders to migrants as hired hands threaten to compromise Canada's long-term national interests (Canadian Council for Refugees 2010b; Alboim and Cohl 2012).

The recalibration of the immigration program has proven contentious (see also Kobayashi, Li, and Teixeira 2012, xxv). One question looms uppermost: Does the customizing (de-massifying) of immigrants along designer, designated, and demand lines reflect a paradigm shift or a program tweak? To one side are those permanent designer immigrants who are deemed to be low-cost and high-yield; to another side, provisional entrants are designated for assignment once they jump the appropriate admission hoops; to yet another side are demand-driven temporary foreign migrant workers whose disposable talents underpin a just-in-time labour market flexibility without incurring long-term costs or corporate responsibility (Piché 2010). A conflict of interest materializes: Demand-driven immigrants may plug immediate economic needs, but their precarious employment position exposes them to marginalization, while obscuring inequities associated with

Canada's neoliberal-leaning immigration program (also Mooers 2005). A commodification of migrant labour also reflects the economics of a customized immigration program that reinforces new patterns of racialized stratification (also Zaman 2006, 2010). Worse still, their value as vital players in Canada building is discredited by a short-sighted strategy in which they are simply hired help to fill labour shortages (Rajagopalan 2011; Omidvar 2013).

The dynamics of customizing immigration and immigrants are re-shaping and restratifying Canada on grounds of residency, status, and contributions. Such a shift is proving double-edged in advancing both benefits and costs, praise and criticism. The number of tempor-ary foreign workers (TFW) has tripled since the early 2000s, with the bulk of the increase to approximately 340,000 by the end of 2012 due to the entrenchment of the Temporary Foreign Worker Program (TFWP) as a labour market necessity (Jason Foster 2012). Time will tell whether Canada can dodge the proverbial bullet in expanding its version of a "guest worker" program without either incurring the wrath of Canadians or compromising its own interests.

CANADA'S IMMIGRATION PROGRAM: THE PREVAILING MODEL

Canada's immigration program is informed by three primary object-ives: to reunite families, promote the economy, and fulfill international obligations and humanitarian traditions with respect to refugees (CIC 2012a; Kenney 2012a). These objectives are implemented through three main admission categories for permanent entry – family class, economic (or independent) class, and refugee class. Moves to offset labour shortages without having to commit to excessive costs reflect the introduction of a provisional stream of provincial nominees, skilled foreign workers with Canadian experience, and international students with postgraduate Canadian degrees. Canada has also ramped up its TFWP to unprecedented levels to address its short-term but increas-ingly permanent labour market needs (Hennebry 2012).

The economic class remains a major source of admission. Prime Minister Stephen Harper confirmed this in his address at the World Economic Forum by emphasizing the centrality of economic and labour force needs in reforming Canada's immigration program (cited in Kenney 2012a). Admissions via this class have undergone several corrections in recent years. Historically, Canada endorsed a labour market/absorptive capacity model of immigration. Matching labour availability with economic needs produced a taps-on, taps-off approach that synchronized immigration levels with business cycles, increasing during boom periods but pared back during the "bust" (Bauder 2008b). This model was eventually displaced in the 1980s by a human capital model, which concentrated on attracting top-quality migrants, most notably the well educated with the flexible, transferable skills that ostensibly flourished in a highly competitive and knowledge-based global market economy (Fleras 2010). Robust levels of immigration were justified in a context of sustainable economic growth, even during economic downturns. The fact that skilled immigrants generate wealth means that their presence (as customers, workers, and entrepreneurs) enables Canada to buy, consume, and work its way out of a recession (Bauder 2008b).

However attractive in theory, the human capital model exposed shortcomings in the selection program. First, there were long delays in processing applications. Second, a disconnect occurred between immigrant qualifications and success in the Canadian labour market, owing in part to time lapses between application and entry. And third, immigrants clustered in the MTV cities of Montreal, Toronto, and Vancouver to the disadvantage of outlying regions. Canada's selection system of federal skilled workers was rebuked as slow, rigid, and passive at best, as sclerotic at worst. Changes were overdue in customizing the program along more responsive lines. As Harper explained during a 2012 interview with *Global News,* "We have been making some fairly profound changes to how we handle immigration. We have traditionally just been a country that passively accepts applications. We are now trying to go out and shape those immigration applications and process those in a way that will serve the labour force holes that are emerging" (quoted in Campion-Smith 2012).

Even the much-vaunted point system elicits criticism for fumbling the challenge. Applicants who are selected on the basis of their human capital quota do not necessarily translate into labour market availability, especially when the economy needs truck drivers, fast-food servers, and bricklayers. Moreover, a human-capital-based point system is perversely illogical: It may block admittance of skilled tradespeople and non-skilled workers, but it treats all skills and credentials as if they were the same, regardless of need or demand (Hawthorne 2007). For example, a PhD in computer design from MIT is equivalent for points purposes to a doctorate in sociology from a small liberal college. A lack of job focus is problematic as well. An applicant's occupation is not taken into account. Instead, admission is assessed on the basis of his or her labour market flexibility related to education, language competence, experience, and age, all in the hope of selecting for capital-rich (both human and financial) individuals with transferable skills and resourceful mindsets (Bauder 2008b).

CUSTOMIZING IMMIGRATION: DESIGNER, DESIGNATED, DEMAND-DRIVEN

Criticism of Canada's human capital/sustainable model of immigration has produced results (Conference Board of Canada 2008b). A more active and strategic approach for admissions was introduced, concentrating largely on labour market readiness in defining who gets in (Lowe 2008; Basok and Bastable 2009). The human capital model as a key admission criterion (flexible and transferrable skills) was dislodged by a labour market focus, with a stronger emphasis on processing and selection, making greater use of technology to improve efficiencies and to offset the growing mismatch between immigrant qualifications and employer needs (OECD 2012; CAPIC 2013). As Box 12 shows, the immigration program was subsequently recast around three additional admission categories based largely on two-step and just-in-time labour models (CAPIC 2013; Boyd 2013), type of work,

12

Customizing Canada's Immigration Model: Three Admission Streams

Permanent admissions	Provisional admissions	Precarious admissions
Designer immigrants	Designated immigrants	Demand-driven migrants
> Labour market ready	> Canadian Experience Class	> Temporary foreign workers
> Labour market	» Postgraduates	(both skilled and unskilled)
preference	» Skilled temporary	> Low-skilled pilot workers
> Provincial nominees	workers	> Seasonal agricultural
	> Live-in caregivers	workers

and patterns of residency – namely, permanent/designer, provisional/ designated, and precarious/demand-driven.

Permanent Admissions: Designer Immigrants

Permanent admissions are now geared to high-yield and low-cost de- signer immigrants. No longer must Canada process all applicants who qualify on a first-come, first-served basis. Nor is it locked into a passive acceptance of those who have sufficient points (67) for entry, regard- less of occupational demand or firm job offer. Instead, it is embarking on a pick-and-choose model consistent with the principle of just-in-time labour market needs (CIC 2012c). Selecting for immigrants of immedi- ate value is grounded in a neoliberal agenda that emphasizes aggres- sive market competitiveness, a flexible labour force, and regulations that work to an employer's advantage (Shields 2003). A commitment to neoliberalism displaces the protectionist model of nation building that framed immigrants as a disruptive form of labour competition at odds with Canada's economic competitiveness at home and abroad. Neoliberalism proposes a proactive international labour program that privileges a market ideology as the ideal mechanism for matching immigrants with jobs, while selecting for newcomers who are unlikely to draw on welfare services or unemployment benefits (Bauder 2008b). Of particular value are relatively young employable individuals whose language competence and marketable skills will make an immediate contribution (Kenney 2012b), prompting Alan Simmons (2010, 85, em- phasis added) to write,

> In effect, the state has shifted toward the admission of "designer immigrants," consisting of individuals who are selected as if they were custom designed to meet the specific criteria of a neo liberal nation intent on *productivity, cost recovery, and immigrant self settle- ment. Immigrants are ideally to have the language and work skills to begin employment soon after arrival. They are to come with savings sufficient to look after their needs until they find employment.*

There are three categories of permanent designer immigrants: labour market ready, labour market preference, and provincial nominees. Im- migrants under the Canadian Experience Class (both graduate students and highly skilled temporary foreign workers) are classified as provi- sional because their entry into Canada comes with strings attached.

Labour Market Ready

The customizing of Canadian immigrants along designer lines involves the removal of unmanageable backlogs and processing delays. Citizenship and Immigration established new rules to restrict the entry of federal skilled workers to those who have an offer of employment, legal residence in Canada for at least a year, or demonstrated skills in one of the listed priority jobs (Alboim 2009; Nakache and Kinoshita 2010). The passage of Bill C-50 in 2008 empowered the immigration minister to prioritize applicants from the Federal Skilled Worker Program in response to labour shortages in select occupations. The processing of applicants outside of these three categories is either delayed or discarded if they are already in the pipeline. This new dispensation constitutes a major change. The government is no longer obligated to automatically process every applicant who meets the 67 point cutoff line, in the process clogging the system with admissions who lack realistic job prospects. Immigration Minister Jason Kenney justified this move when he claimed that "before we changed the system, we had to process every application received. Since many more people applied every year than could be accepted, a backlog was created. Now that we are processing *only those applications that meet specified criteria,* our Government is making significant progress in reducing the backlog" (quoted in *Marketwired* 2009, emphasis added).

In a move that promises to revolutionize the immigration program along more decentralized, demand-driven, and employer-instigated lines (Boyd 2013), Ottawa has proposed a two-stage system (still in the design phase but slated to open in 2015) for selecting federal skilled workers. The introduction of an Expression of Interest system (to be called Express Entry) intends to switch from a passive processing of applicants to a more proactive system for in-demand workers with the skills that employers want and Canada needs (CAPIC 2013; CIC 2013d). The first phase of this New Zealand-inspired model will screen applicants for placement into an expression-of-interest pool (CIC 2012c). Prospective immigrants will indicate their interest to work in Canada by electronically filling out information about their human capital skills and work experience as well as education level and language ability. Those who meet the eligibility criteria will be pre-screened (points assigned and applications ranked) for placement into a pool of candidates (Keung 2014a). The Expression of Interest form does not constitute an application for admission per se, Monica Boyd

(2013) points out; rather, it's an invitation for candidates with valued skills or job offers to apply for a visa (CIC 2013d). In the second stage, the federal government and provinces (not employers, as is the case "down under") will dip into this "employment pool" to select applicants based on local labour market needs or identified by employers with a firm job offer (Mas 2014). Those who qualify will then be accorded priority processing for rapid admission into Canada. Those applicants not selected after a period of time might be removed from the database to prevent a backlog and ensure timely processing (CIC 2013d).

Reaction to the Express Entry system has yet to be fully gauged. For the government, the Express Entry admission model promises to be a game-changer. In allowing greater flexibility and responsiveness to regional labour shortages for which there are no available Canadian workers, this new immigration management system allows stakeholders to select the candidates most likely to succeed in Canada rather than those who happen to be in line first (Canadian Immigrant 2014). The proposed system changes how skilled workers are selected and processed by transforming the current points-based approach into a designer-driven approach with an increased role for employers in deciding who gets in; enhancing Canada's control over the type and number of skilled workers who apply and enter; ensuring a higher level of proactivity in selecting applicants with in-demand skills; and reducing both waitlists and backlogs (AAISA 2013; Boyd 2013). In short, the new system actively matches prospective migrants with labour-hungry employers to advance Canada's national priority of economic growth and job creation (CIC 2013d; Canada News Centre 2014). Canada's growing commitment to a two-tier process of immigrant selection is thus reinforced under the Express Entry route, since newcomers who arrive first as job-ready perform better on the job market (the average income for those with prearranged jobs was $79,200 after three years compared with $44,200 for those without a job placement) (Keung 2014d). Critics are less enthused. The Express Entry approach is criticized as little more than a job bank for government and industry or a "dating site" in which Ottawa plays matchmaker between immigrants and employers (Mas 2014). The danger lies in mothballing the point system as a basis for recruiting newcomers whose long-term commitments are more focused on Canada building rather than simply growing the economy (Beiser and Bauder 2014).

Labour Market Preference

Immigration patterns are increasingly devoted to recruiting people from countries that have track records of success. Customizing the rules for who gets in allows the government to track the performance of newcomers and their children (immigration lawyer Richer Kurland, cited in Gillis 2010). Particularly attractive are immigrants whose "ethnic capital" includes a cultural commitment to excellence, education, and enterprise. Ease of entry is accorded to immigrants from Asia (especially India and China); after all, they and their offspring are most likely to be university educated and employed in high-skill occupations. Children from cultures with in-demand ethnic capital do better than those from cultures that are perceived to be capital-deprived (Wente 2010). For example, 98.3 percent of young Chinese adults who were born or raised in Canada sought post-secondary education by the age of 21 (Laucius 2009). Thus, this demographic is consistent with the government's customized approach to designer immigrants who offer "the biggest bang for the buck." Alan Simmons (2010, 114) says, "While Canada does not officially select immigrants on the basis of country of origins, Canadian policy nevertheless uses socio-economic selection criteria that play an important role in determining the countries from which immigrants come." By contrast, the flow is increasingly pinched for those from less desirable source countries with lower levels of ethnic capital (ibid.). Studies indicate that second-generation youth from the Caribbean and Latin America don't perform as well (they have less education and lower-skilled jobs); as a result, immigration totals from these locales continue to drift downward. In short, labour market preference is oriented toward recruiting immigrants who are easiest to integrate, less socially difficult or costly, culturally compatible, and more economically productive (Jhappan 2009). This prioritizing will invariably draw on immigrants from social class and nationality backgrounds who are labour market ready (Tannock 2011).

Provincial Nominees

The federal government has historically determined who enters Canada. In theory, however, responsibility for admission is shared with the provinces and territories (CIC 2012a). The reality of shared jurisdiction has moved from principle to practice in recent years, with the provinces assuming greater control over admissions. The new arrangement established immigrant admission as a concurrent jurisdiction, with Ottawa exercising authority over numbers and entry criteria, but the provinces actively involved in recruiting workers for local and regional economies (Lawlor 2012). This shift is not surprising; after all, immigration must be responsive to the unique economic needs of provinces and territories (CIC 2010c). Most provinces and territories have implemented both comprehensive and bilateral arrangements to that effect (CIC 2012c). Under the Canada-Quebec Accord of 1991, for example, Quebec exercises nearly absolute control over numbers, selection criteria, and integration services (except for refugees and family reunification, which remain a federal responsibility). It also implements government-funded settlement and integration services (CIC 2010c; Jedwab 2012; Rodríguez-García 2012). Quebec has a number of independent offices abroad for recruiting, screening, and selecting potential migrants.

The Provincial Nominee Program (PNP) is a relatively new and promising subcategory under the economic class (Baglay 2011). All provinces (except Quebec, which has its own quasi-autonomous immigration program) have negotiated an agreement with Ottawa to nominate and recruit prospective immigrants according to their own criteria and priorities, resulting in significant variations in recruitment patterns (Seidle 2012; Boyd 2013). The rationale is unassailable: A centralized intake system may possess certain advantages, but it may prove incapable of properly responding to the diverse and local needs of provinces or employers (ibid.). The PNP does it differently, by decentralizing the formula for linking migrants with jobs. Introduced in the late 1990s as a niche initiative to lure migrants away from the MTV cities of Montreal, Toronto, and Vancouver, the PNP proved a departure from federal immigration programs by allowing provinces to play a direct role in selecting immigrants who were willing to settle in that province for local labour market needs (Alboim 2009; Carter, Pandey, and Townsend 2010). Applicants under the PNP do not require university degrees, a skilled profession, or fluency in an official language. Compare this to federal arrangements, which favour applicants with postgraduate degrees, professional job skills, and exemplary language proficiency. Tradespeople are consequently eliminated from the federal stream because their qualifications fall outside the point grid or they lack English-language proficiency (in 2013, a special program was introduced to expedite their entry). By contrast, the PNP allows provinces to hand-pick tradespeople and semi-skilled workers, often through employer sponsorships or via investor programs that inject thousands of dollars into the local economy (McMahon 2011; Paperny 2011).

In short, the PNP allows the priority processing of overseas applicants and temporary foreign workers already in Canada for the province in which they plan to work and live (Boyd 2013). It circumvents the long delays and red tape of the backlog that clogs the federal pipeline (CIC 2009b). Once nominated, individuals obtain expedited (fast-track) permanent residence without meeting federal point-system requirements, with some provinces providing a direct path to permanent residence, though most provinces offer a two-step path beginning with a work period as a temporary migrant worker (Faraday 2012, 11). To gain entry via the PNP, individuals apply directly to the province or territory and are vetted by provincial officials to determine their compatibility with one of the multiple admission streams established by each province. They must possess the skills, experience, and education to make an immediate economic contribution. Once the province nominates them for permanent resident status, Citizenship and Immigration Canada makes the final decision to accept or reject, based on whether they meet its admission requirements related to health, security, and criminality (Carter, Pandey, and Townsend 2010; Baglay 2011).

To date, the program appears on track to success (Haimin Zhang 2012). The number of provincial nominees has accelerated in recent years from fewer than five hundred in 2000 to just over forty-one thousand (including dependants) in 2012 (Taylor 2009a; Carter, Pandey, and Townsend 2010; CIC 2011c; Canada News Centre 2014). The optics look good at the economic front as well. Provincial nominees tend to have lower levels of education yet almost always have a prearranged job and secure income. As a result, they don't go through the survival job struggle of highly skilled workers who must run the gauntlet of credential recognition and delayed entry into the labour market. The PNP has also contributed to the dispersal of immigrants, as the share of newcomers in the MTV cities has dipped to 75 percent from 90 percent (Friesen 2012a). For example, consider Manitoba, which many regard as the poster child for a decentralized immigration. The province provided the sixteen thousand newcomers who settled there in 2010 with training and support (including matching them with a settlement worker who provided a one-stop shop for settlement and integration). It also targeted immigrants who were more likely to stay because of family ties or an ethnic community into which they could tap (about 85 percent stay); it matched newcomers to unfilled jobs as meat workers, truck drivers, and welders; and it encouraged many to bypass Winnipeg for smaller centres (Ibbitson 2011; Friesen 2012d). Box 13 demonstrates this demographic shift, caused in part by the PNP.

The benefits are laudable (Seidle 2012). According to a PNP evaluation (Paperny 2011), provincial nominees are more likely to stay in the province that "sponsored" them, their earnings in the first year are on par with their federal counterparts (in British Columbia, the mean employment earnings triple those of federal skilled workers [Haimin Zhang 2012]), and their settlement and integration outcomes continue to improve over time (Carter, Pandey, and Townsend 2010). The program is not perfect, of course. For example, investors admitted under one province's PNP can easily resettle in another province, which must then absorb the costs of settlement and services (Collacott 2013). But additional problems with aspects of the Atlantic provincial investor program notwithstanding (McMahon 2011; Paperny 2011), the PNP is now the new face of designer immigration. It reflects a localized, market-responsive alternative to the traditional point system of selecting skilled newcomers, one that matches immigrants to employers while injecting badly needed growth and diversity across Canada (Paperny 2011).

Provisional Admissions, Designated Immigrants

In contrast to permanent admissions, entrants under a provisional status are conditional (their attainment of permanent residency comes with strings attached). They are designated for assignment in Canada on the basis of their provisional status, which may be converted into permanent residency. Designer migrants with the right qualifications may apply for landed immigrant status without leaving Canada to lodge an application. The value of an inland application is inestimable, concedes the Conference Board of Canada (2008a, ii):

> No longer does it make business sense to send skilled and highly sought-after temporary foreign workers back to their home countries so that they can re-apply as permanent immigrants. Today's immigration policies and programs are designed to make the transition from temporary to permanent immigration a much

13 OBSERVATION

Is the PNP Rearranging Immigrant Destinations?

THE PROVINCIAL AND urban destinations of permanent residents continue to shift over time. The 2010 figures reveal that settlement numbers shifted from Ontario, with a corresponding drift toward other parts of Canada. For example, from 1991 to 2006, the Atlantic provinces attracted less than 1 percent of all immigrants to Canada, and Saskatchewan drew only 0.6 percent. In 2011, the Maritime provinces increased their total to 2.7 percent of all immigration, whereas Saskatchewan's total rose to 2.9 percent (Campbell 2012).

PERMANENT RESIDENTS BY PROVINCE AND URBAN AREA, 2010 AND 2006

	2010	2006
Ontario	118,116	125,892
Toronto	92,181	99,289
Quebec	53,591	44,684
Montreal	46,460	38,401
British Columbia	44,176	42,083
Vancouver	37,329	36,299
Alberta	32,640	20,716
Calgary	16,100	11,823
Manitoba	15,803	10,047
Winnipeg	12,340	7,715
Saskatchewan	7,617	2,724
Saskatoon	3,178	1,164
PEI	2,581	565
Charlottetown	2,493	490
Nova Scotia	2,408	2,586
Halifax	1,803	1,966
New Brunswick	2,125	1,646
Saint John	655	547
Newfoundland and Labrador	681	508
St. John's	493	397

more practical, time sensitive, and accessible process for business and international workers interested in such opportunities.

Two classes fall under provisional admissions: the Canadian Experience Class (for international graduate students, highly skilled temporary foreign workers, and the international experience class) and the Live-in-Caregiver Program.

Canadian Experience Class

The launching of the Canadian Experience Class (CEC) in 2008 reflects a move to designate immigrants for reassessment and reassignment. The CEC enables both international students who have graduated from a Canadian university *and* highly skilled temporary workers to apply for permanent residency without having to leave Canada, assuming they possess skilled work experience, legal residence in the country, and competence in English or French. The number of newcomers who were admitted under this program rose to just over 9,353 in 2012 (including spouses and dependants), from under 2,500 in 2008 (Chase 2011). Selection under the CEC is on a pass/fail basis, unlike the point system for selecting federal skilled workers (Picot and Sweetman 2012). More specifically:

> To qualify for permanent residence, TFW must have two years of full-time (or equivalent) Canadian work experience in a managerial, professional, or technical/skilled occupation (for example, in carpentry, welding, and pipefitting). This matching of skill-starved employers with qualified employees frees Canada of training and resettlement expenses. But the program has come under criticism because the transition to permanent residence prevails only at the high-skill end, thus excluding those with lower skill levels (such as meat packers, food plant workers, and kitchen staff). Women tend to be excluded as well: Statistics for 2008 show that about 48 percent of men on temporary work permits qualified for CEC status because of their skill levels, whereas only 19 percent of women did.

> International students in the CEC class are also fast-tracked for admission. Until recently, Canada did not view international students as potential citizens, and a visa for study in Canada was contingent on demonstrating an intent to leave upon graduation. Once in Canada,

students were not allowed to work off campus and had to leave the country to apply for re-entry as landed immigrants. Proposed changes are welcome (Belkhodja 2011). The attractiveness of international students as prospective migrants is understandable, despite some reservations (Alboim 2011a), resulting in intense global competition for their attention and retention (Lowe 2011). They are highly skilled, have Canadian credentials and experience, are likely to be proficient in an official language, and reduce settlement costs due to their familiarity with Canadian society (Simmons 2010). To qualify, foreign graduates from a Canadian post-secondary institution require at least two years of full-time study and one year of full-time (or equivalent) skilled work experience in Canada upon graduation.

> A new entry portal, titled the International Experience Class, enables newcomers between the ages of 18 and 35 with an open permit to work in Canada for up to two years without having a prearranged job. The program, which anticipates as many as twenty thousand admissions in 2014, allows employers to bypass the Labour Market Opinion process (thus removing any need for government approval) while paying less than the prevailing market wage (Canadian Press 2014). Individuals in this category can apply for permanent resident status after one year of skilled work. Bilateral agreements with nearly three dozen mostly European countries resulted in just under sixty-one thousand temporary residents as of December 2011 (exclusion of countries such as India prompted accusations of racism [David Cohen 2013]). This entry portal has come under criticism for usurping jobs from young Canadians (Siddiqui 2013b; Canadian Press 2014).

Live-In Caregivers

The case of TFW in Canada and globally yields insight into the politics and perils of gendered immigration (Hsiung and Nichol 2010). The exploitation of migrants as cheap labour in performing a country's "dirty work" applies to men and women. But only women are expressly imported for gender-specific jobs pertaining to the sex trade, child rearing, and domestic labour (cooking, cleaning, and caring [Pannell and Altman 2009]) (Macklin 1999; Saunders 2014). According to Saskia Sassen (2003), global capitalism prompts the often unauthorized movement of women, including mail-order brides, enslaved sex-trade workers, and undocumented immigrant factory and service employees. Of particular note is the growing legion of women who are recruited for domestic work in economically privileged countries. The dynamics of power are unmistakable here. The off-loading of household duties and the care of children, elderly folk, and persons with disabilities onto foreign domestic workers reinforces how the enrichment of some contributes to the disempowerment of others. That is, one class of women may be freed to pursue professional careers, but households rely on foreign domestic labour to facilitate such options, thus ensuring that care work remains women's work (Benhabib and Resnik 2009). The psychological and emotional burden is significant (Caritas Internationalis 2010). Caregivers are expected to provide love and affection for other people's children in hopes of improving quality of life for their own children. But the untimely and extended separation of family members deprives caregiver children of the basic nurture they require during their formative years. The potential for long-term developmental effects on individuals and costs to society should not be underestimated.

Consider the ambiguities in Canada's Live-in-Caregiver (LIC) Program.[3] The program might allow domestic workers to migrate to Canada, but it also (a) enables affluent households to capitalize on the economic inequalities spawned by globalization, (b) separates mothers and wives from their families, an experience fraught with difficulties in compounding the strain on transnational families, and (c) contributes (however inadvertently) to the marginalization of women through the continued devaluation of domestic labour (Jarrah Hodge 2006). Under the terms of their LIC agreement, foreign caregivers must normally live in their employer's home for at least two years (or 3,900 hours) over a four-year period. Changing employers is possible, although it is discouraged without evidence of abuse or default in terms of the contract (Liston and Carens 2008). As live-in nannies, they are legally classified as temporary workers and subject to deportation upon termination of their contract unless they apply for permanent residency. Receipt of this status entitles them to sponsor their children and partners to Canada. At its peak in 2007, 12,955 individuals were admitted through the LIC program, with the vast majority of LIC workers from the Philippines (Atanackovic and Bourgeault 2014). By 2012, annual admissions had decreased to 6,242 applicants.

The Domestic Worker/Live-in-Caregiver Programs, initiated in 1955, developed in three phases. Caribbean women were designated as live-in domestics to provide affluent Canadian families with cheap home childcare service and domestic labour. As migrant labour, they were granted the right to stay in Canada, provided they remained employed for at least one year after arrival (Satzewich 2000). An initial quota of two hundred domestics per year eventually grew to a thousand by the mid-1960s.

Over time, despite a historical bias against Asian immigration, Filipinas gradually displaced the Caribbean women (Manicom 2013). As well, the 1992 Live-in-Caregiver Program was tightened up by imposing tougher barriers such as stricter education and training eligibility criteria (twelve years of schooling and six months of training) for all domestic workers regardless of their country of origin (Jarrah Hodge 2006).

By the early 1980s, domestic workers on temporary work visas who would otherwise be ineligible to apply for landed immigrant status were accorded the right to apply for permanent resident status from within Canada. Upon completion of their residency requirement (then two of three years or 3,900 hours, ideally with the same employer), they could then sponsor spouses and children whom they had left behind in the care of extended family members (Keung 2011a). In 2014, an estimated total of 17,500 former caregivers and their spouses and dependants are projected for admission as permanent residents (Atanackovic and Bourgeault 2014).

Continuing changes to the program will make it easier for live-in caregivers to qualify for permanent residence status while ensuring that their rights are protected from abuse or exploitation, including workplace conditions that meet national standards (CIC 2011c). As of April 2010, the program insisted on a signed written employment contract to specify all requirements between live-in caregivers and employers (Atanackovic and Bourgeault 2013). The contract must include details of (a) mandatory employer-paid benefits (transportation to Canada and location of work, medical insurance coverage until provincial benefit eligibility kicks in), workplace safety insurance, and all recruitment fees incurred by the live-in caregiver; (b) job duties, hours of work, and wages; (c) accommodation arrangements; (d) holiday and sick leave entitlements; and (e) termination and resignation terms.

Despite safeguards, the potential for systemic abuse exists. Labour laws for the protection of domestic caregivers are a useful start, but the vulnerability of caregivers as "tethered" workers creates an institutionalized power imbalance that puts them at risk for everything from overwork and underpay to sexual assault and social isolation (Atanackovic and Bourgeault 2013). The combination of temporary work permits and the program's "live-in" requirements strips caregivers of the power to complain about punishing work schedules, unpaid wages (especially for overtime work), and unlawful confinement at the hands of employers (Stasiulis and Bakan 1997; Diocson 2005). The provisional (and sometimes precarious) status of live-in caregivers is obvious: They are initially denied citizenship in the countries in which they work and reside. Of course, not all domestic workers are exploited, but as Audrey Macklin (1999) concludes, the potential for exploitation is bolstered by the combination of the unregulated work environment, the constant spectre of expulsion and deportation if they complain, and the perception of employers that they "own" these "indentured" workers. Not surprisingly, the UN regards both female domestic migrants and sex-trade workers as the most vulnerable of migrant workers (Stasiulis and Bakan 1997).

Precarious Admissions: A Demand-Driven "Guest Worker" Program

> *They hand you a soothing cup of Tim Hortons, pack frozen beef in factories, pick blueberries and apples on Abbotsford farms, serve fast-food meals and wipe tables, excavate mines and drill for oil in Western Canada, and raise your kids as if they were their own. Typically paid far less than Canadians, unprotected by labour laws, and disposed of when their contracts end, these migrant labourers have become ubiquitous while remaining all but invisible.*
>
> − KRYSTLE ALARCON (2013)

Temporary foreign workers (TFW) and contract migration schemes are experiencing something of a global revival (Castles 2006; Fudge and McPhail 2009; MacLaren and Lapointe 2010; Piper 2010; Thomas 2010; Goldring and Landolt 2012). Like those in earlier and controversial guest worker programs, TFW are utilized to offset deficiencies in the domestic workforce by matching them with employers across a narrowly defined range of labour shortages. TFW as a just-in-time post-Fordist workforce (Fudge 2011) are attractive for a variety of reasons: (a) They address labour market needs by quickly responding to an expanding economy without incurring the costs of maintaining unemployed workers during a downturn or absorbing the costs of training and settlement; (b) they can be prescreened prior to selection as permanent residents (Thomas 2010); (c) they provide a relief valve that staunches the flow of irregular (undocumented) migrants; and (d) they constitute largely unfree labour to perform the drudge work that Canadians eschew, doing it cheaply and uncomplainingly (Abella 2006; Sharma 2006). Their use also addresses the possibility of permanent labour shortages as a recurrent feature in Canada (or more accurately, a mismatch between skills shortage in those parts of the economy that are hiring, but skills surplus in those parts that are shrinking, though evidence suggests that the Canadian government doesn't know enough about Canada's labour market to assess whether skills shortages are real or which industries are experiencing these shortages (Gross 2014).

Numerous TFW programs (guest worker programs) existed and exist (Jason Foster 2012). For example, migrant work originated in the United States as far back as 1917 to facilitate the flow of menial Mexican labour into America; the legacy of one of them, the 1942 Bracero Program, persists into the present (O'Rourke 2010). Currently, the United States has three major TFW programs, for professionals (H-1B), low-skilled farm workers (H-2A), and low-skilled non-farmworkers (H-2B), in addition to others such as F-visa students (Philip Martin 2008). Australia too has shifted its priorities from settlement immigration to temporary migrants (Hugo 2003). In 2001-02, 340,200 foreigners were granted temporary residence, compared to 88,900 permanent residents, resulting in about 554,200 people who now live as "permanently temporary" residents (Hugo 2004). The number of short-term foreign workers has recently expanded to ease the chronic labour shortage in Australia's booming natural resource sector (Reuters 2012). The use of TFW taps into Canada's historical roots as well. Throughout the nineteenth and twentieth centuries, Canada adopted a variety of TFW programs for jobs that the Canadian-born disdained as too dangerous, dirty, or dull (Siemiatycki 2010). One example is the importation of Chinese sojourners into British Columbia during the 1880s for the dangerous task of laying railway track across rugged terrain.

Of special note are guest worker schemes that flourished in European countries. Germany's gastarbeiter program was launched in the 1950s to accelerate its post-war economic recovery. Eventually, many

Western European countries embraced a program of utilizing low-skilled foreign workers for specified periods to offset job vacancies (Alberta Federation of Labour 2010). Guest worker programs continue to admit probationary workers who rarely possess the right to unify with families, change employers, or remain in the country without renewing work permits and resident cards (Castles 2006; Philip Martin 2008). Finally, the rotating of some 120 million workers in and out of cities puts China in a class of its own. It's the only country with a guest worker system designed exclusively for its own rural citizens (Du, Gregory, and Meng 2006).

Canada itself now possesses a guest worker program in all but name. TFW have existed in Canada since 1973, following the implementation of the Non-Immigrant Employment Authorization Program (NIEAP) (both the Seasonal Agricultural Worker Program and the Live-in-Caregiver Program were inaugurated earlier). NIEAP heralded a structural shift, from temporary programs that targeted specific sectors and occupations such as live-in caregiving and seasonal agricultural labour, to a more general focus that initially recruited the highly skilled and eventually included low-skilled TFW to address widespread labour shortages (Fudge and McPhail 2009). Resolving the shortages would ensure the viability of businesses, whose profitability depended on paying wages at below the going market rate (Worswick 2010). A rotational category of TFW tied specifically to non-permanent employment was established on the basis of time-limited (or closed) work permits, along with various restrictions that continue to inform the core of today's Temporary Foreign Worker Program (TFWP), including (a) work permits tied directly to employment status, (b) the legal right to stay in Canada only during the period of authorized employment (with some exceptions), (c) constraints on labour mobility rights without formal authorization, and (d) restriction on applying for work permits or immigrant status from within the country (Fudge and McPhail 2009; Jason Foster 2012). Not surprisingly, NIEAP was criticized as little more than a scheme of indentured labour, camouflaged as a "bonded forced-rotational system" that effectively prevented TFW from applying for gainful employment or permanent residency (Lloyd Wong 1984; also Sharma 2007; Walia 2010).

In time, NIEAP had bifurcated into two streams: (a) those with highly specialized skills (from academics to engineers to managers) that were in short supply across Canada (Nakache and Kinoshita 2010), and (b) those of lower skills, primarily in construction and the oil patch industry in Western Canada (Gross 2014). Canada's labour market began to rely increasingly on TFW whose time-limited work permits specified location and occupation across an expanding range of industries, from fast-food services to the hospitality industry (Faraday 2012; Taylor and Foster 2014). In 2002, the federal government established the Low-Skill Pilot Project for occupations requiring lower levels of formal training (Fudge and McPhail 2009; Jason Foster 2012; Lenard and Straehle 2012). The project allows employers to hire foreign nationals for a limited time, provided that no qualified Canadian is available. Under the current program, TFW must have authorization from the Canadian government – namely, a Labour Market Opinion (LMO) from Service Canada, acknowledging the need for them to address temporary labour shortages unmet by Canadian workers (those who do not need an LMO enter on the basis of advancing Canadian economic and cultural interests [Corcoran 2014b]). In 2011, an LMO was required for 36.8 percent of TFW entries; of these, 35 percent were in the higher-skilled stream, 22 percent were lower-skilled, 34 percent were in the SAWP, and 9 percent were live-in caregivers. No LMO was required for 49.5 percent of entries (from youth mobility agreements under International Experience Canada to intra-company transfers and spouses [Manicom 2013]). The rest came under provincial nominee programs whose employers do not require an LMO [Gross 2014]). All TFW must satisfy Citizenship and Immigration Canada's (CIC) medical and criminal checks. TFW are issued a two-year work permit, renewable once, but are then ineligible for another permit for four years (Jason Foster 2012). This work visa constitutes a labour contract that restricts them to a particular occupation, location, or employer (though there is some wiggle room to change jobs) (Nakache 2010; Thomas 2010; Hennebry 2012). Some non-permanent residents, such as refugee claimants awaiting a formal hearing, receive open-ended permits to work anywhere in Canada. In theory, TFW with work permits may reunite with family members, provided, of course, that they can demonstrate the financial capacity to support them while in Canada. Needless to say, few low-skilled TFW possess the resources to do so. Even those skilled migrant workers who are entitled to reunite with their families find that the program needlessly separates children from parents, thus impeding their successful integration into Canada (Busby and Corak 2014).

The basic elements of the TFWP incorporate a mix of programs that allows foreigners to work temporarily in Canada (Fudge and McPhail 2009; Austin and Bauder 2012; Curry 2014). The TFWP entails four entry streams (Preibisch 2010; Sweetman and Warman 2010; Faraday 2012). They include the Live-in-Caregiver Program, the Seasonal Agricultural Workers, Pilot Project for Occupations Requiring Lower Levels of Formal Training, and the Agricultural Stream of the National Occupational Classification. All who participate in them confront the potential for precarity, insecurity, and exploitation (Lenard and Straehle 2012), with only the Live-in-Caregiver Program providing a principled path for permanent status (hence its inclusion in the provisional category discussed here). The Seasonal Agricultural Worker Program (SAWP), which originated in 1966, allowed employers to hire temporary workers for up to eight months a year for rural labour shortages (Sweetman and Warman 2010). They must pay prevailing wages negotiated annually, provide transportation to and from job and home, arrange basic medical coverage, and supply acceptable accommodation, though a portion of a worker's wages might be deducted to defray the cost of housing. Workers are generally eligible for provincial health insurance and worker's compensation, in addition to being covered by provincial health and safety legislation, though they are not always able or willing to access these health and compensation services (McLaughlin et al. 2014). However transient and temporary the system, the SAWP has morphed into a structural necessity for the farming industry in Canada and the United States (Grez 2008; Thomas 2010; Hennebry 2012).

The decision to expand the TFWP in 2002 by easing the hiring conditions for low-skilled occupations has transformed the face of Canada's migrant worker program (Curry 2014; Gross 2014). What distinguishes the TFWP from earlier versions of NIEAP is the unprecedented growth in the number of TFW, across a sprawling range of occupations, via entry through various admission portals. In addition, the initial purpose of the TFWP as a mechanism for coping with labour shortages in select (generally higher-skilled) occupations was expanded to include a generally lower-skilled labour supply in a manner that optimizes employer bargaining power (Jason Foster 2012).

TFW are routinely retained as a regular part of the local labour market in construction, hospitality (hotels and cleaning), food services, resource extraction, transportation, and agriculture. The increased reliance on unfree labour as a core employee supply rather than to alleviate short-term localized deficiencies is not without consequences.

The shift from a stable program that plugged short-term labour needs in highly skilled occupations to a broader-based labour market tool for lower-skilled occupations creates a permanent TFW pool reminiscent of European guest/migrant worker programs of the past (ibid.). But unlike conventional guest worker programs that distributed workers across the labour market under a single set of rules, Canada's TFWP restricts job vacancies to in-demand labour market niches (Martin, Abella, and Kuptsch 2005), increasingly customized to meet the specific needs of employers, with a widening range of occupations, from bait worm collectors and oil sands drillers to elder care workers and security guards (Goldring, Hennebry, and Preibisch 2009). Curiously, perhaps, the exponential growth of a pool of cheap migrant labour under the TFWP has occurred without much public discussion or oversight (at least until recently following a series of highly publicized scandals), as program changes are often buried by legislation in omnibus budget bills (Alarcon 2013; Jason Foster 2012).

Over time, NIEAP/TFWP diverged into several streams, each with its own restrictions and obligations, although overall numbers remained relatively small (in the 70,000 range during the 1990s) (Jason Foster 2012). Election of a market-friendly Conservative government in 2006 accelerated the already growing volume of TFW under the TFWP. The figures speak for themselves: With just over 213,000 new admissions in 2012, the number of TFW in Canada stood at 338,189, up from 101,098 in 2002, when an emphasis on higher-skilled TFW exerted downward pressure (Carletti and Davison 2012; Jason Foster 2012; Worswick 2013).[4] In terms of the bigger picture, TFW may account for only about 1 percent of Canada's workforce, but their presence is pivotal in some labour market regions, occupations, and sectors. The ratio between skilled and unskilled temporary workers has shifted as well. Prior to its expansion in 2002, the TFWP was predominantly intended for workers from the global North, with 57 percent of TFW in skilled occupations such as management, university teaching, or engineering (mostly from Europe, the United States, and Japan), whereas 26 percent were low-skilled. By 2009, the number of high-skilled temporary workers had dropped to 37 percent, whereas that of the low-skilled and uneducated leapt to 34 percent (most came from Asia, particularly the Philippines, and Latin American countries such as Mexico). The fastest-growing category are low-skilled staff who work in the fast-food and retail industries as attendants and helpers. Even that most iconic of Canadian institutions, Tim Hortons, admits that without a steady supply of TFW, many stores could not stay open or operate full-time (Carletti and Davison 2012). Construction labourers and light-duty cleaners are also in demand (Jason Foster 2012; Yalnizyan 2012).

Like the number of workers, the range of permissible occupations has increased (there are now as many as two hundred). The time span for advertising job postings in local media was reduced as well, from six weeks to seven days, in hope of fast-tracking recruitment (Goar 2010). More recently, Ottawa proposed to reduce processing times to 10 days for the admission of highly skilled TFW such as engineers, instead of the current 12 to 14 weeks (Yalnizyan 2012). The number of "occupations not stated" doubled during this period (Jason Foster 2012; also Nakache and Kinoshita 2010; Siemiatycki 2010). The vast majority of LMO migrant workers in 2012 originated in the Philippines (48,735), then Mexico (24,175) and the United States (19,910) (Curry 2014). The main source country for non-LMO TFW in 2012 was the United States (36,346), followed by Mexico (20,894) and France (17,454). With 119,903 migrant workers, Ontario had the largest number of TFW (both LMO and non-LMO) present on 1 December 2012, followed by British Columbia (74,219) and Alberta (68,339) (ibid.). Finally, about 40 percent of TFW are women, many of whom are slotted into low-paying and low-skilled sectors, such as caregiving, domestic and hotel work, and entertainment. These occupational ghettos render women more vulnerable to abuse and exploitation while diminishing their chances of permanent residency (Gibb 2010). Box 14 provides a breakdown of temporary foreign worker admissions in 2012 based on 2011 Citizenship and Immigration Canada data provided to Christopher Worswick.

ASSESSING CANADA'S TFWP: RESPONSIVE OR REGRESSIVE?

TFW and contract migration schemes are growing in worldwide popularity (Piper 2010; Thomas 2010). This is hardly a surprise, writes one

14

Entries of Temporary Foreign Workers to Canada, 2012

TFW entries	Number
With labour market opinion	80,615
High skill	28,150
Low skill	51,940
Live-in caregiver program	6,240
Seasonal agricultural worker	25,415
Other low skilled	20,285
Without labour market opinion	132,960
Free-trade agreements	24,485
Provincial/territorial agreements	4,350
Canadian interests	102,120
International experience Canada	59,070
Spouses of skilled workers/students	12,245
Research, education, training	11,305
Intra-company transfers	7,240
Others	12,260
Permanent resident applications in Canada	1,705
Others	300
Total TFW entries	213,575

Note: Figures rounded to the nearest five.
Source: Adapted from Worswick (2013).

critic: "Migrant workers represent the perfect workforce in an era of evolving capital-labor relations: commodified and exploitable; flexible and expendable" (Walia 2010, 76). An equivalent dynamic is true in Canada, where the number of TFW who enter each year now exceeds the number of permanent residents under the Federal Skilled Worker Program (Jason Foster 2012). Canada is now embracing a guest worker model to address labour needs – a kind of just-in-time migration policy for a neoliberal era, one that generally pigeonholes TFW into a particular occupation, location, or employer as a condition of their admission (Thomas 2010). This shift toward a more flexible and competitive labour market constitutes a fundamental departure from traditional notions of immigrants as permanent Canada builders to that of hastily hired fill-ins (Lorne Foster 2012; Omidvar 2013). A preference for permanent residency is understandable as it provides the basis for rights and a pathway to citizenship, whereas impermanence implies a more limited set of rights that are conditional on meeting employer need (Hira, McGrath, and Preston 2013). A reliance on temporary and unskilled foreign workers as "indentured labour" incurs the risk of entrenching an underclass of marginalized individuals whose prospects for citizenship are sharply curtailed (Siemiatycki 2010). Nevertheless, the government maintains its commitment to improving the program to simplify employers' access to TFW, to protect the rights of TFW, and to ensure that Canadians are not deprived of employment opportunities because of TFW (Fudge and McPhail 2009).

Reaction to Canada's TFWP is mixed (Worswick 2010; Canadian Centre for Immigration Policy Reform 2010; Lenard and Straehle 2012). For some, the program of "modern day slavery" (McMurtry 2013) or "indentured labour" (Lenard and Straehle 2012) is so deeply flawed that only a major overhaul will preserve both its integrity and Canada's long-term national interests (Hennebry and Preibisch 2010; Hennebry and McLaughlin 2011; Piché 2011). For others, the principle of the TFWP is defensible, at least in the short run, albeit in need of safeguards to protect workers' rights, including the right to access permanent residency (Faraday 2012). For still others, a better balance is necessary (Conference Board of Canada 2008b). Yes, the contribution of TFW deserves commendation. Yet Canada has gone too far in favouring (a) short-term fixes over long-term solutions and objectives, (b) opting for temporary entrants instead of permanent residents, (c) devolving responsibility for selection to provinces, educational institutions, and employers rather than using a national grid, and (d) prioritizing commodified labour over future citizens (Alboim 2009, 2011b; Alboim and Cohl 2012). The onus is on adjusting the ratio to achieve a balance between long-term national goals and short-term economic interests. As Alboim (2009) argues, immigration works best when immigrants are selected for attributes that are in line with changing economic demands, such as education and language, and when they have access to services and supports that enhance both labour market integration and settlement into Canada. In other words, a reliance on TFW should be a tool of last resort to complement the existing workforce. Otherwise, it may discourage Canadians from entering the job market or dissuade employers from providing training for the Canadian-born (Canadian Centre for Immigration Policy Reform 2010).

For employers, the TFWP is a market solution to a labour problem (Corcoran 2014a, b). Its growth and popularity confirm the value of transforming a slow and cumbersome point-driven system that privileges the principles of human capital to predict employability, into one that is more decentralized and actively responsive to drivers that rely on actual labour market needs (Nakache and Kinoshita 2010). Demand-driven migrant labour secures a solution to Canada's labour shortages by making the system more responsive to the cyclical vagaries of the market (Department of Finance 2006), while minimizing expenditures for education, training, and services in general (Francisco Rico-Martinez, director of a Toronto refugee centre, in Proudfoot 2010). Immigration Minister Jason Kenney acknowledged the necessity of TFW when he explained, "The reality is that there are tens of thousands of Canadian businesses that would go under if they didn't have access to that skilled labour" (quoted in Proudfoot 2010). The convenience and cost of TFW are cast as a business imperative, especially in Western Canada, where employees are lured to lucrative jobs in resource extraction (Deveau 2013). To be sure, the complexities and associated processing expenses, of up to $6,000 per migrant worker, given costs of paperwork, transportation, accommodation, and other necessities (ibid.), may "disincentivize" this labour market route. But many employers have become increasingly addicted to cheap disposable labour for seasonal or cyclical work as a permanently temporary alternative to higher-waged domestic workers (Jason Foster 2012; Hennebry 2012). Their addiction to migrant workers is understandable: "Foreign workers typically won't complain about conditions that would drive the rest of us to rebellion. They work long hours for ridiculously low rates of pay ... In many respects, they're the dream employees – happy to be exploited because bad conditions here are still far better than wherever they came from" (Firby 2014, A-18). Or, as Daniel Kelly, head of the Canadian Federation of Independent Business, explained in acknowledging that migrant workers work harder, work longer, and are more reliable because many Canadians disdain the jobs coveted by those anxious to start a new life in Canada, "if we are not prepared to do these jobs, and we don't want our kids to do them either – yet we still want to go to the mall and find a clean bathroom and we still want someone to clear our hotel rooms – why are we so afraid to allow people to come to Canada to happily do these jobs?" (quoted in Goodman 2014, A-7). The government, too, is enthused about the availability of temporary workers (Blanchfield 2014). The program has proven its value in (a) addressing labour shortages in agriculture, the hospitality industry, food services, construction, and manufacturing, as identified by employers and Human Resources and Skills Development Canada; (b) facilitating staff transfers for multinational corporations with Canadian branch plants; and (c) fulfilling Canada's obligations under foreign trade agreements (such as NAFTA).

For TFW themselves, the assessment is more ambivalent, with costs accompanying benefits. For example, seasonal agricultural workers in British Columbia describe their current employment as "ideal." They appear to be "happy" with their contracts, in part because of moves by the federal government since April 2011 to better assess job offers and to penalize employers who fail to meet wage and housing standards (violators are subject to a two-year ban on hiring foreign workers [Langille 2012]). No less enthusiastic are the sending countries, which increasingly rely on remittances as a primary source of revenue (Ratha 2013). However beneficial the program, it is plagued by downsides: A provisional status (temporary and unfree) combines with precarious jobs to create a pool of vulnerable TFW who are susceptible to abuse or danger (Goldring, Berinstein, and Bernhard 2007). TFW are generally tied to specific locations or jobs, even though such an indentured arrangement is unconstitutional for citizens. Neither the Charter of Rights and Freedoms (which guarantees freedom of labour market and spatial mobility for Canadian citizens and permanent residents) nor the Employment Equity Act applies to those who lack the unfettered freedom to quit their job or switch employment. They represent largely unfree labour who cannot circulate freely within the labour market because of legal restraints that entrench and normalize their low-wage/low-skill/low-rights status by way of restrictions incompatible with Canada's human rights framework (Faraday 2012, 5; Trumper and Wong 2010). Their closed work contract is the sole justification for their presence in Canada, making them doubly indebted to the goodwill of their employer.[5] The fear of deportation or banishment from the program silences complaint and makes it difficult for TFW to exercise their right to challenge dangerous work conditions (Goutor and Ramsaroop 2012; Basok and Ilcan 2013).

Finally, migrant workers may possess many of the same protections and labour standard rights as all Canadians (Manicom 2013).[6] But they must exercise these rights in contexts that are often foreign to them, neither designed to reflect their realities nor constructed to advance their interests. Basic employment protections are in place, though impediments exist for TFW who attempt to use them, thus rendering them somewhat inaccessible (Jason Foster 2012). Migrant agricultural workers in Ontario are not always covered by some of the province's standard regulations pertaining to overtime, holiday pay, and hours of work (Hennebry 2012). Nor are they always informed of the rules or offered health and safety instruction. Moreover, while living, working, and paying taxes in Canada, they are denied access to citizenship, thus reinforcing their status as needed but not wanted (Sharma 2006). They are barred from access to the settlement services that are available to permanent residents, resulting in higher levels of isolation from the wider community (Foster and Taylor 2013; Taylor and Foster 2014) and greater dependency on employer-fed information and services (Jason Foster 2012). Even federal and provincial governments are complicit in the exploitation through payroll taxes. TFW must pay federal and provincial taxes, yet they have no access to federally funded settlement services (Alboim 2011b). They are also largely ineligible for benefits, despite paying into the employment insurance fund and the Canada Pension Plan (Goutor and Ramsaroop 2010).

Critics accuse Canada of abandoning its model of immigrants as citizens-in-waiting (Rekai 2002; Alboim 2009; Siemiatycki 2010; Faraday 2012; Busby and Corak 2014), opting instead to slot guest workers into a particular occupation, location, or employer as a precondition for entry (Liston and Carens 2008; Goutor and Ramsaroop 2010; Thomas 2010). This program of "transient servitude" (Walia 2010) is censured as exploitative and abusive (Faraday 2012; Lenard and Straehle 2012). It is also deemed to be more expensive than permanent hires, when all the true costs are factored in, such as lost productivity due to a revolving door of inexperienced personnel (Connelly 2013). Workers are rendered expendable and threatened with deportation as a disciplinary technique because they are beholden to the short-sighted needs of corporate profits instead of to Canada's long-term viability, with vested interests prevailing over human rights (Alboim 2009; Nakache and Kinoshita 2010; Proudfoot 2010; Basok, Belanger, and Rivas 2013; Taylor and Foster 2014). Criticism intensified with the announcement of a new Accelerated Labour Market Opinion, which enabled employers to pay up to 15 percent below the median wage for a high-skilled occupation and 5 percent less than the median wage for low-skilled TFW (Flecker 2013) (from 2002, employers have been required to pay TFW the median wage for an occupation in a specific region, an arrangement that resulted in some Canadian workers earning less than migrant workers since, statistically, 50 percent of workers are below the median value [Gross 2014]). This measure has since been suspended, but fears are mounting that Canada is becoming the Dubai of the North: Permanent settlement immigration is compromised by an exploitative guest worker program that commodifies low-skilled migrant workers without effective legal protection (Lenard and Straehle 2012), denies them access to entitlements from citizenship status to settlement programs for those transitioning to permament status (Vineberg 2014), and erodes Canadian workers' rights because of a cheap and docile workforce (Faraday 2012). As Harsha Walia (2010, 75-76) explains,

> Migrant worker programs allow for capital interests to access cheap labor that exists under precarious conditions, the most severe of which is being deportable. This ensures a pool of highly exploitable labor, excluded from the minimal protections of the welfare state, and readily disposed of without consequences ... The condition of being deportable assures the ability to super-exploit as well as to readily dispose of especially during moments of labor unrest or economic recession.

Even the integrity of the TFWP is suspect, especially given that thousands of young (and older) Canadians cannot find work (Flecker 2013). With national unemployment figures at just over 7 percent and youth unemployment at just under 14 percent, is there truly a labour shortage in Canada (McQuillan 2013)? Some say yes, there is a shortage, especially in skilled trades (plumbers) and among technicians and engineers in parts of the country (Grant 2009). Others contend that there may be a shortage, but only of those low-cost, high-yield, and just-in-time reliable workers whom employers increasingly crave

(Faraday 2012; Stanford 2014; Goar 2014). To phrase it differently, when employers justify the need for TFW, it's because no one in Canada wants to do certain unappealing jobs for going wages and working conditions. Ross Finnie (2014, n. pag.) puts it smartly when he says, "there is no such thing as a skills shortage, there are only employers who do not want to pay what the market requires for them to attract the workers they need." For critics, the solution is simple enough: The labour shortages that prevail at both extremes of the labour market can be addressed by tapping into the large reserve of unemployed Canadians, including young adults and Aboriginal Canadians, assuming, of course, the introduction of fair wages and decent working conditions.

Additional problems continue to unsettle the TFWP. It appears to be poorly monitored by federal and provincial authorities, thus exposing workers to abuse, fraud, and exploitation (Auditor General Sheila Fraser, cited in Whittington 2009; Trumper and Wong 2010; Smolkin 2013). Recruiters are reputed to charge workers a fee for non-existent jobs, employers are known to overwork and underpay, and many employees are exposed to unhealthy working conditions (Hennebry 2010; Faraday 2012) and threatened with reprisals if they complain or resist (Monsebraaten 2009; Walia 2010). A 2010 audit by Alberta's Ministry of Employment and Immigration visited four hundred worksites and found violations of labour laws on overtime and holiday pay in 74 percent of them (Alarcon 2013). Health risks are a major concern as well. TFW are exposed to harmful pesticides or fertilizers and are untrained in the proper use of farm equipment; they often reside in crowded living arrangements that increase the risk of communicable diseases; and they commonly have limited access to or lack knowledge of health care services and insurance (Goldring, Hennebry, and Preibisch 2009).[7] Their reluctance to complain reinforces the payoff of creating a corporate-friendly labour force that is intimidated and vulnerable (McNally 2006). In short, the presence of TFW may dilute worker bargaining power while introducing an asymmetrical relationship that transfers additional control to employers (Jason Foster 2012).

Permanently Temporary, Temporarily Permanent?

A commitment to TFW has established new patterns of stratification and exclusion (Brownell 2010; Nakache 2010; Siemiatycki 2010). Provisional status and precarious work are rapidly becoming the norm for unskilled TFW in sectors and locations with labour shortages (Goldring, Hennebry, and Preibisch 2009). The few studies that exist indicate that, on average, the weekly earnings of TFW in full-time positions did not match those of Canadian-born workers and established immigrants, although they were higher than those of newcomers who had been in Canada for less than five years (Thomas 2010). A bimodal income distribution is to be expected, given the incorporation of both the highly skilled and the low-skilled as part of the TFW contingent. About 5 percent of those who worked full-time earned $150,000 a year (compared to 2.5 percent of the Canadian-born), whereas 46 percent earned less than $25,000 (compared to less than 25 percent of the Canadian-born). Employment patterns also tend to be racialized. TFW from Europe and the United States were more likely to be working as academics or senior managers, whereas racialized (visible) minority foreign workers tended to cluster in low-skilled jobs.

The creation of a vulnerable and disposable class of workers compromises Canada's integrity as an immigration society (Canadian Council for Refugees 2010a). Most unskilled temporary workers will never become landed immigrants (or permanent residents). Yet many come to Canada with the hopes of staying permanently, a belief nurtured by unscrupulous recruiters and shady consultants who capitalize on Canada's reputation as an easy mark (see Proudfoot 2010). But the gap between aspirations and reality creates a recipe for disaster. Stasiulis and Bakan (2005, 14) acknowledge how refusal to grant permanency and naturalization reinforces the potential for exploitation and expendability:

> The First World state's ability to deny Third World migrants access to naturalization becomes a legal and internationally sanctioned means of discrimination and withholding many basic human rights, and increasing oppression based on race and gender. Denial of citizenship guarantees also intensifies class exploitation, creating pools of labor cheapened and made vulnerable to abuse by threats of deportation, and by pitting recent immigrants against poor and working class citizens.

To be sure, many Canadians may take umbrage at unscrupulous businesses that use the TFWP as a way to replace Canadian staff with lower-paid overseas substitutes (Editorial, *Globe and Mail* 2014a; McQuillan 2013). The potential for an electoral backlash because of this looming crisis has prompted the Harper government to tighten the rules governing the TFWP, by charging employers a fee of $275 per applicant and by imposing restrictions on (a) what language proficiency they can request, (b) expanding requirements for advertising job openings to four weeks in Canada before recruiting abroad, (c) paying the market rate for migrant workers by eliminating an employer option of paying less (between 5 and 15 percent) than the average wage for the same job, and (d) beefing up a questionnaire to determine whether companies are using TFW to bypass or replace Canadian workers (Editorial, *Toronto Star* 2014; Canadian Press 2013b). Yet the benefits and convenience of cheap labour in a commodity society deflate any real resistance or incentive. The program provides significant benefits to the Canadian economy, even when used inappropriately: that is, for employers to bridge the gap between supply and demand in labour-starved industries (Maloney 2013). Furthermore, although the program provides a pathway toward permanent residence for those with Canadian experience and high skills, in doing so it reinforces a hierarchy of rights and privileges that is directly related to education and skill levels (Hennebry 2010; Lowe 2010; Tannock 2011). For critics, this back-door entry, which privileges highly educated TFW, creates a second-class tier of migrants who lack access to the civil rights and social protections associated with permanent residence and citizenship. The end result is a highly stratified and discriminatory system of labour migration (Tannock 2011).

In short, whether by design or accident, the growth of the TFWP accelerates the precarity of vulnerable workers by eroding labour protections and shredding social safety nets. Temporary workers are technically covered by the same provincial and federal labour laws as all workers. Realistically, however, they are unable to exercise their rights and entitlements because of language barriers, lack of information, isolation, and fear of employer reprisals, from immediate dismissal to denial of future employment (Goldring, Hennebry, and Preibisch 2009; Faraday 2012; Jason Foster 2012). TFW may possess the same labour rights and access to health and social programs, but they must confront the challenges of toiling in an environment that is systemically racist, inasmuch as their status in Canada is contingent on maintaining a working relationship with a specific employer, resulting in the persistent threat of abuse or deportation as logical consequences of current arrangements (Ramsaroop and Smith 2014; Editorial, *Globe and Mail* 2014b). Labour standards and access to programs vary from province to province as well, with many requiring a minimum period of work or residence to qualify for benefits (Thomas 2010). Lastly, a confused governance structure intensifies the provisional and precarious status of TFW. The TFWP is part of the federal immigration program, but it is managed and monitored by several government departments and subject to provincial statutes over safety or health. The potential for "passing the buck" or "falling between the cracks" is all too real for those without citizenship status or permanent residency (Walia 2010).

Lastly, many believe that Ottawa has abdicated its responsibilities by devolving its role in selecting future citizens. Provincial governments, employers, and even universities have assumed federal duties in choosing provincial nominees, TFW, international students, and the Canadian Experience Class. But critics dislike the idea of "privatizing" immigration by transferring power to corporations or provinces in determining who gets in (Alberta Federation of Labour 2010). Unlike other countries that are trying to consolidate their immigration program, Canada is moving toward a decentralization by off-loading responsibility and costs of immigrants to provinces, universities, and employers. None of these players have national interests as their mandate or objective; nor do they possess the resources to provide the supports and services for fostering settlement and integration. How ironic: Normalizing the TFWP puts Canada in the same league as the European countries whose misconceived guest worker programs created intergroup tensions and social (integration) cohesion problems that remain unsolved (Omidvar 2009). Or consider the contradiction: TFWP is becoming more permanent, yet individual migrant workers remain temporary as thousands are forced to leave each year upon expiry of their permits, only to be replaced by new migrant workers who often end up working for the same employer (Hennebry 2012; Jason Foster 2012).

THE MIXED IMMIGRATION MODEL: PARADIGM SHIFT OR MARKET CORRECTION?

Canada's immigration program is cresting a transformative wave whose full implications have yet to be realized. Its customization along designer, designated, and demand-driven lines has elicited both praise and criticism. Much of the impetus appears to be fuelled by a neoliberal ideology (Bauder 2008a) that accommodates employer interests by commodifying migrant labour to secure a competitive advantage.[8] Canada's immigration program is tailored to deliver just-in-time migrants to jobs and to transition highly skilled temporary workers into permanent residents (Conference Board of Canada 2008b). Recruiting newcomers solely as workers reinforces the commodification of migrant labour consistent with a neoliberal agenda. Or, to put it more cynically, what's good for the economy may not necessarily be good for workers.

The irony is unmistakable: A small experimental program for those who would otherwise be ineligible for admission burgeoned to the point where it challenges the conventional immigration agenda. But many believe that dangers lurk in constructing an immigration system around short-term results and quick-fix solutions. Problems arise when a system selects for transient hired help rather than permanent residents who have the flexible and transferable human capital skills to adapt to changing economic contexts (Alboim 2009; Nakache and Kinoshita 2010). The consequences should not be trifled with: The Canadian state has gradually moved from a focus on the permanent settlement of citizens as nation builders to an increasing concentration on stop-gap TFW in the service of economic interests. This shift in emphasis may reduce Canada to little more than a temp agency for expediting the delivery of just-in-time workers to employers (Grace-Edward Galabuzi, cited in Shakir 2010).

Is the change transformative, or is the system merely being rejigged? According to the Alberta Federation of Labour (2010, 29, emphasis added), a paradigm shift is impending: "The TFWP is not being expanded to handle a simple labour shortage: It is being wholly transformed into a new kind of migrant worker program that is intended to replace a more thoughtful immigration program." Indeed, now that temporary migration rivals permanent immigration and contingent labour (TFW) is the new normal, many agree with this assessment (Hennebry 2010). The move toward demand-driven migration is criticized as short-sighted and as heralding a drift to a market-oriented micro-management system that is grounded in employer requests, labour market demands, and efficient, flexible, and globally competitive post-Fordist workplaces (Sharma 2007; Shakir 2010). The entire immigration program has become more politicized; after all, attempts to reconcile short-term labour market needs with long-term Canada-building goals are politically driven (Ruddick 2010). Consider the passage of Bill C-50 in 2008, which transformed a relatively transparent system of immigrant determination into a political exercise under ministerial control and discretion, one without parliamentary oversight over whom to select, delay, or deny (Shakir 2010).

Proposing a paradigm shift may overstate the case. What prevails instead may simply be a market correction (a program tweak) (*Economist* 2010b). Canada's immigration program has long endorsed the labour market principle of attracting (designer) immigrants, both permanent and non-permanent (Fleras 2010). For example, consider the importing of Chinese labour during the nineteenth century to work on the difficult section of the transcontinental railway, or the massive importation of Europeans for resource extraction work to bolster a post-war economic boom. In short, when it comes to matters of TFW, the past is not yet dead and buried – it's not even the past (to paraphrase William Faulkner's much-utilized insight). A sense of perspective is useful: Canada is not displacing the centrality of settlement immigration. More accurately, it's superimposing new patterns on conventional forms to create a two-tiered model that hybridizes permanent immigrants with temporary migrants (Haimin Zhang 2012). Hardly a metamorphosis, this is more a case of tweaking the existing agenda. The consequences of this "market correction" reflect and reinforce a paradigm muddle. To one side is the conventional social contract of settlement immigration whose supremacy may be waning but not without a struggle; to the other side is a new social contract involving designer immigrants and designated migrants, albeit without the critical mass appeal to dislodge the existing model.

Admittedly, Canada is not alone in relying on the mixed model to address its labour market demands. Many OECD countries as well as Australia also confront an inescapable challenge that threatens to unsettle around a core question: how to resolve the conflict of interest between a flexible, globalized labour market and traditional citizenship and nation-building arrangements based on permanent residents (Edmunds 2006). For example, curbing the number of migrant workers to give jobless Canadians a break risks jeopardizing the viability of restaurants, retirement homes, and small businesses; not curtailing this flow runs the risk of angering jobless Canadians, young people shut out of the labour market, and frustrated parents and voters (Goar 2013b). A balancing act of negotiated compromises is critical, as expounded by the Conference Board of Canada (2008b, 8):

> Today, Governments face the delicate and often difficult task of balancing three elements: openness to international migration, required so that countries can attract people with the skills needed to satisfy domestic needs; firmness in managing migration inflows to deter the unauthorized movement of some migrants; and the implementation of effective policies to ensure immigrant integration. As with most public policies, the right balance is often difficult to achieve. It requires getting the right mix of immigrants; of temporary and permanent migrants; of professional and entry level workers; and more generally of openness and control.

Perhaps the challenge is not in discarding the TFWP. Proposed instead is a rights-based framework to ensure that the program is employed as intended, as a temporary, targeted, and timely response to short-term labour scarcities in specific industries. But as TFW programs escalate in popularity, people will look to the Canadian model as a best practice, which makes it doubly important to critically examine the program. To put it candidly, as long as migrant workers remain unequal (both legally and de facto), with few if any pathways to permanent residence, touting the Canadian model as an exemplar (Martin and Zurcher 2008, 8) might be undeserved in "a country built by immigrants who become citizens, not visitors who went home" (Editorial, *Globe and Mail* 2014b; also Goldring, Hennebry, and Preibisch 2009).

5

canada's refugee status determination process

CONTROVERSIES, CHALLENGES, CHANGES

FRAMING CANADA'S REFUGEE DEBATES

CANADA'S ENGAGEMENT WITH global refugees is impressive. Many believe that it has one of the world's most welcoming refugee programs (for better or worse), resulting in (a) the largest settlement of refugees per capita of population; (b) the highest percentage of acceptance rates (currently between 35 and 38 percent, compared to the European average of about 10 to 15 percent); and (c) an extremely generous package of benefits for successful claimants (Collacott 2009). In compliance with its international obligations, Canada has implemented a principled refugee status determination (RSD) model, which is both widely admired and occasionally copied. Its attractiveness is bolstered by Canada's reputation for extending fundamental human rights to asylum-seeking non-citizens, including the right to an oral hearing, legal aid (about 85 percent of refugee claimants receive legal aid), a judicial review on points of law, and a promised appeal system that only recently was implemented (see Lamey 2011a). For openness, Canada far outstrips Australia, Britain, and the United States, who rely on detention centres or have outsourced their immigration enforcement (Bernstein 2011; Saunders 2011c; Mainwaring 2012). Andy Lamey (2011b, 48) captures Canada's lofty status as a model to emulate:

Many nations have grown increasingly intolerant of asylum seekers, those who make it to a safe country, and file refugee claims. Yet even as opportunities for asylum dwindle, demand for that protection persists. More than 870,000 claims were filed around the world in 2010 by people running from violence in nations such as Iraq, Somalia, and Afghanistan. The world urgently needs a country to set an example by upholding the rights of these migrants. Given current trends, it won't likely be the United States, Australia, or any European state. Canada, however, has distinct legal and cultural conventions that could enable it to develop a new, more humane asylum system.

To put it bluntly, many countries are struggling to curb the flow of refugees (for Germany, see Hawley and Wilder 2013). Immigrant-friendly Australia is no exception: Asylum seekers who arrive by boat or are intercepted in territorial waters are processed offshore (Billy Adams 2013). Australia pays the tiny Pacific island of Nauru to assess asylum seekers at its detention camps, and successful claimants are subsequently resettled in Papua New Guinea (*New Zealand Herald News* 2013). By international standards, Canada's approach to refugee claimants is relatively transparent, accountable, and humane (Centre for Israel and Jewish Affairs 2013). Also, Canada may well be one of the few countries with an institutional framework and a rule-based protocol to address the questions of "who are refugees?" "how do we find out?" "is the system working?" and "is it fair?"

Not surprisingly, Canada remains a key destination for those who need protection from state persecution and repression or relief from violence, environmental catastrophes, and social chaos. In 1986, Canada won the UN Nansen Medal for its work with international refugees from the mid-1970s to the early 1980s – the first and only country to receive this accolade. It continues to receive kudos for its generosity in welcoming and settling refugees, including the UNHCR's Global Trends 2012 rating of Canada as one of the world's most generous countries based on the volume of refugee admissions per capita (Refugee Council of Australia 2013; Koning 2013). But there is a less flattering picture. Debates and controversies over refugees and the refugee determination process provoke Canadians as few other issues do. In theory, establishing a system that is fair, fast, and final would seem simple enough in a world where millions desperately require protection from persecution (Showler 2006; Jones and Houle 2008). In reality, however, complexities in distinguishing the bogus from the bona fide have exposed the system to relentless scrutiny and withering criticism (Francis 2002; Stoffman 2002; Gallagher 2003, 2008b; Collacott 2009; Bissett 2009b; Grubel 2013).

A sense of perspective is helpful. Yes, Canada sparkles as a beacon of hope for those who need protection, at least when compared with Australia's "Pacific Solution" involving offshore detention and processing of ocean-going asylum seekers (Weber 2014), the hothouse Islamophobia in Europe, and the apoplexy over irregular migrants in the United States (Roman 2013). Yet its reputation might be somewhat inflated. Its overall intake levels are about average for an OECD country, and it accepts fewer refugees than most, relative to its population size and as a share of the entire immigration flow (Kiss 2013). Studies indicate that, in 2010, refugee claimants (those who claim refugee status from within Canada or at its border) comprised only 8 percent of its total immigrant intake, compared to 45 percent for Greece, 40 percent for Sweden, and 35 percent for France (D'Amato 2013; Koning 2013). Canada's intake of refugee claimants per 10,000 of population is 6.6, which puts it 13th among the 34 countries that compose the OECD. Sweden, Norway, and Belgium have the highest rates. This ratio will remain unsettled in light of changes to the refugee system, resulting in a 50 percent decline in admissions (only 7,378 claims between January and September 2013, compared with 20,144 for the same period in 2012, including only 477 cases from the 37 designated safe countries compared with 4,678 claimants from these countries in 2012. The timeline for processing asylum claims in 2013 was significantly reduced from 20 months to three months, while the backlog was whittled down by one-third to 20,500 cases [Keung 2013d; Wingrove 2014a]). A 35-38 percent acceptance rate in recent years of refugee claimants puts Canada as the seventh-most generous in the world, behind Israel, Turkey, and the Netherlands.[1] The frosty reception that greeted the 490 Tamil asylum seekers in 2010 provides additional proof that Canada's generosity is conditional (Mountz 2010; Stuart Anderson 2012). The lustre is further tarnished by opportunists who take advantage of Canada's openness by exploiting program loopholes (Cohn 2010; Editorial, *Toronto Star* 2010). Canada is mocked as a soft touch for securing both permanent residency and benefits, argues Stephen Gallagher (2008b), in effect making it a lucrative destination for asylum seekers, albeit for all the wrong reasons.

Criticism of the RSD system is widespread. Much of the vitriol is directed at asylum claimants (those who have landed without authorization) rather than the lucky few who are sponsored privately or by government decree (Liston and Carens 2008). Critics allege that this "easygoing-to-a-fault" system is too generous and too accessible, accepts too many people, panders to vested interests, is prone to mistakes or is underresourced, lacks a reliable appeal recourse, is hostage to unreasonable laws, and breeds a porosity that poses a security risk (Moens and Collacott 2008; Stoffman 2009a). The imposition of visa restrictions and carrier sanctions appears to have done little to staunch the flow of asylum seekers. Moreover, an overburdened system is incapable of handling large numbers of seemingly frivolous and fraudulent claims (Liston and Carens 2008), resulting in a large backlog and lengthy delays (processing an unsuccessful refugee claim, from application to deportation, consumes an average of four to six years) (Showler 2006). According to the auditor general's report in 2009, the Conservative government's decision to suspend nearly a third of the positions in the Immigration and Refugee Board (IRB) doubled the refugee backlog to sixty thousand (Walkom 2010), though it had subsequently dropped to under forty thousand by March 2012 (Centre for Israel and Jewish Affairs 2013). Some critics are so contemptuous of the system that they would slough it off as a joke were it not life threatening and society destabilizing. Loopholes in the determination process are exploited by desperate refugees, whereas the system itself is subject to abuse by greedy consultants (who coach asylum seekers on how to exploit the system), opportunistic lawyers, ruthless smugglers, gullible refugees, and bungling IRB members (Gallagher 2008b). Rules are so lax and the appeals process so slow that even rejected claimants can put down roots over time. Legal protections enjoyed by non-citizens make it even more difficult to deport rejected cases. (Documents indicate that one 69-year-old man successfully fought deportation orders for 26 years [Chase 2013]).

The public is no less ambivalent about the refugee question. To one side, Canada openly welcomed both Hungarian and Czechoslovakian asylum seekers during the 1950s and 1960s, in addition to Ugandan and Vietnamese refugees in the 1970s, as demonstrated in the timeline below:

1956-57	Canada received 37,500 Hungarian refugees.
1968-69	Canada accepted 11,500 Czechoslovakian refugees.
1972	Canada resettled over 6,000 Ugandan refugees.
1973	Canada took in 7,000 Chilean refugees.
1979-80	Canada accommodated 60,000 Vietnamese, Cambodian, and Laotians.
1999-2000	Canada accepted more than 7,000 Kosovars.

To the other side is an uglier picture. The blistering attacks on the six hundred Chinese "boat people" who landed on the BC coast in 1999 exposed the xenophobia that lurked behind principled excuses (from the unfairness of jumping the queue to swamping Canada's absorptive capacity with regard to health or education services) (Hier and Greenberg 2002; David Cohen 2011). The arrival of two groups of Tamil asylum seekers in 2009 and 2010 prompted a scathing reaction from politicians and sensationalistic coverage from the media (Fleras 2011c). Misleading and disparaging terms, such as "bogus" and "illegal," continue to criminalize refugees, while dissolving public support for their protection (Canadian Council for Refugees 2009d).[2] Spurious distinctions between "real" refugees (who live overseas in camps) and "fake" ones (inland claimants) gloss over a fundamental fact: All asylum seekers have the basic right to due process and protection as stipulated by the 1951 UN Convention on the Status of Refugees. Even those who are smuggled in for seemingly exorbitant sums still deserve a fair hearing; after all, the UN Convention rules that refugees should not be punished for irregular entry or held in detention except as a last resort (United Nations 2011). Nevertheless, the cumulative effect of the negative rhetoric is damaging. It feeds into a more generalized paranoia that does not advance constructive debate.

The conflict of perspectives is palpable: Some see refugees as essentially honest folk who are in genuine need of protection; others perceive them as dishonest opportunists who must be deported as quickly as possible to ensure both the integrity of the system and Canadian control of borders; still others emphasize the need to create a workable framework and a transparent process to expedite decisions. Support is overwhelming for "good" refugees – legitimate victims of state oppression who languish in severely depleted camps (Simmons 2010). But many Canadians balk at the idea of embracing those who (a) appear to be shopping around for the best deal; (b) are smuggled in without documentation; and (c) take advantage of entitlements such as open work permits, health benefits, social welfare, and public housing (Kenney 2012b). Claimants whose racialized characteristics do not align with a Canadian norm of whiteness attract additional antipathy. Perceptions of control appear to be critical. Canadians picture themselves as generous patrons of genuine victims – as long as they determine who enters. But a different reaction greets any departure from the norm, especially when refugees self-select on the basis of their needs rather than those of Canada. Ambivalence prevails: Canadians do not want Canada to become a haven for terrorists because of misplaced generosity or inadequate screening procedures. Yet, while they might bristle at the prospect of being duped by those who cheat, many flinch at refoulment – deporting asylum seekers without due process to a fate of torture or death (Poulton 2010).[3]

Clearly, Canadians are deeply conflicted over the politics of the RSD system. Canada's record may be far from spotless (Stuart Anderson 2012), but it shines when compared with, say, that of Japan, which between 1993 and 2002 accepted an average of 27 refugee claims a year, including just 1 a year between 1994 and 1997 (Lamey 2011b).[4] Those who are content with the existing system (albeit with some fine tuning and additional resources) must contend with growing calls for "a major rethink" and a "complete overhaul" of what many believe is broken (Collacott 2010b). Even supporters are critical: Canada may have a deserved reputation for taking human rights seriously and offering a generous welcome as per international obligations, but its status as a refugee-friendly country is glowing only by comparison to imperfections elsewhere (Canadian Council for Refugees 2010b). The basic recipe for a functioning RSD model would appear to be relatively straightforward: namely, a principled appointment system; a fast and efficient hearing before an independent tribunal; a uniform legal aid system; an effective appeal process based on merits; and prompt removal of failed applicants (Crépeau and Nakache 2008; Waldman 2010; Showler and Maytree Foundation n.d.).

Demands for renewal are one thing. Generating major reforms that are workable, necessary, and fair may be something else. Former immigration minister Jason Kenney explained the tradeoffs associated with a functioning RSD program: "At the end of the day, we need a system that complies with our Charter of Rights and our international obligations, that provides a meaningful and quick protection to real victims, but that stops the incentive for bogus claimants to jump the queue" (quoted in Kohler 2009). Prickly questions and awkward concerns flow from the need to balance national interests with the rights of refugees and Canada's international obligations (Adelman 2004; Gallagher 2008b). These include:

> Why has the public perception of refugees and asylum seekers shifted from the "heroic," as dissidents fleeing communist and despotic regimes in search of freedom, to that of an "unwanted flood" of scheming opportunists (Haddad 2008)?

> This era of so-called bogus asylum seekers and ruthless smuggling rings detracts from reframing people's perceptions of refugees, from a mass of undifferentiated cheaters to a more humanistic understanding of refugees as individuals with needs, desires, capacities, and rights (Buckland 2008; Counterpoint 2010). Moreover, asylum seekers and refugee claimants should not be seen solely as victims, but also as active and creative agents with capacity and resilience (Coleman et al. 2012; Mainwaring 2013).

> Does an affluent country such as Canada have an obligation to be more generous in accepting refugees? Or should priority be assigned to advancing national interests, even at the expense of refugee rights?[5] On what grounds can we justify the exclusion of the less fortunate by way of more rights-restrictive border controls (Stuart Anderson 2012)?

> Do non-citizens have the right to enter a foreign country without authorization if the very act of doing so is deemed unlawful? Few options exist for those whom governments target for persecution and death, in effect making them *personae non gratae* without human rights (Saunders 2011b). A conflict of interest prevails: namely, the universal principles of national sovereignty versus the universality of human rights. Citizens lose their rights when they are banished or compelled to flee, whereas states lose their sovereign right to determine membership if rights are obligatorily extended to non-citizens (Lamey 2011b).

> Has the RSD system proven effective? Is it capable of differentiating between genuine cases and bogus applicants? How can we distinguish real refugees from individuals who are simply seeking economic opportunity, particularly in those grey zones where discrimination is rife and the economy is tanking, thereby making it nearly impossible to separate fact from fiction.

> Is the RSD system efficient? Does it process asylum seekers and refugee claimants in a timely, fair, and transparent manner? Is it subject to abuse, weaknesses, and breakdown, as noted by the auditor general in her annual reports, resulting in a potentially safe haven for terrorists and an expedited channel for queue jumpers (Gallagher 2008b)?

> Should the concept of state persecution as a basis for claiming refugee status be extended to situations where governments are unable or unwilling to protect citizens against third-party (or generalized) violence (Keung 2010d)? Should domestic abuse provide grounds for asylum and sanctuary? Or could such an offer be interpreted as meddling in the affairs of a sovereign nation-state (Lieberman 2011)?

> What does "refugee" mean in the second decade of the twenty-first century? For example, does it include protecting the rights of migrants whose movements are induced by environmental degradation and climate change? The potential for conflict over shortages in food, fresh water, and energy notwithstanding, there is little consensus in defining such migrants or specifying the confluence of environmental factors (Becklumb 2013; Fatima, Wadud, and Coelho 2014).

> What can Canada do to ensure enforcement so that its immigration laws are respected as a deterrent to bogus claimants (Gallagher 2008b)? Is the RSD system fundamentally sound and merely in need of fine tuning? Or is it so dysfunctional that a complete overhaul is mandatory? Will the reforms introduced by Jason Kenney reduce the number of frivolous and fraudulent claims (Tobi Cohen 2013)?

The conclusion seems unassailable: The refugee crisis is real; its impact on countries and the global order is inestimable; and this contested dynamic is unlikely to dissipate in the future. Ambivalence toward refugees appears to unite all Canadians because of anxieties over Canadian values, yet dialogue can remain muted, and the dearth of non-partisan debate is problematic (Grubel 2013). According to critic Stephen Gallagher (2008a), Canada's self-image as an open and tolerant multicultural society makes it difficult to engage in constructive discussion. To the extent that it does exist, debate tends to be dictated more by political expediencies and personal vendettas than by ethics. To one side are organized advocacy and special interest groups who work tirelessly to ensure that the government maintains its pro-refugee course. To the other side are conservative think-tanks who are equally adamant in politicizing the discussion (Grubel 2013). Not surprisingly, most Canadians are confused and uncertain regarding what is going on.

PATTERNS, TRENDS, AND POLICIES: GLOBAL DIMENSIONS

The twentieth (and twenty-first) century may well be commemorated as the age of asylum (Schaeffer 2009). Asylum creation and protection were integral parts of post-Westphalian state building in Europe, applying to French émigrés between 1789 and 1815, and to the nineteenth-century formation of states in Germany, Italy, and France (Betts and Loescher 2011). But the magnitude of the contemporary situation is much greater, and the numbers of "persons of concern" to the UN are staggering. The United Nations High Commissioner for Refugees (UNHCR) annual "Global Trends" (UNHCR 2012) indicated that the number of globally displaced persons in 2011 was more than 42.5 million.[6] This total includes, among others, about 15.4 million refugees (10.4 million under UNHCR mandate and 4.8 million Palestinians registered under United Nations Relief and Agency Works [UNRWA]), 26.4 million internally displaced persons, and another 900,000 asylum seekers awaiting refugee status. In 2012, according to UNHCR (ibid.), the total had reached 45.2 million, including 15.4 million refugees, 28.8 million internally displaced persons, and 940,000 asylum seekers. Between 3.5 million and 12 million persons are estimated to be stateless – that is, not nationals of any country. Almost 5 million Palestinians comprise a large portion of this group, most of whom have lived outside of Israel for their entire lives (Rizzo 2011).

Of the 10.4 million refugees under UNHCR protection, 7.1 million have been awaiting settlement for at least five years, with no foreseeable change in status, given the small number who are vetted and submitted by the UNHCR (92,000 applications) for third-country resettlement. Individuals in protracted refugee situations live in "permanent temporariness," with average wait times for resettlement growing from 9 years in 1993 to 17 years in 2003 (Hyndman 2008). The distribution of refugees is unevenly skewed. Eighty percent of all uprooted persons were sheltered in poor countries (UNHCR 2012; Castles 2013), including 500,000 in a Kenyan refugee camp (Dadaab) – the world's largest, occupying 50 square kilometres of semi-permanent dwellings, stores, hospitals, and schools (Bowness 2013). Compare these totals to the fewer than 100,000 who are admitted annually to Canada, the United States, Australia, Sweden, and Norway (Olivia Ward 2011). The total number of settled refugees among industrialized countries puts Germany first, with 572,000, followed by the United States with 265,000 and Canada with 165,000.

Generally speaking, refugees are people who suffer state persecution or find themselves in need of protection because of breakdowns in the relationship between states and citizens. They have been deprived of homes, livelihood, and rights; are forced to leave their homeland for fear of their lives; and are compelled to cross international borders to seek safety abroad (Betts and Loescher 2011). The gravity of their life-and-death situation has not dissuaded many countries from introducing tougher measures to block the entry of asylum seekers (Samers 2010; Brolan, Hill, and Correa-Velez 2012). Governments that facilitate the flow of trade or finance take a tough stand in staunching the flow of asylum seekers on the grounds that their claims are doubtful, they might overwhelm existing services in health or education, and they may threaten national identity and social cohesion (Lamey 2011b). Managing refugee movements by erecting walls and building barriers might represent the last bastion of untrammelled state sovereignty, as governments reassert control over cross-border movements of trade, investment, and people (Dauvergne 2009; Brown 2014). But the clampdown on migration generates a perverse reaction of unintended consequences. Human trafficking assumes even greater attractiveness when it provides the only route for asylum seekers who confront a closure of legal channels (Samers 2010).

War and persecution remain major contributors to the global refugee crisis. Refugee rights are routinely violated because the least powerful can be readily scapegoated as imagined threats (Canadian Council for Refugees 2010b). Other factors are driving the number of persons of concern to the UN, most notably the emergence of environmental refugees. According to the International Red Cross, climate change disasters (including rising sea levels, increased desertification, weather-induced flooding, natural catastrophes, and a corresponding escalation in food prices) constitute a growing concern for population displacement (Larry West 2010; but see Glennie 2011). Finally, the definition of "refugee" is expanding to incorporate protected persons,

15 FYI

Refugee Sources and Destinations

Nationalities with the largest protracted refugee crises (2011)
> Afghans: host countries (Iran, Pakistan); number, 2.7 million; years of crisis, 29
> Iraqis: host countries (Syria, Iran, Jordan); number, 1.4 million; years of crisis, 4
> Palestinians: host countries (Jordan, Saudi Arabia, Egypt); number, 536 000; years of crisis, 41

In 2012, Afghanistan remained the top source country, with 2.6 million persons, followed by Somalia at 1.13 million. At the end of 2012, the total number of Syrian refugees stood at 728,500, making them the world's fourth-largest refugee group. By the end of 2013, the top three countries of origin for refugees were Syria first, followed by the Russian Federation, and then Afghanistan (UNHCR 2014).

The three major refugee-hosting countries (2011)
> Pakistan (1.9 million)
> Iran (1.07 million)
> Syria (1 million)

At 1.638 million, Pakistan remained host to the largest number of refugees, according to the UNHCR (2012), followed by Iran (868,200), Germany (590,000), and Kenya (565,000). In contrast, Canada hosted 164,000 refugees in 2012, and the United States was home to 262,000.

Countries with the largest number of internally displaced persons (2008)
> Colombia (3 million)
> Iraq (2.6 million)
> Democratic Republic of the Congo (1.5 million)

Canada by the numbers*

Canada received about 10,400 refugee claims in 2013, in part because of changes to its asylum policies, down from 20,500 claims in 2012 (UNHCR 2014). In contrast, the United States continued to be the leading country of asylum among industrialized countries, with 88,400 applications received, second only to Germany's 109,600 new asylum claims. In contrast to 2011, when the top five sources of refugee claims in Canada consisted of Hungary, China, Colombia, Pakistan, and Namibia, the figures for 2013 (from January to September) put China at the top, followed by Colombia, Pakistan, Syria, and Nigeria.

Countries that permanently settled the most refugees in 2012
(total 81,800)
> United States (66,300)
> Canada (9,600)
> Australia (5,900)

* *Source:* Immigration and Refugee Board of Canada; also Ivison (2014).

those who need protection because of internal displacement, stateless-ness, human rights violations, or state failure to shield them from vio-lence or discrimination.

Changing patterns of displacement are no less significant. The fact that 80 percent of the world's refugees are encamped in the global South poses a dilemma. An overwhelming burden is imposed on juris-dictions that are least capable of addressing it (António Guterres in UNHCR 2009). With the vast majority of refugees living in the devel-oping world, the number of asylum seekers across all industrialized countries is smaller than the population of a single refugee camp in northern Kenya (Dadaab) (Grewcock 2013). For example, Pakistan, Iran, and Syria each had refugee populations of over a million, and Kenya was the site of over 500,000 refugees (Lamey 2011b). By con-trast, the total number of asylum seekers in the industrialized nations in 2009 was relatively stable at 377,000, with 51,000 new applicants (a 13 percent increase) for the Nordic countries. Applicants for Southern Europe decreased by 33 percent to 50,100 claims (Briefing Notes 2010). Asia and the Middle East accounted for 45 percent of the asylum seekers to industrialized countries, and Africa was second at 29 percent. Afghanis topped the list of applicants with 27,000 submissions, followed by Iraqis at 24,000 and Somalis at 23,000. The United States remained the destination of choice, with 49,000 applicants, and France came second, with 42,000. (South Africa, with 207,000, may be the largest single destination for individual claims, but it is excluded from the UN definition of an industrialized nation.) Canada ranked third among receiving countries, at 33,000 asylum seekers in 2009, a drop of 10 percent from 2008, followed by a further decline to 23,200 in 2010 (Lamey 2011b) and 10,000 in 2013.[7]

CANADIAN REFUGEE REALITIES

Canada has a long history of offering sanctuary to those who seek protection or flee persecution (Canadian Council for Refugees 2009a). British Loyalists fled north following the American War of Independence, and slaves were offered protection during the pre–Civil War years. But Canada also has a reputation for rejecting those in need, including European Jews just before the Second World War (Abella and Troper 1983). Recent moves to tighten up the system have also drawn criticism for brazenly privileging national interests at the expense of refugee rights (Dauvergne 2013). In 2003, for example, Canada entered into a safe third-country agreement with the United States, which many see as less compassionate than Canada in its treatment of asylum seekers. The US-Canada safe-country agreement rejects the rights of asylum seekers to make a refugee claim in Canada if they have travelled through the United States. Even numbers become politicized: The Canadian Council for Refugees (2010b) points out that Canada has settled about 11,000 refugees annually since 2000, compared to approximately 21,000 during the 1980s and 15,000 in the 1990s. As well, refugees are expected to pay for both their transport to Canada and their overseas medical costs. Loans may be offered by the federal government, resulting in a debt load of up to $10,000 per household even as refugees struggle with the challenges of adapting to a new country.

After the Second World War, Canada accepted a large number of persons who were displaced by the conflict in Europe (the author and

16 CASE STUDY

The Syrian Refugee Crisis: An Unfolding Catastrophe

CASUALTIES ABOUND IN Syria's four-year civil war. They consist of as many as 100,000 dead (*Economist* 2013a), including nearly 1,500 civilians who were killed by chemical weapons on 21 August 2013 in a rebel-held suburb of Damascus (Landay 2013). Up to 10 million refugees and internally displaced persons are experiencing a different kind of dying in hastily constructed camps, struggling to survive without heat, electricity, adequate sanitation, water, food, or hope (Sotloff 2013). Over 2.6 million Syrians have fled the country, according to UN figures, and are encamped as refugees across Jordan, Lebanon, Turkey, and Iraq. With entire villages emptying on a weekly basis, the number of Syrian refugees may rise to 4 million by the end of 2014 (Editorial, *Globe and Mail* 2014b; *Economist* 2013a). Ironically, Syria itself was home to over 1 million refugees in 2011 (Lamey 2011b).

The situation is grim for all the uprooted as agencies and host countries struggle to cope with the catastrophe in the making (*Economist* 2013a). Millions of Syrians are internally displaced, with many living in areas deemed too dangerous for humanitarian agencies to enter. Nobody really knows how many are languishing in the rebel-held north, which remains out of reach to humanitarian aid. Syria simply refuses to allow UN convoys from Turkey to cross borders controlled by the Free Syrian Army (Nebehay 2013). (According to UN rules, relief agencies must follow the strictures laid down by a recognized government. In the case of Syria, President Assad limits aid access to rebel-controlled areas [Kirkpatrick 2013].) The bulk of foreign aid is funnelled into government-controlled areas, prompting rebels to suggest that aid is a weapon in assisting government forces to survive a war of attrition (ibid.). Not surprisingly, the legitimate distribution of aid (including to many armed militia groups, both rebels and loyalists, who use it to buy weapons) has emerged as a pressing international crisis (Khan 2013).

The living conditions for those outside the country are precarious at best, and wretched and dangerous at worst. About 150,000 are crammed into the dusty confines of the Zaatari camp in Jordan, whose 5.3 square kilometres are now the world's second-largest refugee camp and Jordan's fifth-largest city (Zilber 2013). The camp is quickly mutating from a temporary safe haven into an urban jungle with all the problems of any crowded city (Blackwell 2013b). Infrastructure is largely a hit-and-miss affair (see Zilber 2013). Schools and hospitals are packed with pupils and patients, yet understaffed in camps such as Zaatari outside of Syria's southern border, where the 100,000 who live in tents and caravans see their numbers increase by 1,500 daily (Fisher 2013). Residents in the 13,000-strong Atmeh camp, located three hundred metres from the Turkish border, complain of paltry provisions and erratic deliveries. Their two meals arrive at different times each day, and the first is often limited to one piece of bread, a bit of butter and jam, and a few olives. Potable water of substandard quality quickly runs out as residents fill one-litre bottles from water trucks. Another group of asylum seekers arrives each day, putting even more pressure on the meagre resources. The $4,000 daily bill for food, water, and gas is covered by NGO funds, since Atmeh receives no funding from international organizations such as the UNHCR, which is barred by international law from operating in countries without government consent (in this case, the Syrian government in Damascus). There are no aid-sponsored camps in Lebanon, which has close ties with the Syrian regime (Putz 2013), so refugees must seek accommodation in families or rely on the kindness of strangers, from imams to farmers.

The consequences bite deeply. Camps in Iraq and Jordan alternate between extremes: rainstorms or blizzards reduce them to quagmires, and blazing heat and choking sandstorms transform them to deserts (Sherwood 2012). Families live in teeming shantytowns of endless rows of tents or metal huts, with each day an endless and tedious cycle of either queuing for food and water or removing dust and debris (Rudoren 2013; but see Zilber 2013). The situation is so desperate and people are so tired of the heat, filth, tedium, and crime that some are braving the risky return to Syria (Landay 2013). Many of the refugees are children, even unaccompanied minors. Of the 500,000 Syrian refugees in Jordan, about 55 percent are under 18. Witness to killings, subject to sexual abuse, and spending years out of school, they are a lost generation whose lives may be forever blighted (Rudoren 2013). Young refugee girls continue to bear the brunt of violence as they are pressured into forced marriages with other nationals, under the pretext of protecting their virtue (Rahme 2012). Even the once affluent middle class suffers as it exchanges its former lavish lifestyle for the stomach-stretching realities of meagre rations and substandard living conditions, with little to no prospect of reclaiming its abandoned property and valuables (Putz 2013).

Not surprisingly, many of these refugee camps are incubators of unrest, with riots and disturbances one of the few ways of communicating despair (Zilber 2013). In light of this interborder turmoil, neighbouring countries are treading carefully, fearing the possibility of political instability and fallout (from inciting sectarian violence to resurgence of Islamist violence) that often accompanies a refugee influx. Intakes of refugees stretch notions of generosity. For example, Jordan is a poor country, itself dependent on international aid, which puts its vaunted openness to the test as locals compete with Syrian refugees for scarce resources (Blackwell 2013a). Interestingly, given the scale and scope of the crisis, Canada should be doing more to accept and resettle Syrian refugees, but to date it has committed to an intake of only 1,300, few of whom have arrived so far (Editorial, *Globe and Mail* 2014b). Little wonder, then, that the UN has declared Syria the twenty-first century's worst humanitarian crisis – "a disgraceful humanitarian calamity with suffering and displacement unparalleled in recent history" (quoted in Editorial, *Globe and Mail* 2013).

his birth family arrived under this arrangement). Dissidents from communist-controlled countries were warmly welcomed because of Cold War politics. Individuals from countries with close political or military ties to the West had more difficulty in acquiring refugee status (Amnesty International 2009). In 1969, Canada ratified the 1951 UN Convention on the Status of Refugees on the grounds that a civilized international community must protect people in extreme distress (according to the Canadian Council for Refugees 2009a, the signing was not reported by the media). Under the UN Convention, those who were escaping human rights abuses were granted protection (refuge) as a legal right rather than a discretionary humanitarian gesture. But Canada did not articulate a formal distinction between immigrants and refugees until passage of the Immigration Act in 1976 defined refugees as a distinct class of immigrants with a unique status and needs. It also established a refugee status determination system, alongside a program in which Canadians could privately sponsor refugees. The 1986 conferral of the Nansen Medal by the UNHCR confirmed Canada's pivotal role in settling international refugees.

Canada continues to cast its refugee net ever more broadly. A 1986 Supreme Court decision ruled that everyone who landed in Canada had the right to due process when claiming refugee status. All who claim refugee status are entitled to a proper hearing in line with the principle of fundamental justice and guarantees by the Charter of Rights and Freedoms (Canadian Council for Refugees 2009c). The government also instituted an administrative review program that not only sought to reduce a claims backlog, but also amounted to a general amnesty for those with pending asylum applications (Hamlin 2008). Complicating the situation is a growing acceptance of those who do not strictly comply with the UN Convention, including persons who are in refugee-like situations, ranging from environmental disasters to stateless conditions. Canada expanded its definition of refugee status in 1997 to incorporate those who were internally displaced because of war/terrorism or in need of temporary shelter from a dangerous situation.

Reference to the concept of protected persons looms large in contemporary refugee discourses. Protection may be granted to minorities such as the Roma or those who lack state safeguards from open discrimination (Editorial, *Globe and Mail* 2010). For example, Mexican asylum seekers are claiming refugee status on the grounds of "generalized criminality" (Simpson 2009). Gender is also a basis for claims. Female-specific patterns of persecution include domestic abuse, intimidation or exploitation, exposure to mutilation, forced marriage, and victimization by violence in war zones (United Nations 2011). Sexuality is the newest protection platform. At a time when 77 countries continue to criminalize homosexuality, Ottawa has partnered with the gay community and the Rainbow Refugee Committee to defray the cost of sponsoring those persecuted for their sexual orientation (Keung 2011d). Finally, even rejected claimants or those who are inadmissible because they commit a serious crime may elude deportation if they risk harm upon return, fear becoming victims of crime (from gangs to lawlessness), or expose their Canadian-born children to unnecessary suffering because of removal.

Canada is certainly no slouch when it comes to refugee admissions. Over half a million individuals have found sanctuary in Canada since the end of the Second World War (Canadian Council for Refugees 2009a). But refugee issues continue to perplex and provoke. Critics argue that the current system creates a two-tier entry in which those who are chosen for their contribution to Canada and processed overseas are shunted onto the slow track, whereas those who self-select to claim refugee status enjoy access to the fast track (Kohler 2009). The system is also castigated for its seeming inability to quickly distinguish between real refugees and people who are simply taking advantage of Canada's principled approach to processing claims (Carpay 2011). Two projections prevail: Those who criticize government policy as either too restrictive or too expansive tend to see hidden agendas behind every move to expand or constrict. Those who endorse the government policy are reluctant to tamper with success, but they acknowledge that Canada cannot possibly accept all refugees without imploding in the process.

Of course, Canada is hardly alone in confronting this governance challenge (Betts and Loescher 2011; Grubel 2013). Comparable fears pervade many countries in the global North: Anxieties range over too many refugees, too few resources, too ponderously slow and/or too inefficient a process, and too few deported (Showler 2006). Ironically, refugees may be pitied – even embraced – when they first flee a catastrophe; over time, however, they are increasingly demonized as a burden or threat (Samers 2010). These "irregular" movements convince governments to erect new barriers for admission, thereby preventing refugees from seeking the safety they need. Such restrictions invariably fuel a massive rise in the smuggling and trafficking of humans across international borders (Guterres 2007). Similarly, global dynamics are challenging Canada's capacity to cope with the worldwide movements of people; as a result, the process is typified by excess capacity, overworked staff, lengthy delays, and breakdowns in the RSD process (Collacott 2006).

REFUGEE PATHWAYS TO CANADA

Since 1951, or more accurately 1969, when it signed the 1951 UN Convention on the Status of Refugees, Canada has performed admirably in granting asylum and protecting refugees, having officially admitted over half a million persons since the Second World War. Entry under the refugee category falls into two major streams, neither of which require points for entry. One stream consists of sponsored overseas refugees who are selected abroad. Government-assisted refugees are preselected by government officials, whereas privately sponsored refugees are supported by private agencies, individuals, clubs, or church groups, which commit to financially underwriting the initial settlement. To qualify for resettlement, a refugee must be eligible to apply, admissible (no criminal record, security risk, or danger to health), deemed capable of successful establishment in Canada, without reasonable admission options except as a refugee, and supported financially by the government or private sponsors for up to ten years (Canadian Council for Refugees 2009b). Both government and privately sponsored refugees automatically receive permanent residence status (or landed immigrant status) upon arrival in Canada. They also receive assistance through government programs once they arrive, although Ottawa charges for expenses related to medical examinations and transportation to Canada, an outlay that can easily reach thousands of dollars (Showler 2009).

A second stream consists of refugee claimants (also known as in-Canada claimants or inland protected persons). They make a claim at one of Canada's ports of entry or, more commonly, from within the country at an immigration office (Amnesty International 2009). In 1980, refugees sponsored from abroad outnumbered inland claimants by 39,992 to 718. By 1992, inland claimants outnumbered sponsored refugees by 37,152 to 14,726. As of December 2011, according to CIC data, 94,756 refugee claimants whose cases had not been proved resided in Canada, with 35,964 living in Toronto (cited in Outhit 2013). According to the Immigration and Refugee Board (IRB), of the 32,457 refugee claims that were processed in 2010, 38 percent were accepted. By country of origin, the highest success rates were those of Sri Lankans (76 percent of the 672 claims succeeded), followed by Nigerians at 64 percent and Haitians at 55 percent. Canada processed a substantial number of claims from Mexico (5,827), but only 11 percent were accepted. Claims from the United States (1 percent) and Hungary (2 percent) were least successful (reported also in Quan 2011). Acceptance rates have slipped since 2006, from about 47 percent to about 36 percent for 2013. The government believes that the reduction in numbers and source countries can be traced to the passage of a massive refugee reform bill, Protecting Canada's Immigration System Act (Department of Justice 2012), including the introduction of 37 countries that are considered to be unlikely sources of refugees. The claims of individuals from these "designated countries of origin" (DCO) are processed more swiftly, rejections cannot be appealed, and the persons themselves are quickly deported (Tobi Cohen 2013). Source areas have shifted as well (see Box 16).

In short, refugees are admitted along two opposing paths. Those who are stranded in refugee camps are selected in part on their ability to establish themselves in Canada. Inland claimants are admitted because they need protection from state persecution or will encounter life-threatening danger if deported to their homelands. In contrast to sponsored refugees, inland claimants must wait until they acquire permanent residence status before they are entitled to all the benefits and social services that Canadians enjoy, the exception being those who obtain an open work permit for employment anywhere in Canada following clearance to apply as refugees (Thomas 2010).

The definition of a refugee further complicates the debate. In theory, defining a refugee seems easy enough. The 1951 UN Convention on the Status of Refugees (to which Canada is a signatory) defines convention refugees as a class of individuals who cannot return to their country because of a well-founded fear of persecution for reasons of race, religion, nationality, group membership, or political opinion. Signatories to the UN Convention are obliged to ensure the safety of asylum seekers; for example, they must not deport them to unstable (or failed) countries, where they may face persecution. But defining who is a refugee is more complex than ever. Unless they have been explicitly singled out for persecution, individuals may not qualify as convention refugees under international law if they have fled environmental disasters or civil wars, endured atrocities, or suffered the death of family members. Nevertheless, they may be admissible on compassionate grounds. The concept of convention refugees is giving way to rulings involving "persons in need of protection," those who are in danger of cruel and unusual punishment in their homeland or who risk torture or death should they be deported (Showler 2006). Moreover, it's become more difficult to distinguish between outright persecution and ordinary discrimination, institutional harassment and generalized violence, and state hate and public scorn.

Even the distinction between refugee (political persecution) and immigrant (economic opportunity) is getting fuzzier as the threat of political suppression often dovetails with economic hardship. Distinguishing between the voluntary (economic migrants) and the involuntary (politically persecuted asylum seekers) may have worked during the Cold War era, when defecting political dissidents were few and embraced with open arms as a public relations coup for the West. But differentiating the economic from the political is more difficult to maintain in countries (including failed states) that are undergoing rapid change and crisis. Reasons for leaving may be tied simultaneously to conflict, persecution, lack of development, and economic marginalization (Castles and Vezzoli 2009). Finally, developed countries have established increasingly restrictive policies aimed at deterring or limiting access to asylum, with the result that more asylum seekers are moving about as undocumented migrants, further blurring the categories (Grugel and Piper 2007; Alden 2012).

PROCESSING REFUGEE CLAIMANTS:
THE IMMIGRATION AND REFUGEE BOARD

According to the Canadian Council for Refugees (2007), most refugee claims (62 percent in 2006) are activated from within Canada at an immigration office (about a third are handled at the Etobicoke office, which covers Toronto). Only about 20 percent of claims are made at a border crossing. In Canada, a set of refugee determination prompts is activated (see Wayland 2006). According to well-known immigration lawyers Lorne Waldman and Max Berger (Aulakh 2010), the system is relatively simple. A person applies for refugee status, shows identification, and is allowed to go free, provided that he or she is not a health, security, or flight risk or a danger to the public. The individual promises to appear before a hearing to determine eligibility or need for protection and must also submit a "history"/personal information form to the Immigration and Refugee Board (IRB). The hearing occurs within 60 days. In reality, the process is much more complex, with a three-step procedure – eligibility determination, refugee status determination, and permanent residency – that purports to balance fairness and justice with efficiency and effectiveness.

Step 1: Eligibility Determination

Within 72 hours of entering Canada, claimants are photographed, fingerprinted, and interviewed by a Citizenship and Immigration Canada (CIC) official, often with the aid of an interpreter, to solicit information on personal identity, criminality and security risks, and grounds of persecution. This information is used to assess the eligibility of the claim for referral to and evaluation by the Refugee Protection Division of the IRB (about 90 percent of claimants are deemed eligible [ibid.]). Referral may be denied on grounds related to security, human rights violations, serious criminality, and costly health concerns, among other criteria such as refugee status in another country (Showler and Maytree Foundation n.d.). Or admissibility may be revoked if the claimant lied or new information emerges to discredit the application. Also ineligible are repeat claimants and those who have passed through a safe third country (e.g., the United States) en route to Canada (ibid.; Canadian Council for Refugees 2007). To discourage false claimants from entering Canada, the government insists on proper documentation as proof of identity. Without documents, refugees may be temporarily detained until their identification is established. According to a UN report, the number of detainees stood at 4,125 in 2009, down from 5,961 in 2008, with 7.5 percent held in provincial jails for 90 days or more (Keung 2011f). But unless they pose a serious criminal, security, or health risk, or have been previously deported, inland claimants are free to go, pending an IRB hearing to adjudicate their claims for refugee status (Crépeau and Janik 2008). Critics deride this approach as lax and argue that it could enable refugees with terrorist links to evade detection or deportation.

Step 2: Refugee Determination

Once their identity has been established and the CIC or the Canadian Border Services Agency has completed their paperwork, most refugee claimants must attend a formal hearing. Those who are almost certain of entry receive an "expedited hearing," an interview rather than a full hearing, to hasten the process and prevent a backlog, during which claimants can apply for temporary work or study permits. Others, however, must await a formal hearing conducted by the Refugee Protection Division of the IRB. A quasi-independent tribunal and quasi-judicial decision-making body, the IRB is independent of the CIC. Created in 1989, following a scandal involving political and diplomatic interference in the refugee determination process, the IRB is less formal than its judicial counterparts, thus allowing claimants to present their case in a simpler manner (Fleury 2004). Appointed by an Order-in-Council for seven years, IRB members are selected as much for their political connections as their credentials. Following extensive training and access to the refugee documentation centre for assistance in making decisions, they are charged with determining the authenticity of asylum seekers who arrive unannounced. Hearings are conducted by one IRB official, who may operate without the aid of a refugee protection officer (a civil servant who is cognizant of refugee laws) (Bauer 2009). In March 2008, only 104 of the 164 IRB positions were occupied, resulting in a mounting backlog of sixty thousand cases and an 18-month processing time (Kohler 2009; Simpson 2009).

The difficulty of the job should not be underestimated (Showler 2006). IRB members require knowledge of countries of origin, solid legal abilities, and good listening and communication skills for conducting interviews and writing coherent reasons for their decisions (Showler and Maytree Foundation n.d.). Claims are often complex, allegations are commonly difficult to document or verify, and many claimants must speak through an interpreter. Making a claim is a dicey proposition (Jones and Houle 2008). The sole witness is the refugee, and he or she may prove unreliable. Much of the evidence and many witnesses for the defence remain inaccessible in the refugee's home country. Refugees must describe events about which little is known; they are frightened, traumatized, and haunted by their own persecution; they can't remember key events or even find the words to make a credible presentation (ibid.); and they don't understand the legal procedure involved. Although they have the right to legal counsel in some of the provinces, its quality varies from the heroic to the incompetent to the unethical, and few can tell the difference until it's too late. And given the radically dissimilar experiences of IRB members and claimants, the former can have difficulty in distinguishing between the frightened, the confused, the manipulated, and the manipulating (Stadelmann-Elder 2011, 1). Peter Showler (2006, xvi) captures the potential for communication breakdown:

> A vast chasm of potential miscommunication lies between the claimant and decisionmaker. Most genuine claimants experience a profound sense of vulnerability due to their inability to understand the refugee claim process and their fear of being returned to persecution. The process is frightening because it does not make sense to them and because the stakes are so high. The fear is magnified in the hearing room when questions are incomprehensible because of language, different cultural perspectives, or false assumptions on the part of the questioner ... They may be telling the truth as they perceive it, they may be exaggerating, or they may be telling a big fat whopper.

Most cases are decided on the credibility of the claimants, supporting evidence about their country of origin, and the quality of submission by their legal representative (Showler 2006). The IRB member renders a decision, with reasons based on law or evidence, either in writing (in the case of a rejected claim) or orally from the bench. The complexities involved may partly explain a curious anomaly: When the current tribunal members applied for the *same* job in a revamped asylum system under the Balanced Refugee Reform Act, more than half of them failed the qualifying exam and screening (Keung 2011g).

Step 3: Permanent Residency
Conferral of "protected person" (refugee) status entitles claimants to apply for permanent residency. Successful applicants are issued a social insurance number and a record of landing (identity papers), which allow them to open a bank account, apply for employment, and travel freely within Canada. They can also qualify for basic income support, health care, and social services if they possess a valid work permit (although attaining both employment and rental accommodation may

prove difficult because of their insecure status). But others find themselves in a legal limbo, especially those who are accepted as refugees but do not receive permanent resident status, usually because of minor criminality (Showler 2006). They must wait for additional security and medical checks, confirmation of family relationships, and payment of processing fees. Delays in processing can occur for a variety of reasons, resulting in lengthy wait times. The entire three-step process can take about 3 years (Wayland 2006), although 18 months is the average (Showler and Maytree Foundation n.d.).

Not all claimants are successful, with acceptance rates in recent years hovering around the 35-38 percent mark, a figure that is high by global measures but low by traditional Canadian standards (Black 2012). If the IRB rejects an application, the claimant must leave within 30 days or face arrest and deportation. He or she may also appeal by applying for a judicial review in the Federal Court within 15 days, though only on matters of procedure (serious mistakes in law), not the merits of the case. Canada is one of the few industrialized countries that, until recently, lacked an appeal process, although the 2002 Immigration and Refugee Protection Act did make provisions for a Refugee Appeal Division (Fleury 2004). If the Federal Court overturns the IRB decision, which it does for about 13 percent of cases (Showler and Maytree Foundation n.d.), the claim is sent back to the IRB for a new hearing. In theory, those who have exhausted all appeal routes are earmarked for deportation. In reality, they may be exempted on humanitarian and compassionate grounds (if, perhaps, they have married a Canadian and have children who were born in Canada). A pre-removal risk assessment, conducted to determine the probable risks of returning home, may excuse them from deportation (or their own country may refuse to accept them). Only about 2 percent of these pre-removal risk assessment appeals are granted (Showler 2006). Or they may simply slip through the cracks due to administrative bungling. Years can elapse between rejection and removal, during which time no one assumes responsibility for the file (Peter Showler in Keung 2010d), so unless deportees reveal their exit plans, the CIC has no way of confirming who leaves or who stays. In fact, the CIC revealed that in 2008, Canada had lost track of nearly 38,000 people who were slated for deportation (McDowell 2010). It should be noted that Canada's Border Services Agency removed 12,732 persons in 2008, including about three-quarters of all failed refugee claimants, a

17

Three-Step Processing of Refugees in Canada

Initial Citizenship and Immigration
assessment to determine overall eligibility
|
Eligible claims sent to the IRB
(eligibility determination)
|
Hearing at the IRB
(refugee determination)
|

CLAIM ACCEPTED
(permanent residency)
*The claimant is now a
protected person and can apply
for permanent residence*

CLAIM REJECTED
*The claimant has no
protected person status*
|
May apply for judicial review with the
Federal Court on matters of law or to the
refugee appeal division (since late 2012)
|
May apply for a pre-removal risk assessment
or seek exemption on compassionate grounds
|
Removal from Canada

50 percent increase over the 8,361 who were deported in 1999 (Tobi Cohen 2009). Box 17 provides an overview of the processes involved.

Rejected claimants who disappear into the underground instead of leaving Canada default into "non-status," or undocumented status. It is estimated that perhaps 200,000 undocumented people live and work in Toronto alone (including those who overstay their visitor or work visas). They may contribute to Canada as workers and consumers, yet they face numerous barriers in accessing basic services related to health care (hospitals), social (food banks), and educational (schools) institutions. (In early 2013, Toronto became Canada's first sanctuary city, offering safety and services to irregular migrants.) They also live in constant fear of being outed and deported (Wayland 2006). According to the interest group No One Is Illegal (2010), their situation is more precarious than ever because of changes to immigration laws and renewed removal raids.

IRB: A FUNCTIONING DYSFUNCTIONALITY?

How are we to assess the RSD program? Is it a system in disarray, or as good as it gets? Reaction is mixed: Many, including the United Nations High Commissioner for Refugees, congratulate Canada's asylum process as open and generous. For some, this generosity is to be celebrated as a source of pride (Mawani 1997; Showler 2006); for others, it proves that Canadians are being taken for a ride (Collacott 2006). That Canada accepts refugee claimants at six times the international norm reinforces the obvious for critics: The current RSD system is a de facto backdoor entry into the country. As proof of its procedural shortcomings, they point out that claims from citizens of democratic countries such as Israel, the United Kingdom, and the United States are accorded due process. (According to the IRB, about 1 percent of US refugee claims are successful. Canadian officials processed 725 applications from American citizens, but only 7 were granted asylum – in all likelihood, these were American-born children of overseas refugees [Kirby, Geddes, and Weinman 2010].) How else are we to explain why Canada is the only country to recognize convention refugees from Brazil, Costa Rica, Israel, Jamaica (and several other Caribbean countries), the Republic of Korea, and the Philippines (Gallagher 2008b)? Why does Canada recognize more convention refugees from Cuba, Lebanon, Mexico, Pakistan, Peru, and Romania than all other countries combined?

Canada's RSD system might prove a victim of its own success, with fears that it might implode as a result of taking on too much with too little. With a backlog of sixty thousand claims, the IRB may take 18 months to reach a first decision. Finalizing a claim may consume nearly a decade because of delays and appeals (Showler and Maytree Foundation n.d.). A large number of poorly reasoned decisions needlessly clog up the process, which means that thousands of claimants wait to be processed, are lost in limbo, or are awaiting a decision for removal from Canada. To be sure, determining who is a refugee requires close examination of individual cases that may elude assessment by strictly objective criteria (Jones and Houle 2008). Nevertheless, de-

18 FYI

Frivolous Claims

THERE IS A downside to an RSD program that many perceive as liberal: It is vulnerable to claims that appear frivolous. Examples include a German family who home-schooled their children, a homosexual from Mexico (a country that recently approved gay marriage), a white South African who feared violence from the nation's black majority (Editorial, *Globe and Mail* 2010), and, more recently, an accused Florida sex offender who had relations with a 16 year old and faced a 30-year prison sentence in the United States (Clarke 2014a). Perhaps few cases have excited more derision than that of Hollywood actor Randy Quaid and his wife, Evi, who claimed refugee status in Canada on the grounds that they risked being "whacked" by Hollywood conspirators. For critics, such spurious claims not only clog up the resources of the Canada Border Services Agency, but also make a mockery of Canada's refugee determination system. After all, no other country in the world processes applications originating in the United States – least of all individuals who, like Randy Quaid, are in trouble with the law. In early 2013, Quaid's application was rejected by Canadian authorities.

lays hurt legitimate refugees, attract frivolous claims, and rob Canada of its credibility in protecting the deserving. And though Canadians appear to be relatively sympathetic to the plight of refugees, there is mounting frustration over what many regard as abuses in a system that needs renovation (Collacott 2010c).

The numbers elicit sharply differing responses. Of the 95,500 refugees who made claims to the IRB between 1993 and 1997, 42 percent were accepted (down from 84 percent in 1989), 33 percent were rejected, and 25 percent were neither finalized nor eligible. From March 2006 to March 2009, according to the auditor general, 55 percent of claimants were rejected or withdrew or abandoned their claims, whereas 38 percent were accepted (McDowell 2010). The best spin on this relatively high acceptance rate praises Canada's commitment to assist the world's most unfortunate. The worst spin rebukes the RSD system as absurdly dysfunctional. Not surprisingly, the IRB is criticized as the weakest link in Canada's migration management system (Gallagher 2008b; also Keung 2011e).

Operating an inland-refugee-processing system does not come cheaply. That being the case, critics argue, two options prevail. First, why not simply accept all refugee claimants and dispense with the costs and logistics of deporting the few who fail to comply with standards? The savings, time, and energy could then be used to improve settlement or increase overseas sponsorship (Stoffman 2002). Second, the focus must switch to accepting those who are languishing in refugee camps and are officially defined by the UN as legitimate refugees. Government-sponsored refugees do not require expensive and time-consuming processing, are selected on the basis of their value to Canada, and arrive as permanent residents who are ready to make an immediate contribution. Not surprisingly, Ottawa is showing a preference for admitting this type of refugee, including its recent decision to augment their numbers by 2,500 (albeit by siphoning 2,000 from private sponsors) (Scoffield 2010a; but see Canadian Council for Refugees 2009c). Raising the annual total to 14,500 reverses a decades-long decline in the average yearly number of refugees who are settled in Canada from overseas.

Others, such as refugee lawyers and advocacy groups, see the 42 percent acceptance rate as unforgivably low. As one of the world's most privileged countries, Canada is in a position to display more generosity toward the less fortunate. Its RSD system is accused of being racist and exclusionary, both deliberately and inadvertently (Canadian Council for Refugees 2000). Unintentionally negative practices may include an insistence on documentation, a narrow definition of persecution, racial profiling in selection processes, and skewed distribution of visa posts. Nor is there any reason to believe that most refugees are playing fast and loose with Canada's refugee protocols. Catherine Dauvergne (2009) writes accordingly:

> Hundreds of thousands of people are living in fear and in real danger. Some of these people, if they were to reach Canada,

19 OBSERVATION

Critiquing the RSD System

THOSE WHO CENSURE Canada's refugee program focus on two dimensions: the refugees themselves, especially those who make inland claims, and the system that determines their status. Critics argue that, unlike immigrants, refugee claimants rarely make a direct contribution to Canada but impose a costly burden on its various services and programs for settlement and integration (Grubel 2013). Refugees are thought to have less education and lower employment earnings, and to be less likely to speak an official language and more likely to suffer from turmoil-related trauma. They are also seen as economic migrants in disguise, immoral people who make false claims to gain entry (but see Esses et al. 2008; Zimmerman 2011). In addition, the seeming dysfunctionality of the RSD system has prompted condemnation. According to James Bissett (2010; 2013), a prominent critic of the refugee asylum system, the program is in disarray for the following reasons:

> It neither serves the needs of genuine refugees nor enhances Canada's interests.
> It's expensive to operate but inefficient and ineffective.
> Human trafficking is rewarded because of Canada's openness and generosity.
> The system has damaged Canada's bilateral relations by insulting many friendly countries, including the United States, for interfering in their internal affairs.
> The security and safety of Canadians is compromised.
> The system is dominated by special interest groups who rely on taxpayer money to advance more generous asylum procedures.

> Canada is out of step with other countries in curbing the flow of asylum seekers. It allows anyone from any country to claim asylum and apply for refugee status. This commitment to due process can have unwieldy results. Of the 5,800 refugee claims from the European Union in 2011 (more than all claims from Africa and Asia), 4,400 were from Hungary, mostly by Roma. By contrast, the United States received only 47 claims from Hungary. In 2010, Canada received 23 times as many Hungarian refugee claims as all other countries combined (Wells 2012).

> Canada's reliance on the IRB as an independent "first instance" determination process differs from the norm in other countries. For example, administrative officials in Australia initially interview the claimant, thus reserving the procedural guarantees of a tribunal for the appeal stage.

> The IRB produces inconsistent decisions, is administratively unwieldy, overly legalistic, and open to abuse, with numerous loopholes and vulnerabilities that can prove expensive once legal, welfare, and administrative costs are factored in.

> Subjectivity prevails despite the gravity of the situation. Refugee approval rates vary not only from city to city but also from board member to board member, ranging from 100 percent acceptance to 0 percent acceptance (Rehaag 2009). One IRB adjudicator, "DM," rejected all 169 refugee claims between 2007 and 2010. Another seven members had acceptance rates of less than 10 percent. In contrast, a "CF" granted asylum in 100 percent of cases (ibid.; Keung 2011e). Arbitrary decisions remain a problem, including a publicized case wherein one of two nearly identical Palestinian brothers was accepted by a board member, whereas the other was rejected by another board member.

would fit within the narrow range of a refugee. Many would not. But most people do not have enough knowledge of refugee law to figure this out in advance. In fear they flee, and sort things out later. This is not a rampant abuse of a system.

That false and frivolous claims do exist is beyond doubt, but they cannot be exposed without due process – the careful consideration of each one on a case-by-case basis. Even those from so-called safe countries, or designated countries of origin, which normally have high rejection rates, deserve individualized attention (Showler 2006; see also Tobi Cohen 2013; Selley 2013).

A sense of perspective is critical: The RSD system works well because of its intelligence, integrity, and compassion, as Peter Showler (2006) and others argue (see Centre for Israel and Jewish Affairs 2013). But correctable flaws result in poor decisions whose consequences are too important to leave to chance. Of particular concern is the failure to establish an appeal system (despite promises to do so in 2002) to review rejections for bias and error. Overdue as well are improving the selection and training of IRB members, eliminating political patronage from the selection process, and strengthening the criteria for appointment. In short, the system is thought to be slow and cumbersome, encrusted with legalism and red tape, and under-resourced yet overburdened. The appointment of board members is inefficient, lacks transparency, and is often political. Their decisions can be arbitrary and inconsistent. Despite sweeping changes to the IRB that shifted the onus of decision making from political appointees to civil servants, refugee claimants continue to experience substantial discrepancies in the decisions by IRB members, with some rejecting nearly all claims before them and others accepting most claims (Humphreys 2014). The deportation process has too many time-consuming appeal channels. The end result? A huge backlog of over sixty thousand claims (albeit down to just under forty thousand by March 2012) that mocks federal promises of a fast, fair, and final process.

An intermediate position is espoused by those who contend that a paradox ensnares the RSD system. It is subject to criticism for dispensing complicated justice on a high-volume basis (up to 35,000 cases per year, or the metaphorical equivalent of serving haute cuisine in a fast-food outlet, as ruefully noted by some critics). Many believe that it is too quick in processing negative decisions, but not quick enough in weeding out ineligible claims (Keung 2010d). However well intentioned, the RSD system was swamped by the Supreme Court's Singh decision of 1985 (which ruled that everyone who so much as steps onto Canadian soil is entitled to due process). Instead of being efficient, fast, and fair, the system has collapsed into a legal limbo, with numerous avenues of appeal and lengthy administrative backlogs. Contradictions are at play: Canada's refugee determination processes may not respond quickly enough to those who genuinely need protection (the victims of war and oppression, who live in camps), thus inadvertently encouraging the profitable underground migrant smuggling system. Conversely, others argue, it may respond too generously to those who lie and cheat to get in. The final result? The perception that the RSD system is experiencing a "paralysis by analysis" in sorting out who is a refugee. Critics also suggest that the system is less compassionate than in the past because of (a) post-9/11 security concerns; (b) the fact that the Canada Border Services Agency, not the CIC, handles deportation, weakening the balance between compassion and enforcement; and (c) Ottawa's desire to woo the immigrant vote, yet look tough on immigration, especially for queue jumpers (Black 2013).

PHILOSOPHICAL PERSPECTIVES ON ASSESSING REFUGEE CLAIMS

There is much to commend in the RSD system (Showler 2006). Its very existence not only creates a relatively small number of illegal or undocumented populations but also diminishes the major twenty-first-century policy dilemma of dealing with irregular admission and unauthorized (overstayed and underground) migrants (Dauvergne 2009). Nevertheless, there is ample room for improvement. The challenge lies in designing a refugee determination system that matches the real to the ideal in ways that are politically, socially, and ethically acceptable (CIC 2012b). A principled program is required that balances Canada's international obligations regarding those who flee persecution or need protection, with its duty to safeguard its borders and the security of its citizens by controlling irregular migration (Gallagher 2008a). Controversies will need to be addressed, such as whether national sovereignty should trump human rights, resulting in a contradiction in the making: Citizens lose rights if they flee a state, and states lose sovereignty if they are compelled to view rights as universal (Saunders 2011b).

Any hopes of constructive engagement must acknowledge the primacy of two philosophical axis points regarding refugees and their processing under an RSD program (Plaut 1989; Jabir 2013). One perspective advocates a highly restrictive approach. Canada does not share a border with a refugee-producing country, critics contend, eliminating any justification for the arrival of large numbers of asylum seekers. At best, those who arrive without invitation or identification are seen as shameful opportunists who have no qualms about queue jumping. The ease of gaining refugee status attracts economic migrants who may not qualify under the point system or who are unwilling to wait for entry through conventional channels. At worst, they are perceived as potential terrorists who pose a security risk (Hamlin 2008). According to this "guilty until proven innocent" stance, measures are required to thwart the entry of unwanted refugees. After all, Canada has the right to control its borders and consolidate its sovereignty, and to expedite the expulsion of those whose claims are unfounded (Gallagher 2003; Collacott 2006). Consider Box 20, which reproduces an online advertisement for sneaking into Canada as the kind of abuse for justifying tightening up the process. Three options are proposed for ending the gridlock: (a) detain undocumented asylum seekers until proof of person is established; (b) create a firewall, such as a "safe third-country" rule, that excludes as many refugees as possible, and then deal with genuine cases as they arise (Bissett 2009b); and (c) redesign the program to accept only those who languish in refugee camps around the world (Stoffman 2002).

The other mindset disagrees with this restrictive philosophy (see Kaushal and Dauvergne 2011). Proposed instead is a generous acceptance of as many asylum seekers as possible, commensurate with Canada's humanitarian commitments. The assumption is that most asylum seekers are bona fide refugees who are in grave danger. The objective is to cast as wide a net as possible for would-be refugees, then dispose of those who don't comply, based on the merits of individual cases. Under this logic, all refugees should be assumed innocent until proven guilty. They deserve the benefit of the doubt – even if their stories seem far-fetched – by revising and expanding the net for those who need protection (Hamlin 2008). After all, there is no such thing as an illegal refugee, since international law accords everyone

20

A Cheap, Quick, and Effective Way to Come to Canada

THIS ADVERTISEMENT BY Quick Visa Canada, a Canadian firm specializing in fast immigration procedures, appeared online at http://quick visacanada.com. The website was removed on 11 March 2010, after the RCMP launched an investigation. Although it may have been a hoax, it nevertheless reinforced negative attitudes about newcomers who exploit the rules to gain admission.

Do you want to move to Canada now? Come to Canada paying not more than $2,250 USD without going through a long immigration process. Pay only after your [sic] arrive safely into Canadian soil.

You could be in Canada in less than 2 months without going through a long immigration process. Quick Visa Canada could make you travel to Canada as a tourist and when you get to Canada we will help you iniciate [sic] a refugee claim very easily. Do not miss this opportunity.

The steps are very easy. First you have to apply for a tourist visa to come to Canada. You may not even need a visa to come to Canada, if you are from one of the following countries ...

Once you obtain your tourist visa to travel to Canada, we will guide you on how to stay longer once you arrive. The day of your arrival in Canada (or the next day) we will go with you to the immigration office to initiate a refugee claim into Canadian soil in order to stay in Canada for a longer period and to be able to work and to study legally. You could be here in less than two months. The refugee application is a very long process that allows you to remain in Canada while it is under review.

While you are in Canada with a refugee status you can use the following services for free. Unlimited health care; open work permit that allows adults to work anywhere in Canada; monthly economic assistance; free legal services; free education for your children; and free English and French courses for children and adults ...

The next step is to help you find a motive in order to claim refugee status in Canada. We will provide you with a listing of different motives so that you can choose the one that best suits you and we will also give you complete information regarding what kind of documents you will have to obtain in order to make your case strong enough ... For example, many of our clients choose the type of motives in which they claim that they were part of an organization (anti-abortion, human rights, Gay or Lesbian movement, etc. etc.) back in their own home country and that some people were against that movement. This is just a simple example. Our services are so complete that we will brief you before your departure so that your motive is well documented and well verbalized. We guarantee you that the immigration official will not return you to your country. That is what we are here for.

the right to seek asylum, regardless of their mode of entry into the country.

Admittedly, authenticity may be difficult to establish without identity papers. Playing by the rules by patiently standing in a queue is rarely an option for people in distress. Few who fly from persecution and chaos can afford the luxury of asking for an exit visa. The necessity of producing "satisfactory identity documents" for permanent admission into Canada compromises the prospects of those who come from countries that do not issue such paperwork, where no government authority exists to do so, where certain groups such as women or rural residents cannot access it, and where simply requesting it can land you in trouble (after all, identity put the refugee at risk in the first place [Canadian Council for Refugees 2000]). Additional deterrents to flight, which are no less daunting, include preboarding detection barriers, passport and visa controls, and carrier sanctions and fines (Adelman 2004).

In short, refugee claimants as protected persons deserve the benefit of the doubt. The assumption is that it's better to err on the side of generosity – to accept 99 disingenuous applicants rather than incorrectly rejecting a genuine case of acute trauma. As Janet Dench (2006) points out, refugees are people who have no choice except to flee. Canadians, by contrast, do have a choice since they can welcome refugees as human beings who need sanctuary or can abandon them by pulling up the drawbridge. Admittedly, critics insist that the existing system is far from perfect and could benefit from selective changes. Still, Canada's program is better than many alternatives, inasmuch as it gives higher priority to protecting refugees than to rejecting them (Dench 2009). What is required are high-quality first decisions to ensure that claims are assessed by a fully independent, properly resourced, and competent decision maker. Any reform must begin with a foundational premise: Refugee protection is first and foremost a human rights issue because international law recognizes the right to asylum from persecution (Canadian Council for Refugees 2009b; Aspinall and Watters 2010). Box 21 summarizes the arguments of the "less" and the "more" camps.

There is no shortage of recommendations for improving the RSD system. Those of a restrictive bent propose changes that best serve the interests of Canada as well as those of genuine refugees (Collacott 2010b). For Martin Collacott, a harsh critic of the system, radical reforms must include the introduction of safe third-country designations (refugees must seek sanctuary in the first safe country they reach), a major reassessment of the Supreme Court's 1985 Singh decision, which extended Charter rights to non-citizens and non-permanent residents, and Canada's possible withdrawal from the antiquated 1951 UN Convention on the Status of Refugees (which is based on the Cold War dynamics of communism and defectors from the Soviet Bloc). Other reform schemes include (a) imposing an annual limit on the number of refugees (both overseas and in-country, (b) re-establishing Canada's status as a resettlement country for refugees who are selected abroad (as was the case following the Second World War) rather than one that accommodates a large number of inland claimants, and (c) reinforcing a temporary status for asylum seekers (evacuees) until their situation at home improves for a safe return. The expansionist mindset disagrees with this approach (Poulton 2010). Creating a fortress Canada is not a viable option where the free flow of asylum seekers is a

21

Competing Philosophical Perspectives: Refugees and the RSD System

Restrictive/Pessimists	Expansive/Optimists
Claims are bogus (most asylum seekers are fake).	Claims are bona fide (most asylum seekers are genuine).
Claimants are guilty until proven innocent.	Claimants are innocent until proven guilty.
The admission law should be strictly interpreted.	The admission law should be loosely interpreted.
National interests must prevail in determining who gets in.	Human rights take priority in defining who gets in.
Adjudication to determine merits should be on a case-by-case basis.	The net must be spread wide to ensure that no one is excluded.

reality that cannot be curbed. Suggested instead is a system that prioritizes the human rights of asylum seekers throughout the RSD process.

Intermediate perspectives prevail as well. Peter Showler, former IRB chair and now a University of Ottawa lecturer in refugee law, proposes a three-part compromise: (a) ensure good first decisions, by depoliticizing the appointment of IRB members, simplifying the process, and ensuring good legal representation for all claimants; (b) create a reliable appeal process to reduce reliance on judicial review; and (c) promptly remove failed claimants (Showler and Maytree Foundation n.d.). His ideal builds on the strength of the present system: It's accessible, allows claimants to tell their story before an independent tribunal, provides a good first decision, and grants permanent residence to legitimate refugees. Making the process fast, fair, and final would see the creation of a new Refugee Tribunal with two divisions –

the Refugee Claim Division and the Refugee Appeal Division – which would replace the IRB. Their members would be appointed solely on merit. Claims would be decided in 6 months and reviewed/appealed in 4 months; rejected individuals would be removed within 3 months of a negative ruling. The rationale is clearcut: Reducing the process to 13 months would ensure accurate and fair decisions, and prompt removal of failed claimants. Targeting bogus and backlogged asylum seekers for accelerated eviction within a year could also eliminate seemingly pointless appeals, which are both costly and time consuming (Don Martin 2010b).

FAIR, FAST, AND FINAL: REFORMING THE RSD PROCESS

The federal government continues to pass laws and promote initiatives to reform the RSD process. Take, for example, the introduction of the safe third country as part of a broader program to control the border against unwanted migrants (Christopher Anderson 2013). To deter asylum seekers from shopping around for the best deal, Canada defined the United States as a safe third country and a responsible partner in thwarting claims of convenience (CIC 2009c). Asylum seekers who make a refugee claim at the Canada-US border but who initially landed in the United States are returned for processing in the United States as their first safe country of arrival. However sensible this solution (people who seek asylum should be grateful for refuge at the first port of entry), the United States is not necessarily safe for asylum seekers. For example, Canada routinely accepts Colombian refugees, whereas the United States doesn't. Colombians who seek asylum in the United States are likely to be sent home (Satzewich and Liodakis 2013). In short, this Safe Third Country Agreement puts Canada in the position of closing its borders to asylum seekers via the United States, reneging on its refugee protection obligations under international law, unwittingly contributing to the human smuggling crisis, and diminishing human rights protection by making it harder for asylum seekers to lawfully enter Canada and still harder to make their case once they're here (Arbel and Brenner 2013; also Hansen and Papedemetriou 2014).

In recent years, Canada has applied the safe-country concept to all refugee claims, which are sorted into one of two processing streams: (a) those from a designated country of origin (DCO), a democratic country that is deemed to be safe; (b) those from more dangerous domains. Canada posts a list of DCOs, which is based on a combination of rejection/withdrawal/abandonment rates and/or a qualitative checklist to determine the democratic foundations of a country. In mid-December 2012, Jason Kenney listed 29 safe countries (there are now 37), most of them in Europe (Tobi Cohen 2012a, 2013). The initial intent was to reject all claims from DCOs, but this was eventually thought too risky as it would trigger a Supreme Court challenge or run afoul of Canada's international obligations. Safe-country asylum seekers will now be fast-tracked to facilitate a more expeditious removal (they are deported within 45 days instead of the current three years). They still have the right to a full IRB hearing but will be stripped of access to any appeal (such as the promised Appeal Division), except as allowed by the Federal Court on matters of law (Tobi Cohen 2012a).

The Balanced Refugee Reform Act, which received royal assent on 29 June 2010, reinforced a commitment to (a) address the massive backlog of claimants, (b) facilitate the flow of genuine refugees through the system, (c) fast-track claimants from countries that are presumed to be safe, (d) expedite the removal of failed claimants, (e) offer more protection for victims of torture and persecution, (f) create a new Refugee Appeal Division for failed claimants from non-DCO countries, and (g) resettle or sponsor more individuals from refugee camps (McDowell 2010). Other legislative initiatives have proven equally controversial. The Cracking Down on Crooked Consultants Act and the Preventing Human Smugglers from Abusing Canada's Immigration System Act (Little 2010) mandated the imposition of stiffer penalties for smugglers (from shipowners to organized crime smugglers). Asylum seekers who are part of an irregular arrival will be penalized as well – that is, detained without review and put on probation with no right to travel outside Canada, to sponsor their families, or to apply for permanent resident status for five years. Reaction to these seemingly draconian measures is mixed: Critics argue that the acts violate both the Charter and three international treaties that Canada has signed, while criminalizing asylum seekers who are within their rights to stake a claim. Although international law asserts that seeking asylum is not a crime, regardless of the mode of transportation employed, Ottawa proposes to treat asylum seekers as criminals instead of addressing the human rights abuses that create global refugees (Thompson 2011a). Others suggest that these initiatives are a good start in fighting a multibillion-dollar criminal industry that increasingly targets Canada as a "soft" destination whose commitment to the rule of law can be exploited (Collacott 2010a).

Passage of Bill C-31, Protecting Canada's Immigration System Act, which came into effect on 15 December 2012, was intended to hasten the sorting process for those who needed genuine protection and to curb (disincentivize) the number of frivolous and fraudulent claims from EU countries. According to the Centre for Israel and Jewish Affairs (2013), Europeans accounted for 23 percent of refugee claims in 2011, more than those from Africa and Asia combined, although 95 percent of their claims are eventually abandoned, withdrawn, or rejected. The act capitalized on the DCO rule to dissuade people from safe countries from jamming the system to the detriment of those in dire straits.[8] Claimants from DCO countries are now managed through an expedited process, including an initial IRB hearing within 30 to 45 days of their arrival. They do not have access to the newly created Refugee Appeal Division if their claim is rejected, though they retain the right to Federal Court review on matters of law. Medical care benefits under the act have been revised. Most claimants have seen an end to supplemental benefits such as vision and dental care under the Interim Federal Health Program (established in 1957 to provide health care for migrants when universal health care in Canada did not exist [Silnicki 2014]). Three categories of health benefits now include (a) expanded health care coverage for government-assisted refugees and victims of trafficking, which includes vision and dental, and is similar to that received by Canadians on social assistance; (b) health care coverage for most other claimants (except those from DCOs), which is comparable to the coverage received by most Canadians through their provincial plans; and (c) public safety health care coverage for DCO and failed claimants who await deportation. This encompasses the medical services that are necessary to protect Canadians from communicable diseases.[9] Under this new scheme, it is estimated that 14 percent of refugee claimants will receive the same extended care; 62 percent will get basic health coverage; and 24 percent will qualify for coverage only if they pose a public health risk (Keung 2013e). Finally, Bill C-31 established automatic detention for irregular arrivals over the age of 16, who are subject to periodic reviews until a final decision is made that does not imperil the safety and security of Canadians (Centre for Israel and Jewish Affairs 2013). Irregular migrants who are smuggled in are subject to immediate expulsion if their claims are rejected (Department of Justice 2012; Leblanc 2012).

Not everyone concurs with these reforms. Canada's humanitarian tradition is blemished by measures that accelerate the procedure but don't necessarily improve a process that involves more steps and fewer resources yet expects faster results (Dauvergne 2013). What Canada requires are reforms for building an immigration system that improves its economy, demonstrates its compassion, respects international protocols, and strengthens its social fabric. Other criticisms focus on the turnaround time for assessment, appeal, and removal, noting that compassion and thoroughness must not be sacrificed for the sake of speed. For example, under the new dispensation, claimants may have insufficient time to find a lawyer and prepare their defence (McDowell 2010). Finally, crackdowns on bogus claimants, unscrupulous consultants, and human smugglers reflect a punishment-oriented model with a potential for adverse consequences.

Much of the criticism is directed at the safe-country designation. For instance, Mexico is regarded as a safe country because it has a democratically elected government and generally subscribes to international agreements on human rights. Yet many see Mexico as anything but safe, considering its level of gang criminality and generalized violence, which the state seems incapable of curbing (Peter Showler, cited in Galloway 2010b). Nor does it make much sense to call Mexico a safe country yet grant asylum to 568 Mexicans in 2012. The same applies to the 448 Hungarians who were granted asylum despite Hungary's DCO status (Selley 2013; also Tobi Cohen 2013). The attempt to distinguish between claimants from non-safe countries and those from safe countries compromises the legitimacy of asylum claims because of an implicit bias (Janet Dench, cited in McDowell 2010). Even a country's status as democratic does not necessarily preclude the existence of human rights abuses (Showler and Maytree Foundation n.d.).

Curbing human smuggling and trafficking will prove a daunting challenge. According to the UNHCR (cited in Scoffield 2010b), almost all the world's asylum seekers depend on human smuggling rings at some point along the way. Criminalizing the search for asylum is not a solution since it tends to make the process more expensive and dangerous. Moreover, exceptions to refugee law are increasingly common, especially with respect to state security in the post-9/11 era (Kaushal and Dauvergne 2011). In other words, the solution (if there is one) must focus on the root causes that drive asylum seekers into the hands of sophisticated smuggling networks, which are increasingly run by organized crime. No single country can address this problem. Launching a coordinated international effort to target smuggling while helping asylum seekers would be a step in the right direction.

6

american exceptionalism

CONTESTING IMMIGRATION, CONFOUNDING IMMIGRANTS

IMMIGRATION AS AMERICAN EXCEPTIONALISM

CANADIANS MAY REGARD their immigration program as second to none, for Canada welcomes newcomers at rates that are extraordinary by world standards and record setting even by its own past (Leuprecht and Winn 2011). It ranks third-best among 31 advanced countries (behind Sweden and Portugal) for integrating newcomers.

In contrast, when it comes to immigration, the United States is not among the top-ranked "best practices" countries. This seems surprising, because it is the destination of choice for migrants around the world (OECD 2014a). In 2010, 43 million foreign nationals lived on American soil (13 percent of the population), which confirms its status as prime destination, well ahead of Russia with 12.3 million (Perucca 2010). A Pew global study concluded that, if given a choice, 23 percent of overseas respondents would select the United States as their immigration preference, followed by the United Kingdom at 8 percent and Canada at 7 percent. Moreover, its robust status as a destination will remain secure, given the entry of between 1 and 2 million newcomers each year, both legal and undocumented as well as skilled and unskilled. Such a prediction is hardly baseless. For the unskilled, the country represents one last chance to make it big; for the highly skilled, it offers the greatest return on their human capital. This brain gain is of immeasurable value: America benefits from immigrant ingenuity in (a) international commerce; (b) information and communication technologies, with immigrants accounting for a large percentage of high-tech start-ups (25 percent of them, according to *Economist* 2013b); and (c) entrepreneurial enterprises (immigrants account for 18 percent of small-business owners [Editorial, *New York Times* 2012]). The United States also gets top billing on the international stage for the accomplishment of its foreign-born artists, scientists, and athletes (Griswald 2012; Darrell West 2010). Finally, it is a remarkably successful integration machine, with migrants disagreeing on virtually everything except one thing: their belief that they live in the world's greatest country (Hansen 2009).

America's omission from global surveys might not surprise upon closer scrutiny. Immigration and immigrants might be the lifeblood that courses through its veins (McCabe and Meissner 2010), but the United States compromises or discards virtually every criterion for a successful immigration program. The impact of immigrants is subject to acrimonious debate; the integrity of the program (from transparency to accountability) is under fire; long queues and delays for admission are the rule rather than the exception; border control and protection are hit and miss; and enforcement and compliance measures are caricaturized as a joke (Higley and Nieuwenhuysen 2010). The United States may have integrated millions of newcomers without the benefit of a coordinated national program or an official definition of immigrant integration, but what prevails is essentially a laissez-faire philosophy. Newcomers must either rely on their own resources (from family to community) or rummage about for services or information in a patchwork of state and local initiatives (Bloemraad and de Graauw 2013).

America's immigration program is widely condemned as broken. Critics pounce on the presence of between 11 and 12 million undocumented migrants who cross a leaky southern border that apparently cannot be defended. The deportation of unauthorized migrants is proving one of the most contentious issues of the Obama presidency, with removals at a record pace, including two-thirds of the nearly 2 million deportation cases involving people with no criminal record or who committed minor infractions such as traffic violations (Thompson and Cohen 2014). No less scathing an indictment is America's detention system, which warehouses nearly 400,000 migrants per year in prisons or their equivalent as they await deportation or asylum (Editorial, *New York Times* 2011b). A 2007 socio-economic profile of America's foreign-born (Center for Immigration Studies 2007b) reinforced the dicey status of newcomers, noting that

> of adult immigrants, 31 percent had not completed high school, compared to 8 percent of the American-born.
> high rates of poverty, excessive welfare use, and lack of health insurance appear related to low education levels rather than to legal status or unwillingness to work.
> the poverty rate for immigrants and their dependent children is 17 percent, nearly 50 percent higher than for American-born.
> thirty-four percent of newcomers lack health insurance, compared to 13 percent of the native-born.
> the proportion of households that rely on at least one welfare program is 33 percent, compared to 19 percent for American-born households.

The seeming irrationality and/or dysfunctionality of America's immigration program points to a paradox (Susan Martin 2011). The United States may be exceptional as one of the world's most diverse countries because of immigrant-driven changes, but its exceptionality represents a symbol of ruin for some, a sign of renewal for others, and a lightning rod of discontent for still others (MacDonald and Sampson 2012). Americans are highly conflicted and ambivalent about immigration (Cole and Kincaid 2013). Good immigrants are defined as legal and capable of integration, whereas bad ones possess neither of these qualities (see also Kobayashi, Li, and Teixeira 2012). Proponents argue for more immigrants (or at least a path to legalization for those who are undocumented) to offset workforce shortages and improve international competitiveness; opposed are critics who want to increase security, construct a wall between the United States and Mexico, and deport illegal aliens (Darrell West 2010; Kathleen Arnold 2011; Pew Research Center 2013a). Not surprisingly, the US-Mexico border resembles a war zone, with no end in sight to the bluster and bickering (Meissner et al. 2013). The get-tough faction believes that migrants are driving down wages, ratcheting up taxes, stealing American jobs, swamping schools and services, spiking crime rates, and eroding national identity. The pro-immigrant lobby argues that they are indispensable to the economy, doing jobs that other Americans don't want, holding down prices, and generally paying their way. Anti-migrant hysteria and hostility are increasingly pervasive, and a racist backlash against undocumented workers criminalizes Latin Americans as the next potential terror threat. Chacon (2006, 1) writes of the move to militarize borders as the defence of last resort against an invading army:

> Whipping themselves into a frenzy, they prepare for war. The enemy are migrant workers; invisible yet ubiquitous. They lurk in the shadows and pose an imminent threat to the American public. In case you weren't aware of this "invader," armed vigilantes, local politicians, governors, members of both Houses of Congress, and the president are closing ranks to make sure you are afraid. Behind them, a phalanx of media pundits are joining the chorus to awaken a complacent population that immigrants are threatening to wreck society.

Debates over so-called illegal or undocumented/unauthorized migrants tap into America's thorniest public policy issue.[1] No one is exempt: The politics of immigration spans all ideological alignments, including splits among Democrats, Republicans, business, and labour unions (Crook 2007; Sumption and Bergeron 2013). Each successive "wave" of newcomers sparks controversy and calls for tougher enforcement, stepped-up raids, and detentions for non-compliance, followed by a rethinking of the immigration paradigm itself (Sumption and Bergeron 2013). The dearth of clear direction in immigration policy and programs is not without bias or basis. The complexity of international migration in a global economy complicates the prospect of reconciling opposing interests (Bodvarsson and Van den Berg 2009). In an issue that erodes, eludes, or divides, attempts at any kind of compromise solution are often gridlocked (Patricia Smith 2010). Worse still, the principle of "enforcement first" (from building enforcement programs to improving their performance) remains the de facto singular response to undocumented migrants. That enforcement measures cost the country a whopping $179 billion in the 2012 fiscal year attests to the short-sightedness of addressing symptoms instead of root causes (Meissner et al. 2013). Inescapably, America's immigration program is overwhelmed, outdated, and incapable of serving the country's evolving needs (Hansen 2009; Papademetriou et al. 2009). That assessment alone creates an urgency to deconstruct this crisis of confidence with respect to what America is doing or should be doing on the immigration front.

HISTORICAL OVERVIEW: FROM THE HUDDLED MASSES TO THE MASSIVELY HUDDLED

Give me your tired, your poor,
Your huddled masses, yearning to breathe free,
The wretched refuse of your teeming shore.
Send these, the homeless, tempest-tost to me,
I lift my lamp beside the golden door.

— EMMA LAZARUS, "THE NEW COLOSSUS," 1883

Many argue that the history of the United States is largely that of immigration (Handlin 1951; Batalova and Lee 2012). From its inception as an independent country to the present, the United States has received more immigrants than any other country in the world. Its immigration policy and program have varied from a general openness at the time of independence to the more rigid ethnic quota system of the early twentieth century, followed by the current more open framework that dates back to 1965 with modifications in 1990 (Benton 2013), albeit one that is inconsistent and poorly regulated (Bodvarsson and Van den Berg 2009). Changes in immigration policy reflected a complex set of factors related to economic conditions, political developments, vested interests, ideological shifts, and value-based aspirations (see also Kelley and Trebilcock 2010). Not surprisingly, in light of such complexities and contradictions, many Americans remain wary or resentful of immigrants (Patricia Smith 2010). Then, as now, immigrants elicited public concerns about a pending social deterioration embodying a variety of ills related to crime and moral decline. Only the targets have changed (MacDonald and Sampson 2012). For example, in 1882, just four years before the dedication of the Statue of Liberty as a symbol for welcoming newcomers, Congress passed the Chinese Exclusion Act, which literally barred this demographic from admission until 1943 (Darrell West 2010). Chinese sojourners were portrayed as servile, racially inferior, and unassimilable. Lacking political access and leverage in courts, and subject to partisan elections that portrayed them as un-American, they themselves were relatively powerless to resist (Tichenor 2012). In other words, immigrants have often received a surprisingly unfriendly and restrictive reception, despite America's bona fides as a society of immigrants, resulting in the eventual return of many disgruntled migrants to their home country

(Schaeffer 2009). Such a frosty reaction raises the questions of why and how. Sadly, the answers cannot be disassociated from xenophobia, nativism, and racism (Fitzgerald and Cook-Martin 2014).

Four immigration time periods can be discerned: (a) up to the mid-nineteenth century; (b) the 1880s to the 1920s; (c) the post–Second World War boom; and (d) the post-1990s. Americans in 1776 were predominantly white Anglo-Saxon Protestant descendants of immigrants from the British Isles. The population also included large numbers of Dutch and Germans, the latter of sufficient quantity to worry Benjamin Franklin about a possible demographic takeover of Pennsylvania. The Catholicism of newcomers in a staunchly Protestant country was seen as more of a threat than their status as migrants (Bodvarsson and Van den Berg 2009). The nineteenth century produced substantial flows of poor farmers and Catholics from Italy and Ireland (between 1845 and 1855, about 2 million left Ireland for the United States to escape widespread starvation, yet Catholic Irish were despised as one notch above enslaved blacks). This raised fears that immigrants would take jobs away from the American-born or, worse still, that subversive "papists" would eventually control the country (Kivisto and Ng 2005). Northern European groups were advantaged over other migrants since they were culturally recognizable and racially acceptable (Marger 2000). Less lucky were Chinese migrants who first arrived on the West Coast during the gold rush and later disembarked to assist in building the Transcontinental Railroad. Jews fleeing the pogroms in Russia and Eastern Europe were also among the less fortunate.

Relatively few restrictions on admissions existed during the first phase. The relentless demand for labour on farms and in factories and mines saw to that. A trickle of about fifty thousand per year until the 1840s was followed by substantial increases throughout the nineteenth century and beyond, including nearly 9 million between 1901 and 1910 (Bodvarsson and Van den Berg 2009). But as the nineteenth century progressed, especially with the arrival of Irish and Italian newcomers, opposition to non-white and non-Protestant immigration escalated, prompting the creation of a secret anti-immigrant society of nearly one million white Protestant men who called themselves the Order of the Star Spangled Banner. Fears were fuelled by the periodic economic panic and recessions during the 1890s that drew rising numbers of migrants from around the world, with nearly 28 million admissions between 1880 and the 1920s (1.3 million admissions in 1907 alone). The words of nineteenth-century MIT president Francis Walker might have captured the zeitgeist of the times: "The entrance into our political, social, and industrial life of such vast masses of peasantry is a matter which no intelligent patriot can look upon without the greatest apprehension and alarm ... They are beaten men from beaten races representing the worst failures in the struggle for existence" (quoted in Stalker 2009, 96).

Rules for admission were grounded in prevailing prejudices. White Europeans continued to enjoy almost unrestricted entry, without numerical quotas for admissions, but racialized migrants were no longer accepted, culminating in an almost complete ban on Asians, which was designed to preserve the purity, ethnicity, and nationality of the country (Bodvarsson and Van den Berg 2009). During the 1920s, Congress imposed quotas that gave preference to Northern Europeans and sharply reduced the total number of immigrants. This restriction barred millions of Jews and other émigrés from Nazi Germany. The 1930s saw immigration totals fall to just over 500,000, only to rebound after the war and peak at just over 9 million during the 1990s (ibid.). In 1965, America eliminated immigration quotas, resulting in large numbers of entrants from Latin America, the Caribbean, and Asia.

Today, the United States is undergoing its fourth great wave of immigration. Demographic projections suggest that this latest stream of newcomers could prove to be the largest and most diverse. Over 6 million newcomers arrived between 2001 and 2006, reflecting the globalization of economic activity and more accommodative immigration programs (ibid.; Tomás Jiménez 2011). Latin America and Asia remain the top source countries. Immigrants from these areas are highly diverse in terms of socio-economic backgrounds (from wealthy and highly educated to least educated and poorest) and geographical distribution (leaning toward the Midwest and the southern states) (Tomás Jiménez 2011). It is estimated that by 2025, 15 percent of America's population will be foreign-born, exceeding a century-old record of 14.8 percent, which was set in 1890 (Patricia Smith 2010). By 2050, nearly 20 percent of the projected 438 million Americans will claim immigrant status, resulting in re-racialization of the population, with whites forfeiting their majority demographic privilege, as demonstrated in Box 22.

Source countries are equally variable. From 1820 to 2005, 70 million people emigrated to the United States, with Germans topping the

22

US Population Growth

	2005	2050 (projected)
Total population	296 million	438 million
Foreign-born	12%	19%
Racialized groups		
White	67% (65% in 2010)*	47%
Latino/a	14% (16% in 2010)	29%
Black	13%	13%
Asian	5%	9%

* Pew Research Center (2013b).

list at 10 percent of overall numbers, followed closely by Mexicans, who have accounted for 70 percent of migrants since 1980 (Hansen 2009). The top ten ethnicities that passed through Ellis Island were Italians, Jews, Germans, Poles, Scandinavians, English, Irish, Scottish, Slovakians, and French. By 2008, Europeans comprised a modest 13 percent of all immigrants, compared to 53 percent for Latin Americans and 27 percent for Asians. In 2011, the top ten countries of immigrant origin were Mexico, China (excluding Taiwan), India, the Philippines, El Salvador, Vietnam, Cuba, South Korea, the Dominican Republic, and Guatemala (Britz and Batalova 2013). This pattern of racialized immigration is expected to drive and diversify America's future population growth. Box 23 supplies an overview of key dates and statutory developments in the evolution of America's immigration policy and program.

CONTEMPORARY ADMISSIONS

The United States may be the world's foremost immigration destination, but achieving authorized admission into the country is tricky because

23 OBSERVATION

Immigration and the Law: A Selective Timeline

1790   The Naturalization Act allowed any free white person to become an American citizen, provided that he or she was of good character and had resided for 2 years in the United States. The residency requirement was later increased to 14 years and subsequently dropped to 5 years, where it now stands. In 1870, naturalization was extended to persons of African descent but not to Asians.

1875   The Immigration Act, America's first immigration law, sought to bar certain groups from entering the country. Its rationale focused on the immigration of Chinese women, whose children would become citizens under the 14th Amendment. But moves to restrict certain demographics proved tricky because of existing trading partners or treaty relations (Bodvarsson and Van den Berg 2009).

1882   An Immigration Act imposed a 50-cent tax on all foreigners entering American ports. It denied entry to convicts, lunatics, or paupers who were likely to become public charges. The blatantly racist Chinese Exclusion Act of 1882 prohibited all Chinese labourers from entry. The act initially ran for 10 years but was eventually renewed in perpetuity. Targeting Chinese immigration provided a smokescreen for various racist and white supremacist groups (ibid.). It also demonstrated that non-naturalized migrants were largely at the mercy of Congress since they did not enjoy the full constitutional rights of citizens.

1892   A desire to control immigration resulted in the establishment of a processing centre on Ellis Island. Nearly 12 million people passed through the Ellis Island centre before the 1924 advent of the current system, in which applicants are processed overseas at American embassies and consulates (ibid.). Angel Island in San Francisco Bay also processed several hundred thousand people from 1910 to 1949, although its main purpose was to prevent the entry of unauthorized Chinese, East Indian, and Japanese migrants.

1917   The Immigration Act of 1917 denied entry to most East Asians and Pacific Islanders. It also established a literacy requirement for immigrants who were older than 16, imposed a head tax, and expanded the range of the inadmissible (including Mexicans and Filipinos).

1921   The Emergency Quota Act limited immigration to about 350,000 per year and imposed restrictions on migrants from Eastern and Southern Europe.

1943   The Chinese Exclusion Act was repealed, allowing naturalization of Chinese immigrants, but their admission was restricted to 105 per year.

1948   The Displaced Persons Act introduced the concept of sponsorship. Persons or groups who sponsored newcomers assumed responsibility for their welfare lest they become a public charge (Bodvarsson and Van den Berg 2009).

1952   The Immigration and Nationality Act ended all racial restrictions on naturalization. Nevertheless, it maintained a quota system that was first established in 1921. It also bolstered government powers to exclude or deport those of communist sympathies.

1962   Discriminatory selection provisions were eliminated.

1965   The Immigration and Nationality Amendment Act repealed all quotas based on national origin, opting instead for a system based predominantly on family considerations, with employment qualifications lower on the list of priorities. Admission categories were divided accordingly: 80 percent of those who were accepted had relatives in the United States, whereas 20 percent had desirable skills. No numerical limits were imposed on immediate family members (spouse and children) of American citizens (ibid.).

1980　The Refugee Act distinguished refugees (sponsored individuals in overseas camps) from asylum seekers (who entered the country and claimed refugee status). It allowed acceptance of some ninety thousand refugees and five thousand asylum seekers.

1986　The Immigration Reform and Control Act issued a one-time amnesty for unauthorized migrants, resulting in a boom of legal residence status for about 2.7 million foreign nationals residing in the United States (Abella 2012). It also toughened the enforcement of border control and cracked down on employer use of undocumented labour by making it illegal to hire unauthorized workers (Meissner et al. 2013).

1990　The Immigration Act increased the number of visas for priority workers and professionals with job offers. It also created ten thousand permanent resident visas for foreign investors whose net worth of at least $1 million would create employment for at least 10 American residents (Bodvarsson and Van den Berg 2009).

1994　California's Proposition 187 approved laws against the use of false immigration documents in accessing state funding for public social services, publicly funded health care, and public education. Teachers and service workers were expected to inform authorities of those whom they suspected to be undocumented or engaged in fraudulent activities.

2001   The Patriot Act empowered the government to control and deport all foreign nationals who lacked American citizenship. Unencumbered by legal challenges, authorities could exercise power even more arbitrarily across the complex maze of regulations. For those with alleged ties to terrorism, even citizenship could be revoked (ibid.).

2010   The Support Our Law Enforcement and Safe Neighborhoods Act (Senate Bill 1070) mandated Arizona's state and local police to determine the legal status of individuals who were stopped for other infractions. Enforced as well was a crackdown on those who sheltered, hired, or transported undocumented aliens (Medrano 2010; News Batch 2010).

2010   The immigrant share of the American population has varied over time. Between 1860 and 1920, immigrants accounted for 13 to 15 percent of the total population. In 1970, the proportion bottomed out at 5 percent of the total. In 2010, it stood at approximately 13 percent (Batalova and Lee 2012).

2013   The proposed Border Security, Economic Opportunity, and Immigration Modernization Act (Senate Bill 744) represents the most significant restructuring of America's immigration program since 1965 (Sumption and Bergeron 2013). The act is expected to retain a strong, albeit reduced, emphasis on family reunification, with a fourfold increase in skilled immigration. It will reshape the legal immigration system through admission policies that incorporate a merit-based visa and a point grid. Its emphasis will shift from temporarily employed migrants to high-skilled immigrants with permanent jobs, in addition to providing new pathways for middle- and low-skilled workers.

Sources: In part from Bodvarsson and Van den Berg (2009); also Guskin and Wilson (2007).

of the labyrinth of channels that must be navigated, even with the appropriate credentials or connections (Immigration Policy Center 2009; Stuart Anderson 2012). A migrant has little chance of getting in without a job offer, the presence of a family member, an exceptional skill or coveted talent, acceptance at a post-secondary institution, or the luck of the draw (Hansen 2009). This legal restrictiveness impedes lawful entry; unfortunately, it also encourages the influx of unauthorized and undocumented migrants. There are four main legal entry points: family, employment, diversity, and protection.

The family category consists of immediate relatives of US citizens. A legally qualified permanent resident can sponsor eligible foreign-born family members (children, spouses, siblings, and parents) by petitioning for a green card. The sponsoring member must demonstrate an income level above the federal poverty line and must legally commit to supporting family members brought into the country (Immigration Policy Center 2009). This category accounts for about 65 to 70 percent of overall admissions each year. By contrast, Canada's immigration program now restricts family members to about 25 percent, although, until recently, about 60 percent of newcomers to Canada were in the family class, whereas about 20 percent arrived as economic immigrants.

The employment preference involves persons who fit into one of the employment categories (listed below), have a job offer, or rely on an employer for sponsorship and admission (ibid.). Five preferences prevail (Bodvarsson and Van den Berg 2009):

> The first preference (EB-1) targets priority workers who have extraordinary skills.
> The second preference (EB-2) applies to workers with advanced degrees or exceptional abilities.
> The third preference (EB-3) selects for professionals, tradespeople, and skilled workers.
> The fourth preference (EB-4) captures special workers (religious occupation or vocation).
> The fifth preference (EB-5) focuses on employment creation.

A company may apply for a high-skilled (H-1B) visa, which is good for six years, with the option of sponsoring the visa holder for permanent residence. Only 65,000 of these visas are available each year for in-demand skilled workers – a risibly low figure for such an economic powerhouse (Hansen 2009). Most applicants are executives or are in computing, the sciences, and engineering. Few legal channels exist for low-skilled individuals who wish to work in labour-starved industries, including construction, hospitality, and meat processing (only 5,000 low-skilled green cards are set aside for the entire United States). With about 140,000 employment-based green cards available on a yearly basis to qualified immigrants (Immigration Policy Center 2009), visa holders and their dependants account for approximately 15 percent of the annual total of authorized migrants, compared to about 65 percent for Canada.

Most diversity immigrants (5-10 percent of the total) apply to a lottery that is reserved for countries who send fewer than fifty thousand migrants to the United States on a yearly basis or have historically been underrepresented for admissions.

The fourth category, persons who flee their home country due to persecution, constitutes a small percentage of the total. Numbers are determined on a year-to-year basis by presidential decree (News Batch 2010). Box 24 gives the 2012 totals for all four classes.

Authorized immigrants are entitled to the same rights as all citizens, though they cannot vote or hold political office. About 40 percent of

24

US Immigration: Number of Persons Obtaining Permanent Status by Admission Class, 2012

Admission class	Total	
Family-sponsored immediate relatives of US citizens	681,000	(66%)
Employee-sponsored	144,000	(14%)
Diversity	40,320	(4%)
Refugees/asylum seekers/humanitarian	167,000	(16%)
Total	1,032,320	

Source: Sumption and Bergeron (2013).

immigrants become citizens through a process of naturalization. To become naturalized, a newcomer must reside in the United States for five years, demonstrate a passable proficiency in English, and possess a knowledge of American history and government. Many acquire citizenship in part because it enables them to assist overseas relatives to migrate (News Batch 2010). In terms of persons obtaining legal permanent resident status by region of birth, Asia is first, followed by Central America, Africa, Europe, and South America.

IMMIGRATION DEBATES: BROKEN BORDERS OR BUSTED PROGRAM?

Few issues in American politics have proven more fraught than immigration (Moses 2009; Tichenor 2009, 2012; Tomás Jiménez 2011). Hardly any dimension of American life is unaffected by the politics of immigration, whether it's population, jobs, wages, education, health care, or the environment (Kathleen Arnold 2011). Some maintain that the country has benefitted enormously from an immigrant brain gain, including raising the GDP, contributing to tax rolls, establishing new businesses, and filing for patents (Darrell West 2010). Others believe that the United States is badly mishandling an already out-of-date immigration program. Failure to construct a sound and sustainable program harms the economy, diplomatic relations, and national security (see Bush and McLarty III 2009). In between these extremes are moderates such as President Obama who want to balance pro-immigration/pro-amnesty messages with equally tough measures on border security (Saunders 2011a). Those in the middle concede that migrants are hardworking and good for the (global) economy (Semple 2014). But unauthorized migrants have broken the rules for admission while compromising the integrity of America's borders (Cavanagh 2011a). Promises of reform are common, as are pleas to reframe the immigration debate. What transpires instead is more partisan politics, handwringing over the sorry state of affairs, and additional enforcement mechanisms (Cooper and Lopez 2011). Or as Susan Martin (2011, 1) puts it, "As in previous waves, there is a profound ambivalence about immigration among the American public. Historically, Americans have tended to see their migrant ancestors through rose-colored glasses while raising serious concerns about the contributions of current immigrants and the extent to which they will assimilate our values, language and experiences."

25 OBSERVATION

Doing Immigration Differently: Canadian and American Differences

A COMPARISON CAN yield fresh perspectives and inspire a critical awareness of what may be taken for granted (Foner and Bertossi 2011). So how does Canada's immigration program compare to that of the United States? In general, there are striking differences between the two countries in overall numbers, proportions, source regions, types of immigrants, labour market skills, and status (temporary or permanent) (Fong and Chan 2008; Bloemraad 2011; Harell et al. 2012; Kobayashi, Li, and Teixeira 2012; Teixeira, Li, and Kobayashi 2012). For example:

> The average annual level of legal immigration in the United States between 2002 and 2009 was about 1 million (Vengroff 2013). Canada's intake is smaller at about 250,000 per year. But since its population is one-tenth that of the United States, Canada wins hands down when numbers are adjusted on a proportional basis.

> In 2010, immigrants represented 13 percent of the total US population (40 million). The Canadian foreign-born population now stands at about 21 percent (Statistics Canada 2013).

> The US immigration program is guided by a family reunification focus, whereas Canada emphasizes the theme of economy. Most immigrants to Canada (60-65 percent) arrive via the economic class, which is based on a point system that allows a good measurement of labour market needs. Compare this with the United States, where family sponsorship accounts for about 65 to 70 percent of yearly intake (Triadafilopoulos 2006). Canada's economic class puts an emphasis on education, skills, and language proficiency, whereas chain immigration of family and relatives characterizes American immigration patterns (Vengroff 2013). Canada's concentration on the economic (skilled) category did not always exist. A demand for unskilled and family reunification prevailed prior to the 1980s (Zaman 2012).

> Immigrants in the United States are defined as foreign-born with lawful permanent resident status. About 60 percent of those who are granted permanent residency are not new entrants. Already residing in America, they adjust their status from temporary to permanent. In other words, most migrants are already in the country when they receive the right to permanent residency (Hansen 2009). With few exceptions, such as those in the Canadian Experience Class, most would-be immigrants to Canada must apply from outside.

> Canada's immigration program is driven by bureaucracies that stress incorporation, settlement programs, and government commitment to respect diversity. Bureaucracies associated with the US immigration program tend to emphasize policing/surveillance while maintaining an arm's-length distance in facilitating settlement and integration (Bloemraad 2006; Vengroff 2013).

> In the United States, immigration selection, integration, and management are federal responsibilities, with states playing a minimal role except for the settlement and integration of refugees. Canada's system, which is more decentralized, increasingly features a shared jurisdiction between federal and provincial authorities (Vengroff 2013).

> Irregular/unauthorized/undocumented persons account for about a third of immigrants to the United States. In contrast, Canada lacks an asylum-producing border to contend with; as a result, asylum seekers account for about a tenth of its yearly immigration total. About half arrive by crossing the US-Canada border, and the rest come as tourists, workers, or visitors who overstay their visa status. There are slightly different refugee determination processes in place, depending on whether the claim is made at a port of entry or inland (Canadian Council of Refugees 2013).

> Central Americans account for about 55 percent of all immigrants (Mexicans represent nearly a third of the overall total), followed by East/Southeast Asians at about 18 percent and Europeans at about 13 percent) (Kurien 2013). These figures stand in sharp contrast to those of the 1960s, when European sources prevailed (Batalova and Lee 2012). Those from Asia and the Middle East account for about 57 percent of Canada's total (Statistics Canada 2013). Whereas Asian immigrants to Canada tend to be upwardly mobile and of relatively

high socio-economic status, US-bound migrants from Central America cluster at the bottom of the workforce (Vengroff 2013).

> As the largest sending country, Mexico accounts for nearly six times as many immigrants as the next-largest country, China (including Taiwan and Hong Kong), followed by India and the Philippines (Center for Immigration Studies 2007a; also Hansen 2009). The top immigrant-source countries for Canada are the Philippines, India, and China (Harell et al. 2012).

In the past 20 years, many undocumented immigrants have entered the United States, accounting for up to a third of its foreign-born residents. Their presence reflects uncertain economic conditions in Latin America as well as a growing demand for cheap unskilled labour in the United States (Bodvarsson and Van den Berg 2009). Increases in the number of unregulated migrants are grounded in large backlogs and long delays in family reunification applications, as well as ineffective and half-hearted employer sanctions in curbing the hiring of unauthorized foreign workers (Abella 2012). This undocumented factor cannot be underestimated: It's the one issue that never fails to provoke or polarize, with some arguing that the undocumented are bad people breaking good laws, and others seeing them as good people who are breaking bad laws that are out of step with contemporary reality (Dromey et al. 2011). In between are numerous intermediate positions: According to Darrell M. West (2010), public opinion polls indicate that the majority of Americans support an amnesty for unauthorized migrants, if they meet specific conditions (pay a fine, pay their back taxes, pass a background check, and learn English).

The crisis in unauthorized migrants is not without context. It can be traced to the expiration of the Bracero Program, which facilitated the entry of temporary migrants from Mexico for agricultural and menial labour jobs. The program came to an untimely end: Mexicans who did not have advanced education or specialized skills were effectively barred from the United States unless they had immediate family

26 OBSERVATION

Irregular Migrants: "Help Wanted, Keep Out"

AMERICA IS NOT the only jurisdiction confronting a crisis of undocumented immigration. Europe, including the United Kingdom, is also experiencing a crisis of confidence over what to do, as well as a conflict of interest over how to do it (Finch and Cherti 2011). Almost 15 percent of Europe's 56 million migrants are undocumented, with annual arrivals in the vicinity of 500,000 (Hawley and Wilder 2013). In the United Kingdom, it's estimated that undocumented migrants number between 618,000 and 783,000. These include arrivals from both developed and developing countries, most of whom (60 percent) have overstayed or violated the terms of their visa. They also tend to be highly educated (about half have tertiary education). The animating logic behind these flows is economic self-improvement – namely, poor prospects at home – though factors related to persecution and need of protection are also cited. Irregular migrants rely on both formal and informal networks to establish themselves, and most are employed in unskilled and poorly paid jobs in sectors from hospitality to cleaning and construction, but they earn enough to send money home as remittances. Irregular migration is widely perceived as harmful because:

> It damages the credibility and integrity of an immigration program that needs public support to maintain its legitimacy.
> Irregular migrants are in a precarious state, which renders them susceptible to exploitation.
> Irregular migrants may be working and paying taxes without receiving benefits, yet they impose significant costs on society by putting pressure on services and infrastructure.

> The very existence of a large irregular population living in the shadows is seen as inimical to the principles of active citizenship and an inclusive society.

Admittedly, many sectors of the economy rely heavily on irregular migrants, given the dearth of domestic workers or legal migrant labour. Nevertheless, drawbacks and costs are associated with the presence of a large undocumented population. Hardliners would deport all irregular migrants, although this would massively unsettle the economy, which depends on relatively open and flexible labour markets. Besides, many undocumented migrants would rebel against such a move. Having invested emotionally and financially to get into the United Kingdom, they would resent and resist a coerced return, especially when they see themselves as productive members of society who put more into it (taxes) than they receive (services). Many would also dread the prospect of losing face by returning home.

Finally, irregular migration is not a domestic problem. Millions of global migrants are on the move in search of opportunity because of gross disparities of wealth and opportunities between the global North and South. No less conducive to the pattern are ineffective sanctions against employers who hire undocumented migrants, the development of transnational social networks, the pervasiveness of human smuggling rings, and technological advances in transportation and communication (Christopher Anderson 2013). Admittedly, no one has all the answers to this dilemma. Nevertheless, creating an immigration program that controls intake and reduces the number of irregular migrants to manageable proportions would be a step in the right direction.

residing in the country. The fact that the border was largely un-guarded and the economic situation had not changed meant that many former Bracero continued to work illegally, often in their old jobs. Employers were willing accomplices in breaking the law, as were land-lords, retailers, and other economic interests who benefitted from cheap labour (Bodvarsson and Van den Berg 2009).

Reactions to current conditions are uneven: Surveys indicate that most Americans are deeply concerned about the undocumented migrant situation, although business interests continue to support an arrange-ment that supplies a steady and compliant low-wage workforce. A *New York Times*/CBS poll of April 2010 exposed deep fissures: 84 percent of Americans believed that so-called illegal immigration was a serious or somewhat serious problem, whereas only 15 percent thought that it was not serious at all or not too serious. Of particular note are con-cerns over securing broken borders and what to do about the legal status of illegal migrants in light of depleted municipal budgets and penny-pinching state coffers. A focus on migrants as inhuman and an unhealthy threat intensifies the militarization of borders at the ex-pense of all legitimate aspects of immigration identity and dignity (Lopez et al. 2013). Consider, for example, the US-Mexico border as a site of physical, social, and psychological trauma:

> For Latino immigrants, the literal boundary at the US-Mexico border and the physical deterrents it entails shape the immigra-tion journey, leaving particular marks on the psyches and bodies of immigrants crossing the border. These deterrents symbolize the unjustified perception of threat from undocumented immi-grants plotting to rob us of resources, jobs, and culture, while bringing violence, drugs, and disease across our borders. Political boundaries created by policy-makers and the voting public define the qualities of undocumented immigrants that make them "worthy" of citizenship, permanent resident status, and reprieve from deportation without consideration of universal guidelines of health and human rights. (ibid., 6)

Undocumented workers are confused by the cacophony of mixed signals: "needed, not wanted"; "help wanted" but "keep out"; and "mi-gration, not migrants" (Heiskanen 2009). The fact that most of them would not risk entry into the United States without realistic employment

27 DEBATE

Should Unauthorized Migrants Be Offered Amnesty and Legal Status?

NO, amnesty is wrong and costly	YES, amnesty is the only realistic solution
> It's costly, with unauthorized immigrants undercutting the wages and working conditions of American residents while creating a whole new demographic for expensive benefits and overburdened services.	> Unauthorized migrants are here because the unskilled have fewer ways to enter and work.
	> Most are law-abiding, hard-working, tax-paying contributors who generate wealth through consumerism and entrepreneurship.
	> Enforcement, from border patrols to deportation, is costly and doesn't work.
> Rewarding those who break the law is not only wrong but also tends to encourage more deviant actions.	> Legalization would allow migrants to better invest in their communities and contribute to the local economy.
> The ability of a country to control its borders is sharply compromised.	> Migrants are integral to the American economy in general and to specific industries in particular. America needs them as much as they need America.

Sources: See Gans, Replogle, and Tichenor (2012) for the point/counterpoint debate.

prospects opens a new perspective: The problem of undocumented migrants could readily be solved by enforcing existing legislation, most notably on-site workplace monitoring and penalties to employers. Box 27 captures the essence of the debate between those who favour a general amnesty and those who do not.

Almost everyone acknowledges that the current system is flawed. Agreement on how to fix it is more elusive (Patricia Smith 2010). For some, the solution rests with reform of the confusing and counterproductive admission regulations (Immigration Policy Center 2009).

They suggest modifying a family-based visa system to favour more skilled worker visas or, alternatively, instituting a national guest worker program (*Seattle Post Intelligencer* 2010). For others, reform proposals must address the issue of undocumented migrants, with numerous obstacles standing in the way of normalizing their status. Reforms that target irregular immigration pose nettlesome policy challenges because of opposition by powerful organized interests who benefit from the reserve pool of cheap labour. In addition, initiatives have proven politically perilous and polarizing, resulting in narrow bipartisan majorities that are unwilling to negotiate compromises, to the detriment of national interests (Tichenor 2009). For example, both Republicans and Democrats are anxious to attract the immigrant vote. For Republicans, new immigrants provide cheap and docile labour to suit the needs of big business and middle-class families; for Democrats, regularizing undocumented migrants will reap grateful voters at election time (Swain 2007). In other words, the politics of politics creates numerous barriers that often defy rational explanation or deter comprehensive solutions (also Tichenor 2012). Five obstacles stand out: politics, hypocrisy, systemic failure, lack of political will, and optics.

In the world of politics, rival philosophies and interests complicate problem definition while making legislative majorities elusive (Darrell West 2010). Both Republicans and Democrats are reluctant to jeopardize their electoral gains by alienating independents or exposing divisions within the party. Nor is there any political advantage in debating immigration because of its contentiousness. Party members are divided between those who favour immigration reform (business benefits) and those who reject any move to legalize the status of 11 to 12 million unauthorized migrants (Tomás Jiménez 2011). Broadly speaking, conservatives tend toward increased border security and the deportation of undocumented persons; liberals are more amnesty-inclined (Patricia Smith 2010). Cosmopolitans want to expand numbers and improve the status of the most vulnerable; by contrast, nativists want to restrict or reject those who broke the law rather than reward them.

Major reforms entail difficult negotiations that can yield only painful compromise packages. Many sectors of the American economy profit from the exploitation of unauthorized migrants, even as they hypocritically call for restrictions and penalties. But because the American economy is structurally dependent on cheap labour to secure an affluent living standard, any mass expulsion would trigger a huge economic dislocation. Not unexpectedly, migrants are being manipulated by politicians as political pawns and convenient scapegoats for America's economic woes (Cooper and Lopez 2011).

The government's systemic failure to control seemingly porous borders has compounded the problem of illegal migrants. So-called border hawks see illegal immigration as eroding American sovereignty and compromising national security, rule of law, and jobs and services for citizens. The end result is a widespread mistrust and cynicism regarding government incapacity or duplicity. Those who argue that illegal migrants should just join the queue overlook a fundamental reality: For the vast majority of unauthorized migrants, there is no queue to join, especially if they lack close relatives or employment connections in the United States, or do not qualify for refugee status (Hansen 2009; Immigration Policy Center 2009). In short, the crisis does not entail a failure of migrants. More accurately, it's a system failure whose legacy of ineffectiveness is drawn from the past and bodes poorly for the future.

Political will is conspicuous by its absence. Policy initiatives that are designed to meet the demands of one important constituency invariably incur the wrath of others in a never-ending game of whack-a-mole. Inflamed rhetoric on both sides often obscures genuine problems while hindering consensus for effective solutions (Immigration Policy Center 2009). For example, the Comprehensive Immigration Reform Bill of 2007 proposed five main measures: (a) visas for illegal migrants, (b) a guest worker program, (c) workplace enforcement, (d) increased numbers of skilled migrants, based on a point system, and (e) improved border security. But the bill never made it past the Senate floor (Hansen 2009). During an NBC interview, President Barack Obama acknowledged that "fixing our broken immigration system is a top priority" (Gregory 2012), and his administration appears to favour the logic of the 2007 bill. This would entail legalizing unauthorized migrants by imposing fines and payment of taxes, strengthening border security and workplace enforcement by cracking down on employers who hire them, creating a national system for verifying the legal immigration status of new workers, and revising the immigration preference system along more pro-business and pro-labour lines. Brave hopes, indeed, but the politics of politics demolishes any bipartisan consensus (Tichenor 2012). For example, in late June 2013, the Democrat-controlled Senate approved a landmark bill – the Border Security, Economic Opportunity, and Immigration Modernization Act – that would clear the path to citizenship for millions of undocumented people (Sumption and Bergeron 2013). But the Republican-controlled House is determined to kill the bill and focus instead on border security and the removal of "illegals" (Cowan and Ferraro 2013).

Americans may be committed to the rule of law, but they are equally gung-ho about respecting the dignity and rights of the individual. The optics of expelling millions of undocumented migrants are not what America wants to convey to the world (Hansen 2009). Little political capital is to be gained from storylines and images in which crying children are dragged out of school or from their homes and bundled into cargo planes bound for Mexico.

If the problem is to be solved, it must be understood as complex, contested, and beyond a quick fix. It must also be framed as structural and systemic. That is, although the United States itself is constantly changing, the immigration system remains locked in the past, based on legal limits that were set in 1990 and constrained by the 1996 legislation (Illegal Immigration Reform and Immigrant Responsibility Act) (Immigration Policy Center 2009). Moreover, as the Immigration Policy Center (ibid.) notes, the crisis goes beyond the 11 to 12 million unauthorized migrants. A broader range of issues is implied as well, including (a) an insufficient number of worker visas to address America's economy and labour market needs, (b) arbitrary visa caps that create large and lengthy backlogs for reuniting family members, (c) wages and workplace violations by unscrupulous employers, and (d) inadequate government infrastructure that delays the integration of immigrants. In addition, the lack of federal solutions creates a costly enforcement-driven reaction but does little to deter the flow of unauthorized migrants.

In fact, America's immigration program is a paradox. Although the country remains the premier destination for global migrants, its failure to exploit its comparative advantage means that emigrating to the United States is virtually impossible, regardless of skills, educational levels, or language competence, without a family sponsorship, refugee status, a company willing to apply for an H-1B visa, or placement at an educational institution (Hansen 2009; Stuart Anderson 2012). These obstacles are as much an incentive as a deterrent. As Randall Hansen (2009) argues, an exodus of unauthorized Mexican migrants flows

28 OBSERVATION

The Arizona Crackdown: Targeted Solution or Racial Profiling?

THE LACK OF a cohesive and workable federal response to the emotionally charged problem of undocumented migration has created a political and security vacuum. Nor is there any sign of bold new approaches to address the issue. As a result, state and local governments have taken control of the situation, passing legislation that seemingly contradicts the US Constitution and the fundamental rights of both citizens and newcomers, or as Matthew Carr (2010) rephrases it, in a way that acknowledges their less-than-human status.

> After decades of remorseless hostility across continents, undocumented immigrants are in danger of becoming a subcategory of humanity – a target that can be attacked with impunity. And across the world, governments have militarized their borders with new laws, restrictions, and technologies to exclude unwanted migrants. In the United States ... undocumented immigration has been similarly depicted as a threat to national identity, social stability, or a source of unfair economic competition.

In 2010, Arizona passed the Support Our Law Enforcement and Safe Neighborhoods Act (Senate Bill 1070), which criminalized resident foreign-born aliens who lacked the registration documents that are required by federal law. The act mandated police to inquire into the legal status of individuals who were detained for other infractions, in addition to cracking down on those who sheltered, hired, or transported undocumented aliens (Medrano 2010; News Batch 2010). It expanded Arizona's power to eliminate illegal immigration by questioning a person's citizenship, based on the reasonable suspicion that he or she was unlawfully present (Fryberg et al. 2012). Those who lacked proper documentation were deported. Critics say that the act encourages racial profiling; supporters say that it simply enforces existing federal law. In mid-June 2012, the Supreme Court struck down most of the Arizona law as illegal and unconstitutional. The court did leave one provision intact, however – state police are required to check the citizenship status of anyone whom they arrest if they suspect that person of being in the country "illegally" (i.e., without documentation) (Yakabuski 2012). The ruling was seen as a victory in reaffirming the primacy of the federal government in matters pertaining to immigration. Nonetheless, the law received majority support in Arizona and other states such as Colorado, Florida, and Nebraska. A May 2010 Associated Press poll indicated 42 percent in favour, 24 percent opposed, and 34 percent unsure or neither opposed nor in favour. As well, according to a *Christian Science Monitor*/TIPP poll (Medrano 2010), most Americans do not feel that unauthorized migrants should have access to public benefits (from education to assisted housing).

Alabama appears to have pushed the fervour to the limit. Under an Alabama law of September 2011, any undocumented migrant who works or rents a home in the state commits a crime. All contracts involving an undocumented migrant are null and void, and police are required to inspect the papers of those whom they suspect are illegal. Businesses that knowingly employ undocumented workers will lose their licence. Public schools must determine the immigration status of all pupils and report back to the state. And anyone who knowingly conceals or harbours an irregular migrant – from renting an apartment to driving that person to church – could be charged with a crime, in effect criminalizing acts of compassion (Editorial, *New York Times* 2011a).

into the United States because there is no legal alternative for entry. If the border is broken, he concludes, it's because the immigration program is broken.

SHIFTING THE PARADIGM?

The politics of immigration makes it clear that what was once settled is no longer assumed; what was previously a given is now questioned;

and what was off limits is now open to debate. Immigration debates in the United States reflect a set of assumptions by media, government officials, and the beneficiaries of cheap labour. Those who favour liberalizing the movement of people endorse a conventional wisdom that is anchored in five premises:

> Immigration is good; therefore, the more immigrants the better.
> America should be open to everyone; restrictions or distinctions are suspect.
> "Illegal" immigrants are good for the country; therefore, any controls are unjust.
> Immigrants have always melted into becoming American, so programs are not needed to facilitate integration.
> Immigrants have a right to maintain their language and culture without forfeiting their Americanness.

Other Americans challenge these articles of faith. They do not necessarily reject immigration, but they do believe that caution and compromise are required if the legitimacy of the system is to be sustained. They reframe the debate along the following lines:

> Yes, immigration is good, but there is a need to discuss why, how many, and on what basis.
> Yes, America should be open to all legal migrants, but like all countries, it has a right and a responsibility to tailor immigration to its own needs.
> Yes, it's true that undocumented migrants provide a benefit, but immigration laws must be enforced to ensure the integrity of the system and public support.
> Yes, most migrants eventually become Americanized, but programs may be required to facilitate their attachment to their new homeland.
> Yes, everyone has a right to be different, but everyone is also obliged to become American by learning English, adopting core values, and constructing a commitment to the United States.

Indeed, a paradigm shuffle may be in the offing, one that challenges the public discourse and prevailing consensus. Awareness may be mounting that any workable compromise between conflicting viewpoints is doubly elusive when the conflict is between two equally viewpoints or models, in the process rendering any resolution fraught with ambiguity and second guessing. Americans are understandably divided over what principles should be invoked to improve the immigration program (Kathleen Arnold 2011). Questions abound: Is the current system for managed migrants the best framework to address twenty-first-century realities? Who should be admitted? What rights and benefits should be conferred? What are the costs and benefits to society or communities? What do immigrants owe America in return (Swain 2007)? Are there only two solutions to the problem of unauthorized entry? In other words, is the choice limited to (a) enlarging the guest worker program as exploitable labour and offering amnesty to undocumented migrants or (b) militarizing the southern border and imposing harsher punishments on those who are here illegally and who pose a security threat (Kathleen Arnold 2011)?

Whether one paradigm displaces the other remains to be seen. The more liberal-minded may be winning the day but lack the critical mass and political clout to displace the conservative rump, whose time may be numbered but who nonetheless hold sway over wide swaths of the American public. Admittedly, no one should underestimate the fervency of those who rush to the defence of one model rather than the other. But the genie is out of the bottle, and getting it back in again may prove impossible (Renshon 2010).

PART 3

experiencing immigration, immigrant experiences

MANY STUDIES TAKE immigration as a starting point for analysis. They emphasize the deconstruction of immigration policies, the design and implementation of programs, and their impact and implications for society or the economy. Criticism of existing policies and programs is common enough (Bissett 2013). Conflicts of interest (rights of migrants versus rights of the host country) are inevitable when balancing positive policy choices and workable outcomes without succumbing to a purely managerial approach or prevailing media negativity (Cavanagh and Mulley 2013; Rutter 2013). Choosing reactive models to mollify public opinion is a dead end; the challenge lies in constructing a progressive policy that is rooted in reality, public confidence, accountability, and effectiveness (numbers and patterns matter).

However valid and valuable this focus on policy and policy making, such an approach does a disservice. It glosses over the lived experiences of immigrants, which are as varied as they are conflicted and contradictory. Some newcomers have a positive experience; others find it disappointing; and for still others, it combines promise and peril. Of particular note is a growing awareness that the realities of female immigrants differ from those of males (Boyd 2006). Moreover, immigrant experiences do not exist outside a broader social, political, and economic context. The social climate established by Canada's official multiculturalism is critical in shaping the "hospitality dividend." No less important is the role of mainstream media in framing the "warmth of the welcome" (Reitz 1998).

This part of *Immigration Canada* begins by looking at the impact of immigration and immigrants on Canada, in addition to public reaction to both the immigration program and the presence of newcomers. There is convincing evidence that immigration and immigrants have a powerful yet mixed effect on Canada, and vice versa (Clarkson 2011). As a result, concern is rising over the costs and/or benefits of immigration. That makes it especially important to deconstruct the rationale behind competing perspectives. Chapter 7 reframes the contributions and drawbacks of immigration and immigrants by replacing the false dichotomy of "either/or" with the mutuality of "both/and" ("good/benefits" and "bad/costs"). The chapter also contends that public attitudes regarding the subject are mixed at best and indifferent or hostile at worst, with confusion and uncertainty hovering between. It finishes by utilizing a series of multiple responses to deconstruct popular misconceptions about immigration and immigrants.

Chapter 8 explores the range of immigrant experiences in Canada. There is no standard experience, because of differences in gender, racialization, socio-economic status, sexuality, age, and so on (Creese 2011). Nevertheless, there are commonalities in how newcomers cope with the task of settling down and integrating (McDonald et al. 2010; Clarkson 2011). Immigrant experiences are informed by the challenges of making the adjustment from "there" to "here." Or, as Pico Iyer (2001) asks, how does one create a sense of self and home without the aid of conventional cues and coordinates? These lived experiences have changed as well. Severing ties to the home country is increasingly a thing of the past (Bauder 2003; Satzewich and Wong 2006). The experiences of newcomers are examined through the prism of gender, and the role of the mainstream media in shaping a social climate of acceptance is also discussed. The chapter concludes by looking at municipal government efforts to improve the life course trajectory of immigrants in terms of settling down, fitting in, and moving up (also Chappell and Glennie 2009).

Chapter 9, on multiculturalism and immigration, provides a national context for understanding immigrant experiences. It analyzes why some believe that the relationship between multiculturalism and immigration is productive, whereas others see it as dysfunctional, and others yet as simultaneously progressive and regressive. The chapter contends that, despite shifts in emphasis over time, the logic of inclusive multiculturalism as integrative immigrant governance has never wavered in its mission (and myth making). It continues to focus on facilitating the settlement, adjustment, and integration of new and racialized Canadians within the framework of an inclusive country. Yet the rhetoric of official multiculturalism does not always deliver, in the process spoiling the experience of immigrants while shortchanging their contribution to Canada (see Biles et al. 2012). In pursuing its central theme of the politics of inclusion, the chapter deconstructs the integrationist inclusion inherent in Canada's official multiculturalism, contrasts Quebec's inclusive interculturalism with federal multiculturalism, and acknowledges the conceptual value of distinguishing between inclusion and inclusivity as competing immigration governance models. The chapter demonstrates that Canada's multiculturalism – unlike that of other nations – secures the right kind of mindset and infrastructure to bolter this country's status as a vibrant immigration society.

◇◇◇◇◇◇◇◇◇◇◇◇◇◇◇◇◇◇◇◇◇◇◇

7

assessing immigration

COSTS AND BENEFITS, IMPACTS AND EFFECTS, PERCEPTIONS AND REALITIES

SIMPLE QUESTIONS, COMPLEX ANSWERS

IMMIGRATION REMAINS A defining and definitive characteristic of Canada (Ibbitson 2005; McDonald et al. 2010; Worswick 2010; Reitz 2011a). From its earliest days as a colony to Canada's reincarnation as a cosmopolitan player on the global stage, immigration has proven pivotal to its social, economic, and cultural development. The immigrant "other" has long been central to its nation-building imaginary, even if racialized and subject to discriminatory treatment (Haque 2012). Canada has one of the most open and proactive immigration programs in expediting who gets in, how, and why. The program may be far from perfect, but other countries look to Canada for inspirational best practices. Canada also remains one of the most welcoming countries for integrating immigrants along citizenship lines (Transatlantic Trends 2010).

Admittedly, there are worrying changes. The Harper government imposed restrictions on immigration by emphasizing the skilled over the needy, the temporary over the permanent, fast over fair, and the practical over the humanitarian. The government has also toughened the citizenship test, decentralized points of entry, pared back health care benefits for refugee claimants, tightened up the refugee determination process to eliminate abuses (both real and perceived), and securitized the border to reduce the threat of domestic disorder (*Economist* 16

December 2010b; Omidvar 2012a, 2012b; Taras 2012). Yet Canada's pro-immigration stance reflects continuing high levels of admission and a supportive public opinion, albeit it is support with strings attached. Canadians endorse immigration and immigrants as long as Canada controls their admission and they themselves are under control, impose no unnecessary costs or inconvenience, and blend into society instead of retreating behind an illiberal culture or into separate residential enclaves (Reitz 2011a; but see Environics Research Group 2011; and see Angus-Reid 2010b). Immigration Minister Jason Kenney (quoted in Rajagopalan 2011) acknowledged as much:

> We do not have the resources or ability to integrate a million new immigrants each year. We can't teach them English or French. We can't flood our taxpayer-funded services like health care and public education. We don't put such high pressure on housing and real estate markets. We must also be very careful not to jeopardize the generally very positive and welcoming attitude toward immigration and immigrants that Canada enjoys.

Immigration might be one of the most hotly debated and toxic issues of today, less about the facts than about its impact in communities, undermining identities, fraying notions of belonging, eroding social trust, and tolerating questionable behaviour (Malik 2013). Not surprisingly, Canadians have reacted to immigrants and immigration in differing ways. Responses range from enthusiasm and endorsement to resentment and hostile backlash, with indifference, resignation, confusion, and indecision in between. For some, the immigration debate must focus on maximizing benefits for the host country; some feel that migrants must be protected as rights-bearing individuals; and some maintain that national interests must be prioritized without sacrificing those of newcomers (Skrentny, Gell-Redman, and Lee 2012). Those who dismiss immigration restrictions because of their discriminatory overtones tend to espouse the principles of cosmopolitanism – open borders, freedom of movement, and human rights as superseding group/national attachments (see Brock 2013). Others endorse the primacy of a state's sovereign right to regulate admissions on the grounds of preserving mainstream culture and society (Zapata-Barrero and Pécoud 2012). Four classes of reaction can be collated: critics, boosters, pragmatists, and fence-sitters.

There is no shortage of *critics* (see Canadian Centre for Immigration Policy Reform 2010, 2011, 2014; Bissett 2013). They insist on restrictive controls, resent the costs and associated inconveniences, question the need for immigrants, and prefer a reduction in admissions. Immigrants are seen as a burden who swipe jobs and swindle the system, crush existing services, clash with mainstream values, choose to self-segregate, heighten intergroup tensions, and extol extremism (but see Finney and Simpson 2009). Critics point to deeply embedded flaws in selection procedures, rationale, impact, and costs to Canada, and they censure the country for admitting more people than it really needs or can realistically absorb (Grubel 2013). A mismatch between who gets in and who gets to work draws attention to additional weaknesses. Immigrants are unlikely to identify with Canada if they are lured into it by phony promises, only to experience punishing rates of unemployment and underemployment that lock them into poverty and dashed aspirations (Triadafilopoulos 2011). Canada is also accused of promoting mass (as in massive) immigration, a process that negatively affects the country's own living standards by reducing wages, overburdening cash-strapped services, straining public coffers (because of weaker economic performance and higher poverty levels [Grubel 2013]), undermining border defence, and shredding the social fabric while eroding national identity (Moens and Collacott 2008; Bissett 2009a; Grubel 2009; Grubel and Grady 2012). In other words, once Canada discharges its obligations by accepting its share of the world's refugees (and distributing foreign aid as a disincentive for migration), the program should transition to promoting national interests rather than satisfying the desires of either business for cheap labour or vote-hungry politicians (Gibson 2009; Canadian Centre for Immigration Policy Reform 2014).

No less vociferous are the *boosters*, who embrace immigrants as positive contributors to society and Canada building (Bloemraad 2012; also Goldin, Cameron, and Balarajan 2011). For the "bigger is better" crowd, the economic, demographic, cultural, and social benefits of immigration outweigh any minor costs or inconveniences (Li 2003; Conference Board of Canada 2008b; Legrain 2006; see Guskin and Wilson 2007 for the United States). Framing immigrants as exceptional people who provide a solution rather than pose a problem, pro-migrant boosters emphasize their benefits, propose expanding the level of entry, and want to maximize their numbers (also Finch and

Mulley 2009). Popularity and support for immigration and immigrants reflect the economic benefits of immigrants, as well as the success of multiculturalism in reducing the risks of their integration (Reitz 2011a; also Kymlicka 2012). Benefits are further enhanced when immigration is controlled and managed in a way that commands public confidence and respects the rule of law (Finch and Mulley 2009). Nothing is perfect, of course. Immigrants continue to encounter barriers that deny or exclude. They are not second-class citizens under the law but may be so in fact, in part because they live in a Canada that was neither constructed with them in mind nor designed to advance their interests. In short, Canada's record in integrating immigrants may not be spotless, but in striving to reach its ideals, Canada is less imperfect than other countries.

In between are the *pragmatists,* who acknowledge both costs and benefits of immigrants and immigration. After all, benefits (from entrepreneurship and international linkages to investment and creativity) are unlikely without attendant costs, including traffic congestion, overload of services, welfare costs, labour market disruptions, and divided loyalties (Reitz 2006; Friesen 2012a). Benefits and costs must be evaluated on the basis of context, criteria, and consequences instead of being pigeonholed into opposing categories or shoe-horned into preconceived notions (Alboim 2009; Fleras 2009b). For example, even the very advantages that are associated with newcomers (such as creative thinking) may unintentionally generate cultural clashes. Or consider how countries of the global South benefit from sending skilled migrants to the global North despite the costs associated with a brain drain. Benefits for receiving countries as a whole may be offset by negative impacts at local levels; parts of the economy prosper, whereas other parts sag because of immigration; some segments of society benefit from newcomers, some parts are penalized and threatened, and others remain relatively untouched (Goldin, Cameron, and Balarajan 2011).

Finally, many are confused and uncertain because of politically correct silence over immigration issues. *Fence-sitters* are unsure of where they stand or what to say, owing to a lack of balanced and honest information. As Stephen Gallagher (2008a) observes, Canada may be the only country in the world where so-called mass immigration constitutes an article of faith, a policy norm, and a key to national identity. Such a lofty status exempts it from criticism so that anyone who dares to question immigration or government policy is deemed a narrow-minded bigot (McCullough 2013). Political suicide awaits anyone who dares question the benefits of immigration, despite attendant political, economic, social, and cultural costs and tradeoffs. Politicians won't discuss immigration because they are looking for votes rather than looking for trouble (being demonized as racists) on topics that are too taboo to address (Gibson 2009; Weld 2009; Simmons 2010).

Yet too much of what passes for debate lapses into one-sided polemics (a dialogue of the deaf) between ideologically opposed camps that either criticize or endorse, with little or no room for nuance or compromise (Gibson 2009; but see Finch and Mulley 2009). For example, the current minister of immigration, Chris Alexander, might have expounded his predecessor's reforms as popular, productive, and consistent with Canadian values, but Haroon Siddiqui (2013b) criticized both by condemning Kenney's reforms as ideologically driven disasters that were unpopular, unworkable, anti-family, anti-refugee, and unhelpful to unemployed Canadian-born. The resulting dearth of balanced information is deafening, as Madeline Weld (2009) writes:

> The subject of immigration to Canada is addressed from an almost complete ideological and emotional perspective with no serious analysis of the real benefits versus costs to Canadians. It is based on the paradigm of perpetual economic growth and all tied up with our official embrace of multiculturalism and diversity as well as our feelings of guilt for real and perceived wrongs towards immigrants in the past.

To put it simply, the immigration issue remains one of the most elusive and/or polarizing on the public agenda (Wilkes, Guppy, and Farris 2007).[1] For some, Canada's immigration and refugee programs represent the epitome of Canadian values and its maturity as a nation. Immigrants and refugees erected this country, and its prosperity and identity will continue to flourish because of their contribution. Others point out that arguments in defence of immigration neither stand up to empirical scrutiny nor follow a logical basis (Stoffman 2002; Gallagher 2008a; Grubel 2009; in particular, see debates by Javdani and Pendakur 2011 versus Grubel and Grady 2012). For critics, immigration is essentially an investment option for Canada, to be evaluated along cost-benefit lines (Bissett 2008). If the costs are too high, pare back or bail out. For example, Grubel and Grady (2012) suggest as much when they argue that *recent* immigrants cost Canada an average of $6,000 each per year, cumulatively adding up to $23 billion annually (based on calculating the difference between income-based taxes and services received) (also Grubel 2013; but see Javdani and Pendakur 2011).[2] For others, confusion reigns: People feel increasingly vulnerable to factors beyond their control. Sensationalistic media coverage reinforces a fear of others, with immigrants increasingly targeted by the xenophobia and insecurities of the post-9/11 era (Brinkerhoff 2009).

Conflicting responses await the following questions: Do immigrants – or do they not – take jobs from the Canadian-born, depress wages, strain services, create health risks, and erode mainstream cultural values? Are they necessary – or not – for economic prosperity, from filling labour vacancies to offsetting the spiralling costs of servicing an ageing population? Do they – or do they not – contribute more in taxes than they "withdraw" in services (see Bissett 2009a; Grubel and Grady 2012)? How are we to explain the gap between the immigration program and the needs of the labour market? Does it exist because laws are not enforced, because the program is not tailored to the realities of the labour market, or because vested interests suppress public debate about what is really going on (Pannell and Altman 2009)? How many immigrants can Canada absorb? How much is too much? Can this capacity be exhausted or stretched indefinitely? And how will Canadians know when it is attained? Is Canada's immigration model working? In overall rates of naturalization, immigrant participation in politics, and measure of satisfaction or integration, Canada fares well (Kymlicka 2012). But its sparkle tarnishes when economic indicators for immigrants during the past 30 years are evaluated (Triadafilopoulos 2011; Grubel and Grady 2012). Do Canada's immigration policies still serve the needs of employers or of immigrants (Deloitte 2011)? With critics and supporters aligned on one side or the other in never-ending tussles over benefits and/or costs, Canadians are understandably baffled.

BENEFITS AND COSTS: DUELLING DISCOURSES, OR DIALOGUES OF THE DEAF?

In the parlance of sociologists, Canada is an immigration society. That is, like New Zealand and Australia, it has a principled framework to regulate the intake of newcomers, sees them as assets, expects permanent residency and encourages citizenship, and assists in settlement and integration (Fleras 2012e). It is also a society of immigrants. Newcomers have always contributed to Canada and have proved pivotal in securing its quality of life. A playful inversion involving who needs whom seems apropos: Canada has evolved into a society that needs immigrants more than they need it.

Yet Canadians harbour mixed feelings regarding immigration programs and flows, with an ambivalence that borders on a "love-hate" relationship (also Bygnes 2012). Yes, immigrants and immigration are perceived as good for the country, but many criticize its immigration program for failing to exclude the unwanted and delaying the arrival of the preferred (Gallagher 2003). Ambivalence often pivots around immigration as benefit or cost.

Benefits

Studies in Australia, New Zealand, and the United States confirm what many already believe: On balance, immigrants are net contributors to society – demographically, socially, culturally, and economically (Castles and Miller 2009; Fleras and Spoonley 1999; Hiebert and Ley 2003; Spoonley and Bedford 2012). Similar conclusions apply to Canada (Reitz 2011a): Immigrants create more jobs than they take; they buy Canadian goods; they start businesses (also Editorial, *New York Times* 2012); they are well educated; they offset the effects of an ageing population and declining birth rate; and they pay more in taxes than they accept in social services (but see Grubel and Grady 2012). They do the country's drudge work and they ease labour shortages in certain regions and industries (especially mining, oil, and health care). Immigrant admissions since 2011 have accounted for all new labour market growth, and by 2017 overall population growth will be largely immigrant-driven. According to Cameron and Goldin (2012),

> The truth is that migrants are, as a population, exceptional people. And it is the qualities of migrants – not just their education and skills – that benefit our economy and society. Those people who elect to move abroad are, by nature or by choice, often willing to tolerate more risk and ambiguity in pursuit of opportunity. In their Canadian workplaces, they are "divergent thinkers" whose different ways of viewing the world can challenge the status

quo and stimulate new approaches to problems. Migrants often bring cross-cultural skills and international networks, assets to Canada's economy in an age of global integration.

Former immigration minister Jason Kenney (2012a) is no less effusive:

> The vast majority of these newcomers have deeply impressed me with their determination to succeed, with their desire to help us build Canada, and with their amazing bottomless work ethic. In fact, I am often reminded when I meet these newcomers, and I see the ambition in their eyes, that they bring to this country the sort of founding virtues which helped to make this a land of prosperity and productivity.
>
> When I meet with employers across the country who depend on new Canadians, they tell me again and again that the newcomers are raising the work ethic, the level of productivity, and a positive attitude that they bring to work.

Finally, financial outlays and consumer purchases related to initial settlement in Canada will keep the economy afloat so that Canadians can retire comfortably (Hiebert 2006).

In general, rather than crippling the economy, immigrants inject a much-needed kick-start, thanks to their commitment, connections, and cash. According to a study for the Metropolis Project (see Dungan, Fang, and Gunderson 2010; Fang, Gunderson, and Dungan 2011), raising annual immigrant numbers by 100,000 would significantly boost Canada's GDP over a ten-year span, spur investment in housing (and consumer spending), add billons to government coffers through taxes, and create a critical mass of Canadians with more global political clout (but see Grady 2011 for critique). Moreover, temporary foreign workers are so embedded in Canada that its quality of life would be compromised without them (Michael Austin 2009).

Admittedly, not all economic benefits are distributed equally; some regions and sectors receive a disproportionate share of both costs and benefits. For instance, real estate and immigration lawyers may benefit from immigration, whereas manual workers may suffer (Stoffman 2002), but the average person may remain largely unaffected. The affluent rely on immigrants, from domestic help to cheap agricultural labourers, to raise their standard of living; those at the bottom of the socio-economic ladder may have to compete with immigrants for survival jobs. Certain immigrants provide immediate benefit (especially those in the economic class), some may not (such as the refugee class) because of their circumstances, and others do so indirectly or over time (family class) (Li 2003). Finally, benefits are selective: Migration may be good for the host country, but it may sap the sending country of resources and resourcefulness (Pécoud and de Guchteneire 2005). Such a complex assessment makes it doubly important to appreciate the simultaneity of benefits *and* costs.

Lastly, simply framing the benefits of immigration and immigrants along economic lines would be a mistake. Their presence is transforming Canada's social and political landscape in barely anticipated ways. In *The Big Shift*, Bricker and Ibbitson (2013) demonstrate how immigration is profoundly changing Canada's political contours. The collectivist and big government concerns of the Laurentian Consensus (political, business, and media elites in Toronto, Ottawa, and Montreal) no longer control the national agenda as they once did, in large part because the Canada they knew doesn't exist any more. The Laurentian Consensus embraced a specific reading of Canada as a fragile and insecure country that was grounded in British and French colonialism; the exploitation of Aboriginal peoples, racialized minorities, and women; Canada building by appeasing Quebec nationalism; equalization payments to have-not provinces; economic protectionism; national social programs; an arm's-length distance from the United States; moral superiority on the global stage; and official bilingualism and multiculturalism. But Canada's traditional agenda and power base are increasingly displaced by a new influential coalition that is based in the West and supported by newcomer voters in Ontario who lean toward economic issues rather than those of social justice or cultural concerns. The key economic and political drivers include a growing population of new arrivals, suburban middle-class foreign-born (who are turning Ontario into a Pacific-oriented province), and first-generation citizens whose political values and voting tendencies are thought to be more socially conservative in terms of lower taxes, less bureaucracy, and less government spending, with a more market-oriented mindset toward hard work, ambition, thrift, and self-reliance. The potential to grow Canada in a new direction should not be underestimated.

Costs

For critics, large-scale immigration exacts more costs than benefits (Bissett 2008). They dispute studies that link immigrants to economic benefits as lacking empirical evidence or as ideologically slanted (Paquet 2011). If anything, argues Herbert Grubel (2009, 2013), immigrants received $18.3 billion more in government services and benefits between 1990 and 2002 than they paid in taxes. In 2005-06, every immigrant received an excess in benefits of $6,051 over taxes paid, partly because of lower incomes and smaller tax payments from underemployed recent newcomers. The net result is a national fiscal burden of between $16.3 and $23.6 billion (Grubel 2012). Others disagree with these figures and suggest that the total transfer from Canadian-born to immigrants is closer to $450 per person per year (Javdani and Pendakur 2011; also Lenard 2013; and Grubel and Grady 2012). It's possible that, when immigrants possess an unfavourable net fiscal position, they might contribute less because they tend to be un/underemployed or work for lower wages on average (OECD 2013, 2014b).[3]

Long-term gains may be undeniable, but short-term costs are inevitable. Yet Ottawa prefers to off-load settlement costs to provinces, municipalities, and institutions. Even economic justification can be problematic. Canadians may rationalize the value of immigrants or temporary foreign workers (TFW) for jobs that they themselves won't do, but reality is less flattering. Canada wants immigrants and TFW because they have no choice but to accept substandard wages and working conditions (Gallagher 2008b). Also criticized is the oft-touted view that immigrants can offset the rising costs of an ageing population (Stoffman 2002). Not only is this patently untrue, critics argue, but countries such as Japan have managed to maintain a high standard of living without resorting to immigration for wealth creation. Worse still, critics contend, is the phenomenon known as chain migration. Collacott (2009) draws attention to the perils of chain migration via parental sponsorships:

> In some immigrant communities, sponsoring one's parents is particularly popular because they're allowed to bring with them their unmarried children without the latter having to have any of the qualifications for employability, language fluency, etc. needed to be admitted as an independent immigrant. When the

29 OBSERVATION

Daniel Stoffman: Critic

ONE OF THE MOST vocal critics of Canada's immigration program is Daniel Stoffman (2002, 2008). He does not see himself as anti-immigrant, preferring instead to self-define as a concerned citizen who wants a win-win system that benefits Canada while maximizing immigrants' chances of success. Stoffman begins by disposing of two myths – that immigration is necessary for economic growth and that it compensates for the declining birth rate. Yes, immigration might make the economy grow because it increases the number of producers and consumers, yet the average person rarely becomes any richer as a result. As well, any demographic changes because of immigration would require substantially larger numbers than Canada could possibly absorb. The current system persists because it provides (a) a cheap and disposable workforce, (b) a lucrative revenue source for immigration lawyers and consultants, and (c) electoral advantages for whatever party plays it best. But high immigration levels do little to help Canadians in general, advance national interests, alleviate the fiscal burden of beleaguered cities, or assist in the settlement of bona fide newcomers. The refugee claim system is further compromised by the largely false claimants who skirt conventional immigration protocols. Despite this, Stoffman argues, all political parties support mass immigration for various self-serving reasons, and anyone who dares to criticize the system is hung out to dry (McCullough 2013).

offspring are old enough, they, in turn, sponsor spouses from their homeland whose families will pay large sums so they'll be able to launch a chain of family-class sponsorships of their own. Bringing in one's parents, therefore, can be a very profitable enterprise.

In addition, immigrants are *thought* to create certain problems. These include loan-sharking, extortion rackets, prostitution and human trafficking, smuggling human cargo into Canada, and manipulating their ties abroad to establish illegal international distribution systems for contraband drugs. The myth of immigrant criminality (Wortley 2009) persists as well, despite evidence that newcomers are no more criminally oriented than the Canada-born, although some groups are significantly overrepresented in official crime statistics (admittedly, statistics may say more about policing strategies and public visibilities than about criminality per se [Rankin and Winsa 2013]). Even the geographic distribution of newcomers evokes disapproval. Nearly all immigrants once settled in urban centres (primarily Montreal, Toronto, and Vancouver), shunning large areas that badly needed what they had to offer. That immigrants and refugees are drawn to large urban regions is understandable (Hiebert and Ley 2003). Cities provide the networks, supports, and resources to facilitate their adjustment and integration. This, in turn, proves an irresistible magnet for incoming immigrants and refugees. For example, about half of all Toronto-bound immigrants cite family and community as instrumental in their choice of destination (only about a quarter invoke economic or work reasons). To date, moves toward a more geographically balanced distribution of migrants across Canada have proven erratic, despite proposed government incentives and some impressive gains under the Provincial Nominee Program. Lastly, it's widely assumed that the bar for entry and settlement will continue to rise for permanent residents, asylum seekers, and would-be citizens in light of Ottawa's robust labour market agenda and enforcement mentality (Keung 2013a). Box 30 demonstrates how benefits and costs often constitute two sides of the same coin.

CRITIQUING THE CRITICISMS

Who's right? Who's wrong? Is immigration of benefit or a cost? Do immigrants contribute or detract? A sense of proportion is helpful in sorting out the responses. Somewhere between the "yeas" and the "nays" are those who see the interplay of costs *with* benefits as central to any interpretation. The in-between sector takes a practical stance on immigration. A degree of friction and annoyance is inevitable in a Canada that accepts approximately 250,000 people each year, many

30 OVERVIEW

Putting Costs and Benefits into Perspective

COSTS (immigration as problem)	BENEFITS (immigration as solution)
Settlement costs (estimated at nearly $900 million for federal government alone).	Immigrants generate economic benefits both directly (paying taxes, consumer purchases) and indirectly (providing childcare for working parents).
Costs of providing services – from education to health care – amount to more than immigrants pay in taxes.	Established foreign-born pay their share of taxes. It's the economy's/employer's fault if highly skilled newcomers are under- or unemployed and underpaying taxes. Even here, there is a silver lining: pressure to do more with less may stimulate more creative and effective delivery of services, such as creating community-private partnerships.
Wage cutting/more job competition.	Addresses skills shortages and filling of drudge jobs.
Money drains from Canada due to high remittance levels.	Improves wealth creation through innovation, spending on settling down, and productivity and entrepreneurship. Enlarges trade links via international networks.
Erodes social fabric by undermining values, cohesion, trust and national identity.	Bolsters a more interesting, diverse, and cosmopolitan lifestyle. Differences mesh to create a more organic solidarity.
Contributes to deterioration of standard of living - congestion, sprawling urban blight, environmental destruction.	Enhances quality of life via creative and talented people.

Source: Adapted from Friesen (2012a).

with radically different cultures, experiences, and expectations who compete with the Canadian-born for jobs and resources. No less likely is crowding, pressure on existing services, inflated housing markets, and congested roads. Costs cannot be ignored, even if many suspect that Canadians would prefer an immigration program without actual immigrants. No country can possibly expect immigration-driven economic growth without some identity disruptions, cultural clashes, social tensions, and economic repercussions. Lastly, although many believe that healthier immigration patterns prevailed in the past and that current migrants make incessant demands, impose exorbitant settlement costs, and refuse to integrate, evidence suggests otherwise: Each new migrant cohort will be Canadianized over time (Bunting 2007).

In brief, if Canadians value the cultural and economic benefits associated with immigration, they must be prepared to shoulder the accompanying costs. A step back from the fray reminds us that immigration *is* a benefit that invariably has a cost for someone, somewhere, sometimes. For example, few would dispute the value of Canada's principled approach to immigration. But a proliferation of rules to address high volumes can also create a stifling bureaucracy, endless red tape, and inflexibility, in the process eliminating room for discretionary decisions except at political levels, where such interference can prove costly. For the in-betweens, then, immigration is neither a sacred cow to worship nor a convenient scapegoat to skewer. Those who occupy an informed middle ground acknowledge the partial yet simultaneous validity of arguments both for and against.

There seems to be no objective way of determining who is right, which reinforces the primacy of perceptions in defining benefits and costs. Thus, reframing the debate in terms of complementary discourses seems apropos. Also, it would appear that benefits invariably accompany costs, as Cameron and Goldin (2012) point out: "In short, the key innovation advantage conferred by higher rates of immigration is also its greatest risk. Migrants are disruptive. They often bring different ways of thinking, different ways of doing things, and an aspirational drive. These qualities make migration essential to the future prosperity of Canada, but they also point to the stabilizing effect of rapid change." In the final analysis, answers to questions about costs and benefits are both right and wrong, depending on the context, criteria, and consequences.

PUBLIC ATTITUDES TOWARD IMMIGRATION: SURVEYING THE SURVEYS

Surveying public attitudes toward immigrants and immigration is hardly an idle exercise. Nor is it much of an exact science. Public attitudes may influence public policy, shape the social climate in advancing immigrant successes and failures, and determine the collective vision of national identity and belonging (Esses, Dovidio, and Hudson 2002). Attitudes themselves reflect an interplay of personal and contextual factors (Wilkes, Guppy, and Farris 2007; Wilkes and Corrigall-Brown 2011). According to Wilkes, Guppy, and Farris (2007), determinants of attitudes vary with differing levels of education, socio-economic status, official language competence (those whose first language is French or English tend to be less supportive), and political orientation (more conservative leanings equate to more disapproval). Even the notion of Canada-wide attitudes is a misnomer since public perceptions regarding immigrants fluctuate across provinces (Bilodeau, Turgeon, and Karakoc 2012; EKOS Politics 2013a; Graves 2013). Finally, individual attitudes can change over time because of the social context, including economic downturns, ideological shifts (including neoliberalism), and political conservatism.

But assigning importance to attitudinal surveys is one thing. Interpreting their results or significance may be something else. Surveys about immigrants and immigration are blunt instruments that conceal more than they reveal. For example, respondents may support immigration in principle but dislike immigrants themselves, or vice versa. Public attitudes do not necessarily coincide with hostility toward the immigration program (Ceobanu and Escandell 2010). Survey data have difficulty in determining what respondents like or dislike about immigrants or about the immigration program itself (Graves 2013). Do those who favour immigration support all immigrants or just those whom they see as good immigrants (or good refugees)? Are critics of immigration dismissive of all immigrants or only those who bend the admission rules? Contradictions abound: Immigrants are accused of not wanting to work but are also castigated for snatching jobs from the Canadian-born (Broadbent 2012). In other words, surveys that measure public attitudes need to be handled with caution.

To date, surveys indicate that Canadians are generally suppo[rtive] of immigration and the benefits that immigrants bring (see [

Guppy, and Farris 2007; Harell, Soroka, and Andrew 2011; Reitz 2011a; Bloemraad 2012). Canadians tend to agree that immigrants have a positive impact on the economy and to disagree with claims that too many immigrants take jobs from Canadians (Lawlor 2012; but see Siddiqui 2013b). Yet this support is conditional or contradictory (also Nielson 2009). For example, a 2010 Angus-Reid online survey of 1,007 adult Canadians concluded that the benefits of immigration are increasingly questioned (46 percent of respondents said that immigrants had a negative effect, 34 percent said they were beneficial, and 20 percent were unsure) (2010b). An EKOS Politics (2013a) poll, which used an interactive voice response method to track the attitudes of over 4,500 adult Canadians in early April 2013, also indicated growing opposition to immigration ("too many").[4] Antipathy grew from 25 percent in 2005 to 40 percent in 2013, with provincial anti-immigration responses ranging from 47 percent in Alberta to 28 percent in Manitoba. Nevertheless, a sense of perspective is handy. Compared to other jurisdictions, where newcomers routinely confront anti-immigrant parties and xenophobic attitudes, Canada is a paragon of virtue (*Economist* 2011). Box 31, which summarizes attitudes in Canada, the United States, and the United Kingdom, is instructive.

Other surveys reflect a high degree of ambiguity (Graves 2013). According to a 2010 Environics Survey for Focus Canada, 40 percent of respondents believed that there was too much immigration in Canada, up from about 35 percent in 2008. When asked if immigrants were adopting Canadian values, 66 percent said no, and 46 percent believed that immigration controls were ineffective in thwarting criminals. However, 80 percent agreed that immigrants had a positive impact on the economy; 24 percent believed that they took jobs from Canadians; and 92 percent felt that non-whites should be allowed to immigrate to Canada. A November 2010 EKOS survey commissioned by the federal government also exposed a streak of hostility toward newcomers (Mary Jones 2010). About 48 percent of the 1,500 respondents thought that immigration was bad for their community, 36 percent felt that it increased joblessness among the Canadian-born, and only 23 percent stated that immigrants from diverse origins would strengthen Canadian culture. Nevertheless, 71 percent believed that immigration was positive for Canada.

31

Attitudes toward Immigrants and Immigration in Canada, the US, and the UK

	Canada	US	UK
Approval of government management of immigration/integration (last 6 months).	Yes (54%)	Yes (39%)	Yes (48%)
Are there too many immigrants?	Yes (17%)	Yes (37%)	Yes (59%)
Is immigration more of a problem than an opportunity?	Yes (27%)	Yes (52%)	Yes (65%)
Do immigrants take away jobs? Bring down wages?	Yes (32%)	Yes (56%)	Yes (58%)
Immigrants in general are integrating well?	Yes (65%)	Yes (59%)	Yes (43%)
Muslim immigrants are integrating well?	Yes (45%)	Yes (45%)	Yes (37%)
Do legal immigrants increase crime?	Yes (25%)	Yes (32%)	Yes (33%)

Source: Transatlantic Trends (2010).

The variation in responses may reflect the wording of survey questions or the frame of reference employed. For example, a survey conducted by Forum Research for the *National Post* in early March 2013 found that, of the 1,755 adults polled, 73 percent supported limits on immigration, including 58 percent of the foreign-born (Ligaya 2013). However, the question was misleading, and the methodology was flawed.[5] According to Jack Jedwab (2014), an Association for Canadian Studies poll that was conducted during the same period yielded a different result. Fifty-nine percent of respondents were not worried about the number of newcomers, including 71 percent of those who were not born in Canada. In the Forum Research poll, nearly half (percent) indicated a preference for newcomers who shared Canad

32 OBSERVATION

Transatlantic Differences in Attitudes toward Immigrants and Immigration: Patterns and Trends

> Compared with citizens of other countries, Canadians are more favourably disposed toward immigrants and immigration. Canadians see immigration as an opportunity and asset. Majorities in the United States, the United Kingdom, and Spain see it as a problem, whereas French, German, Dutch, and Italian respondents are divided. The worst-case scenario equates immigrants and multiculturalism with the destruction of Europe (Breivik 2011).

> Canadians are less likely to see immigration as a problem (27 percent), compared with 65 percent of UK respondents. Still, a significant number are critical of Ottawa's immigration program and question the value of immigrants.

> Only 32 percent of Canadian respondents believe that immigrants take jobs away from the Canadian-born or naturalized citizens, compared to a European average of 35 percent. Respondents in the United States (56 percent) and the United Kingdom (58 percent) agree that immigrants take jobs.

> Canadians are in slight agreement with government management of immigration (54 percent versus 43 percent). Majorities in all the other countries (listed here) disagree, including 39 percent in the United States who believe that the government is doing a poor job of managing immigration.

> Canadians (65 percent) believe that immigrants are integrating well, followed by the United States (59 percent) and Spain (54 percent). All other European countries held unfavourable views of the state of immigrant integration.

The 2011 Transatlantic Trends survey (which did not include Canada) concluded that US and UK attitudes toward immigration remained relatively stable despite the continuing economic crisis and the aftermath of the Arab Spring. Key findings of the 2011 survey indicated a strong preference for highly educated immigrants, sympathy for those who were forced to migrate, continuing worries about so-called illegal migrants, optimism about integration, respect for law and political institutions as a basis for citizenship, and persistent views of government mishandling of immigration issues.

> An Ipsos MORI Poll (2012) of 24 countries found that 7 of the 9 EU members thought that immigration had a negative impact and preferred to reintroduce border controls (Sweden and Poland were the two exceptions).

Source: Based on the key findings from Transatlantic Trends (2010).

values, and a majority of 62 percent believed that immigrants should abandon cultural values that were not compatible with those of Canada. In yet another survey, the 2012 CIC annual tracking survey, 56 percent of respondents stated that immigration was good for the economy, down 10 percent from 2010, and 40 percent believed that it had a positive effect on Canadian culture, down between 16 and 18 percent from 2010. Even support for immigration levels is shifting. Since 2004, it has hovered consistently in the 50 percent range, though when respondents were told that Canada admits 250,000 immigrants annually, up to 14 percent changed their minds, asserting that the number was too high (Levitz 2012a).

The conclusion seems inescapable: Attitudes toward immigrants and immigration are generally positive yet riddled with ambiguity and inconsistency (Bloemraad 2012). This should come as no surprise. No critic or nativist, no matter how opposed to immigration, is without some sympathy for the world's poorest. Similarly, regardless of pro-immigrant sympathies, no one can deny that mass immigration has a negative impact on some sectors of society (also Millman 1997). Canadians are comfortable with newcomers who are poor, grateful, prepared to start at the bottom, and willing to acknowledge that immigration policy must advance national interests rather than cater to minority demands (Nanos 2008). Sympathy prevails for the unfortunate souls who have fled their homes, only to find themselves struggling to survive through minimum wage employment (Kazemipur and Halli 2003; also Montreuil and Bourhis 2004). Canadians are less sure of how to engage those who are affluent, confident, assertive, and highly qualified; allegedly finance or finagle their way into the country; refuse to put up with slights or slurs as the price of admission; and, as professional transnationals, are willing to shop their talents wherever they please. This so-called uppityness elicited a sharp rebuke from George Jonas (2011):

> It was only in the last thirty years that a new type of immigrant emerged: the immigrant of dubious loyalty ... The new immigrant seemed ready to share the West's wealth but not its values. In many ways he resembled an invader more than a settler or refugee. Instead of making efforts to assimilate, he demanded changes in the host culture. He called on society to accommodate his linguistic and religious requirements.

Such mixed messages make it clear that the complexities, inconsistencies, and fluidity of Canadian attitudes toward immigrants and immigration should neither be underestimated nor taken for granted.

POPULAR PERCEPTIONS, RECURRENT CONTROVERSIES: PUTTING THEM TO THE TEST

The domain of immigration and immigrants/refugees is littered with popular misconceptions and partial truths (also Broadbent 2012; also OECD 2013). These pseudo-truths range in scope from exaggerated claims, wish fulfillments, and unfounded beliefs, to a host of myths, projections, and misconceptions that are difficult to operationalize and quantify, reflect doctrinaire beliefs that are difficult to dislodge, and conceal and distort more than they reveal or inform. But separating fact from fiction has proven tricky. Supporters of immigration tend to be just as polemical and ideologically slanted as critics, with both camps disingenuously selective in defining and defending their positions. To be sure, the popular perceptions are not entirely without foundation; rather, they are rooted in how data are collected and interpreted (EKOS

Politics 2013a; Graves 2013). Criticism and support should not be slotted into the categories of right or wrong. More accurately, they should be viewed as alternative conceptual frameworks for examining the same phenomena (the flipsides of a coin) (Satzewich and Liodakis 2013). As a result, the responses that inform the topic are more complex, multi-dimensional, and nuanced than conveyed by critics or supporters.

There is considerable value in debunking the myths that supporters and critics endorse. A constructive and critically informed debate on immigration and immigrants cannot begin without an intellectually sound foundation. To put this assertion to the test, thirteen popular perceptions about immigration and immigrants are listed below, followed by various responses, each of which is partially correct (see also Finney and Simpson 2009; Royal Geographical Society 2009). The fact that these perceived realities can elicit multiple responses confirms that there is no single correct stance, although the weight of evidence may support one line of inquiry over others.

Perception No. 1

Immigrants are an economic burden and a drain on society, especially family class entrants, who add minimal value to the economy and rely disproportionately on government transfers.

Response A

According to the Canadian Council for Refugees (n.d.), immigrants contribute positively to the economy: They create jobs, engage in consumer spending, establish entrepreneurship, and increase government revenue (Reitz 2011a). Immigrant and diasporic networks constitute an invaluable resource that secures a competitive edge for Canada in global markets (*Economist* 2011). Immigrants are also consumers who spend thousands settling into Canada, including contributing to a prolonged boom in the housing market. Furthermore, family class immigrants may make an indirect contribution as caregivers and community volunteers.

Response B

The economic benefits of immigration are mixed at best. Empir
evidence is inconclusive regarding the costs of immigration in
of dampening wages and competition for jobs, and studies sh

immigrants have a minimal impact on public finances, employment and wages, and demographic shifts (Jurado and Bruzzone 2008; but see Grubel and Grady 2012; Paquet 2011). A 1991 study by the Economic Council of Canada concluded that immigrants add little to the economy (see also OECD 2013; Jolly 2013). More recent studies indicate a growing net deficit (Grubel and Grady 2012). Moreover, immigrants may be good for some sectors of the economy and bad for others, but they are largely inconsequential outside the main urban hubs. In assessing benefits, we must also determine whether they are direct or indirect, temporary or more permanent, and whether they serve vested interests or Canada as a whole.

Response C

Nearly 80 percent of newcomers to Canada are not tested for their economic contribution (from education levels to experience to language competence). Their risk of becoming an economic burden (from reliance on welfare to taxing existing services) cannot be casually dismissed (Grubel and Grady 2012).

Response D

Canadians have been deliberately misinformed by the government and the media about the impact of immigrants on the economy and their benefit to Canada's common public culture. There is no proof or meaningful argument (except to capture newcomer votes) to justify faith in the long-term benefits of high levels of immigration (Paquet 2011).

Response E

Immigrants provide overall economic benefits by doing work that Canadians shun or by filling value-added jobs that locals aren't skilled enough to do. The benefits go beyond net fiscal impacts, but include positives such as fuelling economic dynamics, capital formation, labour market flexibility, and fostering creativity and entrepreneurial activity. The challenge arises in trying to calculate the nature of these benefits and in determining whether or not they are outweighed by costs (Royal Geographical Society 2009).

Response F

fear that immigrants weaken the welfare state by exerting pressure social services such as health care and education. This fear may be overblown, given that immigrants do pay taxes and many work as doctors or hospital aides (OECD 2013). Where immigrants do compete with the local population for scarce services, the problem may arise from misguided local and regional policies that create poor planning and resource mismatch (Royal Geographical Society 2009).

Response G

The immigration program is not designed for the benefit of average Canadians. To the contrary, it is beholden to the principle of economic growth at all costs, is hostage to immigrant lobby groups and industries (such as consultants), and is designed to attract immigrant votes in swing ridings (Weld 2009). How else can we explain that high levels of immigration persist despite serious unemployment everywhere in Canada (Stoffman 2009b)?

Response H

Why is it that highly skilled and educated immigrants have difficulty finding work in their fields, yet employers can't find the people they need, despite large numbers of highly educated young Canadians who can't get a job (Alboim 2009)? In other words, we now live in a Canada where there are workers without jobs and jobs without workers, at a time of high immigration yet chronic labour shortages. Perhaps the problem lies in the failure of employers to create wages and working conditions that will appeal to the Canadian-born.

Response I

Family reunification is an important tool in attracting skilled economic immigrants. If people can't bring their families to Canada, they may not stay (or even come at all). Parents and grandparents provide valuable support and save money for working families, and reunification creates more stable and happier homes (Lafleur 2011). In other words, immigrants are more likely to make a healthy adjustment in the company of their family.

Response J

Immigration costs are more narrow than many believe, but the bene fits are more widespread. Even unauthorized immigrants pay sales t or property tax when renting or purchasing a home (Darrel West 2 Goldin, Cameron, and Balarajan 2011).

Perception No. 2

Immigrants take jobs from the Canadian-born and drive down wages.

Response A

According to the Canadian Council for Refugees (2010a), immigrants create jobs by starting companies, consuming goods, and investing capital. In taking on the dirty, dull, and dangerous jobs, they also complement the skills of the Canadian-born. Wage levels of Canadian-born workers are not significantly affected by increased immigration. Besides, job losses are caused by the profit-driven market dynamics of downsizing or outsourcing.

Response B

Canadian-born workers with few skills and low educational levels may find themselves competing with newcomers who must accept whatever entry level jobs they can get. Young people who are entering the labour market and some racialized minorities may suffer because of competition from immigrants who will work for low wages and in poor conditions (George Borjas concluded this for the United States as well) (Weld 2009). In a buyers' market, the diminishment of wages is a real possibility for the unskilled and undereducated, especially when supply exceeds demand. Finally, evidence suggests that immigrants are competing against each other in the labour market and economy (from entrepreneurship to employment) rather than against the Canadian-born (Hiebert 2006).

Response C

Evidence reveals that employers prefer workers with Canadian experience, credentials, and language skills. This requirement (which may or may not be justified [Sakamoto et al. 2013]) puts newcomers at a decided disadvantage, despite evidence that global experience and connections are increasingly good for business (Deloitte 2011).

Response D

The idea that foreigners are taking new jobs is misleading because of how the issue is framed. Every year thousands of new jobs are created or become vacant. Canadian-born individuals – from neophytes to those who are re-entering the labour force – are likely to fill these vacancies. Immigrants, in turn, may well account for most of the net increase in employment (Cavanagh 2011b).

Response E

Canada's changing demographic profile will generate a dependency ratio in which a smaller percentage of working people must support an ageing population. Evidence indicates that a replacement intake of younger (working-age) immigrants may partially offset the effects of this dependency ratio (Royal Geographical Society 2009).

Response F

Canada's brain gain (again at the expense of Canadian-born workers) represents a serious brain drain for developing countries of the global South. They lose skilled and much-need personnel (such as doctors, nurses, and engineers), must absorb the cost of training these individuals, and cannot benefit from the taxes they would have paid. Others argue that this "brain circulation" has benefits, including badly needed income through remittances, transfers of knowledge to the country of origin, and an impetus for development projects to foster economic growth and poverty reduction (ibid.).

Perception No. 3

The inability or reluctance of immigrants to speak English or French may delay their integration into society and exert pressure on costly ESL programs.

Response A

According to the Canadian Council for Refugees (2010a), the vast majority of immigrants (75 percent) either speak one of the two official languages or acquire competence in due course.

Response B

According to Alan Simmons (2010), about 43 percent of newcomers speak neither French nor English as their mother tongue. Admittedly, this figure includes children of immigrant parents, who quickly learn one of the official languages. For adults, the major stumbling block t success in Canada remains poor language skills, and immigrants w lack access to ESL classes will have difficulty integrating into the omy (for details, ꭥe Chapter 8).

Perception No. 4

Immigrants are not integrating into Canada, preferring to live in cultural clusters known as ethnic enclaves.

Response A

Over 85 percent of newcomers eventually become Canadian citizens (Statistics Canada 2011).

Response B

The integration of newcomers is delayed by the significant growth of ethnic/immigrant enclaves in urban Canada (an enclave is a census tract in which at least 30 percent of the population is of a single ethnicity). But ethnic enclaves are not ghettos, which are downward-spiralling communities of poverty and powerlessness. Escape from the ghetto is difficult, but enclaves consist of individuals who prefer to be with their own cultural, linguistic, and religious kind without sacrificing involvement, integration, and commitment to the mainstream. They belong to and identify with Canada through their ethnicity. This enclavization is partly a response to the housing market – newcomers opt for relatively inexpensive accommodation until they can move out and up (Qadeer and Kumar 2006).

Response C

Who's avoiding whom? Newcomers may keep to themselves for a variety of reasons. They may choose isolation in reaction to the loss of reassuring social and cultural certainties, because they detect an avoidance attitude in the mainstream, by default because of white flight from neighbourhoods that are undergoing ethnicization (Scheffer 2010), or simply because they can, thanks to sufficient levels of human and social capital.

Response D

Robert Putnam's "E Pluribus Unum" (2007) underscored the negative consequences associated with immigrant-driven diversity, including loss of the social capital that is crucial to the functioning of society (e.g., trust, cooperation, civic engagement, and solidarity). According to Putnam's constrict hypothesis, ethnic diversity not only hampers intergroup relations but also induces ethnic inwardness and isolation. Everyone agrees: Those who espouse the contact hypothesis argue that intergroup contact reduces prejudice over time, while reinforcing positive out-group attitudes and relations (Allport 1954).

Perception No. 5

Immigrants – especially so-called illegal immigrants – commit more crimes.

Response A

Proof is sparse that immigrants commit more crimes than anyone else (Wortley 2009). However, it's possible that because of their visibility and poverty, racialized immigrants are arrested, charged, and incarcerated more often than the general population. When applied to asylum seekers, even the label of "illegal" is a misnomer; after all, the Criminal Code does not list asylum seeking as a crime. Perhaps the focus should be on Canada's criminality in perpetuating the overseas conditions, from military action to corporate expansion, that prompt people to flee for their lives.

Response B

Immigrants come to Canada to pursue opportunities and build a better life for themselves and their children. As a result, they (and especially undocumented individuals) have little to gain but much to lose by breaking the law (see also Haas 2007, 2008). If criminality does exist among some, it arises from adverse social and economic conditions rather than inherent lawlessness (Scheffer 2010). Evidence also indicates that newcomers are generally unlikely to import conflicts into this country to the detriment of social cohesion and public security; as well, most overwhelmingly reject the use of violence to resolve intergroup issues in Canada (Monahan, Berns-McGown, and Morden 2014).

Response C

Canada's immigration program is influenced by organized crime, including corruption and influence peddling at Canadian consulate (Weld 2009).

Perception No. 6

Canada receives more than its fair share of refugees, result
unmanageable deluge

Response A

According to the Canadian Council for Refugees (n.d.), many Western countries receive more refugee claimants than Canada, in both absolute and relative numbers. Moreover, the number of asylum seekers who make refugee claims in Canada and the West is much smaller than in many other countries. Eighty-three percent of asylum seekers go only as far as a neighbouring country, and thus most of the top 10 refugee-hosting states are in the developing world; 33 percent of all refugees remain in Asia. The total number of refugee claimants in Canada – though impressive in some ways – is modest compared with that of some developing countries in the global South. Syria is host to over a million Iraqi refugees (Canadian Council for Refugees 2007), yet it is estimated that by the end of 2013, 3 million Syrians will have fled to neighbouring countries to escape sectarian violence. Numbers in Canada may vary from year to year, though a sharp decline is clearly evident (e.g., there were 45,000 claims in 2001, 20,000 in 2005, and about 10,000 in 2013).

Response B

Until recently, Canada accepted between 40 and 45 percent of claimants, far more than all other OECD countries, which annually average about 10-15 percent. Canada's acceptance rate dropped to 38 percent in recent years.

Response C

Is it morally acceptable for affluent countries of the global North to ignore the less fortunate who need protection or escape from grinding poverty?

Response D

The vast majority of refugees flee to neighbouring poor countries and tend to remain in their region of origin (up to 90 percent, according to the Royal Geographical Society 2009). Like Canada, most wealthy countries possess a relatively small proportion of refugees per head of population, a proportion that continues to decline because of increased militarization of their borders and securitization of admission.

ption No. 7

is thought to accept almost everyone who claims to be a refu-
as those who are rejected have numerous avenues of appeal.

Response A

Fewer than half of all claimants are successful (in 2013, the figure stood at 36 percent). Until recently, failed claimants could appeal their cases only to the Federal Court, though solely on points of law. They can also ask for a pre-removal risk assessment, but according to the Canadian Council for Refugees (n.d.), 95 percent of them do not succeed.

Response B

Failed claimants may lack access to an official appeal court, but they can pursue their claims in the Federal Court, insist on a pre-removal risk assessment to determine whether it's safe to return, or request a stay of refugee status on humanitarian/compassionate grounds.

Perception No. 8

Refugees who use false documents to enter Canada are bogus (or illegal) and should be rejected.

Response A

For many refugees fleeing persecution, a false travel document is the only means of escape. They are rarely in a position to acquire authentic paperwork, and governments may refuse to issue passports to known dissidents or may imprison them if they apply. According to the Canadian Council for Refugees (n.d.), the UN Convention on the status of Refugees (which Canada signed in 1969) prohibits governments from penalizing or delegitimizing claimants who use false documentation or gain entry illegally. To staunch the flow of refugees from seeming safe countries, Ottawa requires travellers' visas, intensifying the demand for false documents. The end result of tougher laws is greater reliance on smuggling rings.

Response B

There are fears that some claimants are actually economic migrants who carry fraudulent documents and have been coached by unscrupulous consultants on how to apply for refugee status (McMahon 20

Response C

There is no such thing as an illegal refugee. All asylum s
·ithin their international rights to apply for refugee stat·

if their claim is rejected and they refuse deportation, they may be defined as illegal. But then, they are no longer refugees. Alternatively, illegality exists if an individual goes underground once his or her tourist or worker visa has expired. The No One Is Illegal Movement in Canada argues that overstayers and rejected claimants are entitled to all rights and citizen services simply because they are human beings.

Perception No. 9

Refugees in overseas camps are more deserving of sanctuary than those who self-select to register a claim in Canada.

Response A

Regardless of how they arrive or apply, all refugees are equally deserving of protection from human rights abuses. Besides, is it fair to expect at-risk people to wait in a queue for someone to help them? As well, under the UN Convention on the Status of Refugees and the Convention against Torture, Canada has specific obligations toward all refugees on its soil.

Response B

Squandering time and money on often fraudulent claims is a losing proposition. We should concentrate on offering sanctuary to people who are in overseas camps and should drastically reduce our openness to claimants who have landed in Canada, except as absolutely necessary (Collacott 2010c). These changes would make the process more humane, less costly, and of greater benefit to Canada.

Perception No. 10

Refugee claimants pose a security risk, especially because they are allowed freedom of movement once they promise to attend a formal hearing to determine their status.

Response A

ose who are intent on terrorism would not expose themselves to the ; of the refugee determination process. Since November 2001, all nts have been required to undergo a security screening process, fingerprinting, interviews, and security checks by CSIS MP. The 2002 Immigration and Refugee Protection Ac excludes claimants on the basis of security, serious or organized criminality, or human rights abuses. They may be detained if they are deemed a flight risk, a danger to the public, or a security threat.

Response B

Migrants may use the host country for recruitment, fundraising, and as a staging ground for terrorist attacks, both abroad and at home (Moens and Collacott 2008).

Perception No. 11

Canada's excessively generous refugee program rewards those who jump the queue at the expense of immigrants who wait patiently in line.

Response A

The refugee and immigration programs run on two separate tracks. An increase in the number of successful refugee claimants will not necessarily disrupt the processing of immigrants. True, asylum seekers who have cleared security, health, and criminal checks, and who are entitled to make a refugee claim, do receive a lump sum (about $2,500 for a family), access to basic social services, emergency health care, education for their children, and a work permit. How else should we proceed? What is the point of accepting people only to let them starve to death in the promised land (Canadian Council for Refugees 2007)?

Response B

Government-sponsored refugees are expected to pay both the administrative fee and transportation costs of their relocation. Ottawa also assists in defraying the expense of immigration settlement.

Perception No. 12

Canada should accept more refugees and immigrants because it's underpopulated.

Response A

Claims regarding underpopulation are misapplied. The vast ity of migrants choose to settle in Canada's 12 largest cities to a rapid and unplanned growth that results in problems fr to smog (Weld 2009)

Perception No. 13

Despite its claims to colour-blind admission, Canada's immigration program is racist.

Response A

The vast majority of Canada's immigrants come from non-Western countries, and no one is excluded because of nationality or race.

Response B

The program may claim to be colour-blind, but it's deeply racialized (and gendered and classed). For example, the locations of the 44 immigration visa offices and their numbers of staff reflect a bias that could be interpreted as racialized (Satzewich and Liodakis 2010).

Response C

Immigration and immigrants continue to be framed as a social problem. Immigrants may have been perceived as Canada-building assets because of their economic, cultural, and social contributions, but racialized newcomers from non-preferred sources are denounced as a potential problem in need of containment. As well, much of the political and public discourse is grounded in the unspoken assumption that immigrants are a burden and that their cost must be minimized through immigration controls and complex regulations governing the acquisition of residency rights and citizenship (Triadafilopoulos 2010). Because they are often perceived as a threat to jobs, security, social services, cultural homogeneity, and national unity, immigrants continue to be scapegoated for economic problems that are largely beyond their control.

8

immigrant experiences

THE GOOD, THE BAD, AND THE HOPEFUL

SURVEYING IMMIGRANT EXPERIENCES

TO SAY THAT Canada is a destination of choice for international immigrants is surely an understatement. The Immigration Public Opinion Survey by Washington-based Transatlantic Trends (2010) concluded accordingly: Canada may be the most welcoming society in the world for newcomers (also Banting and Kymlicka 2010). No less effusive was an international survey commissioned by the Historica-Dominion Institute in partnership with the Munk School of Global Affairs and Aurea Foundation, entitled "What the World Thinks of Canada: Canada and the World in 2010. Immigration and Diversity" (Friesen 2010). Of the 18,600 adult respondents from the 24 leading economies, more than 53 percent said that they would abandon their homes and move to Canada if they could, including 77 percent of Chinese respondents and 71 percent of Mexicans. Respondents also expressed positive attitudes toward Canada's immigration welcome mat:

> Eighty-six percent believed that rights and freedoms were respected in Canada.
> Seventy-nine percent believed that Canadians were tolerant of th
> from different backgrounds.
> Seventy-nine percent believed that Canada had one of the best
> of-life standards.

> Seventy-one percent believed that Canadians were welcoming of newcomers.

The report duly noted the absence of an anti-immigration political party in Canada and its dearth of popular racist skinhead movements. Furthermore, most immigrants were relatively satisfied with their decision to come to Canada despite uneven economic prospects and sometimes unwelcoming sectors. According to the Longitudinal Survey of Immigrants to Canada (Jedwab 2012), four years after their admission into the country, 84 percent of respondents said they would repeat their decision to migrate (in terms of admission categories, 80 percent of the economy class, 88 percent of the family class, and 93 percent of the refugee class voiced this opinion). A similar study by Statistics Canada in 2005 (ibid.) revealed that three-quarters of recently arrived immigrants were satisfied with life in Canada; four years later, two-thirds of the study participants said that their expectations were met or exceeded. Finally, Canada's success in integrating newcomers is of sufficient merit in a global context to earn the sobriquet of a "Canadian exceptionalism" (Bloemraad 2012; Jeffrey Reitz in Ho and Natt 2012).

Other surveys are positive as well, albeit more guarded in their praise. The Migration Integration Policy Index (2010), based on 148 policy indicators, ranked Canada third in integrating migrants – just behind Sweden and Portugal – among 31 North American and European societies. Canada may have earned top marks for granting equal rights, responsibilities, and opportunities, including labour market entry, education access, and family sponsorship, but it was denied a first place finish for its failure to provide newcomers with voting rights and input into policy matters (Keung 2011a). Another study by the Migration Integration Policy Index (2007) for best practices among immigrant-receiving countries put Canada even farther behind. Of the 28 countries surveyed, Canada tied with Finland for fifth, behind Sweden, Portugal, Belgium, and the Netherlands. It received perfect marks on several counts, including commitments to dual citizenship, automatic citizenship for Canadian-born children of immigrant parents, employment rights and civil liberties for immigrants, eligibility for family reunion, and equality and anti-discrimination policies. It poorly because of its long-term residence policies and lack of participation for newcomers (Taylor 2009c). Lastly, the

time-differentiated (Satzewich and Wong 2006). The end result is a range of responses. To one side, hybridic identities are freefloating and flexible. To the other side, the discord and confusion associated with such fragmentation may entail the loss of cultural certainties as both newcomers and the native-born struggle to reclaim contested social blueprints (Scheffer 2010).

Immigrant experiences commonly entail a complex and drawn-out transformational process involving a host of political and social factors, against a backdrop of global and transnational dynamics, with economic and cultural consequences for both the sending and receiving countries (Castles and Miller 2009; Simmons 2010). Social networks across two or more countries are key components in the migration process, from the choice of a particular destination to the quality of the settlement experience (Poros 2010). In other words, the immigrant experience does not commence upon arrival in the host country. To the contrary, it begins long before departure and continues well afterward (Segal, Mayadas, and Elliott 2006). The adjustment process can be envisaged as moving along a continuum, from the preparation phase to the post-migration integration phase, with transitional phases of settlement and adaptation in between. Integration can also be framed as a "nested" process whereby immigrants first adjust to family, then to neighbourhood, ethnic subcommunity, ethnic community, city at large, and then the wider society (Liston and Carens 2008; Poros 2011). Or to put it somewhat differently, once a decision to move is made, immigrants may undergo a life course transition of settling down, fitting in, and moving up, as demonstrated in Box 33 (Kunz 2005; also Segal, Mayadas, and Elliott 2006; Local Immigrant Partnership Council 2010).

The micro-politics of entry may vary as well. Common enough is a romanticized image of migrants as the personification of an increasingly globalized and mobile world. But migrants move for a variety of reasons, most often to escape deplorable living conditions in their homeland (Scheffer 2010). Yet the transition process is proving more difficult than many imagine in shaping immigrant experiences. Despite destinations that consist of networks of relatives who provide a buffer or opportunity (Poros 2011), immigrants must deal with uncertainty and risk in coping with situations that differ markedly from those at home. They are uprooted from a familiar social world and transplanted into a society and culture with unfamiliar concepts of the normal,

Immigrant Experiences as a Life Course Transition

Premigration	→	Settlement (settling down/short-term transitional adjustment)	→	Adaptation (fitting in/ self-sustaining)	→	Integration (moving up, a protracted process of mutual accommodation)
> Conditions in homeland (political, economic); reasons for leaving > Status and experiences in home country (social class, education level, resources, resourcefulness) > Skill sets (labour, entrepreneur, professional) > Kin and communities support emigration of their own > Necessary attributes: motivation to move, resources to do so, admissibility > Transition experiences: planned, voluntary, legal, direct		> Basic language > Housing > Employment > Education > Social services > Readiness of receiving country (policies, programs, labour opportunities, social services) > Networks link migrants to kin/ community and provide buffer and opportunities > Immigrant resources, including psychological strengths, language competence, social supports, race, professional skills, and economic resources		> Language skills > Career > Networks > Community > Sense of identity > Knowledge of Canada + > Begin flow of remittances to kin/community of origin, in the process connecting both kin and community to the expat's new home		> Citizenship > Participation in politics and civic life + > Begin significant investments in their adopted homeland, resulting in increased clout in local affairs

Source: Adapted from Fleras (2012a; also Kunz 2005).

desirable, and acceptable (Breton 2012). Admittedly, those who enter a developed country for the first time do not always plan to stay (Simmons 2010). They may intend to overcome economic problems at home by working abroad temporarily, generating sufficient collateral to diversify risks, accumulate cash, and finance local production and consumption. They may opt for a more permanent arrangement as they acquire foreign experiences and exposure to new lifestyles, both democratic and consumerist. Even those who emigrate because of economic upheavals do not act entirely from self-interest. They choose destinations to which their home country is already linked economically (via trade), politically (treaties or colonial links), or socially (social ties, from student exchange programs to tourist travel) (Poros 2011).

The transition process may be one thing; adjustment may be quite another. Getting in can be complex and costly, but settlement, adaptation, and integration can prove substantially more difficult because of often hidden barriers, ranging from systemic bias to the uncoordinated nature of available services (TD Economics 2012). As this chapter demonstrates, a focus on a life course as a theoretical lens reveals a complex and challenging process, with varying levels of success, depending on the interplay of agency and structure. Some immigrants are primed for success and rapid integration, especially those with prearranged jobs, Canadian experience, and fluency in an official language. Some are being painted out of the picture because they lose traction in coping with Canada, and others are just muddling through as best they can. A few find the transition to be relatively smooth, thanks in part to the settlement support services that have been in place since 1974 (Vineberg 2012, vii). But most encounter periods of confusion, conflict, and uncertainty as they grapple with the realities of becoming "compatriots in a strange country, yet strangers in their own" (Scheffer 2010, 2). Their experience may prove less gratifying and more ambivalent than originally anticipated, especially as the strong sense of attachment to Canada shown by first-generation immigrants might diminish as time elapses for children and grandchildren of immigrants (Wong and Simon 2010). A mood of social dislocation may prevail as dreams of making it big evaporate, the generations drift apart, younger women chafe at traditional roles and paternalism, male household heads are stripped of their authority, and educated elites become estranged from the community at large (Handa 2003).

NEWCOMER PATHWAYS

> *Every act of immigration is like suffering a brain stroke: One has to learn to walk again, to talk again, to move around the world again, and, probably most difficult of all, one has to learn how to re-establish a sense of community.*
> — VIVIAN RAKOFF, QUOTED IN FULFORD (2003)

Canada's immigration program emphasizes the settlement and integration of newcomers (Fleras 2012c). Settlement itself involves a three-stage adjustment process: Immediate needs for assistance and reception (settling down); intermediate needs for accessing the labour market, housing, health services, and so on (fitting in); and long-term needs, including full integration into society and the economy (moving up) (Wayland 2006). Also implied is a two-way process of mutual accommodation. Canada expects immigrants to identify with its core cultural values, make a positive contribution, participate through involvement, and abide by its laws. Immigrants, in turn, expect Canada to behave with fairness by removing discriminatory barriers, conferring citizenship rights, creating welcoming communities and equal opportunities, and respecting their contributions and cultural traditions. In short, coming to Canada activates a reciprocal social contract in which immigrants accept obligations and trade their talents for security and rights.

Settling Down

Equipping migrants with the tools to settle down entails a financial outlay. The federal government allocated just under $600 million in settlement services in 2011-12, down slightly from the previous year ($651 million), with Ontario receiving approximately $44 million, or about $3,400 per immigrant (Pagliaro and Mahoney 2010). Nonetheless, Canada lacks a unified approach for newcomer services and programs, in large part because health, education, and social services are provincial responsibilities. Provinces such as Quebec assume direct responsibility for the design, administration, and delivery of social services. As well, all levels of government and the non-profit sector offer language training, employment counselling, and translation services. Settlement services, which are predominantly delivered by groups such as the Kitchener-Waterloo Multicultural Centre, rely heavily on government funding to defray their costs, from translation services to job networking. But the services are a hodge-podge (Vineberg 2012, 2014). In most provinces, they are available only to permanent residents or convention refugees; thus, years of residence in a legal limbo may be required before eligibility (Wayland 2006). Conversely, some programs are off limits to those who have citizenship status.

For some immigrants, settling down is filled with hope and opportunity; for others, it is fraught with danger and disappointment; still others cope as best they can with difficult circumstances and limited resources (Fleras 2012e). Life for newcomers may prove a disappointment, resulting in feelings of hopelessness that may induce violence turned inward (suicide) or outward. As Debbie Douglas, executive director of the Ontario Council of Agencies Serving Immigrants, states, "The acculturation process is very difficult, whether you come by choice or not. It's about developing a sense of belonging and being able to integrate economically, socially, and politically into society" (quoted in Keung 2009). Racism remains a problem. For example, the Association for Canadian Studies and Canadian Race Relations Foundation commissioned a survey of 1,522 Canadians, which was released just before the 21 March 2012 International Day for the Elimination of Racial Discrimination. More than half of the respondents believed that Muslims couldn't be trusted, and nearly as many thought that Muslims themselves were to blame for any discrimination they experienced (see also Saunders 2012a). Or consider that the racialization of Markham, Ontario, remains a demographic success story (immigrants and racialized minorities constitute 72 percent of its population), yet the "white" (flight) population dropped 12 percent between 2001 and 2011, despite a 60 percent overall population increase. So much for living together with differences (also Forum Research 2013). Even Canada's much ballyhooed multiculturalism may confuse new Canadians. For example, in Rabindranath Maharaj's *The Amazing Absorbing Boy* (2010), exposure to diversity may prove both comforting and perplexing. Newcomers must learn to navigate the social patterns and diverse cultural norms of Canadian society. They must also learn to embrace the fragments of various ethnic communities, with the result that there is no monoculture or single body with which to affiliate (see also Soto 2012). The words of Constance Inju Tendoh (2009) capture the dilemmas of settling down:

Foreign policies of the West on immigration require total integration of immigrants in their host countries. In the eyes of the capitalist society, the immigrants are threats and need to either cooperate with their host societies or return to their countries of origin. From the immigrants' perspective, the host community talks of integration yet they make integration impossible. They have drawn lines of divide separating the included from the excluded. Despite the fact that immigrants work for the welfare of their host societies, they have been identified as the excluded and the undesired others. The word *immigrant* in capitalist societies is connected to marginality, inferiority, illegality, poverty, rejection etc. Most immigrants do not feel at home in their host countries as they have become subject to discrimination, yet they cannot return because of life uncertainty in their homeland and many blame the West for this ... Government's policies insist on the return of immigrants with the logic that immigrants are dangerous. It is their nation-state and they have the right to decide who enters or leaves within the territorial boundary of their nation-state. Yet they should not forget history.

Immigrants invariably want to improve their economic lot, but they encounter many barriers (Constant, Kahanec, and Zimmerman 2009). Those who speak neither French nor English may retreat into ethnic enclaves, according to a federal government document obtained by Richard Kurland (O'Neil 2012), where they earn less than other Canadians because of difficulties in adjusting to the economy. They must also internalize those subtle codes that inform a Canadian way of doing things if they hope to achieve success and acceptance (Derwing and Waugh 2012). Not surprisingly, glitches mar the integration process. The 2002 Ethnic Diversity Survey, which conducted forty thousand interviews, asked questions regarding "sense of belonging," "trust in others," "feeling Canadian," "becoming a citizen," "participating in voluntary activities," "voting in Canadian elections," and "life satisfaction." It concluded that racialized immigrants were less integrated into Canada than their white counterparts (Reitz 2012b). Moreover, the gap persisted and sometimes increased, not only for those with longer experiences in Canada but also for Canadian-born children of immigrant parents who possessed high levels of education and employment success. Burton and Phipps (2010) and Wong and Simon

(2010) argue that immigrants and their children have lower self-reported life satisfaction and a weaker sense of belonging to their local communities than their Canadian-born peers. Others, such as Wu, Schimmele, and Hou (2012), contend that the level of newcomer integration – based on a sense of belonging and feelings of discomfort about the host society – is situational. That is, it depends on numerous factors, including age, gender, level of education, city of settlement, and neighbourhood characteristics. The sense of belonging is higher for South Asians than for Canadians of British origin, but lower for Chinese and similar for both Aboriginal people and blacks. Notions of belonging do not change across immigrant generations. Wu, Schimmele, and Hou (ibid.) conclude that feelings of discomfort are highest for first-generation racialized persons and whites, and that discomfort decreases over time and across generations.

For others, the immigrant experience provides a payoff, albeit one with strings attached. Newcomers strike a Faustian bargain in which they relinquish much of their valued past as the price of admission (also Scheffer 2010). Many quickly realize that the lure of abundance may also tarnish memories of their homeland (ibid.). Andrei Codrescu (1995, 47) writes of the near-death social experiences of his Romanian mother:

> Most people come here because they are sick of being poor. They want to eat and they want something to show for their industry. But soon enough it becomes evident to them that these things are not enough. They have eaten and they are full, but they have eaten alone ... This time they are lacking something more elusive than salami and furniture. They are bereft of a social and cultural milieu ... Leaving behind your kin, your friends, your language, your smells, your childhood, is traumatic. It is a kind of death. You're dead for the home folk and they are dead to you.

Culture shock may be unsettling because of exposure to radically different lifestyles, mixed messages and conflicting expectations, rapid social change, and an inhospitable climate that tolerates cultural differences in the abstract yet rejects specific practices if they are at odds with mainstream norms (a classic case of supporting diversity as principle, but rejecting diversities as realities). For example, securing a place in a new country often compromises family traditions:

Many of us were greeted with a myriad of challenges when we arrived, but we decided to take things one day at a time. We missed our home countries but then we find opportunities here that we may not have had back home. There are some values here that we appreciate and would like to add to the values back home that we still hold on to. On the other hand, many of us still cannot help missing home because there are certain values over there that we just cannot find here. Sometimes acceptance and closeness become very limited to us. We have friends here but even when you get close, it does not feel like the closeness back home. This makes you wonder if it is your imagination or whether you are unconsciously holding back, apprehensive about giving your all. We try hard to make adjustments taking on the values here that we like and at the same time holding on to some values from home, trying to have the best of both worlds. (Phyllis Peprah 2005)

Ambivalences rule. Consider access to health care. Canada's "universal" health care does not cover newcomers for the first three months. They must pay cash for hospital care and will receive a bill in the mail for emergency care (Morris 2009). Some groups, such as refugees and refugee claimants, are covered under the Interim Federal Health Program, although Ottawa has recently scaled back benefits for failed refugee claimants and those who arrive from a designated country of origin or through a safe country. Others, such as temporary foreign workers and live-in caregivers, are excluded from immediate health care provisions, and hundreds of thousands of undocumented workers are permanently barred (Keung 2013c). It remains to be seen if Canada can accommodate those "halfway" people, who are halfway between the life they left behind and the life they have chosen. Toronto's decision to become a "sanctuary city" (to provide services, no questions asked, to the undocumented [*CBC News* 2013]) is a step in a more inclusive direction.

Canada may be a favoured destination because of its democratic reputation and high standard of living, but many immigrants find it difficult to make big money there. As a result, it is increasingly seen as a great place to retire or to raise children rather than a viable place to live or work (MacKinnon 2012). The outflow of newcomers is no less an indictment of making it in Canada. According to Aydemir and

Robinson (2006), about 35 percent of working-age males, many with professional skills, leave Canada within 20 years of their arrival. There is also a flipside to immigration that exposes newcomers to challenges and contradictions. Naheed Mustafa (2007) writes in response to the death of young Brampton-based Muslim women:

> To say immigration is transformative is a gross understatement. Families leave everything and everyone they know and move to a foreign place where they become blank slates. The support of the extended family is gone, the cocoon of well understood social norms is cast off and parents and their children stand out in the open waiting for a new life to start ... But while parents want economic opportunities and a solid education for their children, they are wary of the siren call of the "West." They want change but not too much change. But for kids the desire to fit in, to be "normal," is tough to ignore.

For refugees, the situation is decidedly grimmer. They have complex needs, reflecting widely varying educational and literacy levels, with much to learn in a relatively short time, including awareness of community support agencies and the issues of abortion, contraception, same-sex relations, domestic violence, child supervision, divorce, and child custody (Goodwin 2010). Traumatized by emotional and psychological abuses en route to Canada, they must adapt to its unique social, cultural, and geographic climate. Worse still, refugee families may remain separated for lengthy periods due to delays in acquiring permanent residence for the sponsoring family member or an increase in the processing fee for each application (Wayland 2006). The transitional stresses that accompany refugee claimants are compounded by language difficulties, shame at their inability to work and provide, and low self-esteem due to loss of control over authority or destiny. Media coverage is rarely helpful: Asylum seekers and refugees are routinely stereotyped as criminals, cheaters, and scapegoats, often within contexts of moral panic related to threats, conflicts, or crises (Chan 2014; see Philo, Briant, and Donald 2013). As expressed by one Central American refugee who fell into an abusive relationship, "I was from a country where I was the daughter of a middle-class professional. Here, I was no one. *Refugee* is such a negative word. People saw me as garbage" (quoted in White 1999).

To be sure, many new Canadians appear to be relatively satisfied with life in Canada (Monohan, Berns-McGown, and Morden 2014, 100; Michael Adams 2007).[1] They appreciate the opportunities and services that are available to them and their children, the promise of human freedom, and the market transparency that enables them to achieve modest economic success (see also Raleigh and Kao 2010; Lewin et al. 2011). A *Globe and Mail* article by Mark MacKinnon (2012) explains Canada's appeal:

> For young and well educated Chinese like Emily Gao, the lure of immigration to Canada is obvious: Clean air, public health care, and a strong education system are all draws compared to living in a country without them. Add the large Chinese communities that already exist in places such as Vancouver and Toronto, plus relatively cheap real estate (compared with prices in some Chinese cities), and you have something close to a dream destination.

The 2006 census indicated that 84 percent of immigrants aged 15 and up were positive about their decision to immigrate after four years of living in Canada; two-thirds said that life in Canada had met their expectations; and 85 percent of the eligible foreign-born had become citizens (Statistics Canada 2008b; also Wong and Simon 2010). In another study for the Mosaic Institute by Monohan, Berns-McGown, and Morden (2014), 94 percent of 4,498 respondents reported feeling attached to Canada, 86 percent reported feeling as though they belonged to Canada, and 85 percent indicated they were proud to be Canadian. Studies also indicate that, on average, children of immigrant parents are doing as well as or better than those of Canadian-born parents, based on unadjusted unemployment and income data, though second-generation members of some racialized minorities tend to have greater employment difficulties (Picot and Hou 2011).

Canada has a lot to offer newcomers: According to the 2005 Longitudinal Survey of Immigrants to Canada (see Schellenberg and Maheux 2007), they liked its climate and physical environment (19.1 percent of the respondents), cultural aspects (freedom, rights) (14.4 percent), safety (11 percent), peace and political stability (10.4 percent), and educational opportunities (9.9 percent). Ironically, what they most disliked (except for the 19 percent who seemingly liked everything) were climate/physical environment (26.7 percent), lack of employment opportunities (17.4 percent), and high taxes (11.1 percent). Their material well-being and quality of life were perceived as better than in their homelands. But many were disillusioned because of problems that accompanied them into Canada. Or they encountered obstacles upon entry and settlement that few could have anticipated: "Let's face it, a lot of 'us' never considered, when we decided to emigrate, what it would really be like once the dust of moving had settled – especially the psychological adaptions that would be required of us, our children, and future generations" (Singh 2000, 25).

Problems may arise due to culture shock, loss of economic well-being, isolation, lack of political power and support from the homeland, and discriminatory barriers that preclude entry or acceptance (also Lewin et al. 2011; Spoonley and Bedford 2012 for New Zealand). Surveys repeatedly indicate that securing employment (preferably in their field of expertise) is the foremost settlement-related problem for new Canadians (Wayland 2006). The employment level for core-aged immigrants in 2011 was 75.6 percent, compared to 82.9 percent for the Canadian-born, although rates were better for settled immigrants (living in Canada for more than 10 years) (Statistics Canada 2012). Immigrants not only constitute a higher share of Canadian residents with a university degree, but those with higher education levels also enjoy higher employment rates than immigrants with lower education levels, regardless of length of residency in Canada, though their employment rates consistently fall below the employment rates of the Canadian-born (Bollman 2013). Other common obstacles include learning a new language, adjusting to the weather, adapting to new cultural values, and accessing language training, housing, and health care services (Schellenberg and Maheux 2007). The persistence of immigrant enclaves has raised questions about the warmth of Canada's welcome. To what extent are these enclaves the result of racist and exclusionary practices such as housing discrimination? Or do they reflect an immigrant preference for familiar community and culturally grounded experiences? In either case, Canada must contemplate the prospect of creating more spaces for interaction and dialogue as newcomers may gravitate toward the relative isolation of suburban enclaves (Reinhart 2007; Siemiatycki 2005).

In general, the primary concerns of new Canadians are practical and survival-related. This pragmatism stands in contrast to the demands of Canada's founding (Aboriginal) peoples for self-determining autonomy over land, identity, and political voice (Maaka and Fleras 2005). Sociologically speaking, immigrants constitute "voluntary people" who are looking for ways of getting in and settling down, unlike forcibly incorporated Aboriginal peoples who want to get out of political arrangements and social structures that are neither of their making nor a benefit to them (Fleras 2012e). Immigrants insist on integration into Canada, albeit through their ethnicity and on their own terms, even if this means (a) opting for residence in an ethnic enclave because of convenience or comfort, (b) pressuring institutions to accommodate their difference-based needs and religious identities, (c) ensuring respect for a language and culture with which their children can identify, and (d) putting down roots without necessarily severing ties to their cultural tradition. More specifically, immigrant needs can be itemized as follows:

> meaningful employment in a workplace with opportunity but without discrimination;
> expanded opportunities in the labour and education markets as well as access to housing, government institutions, and social services;
> conferral of full citizenship rights, including the right to move, participate, and criticize;
> access to the best that Canadian society has to offer without diminishing their children's sense of cultural distinctiveness;
> the capacity to express their identity without paying a penalty; and
> respect for their differences as a legitimate and valued part of society.

In a word, immigrants and their descendants want to capitalize on the best of both worlds (Fleras 2012e). They want to be treated as individuals, not lumped into an inchoate mass. Conversely, they also want respect and appreciation for who they are, culturally speaking, without sacrificing meaningful involvement in society, in effect prompting the plea "Don't judge me by my background but never forget where I came from" (Scheffer 2010, 17). Full citizenship rights are important, yet so too is recognition of their cultural worth as humans with a meaningful past. Successful integration is contingent on managing change on their own terms, including mainstream acceptance of faith and spirituality as a positive dimension of difference. Relationship building within their communities is important in easing the transition and the integration process (Griffith 2013). Maintaining a strong immigrant identity is also critical in making the move from there to here. It provides a buffer of confidence and self-respect for facilitating a sense of belonging (Bunting 2007; Couton and Gaudet 2008).

But what newcomers want is not necessarily what they get. They are experiencing a marked decline in economic fortunes as corporate Canada fumbles the challenge of integrating them into the workforce (McDonald et al. 2010; Noorani 2011). In a risk-averse corporate world, their qualifications continue to be dismissed, education degrees devalued, and overseas experience discounted as virtually worthless. Foreign education counts for about half the value of Canadian schooling in terms of earning power, and foreign experience has little market value in Canada (one year overseas equates to a third of a year in Canada). The refusal to recognize the credentials of new Canadians costs Canada billions in lost revenue (Conference Board of Canada 2004; RBC Economic 2011). Paying immigrants comparably to the Canadian-born would add $30.7 billion (or 2.1 percent) to Canada's GDP and would translate to about forty-two thousand new jobs. The paradox is all too real: Immigrants may be selected for their skills, credentials, and work experience, but their economic marginalization reflects the very factors that presumably got them into Canada in the first place. The observations of Jason Kenney (2012a) seem apropos:

> For far too long, the archetype of immigration to Canada has been that of an education [sic] professional arriving from a developing country only to find seemingly impenetrable barriers to getting licensed to practise in their profession, unable to find a Canadian job because, ironically, they don't have Canadian experience ...
>
> And here's the paradox. While that educated immigrant is disappointed and often goes into a downward spiral of disappointment and depression ... in other parts of the country, in other parts of the economy, employers are desperate for skilled workers ...
>
> We are bringing in historic high levels of immigration, the highest relative levels in the developed world, yet many of them

are facing unemployment or underemployment in an economy
with huge and growing labour shortages.

Something's broken and needs to be fixed.

Not surprisingly, as labour sociologist Jeffrey Reitz (2005) puts it, the
success of Canada's immigration policy will ultimately be measured
by initiatives and institutions that link workers to jobs by facilitating
an international transferability of skills, credentials, and experience.

The much-hyped reference to Canada as immigrant-friendly cannot
conceal the obvious. Thousands of immigrants can't find gainful employment (Galabuzi 2007; McDonald et al. 2010; Picot and Sweetman
2012; Frank 2013). During the past 30 years, economic outcomes for
new immigrants (from higher unemployment to lower wages despite
higher education levels) have spiralled downward, relative to the
Canadian-born (Bonikowska, Hou, and Picot 2011; RBC Economics
2011). The most commonly cited barriers to accessing skill-appropriate
jobs include (a) a dearth of Canadian work experience, (b) lack of recognition of foreign credentials and work experience, (c) minimal
knowledge of the Canadian economy and the unwritten labour market
codes that take time to learn (Derwing and Waugh 2012), (d) a deficit
of "soft social skills" related to official language proficiency, and
(e) increased competition with an educated Canadian labour force
(Alboim and McIsaac 2007; Sweetman 2011). Highly skilled newcomers
find themselves segregated in menial and unskilled occupations with
minimal job security or prospects for promotion. Even here, problems
prevail because of the dampening effects of globalization in eliminating or outsourcing manufacturing jobs. Structural adjustments have
further depressed the earnings of new labour market entrants, both
foreign- and Canadian-born (Biles, Burstein, and Frideres 2008). The
combination of underemployment and precarious work is especially
hard on newcomers who have been misled or misinformed (Jackson
2011). As Sarah Wayland (2006, 77) notes, "Many individuals feel
they were duped into coming to Canada, but do not want to face the
shame of returning to their homelands. They settle for underemployment and hope that their children's luck will be better. Other migrants
move to the United States where accreditation processes are perceived
to be swifter."

No less harrowing for professionally trained immigrants is the
closed-shop mentality of licensed occupations that impose restrictions

and deny accreditation. Accrediting foreign certificates and establishing equivalences in qualification is a complex and time-consuming process (Deloitte 2011). This holds true for more than 440 regulatory bodies governing 55 industries, (about 20 percent of jobs in Canada require licensing by a professional regulatory body [Keung 2011b]). The resulting bottleneck bars professionals from gainful employment and reflects a fundamental disconnect between admission criteria and employment qualifications. The federal government controls immigration admission, but the provinces control the licensing of professional bodies who, in turn, control who gets licensed. Nowhere is the crisis more acute than in the case of foreign-trained doctors, as Box 34 demonstrates.

Fitting In

The challenges of fitting in are inseparable from those of settling down (Toten 2011). Yet fitting in goes beyond simple survival. It involves a combination of social capital (connections) and human capital (skill sets) for integrating into Canada without necessarily relinquishing cultural and religious distinctiveness. Immigrants must be comfortable in managing adjustments on their own terms for successful integration. Maintaining a strong identity provides them with the confidence and self-respect to move forward (Bunting 2007). Diverse migrant groups encounter differing challenges. Minorities such as Muslims are seeking ways of engaging with the secular world of Canada, albeit on their own terms. Multiple identities are the result – they are citizens of Canada who belong to the global Muslim community as well as a specific Islamic sect (Karim 2009a). The challenge for followers of Islam is formidable: how to remain Muslim while becoming Canadian (Anderssen 2009).

The task of fitting in along gender lines is particularly acute (Andrew 2009). Men may have trouble getting work; the jobs they do find tend to reflect less respect, prestige, and income than their employment in the homeland; and they lose status, both in society at large and in their households. The position of immigrant women is equally complex and contradictory (Boyd 2006). No one denies that they are often limited to precarious, part-time work or that their credentials go unrecognized. But opportunities also exist, including (a) employment openings in a Canada that commits to the principle of gender equality, (b) increased status in households and the community

34

Accrediting Immigrants, Discrediting Canada: The Politics and Perils of Accreditation

Q. Where's the best place to have a baby in Toronto?
A. In a taxi: there's a good chance the driver is a foreign-trained doctor.
— COMEDY LINE MAKING THE ROUNDS IN TORONTO

Canada has the best educated pizza delivery guys in the world.
— COMMENT ON ADAR AIHIL'S CANADA IMMIGRANT'S BLOG
(QUOTED IN "OH CANADA," *THE WALRUS,* DECEMBER 2010)

I saw the funniest thing last week, a white guy driving a taxi.
— COMEDY LINE

HOW MANY TIMES have we heard comments like these? New Canadians with professional and medical degrees are driving taxis. Or delivering pizzas. Or mopping floors. (In California's Silicon Valley, by contrast, it is estimated that immigrants and their children account for 40 percent of start-ups.) But Canada's proverbial immigrant taxi driver with a doctorate is no laughing matter. It results from a key contradiction in our immigration trends – the discrepancy between admission criteria (*foreign* education and work experience) and employment criteria (*Canadian* education and work experience) (Somerville and Walsworth 2010). Immigrants may be increasingly skilled and highly educated, but many are penalized by the very qualifications that gained them entry in the first place (Kunz, Milan, and Schetagne 2001; Lorne Foster 2012). This untapped potential of underutilized labour notwithstanding, Canada is experiencing a skills shortage that borders on the unfathomable. For example, thousands of foreign-trained doctors cannot gain accreditation to practise in Canada, even as millions of Canadians are suffering from gaps in health care delivery, including those who cannot find a family doctor but must rely on emergency services or walk-in clinics (see Rampell 2013 for the United States).

To be sure, Ontario licensed more foreign doctors in 2006 than ever before. They were granted fully 42 percent of its 2,961 new licences, but only 469 of them were certified to practise medicine, with the rest receiving education licences to teach (Mahoney 2007). In 2010, 41 percent of the 3,708 doctors who were licensed in Ontario were foreign-trained (Brown 2011). Nevertheless, a licensing bottleneck persists because accrediting institutions such as the Ontario College of Physicians and Surgeons seemingly lack the resources to increase residency spaces (Urbanski 2004). Foreign-trained doctors encounter frustrating obstacles on the road to professional accreditation. These range from costly retraining programs to a restricted number of residencies (from two to seven years of training in hospitals upon graduation), despite a doubling of residency positions in Ontario for them (Neiterman and Bourgeault 2012). Consider the licensing process for international medical graduates, according to the Association of International Physicians and Surgeons of Ontario:

Step 1 An acceptable medical degree from a list of Canadian and international schools

Step 2 Equivalency exams: must pass the Medical Council of Canada evaluating exam

Step 3 Post-graduate training: entry into a residency training spot (internship)

Step 4 Licentiate of Medical Council of Canada: must pass qualifying exams 1 and 2, and an evaluation exam

Step 5 Specialty certification: upon completion of residency, graduates must pass certification to become either a family physician or a specialist

Step 6 Ontario registration: must be registered/certified by the College of Family Physicians or the Royal College of Physicians and Surgeons of Canada

Not all foreign-trained medical graduates must jump hoops to practise in Canada. For example, those from the so-called Category 1 countries (New Zealand, Australia, South Africa, England, and the United States) may bypass the internship requirement and, after an evaluating exam, practise medicine immediately. All other foreign-trained doctors must pass equivalence and evaluating exams before applying for an internship/residency position (Neiterman and Bourgeault 2012). Ironically, Canadian-born students who have trained abroad are defined as foreign-trained by Ontario's medical authorities. They, too, must compete with the foreign-born for the coveted residency spots at university teaching hospitals (Carey 2004). To add insult to injury, many who pass all the required exams cannot practise in Ontario but are assigned teaching-only placements (Mahoney 2007). Even graduating doctors in Canada cannot find work in understaffed fields such as oncology (cancer). The reason may be simple: Hospitals and health regions lack the money to hire them (Blackwell 2011). For example, there was no full-time employment for 22 of the 31 radiation oncologists who finished training in 2009 and 2010, despite an obvious need for their services.

Physicians are not the only ones who must run a gauntlet of pre-internship and internship training "modules" that are designed to evaluate and upgrade their clinical skills (PROMPT 2004). Foreign-trained dentists must pass a taxing certification exam and then complete a two-year qualifying program at one of the five Canadian dental schools that will accept them (Nazir 2004). Similarly, foreign-trained lawyers must return to school for up to two years, article with a law firm, and then enter a provincial bar admission program. Engineers from "non-accredited" universities must also demonstrate a fixed period of satisfactory practical experience and completion of exam requirements (George et al. 2012).

Of course, professional and regulatory bodies exist to ensure competency and to protect the public (Hagopian 2003; Rampell 2013). They also ensure that the supply of high-priced help never outstrips demand. But the recertification process seems unduly harsh and punitive, especially when rules for qualifications and standards of practice vary from province to province (Perkel 2008). Foreign-trained professionals may be poorly informed about accreditation procedures prior to entering Canada, with each province setting a different standard for certification. Many must repeat the educational requirements and undergo costly and time-consuming retraining (also Rampell 2013). Risk-averse Canadian employers are reluctant to hire newcomers because of a perceived gap in their professional knowledge or lack of language skills (Taylor 2005). Not surprisingly, many are trapped in a vicious Catch-22 cycle of systemic bias, or as John Samuel (2004) contends, "Employers do not hire foreign-trained people unless they have attained membership in appropriate professional associations while professional associations do not grant membership unless the individual applicant has some proven amount of Canadian work experience." To put it somewhat differently, "You can't get a job in your field without Canadian experience, and you can't get that experience without a job" (Naomi Alboim, Queen's University School of Policy Studies, quoted in Taylor 2005, 34).

To its credit, Ottawa has unveiled a series of initiatives to expedite the entry of new Canadians into the job market. The Canadian Immigration Integration Program was established in 2007 to prepare immigrants who were still resident in their country of origin. Four years later, 62 percent of participants had found employment within six months of arrival, up from 44 percent in previous years (Keung 2011b). In its 2007 budget, the federal government also set aside $30 million over five years for a Foreign Credential Referral Office to provide prospective immigrants with information about the Canadian labour market and to help those with overseas training to bring their credentials up to par with Canadian standards (Alboim and McIsaac 2007). The creation in 2010 of the Pan-Canadian Framework for the Assessment and Recognition of Foreign Qualifications established principles for assessing foreign credentials in cooperation with the provinces and territories. This Economic Action Plan Framework streamlined applications into eight priority occupations, such as engineering and architecture, to ensure recognition within a year. As well, business leaders have vowed to hire more immigrant recruits because, as the Royal Bank's CEO commented, "Governments can attract skilled immigrants to Canada but, once they arrive, businesses have to pick up the ball. And to date we have not. In fact, we are dropping it" (quoted in Abraham 2005).

But the situation has not appreciably improved, despite perceptions that, unlike the United States, where the licensing process for physicians is unduly restrictive and time consuming, Canada has acknowledged the value of more "high quality training programs done abroad" (Rampell 2013). Notwithstanding government promises that the licensing practices of regulatory bodies will be "transparent, objective, impartial, and fair," immigrant professionals are still experiencing difficulties (Jackson 2012). The end result should come as no surprise: According to the Office of the Fairness Commissioner, the earnings of skilled immigrants are about half those of their educated Canadian counterparts; only 25 percent have obtained a licence to practise in one of Ontario's 37 regulated professions, compared to 60 percent of Canadian-trained; and 1 in 10 have given up trying to get professional recertification (Keung 2010b). None of this augurs well for Canada's future as a country where immigration works because immigrants work (Hansen 2014).

Much is made of Canada's brain drain to the United States. Nevertheless, Canadians are less aware that Canada receives a brain gain, thanks to an immigration policy that often poaches from countries that cannot afford to lose their brightest stars. For example, a stunning percentage of skilled nationals from poor regions reside in the global North, including 41 percent from the Caribbean and 27 percent from West Africa, in effect dooming these areas to poverty and poor health (Kapur 2005). That the island of Grenada must train 22 physicians to secure the long-term services of 1 is surely an indictment of global talent poaching. Researchers who studied nine sub-Saharan countries also found that they spent nearly $2.2 billion in training doctors who left for Canada, the United States, Britain, and Australia, thus saving these four rich countries the tidy sum of $4.5 billion in education costs (Mills et al. 2011). (To compensate for this brain drain, economics professor Jagdish Bhagwati proposed that homelands tax the earnings of their skilled and professional expats, who would thus pay back the benefits they receive due to their education and training in their home country [Freitas, Levatino, and Pécoud 2012.]) In theory, Canada could reframe this migrant diaspora along development partnership lines that entail a two-way flow of mutual benefits to facilitate economic and social development in the global South (Crush et al. 2013). In reality, it doesn't, which does not bode well for the principle of bilateral cooperation.

In short, Canada practises its own version of a great brain robbery. It poaches medical talent from countries that can least afford its loss, yet leaves little in the way of compensation (Mills et al. 2011). Worse still, these medical skills may be wasted once migrant health care professionals reach Canada (Conference Board of Canada 2004; Editorial, *Toronto Star* 2011). What an inexcusable squandering of human talent, to entice the highly skilled into Canada and then deny them access to employment (Editorial, *Globe and Mail* 2011a). Soon word will leak out that the welcome mat is not what it seems. Canada may be good at attracting migrants, but it's poor at putting them to work in their chosen fields. In the end, Canada's underutilized brain gain will inevitably yield another brain drain (Kapur 2005).

Source: Adapted from Fleras (2012a).

---

35 FYI

Highly Recommended

THE BIG WAIT, an OMNI Television/Big Read Media documentary (Jackson and Osborne 2012), focuses on how Canadians in general, and small towns in particular, are desperate for family physicians. Yet thousands of international medical graduates who are equally desperate to practise are thwarted from doing so because they lack access to the residency program.

at large, and (c) greater involvement in mobilizing communities to provide services for immigrant women.

Immigrant and refugee schoolchildren are subject to a host of conflicting demands and pressures, which may be intimidating (Handa 2003). They must adjust to a new country, cope with prejudice and racism during their formative years, create routines and friendships, and learn a new language quickly enough to finish high school and compete with the Canadian-born for post-secondary education (attaining English-language proficiency generally takes five to seven years). They also confront a host of barriers, from stereotypes to curricula and textbooks that are at odds with their experiences, to a lack of positive role models among school staff and low teacher expectations. Others have the opposite problem: Inflated teacher expectations of brainy immigrant children mean that anything less than perfect is a disappointment (Hammer and Friesen 2011; also Gilmour et al. 2012). Finally, both immigrant youth and Canadian-born children of immigrants must navigate the byzantine demands of mainstream peer culture, whose values often conflict with those of family and community (Anisef and Kilbride 2003; Handa 2003; Kobayashi and Preston 2014). Cast as the moral guardians of the culture and the nation, young women are particularly vulnerable to restrictions, as Rajiva (2005, 27) notes:

> Girls are expected to maintain cultural practices that are sometimes no longer relevant in their homeland countries, and are certainly not widely accepted in Canadian society. This includes concerns with dress and behaviour; peer socializing (at night, at parties, and school dancing); growing independence at adolescence (which is often not part of immigrant community understandings of adolescence); and perhaps most importantly, interacting with members of the opposite sex and having romantic relationships with boys who are not part of the community.

Intergenerational tensions are inevitable as parents and offspring struggle to find a working balance between Canada's permissiveness culture and the more conservative traditions (Handa 2003; Wu, Schimmele, and Hou 2012). Consider, for example, fate-based cultures, where everything from class, religion, experiences, and opportunities is seen as largely set in stone. Contrast this fatalist attitude to the optimism of Western liberal universalistic societies, where life is embraced as an ongoing initiative to disprove fate (from biogenetics to cultural tradition). The challenge is straightforward: how to reconcile the Western mindset, in which the concept of fate is discarded, with that of other cultures for whom fate is real (Scheffer 2010). A culture clash is inevitable, as French historian Gerard Noiriel explains: "On top of the shock of transplantation and the discovery of a new universe characterized by the speed of the assembly line and the complex topography of metro tunnels comes incomprehension in the face of new dominant norms" (quoted in ibid., 10). The case study in Box 36 is highly instructive of these dilemmas, divisions, and delusions.

Two broad narratives can be discerned in the intergenerational crisis: To one side, adult immigrants who falter in making the transition from there to here; to the other side, their offspring, who tend to quickly adapt (Sykes 2008). Immigrant parents may feel alienated from a language and culture that confuses or diminishes; by contrast, their children assimilate rapidly, assuming an assertiveness and independence that invert conventional status/roles between parents and children. Parents are trapped in a culture crossfire: They insist on a better future for their children, but attaining it may prove too much of a good thing if it undermines cultural tradition, family cohesion, and their own authority. Immigrant women may be the real victims when push (literally) comes to shove, and worse (Rajiva 2005). Many are caught between the old world of male-dominated submissiveness and a new world of independence, assertiveness, and opportunities, but they often lack the resources, skills, or support to make the transition from one to the other. Not surprisingly, thousands of new Canadians may be fuming in desperation and depression, suffering in silence behind walls of social alienation, financial pressure, family turmoil, and cultural values that isolate and foreclose avenues of help (Reinhart and Rusk 2006).

Moving Up

The challenges of moving up are equally demanding (Fleras 2012e). Unlike settling down and fitting in, it entails a fuller incorporation and participation in Canadian society (Landolt, Goldring, and Bernhard 2011). Yet what should be a relatively straightforward process may prove complex and confusing. On arrival, immigrants may well keep to themselves, not necessarily because they want to re-create transplanted homelands, but because mainstream discrimination pushes

36 CASE STUDY

South Asian Youth in Canada

IT'S TOUGH ENOUGH being an adolescent in a society that both reveres and reviles youth (Anisef and Kilbride 2003; also Fleras 2007d). It's tougher still for second-generation immigrant youth who must negotiate their way through Canadian society without trampling on parental tradition (Handa 2003; Shariff 2008; Naji 2012; also Biswas 2003; Garroutte 2003; Beyer and Ramji 2013). The process of identity formation is especially vexing for immigrant youth who must cope with the competing demands of school, family, friends, peers, and the labour market (Nazroo and Karlsen 2003). For them, fitting in and settling down can come at a price. The killing of Aqsa Parvez in December 2007 by her father attests to the perils of wanting to fit in. No less devastating were the 2009 murders in which four female members of the Shafia family died at the hands of their immediate relatives, some of them ostensibly for dishonouring the family name by adopting Western dress and mainstream behaviour. Admittedly, references to the clash of cultures are misleading (as are those to "honour killings"). What transpires is not a culture clash per se; after all, such a reference tends to reify cultures as static (essentializing) and to assume an equivalence between them. What prevails instead is a negotiated process involving selective aspects of modernity and tradition within contexts of power (Handa 2003).

The Precarity of Immigrant Youth

Immigrant youth confront formidable oppositional dynamics (Fleras 2007d). They must balance the demands of home, family, and tradition with the challenges of performing well at school, forging healthy relations with peers and friends, developing a sense of belonging, and seeking employment. They are also pushed to identify with the mainstream, thus compromising their relationship to parents, who may want them to become Western but not so much as to lose respect for tradition and family values. In addition, they must also resist, even rebel, against identifying too closely with the norms of mainstream society for fear of being accused of selling out (Anisef and Kilbride 2003). Compounding the difficulties is the creation of diverse social strategies and psychological mechanisms for coping with disadvantage and discrimination in culturally appropriate ways (Ghuman 2003). For example, spending time with one's "own ethnic kind" can provide a sense of identity and belonging because of shared perspectives on issues, experiences, and aspirations (Johal 2003), but too much of this in-group security blanket can also prove a social death knell.

In short, immigrant youth and Canadian-born children of immigrants confront some tough challenges in living between two cultural fragments (Desai and Subramanian 2003; Zine 2008; Kobayashi and Preston 2014). They are seen by some as having problems because of adjustment difficulties, by others as creating problems due to their tendency toward anti-social or un-Canadian behaviour, and by others still as victims of circumstances beyond their control (Rathzel 2003). Problems also arise from conflicting expectations: children of racialized immigrant parents may be fluent in the official languages and share educational attainments yet must endure prejudice and discriminatory barriers, resulting in greater alienation from Canada (Reitz and Banerjee 2007; Ali 2008). The conflict of interest is tangible: Immigrant youth may want to maintain a connection with their parents and cultural tradition but not at the cost of full participation in society. Conversely, most want to identify with mainstream Canada as long as this does not entail wholesale abandonment of what makes them distinctive and authentic (Berry 2006). For some, engaging with the demands of opposing value systems is exciting and rewarding, but others find it confusing and frustrating. As aptly articulated by Puneet Parhar, "We grow up in the confusion of different morals, different values, and the fear of another culture" (quoted in Sandhu 2003).

Navigating Lived Identities in a Multicultural Context

Consider the promises and perils of growing up Canadian for a South Asian youth whose parents migrated to Canada in search of opportunity (Handa 2003; Fleras 2007d; Sodhi 2008). As is often the case, second-generation South Asian youth are better off than their parents – materially, socially, and mentally. Many are relatively free from the fears and frustrations that their parents endured, including an obligation to support family back home. They are also less likely to ruminate about the politics of belonging to Canada since most have no interest in relocating to their parents' homeland. Riad Saloojee, executive director of the Council on American-Islamic Relations in Canada, acknowledges an emergent and positive Muslim Canadian youth identity: "They see themselves as being firmly entrenched here. There are less emotional ties to the home country, in some cases none at all. They have a distinct Canadian and Muslim identity and many people see that as being perfectly compatible and harmonious" (quoted in Alan Martin 2004).

However, South Asian youth confront unique and baffling problems that their parents did not encounter. Growing up in a multicultural society is fraught with pitfalls and paradoxes in finding answers to the question of "Who am I?" (Ghuman 2003). Whereas parents may be secure in their personal and social identities because of a rootedness in tradition, their offspring may confront a bewildering host of choices as well as constraints and criticism. South Asian youth must constantly compare themselves to others in gaining acceptance and must worry about appeasing parents while saving face among peers (Johal 2003). They may have little choice but to compartmentalize language and culture by speaking English to friends but reverting to their heritage language at home. For some, this code switching is no problem, but others find it a nerve-racking affair.

Many of the challenges awaiting young South Asians arise from tensions between competitive value systems, primarily those of home and community versus those of school and society at large. The former emphasize the religion, culture, and tradition of the sending society, whereas the latter stress mainstream norms, beliefs, and values. One endorses customs and traditions such as extended family values or a preference for arranged marriages, whereas the other promotes a competitive and freewheeling individualism whose virtues are endorsed by parents as keys to success yet seen as threats to tradition. To be sure, the social conservatism of immigrant parents and their communities is difficult to assess (see Bricker and Ibbitson 2013). It may reflect a reaction to the loss of social routines and cultural certainties because of migration disruptions, resulting in contradictory demands on South Asian youth. These include deference to parents versus conformity to peer groups; the paradox of obedience (parents want them to obey and be deferential without losing their initiative and drive to succeed); retention of parental culture against the backdrop of Canadian expectations and normative standards; and coping with parental ambivalence toward success (be successful but not too successful if this eclipses a sense of who you are or where you came from).

Clearly, South Asian youth are caught on the horns of a dilemma. They are confronted by the sometimes conflicting challenges of integration and full participation in the host culture at the expense of losing their religious and cultural identities (see Alvi, Hoodfar, and McDonough 2003). They often wish to participate in activities, such as dating or parties, that frighten or repulse their parents. But they don't want to antagonize their parents through rash actions. Conflicts between parents and offspring are inevitable. Parents are perceived as out of touch with the realities that children encounter on a daily basis. Youth, by contrast, rarely consider their parents' experiences in a secular and liberal Canada that frequently devalues their skills, culture, and values. Parents, who often have little choice but to make sacrifices, sometimes project their hopes for success upon their children (Anisef and Kilbride 2003).

The end result is nothing short of confusing or infuriating. What constitutes proper behaviour is constantly compromised by mixed messages about irreconcilable differences between "the here" and "the over there" (Ghuman 2003). Youth identities must be negotiated in relation to "whiteness" as the normative reference point. South Asianness may be officially tolerated in Canada's multicultural matrix, but exhibiting too much difference may compromise mainstream acceptance. Yes, South Asians have the same rights as all Canadians. Yet they must exercise and negotiate these rights within contexts and rules that they did not create. The challenge lies in finding a middle or hyphenated way, one in which there is a fusion or synthesis of two cultures (hybrids) without discarding the realities of both.

Double Lives as Double Standards: South Asian Females

Not all South Asian youth confront the same obstacles. Girls tend to experience additional difficulties in negotiating identities because of differences in gender expectations between the home in which they live and the wider society in which they participate (Ghuman 2003; Tastsoglou 2008). Due to the double standards of a patriarchal society (Papp 2011), they do not enjoy the freedom of their brothers and boyfriends. South Asian families in Canada tend to be more indulgent with sons, even to the point of overlooking social taboos related to dating, curfews, partying, drinking, food preferences, and dress codes. Yet daughters and sisters, who are perceived as the custodians of culture and traditional morality, are expected to conform and must be protected from the polluting influence of the modern. Notions of female sexuality related to innocence, purity, and modesty in dress, behaviour, and body functions are employed as a proxy for marking the boundaries between the East and the West. Due to parental "paranoia," young South Asian women have less autonomy than their white classmates. Middle-class Canadian parents may routinely accept dating and premarital sex as part of their teen's maturing process, but South Asian parents condemn such behaviour, fearing sexually transmitted diseases, exploitation, family dishonour in the case of unwanted pregnancies, and difficulties in subsequently finding a suitable South Asian husband (Hai 2003).

The consequences of this protectiveness may prove awkward. To safeguard their reputations, young South Asian women must create a comfort zone in which they uphold family and community honour by the constant masking of truths (Handa 2003). South Asian codes of femininity and femalehood are narrowly prescribed, resulting in little wiggle room for crafting an identity that captures the complexities of living in a modern Canada. Yet peer pressures constantly urge immigrant youth to "move with the times." As one young South Asian woman put it, in dismissing the old-fashioned notion of saving virginity for marriage, "Sex is part of our culture now. Plus, there's a lot of pressure from the boys" (quoted in Hai 2003).

Double standards complicate life for South Asian girls. They must quickly learn what's acceptable for "good" daughters. They know that their behaviour, especially in sexual matters, will affect how they and their families are viewed by the community members who monitor their reputation and the family honour. Thus, they have little recourse but to wear masks, hide secrets, tell "white" lies, protect their reputations, and generally engage in subterfuge. Admittedly, they may feel guilty about lying, but as one 18-year-old commented, "We live in fear of upsetting our parents, but we have to get on with life. We can't become isolated like your generation was" (quoted in Hai 2003).

To say that they are experiencing an identity crisis is an understatement. Within a predominantly white context of power, inequality, and racism, they must construct identities that balance the modern with the traditional. They may have difficulty in achieving that balance – belonging to a particular religion and culture as citizens of a Canada that continues to harbour colonial perceptions about South Asia against the backdrop of extremism in the Muslim world (Alvi, Hoodfar, and McDonough 2003). Of course, no one said that growing up South Asian in Canada would be easy. But some have more difficulty than others in navigating the tricky shoals of becoming a hyphenated Canadian.

them into an ethnic corner (Scheffer 2010). They continue to experience barriers that deny or exclude, not because they are second-class citizens under the law, but because they must survive and succeed in a society that is organized along Eurocentric lines (Valverde 2012). Canada may not be overtly prejudiced, but it may practise a gentler version of benevolent racism that combines passive tolerance with politely coded biases (Henry and Tator 2010). Such mixed messages reflect badly on its reputation as an immigration society that abides by multiculturalism principles as a basis for living together with differences.

Economic fortunes related to income and employment levels have declined in recent years (Pendakur and Pendakur 2011; Jedwab 2012). Immigrants in general earn less than the Canadian-born, have lower employment rates, and are not compensated for foreign education or credentials (Javdani, Jacks, and Pendakur 2012). They once spent several years earning less than the average Canadian but would achieve or surpass the average over time (Ley and Hiebert 2001). For example, according to a special report by TD Economics (2012), within five years of their arrival during the 1970s, immigrants earned 80 percent of what Canadians earned. The gap was virtually closed after 20 years (Tal 2012). But those who arrived between 2000 and 2004 earned just 61 cents on the dollar relative to the Canadian-born, with the result that they faced the prospect of working their entire lives to match Canadian-born incomes. In a 2011 study by Statistics Canada utilizing data from the 2010 National Household Survey, male immigrants earned about $7,000 less than did Canadian-born males, whereas female immigrants earned, on average, $4,000 less than Canadian-born women. Male immigrants with university degrees earned almost $17,800 less than Canadian-born males, and female university graduates earned about $13,700 less than their Canadian counterparts. Furthermore, male immigrants who arrived between 2006 and 2010 with degrees earned $34,200 less than Canadian-born males; the figure for female immigrants with university degrees was $28,800 compared with Canadian-born females (Pathways to Prosperity 2014). Clearly, then, a distinction between recent and long-term immigrants yields different results. Newcomers also lost their jobs at more than three times the rate of Canadian-born workers during the Great Recession. Employment for the Canadian-born fell 1.6 percent between 2008 and 2009, compared to 5.7 percent for those who had

37

Economic Indicators: Recent Immigrants and Canadian-Born (ages 25-54), 2010

	Recent immigrants	Canadian-born
Percentage of unemployed	14.7%	6.1%
Employment rate percent	63.5%	82.4%
Average hourly earnings	$18.74	$25.04
Percentage of those with average earnings under $20/ hour	67.1%	37.9%

Source: Adapted from Jackson (2011), based on data provided to the Canadian Labour Congress by Statistics Canada.

lived in the country for five years or less. Newcomers who had lived in Canada for 10 years saw their employment level drop by 3 percent. Box 37 indicates gaps in economic status between recent immigrants (less than five years in Canada) and the Canadian-born.

Recent recessions suggest that immigrants suffer longer-lasting repercussions. Many have greater difficulty re-entering the labour force, even when the economy rebounds. For those who are compelled to accept jobs below their qualifications, the damage to careers may be permanent – a process called the "scarring effect" (Grant and Yang 2009). Others survive by participating in parallel (or informal) economic activities or by working under the table, often under substandard work conditions, including patterns of exploitation or harassment (Akter, Topkara-Sarsu, and Dyson 2013). As well, studies reveal the prevalence of employer discrimination against immigrants with foreign-sounding names or with overseas work experience (Oreopoulos 2009). In other words, foreign credentials matter. But employers are more interested in the competencies for which qualifications often serve as a proxy. Not surprisingly, the strongest predictors of economic success are neither credentials nor degrees but relative youth and proficiency in English or French (CIC 2012a; Derwing and Waugh 2012). And this goes beyond basic French or English skills in reading and writing to a level of sophistication and nuance for solving problems, working in teams, and deciphering coded workplace messages (Banting, Courchene, Seidle 2007).

Clearly, then, the picture is more complex than generally imagined. Age at immigration plays a key role. Individuals who came before the age of 18 have better labour market outcomes (Boulet and Bourdarbat 2010). For example, according to Statistics Canada (Black 2011), in terms of employment prospects and income levels, the children of immigrants are doing well, compared to those of Canadian-born parents. But the children of racialized immigrants are subject to a wage gap, particularly male blacks, who earn 20 percent less than the average wage (Picot and Sweetman 2012; also Kelly 2014). Studies indicate that immigrants with a university degree earn 29 percent less than their Canadian-born counterparts, whereas those without a degree experience only a 15 percent gap (Jedwab 2012). Admission categories seem to make a difference. Those who arrive as economic migrants (both male and female) consistently demonstrate the highest median annual income per category, prompting calls to reduce the size of this category during periods of economic decline and high unemployment (Abbott and Beach 2011). Those in the Federal Skilled Worker Program who are proficient in an official language are 50 percent more likely to find a job (and earn 40 percent more) than individuals in the program who do not speak English or French (Tal 2012). Evidence indicates that minorities with at least one degree from Canada and another from abroad have a significant income premium, even when compared to white immigrants with the same credentials. Immigrants of colour with only a foreign degree do poorly in comparison with similarly educated white immigrants who earn substantial returns on their schooling. In contrast, whites and non-whites who hold a Canadian university degree earn about the same, regardless of whether they are immigrants or Canadian-born (Alboim, Finnie, and Ming 2005; Lorne Foster 2012).

How are we to explain these disparities? Some argue that labour market conditions account for 40 percent of the decline in earnings since the 1980s (from local labour market supply and demand to diminishing returns on educational qualifications and overseas work

38

Median Earnings in Canada, 1995-2005

	1995	2000	2005
Canadian-born			
With university degree	$48,805	$50,668	$51,656
Without university degree	$30,526	$33,101	$32,499
Overall immigrant population			
With university degree	$40,394	$40,343	$36,451
Without university degree	$27,115	$29,142	$27,698
Immigrant arrivals			
With university degree	$24,368	$30,222	$24,643
Without university degree	$18,347	$20,840	$18,572

Sources: Adapted from Statistics Canada (2008b); Jedwab (2012).

experience to a mismatch of immigrant skills with the needs of a changing economy) and that 60 percent is related to the human capital of immigrants (from language skills to lack of Canadian experience) (Jedwab 2012). Others prefer an alternative narrative – if immigrants are doing badly, the fault is Canada's. Their credentials aren't recognized, they are held back by subtle discrimination, including insistence on Canadian experience, and so on. No doubt there's substantial truth to this claim as demonstrated by the following structural factors: the changing composition of immigrants; the racism that accompanies diversity; the inability of employers to evaluate foreign credentials and educational degrees (credential devaluation); the corresponding discounting of foreign skills because of more intense competition with Canadian-born workers (skills discounting); the lack of fit; and changes in the labour market because of economic globalization and knowledge-based economies (Biles and Burstein 2003; Lorne Foster 2012). Lower entry-level earnings for newcomers are determined as much by institutional structures and the protectionism of employers and professional bodies as by prejudicial attitudes and lack of immigrant human capital (Reitz 1998). Moreover, management may be unable to hire skilled workers with overseas experience due to collective agreements that insist on "in-house" seniority when filling positions (James 2005).

Whatever the reasons, the consequences are unacceptable: Immigrants are pivotal to Canada's growth and innovation. They bring enthusiasm, energy, skills, and connections. But achieving success in a post-industrial knowledge-based economy isn't easy without sophisticated language skills, along with knowledge of social networks, that often elude the grasp of newcomers (Wente 2010). Yet mishandling the diversity dividend is both counterproductive and counterintuitive (Deloitte 2011). Immigrants are robbed of what they can offer to Canada; Canadians, in turn, are shortchanged in terms of immigrant talents, optimism, and linkages. Clearly, a rethinking is required.

WOMEN AS IMMIGRANTS, IMMIGRANTS AS WOMEN: ENGENDERING THE EXPERIENCE

> *Failure to understand immigrants as gendered subjects who are differently located with respect to identity construction, experiences, and opportunity and outcomes is seriously flawed.*
>
> — EVANGELIA TASTSOGLOU, BRIAN RAY, AND VALERIE PRESTON (2005)

The study of immigration and immigrants has historically ignored gender as a key variable throughout the transitioning process (Vickers and de Sève 2000; Willis and Yeoh 2000; Lutz 2010 but see Piper 2008). Immigrants were assumed to be gender-neutral beings with respect to legal positions (entry status and citizenship), migratory patterns, and settlement concerns (from family reunification to employment prospects). Both policies and studies focused on the male migrant as the norm or standard, thus reinforcing a perception of migrant women as maternal-domestic dependants or male extensions (as wife, daughter, or sister) rather than as active agents in their own right (Bach 2009; CIC 2012a). A tendency to aggregate data on immigrants further obscured the realities of female migrants, thus buttressing the gender bias in both scholarship and public policies (Freedman 2012).

Such an omission was puzzling; after all, immigration and immigrants are neither gender-neutral nor gender-passive. The lives and life chances of migrant women are fundamentally gendered by way of asymmetrical relations, conflicting identities, diverse experiences, and differential outcomes (Boyd and Pikkov 2008). Immigrant and refugee women experience reality differently than their male counterparts with respect to behaviour, opportunities, family circumstances, risks and challenges, and vulnerabilities to violence and discrimination (Caritas Internationalis 2010), in the main because of who they are, what they want and need, and where they stand in the wider scheme of things (Epp, Iacovetta, and Swyripa 2004; Boyd 2006; Piper and French 2011). Racialized immigrant and refugee women experience reality differently than their white counterparts because they are uniquely located with respect to the devalued statuses of race, class, and ethnicity (Fleras 2012b). Finally, despite commonalities due to racism and discrimination, immigrant and refugee women differ from racialized women of colour because of their status as "outsiders within." A belated recognition of these differences within differences is taking hold. Hondagneu-Sotelo (2003, 9) captures this surge in scholarly interest:

> Research is beginning to look at the extent to which gender permeates a variety of practices, identities, and institutions implicated in immigration. Here, patterns of labor incorporation, globalization, religious practices and values, ethnic enclave businesses, citizenship, sexuality, and ethnic identity are interrogated in ways that reveal how gender is incorporated into a myriad of daily operations and institutional political and economic structures.

Feminist scholarship has exposed the gendered assumptions that historically informed both patterns of immigration and immigrant realities. That alone makes it doubly important to understand immigrants as gendered subjects who are differently located with respect to identity construction, lived experiences, and opportunity (Tastsoglou, Ray, and Preston 2005). Prioritizing gender as a key explanatory variable in defining immigration and immigrant experiences puts the onus on dual obligations. First, we must examine the politics of immigration through the conceptual lens of gendered immigrants but we must also scrutinize the politics of gender through the prism of immigration as program and dynamic. Second, we must determine how gender intersects with immigration to create interlocking systems of inequality and we must also explore how immigration intersects with gender to intensify differing processes and unequal outcomes. According to this line of reasoning, gender intersects with immigration to shape women's incorporation into a system of global capitalism and an international division of labour. It also interacts with other axes of identification in shaping women's migratory experiences and relations in both host and sending countries, and it defines the complex ways in which migrant women accommodate, resist, and engage with gendered institutions and values as individuals and in groups (Gaetano and Yeoh 2010).

The gender concept is now well established as a constitutive element of international migration (Nawyn 2010; Palmary et al. 2010; Gu 2012). Gender is essential to understanding the causes, characteristics, and consequences of international migration (Piper 2008; Pierce 2011). Migration is a gendered process in the sense that women (a) confront certain barriers along the migratory movement, from departure to settlement and integration, (b) must negotiate the private-public continuum, and (c) must construct, deconstruct, and reconstruct notions of identity, belonging, and boundaries (Tastsoglou 2011). Policies and programs, as well as laws and theories of citizenship and sovereignty, must grapple with the politics of gender – that is, with how gender-based biases influence the conceptualization and implementation of rights, opportunities, and burdens (Benhabib and Resnik 2009). Migration affects men and women differently (Ray and Damaris 2012), as the Strategic Workshop (2002) explains:

> Migration affects women and men differently depending on the context (social, political, cultural) of the migration decision, the migration journey itself, as well as the settlement experience. Not only does gender differentiate physical movements across borders, but gender relations also are reaffirmed, negotiated, and reconfigured in their transnational contexts. Gendered processes also lead to differences in people's interactions with settlement and other service delivery institutions. They may also lead to divergent interests in return migration.

Gender as a key determinant of migration patterns is also driven by the demand for female labour, from caregivers to sex-trade workers. For example, Canada once offered "entertainer" visas for women from Asia or Europe to work as exotic dancers – a practice that was conducive to exploitation and abuse (Goldring, Berinstein, and Bernhard 2007). Women may migrate in hopes of escaping dependency, especially in societies with culturally restrictive traditions and social conditions (Segal, Mayadas, and Elliott 2006). Their decision to leave may reflect exposure to violence, from domestic abuse to persecution (from female genital mutilation to so-called honour killings), together with a government's unwillingness or incapacity to protect them. In addition, immigration laws and policies affect women and men differently, resulting in both gendered patterns of immigration and gendered outcomes. The feminist turn in migration studies also recognizes the centrality of changing gender roles as women increasingly take the initiative to migrate.

Modes of entry into Canada are gendered as well (Boyd and Pikkov 2008). Recent research highlights the gendered dynamics underlying Canada's admission requirements (criteria for entry tend to favour male domains and qualifications [CRIAW 2003]), access to skills training and employment, and definitions of family and sponsorship (Hyndman 1999). Historically, women arrived as the wives or dependants of the men who sponsored them (CRIAW 2003); in recent years, however, they are much more likely to be admitted as autonomous labour migrants, highly skilled professionals, or primary "breadwinners" whose status is beyond that of "dependants" or "spouses" (Khoo, Hugo, and McDonald 2008; CIC 2013b). Settlement programs for integrating immigrants into society also differ along gender lines as eligibility may be restricted to the (presumably male) head of the household (or breadwinner). Yet rules that bar persons from sponsoring family members to Canada tend to disproportionately disadvantage women, given their socio-economic status, although they are most in need of family support and networks (CRIAW 2003). Female migrants also encounter a gender-stratified labour market that diminishes their credentials and expertise, and pervasive stereotypes cast them as suitable only for "women's work" (Khoo, Hugo, and McDonald 2008; McDonald and Worswick 2010). The conclusion is unavoidable: The politics, policies, and practices of immigration are gendered, as gender intersects with other social indicators and devalued markers of identity such as class and race to create complex systems of inclusion and exclusion that cut across origin, transitional, and destination societies (Piper 2008).

In short, gender permeates a variety of dimensions in immigration. Those who ignore it as an explanatory variable do so at their own peril, for failure to acknowledge its centrality compromises our understanding of the immigration process. The growing feminization of migration has intensified this fact. Between 2002 and 2011, women represented slightly more than half of all new permanent residents in Canada (CIC 2012a). In most admission categories, the balance between male and female entrants is close, including the economic class, with the exception of the family class (58 percent are women), the Live-in-Caregiver Program (97 percent are women), and those who apply as principal economic migrants (41 percent are women). For example, in 2012 (CIC 2013b), female permanent residents outnumbered male admissions (131,430 to 126,457), and 59.4 percent of them arrived via the economic class (both as principal applicants and as dependants), compared to 62.4 percent of the men. Even the Temporary Foreign Worker Program is experiencing a gender shift. Between 2001 and 2009, the proportion of female temporary foreign workers increased from 25 percent to 41.4 percent (CIC 2012a).

The emergent reality of gender as social variable and immigration discourse is paying dividends. In response to a challenge by the 1995 Beijing Platform on Women, Ottawa endorsed a policy-making commitment to gender equality (Fleras and Maaka 2009). Its gender-based analysis (GBA) framework compels federal departments and agencies to assess the impact of relevant legislation to women (NWAC 2004). GBA focuses on detecting and correcting systemic biases in government policies and programs, thus ensuring that women have a key role in designing and coordinating meaningful and inclusive participation in line with the principles of democratic and participatory governance. Acknowledging the significant differences in the social location of men and women reinforces that policy cannot be divorced from social context. A GBA framework examines existing and proposed policies to ensure that they produce fair results (CIC 2008). It is proactively applied to the policy-making process and is not a reactive add-on after the fact. As a result, attention is directed at outcomes and outlooks as well as concepts and language for putting gender back into the big picture. GBA assesses the impact of proposed policies on women and men, and responds with options and strategies.

Take, for example, how Health Canada (2000) formally incorporated the principles of GBA, seeking to understand and correct the ways in which biases within the health care system affected the health of women (and men). Its implementation of a dual-track GBA (one centred on women, the other on gender differences) to improve health impacts for women proved empowering. It resulted in a principled approach to developing policies, programs, and legislation; conducting research and data collection; and day-to-day planning and operations in the hopes of identifying the conditions, inequities, and experiences that affect women's health status and their access to, and interaction with, the health system. The decision to apply a dual-track approach is not without justification, when it comes to evaluating health outcomes. Prior to approval of a new drug in Canada, manufacturers must scientifically prove its safety through clinical trials. Historically, however, the trials have tended to use male subjects. Women were excluded to avoid risks and because of research complications related to reproductive biology. This omission (or methodological bias) put women at risk because the male-only findings were applied to them. The approval of new drugs also exhibited a gender bias by uncritically incorporating male bodies as the tacitly assumed norm for measuring health research and treatment options. To offset any systemic gendered bias against women's unique experiences and biologies, Health Canada (2000) now insists that both genders are included in clinical trials (unless the drug is intended for one gender only), in the process securing both better science and safer treatment.

Passage of the 2002 Immigration and Refugee Protection Act (IRPA) prompted Citizenship and Immigration Canada (CIC) to commit to a GBA of its policies and programs – the 2005 Strategic Framework for Gender-Based Analysis (CIC 2012a). In the context of the IRPA, the GBA constituted an evidence-based assessment that incorporated gender and diversity considerations related to the impact of policies, programs, and services on women and girls (as well as men and boys). It recognized the following truths: (a) that equal opportunity within unequal contexts does not always lead to equal results; (b) that female differences will be ignored or devalued in a male-dominated world; and (c) that any move toward inclusion must incorporate the intersection of gender with other diversity factors and identity markers (ibid.). The CIC's strategic framework was in place until 2010, and a new policy on GBA was launched in 2011, which applies to all facets of CIC business, from policy development to program implementation. For example, a GBA was conducted to assist in the design of selection criteria for the new Canadian Experience Class to determine their differing impacts on men and women. As a result of the analysis, the minimum work experience requirements were adjusted to include an equivalent accumulation of part-time labour (based on the premise that women had difficulty in obtaining full-time continuous employment because of pregnancy, childcare responsibilities, and the care of elderly parents). GBA identified additional areas of concern with respect to differential gender, including minimum language requirements (women may not have equal access to language training) or full-time study requirements (CIC 2009b). Clearly, then, immigration is a gendered experience, and failure to take engendered immigrants into account does a disservice by excluding half of humanity as agents of action, change, and outcome.

FRAMING IMMIGRATION, MEDIATIZING IMMIGRANT EXPERIENCES

Of those factors that influence the quality of immigrant experiences, few can match the mainstream media. Positive coverage of newcomers creates a warmer welcoming mat, whereas negative reporting generates a more frosty reception. Nowhere is this ambivalence more tellingly expressed than in news media coverage of immigrants and immigration (Fryberg et al. 2012; also Spoonley and Bedford 2012; Chan 2014). According to Rodney Benson (2010), news media coverage of immigrants employs ten recurrent frames: three victim frames (global economic injustice, humanitarian violations, racism/xenophobia), three hero frames (cultural diversity, integration, and good workers), and four threat frames (job threat, public order/illegal/security threat, fiscal threat, and national identity/culture threat). Nevertheless, a steady diet of stereotypes and distortions heightens public anxieties and fears associated with negative media coverage (Chan 2014):

> First, mainstream media often portray newcomers with broad brush strokes, employing sensationalist and simplistic frames (Hennebry and Momani 2013). But migration is a complex and changing issue

that needs balanced and accurate coverage, if only to foster democratic debate while smoothing Canada's welcome mat (Blion 2011;
Dujisin 2011).

> Second, coverage is conditional (Inouye 2012): "Good" immigrants
are presented as positive contributors to Canadian society, and "bad"
immigrants and refugee claimants are labelled as troublesome constituents who create costly or inconvenient problems (Sakamoto et al.
2013). News media portray immigrants as threats to mainstream values and practices (Bauder 2008c; Fleras 2010; Bradimore and Bauder
2011). Immigration programs and the asylum process come across as
dysfunctional, prone to abuse, badly out of touch with contemporary
realities, and in desperate need of repair.

> Third, immigrants make headlines when they are associated with
crime or controversy, crisis or catastrophe, in the process reinforcing
negative stereotypes or generating public ill-will (Chan 2014). Paradoxically, those who comply and cooperate receive only token coverage, or none at all, in the process privileging the logic of negativity as
the preferred discourse ("only bad news is good news") (Suro 2008).

Negative news media frames are anything but harmless or innocent. Framing as a process for organizing information encourages a
preferred reading in (a) defining what counts as a problem or what
problems count; (b) restricting the range of issues to be debated
(whose voices will be heard and whose will be silenced); and (c) proposing solutions to problems (Lakoff and Ferguson 2006; Timberlake
and Williams 2012). Yasmin Jiwani (2012b) explains the potency of
media framing like this:

> As a major institution in society, the media play a crucial role.
> They provide us with definitions about who we are as a nation;
> they reinforce our values and norms; they give us concrete
> examples of what happens to those who transgress these norms;
> and most importantly they perpetuate certain ways of seeing the
> world and peoples within the world ... [They also] provide with
> images of prescription and description. They tell us how society
> sees us and at the same time, tell us how to behave in society.
> They promote a notion of consensus ... Through coverage of those
> that deviate from the consensus, we are constantly presented with
> the threat of a lawless society where chaos could reign.

The filtering of immigrants and refugees through the discourses of negativity (Sakamoto et al. 2013) emphasizes their ambivalent status as the outsiders within (Jiwani 2006). That kind of agenda-setting power reinforces the importance of analyzing news media coverage, especially in terms of brokering relations between Canada and new Canadians (also Spoonley and Butcher 2009). Does the coverage of immigrants and refugees improve their chances of settlement, accept-ance, and integration? Or does it undermine their self-esteem as vulnerable persons in search of safety or opportunity (DiversiPro 2007; Murray 2009, 681; Fleras 2011c)? Do mainstream news media have a responsibility to foster the integration of immigrants in a multi-cultural Canada that claims to be inclusive? If yes, should the media facilitate integration through supportive coverage, resocializing the mainstream toward positive acceptance, or offsetting negative coverage by emphasizing commonalities and/or positives? If no, what constitutes the ideal (accurate and impartial) in defining what to cover and how? Who decides and on what grounds?

To date, assessments of the news media role in setting the immigra-tion agenda have fluctuated. For some, the news media discharge their responsibilities fairly and objectively in shaping public discourses. For others, however, the flames of intolerance are fanned by news stories that conflate immigrants and refugees with illegality, crisis and con-troversy, and program failure (Metropolis Presents 2004; Suro 2008). But the real issue is not media coverage per se. More accurately, it's the public perceptions and political reactions that are derived from "mediatizing" immigrants and immigration (Adeyanju 2011). Indeed, what most Canadians know about immigrants and immigration rarely comes from first-hand experience. For many, the media are the primary or preliminary source of information about the world (also Georgiou 2012). Such a status exerts pressure on the news media to portray im-migrants beyond the themes of security, danger, and illegality. Both informed public debate and sound policy decisions depend on such a commitment in advancing an inclusive multicultural society (Lakoff and Ferguson 2006; Bauder 2008c). Yet neither consensus nor con-viction are in abundance for improving the representational basis of news media-newcomer relations.

Clearly, therefore, news media coverage of immigration and immi-grants is prone to paradox. The media are known to play contradictory roles in securing an imagined national community in terms of who belongs (Bourbeau 2011). Yet they also provide spaces that foster diversity and multiple identities, while galvanizing attention and mobilizing activity (Cottle 2005; d'Haenens and Mattelart 2011). But news framing can prove deceptive. To the extent that it exists, coverage tends to be piecemeal, without much context, crisis-driven, and long on generalizations and stereotypes (James Adams 2013). Not surprisingly, coverage is accused of selectiveness (Surette 2007). For example, violent crime receives more attention than property crime, even though the latter predominates in police data. Other critics accuse the news media of transforming the least common aspects of criminality and criminal justice into the most enduring images (Fleras 2003; Perlmutter 2000). This misrepresentational bias has become even more accentuated in light of the ever shorter, more intense, and more competitive news cycles that are popularized by cable television and the Internet (see Suro 2009). Misinformation comes with costs: When the media celebrate immigrant pageantry or denounce immigrant criminality, with little else in between, they perform a disservice in mishandling the lived experiences of migrants and minorities.

Similarly, the American and European news media have tended to mischaracterize the politics of immigration and the nature of immigrants (Geissler and Pottker 2005; Suro 2008). The public is conditioned to seeing immigration in negative terms, a process that contributes to polarization and distrust (Akdenizli, Dionne, and Suro 2008). For example, a computer-aided analysis of fifty-eight thousand news stories that appeared in Britain's 20 national dailies and Sunday newspapers between 2010 and 2012 noted that "illegal" was the most common modifier of the word "immigrants" and that "failed" was the most common modifier of "asylum seeker" (Migration Observatory 2013). In reality, however, most migrants arrive through legal channels, want to make new lives without public fanfare, and have achieved a modicum of success in their new homeland. Yet news coverage fails to keep pace, preferring instead to traffic in conflict, negativity, and the abnormal. Coverage is invariably patchy and episodic rather than contextual and thematic, and is fixated on human interest stories involving drama and spectacle (Suro 2009). Dominant narratives focus on the actions of individuals, law enforcement, and policy makers at the expense of contextual factors that influence the movement of people in search of escape or opportunity. The depiction of immigration as a sudden crisis reflects and reinforces practices that are deeply ingrained in the news media's foundational principles (ibid.).

News media coverage of immigrants and immigration reflects an ideological shift. Minorities and migrants are no longer criticized on the basis of physical inferiority (race). They are more likely to be critiqued as culturally inferior or socially deviant for violating mainstream values. A categorical dislike is replaced by a situational dislike, which is grounded in the premise that newcomers are culturally incompatible or socially uncontrollable (Liu and Mills 2006). A politely racialized discourse identifies and rationalizes patterns of bias, exclusion, and discrimination. Glaring inconsistencies abound because of racialized messages that "normalize invisibility," while "problematizing visibility" (Henry and Tator 2002). To one side is the problem of underrepresentation – a tendency to normalize the invisibility of migrants and minorities in domains that count (politics or business). To the other side is an overrepresentational inclination to problematize visibility in areas that don't count (crime or welfare dependency). Migrants and minorities are inferiorized by association with negative news contexts, including (a) crime, public disorder, and deviance; (b) their so-called reverse discrimination against whites; (c) religious fundamentalism; (d) home country troubles; and (e) asylum seekers and illegal immigration as security risks (Cottle 2005; ter Wal, d'Haenens, and Koeman 2005). Such racism-by-association inflates minority overrepresentation in problematic domains, while deflating immigrant presence in positive stories (Perigoe 2006). In some cases, this bias is deliberate (systematic institutional bias). In other instances, it is simply part of the normal functioning of the news media rather than a conscious attempt to deny or defame (systemic institutionalized bias).

Yet a blanket condemnation is unwarranted. Consider the paradoxes of sorting out "good" Asian immigrants from "bad" ones (Sakamoto et al. 2013). The former embrace capitalist and liberal values by exerting themselves and establishing productive families that contribute to communities and to the nation. Dedicated to their new home and successful within it, they legitimize the myths and virtues of meritocracy. The failure of bad Asian immigrants is individualized instead of being framed as structural or systemic. They are thought to exploit the generosity of the nation and are accused of creating social divisions by remaining loyal to their homeland/ethnoculture by cloistering themselves in enclaves. Hijun Park (2011, 646) describes the ambivalence at play in media coverage of model minorities:

> Asians are admired for their perceived economic efficiency and intelligence and feared for their frugality and cunning; revered for their exceptional work ethic and vilified as unknowable due to their inhuman inability to withstand hardship; respected for their family values and perpetually suspect due to their fierce loyalty to home, ethnic community, and foreign nation. Rather than being perceived in an either/or linear dichotomy, Asians can be both good and bad as they bolster national mythologies while simultaneously endangering the status quo.

Let's put this into perspective: Migrants and minorities continue to be ignored, stereotyped, and miniaturized by negative images that distort who they are and what they want (Weston 2003). This negative portrayal is based on the actions of a few malcontents or extremists. Paradoxically, despite accusations of media racism and racist coverage, they do not necessarily suffer from news stories that are deliberately misleading, slanted, or malevolent (van Dijk 1991, 2011; Henry and Tator 2002; Mahtani, Henry, and Tator 2008). To the contrary, they must endure coverage that is systemically biased because of a business model that purports to treat everyone in the same manner (negatively) regardless of the impact on the vulnerable. A controlling/biasing effect is created precisely because of the one-size-fits-all preoccupation with the negative as quintessentially newsworthy. Admittedly, this focus is not confined to minority coverage. Newsworthiness in general reinforces the notion that "only bad news is good news" (also ter Wal, d'Haenens, and Koeman 2005). But the framing of vulnerable migrants and minorities in exclusively negative terms exerts a significant impact, primarily because they lack the institutionalized power to deflect or to neutralize a pro-white discourse about what is normal and who is acceptable.

A similar assessment can be applied to Canada (Fleras 2003). Like other institutions, Canada's mainstream media are bound by a multicultural commitment to institutional inclusion (to ensure that no one is excluded for reasons beyond their control). Until recently, however, the media misfired in this respect. Depictions of migrants and minorities were openly racist and demeaning because of unbalanced and biased coverage, resulting in defamatory images and derogatory assessments of new and racialized Canadians (Fleras and Kunz 2001; Mahtani 2002; Jiwani 2006). A media fixation with the sordid and the sensational obscured the normal and the routine. Notwithstanding modest improvements in reporting, racialized minorities and Aboriginal people remain vulnerable to questionable coverage in which they are (a) miniaturized as irrelevant or inferior, often by being placed solely in sports or entertainment stories; (b) demonized as a social menace; (c) scapegoated as the source of all problems; (d) othered for being too different or not different enough; (e) refracted through the prism of Eurocentric fears and fantasies; and (f) caricatured by exposure to double standards that lampoon them regardless of what they do or didn't do. All of this simply fortifies the exclusion and demonization of immigrants as the other within (Mahtani 2008; Hennebry and Momani 2013).

In short, immigrants are harshly victimized by questionable media coverage (O'Doherty and Augoustinos 2008; also Saunders 2012a; Chan 2014). They are routinely framed as posing security risks, stealing jobs, cheating on the welfare system, clogging public services, creating congestion and crowding, compromising Canada's quality of life, exploiting its generosity, engaging in crime, and imperilling national unity (see Li 2003). Admittedly, Canadian news coverage may be more progressive (muted) than that of the British tabloids, which routinely sensationalize and scandalize. The Canadian media are loathe to openly criticize migrants or government minority policy for fear of disturbing a national consensus or arousing a chilly reaction (Masood 2007). They avoid explicitly vilifying immigrants, often by downplaying race or religion when they are unnecessary to the story, while emphasizing the loyalty and law-abidingness of most members of a devalued group (Silk 2008). Nevertheless, any positive emphasis on the economic, demographic, and cultural utility of model migrants cannot offset the preponderance of negative coverage. Seemingly neutral language disguises dislike through snide asides ("jumping the queue"), mocking references ("Allah of the people"), politely coded subtexts ("those people"), and "fish out of water" stories (consider how a positive story involving the racialized inhabitants of Toronto's Jane-Finch area may perversely serve as a reminder of how bad things really are).

Asylum seekers and refugees are no less negatively framed. Not all of them, of course. Those who flee repressive regimes (from communism to Islamic countries) are perceived as deserving because they confirm Canada's moral superiority and progressiveness (see Jenicek, Wong, and Lee 2009). In contrast, bad refugees are stigmatized as cheating or manipulating their way into Canada. Their labelling as problem people is compounded by a fascination with illegal entries, security risks, and the corresponding costs of processing and settlement (Hier and Greenberg 2002). But news media preoccupation with undocumented refugees is selective. It fixates on the immediate or precipitating causes of refugee movements rather than the root causes – global inequality, structural adjustments, ethnic conflict, environmental destruction, and human rights abuses. It also glosses over the traumas of seeking asylum, the difficulties and dangers in securing a passage to Canada, and the perils of adjusting to a new and complex environment. Exaggerated and negative coverage of bad refugees may not intend to invoke public fears and hostilities, but the process of making newsworthy news may lead to such results (also Wilkes, Corrigall-Brown, and Ricard 2010). Thus, an already edgy public may be stampeded into supporting policies and programs that serve elite interests or intensify state surveillance (Hier and Greenberg 2002; Chan 2014).

MUNICIPALITIES AND IMMIGRANT EXPERIENCES: LAYING DOWN THE WELCOME MAT

Cities around the world are now central nodes of economic growth and immigrant settlement (about half the world's population currently lives in cities). Because immigrants tend to integrate into communities first and with society later, municipal governments, agencies, social groups, infrastructures (from schools to libraries), and civic organizations are more influential than ever in shaping their integration and inclusion (Ray 2003; Perrault 2009; Tossutti 2012; Vineberg 2012; Tolley et al. 2013). Cities and municipalities have increasingly assumed responsibilities for securing immigrant-friendly environments, despite the fact that many national and sub-national governments do not have a specific urban policy agenda. Many urban management techniques have been introduced, from policing to housing to transportation, that secure positive outcomes for newcomers through initiatives that are not normally associated with immigration integration programs. Cities and municipalities are also responsible for organizing and regulating the routine aspects of urban life that affect newcomer experiences. These include enforcing building codes, managing social housing, ensuring public transportation, and supporting fledgling immigrant community centres and daycares. In other words, cities are sites of the seemingly mundane concerns that rarely attract national policy attention but are nonetheless influential in shaping the adjustment experience.

What is globally true is no less applicable to Canada. Its social health, economic prosperity, and political future may depend on its ability to attract and integrate immigrants (Kenney 2012d). Increasingly diverse communities confront a raft of challenges in co-existing with cultural diversities, managing inter-ethnic interaction among groups and institutions, establishing public spaces for positive encounters between groups, and dealing with inequities and discrimination in access to public services (see also Kymlicka and Walker 2012). Questions arise with respect to integrating newcomers: Should municipalities develop differentiated programs and adapt their services in response to newcomer needs? Or should newcomers be the recipients of universal services that apply to everyone? That responses to these questions are varied adds to the uncertainty.

Cities remain the destination of choice for most immigrants. The quality of their welcome is key to their adjustment. Nor should anyone be surprised that the size and structure of cities differentially affect immigrant experiences and outcomes (Frideres 2006). But newcomers increasingly opt for smaller towns (Tolley et al. 2013), a "regionalization of immigrants" that spells demographic doom for the MTV cities of Montreal, Toronto, and Vancouver: In 2001, they attracted 77 percent of all newcomers and 63 percent in 2011 (Statistics Canada 2013). By contrast, Calgary, Winnipeg, and Edmonton saw their share double from 7.4 percent to 14 percent. Provincial rates have varied as well. Ontario receives the largest number of newcomers; as a result, its cities remain a hub of diversity (Andrew et al. 2013). But a shift is discernible. Ontario accounted for nearly 60 percent of immigrants in 2001 but for only 40 percent in 2012, whereas Manitoba, New Brunswick, and Saskatchewan more than doubled their share (Federation of Canadian Municipalities 2011). To assist in enhancing settlement by connecting newcomers to community services and language- and job

39 CASE STUDY

Doing Immigration Integration the "Waterloo Way"

WATERLOO REGION IS a prosperous and progressive community.* Located just west of Toronto and home to RIM/Blackberry, it is Canada's fifth largest in terms of foreign-born per capita, with newcomers in 2011 accounting for 23.1 percent of its 550,000-plus population, according to the National Household Survey. Like other communities across Canada, Waterloo Region is increasingly reliant on an immigrant workforce to enhance productivity, innovation, and entrepreneurship. But its immigrants underperform its general labour force: in 2001, 14 percent of recent immigrants in the Waterloo Region were unemployed, compared to 5 percent of the Canadian-born. Newcomer underemployment is also a problem despite generally higher educational levels. Many work in survival jobs (low-paying, part-time, and menial) that underutilize their skills, and others return home in desperation or move to other jurisdictions for opportunity. The paradox is unmistakable: a depleting pool of skilled workers is offset by under-resourced migrant labour, even though municipal prosperity depends on the productivity of engaged newcomers (Maytree Foundation 2011).

Waterloo Region has introduced a series of initiatives and services to improve its integration agenda (Jantzen, Roberts, and Ochocka 2013; Reyes, Walton-Roberts, and Hennebry 2013). The Waterloo Region Immigration Partnership (WRIP) provides a community-wide collaborative strategy for the settlement of newcomers. It assumed that successful settlement and integration entailed a mutually beneficial process of learning, communication, and adjustment. It focused on what it called "the Power of Three": (a) settle (short-term transitional needs, from interpreters to housing to accessing/understanding needed services and systems), (b) work (finding work consistent with skills and education), and (c) belong (a more long-term process leading to integration and involvement in the community). Fostering newcomer placement in a more inclusive Waterloo Region also entailed a different set of collaborative strategies, including improving access and coordination of services and programs, enhancing access to the employment market, and bolstering the region's capacity to integrate increased numbers of people.

Creating general support groups such as the Immigrant Support Working Group provided a good start. The Waterloo Region is also exploring ways to connect employers with immigrant workers in the hope of utilizing immigrant skill sets to offset shortages of skilled workers in its high-tech-driven economy. In 2002, interested stakeholders (funders, education, governments, community-based organizations, and new Canadians) began collaborating on a cross-sectoral basis to forge a region-wide response to immigrant employment issues (Jantzen, Roberts, and Ochocka 2013). The Waterloo Region Immigrant Employment Network (WRIEN, pronounced "Ryan" and modelled somewhat after Toronto's TRIEC program [Hepburn 2014]) espouses three objectives: strong lives, strong economy, and strong and inclusive communities. Proposed outcomes incorporated the following goals: (a) provide immigrants with networking skills, (b) promote a credential recognition and assessment program of relevance to both employers and newcomers, (c) ensure that employers attract immigrants with the appropriate skills and expertise for the local labour market, (d) secure enhanced regional service delivery and immigrant support groups, (e) improve effectiveness and collaboration through reliable data collection, and (f) assist employers in hiring immigrants and integrating them into the workplace (ibid.).

WRIEN's preliminary results have been encouraging. These include (a) a collaborative governance model that facilitates the cooperation of six stakeholder segments and broad-based community engagement; (b) increased resources for labour market integration initiatives; (c) enhanced region-wide advocacy on behalf of immigrant workers and better lobbying of senior governments; (d) a planned or implemented mentorship program, internship program, employer engagement strategy, web portal for the Waterloo Region, and immigrant loan program to verify foreign credentials; (e) a partnership-in-programming initiative that prompts stakeholders to assume sustained leadership and responsibility for each initiative, with a corresponding commitment to connect across a different nexus of stakeholders beyond the three-year mandate of WRIEN (extended indefinitely beyond 2009), and (f) an awareness that finding local solutions to problems not only increases the probability of successful outcomes, but also enhances the "worth" of the welcome.

* The Conference Board of Canada in its report, *City Magnets III: Benchmarking the Attractiveness of 50 Canadian Cities,* 18 September 2014, assigned an *A* to Waterloo as one of the six most attractive Canadian cities for newcomers to live in.

training, Ontario's Immigration Strategy's Newcomer Settlement Program provides support for 98 organizations across the province.

Municipalities with large immigrant populations are experiencing pressure to accommodate their settlement and integration (ibid.; CCMARD 2012; Tossutti 2012; Andrew et al. 2013; Fong, Chiang, and Denton 2013). Municipal social and community services must respond to immigration-generated demographic changes by ensuring the availability, accessibility, and appropriateness of programs (that are reflective, respectful, and responsive to minority needs) related to income and employment support, poverty reduction strategies, housing, childcare, community development, and neighbourhood building. Clearly, immigrants depend on a much broader range of services than are provided by federal and provincial governments – namely, orientation, language training, and employment.[2] Their top priorities include proximity to family and friends, homeownership (or at least a decent place to live), establishment of community-affirming organizations, employment prospects, and affordable and reliable public transportation, some of which tie into municipal services. And when they don't succeed, local services such as shelters and food banks take on added importance (Federation of Canadian Municipalities 2011).

However critical their role, municipalities confront a conflict of interest. They want to attract and integrate newcomers, but many lack the revenue base to do so. For example, migrants increasingly settle in suburbs rather than inner cities, yet many suburban neighbourhoods possess neither the experience nor the resources to manage cross-cultural relations and to foster social and economic inclusion (Ray

2003). Federal immigration programs tend to ignore the input of municipalities when setting urban agendas, despite their front-line status for newcomers (Vrbanovic 2011). In funding settlement services to permanent residents (generally for three years after arrival), Ottawa allocates just under $600 million annually to provinces and territories, but the 250,000 temporary foreign workers and those in the foreign student class receive none of it, even though they depend on municipal services for housing, public transit, leisure, and libraries (Federation of Canadian Municipalities 2011).

In short, cities and municipalities are the preliminary and primary point of contact for newcomer settlement and integration. Of necessity, and in recognition of the value of immigrants, they must budget for their needs. Yet they must dig ever deeper to meet the growing demand for services (ibid.). Despite this financial crunch, they rarely play a pivotal role in policy making or the funding allocations that affect them directly. Clearly, if some kind of robust partnership arrangement with the federal government is not reached, their role in integrating immigrants will remain contested (Vrbanovic 2011).

9

integrating immigrants

INCLUSIVE MULTICULTURALISM
AS IMMIGRANT GOVERNANCE

THE PARADOXES OF CANADA'S MULTICULTURALISM

THE INTERPLAY OF immigration and multiculturalism yields the notion of Canada as an immigration society of immigrants. Canada is composed of distinct cultures who live in shared social spaces of mutual tolerance, with a corresponding distaste for open violence and a respect for the rule of law, the primacy of politics for dispute resolution, and a proclivity for complex and unconventional political arrangements to accommodate these diversities (Letourneau 2013). But the remarkable transformation of Canadian society along immigrant lines poses a challenge – namely, balancing immigrant accommodation and integration with social cohesion, liberal-democratic values, and national unity (Ferguson, Langlois, and Roberts 2009; Seidle 2013). Former immigration minister Jason Kenney (2010) captures a sense of the challenges in store for his government:

> I want to see an integrated society based on active and engaged citizens, not a series of separated ethnocultural silos. I want Canadians, whether they have been here for a few months or all of their lives, to embrace our shared values, our shared history, and institutions. I want newcomers to integrate into our proud and democratic Canadian society and I want us all to work together

to invest in and help strengthen the prosperity of a country that continues to attract newcomers.

Needless to say, Canada shares many of the same unity challenges as other countries. No one should underestimate what's entailed in transforming a culturally diverse range of newcomers into a community of consensus, conviction, cohesion, and commitment (Banting 2010; Triadafilopoulos and Young 2011). The enormity of this challenge is compounded by the interplay of global dynamics with the demands of increasingly politicized minorities, the diversification of diversity, and deep economic cleavages. But unlike other countries, Canada is one of several democratic societies to have capitalized on multiculturalism as a principled governance for living together with immigrant differences. That it has managed to achieve the once seemingly impossible – to forge a working unity from its disparate parts without invoking repressive measures or spiralling out of control – is worthy of praise and emulation (Michael Adams 2007; Bertossi and Duyvendak 2012).

There's a saying that people often use the same words but speak a different language. The term *multiculturalism* is a good example of communicating past each other. Canada's commitment to an inclusive multiculturalism and a multicultural model of inclusion differs from the approach of European countries in which multiculturalism and integration are often seen as mutually exclusive (see Reitz 2012b). The logic at the core of multiculturalism seeks to shore up immigrant integration by eliminating both inherited inequality and the patterns of exclusion that are commensurate with the advancement of "white Canada" (Thobani 2007). But an inclusive multiculturalism that persists for the purpose of harmonizing competing ethnicities without relinquishing overall control bears a less flattering interpretation: multiculturalism as hegemony. Canada's official multiculturalism originated as a political act to achieve political goals in a politically acceptable manner (also Abu-Laban 2014). Its tainted status as a hegemonic governance by "ruling elites" for controlling "unruly ethnics" rendered immigrant ethnicity less threatening to the dominant sector (Banting et al. 2007). Depoliticized multiculturalism also proved a Faustian bargain for newcomers – a kind of *opiate for narcotizing the immigrant masses* to distract from more fundamental issues related to racism and power (Lentin and Titley 2011b). In other words, immigrants acquired a right to saris, samosas, and steelbands but not to a share of power (Uzma Shakir, executive director of Council of Agencies Serving South Asians, cited in Aliweiwi 2006). The depoliticization of diversity also contributed to a superficial national narrative that whitewashed the racism and exploitation related to Canada building (Dei 2007; also Jakubowicz 2007). Sunera Thobani (2007, 160) writes accordingly:

> Multiculturalist policy and its after-effects on popular culture eroded the salience of anti-racist politics and discourses; it disguised the persistence of white supremacy and power in the new constitution of whiteness as signifying "tolerance." Multiculturalism avoided recognition of the critical intersection of institutional power and interpersonal forms of racism, demanding only tolerance at the interpersonal level of interaction. Knowledge about the nature of racism, and the role it has historically played in Canadian nation-building, has thus been made peripheral.

Others disagree with this uncomplimentary interpretation (Michael Adams 2007; Reitz 2009; Kymlicka 2010a). The inception of multiculturalism as a society-building enterprise reflected a logical extension of the human rights revolution that (a) upended entrenched ethnic and racial hierarchies, (b) sought to defuse dangerous ethnonational conflicts while improving the collective status of immigrants, and (c) promoted the goals of peace, democracy, and good governance as compatible with diversity (also Baubock 2008b). The origins of Canada's official multiculturalism cannot be divorced from a broader national agenda in constructing an inclusive country, including initiatives ranging from passage of the Official Languages Act in 1969 to the entrenchment of the Human Rights Act in 1977. Both the Liberal government's 1971 policy statement on multiculturalism and Canada's 1988 Multiculturalism Act were designed to promote inclusion through removal of prejudicial attitudes and discriminatory barriers (Fleras 2009a). They also sought to redefine Canada's symbolic order and its national identity, from that of Britishness to one of a mosaic cosmopolitanism (Bloemraad 2012). Admittedly, the unintended impact of official multiculturalism or its manipulation by vested interests may be the ideological masking of racial hierarchies or the exacerbation of racialized inequities. But increased recognition of immigrant cultures and a responsiveness to minority needs under the multicultural umbrella have aligned newcomers more closely with Canadian society (Wright and Bloemraad 2012).

The implementation of multiculturalism as an immigration governance model is reaping rewards (Ryan 2010). Canada is globally admired. Kudos range from high-flying celebrities such as Bono of U2, who claims that the world "needs more Canada," to personalities such as the Aga Khan in praising Canada as the world's most "successful pluralist society" (see Biles, Ibrahim, and Tolley 2005, 7; Masood 2007). Canada's multicultural project is deemed by some, including UBC professor Leonie Sandercock (2006), to represent one.of the four great animating ideas for revolutionizing the organization of society:

> the American Revolution (with its liberal-democratic ideals of life, liberty, and freedom);
> the French Revolution (with its republican commitment to liberty, equality, and fraternity);
> the Russian Revolution (which ushered in the principles of socialist equality); and
> Canada's quiet multicultural revolution (in proposing a new governance framework for living together by integrating newcomers into the urban-rich and multi-ethnic realities of a globalizing world order).

Canada's official multiculturalism provides a working strategy to integrate immigrants and racialized minorities in ways that are deemed to be workable, necessary, and fair (Kymlicka 1998, 2008; Reitz 2009; Berry 2011; Wright and Bloemraad 2012; Banting 2012; Biles 2014). It advances an inclusive Canada by capitalizing on a commitment to social justice and cultural identity, while prescribing a proactive role for discrediting prejudice (Hyman, Meinhard, and Shields 2011). National interests are secured as well by facilitating intergroup relations through promotion of cultural respect, economic equality, and full participation (Ley 2007; also Jupp and Clyne 2011). In that Canada's national narratives pivot around its status as a multiculturally inclusive society (Moosa 2007), few will dispute the centrality of multiculturalism to Canada building via immigrant integration.

Yet theory is one thing, given the tendency of political philosophers to dwell on normative accounts of living together (Kymlicka 2011a;

Murphy 2012). Practice has proven yet another. Canadians appear better at "talking the walk" than "walking the talk" (see Bloemraad 2011, 1132). The complexities and contradictions of making multiculturalism a reality yield two competing yet powerful discourses: To one side is a pro-diversity narrative as grounds for cooperative co-existence; to the other side is a commitment to cultural and racial uniformity as the basis for society building (Forrest and Dunn 2010). No matter how revered or vilified, official multiculturalism is prone to a governance enigma: how to establish a rules-based framework to engage immigrant differences as different yet equal without forfeiting the goals of unity, identity, and prosperity in the process (Banting 2010; Harell and Stolle 2010; Lenard 2012). In other words, how are we to construct a multicultural governance that makes Canada safe "for" immigrants (that maximizes benefits), yet safe "from" immigrants (that minimizes costs) (see Schlesinger 1992; Samuel and Schachhuber 2000; Pearson 2001)? Questions abound in aligning principles with practices to the satisfaction of all Canadians, especially when security concerns trump a commitment to diversity and minority rights in the post-9/11 era:

> Is multiculturalism as a governance for managing immigrants based on solid premises or, alternatively, on assumptions that buckle under closer scrutiny (Reitz 2009)? Is it still viable, or are we witnessing the exhaustion of a paradigm that has formed the heart of the Canadian project for the last 40 years (Letourneau 2013)? Does promoting immigrant diversity foster an integrated unity? In what way does a positive attachment to immigrant cultural identity reflect, reinforce, and advance a positive identification with Canada? Or will it exacerbate deeper divisions by encouraging a wallowing in nostalgia, a smoke-screen for illegal actions, a revival of ancient grudges, or perhaps an anything-goes relativism that justifies illiberal practices in a liberal society (Ryan 2010)? Multiculturalism is criticized for allowing extremism to flourish, according to Ujjal Dosanjh, one-time BC premier (cited in Ibbitson 2010), partly because politically correct Canadians seemingly countenance anything in the name of tolerance and inclusion. That, in turn, poses the prickly question of how far liberal states should go in adjusting their institutions, values, and laws to accommodate minorities (Triandafyllidou 2011).

> Do continuing immigrant attachments and transnational linkages hinder or assist integration? Can a territorially grounded multiculturalism be stretched to incorporate newcomers who define themselves along crosscutting lines of ethnicity or religion as well as across borders and nationalities (Friesen and Martin 2010; Carruthers 2013)? Is it possible to reconcile a rooted multiculturalism with an increasingly cosmopolitan world of diasporic linkages, transnational networks, transmigrant identities, and translocal contexts (Karim 2007)? Can state-based multiculturalism connect to modes of otherness whose multiple identities and splintered belongings transcend the confines of the nation-state (Shome 2012)?

> Does multiculturalism assist in the integration of immigrants by removing barriers to participation while forging a sense of "welcoming into Canada" (Banting 2012)? Or does it promote an inward-looking ghettoization or a balkanized governance, both of which emphasize differences rather than commonalities? Are newcomers encapsulated into self-contained silos that essentialize their cultural differences as little more than frozen-in-time museum curiosities for display or distraction (Bissoondath 1994)? Studies have proven inconclusive, partly because of the way in which the issues were framed. Some contend on the basis of 2002 Statistics Canada data that racialized immigrants feel less Canadian and are slower to integrate than their white counterparts, and that their offspring profess a more profound sense of social exclusion than they themselves (Reitz and Banerjee 2007). Whereas some suggest that multiculturalism as integration isn't working as well for recent immigrants and their children, others argue that there is little evidence that it erodes newcomer affiliation with Canada or that newcomer identities are mutually exclusive (Jedwab 2014). In 2008, the Association for Canadian Studies commissioned a survey of new Canadians in the MTV cities. Most respondents expressed a powerful sense of belonging to Canada (87 percent said that they felt a strong or somewhat strong attachment), which outweighed their attachment to their native language (66 percent), ethnicity (65 percent), and regional identity (78 percent) (Canwest News Service 2008). EKOS Politics (2013b) also allayed fears regarding multiculturalism by confirming people's vigorous attachment to Canada (86 percent said that it was moderately or very strong, down slightly from 90 percent in 1998),

to their province (81 versus 90 percent in 1998), and to their ethnic group or national ancestry (66 versus 81 percent in 1998) (Graves 2013). Interestingly, family belonging was strongest, at 94 versus 98 percent in 1998. Additional evidence reveals that second-generation newcomers express high levels of pride in Canada on par with the Canadian-born (Will Kymlicka in Marina Jimenez 2007). Most newcomers take out citizenship and identify positively as Canadian citizens, according to a global survey (Gilkinson and Sauve 2010).

> Does too much multiculturalism create a topsy-turvy world that leaves society without a centre to hold it together? Does too little of it forge a monolith that stifles creativity and growth? Or does it foster a paralyzing political correctness that refuses to criticize minorities or government minority policies for fear of being labelled a racist? What exactly is the right amount of multicultural accommodation in advancing an inclusive governance? Can it be operationalized? Is the goal measurable? A conflict of interest may be inevitable: Higher levels of immigration further justify a need for multiculturalism as integration governance. Yet increases in immigrant numbers, differences, and needs will also generate controversy over how much and what kind of multicultural governance is best for integrating immigrants (Parrillo 2009; Jupp and Clyne 2011).

There is much of value in multiculturalism. Widely applauded, occasionally detested, it is not perfect by any stretch of the imagination but it is demonstrably better than global alternatives (Fleras 2009a). Admittedly, the perils of balancing unity (commonality) with diversity are all too obvious: Too many immigrant differences and not enough national unity may cripple a governance to the point of dismemberment. Too little difference but too much unity can create a one-size-fits-all leviathan that smothers as it standardizes (Fish 1997; Reitz 2009). Reference to the appropriate amount of accommodation raises the question of how much and what kind of immigrant diversity is tolerable without repudiating Canada's democratic institutions and unsettling social cohesion. No less challenging are questions of how to construct a tradeoff between the seemingly contrastive domains of diversity and equality. This paradox – multiculturalism as progressively inclusive yet systemically exclusionary – makes it doubly important to critically distinguish what official multiculturalism "says it's doing" from "what it's really doing, how, and why" (Dupont and Lemarchand 2001; Wood and Gilbert 2005).

The link between immigration and Canadian multiculturalism is irrefutable. As emphasized earlier, an immigration society provides an inclusive framework for improving the settlement and integration of immigrants. Multiculturalism is a tool to foster social inclusion through the removal of prejudicial barriers, while promoting respect for cultures without reneging on a commitment to Canadian values and good citizenship (Reitz 2011b). Immigrants are no less inclined to see multiculturalism in ambivalent terms, based on personal experiences and group expectations (see Fries and Gingrich 2009). Multiculturalism secures a platform for staking out immigrant claims while articulating their demands alongside those of the mainstream (Fleras 2012a). An otherwise powerless sector is thus empowered to prod or provoke central policy structures by holding them accountable for failure to close the gaps between multicultural ideals and everyday results. Appeals to official multiculturalism are thus calculated to extract public sympathy and global scrutiny, in the same way that indigenous peoples have relied on international fora (such as the UN) for leveraging concessions from the federal government.

OFFICIAL MULTICULTURALISM: A PROJECT IN PROGRESS

To say that Canada is the poster child for multiculturalism is stating the obvious. From its inception in 1971, when it barely garnered a paragraph in Canada's national newspaper, official multiculturalism has evolved to become a definitive component of Canada's national narrative. It originated as part of a broader overhaul of Canada and Canadian national identity by harnessing the power of the state for advancing a new Canada (Peter Ward 1990). It altered how Canadians think about themselves and their relationship to the world, and the more than four decades of its sway also orchestrated a national consensus in the art of living together with differences (Biles 2014). Multiculturalism originated as an inclusionary framework for European newcomers (Kunz and Sykes 2008). That is, it dealt mostly with white Christian ethnic groups whose demands focused on equal opportunity and preservation of language and culture (Jupp 2011; Haque 2012).

That it continues to persist for precisely the same reasons, albeit with different demographics, speaks to the politics of politics. To put it bluntly, multiculturalism is a political project in reframing the relationship of the state to immigrant Canadians along more inclusionary lines (Kymlicka 2010a). Only the means for achieving this goal have changed because of demographic upheavals and political developments, with ethnicity-based solutions giving way to equity-grounded reforms and, more recently, the promotion of civic belonging and cohesive integration as organizational frameworks.

Despite (or because of) its centrality, references to multiculturalism rarely yield a singular meaning (Karim 2009b). It is a slippery and elusive concept with a tendency to skitter off in different directions, in the process becoming a conceptual grab bag of spongy associations and infuriating misconceptions (Lentin and Titley 2011a, 2011b; Murphy 2012). The existence of many different multi-culture societies generates an additional array of diverse multiculturalisms (Ang 2010). Not surprisingly, the question "Is Canada a multicultural society?" prompts a variety of answers, depending on the intended level of meaning. Failure to acknowledge the different semantic levels associated with multiculturalism – as *demographic fact,* as *ideology,* as *governance practice,* and as *official policy and program* – often yields confusion and misunderstanding.

First, Canada is multicultural in terms of demographic fact. According to the 2011 census, just over 20 percent of its population is foreign-born (only Australia, at 24 percent, has a higher number), and just under 20 percent identify as racialized (visible) minorities. This multicultural diversity is expected to expand in the future because of immigration patterns. Multiculturalism as a fact is also expressed at the level of everyday interaction and communication between individuals of diverse racialized backgrounds (Ho and Natt 2012).

Second, Canada is multicultural because of an ideology that embraces the values of tolerance, respect, social justice, and redistribution. With multiculturalism, immigrant cultural differences are entitled to public affirmation and respect as a minority right and fundamental justice (Nagel and Hopkins 2010). In addition, the multicultural ideal acknowledges the right of migrants and minorities to social equality and full participation through removal of prejudicial barriers. Multiculturalism is also promoted as an integral component of national unity and identity (Kymlicka 2008). A multicultural Canada is ideally a better and more productive place to be, one that is preferred to places whose systems endorse uniformity, on the grounds that a society of many different cultures is possible, provided that rules are in place. Compare this ideal with that in Europe, where the ideology of multiculturalism is criticized for undermining integration and fostering extremism (Cramme and Motte 2010).

Third, Canada is multicultural because of its insistence on putting multicultural principles into practice at institutional levels. Mainstream institutions are expected to be inclusive of diversity by (a) improving workplaces to make them more responsive to diversity, (b) redefining institutional rules of reward, (c) expanding procedures for hiring and promotion through removal of discriminatory barriers, and (d) ensuring delivery of services that are available, accessible, and appropriate (Fleras 2012b). Conversely, migrants and minorities rely on multiculturalism as social capital to bond (inward) and bridge (outward) as part of settling down, fitting in, and moving up. Finally, multiculturalism as practice acknowledges the reality of everyday multiculturalism, as those in urban areas are routinely called upon to navigate among ethnocultural groups (Wise and Velaythum 2009).

Fourth, Canada is multicultural at official levels. Few policy initiatives have greater potential for the lives and life chances of newcomers than multiculturalism (Fries and Gingrich 2009). Originating as an all-party policy agreement in 1971, it was subsequently entrenched in the 1982 Constitution Act as an interpretive principle: That is, nothing in the Charter of Rights and Freedoms will be interpreted in a manner that detracts from the enhancement and preservation of Canada's multicultural character. In 1988, with passage of the Multiculturalism Act, it was finally accorded statutory standing. That Canada remains the world's only officially multicultural country (in statutory and constitutional terms) speaks of its commitment and convictions. But just as Canada has evolved, so too has multiculturalism in response to shifting realities. Four overlapping policy stages can be discerned in describing multiculturalism as an evolving governance framework: ethnicity, equity, civic, and integrative.

Ethnicity Multiculturalism

Ethnicity multiculturalism initially focused on advancing the concept of Canada as an ethnic mosaic. Multicultural discourses were rooted in an almost essentialized understanding of immigrant ethnicity as primordial and immutable rather than flexible, dynamic, and relational, with members locked into hermetically sealed groups (according to tabled documents, however, the government flatly rejected the principle of assisting any immigrant group that disengaged from the rest of Canada [Kruhlak 2003; Fleras 2012a]). But a focus on cultural preservation and the celebration of diversity did not persist beyond the early stage, when powerful ethnic lobbyists initially prevailed and when diversity applied to established European ethnicities rather than racialized newcomers (Haque 2012). Yes, immigrant ethnicity was important and not necessarily divisive if managed properly – that is, if it (a) was confined to the private and personal; (b) contributed to society but did not constitute the raw material of nation building; (c) involved acceptance of certain values such as those related to liberal universalism; (d) entailed acquisition of official language to ensure participation, opportunity, and success; (e) acknowledged the benefits and obligations of national citizenship; and (f) promoted a spirit of sharing and interaction (also Jupp and Clyne 2011).

The goals of ethnicity multiculturalism were twofold. *First,* it sought to eliminate discriminations anchored in ethnocultural prejudices. It sought to make immigrant ethnicity irrelevant as either an indicator of success/failure or a predictor of entitlement (Kruhlak 2003). Ethnicity would no longer be used to rank Canadians or to exclude them because they lacked so-called founding-nation status (English and French). The inception of ethnicity-infused multiculturalism altered people's conception of who was Canadian; it also dispersed power relations beyond the French-English axis. The combination of official bilingualism (implemented in 1969) with official multiculturalism was designed to wean Canada away from its former essentialist conception of Britishness (and Frenchness), while differentiating its minority governance from America's melting-pot assimilationism (Haque 2012).

Second, ethnicity multiculturalism created a new symbolic order of governance that respected immigrants' ethnicity differences as the basis for improving their integration (Reitz 2012b). This commitment was predicated on the assumption that migrants and minorities were more likely to emotionally embrace Canada if they took pride in their cultural traditions without fear of penalty or exclusion (Adams 2007; Reitz 2009; Berry 2014). With multiculturalism, in other words, immigrant Canadians could belong to and identify with Canada through their ethnicity if they so chose.

Equity Multiculturalism

Official multiculturalism changed significantly during the late 1970s and early 1980s, as the emphasis on inter-ethnicity gave way to an equity multiculturalism that embraced the more pragmatic concerns of racialized immigrants. The often diverse requirements of immigrants from so-called non-convention sources proved perplexing since their visibility complicated the prospect of settling down, fitting in, and moving up (Fleras 2009a). Migrant and minority concerns shifted accordingly: For new immigrants, dismantling racial barriers to opportunity superseded concerns over culture and language preservation. The earlier emphasis on ethnicity and identity as keys to integration was jettisoned in favour of a commitment to equity, social justice, and institutional inclusiveness (Donaldson 2004). Funding allocations changed as well. Rather than simply doling out money to ethnocultural organizations or events, as had once been the norm, authorities channelled spending into equity goals of anti-racism, race relations, and removing discriminatory barriers at institutional levels.

Passage of the Multiculturalism Act in 1988 consolidated Canada's status as a premier multiculturalism society. The act sought to respect cultures, promote a shared citizenship to ensure inclusion, foster participation, reduce discrimination and combat racism, encourage ingroup bonding as a precondition for outgroup bridging and cross-cultural understanding, and accelerate institutional accommodation of racialized minorities at the federal level (Fries and Gingrich 2009; also Jupp and Clyne 2011).[1] This commitment to integration over separation, interaction over isolation, and participation over withdrawal persists into the present. But the logic behind an integrative multiculturalism is more openly attuned to the narratives of cohesion, solidarity, and value consensus (Michael Adams 2007; CIC 2011a; Fleras 2012a).

Civic Multiculturalism

Another adjustment in emphasis emerged in the mid-1990s, as a combination of factors fostered a renewal in federal multiculturalism. A major review of program priorities in 1997, in part to safeguard Canadian unity in the aftermath of Quebec's 1995 referendum scare

(Winter 2011), resulted in a shift toward (a) support of economic and social objectives, (b) initiatives regarding youth at risk, and (c) promotion of intercultural understanding and the Canadian value of democracy (CIC 2009a). A civic-oriented multiculturalism focused on fostering a sense of belonging, an active involvement in community life and society, and a shared awareness of Canadian identity against the broader backdrop of Canada's national interests (also Simon-Kumar 2012). It also concentrated on "break[ing] down the ghettoization of multiculturalism," according to former multiculturalism minister Hedy Fry (1997, 1): "As a national policy of inclusiveness, multiculturalism's activities aim to bring all Canadians closer together, to enhance equal opportunities, to encourage mutual respect among citizens of diverse backgrounds, to assist in integrating first-generation Canadians, to promote more harmonious intergroup relations, and to foster social cohesion and a shared sense of Canadian identity."

This change was formalized with the renewal of the multiculturalism program (CIC 2009a). Three strategic goals prevailed: social justice (to ensure fair and equitable treatment), cultural identity (to foster a Canada to which all Canadians could commit or belong regardless of their ethnic background), and civic participation (to improve citizen involvement in community and country). Priority objectives have shifted over time, including a commitment to institutional change (inclusiveness through removal of discriminatory barriers), federal institutional change (incorporate diversity into policies, programs, and services), combatting hate and racism (anti-racism programs, cross-cultural understanding, and removal of discriminatory barriers), and civic engagement (promoting active and shared citizenship and building capacity to improve minority participation in public decision making) (CIC2009a). Three new policy objectives eventually informed the multiculturalism program, including removal of barriers to full participation, especially in federal institutions; nurturing intercultural understanding; and promoting Canadian values at home and multiculturalism abroad (CIC 2011a).

Integrative Multiculturalism

A new integrative multicultural agenda has taken shape in reaction to global security concerns, from 9/11 to the Toronto Terror Scare in June 2006 (when 18 men were apprehended on suspicion of fomenting terror) (Griffith 2013). Integrative multiculturalism supports government efforts to build an integrated and socially cohesive society by fostering intercultural/interfaith understanding, civic memory and pride in Canadian history and society, respect for core democratic values, and equal opportunities for all Canadians through removal of discriminatory obstacles (CIC 2013a). Its intent is to neutralize the threat of ethno-religious extremism (Freeze 2008; Kunz and Sykes 2008; Abu-Laban 2014) in the hopes of securing a safe and cohesive Canada based on shared values and common identity. It promises equality of opportunity for all Canadians regardless of their immigrant status. It seeks out lasting relations with ethnic and religious communities, recognizes the contribution and potential of all Canadians, focuses on newcomer duties and responsibilities, and encourages their participation in Canada's social, political, and economic affairs (CIC 2013a). An integrative agenda was reinforced by Jason Kenney (CIC 2011e, emphasis added) in celebration of Canadian Multiculturalism Day (27 June):

> Canada is one of the most ethnically, culturally, and religiously diverse countries in the world ... formed by citizens from many cultural backgrounds who have come to live together in harmony in this free land ... Canadian Multiculturalism Day is an opportunity to reflect on both the contributions of Canada's various cultural communities and the *values that we all share*: freedom, democracy, individual rights, and rule of law. Canada's future depends on us growing together. *That is why our multiculturalism programs continue to encourage all Canadians to embrace our shared values, history, and institutions and to build a strong, integrated society.*

Certainly, an integrative commitment is not altogether different from past priorities. Multiculturalism has historically sustained this focus (Ley 2007) despite criticism that it promotes divisiveness or extremism (perhaps inadvertently). Only its bluntness differs. In this sense, the shift toward integration as an explicit immigrant governance reflects parallel developments in Europe and the Antipodes toward a neo-assimilationist code of social cohesion and national (comm)unity (Fleras 2012e).

40 OBSERVATION

Deconstructing Integration: A Governance Model in Search of Grounding

THE RE-EMERGENCE OF integration as a preferred governance framework has not made it any easier to define or operationalize. Three distinct discourses can be discerned: the social, the cultural, and as governance. Technically speaking, integration as a social concept is diametrically opposed to segregation. Integration here refers to the full and equal incorporation of individuals who were formerly excluded through no fault of their own. Integration in the cultural sense entails a fusion (like mixing different paints in a bucket) to create a new hue from the originals. The American concept of the melting pot is a good example of this. Finally, integration as governance from a political perspective involves a process of mutual adjustment, in which immigrants and society both adapt and adopt through reciprocating obligations, responsibilities, and respect (Biles and Frideres 2012).

Not surprisingly, no clear definition of integration exists. It is often employed as a default or catch-all term, applying to belonging, participation, inclusion, recognition, and legitimacy (Neerup 2012). It remains a problematic concept because of difficulties in (a) pinpointing its limits (where does assimilation end and integration begin?), (b) measuring its attainment (how can we tell when immigrants have integrated?) (Bloemraad and de Graauw 2012), and (c) applying it to real-world problems (Spoonley and Tolley 2012; Tolley and Spoonley 2012). Differing dimensions prevail as well, making it important to distinguish between economic, political, social, and cultural integration. For example, according to Will Kymlicka (in Marina Jimenez 2012), Canada may be doing poorly on the economic integration front but it is performing well on the other dimensions. As might be expected, settler countries such as Canada and Australia tend to be better at integrating immigrants than many European countries.

The combination of a relatively open mindset regarding immigrants and immigration with a principled admission and settlement framework tends toward a higher proportion of educated and skilled migrants (better job of balancing labour, family, and humanitarian streams) (Thoreau and Liebig 2012).

The lack of consensus regarding the meaning and scope of integration results in disagreement over how to measure it (Jentsch 2007; Saggar and Somerville 2012). Nevertheless, there are models that attempt to operationalize the concept. In Canada (Banting and Kymlicka 2010; Hyman, Meinhard, and Shields 2011), the indicators of integration include high levels of citizenship and political involvement on the part of newcomers, language acquisition, dispersed residential location, intermarriage, and mutual acceptance between newcomers and the Canadian-born. Others refer to a sense of belonging (Reitz and Banerjee 2007), trust in the other, identification with society at large, acquisition of citizenship, life satisfaction, a spirit of volunteerism, and exercise of voting rights. The European Council also adopted a commitment to integration in 2004 whose principles are paraphrased below (for critique, see Joppke 2010; Fleras 2009a):

> Integration is a dynamic two-way process of mutual accommodation by immigrants and the host country.
> It implies respect for the basic values of the European Union.
> Employment is a key part of the integration process for immigrants and the host country.
> Basic knowledge of the host country's language, history, and institutions is indispensable to integration.
> Access to education is critical to the integration of immigrants.
> Integration requires full and non-discriminatory access to institutions and public and private goods and services.
> Frequent encounters and creative interaction between immigrants and host country citizens secure successful integration.
> Integration is predicated on respecting diverse cultures and religions, provided that these do not conflict with rights or laws.

> Immigrants' participation in the democratic process is critical, especially in the formulation of programs and policies that affect their lives.
> Integration is contingent on mainstreaming (making more inclusive) polices and measures in all relevant portfolios and levels of government and public services.
> Clear goals, indicators, and evaluation mechanisms must be in place to adjust immigration policies and to evaluate progress.

In summary: Canada's official multiculturalism constitutes a complex and contested governance policy that has evolved over time in response to social changes and political challenges. Box 41 compares its ethnicity, equity, civic, and integrative stages. Keep in mind the inevitability of (over)simplification when comparing ideal-typical categories in a world that is contextual rather than categorical.

Shifts in emphasis notwithstanding, official multiculturalism has never strayed from its foundational rationale: *to create an inclusive Canada by integrating migrants and minorities without disrupting the status quo.* A threefold commitment is implied: (a) no one should be excluded from full and equal participation and the exercise of citizenship rights for reasons of race, ethnicity, or nationality; (b) a Canada of many immigrant cultures is possible as long as rules are in place to regulate interaction and distribution in the public domain; (c) integration is to be facilitated via a framework to remove discriminatory barriers. Everyone is treated in the same manner under a liberal-leaning inclusive multiculturalism because people's commonalities as rights-bearing individuals supersede any group-based differences, at least for purposes of recognition and reward. But although equal treatment is the goal, the lived experiences of migrants are also accorded recognition if necessary. In certain situations, migrants may be treated differently, provided that this exception is temporary, needs-based because of differences rather than based on race or ethnicity per se, and individual-focused not group-oriented.

41

Policy Shifts in Canada's Official Multiculturalism

	Ethnicity (1970s)	Equity (1980s to mid-1990s)	Civic (mid-1990s to mid-2000s)	Integrative (mid-2000s onward)
Dimension	Cultural	Structural	Social	Societal
Focus	Respecting differences	Fostering equality	Living together	Cohesion
Mandate	Ethnicity	Race relations	Civic identity	Citizenship
Magnitude	Individual adjustment	Institutional accommodation	Engagement	Safety/security
Problem	Prejudice	Racism/ discrimination	Exclusion	Segregation/ extremism
Solution	Cultural sensitivity	Remove barriers	Inclusion	Shared Canadian values
Outcomes	Cultural capital	Human capital	Social capital	National (comm) unity
Key metaphor	Mosaic	Level playing field	Belonging	Promoting integration

Source: Fleras (2012e).

INTERCULTURALISM AS IMMIGRANT GOVERNANCE IN QUEBEC

Federal multiculturalism is not the only governance game in Canada. Every province has its own policies, laws, advisory boards, or commitments, which often overlap with those of Ottawa. Few have attracted as much attention or notoriety as the Quebec model. Called interculturalism (or transculturalism), it is arguably similar to its federal counterpart, but it differs in tone and emphasis (Gagnon and Iacovino

2007), though some assert that the two governance agendas are diametrically opposed, whereas others dismiss differences as largely semantic (Fleras 2012a), as moving targets difficult to define (Weinstock 2014), and as regimes of pluralism that have developed in "distinctive, related, and contradictory pathways" (Nootens 2014, 175).

Quebec first articulated its commitment to interculturalism in the 1990 Policy Statement on Immigration and Integration. This acknowledged the value of cultural differences without compromising the priority claims of a founding society, and it promoted the metaphorical equivalent of an "arboreal" model – that is, the tree trunk is unflinchingly French in language and culture, and minority cultures represent branches that are grafted onto the trunk. According to the tree-trunk tenets of interculturalism, immigrants and their contributions are welcome. But their entry activates a "moral contract" involving a reciprocal exchange of rights, duties, and obligations between newcomers and the people of Quebec. Immigrants must accept the primacy of French language and culture, observe the prevailing cultural norms and rule of law of a democratic society, actively participate as citizens in Quebec's secular and pluralist society, become involved in community dialogue and exchanges, respect other differences, and obey constitutional principles and practices related to gender equity (Gagnon and Iacovino 2007; Hamilton 2008; Chung 2009). With interculturalism, in other words, limits are explicit, including a commitment to values, institutions, and norms as set out in laws and the constitution.

Clearly, then, both federal multiculturalism and Quebec's interculturalism share a core theme – a common commitment to an inclusive governance by integrating newcomers into the larger community (Banting, Courchene, and Seidle 2007; Gagnon 2008; Reitz 2009). Two broad governance agendas prevail (Banting, Courchene, and Seidle 2007):

> a difference agenda that encourages migrants and minorities to express and share their cultural identities without sacrificing inclusiveness; and
> an integrative agenda to incorporate migrants and minorities into the mainstream without discrediting a respect for cultural differences.

Differences between multiculturalism and interculturalism are subject to debate (Fleras 2012a). For some, the major difference lies in

Quebec's willingness to be explicit about what is expected of migrants and what they can expect in return, what constitutes the limit of acceptable behaviour, and the unassailable primacy of French language and culture as national identity. For others, the two models reflect distinctive society-building projects (Maxwell et al. 2012). Multiculturalism aims at constructing a unitary citizenship based on nominal recognition of diversity and difference. In promoting the principle of unity within diversity, it resembles a planetary model – that is, minority cultures spin in varying orbits around a mainstream centre. (You can be Haitian and Canadian as long as you obey the laws, don't deprive others of their rights, and respect core constitutional values.) By contrast, Quebec's arboreal model aims at articulating a distinct political community whose cultural and language priorities supersede ethnic diversities – you can be Haitian but always a Haitian in Quebec. Interculturalism cultivates a pluralistic notion of society that is sensitive to immigrant rights; preserves the creative tension between minority and migrant difference and the continuity and predominance of the French culture; and emphasizes the centrality of integration and interaction (Bouchard-Taylor Commission 2008). That's the theory, but reality is different, as is revealed by the intense debate over the proposed Charter of Quebec Values, which would uphold strict secularism in the public domain.

The seemingly disparate logics behind multiculturalism and interculturalism mean that the two models are difficult to mix or merge. According to the Bouchard-Taylor Commission (2008), multiculturalism cannot be duplicated in Quebec. English Canada can afford a looser concept of multiculturalism as governance because it has (a) fewer anxieties over English as a threatened language, (b) fewer insecurities because English Canadians are a majority, and (c) less concern for protecting a founding nation (those who identify as British descent constitute only a third of Canada's population). Not surprisingly, Quebec's view of federal multiculturalism is tainted by association with negative and extremist views. It's criticized for ostensibly granting licence to illiberal practices, encouraging a radical relativism that defines all cultural practices as equally valid, and fostering the creation of ethnic ghettos at the expense of social cohesion (Rodríguez-García 2012). Moreover, the paradoxicality of Quebec's majority/minority status – the Québécois are a majority in Quebec but a minority in Canada and North America – militates against any move toward Canada's so-called laissez-faire multiculturalism. Such a move would be tantamount to linguistic and cultural suicide. Quebec's growing pluralism can flourish only within the limitations imposed by its status as a beleaguered cultural minority that is about to be swamped in a sea of English-speaking North Americans (Bouchard-Taylor Commission 2008). Or as the Bouchard-Taylor Commission concluded when acknowledging that Quebec and English-speaking Canada are playing by different rules, "French-speaking Quebec is a minority culture and needs a strong identity to allay its anxieties and behave like a serene majority." In other words, Quebecers should continue to support the interculturalism principles of pluralism, equality, and reciprocity. The emphasis on immigrant integration (rather than accommodation) around a common culture, a moral contract, and the centrality of French secures the status of interculturalism as governance in advancing Quebec's survival as irrevocably French yet ostensibly cosmopolitan.

PUTTING MULTICULTURAL COMMITMENTS INTO INSTITUTIONAL ACCOMMODATION

The inception of official multiculturalism markedly improved institutional responsiveness. Immigrant differences are no longer disparaged as a bothersome anomaly with no redeeming value outside a personal or private context. Difference-based needs are no longer trivialized as a problem to solve or a challenge to surmount. They are promoted instead as an integral part of Canada's social fabric, with untapped potential for improving national wealth and international standing. Putting multiculturalism to work at institutional levels promotes diversities as an asset for improving the bottom line, enhancing the workplace climate, or improving the delivery of social services.

Few contest the necessity for more multiculturally responsive institutions. Only the pace or scope of adjustments remain open to debate. Public and private institutions are increasingly anxious to enhance overall effectiveness by maximizing the talent and creativity to contribute. For service organizations that wish to improve delivery quality, a commitment to multiculturalism can reap rewards by easing workplace tensions, generating creative synergies, and facilitating community access. For private companies, the inclusion of diversity is

42 OBSERVATION

Deconstructing Multiculturalism: An Inclusive Multiculturalism, a Multicultural Model of Inclusion

TO UNDERSTAND the logic behind Canada's official multiculturalism, it's not enough to focus solely on what it says it will do – to integrate newcomers, respect differences, encourage more responsive institutions, facilitate interaction and participation, and remove discriminatory barriers. Digging beneath the surface of federal and bureaucratic statements reveals that the logic is grounded in five themes – multiculturalism as political act, as inclusion, as depoliticizing differences, as managing the mainstream, and as Canada building. Their articulation exposes popular myth-conceptions about multiculturalism while deconstructing the reality behind it:

> *Political Act.* Multiculturalism originated in Canada as a political act to achieve political goals in a politically acceptable manner. That it continues to reflect and reinforce this fundamental logic is central to any understanding of it as inclusive immigrant governance. As a political act, multiculturalism constitutes an instrument of the state in defence of the status quo; its goal is to construct an inclusive Canada by integrating migrants and minorities, and as a political astute act, it capitalizes on Canada's traditions of individualism, tolerance, and freedom. It is consistent with the ideology that our commonalities as morally autonomous and rights-bearing individuals supersede group-based differences as the grounds for recognition and entitlements. Accordingly, everybody must be treated the same, regardless of race or ethnicity, not only because everyone is equal before the law, but also to smooth interaction in the public domain without prejudice, undue privileges, or ethnic entanglements. Differential treatment is permissible as long as it is need-based rather than ethnicity-driven.

> *Inclusion.* Multiculturalism is about inclusion (Ley 2007) and enhancing active participation and democratic citizenship while respecting

minority rights to culture and identity (within limits) (Hyman, Meinhard, and Shields 2011; Kymlicka 2012; Jedwab 2014). It provides an aspirational framework (it has no compliance or enforcement powers) for improving integration by establishing a social climate of relatively neutral public spaces and a responsive institutional framework, while equipping newcomers with the resources and resourcefulness to integrate into the system.

Canada's approach to the diversity of migrants and minorities has traditionally balanced two objectives: to encourage immigrant inclusion and to ensure an inclusive Canada (CIC 2010a). In that sense, an inclusive multiculturalism model focuses on integrating all Canadians into the existing societal framework, whereas a multicultural model of inclusion acknowledges the right of newcomers to become Canadian on their own terms (within limits and with strings attached). This inclusive dimension applies to immigrants and their descendants, not to Aboriginal peoples and the Québécois, whose interests are aligned along nationhood narratives.

> *Depoliticizing Differences.* Multiculturalism is not about celebrating differences or promoting minority groups per se. It does not insist that all cultures are equal solely so that everyone has the right to practise his or her culture or ethnicity, have it recognized in public, and be represented in all social institutions. Rather, it is about depoliticizing differences by (a) removing difference-based disadvantages, (b) respecting ethnocultural differences as contributions to Canada, (c) ensuring that individuals will not be penalized for identifying with their ethnicity, (d) promoting the expression of ethnocultural identity at the personal and private level to abort the possibility of messy ethnic entanglements in the public domain, (e) embracing the ethnicity principle (those who are confident in their ethnicity are more likely to be tolerant and accepting of others), (f) acknowledging an immigrant's right to belong to and identify with Canada through his or her ethnicity (e.g., one can be Tongan and Canadian but always a Tongan in Canada), (g) sharing and exchanging cultural traditions rather than retreating into enclaves, and (h) transforming differences into discourses about social justice, equal opportunity, and human rights.

Of course, multiculturalism is not about eliminating differences but about respecting an individual's right to be different. Nor does it condone an "anything goes" mentality. It draws the line regarding the acceptable: you can be different, but differences must be freely chosen and cannot break the law, violate rights, preclude involvement in Canadian society, or contravene core constitutional values such as gender equity. In short, multiculturalism is about respecting cultural differences *within* the parameters of Canadian society, including adherence to the rule of law, parliamentary democracy, citizenship rights and obligations, freedom of speech and religion, tolerance, and gender equality.

> *Managing the Mainstream.* Multiculturalism is widely perceived as something for and about migrant "others." As integrative governance, it is more concerned with removing disadvantages to ensure an inclusive Canada. A commitment to redistribution embraces a social justice ideal that addresses the needs of those whose differences are disadvantaging in a particular context (Fries and Gingrich 2009; Kymlicka 2012). However, achieving this goal entails removing prejudicial mindsets and barriers from mainstream society. This focus on changing the mainstream reinforces the obvious: official multiculturalism is as much about managing the mainstream as it's about engaging the "them."

> *Canada Building.* First, multiculturalism is not about diversity, ethnicity, minorities, or even inclusion. To put it plainly, it's about building a productive and governable Canada without disrupting the status quo and corresponding distribution of power and privilege (see Haque 2012). As a Canada-building component, multiculturalism improves the lives of Canadians in general and enhances Canada's economic interests at home (via immigrant entrepreneurs) and abroad (through capital linkages). Second, multiculturalism is not about transforming Canada by challenging its constitutional liberalism (with its obligation to protect individuals from state intrusion). It eschews wholesale structural changes to society, choosing to modify attitudes and reform institutions to improve newcomer accommodation and integration without disturbing the status quo. Its purpose is to build a

country that is safe from immigrant differences, yet safe for these differences, by forging unity from diversity, fostering a sense of community and commitment among migrants and minorities, and depoliticizing differences to neutralize their potency to disrupt or challenge.

Can we construct a model that describes and explains Canadian multiculturalism?* Consider the complexities of such a task: any model must be gleaned from (a) the various levels of meaning that are associated with multiculturalism, (b) both the 1971 Liberal government's multicultural policy statement and the 1988 Multiculturalism Act, (c) Canada's status as an immigration society, (d) a close reading of official documents such as Citizenship and Immigration Canada's Annual Reports, (e) constants that weave throughout the various policy stages, and (f) an acknowledgment of the significant disparities between what multiculturalism purports, what it's actually saying, and what it can realistically say or do as a state-sponsored initiative.

Ultimately, Canada's multicultural model can be read along three narrative lines – integrative, disintegrative, and hegemonic. The integrative narrative sees multiculturalism as a relatively progressive framework for respecting differences while removing ethnicity-based disadvantages so that no one is excluded from full participation in society (Banting 2012). Admittedly, achieving this goal is complex. How are we to reconcile an increasingly cosmopolitan world with a multiculturalism that is located in the context of the nation-state and grounded in the idea that migrants undertake a one-way trajectory toward a final destination (Karim 2007)? The disintegrative narrative argues that regardless of policy intentions, multiculturalism results in a host of negative consequences for Canada and Canadians (Paquet 2008; Mansur 2011; also Malik 2013). According to this narrative, which is concerned with illiberal practices in a liberal-democratic society, multiculturalism undermines Canadian unity and identity, and could even function as a smokescreen for terrorism. The hegemony narrative

---

* Models provide explanatory frameworks, but care must be exercised because their content tends to be static and simplistic. In addition, they ignore internal variation and are too normative by virtue of representing an ideal rather than reality (Finotelli and Michalowski 2012).

defines multiculturalism in terms of control, perceiving it as an opiate of the masses that gives the illusion of inclusion but that actually serves the government and the interests of the status quo without taking any meaningful action to challenge and change (Thobani 2007). How, then, can multiculturalism be taken seriously in a Canada that has evolved from a white settler society to a society of "settled whiteness" wherein whiteness and Eurocentricity remain the hegemonic norm in both principle and practice (Zine 2009)?

NARRATIVES OF MULTICULTURALISM:
INTEGRATIVE, DISINTEGRATIVE, HEGEMONIC

	Integrative model	Disintegrative model	Hegemonic model
Framework: multiculturalism reflects	Policy intention	Policy effects (unintended)	Hidden agenda (political act)
Objectives	Integration	Marginalization and division	Illusion of inclusion
Means	Remove discriminatory barriers through reasonable accommodation	Pluralism: > tolerate anything-goes relativism > smokescreen for illiberal practices	> Pretend diversity/impression management > Nullify troublesome constituents
Outcomes/consequences	Canada building: cohesive and inclusive	Canada destabilizing: > divisive (us versus them) > foster illiberalism > home-grown extremism	> Vested interests > Canadian capitalism
Underlying assumptions	Liberal universalism	Ethnic particularism	Opiate of the masses
Status of diversity	Beneficial	Costly, disruptive, delays integration, undermines Canada	False consciousness (distraction) and class fractions
Core slogan	Unity in diversity	Disunity in disarray	Ruling elites controlling unruly ethnics

tantamount to money in the bank (RBC Financial Group 2005). Corporations increasingly rely on the language skills, cultural knowledge, life experiences, and international connections that diversities bring to the table. Diversity connections can also be the catalyst for internationalizing domestic businesses as grounds for improving competitive advantage in global markets.

A commitment to inclusiveness entails a rethinking of "how we do things around here." It involves a process of modifying institutions through adjustment (in design, values, operation, and outcomes), making them more reasonably accommodative of difference – both within the workplace and outside it (Fleras 2012a). Yet efforts at putting multiculturalism to work have proven uneven. The commitment may be there, but it may collapse due to a lack of political will or an inadequate resource base for implementation, in effect experiencing a slippage between rhetoric/theory and reality/practice. Resistance to institutional inclusiveness reflects the deep ambiguities that surface in the attempt to be both culture-blind and culture-conscious (see also Bleich 2006). This gap should come as no surprise. Institutions are complex and often baffling landscapes of power and control, frequently pervaded by prejudice, nepotism, patronage, and the "old boys' network." Moreover, moves to inclusivize are rarely simple or straightforward; rather, they routinely encounter individual resistance, structural barriers, and institutional inertia. Conventional views remain firmly entrenched, especially when vested interests balk at discarding the tried and true. Newer visions may be compelling, but they often lack the clout to scuttle traditional ways of "doing business." All this can prove disruptive as institutions are transformed into "contested sites" involving competing worldviews and hidden agendas.

Public-service-oriented institutions such as the media, education, health, and policing are under pressure to move over and make institutional space (Fleras 2012a). Their mandate as agencies of socialization and social control exposes them to greater demands for accountability and transparency in decision making. No one should be surprised by this commitment and these demands. Both processes strike at the hub of social existence and influence the degree to which people are in harmony with their communities or alienated from them. Media and education furnish the "blueprint" for acceptable behaviour; in turn, policing and health services manage unacceptable behaviour by enforcing the rules. Consider these developments in doing multiculturalism by capitalizing on inclusiveness initiatives:

> Educational institutions have responded to the challenges of multiculturalism by realigning schooling along inclusiveness lines. Various levels of multicultural education can be discerned in engaging difference, including enlightenment, enrichment, and empowerment (Fleras 2012a). Anti-racist education transcends the principles of multicultural education by acknowledging the structural barriers that underpin inequality in schools and workplaces (Dei 2007).
> The criminal justice system has also taken steps toward more inclusiveness. Both the courts and the prison system have modified procedures and structures to become more diversity friendly. Of particular note is the policing service, which has embraced the principles of inclusive community policing (power sharing, partnership, prevention, problem solving) alongside those of conventional police work (Cryderman, O'Toole, and Fleras 1998).
> Mainstream media have risen to the challenge of inclusion by way of programming and coverage that bodes well for the representational basis of media-minority relations (Fleras 2011a). But, though the quality and quantity of minority representations have improved on television and advertising, other media processes such as newscasting continue to frame racialized minorities and migrants as problems (Fleras and Kunz 2001; Chen 2014; also Philo, Briant, and Donald 2013).
> Health services in Canada are equally cognizant of providing a range of services (from prevention to treatment to rehabilitation) that are accessible, available, and appropriate for an increasingly diverse population. Particularly relevant is the challenge of constructing community-based and culturally responsive social work services and mental health supports for assisting often-disoriented immigrants and traumatized refugees (Fleras 2006; Cooke et al. 2007).

Clearly, then, mainstream institutions are under pressure to advance a more inclusive Canada. Some have enthusiastically taken up the challenge. But not all are jumping on the inclusion bandwagon, resulting in gaps between multicultural ideals and monocultural practices. To be sure, there isn't much consensus regarding what constitutes inclusion or reasonable accommodation. Consider the options: Should reform be directed at changing the institutional culture or revamping patterns of power? Should efforts aim at changing personal attitudes or reshaping institutional structures? Should programs and services be customized for particular cultural needs, or should a one-size-fits-all approach prevail to ensure common standards? How far should institutions go in making reasonably accommodative adjustments?

Responses vary depending on the preferred model of multiculturalism as immigration governance (Fleras 2009a). Some believe that a Canada of many cultures is possible as long as people's cultural differences do not impede full and equal participation in society. Cultural differences are deemed as largely irrelevant under an official multiculturalism; after all, true equality and inclusion arise from treating everyone equally regardless of their differences. The objective is to create as neutral an institutional space as possible in hopes of averting ethnic entanglements. Others believe that a Canada of many cultures is possible, but only if difference-based needs are taken into account when necessary. As noted earlier, all Canadians may possess formal equality by virtue of being equal before the law. But newcomers must exercise this equality and achieve success within a framework that neither reflects their realities nor advances their interests. In other words, inclusive institutions and societies will arise when people's lived experiences and difference-based disadvantages are taken into account to improve equal opportunity and equality of outcomes.

RETHINKING IMMIGRANT INTEGRATION, INSTITUTIONAL ACCOMMODATION: INCLUSIVITY VERSUS INCLUSION

Immigrant integration remains one of the more prominent issues in political and policy analysis. Yet achieving it – through a balancing act of respecting diversity, fostering unity and belonging, and promoting equality (Joppke and Siedle 2012) – is proving more difficult than many imagined (Breton 2012; Jedwab 2012; Poisson 2012). It is not simply a top-down state-run project that conceptualizes immigrants as passive recipients of services. Immigrants are known to participate in the deliberation, creation, implementation, and consumption of programs (Schmidtke 2012; also Wu, Schimmele, and Hou 2012). Moreover, the dynamics of transmigration and transnationalism are altering the nature of integration. The sequential process of adaption and assimilation into a nationally defined society is giving ground to more complex and dynamic models involving unintended consequences, fluid realities and experiences, and multiple loyalties (Schmidtke 2012). Finally, numerous factors influence integration (Spoonley and Bedford 2012; Spoonley and Tolley 2012; Biles and Burstein 2013), including the policies of the host government (restrictive or expansive), the condition of the labour market (strong or weak), the characteristics of the settlement community (ethnic enclaves or generalized), and the attitudes of wider society to newcomers.

A central paradox underpins the integration politics of immigrant governance: How can we engage immigrant differences as different yet equal without eroding the goals of unity, identity, and prosperity (see also Modood 2011)? In other words, how are we to construct an integration governance model that makes Canada both safe for and safe from differences (see Schlesinger 1992)? Should we focus on creating a level playing field for everyone? Or is true equality to be reached by taking immigrant-based needs and disadvantages into account through institutional adjustments? How effective is a compromise initiative, one that treats everyone the same but takes differences and needs into account when necessary?

The perils of balancing unity (commonality) with diversity are all too obvious: Too much difference may fatally destabilize integration governance, whereas too much unity can create a stifling one-size-fits-all leviathan (Fish 1997). This paradox is accentuated by the politics of transmigration, which challenge conventional forms of immigrant integration. In classic integration theories (Brown and Bean 2006), white European newcomers worked at low-end jobs (Hernandez 2009) and achieved success by adopting mainstream norms, with those of longest residence attaining the biggest gains. Their children moved up the occupational ladder thanks to education and socialization into mainstream values. Newer models concede higher levels of complexity and fluidity in integrating migrants, especially for highly educated and professionally trained middle-class individuals.

Ultimately, does it still make sense to talk about integration along place-based lines in a diasporic world of transmigration and transnationalism (Fleras 2011c; Kymlicka and Walker 2012; Carruthers 2013)? Some say no and point to the emergence of global and border-busting forces that make a mockery of the nation-state. Others assert the ongoing salience of the nation-state as a unifying authority of last resort in the context of superdiverse differences. A playful inversion might help in sorting out the dilemma. The challenge of accommodation goes beyond the integrative principle of making society safe for, yet safe from, diversities. More importantly, it entails a governance shift toward the principle of inclusivity – that is, making immigrant diversities safe from society yet safe for society, in part by acknowledging the need to accommodate different ways of accommodating differences within differences (see also Chapter 12).

Debates over integration as a preferred governance model are shifting toward the principle of inclusivity (Fleras 2012d). Inclusivity can be defined as a process and framework for modifying society and institutions, including their design, organization, assumptions, operations, outputs, opportunity, and reward structures – in the hope of reasonably accommodating the needs of the historically disadvantaged. More specifically, a commitment to inclusivity as integration involves a two-way process of mutual adjustment for improving immigrant access, representation, and equity – by creating a workplace that is *reflective of, respectful of, and responsive to* immigrants' needs and differences, in addition to delivering community services that are accessible, accountable, and appropriate (Fleras 2012e). Pursuing a dual strategy that balances the reactive (removing discriminatory barriers) with the proactive (compensatory measures) is critical in advancing an inclusivity model that proposes a commitment to equal treatment (the culture-blind approach) alongside treatment as equals (the culture-conscious approach).

Inclusion versus Inclusivity: Models of Integration/Accommodation

Often used interchangeably, inclusion and inclusivity may be analytically separated to contrast distinct yet related integration governance models (Fleras 2012d, 2014b). "Inclusion" is used in contrast to "exclusion" (no one is excluded from consideration or participation for reasons beyond their control). Inclusive models of integration assume that something about the person or community must be fixed to ensure their fit into the existing system (Harmon n.d.). To the extent that differences are recognized – and many do see integration as a two-way process (Biles and Frideres 2012) – they tend to be framed via a mosaic metaphor. Like tiles, differences are firmly positioned into place by a mainstream grouting, in effect boxing ethnocultural groups into parallel communities and essentialist cultures.

By contrast, inclusivity (not to be confused with inclusion) models entail a fundamentally different principle: Whereas inclusion is about including everyone by fitting them into the existing system, inclusivity modifies the system itself to ensure that no one is excluded. The focus is on changing the system to accommodate the needs of an internally diverse and fluctuating demographic (Council of Europe 2008). Proposed changes must be structural in nature; after all, cosmetic changes such as hiring minorities or sensitivity sessions are unlikely to dislodge the foundational rules that reinforce power structures and institutional culture. In short, a commitment to inclusivity proposes the creation of a new game with a different set of rules for belonging *in* (not just to) society. Pressure is exerted under inclusivity for doing things differently by contesting the rules that refer to the conventions instead of simply tweaking the conventions that inform the rules.

Notions of equality differ as well. With inclusion as integration, people tend to be treated in the same manner on the assumption that everyone is equal before the law. According to a formal equality model, the emergence of a level playing field in a post-racial Canada means that any achievement gaps are the result of individual choices rather than structural barriers. To the extent that adjustment is required, it's predicated on a one-size-fits-all model that normalizes the accommodation of migrants and minorities into existing or desired hierarchies of power. With inclusivity, however, people must be treated as equals or equitably (similarly) rather than equally (the same). A commitment to an inclusivity model invariably draws attention to the principle of differential accommodation – accommodating different ways of accommodating differences. The contrast is unmistakable: Integration tends to frame diversity as an obstacle to surmount (put bluntly, how to incorporate differences so they no longer constitute a problem [Modood 2011]). A commitment to inclusivity endorses the value of diversity and diversities. Neither a problem to solve nor a challenge to surmount, they are embraced as an asset for improving workplace climate and the delivery of social services – one in which both workers and clients feel recognized and respected rather than excluded or at risk (Fleras and Spoonley 1999). Finally, inclusivity is about building relations with a wide range of stakeholders through "listen and learn" dialogues, including a bottom-up approach involving a two-way process of mutual adjustment ("you adapt, we adjust; we adopt, you adjust").

A commitment to inclusivity proposes a difference model that questions existing arrangements, posits a relational and multiversal view of culture, and frames diversities within contexts of power and inequality (Glasser, Awad, and Kim 2009). Access to services is rooted in rights rather than needs or cultural differences, so that the focus is on mainstreaming equitable provisions rather than applying perfunctory add-ons to mainstream services. Particularly noteworthy is a distinction between the principles of differences-in-society versus society-in-differences (Sandercock 2003). An inclusion model is likely to pose the question "What is the good society?" and then accommodate differences according to that vision (differences-in-society). By contrast, an inclusivity model will begin with the primacy of diversities and differences as good and then adjust society accordingly (society-in-differences). Box 43 captures the distinction between inclusion and inclusivity.

To be sure, neither inclusion ("fitting in") nor inclusivity ("adjusting to") needs to be mutually exclusive of the other. Inclusion as commitment provides a useful first step in the integration process (i.e., "ensuring that no one is excluded because of his or her differences"), whereas inclusivity with its commitment to accommodation takes it to another level ("ensuring that everyone is included precisely because of his or her differences"). Admittedly, putting inclusivity principles into the institutional mix is easier said than done. Mainstream institutions are neither neutral in design nor value-free in process or outputs. Rather, they are ideologically loaded with ideas and ideals about normalcy, acceptability, and desirability that are deeply entrenched within the foundational principles of the constitutional order (from institutional design and organization to operations and outcomes). As socially constructed conventions, they tend to reflect and reinforce the priorities and agendas of those who created or control the process. Majority interests and mainstream priorities are routinely and systemically advanced without much awareness or resistance ("hegemony") (Wallis and Fleras 2008).

MULTICULTURALISM AS INCLUSIVE IMMIGRANT GOVERNANCE: A CANADIAN WAY

> *There are now two major challenges for humanity in the twenty-first century. One is how to live with our planet. The other is how to live with each other.*
> — COMMISSION FOR RACIAL EQUALITY (2007)

43

Models of Immigrant Integration Governance: Inclusion versus Inclusivity

Inclusion models	Inclusivity models
People must fit into existing system	System must change to accommodate diversities
One-way process of adjustment	Two-way process of mutual accommodation
Diversities are a problem	Diversities are assets
We/they mentality	Us/our mindset
Living together with diversity (multiculturalism)	Living together in/with/through diversities (post-multiculturalism)
Make society safe from, safe for, differences	Make differences safe from, safe for, society
Differences-in-society	Society-in-differences
Diversity/diversities/differences	Difference and diversities
Incorporating (whitewashing) differences translates to one-size-fits-all colour-blind treatment	Accommodating differences within differences translates to colour-conscious customizing treatment
Everyone is treated the same (equal treatment)	Need-based differences taken into account
Minority hires and sensitivity training create the right change	Structural changes through removal of discriminatory barriers
Change conventions that refer to rules	Change rules that inform conventions
Top-down approach to decision making (we know what's best)	Bottom-up decision making (listen and learn dialogue)
Modernist bias	Postmodernist bias
Modern nation-state	Postnational society

Source: Fleras (2014b).

Many European countries are experiencing a media-hyped moral panic over multiculturalism as the enemy of integration governance (Vasta 2010; Fleras 2009a). Multiculturalism in Canada entails a relatively benign philosophy and program for accepting and recognizing immigrants as legitimate stakeholders in society. But European multicultural models of immigration governance are perceived to have failed by tolerating inferior or incompatible values (but also Lentin and Titley 2011a, b). In Europe, multiculturalism is dismissed as an "alien import" at odds with a tradition of nationalism in which every state was to coincide with a particular nation (and ideally, vice versa), together with a duty to protect a national culture. To the extent that multiculturalism prevailed, it did not spring naturally from geopolitical developments (unlike in Canada, which needed settlers to domesticate the frontier). It was uncritically transplanted without due consideration of the devastating impact in violating established cultural codes, political and historical traditions, and existing social patterns (Sofos and Tsagarousianou 2012). Europe's experiment with multiculturalism is also criticized for fostering social exclusion because of communal segregation, mutual incomprehension, immigrant exclusion, and gender oppression by sacrificing women's rights in immigrant communities (Council of Europe 2008).

Not unexpectedly, two trends have emerged in Europe. The first openly rejects multiculturalism as a governance framework for integrating immigrants. (Keep in mind that a decline in political support for multiculturalism or a prevalence of anti-multiculturalism do not necessarily invalidate strong levels of support for cultural diversity or inclusiveness initiatives [Fleras 2009a; Forrest and Dunn 2010].) The second trend seeks to rebrand multiculturalism along more inclusionary lines in hopes of nurturing social cohesion and common identity (Vertovec and Wessendorf 2009; Fleras 2012a; Banting and Kymlicka 2012-13). In contrast, the Canadian situation is relatively stable. There is growing evidence of Canada's success in integrating immigrants, including adopting a Canadian identity, participation in Canadian institutions, learning an official language, and forging inter-ethnic friendships (Kymlicka 2010a; Berry 2011; Reitz 2011a; Kymlicka 2012; Wright and Bloemraad 2012). Multiculturalism is singled out as instrumental in facilitating integration, with the following indicators "proving" that it is working:

> A high level of mutual identification and reciprocal acceptance exists between immigrants and the Canadian-born (Transatlantic Trends 2010). International studies consistently rank Canada as the most tolerant country; for example, a study titled Love Thy Neighbour surveyed 32,900 individuals in 23 countries about their views toward other groups. Respondents were asked whether they would want immigrants or people of a different race living next door. Canada scored highest as a welcoming nation, especially toward Muslims, with fewer than 5 percent responding negatively to the question (*Canadian Immigration News* 2007). For their part, immigrants display high levels of pride in Canada (Michael Adams 2007), with the vast majority obtaining citizenship (Bloemraad 2006).

> Compared to those in other countries, naturalized immigrants in Canada are much more likely to be involved in the political process as voters, party members, and candidates who are actively recruited by political parties (Howe 2007).

> Children of immigrants in Canada score better educational outcomes than in any other Western democracy, and second-generation Canadians outperform children of the Canadian-born.

> The absence of immigrant ghettos in Canada suggests high levels of social/geographical integration. Indeed, immigrant/ethnic enclaves are common, but unlike ghettos, they are chosen, not imposed.

> Increasing levels of inter-racial marriage and offspring also attest to growing integration.

That Canada outperforms other countries on such a wide range of measures can be attributed in part to multiculturalism (Wright and Bloemraad 2012). Its positive effects operate at two broad levels: national identity and institutional inclusion (Kymlicka 2010a). In terms of identity, Canada's commitment to multiculturalism embraces immigrants as a constituent part of Canada building, including construction of a national identity and unity. Multiculturalism also provides the bridge by which immigrants come to identify with and take pride in their new country, in effect bolstering their self-esteem while providing a buffer between here and there. Because multiculturalism promotes tolerance and social equality, it has a positive effect in advancing immigrant settlement and integration (Reitz 2009). Multiculturalism (and related programs such as Employment Equity) also plays a central role in constructing inclusive institutions that are responsive to immigrants, reflective of their presence, and respectful of their differences (Fleras 2009a). The conclusion is obvious: In Canada, multiculturalism promotes immigrant inclusion by encouraging healthy attitudes toward others and establishing responsive institutions that include rather than exclude in building an inclusive country (Wright and Bloemraad 2012).

Canada's multiculturalism model is arguably themed around the goal of inclusive nation building (Kymlicka 2007a). It concentrates on constructing an inclusive governance that advances both national and vested interests. It also reinforces a commitment to inclusiveness through the promotion of social justice, identity, and civic participation (also Duncan 2005). It affirms the value and dignity of all citizens, regardless of origins or ethnicity. In the words of Citizenship and Immigration Canada (2012d, 1),

> Canadian multiculturalism is fundamental to our belief that all citizens are equal. Multiculturalism ensures that all citizens can keep their identities, can take pride in their ancestry, and have a sense of belonging. Acceptance gives Canadians a feeling of security and self confidence, making them more open to, and accepting of, diverse cultures. The Canadian experience has shown that multiculturalism encourages racial and ethnic harmony and cross-cultural understanding, and discourages ghettoization, hatred, discrimination, and violence. Through multiculturalism, Canada recognizes the potential of all Canadians, encouraging them to integrate into their society and take an active part in its social, cultural, economic, and political affairs.

Of course, multiculturalism is not without limits and costs (Frideres and Biles 2012). It is concerned with integrating people into the framework of an existing Canada rather than bringing about transformative social change (Hansen 2014). An integrative agenda tends to endorse the principles of liberal universalism and to dismiss differences as irrelevant, inferior, or threatening (a pretend pluralism). But what if immigrant minorities wish to go beyond this agenda, not only in demanding equality and non-discrimination (redistribution), but also in insisting that their collective identities be made a matter of public record (recognition) (Bhabha 2009)? With multiculturalism, however, the disruptiveness of difference is depoliticized by the simple expedient of institutionalizing differences or, alternatively, by privatizing them into the personal. Differences are stripped of their potency by channelling potentially troublesome conflicts into the harmless avenues of identity or folklore. They are further depoliticized (or neutered) by treating them as if they are all the same, ensuring that central authorities continue to define them and to circumscribe their outer limits, while removing culturally charged symbols from public places.

Two spins are possible. First, far from being a destabilizing threat to the social order, Canada's multiculturalism is a hegemonic discourse that defends dominant ideology (Abu-Laban 2014; Day 2014). Depending on where one stands on the political spectrum, this is cause for concern or contentment. Second, multiculturalism remains a governance of necessity for a changing and diversifying Canada. As a skilful blend of compromises in a country that is constructed around compromises, it symbolizes an innovative if imperfect social experiment for living together differently and equitably. It has extricated Canada from its colonialist past, in the process encouraging immigrant women and men to participate in their communities, build productive lives, and contribute to society (Jedwab 2014). Under the circumstances, the question is not whether Canada can afford multiculturalism. Perhaps it's more accurate to say that Canada *cannot not* afford to embrace multiculturalism in its constant quest for political unity, social coherence, economic prosperity, cultural enrichment, and societal survival.

PART 4

repositioning immigrant governance

NEGOTIATING A NEW GLOBAL MIGRATION ORDER

LARGE-SCALE IMMIGRATION and its corresponding diversities are transforming communities by challenging conventional notions of national identity and societal unity (Ferguson, Langlois, and Roberts 2009; Grubel 2009). This rapid change has coincided with a host of deeper challenges, including the most severe economic downturn in decades, putting pressure on political leaders to "navigate a tangled web of complex policy dilemmas" (Papademetriou 2012, 1). Immigration-related drivers of anxiety, public unease, and social unrest revolve around the following themes: (a) loss of control over markers of identity (culture); (b) disruption to familiar patterns of interaction (social); (c) the perceived high cost of immigrant settlement (economic); (d) loss of confidence in the state's ability to curb unwanted migration (political); and (e) fears of extremism and terrorism (security). A commitment to multiculturalism as immigrant governance has come under criticism as well, in part for overemphasizing difference and separation rather than community and society building, in part for underemphasizing the accommodation of differences within differences in the immigrant community. Not surprisingly, as the social fabric frays because of dynamics beyond individual control, people tighten their grip on what they cherish (identity, citizenship, culture), impose more rigid patterns of conformity, and restrict migrant rights to residence and citizenship (ibid.).

Part 4 of this book, on rethinking immigration governance in the context of the new global migration order, provides a fitting finish. The internationalization of immigration is transforming the social landscape of both immigration societies and societies of immigrants. Newcomers are younger and more diverse, more global in scope, increasingly transmigrant in connections, and more influential in their impact on domestic and international politics (Castles and Miller 2009). The geopolitics of a flexible migratory labour force under global capitalism and transnational migration (Webb 2010; Simmons 2010) places an onus on theorizing how immigration no longer respects national borders or is contained within the framework of state sovereignty. Or, as Bridget Anderson (2013) observes, there is no real "outside" anymore. Global processes associated with free trade, financial markets, production supply chains, and free-floating migrant workers have transformed the world into one vast "inside," with the relatively privileged continuing to exercise control over the movement of the mobile poor. Immigrant-receiving countries are no less conflicted and challenged by the dynamics and demands of newcomers. That many national governments are poorly equipped to address the complex global issues that are associated with international migration (Gogia and Slade 2011; Malloch-Brown 2011) is hardly a hopeful sign.

The globalization of migration draws attention to the politics of trans-immigrant governance in a diversifying and postnational Canada. The challenges are readily evident in a connected and colliding world where what happens elsewhere affects the here, so that the "there" and the "here" are rarely where people think they are (Shome 2012). Chapter 10 delves into the reasons why and how, concentrating on two themes. First, it discusses various governance models for managing immigrants – monocultural, multicultural/national, and multiversal/transnational. A commitment to an inclusive multiculturalism may facilitate the integration of newcomers, but the advent of immigrant "superdiversities" suggests a drift toward a post-multicultural model of immigrant governance. Second, awareness is mounting that the macro politics of the global migration order require the establishment of new patterns of immigrant governance that are anchored in the principles of transmigration, inclusivity, and multiversality. A discursive shift toward Canada as a postnational society is shown to be commensurate with a transnational immigration model that, in turn, plays into a model of differential accommodation – a commitment to accommodate different ways of accommodating differences within differences (Fleras 2011b).

Notions of citizenship are increasingly debated in a globalizing world of transmigration and transnationalism. In addition, references to citizenship practices, discourses, and policies have devolved into debates over securitizing society by disciplining migrants. Canada remains a governance outlier in this respect. In much of the world, fears are mounting over transmigrant belonging and multiple identities, but Canadians are relatively free to follow paths of citizenship as they see fit (Conference Notes 2011). Yet the concept of citizenship as a disciplinary (resocializing) tool is no less evident in federal moves to tighten up the process of becoming Canadian. Chapter 11 capitalizes on this oppositional dynamic by exploring the politics of citizenship within the framework of a postnational/transnational Canada. Of particular note is the rethinking of citizenship from a singular (one-size-fits-all) model to a more inclusive model that customizes patterns of entitlements for new Canadians.

The final chapter provides an overview of the volume. It addresses the core themes of the book, including (a) new migrant trends and patterns, (b) the demands that these dynamics impose on both sending and receiving countries, (c) their impact and implications for migrants themselves, and (d) how people should think and talk about immigration and immigrants in light of twenty-first-century realities. Failure to rethink immigration and reframe immigrants, the chapter concludes, does not bode well for living together differently in an immigration society of immigrants.

10

rethinking immigrant governance

THE CHALLENGES OF COMPLEX DIVERSITY

UNSETTLING IMMIGRATION GOVERNANCE

TO SAY THAT we live in provocative and perplexing times is (to borrow a phrase) a cliché of understated proportions. The border-busting dynamics of transmigration and transnationalism are contesting conventional notions of nation building and national unity.[1] Orthodox notions of belonging and identities are increasingly up for grabs in a diasporic world of crossings and connections (Geislerova 2007; Fleras 2012c). No less challenging is the emergence of cosmopolitanism as a global governance principle.[2] Its humanistic notion of a universal social justice in advancing a global citizenship without borders adds yet another layer of complexity to an already complex world (Fleras 2011a). The interplay of these factors raises an intriguing question: Does a place-based model of immigrant governance still make sense? Is it possible to dwell together in a spatialized location if immigrant notions of identity and belonging are increasingly uncoupled from place?

The prospect and the politics of immigrant integration are now a major global governance challenge (Garcea, Kirova, and Wong 2008). The movement of people is ramping up global anxieties over a "coming anarchy" in unsettling long-established patterns of identity and belonging, unity and security (Bourbeau 2011). National jurisdictions in the post-9/11 era are looking to discipline differences by tightening up conditions for naturalization, introducing tougher language/value requirements as a precondition for integration and citizenship, and deterring unwanted immigration flows via robust border enforcement and multi- and bilateral agreements (Ang 2010; Carr 2010; Laegaard 2010; Rygiel 2010). This combination of increased securitization and transmigratory dynamics poses prickly questions about an inclusive immigration governance. The politics of transnationality are known to (a) blur a defence of territorial boundaries, (b) encourage cross-border movements of migrants in search of safety or success, (c) undermine patterns of multicultural governance, (d) transform public space, (e) direct identities away from a strict national focus, and (f) exert pressure for alternative political arrangements to manage diversities without reneging on a sense of community and commitment (Birt 2007; Jedwab 2007-08; Ang 2010).

These emergent realities raise additional questions about the relevance of an official multiculturalism as a territorially based model of immigrant governance within the seemingly opposed contexts of an inhospitable national yet the uninhabitable transnational (Vertovec and Wessendorf 2004; Ang 2010). Can Canadian multiculturalism be unbound from the myopic monoculturalism of a mosaic universalism and relinked along lines that respect the complexity of diversities in a transmigrant world (Walton-Roberts 2011)? Is it possible to conjoin oppositional dynamics in a creative synthesis that aligns the realities of porous borders with a bounded nationalism and complex diversities (Birt 2007)?[3] These challenges make it doubly important to rethink the immigration/multiculturalism/citizenship nexus when it contests conventional notions of sovereignty, territorial integrity, border control, and immigrant governance. This chapter examines three models of governance – monocultural, multicultural, and multiversal – which Box 44 presents in simplified terms.

WHAT IS MULTICULTURALISM TO DO IN A TRANSNATIONAL WORLD?

The world is an untidy and unruly place. Societies are no longer the orderly jurisdictions that many imagined or that they themselves aspired to be. To the contrary, they are complex, inconsistent, and overlapping, with many identities, perspectives, and sites of action, including multiple universes within universes (multiverse) that cross

44

Aligning the Models of Governance,
Immigration, Society, and Citizenship

	Model A	Model B	Model C
Governance model	Monoculturalism	Multiculturalism	Multiversal (post-multiculturalism)
Immigration model	National/European	National/European	Transnational
Model of society	Premodern	Modern	Postmodern/postnational
Citizenship model (see Chapter 11)	Exclusive	Singular/common	Customized

Source: Fleras (2014b).

borders and collapse notions of time and space (Latham 2008). Nation-states confront the challenge of maintaining their integrity, unity, and identity in the face of increasingly disruptive dynamics over models of immigrant governance (Ang 2010). The interplay of trans-migration (transnationalism) with cosmopolitanism and diaspora may subvert the salience of multiculturalism as an immigration govern-ance model. A static and categorical multiculturalism will no longer suffice due to its inability to capture the immensely complex social re-alities of immigrants within a context of differences-within-differences (multiversality) will see to that (Fleras 2012c). Or to phrase it more emphatically, Canada's urban centres are outgrowing both the trad-itional model of multiculturalism and the language that was once used to describe Canadian society (Sandercock 2006). Evolving instead are superdiverse (multiversal) realities that fundamentally alter the way in which people see, interact, and communicate (Ley 2005; Habacon 2007; Fleras 2011b). Writing of a pending post-multiculturalism, Ang (2011, 29) points out that nation-states are de facto diverse in ways that can no longer be contained within the neat model of unity in diversity. After many generations of immigration history, migrants and their descendants are no longer containable within a fixed and internally homogeneous category of "ethnic community," as tended to be assumed in the formative years of a state-sponsored multiculturalism. Witness the second, third, and fourth generations, whose ethnic identities are increasingly fluid, hybridized and Westernized. Nor has there been a smooth process of integration of migrants into the national community, not because multiculturalism encouraged them to lead parallel lives, but because differences between people(s) – racial, cultural, religious – are very resistant to erasure: processes of inclusion and exclusion, the differentiation of the self and other, and the drawing of dividing lines between us and them are an enduring feature of the human way of life.

In a postnational Canada, established rules, values, and institutions are struggling to construct more fluid and flexible models of immigrant governance that have yet to gain mainstream traction (ibid.). To one side is the proliferation of identity politics and the politicization of faith-based communities whose inward-looking commitments complicate and confuse. Pressure is mounting for differences to be taken seriously, even though official multiculturalism is ill-equipped to do so except in the most superficial way. To the other side are those globalizing processes whose transmigratory forces threaten to decouple multicultural governances from a place-based model of immigrant integration (Ferguson and Mansbach 2012). A mosaic model of multiculturalism is problematic, especially for those Canadians whose ethnicity is not all-consuming. Yes, ethnicity may inform their identity across multiple cultural spaces, yet it should neither define who they are nor box them in (Milton Wong 2007). As well, multicultural discourses are often limited to issues and arrangements within a particular nation-state, a clearly bounded territory, and on a nationalist frame of reference (Ang 2010). But what happens when nearly 9 percent of Canada's population live and work overseas? Are they "real" Canadians in need of innovative arrangements? Or are they Canadians of convenience who deserve to be scorned (Ignatieff 2011)? Or consider how 250,000 new Canadians each year no longer automatically identify exclusively with Canada but may nurture transmigrant linkages because of communication technology and transportation ease.

Clearly, ours is a profoundly post-multicultural era. The mosaic concept has given way to the rearticulation of individual identity and belonging along multi-diverse, fluid, and hybridic lines within a changing, diverse, and confusing world. A post-multicultural world draws its legitimacy from a postnational society, which in turn beckons the postmodernist principle of "doing things differently." The emergence and growing awareness of a differences-within-differences framework as the basis for diversity governance mean that it's futile to endorse modernist goals of clarity, coherence, centralized authority, commonality, and consensus. The lofty position of a monocultural nation-state as the privileged unit of sovereign identity and agency is contested by rampant internal fragmentation, instability and contestation, and potentially porous borders. To put it bluntly, a globalizing world of capital flows and transmigrant movement may be slowly eroding the salience of the nation-state as the exclusive governance space for fostering security, community, identity, and belonging.

To be sure, the nation-state is proving resistant as a site of immigrant integration. Doomsday naysayers notwithstanding, it is unlikely to disappear as an organizing principle or lose its influence or legitimacy, but it will no longer be absolute. It is more likely to operate as one of many nodes of socio-spatial power, as its territory is transversed by the flow of cross-cutting border dynamics (Ang 2010; Rygiel 2010). The end result is nothing short of contradictory. On the one hand, nation-states are disorderly and permeable social spaces, but they continue to define who gets in and who gets what. On the other hand, postnational notions of identity and transnational concepts of belonging are emerging that supersede territorially based versions of citizenship and integration (Ang 2011).

The interplay of unsettled boundaries, transnational loyalties, and multiple identities has proven consequential in deconstructing the monocultural ideal of a unitary nation-state. International migration poses a governance challenge in confronting the concept of the nation-state with respect to borders, organization, identity, services, and "belongingness" (Consterdine 2013). National governments are no longer equipped to address complex global issues and multiple identities associated with transmigration and multiversality. Nowhere is this

challenge more sharply contested than in debates over multiculturalism as a model of immigrant governance in a trans-world (see Reitz
2009; Ryan 2010). For some, a commitment to multiculturalism con-
jures up the spectre of condoning multiple identities at the expense of
common values (Paquet 2008; Mansur 2011). The political philoso-
pher Roger Scruton conveys a sense of the dilemma: Can any cultural
or immigrant group whose laws, social identity, absolutism, and blind
loyalty emanate from a religious or tribal source possibly co-exist with
a Western political culture or membership in a multicultural society
(cited in Boswell 2011)? Consider, for example, that the challenge of
integrating Islam into a secular and multicultural governance has unleashed debate over "whose governance rules rule" – as Ghassan Hage
(2006) cogently puts it:

> For multiculturalism was always about finding a space for the
> culture of the other, insofar as that culture does not claim a
> sovereignty over itself that clashes with the laws of the nation ...
> Multiculturalism has always had capacity to find a space for such
> minor laws within an all encompassing national law. This is part
> of what defines it. However, for people who take their religion
> seriously, this situation is reversed. The laws of God are all en-
> compassing, and the national laws of the host nation are minor.
> For a seriously religious Muslim migrant, to integrate into the
> host nation becomes a matter of finding space for these national
> laws within the all encompassing laws of God. We then see how
> the very relationship between encompassing and encompassed
> cultures, on which multiculturalism is based, is here inverted.

A conflict of interest is inevitable (Blond and Pabst 2008). The Islamic
presence poses a governance threat by seemingly challenging the notions of governance that historically privileged the monocultural (and
often secular) state to define what differences count and what counts
as difference. The state, it would seem, does not take kindly to such af-
fronts to its authority.

Anxieties are accelerating over the politics of immigrant identities
and integration within a shared political space and human rights
framework (Berkeley 2011). Questions focus on the viability of multiculturalism as an immigration governance model in a globalizing and
increasingly postnational world (Pieterse 2006). A *national* model of

immigration governance envisions immigrants as moving along a one-off trajectory of severed affiliations and singular commitments (Karim 2007). A commitment to multiculturalism, official or otherwise, is thought to be consistent with this arrangement. But the dynamics of transmigration in a *transnational* world of movement and connections eclipse this model, with multiculturalism shouldering the blame for perpetuating often diametrically opposed trends. More specifically, three lines of argument prevail in assessing the salience of a "rooted" (bounded) multiculturalism in an increasingly "rootless" (unbounded) world (see also Kymlicka and Walker 2012):

> For some, any multiculturalism that is bounded by the state is deeply flawed (Pieterse 2007). The inwardness of multiculturalism as a society-building project renders it increasingly irrelevant in a globalizing world of fluidity, border crossings, and multiplicity. Transnational relations are no longer simply a transfer point between host and home country. A criss-crossing of diasporic communities occurs instead across multiple continents. In brief, nation-states are no longer the exclusive container of identities and belonging; nevertheless, most mindsets still fixate on multiculturalism within the framework of a national arena (ibid.; also Kymlicka 2007c).
> Others see state multiculturalism as facilitating unhealthy political loyalties by tolerating transmigratory ties and old world conflicts (Granatstein 2007; but see Satzewich 2007-08; Vasta 2010). A commitment to multiculturalism ostensibly encourages transmigrant social practices and transnational social identities that many believe reinforce un-Canadian values, segregate newcomers into isolated communities (Paquet 2008, 2011), devalue citizenship, preclude integration into society, and legitimize dual political loyalties (Mansur 2011). Worse still, the wrong message for living together with differences is transmitted: It's acceptable for migrants to live in distinct communities, with their own set of socio-cultural values, but political correctness ensures that it's not acceptable for the mainstream to criticize objectionable cultural practices (Stoffman 2009a).
> For still others, a sense of nuance is critical (see Reitz 2010a). Domestic affairs cannot be divorced from global contexts. Globalization has fundamentally altered people's lived experiences at the level of social structures, organizational contexts, and interpersonal relations (Negi and Furman 2010). A commitment to state multiculturalism for

managing immigration governance is thus experiencing an identity crisis of confidence because of borderless trajectories and splintered identities. But because globalization is not a zero-sum game (Gelernter and Regev 2010) – it's more of a mutually constitutive process involving an interplay of local, national, and global – multiculturalism is conceivably a logical extension of transnationalism yet simultaneously occluded (Satzewich and Wong 2006).

The paradox of a multiculturally based immigration governance cannot be underestimated (Ang 2010). A commitment to multiculturalism may foster a more secure basis for reconciling the micro politics of immigrant diversities with the demand for national unity, but a landscape littered with the internationalized, transmigratory, and globally interpolated raises key questions that challenge the politics of immigrant integration (Walton-Roberts 2011). Immigration has moved from a domestic policy for nation building under the control of a sovereign state to a multi-contested site that (a) involves international competition for talent; (b) must neutralize border-busting dynamics, from communication technologies to sophisticated smuggling rings; and (c) is increasingly monitored by international human rights organizations. Canada is no longer just a country of immigrants; to the contrary, it is but one operational node in a transnational world. Or, as Margaret Walton-Roberts (2011, 119) writes, "Discussions of multiculturalism must continue to consider the ways in which it engages not only with domestic preoccupations regarding Canadian identity, but also with the realities of global migration and labour circulation which are structured by the global system of inequality." Society is caught between the proverbial rock and a hard place. For fear of looking inflexible, it can't uphold a fixed national identity; nor can it espouse a no-holds-barred commitment to diversity without eroding borders or eclipsing sovereignty. The tensions associated with this balancing act may, if left unchecked, threaten to destabilize the boundaries and integrity of the nation-state.

CONCEPTUALIZING IMMIGRANT GOVERNANCE MODELS

Reference to governance has progressed from relative obscurity to an obligatory slogan in less than a decade. Despite its popularity at conceptual and practical levels, the concept is prone to uncertainties over definition and characteristics (Fleras 2012a). For our purposes, governance is a framework of rules that establishes a principled relationship between ruler and ruled, with a corresponding distribution of power and an exchange of rights and obligations. The governance framework addresses how authority is divided, power is distributed, policies are formulated, valued resources are allocated in a given jurisdiction, priorities and agendas are set, decisions are made, accountability is rendered, implementation is secured, and rules of the political game are respected to prevent conflict and promote cohesion (Turton et al. 2007; also Fox and Ward 2008). Three governance models – monocultural, multicultural, and multiversal – manage immigration and immigrant diversities.

Monocultural Governance

Monocultural governance embodies a Westphalian model of society building. Nineteenth-century nationalist ideologies sought to conflate the notion of a nation with a sovereign state in striving for unity through uniformity by rejecting any differences as contrary to successful governance (Coleman 2011). This Westphalian commitment to monocultural governance and national homogeneity as the first modernity was organized along the lines of a centrist state that embraced an essentialized and uncontested concept of national unity and identity (Ben-Eliezer 2008). According to the core doctrine of nationalism, the nation is the sole source of political power (Anthony Smith 2013). Each nation is entitled to its own sovereign status and state, with a corresponding right to protect its destiny by coupling statehood with collective identity (Koenig and de Guchteneire 2007). The ideology of monocultural nationalism focused on unifying an otherwise disparate population around a shared sense of national identity, political unity, and cultural homogeneity (Parekh 2005; Guibernau 2007). To the extent that the concept of citizenship even existed in a nationalistic context where the primary loyalty dovetailed with the nation-state, it was (a) restrictive and difficult to access, (b) assigned by blood at birth with only one citizenship possible, and (c) revoked upon naturalization in another jurisdiction (Faist 2008; Weinstock 2008).

In short, the mononational state possessed and was possessed by a dominant national group that manipulated its hegemonic powers to control and contain. Membership in the nation under nationalism was the precondition for the trust and relationships that would organize and secure the basis for society (Bridget Anderson 2013). Those who didn't belong to the group were subject to annihilation or expulsion, discrimination or assimilation (Kymlicka 2007b). The consequences of this monoculturalism persist into the present, as Parekh (2005, 8-9) writes:

> Contemporary multicultural societies have emerged against the backdrop of several centuries of the culturally homogenising nation-state ... Since the state required cultural and social homogenization as a necessary basis [for a new kind of societal unity], it has for centuries sought to mould the wider society in that direction. Thanks to this, we have become so accustomed to equating unity with homogeneity, and equality with uniformity, that unlike many of our premodern counterparts we feel morally and emotionally disoriented by, and do not quite know how to accommodate, the political demands of a deep and defiant diversity.

Multicultural Governance/National Immigration Model

Monoculturalism as governance was eventually discredited on the grounds that it reflected a false view of human ideals; became tainted by association with nationalism, fascism, and war; and was needlessly repressive of individuality and human rights. A multicultural model emerged instead that embraced the principles of universal personhood and the practices of active citizenship, while challenging conventional notions of belonging and identity, especially those that relegated minorities and migrants to second-class status (Berns-McGown 2007-08). Multicultural governance rejected any explicit endorsement of a state-sponsored ethnicity or religion. Advanced instead was the principle of separating church from state as governance framework – that is, the state does not interfere in the activities of ethnic communities. Conversely, ethnocultural groups are expected to stay out of state business. The end result is a multicultural state that (a) remains ostensibly neutral and impartial when engaging its constituent individuals and communities; (b) sees the state as belonging to all of its citizens, not just a single national group; (c) embraces the rights of all migrants and minorities to full and equal participation without forfeiting the right to identity and equality; and (d) ensures that all citizens have the same institutional access as the national group (Kymlicka 2007b).

The introduction of multicultural governance was premised on an integration promise. Members from diverse ethnocultural groups would co-exist with each other through a process of national integration – a kind of unity in diversity that was paralleled at the global level by the United Nations. There, each nation-state member has its own seat at the table to maintain its distinctiveness, yet all must abide by common rules (Ang 2011, 28). But principles are one thing in defining a framework for living together with differences. Putting them into practice is quite another. Bhikhu Parekh (2005, 343) captures a taste of the contradictory and the contested conveyed by multiculturalism, albeit within a different context:

> Multicultural societies throw up problems that have no parallel in history. They need to find ways of reconciling the legitimate demands of unity and diversity, achieving political unity without cultural uniformity, being inclusive without being assimilationist, cultivating among their citizens a common sense of belonging while respecting their legitimate cultural differences and cherishing plural cultural identities without weakening the shared and precious identity of shared citizenship. This is a formidable political task and no multicultural society so far has succeeded.

Predictably, fears of extremism or separation/isolation in the post-9/11 era have prompted assimilationist pleas for additional control. The growing securitization of society and the militarization of borders also challenge the salience of multiculturalism as a framework for fostering integration, social cohesion, and loyal citizenship (Ang 2010).

One way of conceptualizing multicultural governance is by playing it off against its conceptual opposite. Whereas monocultural governance suppresses diversities, multiculturalism acknowledges them (Panossian, Berman, and Linscott 2007; also Ang 2010). Monocultural governance embraces assimilation and/or segregation, but multicultural governance focuses on adjustment and inclusion, at least in principle. Monocultural governance expects migrants and minorities to accept their subordinate status, whereas contemporary multicultural governance no longer dismisses them as irrelevant, unequal, or marginal. They are perceived instead as legitimate and integral components of society with membership based on (a) residency rather than ancestry, (b) a commitment to liberal-democratic values, (c) a belief in a shared (civic) future rather than a common (or ethnic) past as the basis for belonging and identity, and a (d) relatively easy process of naturalization with the possibility of multiple citizenships (Weinstock 2008).

Canada's official multiculturalism as national governance for immigrant settlement provides an ideal template. Shifts in emphasis notwithstanding – ranging from ethnicity to equity to civic to integrative (Fleras 2012e) – it has never wavered from its central mission of constructing an inclusive Canada without disrupting the status quo in the process. As might be expected of any state program with hegemonic overtones, it does not extol (a) celebrating differences, (b) promoting ethnic minorities or group rights, (c) fostering parallel communities, (d) transforming structures or challenging liberal-democratic principles, (e) addressing politicized or deep differences, or (f) an anything-goes relativism whereby all cultures and cultural practices are accepted. Of course, no one is suggesting that a commitment to inclusiveness is beyond politics. Rather, it is consistent with state multiculturalism's unofficial status as a political act to achieve national unity and identity (Peter 1978; also Clark 2009).

Multiversal Governance/Transnational Immigration Model

A multiversal governance model builds upon but goes beyond its multicultural counterpart (Fleras 2014b). It achieves this by acknowledging the principles of a postnational society and the primacy of transnational immigration models within a governance context that not only recognizes the reality of differences within differences, but also accepts the corresponding necessity to accommodate different ways of accommodating differences. The politics of multiversality are looming large. In contrast to the liberal principles of state multiculturalism whereby the dominant group establishes the agenda for minority participation while circumventing dialogue for belonging and identity, a commitment to multiversality does it differently. A multiversal governance seeks to delegitimize the barriers to hyper-different ways of being and becoming (superdiversity), in the process making it compatible with a wide range of transmigrant belongings and transnational identities.

What is multiversality and how does it embody a post-multicultural model of immigrant governance? According to Robert Latham (2007-

08), the word "multiverse" conveys the idea of multiple social universes. Differences in a multiverse persist across many overlapping and intersecting universes, resulting in a proliferation of *fissions, fissures,* and *fusions.* Fissions within migrant and minority communities are increasingly compounded and crosscut by new axes of differentiation, distinction, and demands related to legal status, religion, gender, age, nationality, and class (Vertovec 2010; also Vertovec and Wessendorf 2004). Fissures within migrant and minority communities reflect social cleavages, both temporary and permanent, because of internal politics, conflicting agendas, and variable socio-economic statuses. Cue fusions: Thanks in part to Canada's immigration program, its cities now exhibit superdiversity, according to Daniel Hiebert, a co-director of Vancouver's Metropolis Project (*Globe and Mail* 2011a) – namely, a vibrant fusion of cultures, religions, homeland linkages, sexual orientations, and everyday experiences (also Ley 2005). Unlike a mosaic model that manacles people to their ethnicity and ancestry, a multiversal model acknowledges ethnicity as one component of a multi-dimensional identity (Ang 2011).

Canada is much more than a multicultural social formation. It is also aligned along the crosscutting lines of multiracial, multiclass, multigendered, multisexual, multilingual, multireligious, multigenerational, multihistorical, multicitizenships, and so on (Latham 2008, 2009). This complex co-existence reflects a dizzying range of differences and entitlements, not only between identifiable groups and communities, but also *within* groups and *across* spaces and borders. The politicization of differences within differences, ranging from identity politics to demands for public recognition of religious differences, demands more complex responses than are offered by multiculturalism. Faisal Bhabha (2009, 48) speaks to the prospect of living in what amounts to a post-multicultural (multiversal) Canada:

> Controversies surrounding multiculturalism are neither unique to Canada nor new. However, the recent prominence, and growing hyper-consciousness of culture in the public realm, reveals the profound underlying social cleavages of our modern, multi-ethnic society. Members of minority cultures are increasingly demanding not only equality and non-discrimination when integrating into the dominant culture but also that their collective identity be made a matter of public importance and accommodation.

Claims can be complex and confusing; distinctions between groups and individuals are often muddled. For instance, during the now infamous sharia controversy in Ontario, the most acute debate raged between different factions of the same minority community ["devout" Muslims versus the "silent majority" of moderate Muslims].

The politics of multiversal governance are not new to Canada but embody the logic behind its difference model (Fleras 2012c). Canada may be the only country in the world that simultaneously addresses the realities, agendas, constitutional status, and aspirations of three major difference projects – namely, Aboriginal peoples, English and French Charter groups, and multicultural minorities (Kymlicka 1998). The genius of a multiversal arrangement is its willingness to embrace the need for these three broadly exclusive platforms (silos). It also accepts that (a) the three difference sectors possess fundamentally divergent agendas and priorities, given their varying historical status, corresponding entitlements, patterns of belonging, and aspirational objectives; (b) any policy solutions must reflect a sociological distinction between voluntary (immigrant) minorities and forcibly incorporated Aboriginal peoples; and (c) proposed outcomes must coincide with the constitutional status of each sector without breaching a commitment to the principle of unity within diversity. Three levels of difference governance reflect and reinforce a commitment to the principles of inclusivity, albeit at macro levels:

> At one difference level are Aboriginal peoples' claims to be sovereign nations with rights of self-determining autonomy over land, identity, and political voice (Maaka and Fleras 2005). A package of priorities is suggested whose foundational premise advances the principles of power sharing and a partnership commensurate with a government-to-government relationship. Canada is grappling with decolonizing its relationship with the descendants of the original inhabitants, in part by promising a more positive alternative that is consistent with a new postcolonial social contract.

> The second level addresses the concerns of the Québécois, who, like Aboriginal peoples, claim sovereignty as "nations within." This entails the acknowledgment of (a) a compact/covenant view of Canada, (b) Quebec's sociological status as a forcibly incorporated minority

that wants to get out of existing political arrangements, and (c) its demands as a distinct society to exercise mastery over its own house. English-speaking Canada appears to be moving in the direction of a more flexible federalism, one that recognizes Quebec as more than a province but less than a separate nation-state, although there is reluctance to constitutionally entrench this shift for fear of demolishing the fictions that paper over Canada's contradictions.

> The third level acknowledges the rights of Canada's immigrant and multicultural minorities to be different (recognition) yet equal (redistribution) and the same (citizenship) without paying a penalty in the process (James 2005; Jedwab 2014). The combination of initiatives, from anti-racism to employment equity, reinforces the notion of Canada as a society of many cultures in which people's cultural differences cannot preclude full participation and equal citizenship rights, while still acknowledging that need-based differences may be incorporated when necessary.

Canada's difference model of governance has proven its potential in managing complex diversity. The next step is to ratchet up the reality and centrality of diversities within diversities in constructing a post-multicultural governance model. This line of reasoning can be applied not only at national levels but also in a globalizing and transmigratory world where notions of identity and belonging are increasingly cast adrift from the fixed moorings of the nation-state. A new type of immigrant and immigrant experience is emerging in light of these complex diversities, one that neither severs ties with the home country nor passively assimilates into the host country, yet thrives in the positives of such complexities. The following passage, with its portrait of a super-diverse Canadian, is instructive of the micro politics at play:

> My name is Sophie and I am Canadian. And what does that mean? According to Canadian census, it means: I am third generation Canadian on my mother's side and second generation Canadian on my father's side. My maternal grandparents are Canadian and British. My paternal grandparents are Senegalese. My aunts and uncles come from Canada, Thailand, Senegal, and the Ivory Coast. I am Muslim by birth, my father is Muslim and my mother is Roman Catholic. Our family celebrates Aid El-Fitr and Eid Al-Adha, as well as, Christmas and Easter. I have multiple

citizenships; British, Canadian and Senegalese. I attended French primary and secondary schools and then went on to university in both English and French. At home I spoke English with my mother and French with my father. I don't remember which language I learned first ... At the moment ... I divide my time living between Abbotsford and Dubai, while working for three separate companies headquartered in Hong Kong, South Africa and Guatemala. My taxes are paid based on the amount of time I spend in each of my residences. (quoted in Gaye 2011)

Trans-immigrants participate simultaneously across many spheres of life in both host and home countries. They identify with and hold onto multiple identities across national borders as they settle into their new homeland; they construct diasporic communities that offer solidarity, support, information, and identity; and they participate across multiple universes without necessarily dissolving attachment to the host country (Pieterse 2006). Finally, notions of citizenship are shifting as well. References to a nationally bounded citizenship that tether individuals to one nation-state are giving way to the concept of postnational (multiversal) citizenship that acknowledges immigrant claims for rights, identity, and belonging across numerous domains (Ehrkamp and Leitner 2006).

TRANSNATIONAL IMMIGRATION IN A POSTNATIONAL CANADA

The world is engulfed by three mutually exclusive yet inextricably linked forces. First, a freewheeling global market economy exerts a universalizing (and homogenizing) strength. Transnational movements of goods and services are conducted with seemingly minimal regard for societal boundaries (Castles and Miller 2009). Advances in information technology tend to render national borders increasingly porous and difficult to monitor and control. Second, the fragmenting forces of insurgent ethnic identities are poised to dismember and destroy. Radical ethnicities and ethnic nationalisms appear to be largely indifferent or hostile to the legitimacy of the nation-state, regardless of consequences (Ignatieff 1994). Third, the nation-state is resilient in preserving its sovereignty, territorial integrity, and border crossings. In a global world fraught with ethnic tensions and global movements, this interplay of centrifugal (push out) and centripetal (pull in) factors is reshaping the political contours of societies large and small, in the process contesting the concept of what society is for.

Canada appears to have successfully balanced these global dynamics with national interests and minority rights. Although its juggling act is sometimes wobbly, its achievement in Canada building cannot be scoffed at, given the enormity of the challenges. Unlike the more complete (or civilizational) societies of Europe (Castles and Miller 2009), Canada *represents* an idea and a set of ideals rather than a single people with a history, language, and culture. It is precisely this fundamental ambiguity that underscores the contradictions in Canada building. "Canada is not a real country," as Quebec premier Lucien Bouchard (27 January 1996, cited in Beiner 2003, 171) once taunted English-speaking Canadians, but a collection of shreds and patches, with no raison d'être (historical or cultural) to claim nationality or peoplehood. Outside of Quebec, Canadians have little in common – no shared ancestors or gene pool, no origin myths, and few common rituals, except perhaps a commitment to public institutions such as universal health care (Fleras 2012a). To rephrase it, Canada is not so much a mosaic of culturally distinct tiles, but a complex matrix of wiggly lines and contested angles in response to the demands of multiple identities and competing sovereignties under a single polity.

This assessment of Canada may not flatter, but the persistence of these very vulnerabilities may yield a host of possibilities for crafting a new kind of country. Canada may be poised on the brink of becoming the world's first postnational society, even if nobody can agree on exactly what this means (Florby, Shackleton, and Suhonen 2009). Consider the contrasts. A "national" society embraces the principles of modernity as the basis for migrant governance. As an Enlightenment project, modernity rejected religion (and race/ethnicity) as a legitimate form of social authority, embraced reason and scientific inquiry as the organizing principle of social life, sought to develop universal categories of explanation and rationalization, strove to attain absolute truth (universally valid foundations for human knowledge based on reason and science), and conceived of history as having direction or purpose (Dustin 2007). Applied to society, an embrace of modernity reflected the ideals and attainment of a unitary, centralized, and homogenized nation-state. The nation-state was possessed and governed by a dominant national group, which expressed its nationhood through language, culture, history, and symbols (Kymlicka 2007a, 2007c). It also entailed a commitment to a master narrative (uniformity), a coherent state identity (homogeneity), universalism (rules apply to all), centrality (to ensure conformity and control), clarity (rather than ambiguities), a low threshold for uncertainties, and a belief in merging nation (peoples) with state (a people) (Dustin 2007). Or, to rephrase it in the vernacular of the twenty-first century, it pursues a "McDonaldized" efficiency, predictability, and standardization (Ritzer 2008).

A postnational society reflects the postmodernist principle of doing it differently. An era of politicized difference and multiversal differences challenges the foundational principles of a conventional societal order; it also demonstrates the futility of defending the modernist goals of clarity, coherence, centralized authority, commonality, and consensus when confronted by fluidity, contestation, and superdiversities. A centralized and fixed mono-uniformity is displaced by a more fluid sense of impermanence, fragmentation, and mutability, thus reflecting a radically skeptical world where everything is relative and contested because nothing is absolute and definitive (Dustin 2007). Traditional criteria for defining a nation-state are contested, such as the goal of matching a bureaucratized state with culture, identity, a people, and history. A postnational society embraces a plurality of identities and ethnicities within the context of a national community; as a result, belonging to society is not contingent on affiliation to a specific (and usually dominant) ethnocultural group (Wilton 2009). A society and governance model is proposed based on a fundamentally different set of ideas and ideals, as *Globe and Mail* editor Edward Greenspon (2001) aptly stated:

> Increasingly, we are cultural Canadians: Canadian by willpower rather than by policy. We feel attached to Canada because we like the smell of it. It is an affair of the heart. The process is ephemeral, not mechanical, but no less real. Get used to it. We live in an age of intangibles, and our love of country is as intangible as it is profound.

Put succinctly, a commitment to diversities within diversity does not preclude good governance; to the contrary, good governance is impossible without it. With postnationality, in other words, weaknesses become society-building strengths; conversely, strengths may prove to be weaknesses when contexts undergo transformative changes.

Postnationality challenges the rules upon which convention is based rather than simply modifying the conventions (or practices) that refer to the rules (Angus 2002). A postnational society proposes a new governance game, along with different rules for belonging, identity, and loyalty. This logic applies to a Canada that excels in managing the politics of differences within differences without splintering apart in the process. Reference to Canada as a nation – an entity with a shared history, geography, or ethnicity – is displaced by the "notion" of Canada as an ongoing socially constructed convention, created and evolving, relative to a particular time and place, and subject to reformative change. Or as John Gray writes, "Canada is a kind of model for the twenty-first century, in which a nation defines itself not as a piece of geography or a race of people but as a political and cultural and existential concept" (quoted in Whittington 1998). Box 45 summarizes the contrasts between the competing models of society.

IMMIGRATION MODELS: FROM NATIONAL TO TRANSNATIONAL

Two models of immigration policy and integration prevail: national and transnational. To some extent, they correspond to multicultural models of governance in national societies and multiversal governance models in a postnational society. A national model theorizes immigration as a fixed field of location between "a" and "b." It positions immigrants as people who have permanently severed ties with their home country and embarked on a fresh life in their new homeland. Governments and host communities imposed certain obligations on them, including undivided identification with and political loyalty to a single national community (Ehrkamp and Leitner 2006). Multiple allegiances and divided attachments were seen as impediments to the governance process (Baron 2009). Attainment of citizenship proved that newcomers had transferred their loyalty from "there" to "here" (Spoonley and Bedford 2012). In brief, society building was predicated on including/excluding populations from the national community through restricted modes of incorporation that twinned national belonging to spatial locations (Landolt 2007).

But national models of immigration and immigrant integration are increasingly contested (Satzewich and Wong 2006; Spoonley and

45

Contrastive Models of Society: National versus Postnational

National model (nation-state)	Postnational model (nation-state)
Society as striving for completion	Society as ongoing social construction/project in progress
All-encompassing narrative: "We are all one people"	Multiple voices, identities, and loyalties
One-way adjustment: "Our way, the right way"	Inclusive two-way adjustment/reasonable accommodation: "You adjust, we adapt; we adjust, you adapt"
Commitment to inclusive integration	Commitment to integration via inclusivity
Coherent and singular national identity (totalizing, rationalistic, and universalistic)	Splintered and contested national identity (diffusion, fragmentation, fluidity, relativistic)
Conformity and standardization: "Treat everyone equally"	Diversity within diversity: "Treat others equally and as equals," and accommodate different ways of accommodating differences
Centralized command and pyramidal control	Decentralized and devolved (flattened) control
Conflate nation with state, including universal model of belonging, entitlement, and peoplehood	Society as a nation of nations, community of communities, collection of individuals
Modernist (unitary) citizenship	Postmodernist (customized) citizenship
Society building is a problem to be solved	Society building is a tension to be managed/negotiated
A commitment to a nation (common history, cultures, peoples, fixed borders, and territory)	A commitment to a notion (a set of ideas and ideals)

Source: Fleras (2014b).

Bedford 2012). The transnational model acknowledges new social spaces for integration and settlement,[4] in addition to redefining notions of belonging and identity along geographically discontinuous lines (Lloyd L. Wong 2007-08; Faist 2010). Conventional notions of migrant identity, attachment, and belonging have become unsettled by the combination of low-cost travel, digital technologies, and the aggressive recruitment of skilled professionals (Spoonley and Bedford 2012). Transnationalism reconceptualizes the discursive frameworks associated with migration and migrants. Its focus on a complex, dynamic, interrelated, and multidirectional process displaces the primacy of a single-society framework (either sending and receiving) (Inglis 2007). Immigration is conceptualized as a dynamic of flows and linkages (a process, not a thing) involving diasporic networks of numerous actors, across diverse domains, and differing levels of connectedness and involvement (Simmons 2010). Priority is assigned to the networks that transmigrants retain and cultivate with overseas families, institutions, and political systems. They include multiple border crossings and multifaceted dimensions of identity and belonging, all of which pose a unique challenge for establishing the legitimacy of place-based governance models (Negi and Furman 2010).

At the core of this debate is the question of whether a place-based multicultural governance can connect to modes of belonging and identity that transverse the nation-state (Shome 2012). Ongoing debates over migrant integration in a transmigratory world are contesting the legitimacy of binary analysis. Even binary notions that dichotomize sending and receiving countries are increasingly challenged (Berns-McGown 2007-08). Too often, identity and belonging are viewed in zero-sum terms in which the local invariably detracts from the translocal and vice versa (Jedwab 2007-08). Yet they need not be mutually exclusive. For example, migrants may capitalize on their local connections to carve out an identity and belonging consistent with the principle of a multicultural governance, while capitalizing on translocal links to offset incidents of racism and discrimination in the host country (Akesson 2010). In short, consensus is mounting that transmigratory linkages and incorporation into the receiving country are not necessarily contradictory. The fact that they may occur simultaneously in a mutually reinforcing fashion speaks to the challenges in store.

That individuals possess multiple identities, from the social, personal, and humanistic (Parekh 2007; Lloyd L. Wong 2007-08) to the national, diasporic, transmigratory, or cosmopolitan is unremarkable but significant. Conceptualizing identities and belonging along transnational lines puts the onus on rethinking the in-between spaces and hybridic lifeworlds as portals for understanding international migration and migrant transnationalism. As Tendoh (2009) suggests,

> Migrants are people who, for one reason or the other leave their country of birth to live in another country. They carry with them their cultural identities and other traditional values which they maintain in their new land. They are not uprooted persons as the capitalist society perceives them. Most immigrants live their lives as cross border citizens. While they settle in their host countries, they maintain and create links of networks with their homeland. Migrants maintain very strong circuits of connection with their countries of origin. They do this with the help of present technological developments that we do experience in this age of globalization. About 90 percent of my informants think they can never abandon or cut off transnational circuits. For them, remaining attached to one's homeland is a responsibility one owes to his/her ancestors. They believe they live and survive because of the strength of the immobile structures that link them to their country of birth. For these immigrants, home is home. While some think home is in the mind's eye and can be made anywhere depending on the circumstances, for others, home is their roots, the land of their ancestors and no matter how long they stay abroad, they will always turn back to home. They will always remain attached to this place by race, language, and family ties.

11

customizing citizenship

RECALIBRATING IDENTITY AND BELONGING
IN A POSTNATIONAL CANADA

TOWARD A POSTNATIONAL CITIZENSHIP IN
A TRANSNATIONAL AGE

NOT LONG AGO, everyone knew what citizenship meant. Its meaning was forged in the crucible of nationalism, with corresponding nation-state assumptions about belonging and identity (Lyons and Mandaville 2008). The core doctrine of nationalism assumed that a person's primary loyalty and source of freedom belonged exclusively to one nation-state (Anthony Smith 2013). Citizenship was acquired through birth or by choice (naturalization). It entailed rights and obligations that applied equally to everyone. Everybody was equal before the law because every citizen belonged in the same way. Differential recognition or preferential treatment was out of the question. Acquisition of citizenship for the foreign-born symbolized commitment to their new country and a clean break with the past. The assimilationist intent and integrationist logic behind this form of citizenship was subtle yet unmistakable: to transform an inchoate mass of newcomers into citizens whose sense of commitment, community, and conviction could be marshalled into nation-state building.

But singular citizenship is losing its lustre (Janoski 2010; Samers 2010). Migrant movements, motivations, and destinations are much more diverse and complex than in the past, as Lyons and Mandaville

(2008, 2) explain, and linkages are produced and sustained through an expanding web of social networks that criss-cross the globe. Singular citizenship takes a tumble when (a) the body politic is increasingly mobile; (b) national commitments (including identity, loyalty, and belonging) are delinked from geographical proximity; (c) the nation-state is no longer the exclusive mediator between political communities; (d) competing spatial forms (territorial versus residential) complicate the governance challenge; and (e) translocal constituencies reside outside the state (ibid.). The frictionless spread of information and the expansion of personal-to-global networks tend to unsettle linear models that once informed people's sense of identity and belonging, in the process eroding the simple categorizations that framed citizenship discourses around rights and obligations (Safian 2012). And yet the permeability of borders poses additional challenges for citizenship building. The risk-averse post-9/11 era renders it absurd to rhapsodize about an unfettered movement of people, given the increased securitization of the mobile poor or "other" (especially the disciplining of Tamils or Muslim/Arab populations as security risks in need of surveillance and control) (Mawani 2008; van Munster 2010).

Citizenship in the new global order entails contradictions and tensions that are unlikely to quietly go away. Of particular note are the transnational webs of connection that challenge the legitimacy of an exclusively national framework for defining citizenship (Mawani 2008; Castles and Miller 2009; Akesson 2010). The national model may have prevailed in the past, when notions of identity and belonging were inextricably meshed into a single nation-state (Anthony Smith 2013), but the dynamics of the *transnational/postnational* world are contesting its relevance. Cross-national linkages increasingly inspire more complex transmigratory networks (Karim 2007) which, in turn, give rise to dual and multiple citizenships. Concepts of belonging and identity are stripped of their national meaning and transformed into a resource or property (embodied in a passport) for pragmatic reasons (Harpaz 2013). Likewise, there is growing pressure to customize citizenship by rendering it more inclusive of the differences within differences that inform a postnational world. Not surprisingly, debates over citizenship will remain near the top of the political agenda in a world where borders are not necessarily crossed as much as transcended, contested, delocalized, and diffused (Rygiel 2010).

A conflict of interest informs the politics of citizenship. First, pressures prevail to expand access to citizenship by extending it to any resident of a country regardless of his or her legality (Austin and Bauder 2012). Second, pressure is escalating to tighten up citizenship requirements and entitlements in hopes of disciplining immigrants through integration tests and swearing-in ceremonies (Lyons and Mandaville 2008). Third, how does the state continue to morally justify its right to exclude (Fine 2013)? Why do people tacitly accept its right to restrict immigration, control the entry and settlement of non-citizens, and establish the conditions for citizenship? The cacophony of responses to these questions is nothing short of revelatory. The ambiguities of national citizenship as immigrant governance in the transnational context expose certain paradoxes beyond the scope of conventional models of identity and belonging (Joppke 2010; Rygiel 2010). Fleischmann, van Styvendale, and Maccaroll (2011, xx) write accordingly:

> Citizenship both alienates and assimilates, ostracizes and "equalizes." It rests upon its own categories of exclusion. It is a highly problematic, contested, and contestable category, composed as much of negative as positive content, of absence as much as presence, especially for members of the uncountable demographics who find themselves other-than-naturalized. Persons from diaspora and Indigenous groups are often engaged in protracted struggles to define which of the most basic of human rights should be accorded them by countries that demand their assimilation while insisting upon their separation and, in extreme cases, internment or expulsion.

The role, relational status, and relevance of citizenship in a postnational era are vigorously debated (Bevelander and Pendakur 2012). Particularly rancorous are arguments over the status and rights of would-be citizens in an increasingly postnational world. The controversy is embedded in a core question: Is a grounded citizenship as a society-building device relevant – or outdated – in a disembodied world of "here," "there," and "everywhere"? Do the politics of deterritorialization disrupt the Canada-building project by uncoupling notions of citizenship from a national policy framework? How do previous definitions of citizenship align with new notions that are related to the micro politics of identity and belonging? That these questions generate conflicting answers intensifies the need to figure out what's going on.

Immigration and citizenship rank among the most important issues in the contemporary world (Glover 2011). The twinning of immigration with citizenship is even more contested and complex in the context of global security concerns, humanitarian crisis, skill shortages, and increasingly diverse movements (Samers 2010). Newcomers challenge prevailing notions of identity and belonging as a basis for citizenship governance (Bilodeau, Turgeon, and Karakoc 2012; Citrin, Johnston, and Write 2012), and the diversification of immigrant diversities disrupts the commonality of singular citizenship (Schmidtke 2012). This chapter examines the politics and politicization of citizenship as immigrant governance in a postnational Canada.

CONCEPTUALIZING THE CITIZEN IN CITIZENSHIP

Debates over immigration and immigrant governance are infused with the politics of citizenship, and vice versa (Spoonley and Bedford 2012). This interconnectedness is not surprising; after all, the relationship between immigration and citizenship is incontestable, a link that is symbolized by folding immigration and citizenship (and more recently, multiculturalism) into the federal Department of Citizenship and Immigration Canada. In general, citizenship refers to membership in a specific nation-state (or to supranational citizenship, as in the European Union), together with the formal rights, obligations, status, and identity that membership entails (Gilbertson 2006). Possession of citizenship activates a range of benefits, such as (a) access to government entitlements, including mobility rights to come and go; (b) protection at home and abroad from unlawful detainment; (c) membership in a national community, with corresponding rights and safeguards; and (d) legitimacy as insiders who cannot be arbitrarily excluded or subjected to expulsion (Bloemraad 2007; AMSSA 2014). Citizenship in a multicultural society goes beyond the legal protocols that naturalize foreign nationals. It also entails a social dimension for advancing (a) the society-building goals of community, consensus, and commitment; (b) the personal goals of identity, belonging, and affiliation; and (c) the justice goals of inclusion, equity, and participation. A non-exclusionary citizenship secures a governance for bonding strangers into a common political body, while building bridges to ensure legal guarantees for equitable access, reasonable accommodation, protection from discrimination, full participation, and expression of democratic rights.

Citizenship can be assigned along several lines: (a) by blood or genealogy (it is restricted to those who share a common descent, as is the case in Germany); (b) by soil or territory (open to all who were born in a certain area, such as the United States or Canada); (c) by ideology (for those who share values); (d) by colonialism (open to members of a former empire, such as that of Great Britain) (Castles and Miller 2009; Buckley 2013); and (e) by residency (based on an individual's residential location) (Austin and Bauder 2012). For example, the No One Is Illegal Movement is predicated on the principle of universal rights of citizenship and entitlements for anyone who is on Canadian soil (Abji 2013). People can acquire citizenship in two ways: at birth and by naturalization (Macklin and Crépeau 2010; AMSSA 2014). Citizenship by birthright is restricted to those who share a common bloodline or who can trace their descent to a citizen.[1] Such a narrow definition creates unsettling restrictions such as in Germany, where Turkish guest workers and their children rarely possessed a clear path to citizenship (Samers 2010). Admittedly, citizenship prospects for newcomers to Germany have improved a great deal. But its failure to integrate minorities is hardly the fault of multiculturalism, as Chancellor Angela Merkel famously opined. In a country that never endorsed multiculturalism in the first place, integration failures may be better attributed to the denial of citizenship to guest workers (Adams and Omidvar 2010).

Citizenship by birthright is acquired from birth within the territory of the citizenship-conferring state. All states allow parents who are citizens to automatically pass citizenship to their children, although most countries vary in the number of generations across which a citizen living abroad can transmit citizenship by descent. A few countries (such as Canada and the United States) allow for automatic and unconditional citizenship due to birth in their territory, regardless of the lawful resident status of the parents (McCabe and Meissner 2010). The concept of citizenship by birth within territory may also extend to members of former colonies (Bell 2004). Citizenship by naturalization

46 OBSERVATION

Reinvigorating Germany's Citizenship Agenda

CANADA ACKNOWLEDGES ITS normative status as an immigration society. But countries such as Germany historically denied the need for immigrants while rejecting their status as immigration societies. If anything, they saw themselves as "complete societies" (Castles and Miller 2009), ethnically based *nation*-states with a shared sense of history, culture, and destiny. They had an elitist concept of citizenship that excluded outsiders and a belief in their right to export their surplus populations (Sykes 2008, 11; Zick, Pettigrew, and Wagner 2008). Immigration was perceived as an anomaly whose economic value was appreciated but largely irrelevant in advancing national identity. Foreigners and their children were generally excluded from citizenship, even if they were born and raised in Germany. Those of German parentage (ancestry) were automatically granted citizenship regardless of how long they strayed from the homeland (Austin and Bauder 2012).*

To be sure, this mindset is changing across Europe. Anti-immigrant countries are now under pressure to embrace immigration to offset the effects of an ageing population, a tumbling birth rate, costly welfare programs, the shortage of skilled professionals, and obligations under EU membership (Munz and Ohliger 2005). Since 2000, children born to lawfully resident foreign parents have received German citizenship (Macklin and Crépeau 2010). Passage of Germany's 2005 Immigration Act also established provisions under a single statutory framework for managing immigration into the country, including the Residence Act, for regulating the domestic status of foreigners. But many proposed changes were amended or watered down to the point of irrelevance (Bauder 2011; Jacoby 2011). Admittedly, Germany has made substantial progress in terms of accommodating and integrating newcomers into society (Bauder, Lenard, and Straehle 2014; Kolb 2014). In short, for Germany, any significant transformation from a society of emigrants to an immigrant society will prove challenging.

Collective mindsets and institutional arrangements must rethink the paradox of needing immigration but disliking immigrants (*Economist* 2010a). And this rethinking cannot come too soon, because immigration to Germany is no longer about cheap menial labourers but about highly educated and skilled migrants from the European Union (Hawley and Wilder 2013).

* In his review of Ayelet Shachar's *The Birthright Lottery,* Andrew Coyne (2009) makes an interesting comparison. Canadians may find it odd that a person must be born of German parents to obtain German citizenship. How, they wonder, can citizenship be determined by an accident of birth, especially if the parents are living abroad? But Germans might find Canada's system to be equally odd. Bloodline is irrelevant; simply being born in Canada automatically confers citizenship, even if the parents have never lived there but were simply in transit. In other words, Canada's citizenship status is no less contingent on an accident of birth.

involves formal acquisition of nationality by those who were born elsewhere (Statistics Canada 2011). A naturalized citizenship is offered to newcomers who are legal residents, fulfill certain residency requirements, make an effort to put down permanent roots, and acknowledge a commitment to the rule of law and shared values of the country in question. A citizenship by choice suggests the possibility of dual (or even multiple) citizenships, although some countries require that prospective citizens renounce their citizenship in another country. Box 47 lists Canada's rules for citizenship.

The citizenship concept can be deconstructed along two lines: the legal (membership and rights) and the social (belonging, entitlements, and identity) (Fleischmann, van Styvendale, and Maccaroll 2011). In legal parlance, citizenship entails formal membership in a politically constituted community, with a corresponding contract of mutual rights and duties (Hebert and Wilkinson 2002; Squires 2007; Rygiel 2010). Canada has a duty to accommodate and protect newcomers; for their part, new Canadians are expected to integrate and contribute while relying on the state to protect their rights and freedoms. Citizens' rights include equality rights, democratic rights, legal rights,

47 OBSERVATION

Canadian Citizenship: Who Can Become a Canadian Citizen?

> **Oath of Citizenship**
> I Swear (or affirm)
> That I will be faithful
> And bear true allegiance
> To Her Majesty Queen Elizabeth the Second
> Queen of England
> Her Heirs and Successors
> And that I will faithfully observe
> The laws of Canada
> And fulfill my duties as a Canadian Citizen.*

> Those who are born in Canada automatically become citizens, regardless of their parents' status (Liston and Carens 2008; Kobayashi, Li, and Teixeira 2012). Canada and the United States are the last two major countries to grant citizenship in this manner (Bell 2013a).

> Anyone who has permanent resident status can become a citizen. To qualify, one must be 18 or older; have lived in Canada for three of the four years immediately prior to application; demonstrate an ability to communicate in French or English; and possess a knowledge of Canada, including rights and obligations. Everyone must take a citizenship test or do an interview (except those over 55 years of age) to assess their knowledge of the rights and obligations. Individuals cannot become citizens if they are (or were) in prison, on parole, or on probation for one year or more during the past four years; convicted of an indictable offence or crime in the three years preceding application; under investigation or charged with a war crime or crimes

against humanity; or have had their citizenship revoked during the past five years.

> Anyone born outside Canada to one parent who is a Canadian citizen becomes a citizen. After 17 April 2009, citizenship by descent was limited to the first generation born (or adopted) outside Canada. This limit does not apply to children born outside of Canada to a parent who is employed by the federal/provincial/territorial government or is in the Armed Forces.

> In February 2014, the federal government tabled Bill C-24, the Strengthening Canadian Citizenship Act. The act will increase both residency requirements (applicant must reside for four of six years prior to application, including being physically present in Canada for six months in each of the four years) and language and knowledge skills (those between the ages of 14 and 64 must demonstrate proficiency in either official language and pass a citizenship test in that language). The act also grants the immigration minister authority to revoke the citizenship of those found guilty of major crimes. For some, this legislation addresses legitimate concerns about divided loyalties and attachments of convenience; for others, it transforms citizenship into a reward for good behaviour rather than a tool of integration – an extra layer of punishment for dual citizens – and delays the engagement and contribution of new Canadians (the sooner people get citizenship, the more fully they invest of themselves in their adopted country) (Adams, Macklin, and Omidvar 2014). In other words, Canadian citizenship is an investment ("solution"), not a deficit ("problem") – a sign that Canada is invested in the integration of newcomers and that immigrants are invested in Canada (ibid.).

---

* Adapted from Citizenship and Immigration Canada (2011f). Canada is a constitutional monarchy, so people profess loyalty to the person who represents the country (the sovereign of England) rather than to a document, constitution, flag, or the country itself.

mobility rights, language rights, and a right of return to Canada from overseas travel. They also extend to freedom of religion, of expression, and of assembly and association. (According to the Charter, only three rights are reserved exclusively for citizens: the right to vote and stand for election; the right to an education in English or French; and an unrestricted right to enter and remain in Canada [Macklin and Crépeau 2010]). In return, the state expects certain things from citizens. They are obliged to obey Canadian laws, participate in the democratic process, respect the rights and freedoms of others, and recognize Canada's linguistic duality and multicultural heritage. Recent changes to Canada's citizenship guide are instructive. Greater emphasis on Canadian history, its military, and the monarchy; introduction of a more demanding citizenship test and language requirements; and enforcement of the rule that all candidates must uncover their faces might well herald a "renationalization" of Canadian citizenship wherein nation-specific definitions of citizenship prevail alongside those common to most liberal democratic societies (Winter 2014).

Citizenship's social dimension goes beyond the legalities of state membership to involve the redistribution of resources, based on needs and rights. Just as terms such as "refugee" are not simply descriptive of legal status but also of status in the sense of worth and respect, so too is the concept of citizenship more than a legal status; it is also about membership in a community of value and values (Bridget Anderson 2013). According to this dimension, everybody, including citizens and non-citizens, should be entitled to a basic level of social and economic services related to work, welfare, housing, education, and health (Humpage 2011). This dimension focuses on citizenship as lived experiences and does not gloss over the particularistic and the situational. It also incorporates notions of belonging, identity, and entitlements, not just in the formal sense (theory) but also in the substantive sense (practice) of everyday realities. Issues of pertinence to social citizenship include who can belong as citizens; whether they can differently belong; the range of identities they can espouse; and the kind of entitlements (rights) that flow from this relationship. The end result? Social citizenship is a contested field of political struggle for rights, status, and recognition, mediated in part by a person's membership in groups and networks beyond a singular nation-state (also Andrew 2009).

RECALIBRATING CANADIAN CITIZENSHIP: FROM SINGULAR TO CUSTOMIZED

Canadians take quiet pride in themselves as citizens of a widely admired society (Environics Institute 2012). Newcomers are no less excited about Canada, judging by the numbers who become citizens. In 2013, 128,936 newcomers were granted citizenship, a slight increase from the previous year, but sharply down from the 181,339 in 2011; for the first two months of 2014, the number of new citizens (about 41,000) is double the total for the same period in 2013 (CIC 2014b). Just over 85 percent of all permanent residents eventually take the oath of citizenship, in effect putting Canada at the forefront of the global citizenship sweepstakes (AMSSA 2014; Kymlicka 2003; Tran, Kustec, and Chui 2005; Statistics Canada 2011). Compare Canada's naturalization rate to that of Australia, where 74 percent of its foreign-born were naturalized in 2011; the United States trails behind with a rate of just under 44 percent (Statistics Canada 2011). Such a commitment is hardly surprising: Canadian citizenship entitles its bearer to certain rights and privileges in what many regard as one of the best places to live. And yet, until passage of the Citizenship Act, which came into effect on 1 January 1947 (Bloemraad 2007), Canadian citizenship per se did not exist, apart from a Commonwealth context. "Canadians" were defined as British subjects who happened to reside in Canada as a subset of British subjecthood, with a corresponding obligation to conduct themselves in a manner consistent with the language, culture, and identity of the British Empire (Macklin and Crépeau 2010).

Passage of the Citizenship Act announced that Canadians were no longer simply transplanted British expats. With the Citizenship Act, Canada became the first Commonwealth country to create its own class of citizenship distinct from that of Britain (CIC 2006). Canadian citizenship acquired autonomous status and legal existence, although Canadians remained de jure British subjects as well (British subjects with Canadian domicile were automatically conferred Canadian citizenship [CMIP 21 2014]), a situation that prevails into the present under Canada's constitutional monarchy, with the queen of England as head of state (Bloemraad 2007; Macklin and Crépeau 2010). A common citizenship asserted independent nationhood by fostering a sense of community and commitment. It also embraced the realities of life in Canada rather than those of the United Kingdom.

Canadian citizenship was automatically conferred on those born in Canada (or even those born outside Canada if their father was Canadian-born), whereas immigrants could apply for citizenship after five years of residence, provided that they were of sound character and possessed an adequate knowledge of French or English (CMIP 21 2014). Removing any distinction between Canada-born and foreign-born as a basis for belonging negated provisions of the 1923 Immigration Act, which had created three classes of subjects: natural-born, naturalized, and those with special certificates (Pon, Gosine, and Phillips 2011). The Citizenship Act sought to integrate all Canadians into a single body politic, redefined what it meant to be a Canadian, enabled married women to control their nationality status, secured the right to full participation for all citizens, and specified their rights, duties, and obligations.

Clearly, Canadian citizenship reflected the primacy of universality as grounds for belonging and entitlement. A singular (or universal, also common or unitary) citizenship treats all citizens in the same manner since everyone possesses the same rights and obligations, is equal before the law, and must belong in the same way. All citizens are entitled to the same benefits and rights because they stand in the same relation to the state, regardless of race or ethnicity. Entitlements because of difference are ignored under the commonality of singular citizenship; after all, just as people's differences cannot be invoked to exclude, so too should their differences preclude any special treatment. A singular citizenship also rejects any type of entitlement that is rooted in collective or group rights as contrary to the principle of individual equality before the law. Promotion of group differences on racial or ethnic grounds, even in the spirit of inclusiveness and progress, can erode the bonds of loyalty, unity, and identity.

The singularity of this unitary embrace cannot be underestimated. In an era when differences invariably denoted exclusion or inferiority, passage of the Citizenship Act broke ranks by including all citizens regardless of who or where they were. Even permanent residents without citizenship status were eventually recognized as full members of Canadian society, with the same rights and social benefits as citizens except the right to vote or hold public office and to work in federal civil service positions involving high-level security clearance; they were also subject to deportation if found guilty of a serious criminal offence (Liston and Carens 2008). But the interplay of transnationalism with the politics of superdiversity has taken a toll on assumptions about citizenship. This transformation makes it doubly important to rethink what it means to be a citizen in a new global migration order. It also puts pressure on redefining patterns of entitlements and belonging because of ongoing social changes related to (a) the primacy of the nation-state, (b) the right of individuals to negotiate their sense of identity and belonging in a local and transnational context, and (c) the relative cohesion and universalism of citizenship (Ommundsen, Leach, and Vandenberg 2010). Rygiel (2010, 6) points to reconfigured citizenship as a tool for spanning the gap between a deterritorialized global economy and territorialized political systems: "Despite the criss-crossing and transgression of territorial state borders and the reconfiguration of the state as a result of globalization, citizenship as a form of governing has been strengthened through innovative strategies and technologies of power, becoming an increasingly effective way of controlling populations in a globalizing environment."

However enlightened for its time, singular citizenship has come under attack (Bosniak 2000; Kernerman 2005; Harty and Murphy 2005; Yuval-Davis 2007; Fleras 2012a). Citizenship frameworks based on a modernist paradigm of unity and uniformity cannot possibly address the highly politicized and collective claims of national minorities and indigenous peoples. A postnational world of transmigration and multiple identities renders as increasingly antiquated and counterproductive the idea of a common citizenship, although arguably, it may be more salient than ever in a diverse and changing world (Kymlicka 2003). Others criticize singular citizenship as inherently unfair because it reinforces inequality in unequal contexts. All citizens, regardless of their difference-based disadvantages related to race, class, or gender, become miniaturized to the level of disembodied individuals in the abstract and are not seen as disadvantaged minorities in a real world. Treating everyone the same in unequal contexts tends to freeze the status quo (treating unequals equally creates even more inequality), alongside a prevailing distribution of power, privilege, and productive property. Proposed instead is a customized citizenship that combines the rights of unitary citizenship with the multiversal claims of Aboriginal people, national communities, and multicultural minorities (Harty and Murphy 2005). Indeed, Thomas Franck (2006, 37) sees it as "humanity's best answer to the most complex puzzle of the twenty-first century: how to accommodate, within a functioning persona, the multiple identities layered on each person in an era in which responsibility to the global must coherently contend with the loyalties to the nation and the local."

A customized (or inclusive) citizenship endorses five types of entitlements pertaining to identity and belonging: equity, multicultural, self-determining, transnational, and postnational. Each of these admittedly ideal types reflects a reading of Canada as a deeply divided and multiversal society that must address the realities and challenges of differential accommodation (Fleras 2012a):

> *Equity Entitlements:* Immigrants and their descendants who have historically been disadvantaged because of their differences may require a different set of entitlements to ensure full citizenship rights. Equity citizenship entitlements are aimed at improving institutional access and societal integration through removal of discriminatory barriers or the introduction of proactive measures such as employment equity. Canada's Employment Equity Program represents one such initiative.

> *Multicultural Entitlements:* Both racial and cultural minorities may require some degree of official protection of their ethnocultural heritage. Notions of (multi)cultural citizenship go beyond a demand for cultural rights or acceptance of cultural differences as a value. Rather, new forms of inclusion involve recognition and promotion of previously marginalized cultures on the assumption that membership in a living and lived-in cultural reality secures meaning and meaningful choices (Kymlicka 1995; Allegritti 2010). In contrast to the liberal universalism of a unitary citizenship, an inclusive (or customized) multicultural citizenship insists on recognizing the cultural embeddedness of citizenship (Tully 2005; Allegritti 2010).

> *Self-Determining Entitlements:* Another type of citizenship entitlement applies to Aboriginal people and the Québécois, who have certain group-specific needs related to aspirations and history. Their distinct constitutional and sociological status as forcibly incorporated occupants challenges the hegemonic norms of a unitary citizenship. Liberal universalism under a unitary citizenship rejects the notion of taking

differences seriously by refusing to take differences into account when necessary. The entitlements of Aboriginal people go beyond those of a common citizenship, such as political representation or institutional accommodation. They incorporate (a) claims upon the state for self-determining autonomy and control of land, culture, language, and identity; (b) the right to self-government and jurisdiction over matters of direct relevance; (c) recognition of Aboriginal title and treaty rights; and (d) a transfer of power from central authorities as consistent with their pre-existing status as sovereign political communities. Their status as sovereign peoples with citizens-plus rights (Cairns 2000; Fossum, Poirier, and Magnette 2009) entitles them to spurn the principle of direct Canadian citizenship (Blackburn 2009; Coleman 2011). Belonging to Canada is indirect – that is, it occurs through membership in self-determining First Nations communities rather than through common citizenship. As a result, citizenship entitlements must be customized to reflect, reinforce, and advance their status as the "sovereigns within" (Fleras and Elliott 1992; Maaka and Fleras 2005). A similar logic applies to Quebec, where Quebecers define their place in Canada through a collective lens that extols a distinctive citizenship space as a basis for belonging (Iacovino 2013).

> *Transnational (Transmigratory) Entitlements:* The age of migration exposes the inescapable. Although more than 215 million people are living outside their homeland, connections are only a click away. Immigrants in the past may have severed their ties to the homeland, but return or intermittent migration is now a real possibility, with a corresponding greater likelihood of multiple loyalties and belongings (Squires 2007; Yuval-Davis 2007; Castles and Miller 2009). A commitment to a transnational citizenship is predicated on three realities: the eroding sovereignty of states, less constraining geography because of technology, and the capacity of people to maintain multiple links across borders (Simmons 2010). The end result is that transmigrant patterns of citizenship, identity, and belonging may reflect a simultaneous loyalty to the home country and the adopted one (Cuccioletta 2001-02).

> *Postnational Entitlements:* Postnational scholars who adhere to global human rights discourses and the principle of cosmopolitanism believe that the logic of personhood precedes that of national or legal citizenship

(Abji 2013). Postnational citizenship challenges the dominant understanding of citizenship as a formal relation between a person and a state, which by definition requires the exclusion of some migrant others as constitutive of the nation. It also calls into question the historical privileging of the nation-state in conceptualizing and determining citizenship. Proposed instead is a postnational (or cosmopolitan) citizenship as a set of rights that stem from personhood (inherent to a person as a right) rather than political membership in a national community (Bloemraad 2007; Abji 2013). The challenge of citizenship in an era of cosmopolitanism is no less daunting.

To be sure, a customized citizenship does not reject a singular citizenship. All citizens possess common rights and universal entitlements, regardless of who or where they are. Suggested instead is what Lister (2003) calls a differentiated universalism in which the singular and the customized stand in a creative tension to generate an inclusive citizenship (also Basok and Ilcan 2013). Citizenship is visualized as a rope of interwoven strands. One strand emphasizes the singular citizenship rights of individual equality and equality before the law. Another strand takes differences into account in defining identity, belonging, and entitlements. The rationale is fairly straightforward: Just as Canada's difference model acknowledges the principle of accommodating differences in differing ways, Canadian citizenship can be customized along inclusivity lines (Fleras 2012a). Just as a commitment to multiversalism recognizes the legitimacy of differences within differences across shifting domains, so too does a customized citizenship concede the value of different ways of valuing citizenship differences. That is, a person can belong to and identify with Canada through his or her ethnicity or nationality. Moreover, just as Canada's official multiculturalism acknowledges everybody's right to full democratic citizenship, a customized citizenship recognizes the right to equal recognition and entitlements as a matter of course, but without necessarily reneging on the right to special treatment when necessary. Note that it does not promote a differing set of citizenship rights for various groups of citizens. More accurately, it's about the possibility that certain groups of Canadians are differently entitled (including distinctive claims to identity and belonging), thanks to differences in sociological status, normative aspirations, and historical experiences.

48 OBSERVATION

Unbounded Cosmopolitanism, Bounded Citizenship: A Governance Conundrum

THE CHALLENGES OF immigrant governance never cease to amaze: in the face of deterritorialized identities and belongings, how are we to transform a society of newcomers into a community of conviction, commitment, and consensus (Soutphommasane 2012)? Cosmopolitanism is no less disruptive to the multicultural governance project. Renewed interest in the subject is inevitable in light of globalization and its discontents, including the inability of nation-states to address global problems (from international migration to environmental degradation) that demand a global frame of reference that applies to community, responsibility, and governance (Trepanier and Habib 2011; Kymlicka and Walker 2012). Neither the nation-state as the exclusive locus of identity and belonging, nor people's attachment to specific ethnic traditions, should supersede the primacy of the moral imperatives that are related to universal human rights, global justice, and international law. Or as Trepanier and Habib (2011, 1) put it slightly differently,

> Cosmopolitan is a term often used to describe a citizen of the world: an enlightened individual who believes he or she belongs to a common humanity or world order rather than to a set of particular customs or traditions. Cosmopolitans consequently believe that peace among nation-states is possible only if they transcend their parochial identities and interests in the name of a global state or consciousness.

Cosmopolitanism can be defined as the belief that we are all subject to universal justice because of our common membership (citizenship) in the human community (Nussbaum 2012). All humanity belongs to the global community of human beings that transcends the specifics of local affiliation (Kymlicka and Walker 2012). Martha Nussbaum

(2006, 324) expands on the concept of world citizenship in what is tantamount to a global village:

> If our world is to be a decent world in the future, we must acknowledge right now that we are citizens of one interdependent world, held together by mutual fellowship, as well as the pursuit of mutual advantage, by compassion as well as by self-interest, by love of human dignity in all people even when there is nothing we have to gain from cooperating with them.

Under a cosmopolitan citizenship, the objective is to transcend particular traditions by disallowing local obligations to crowd out distant responsibilities (Brock 2013). The focus is on norms inherent in humanity itself while embracing a whole-of-the-world approach as a moral concern. With cosmopolitanism, all humans have equal moral standing and inherent rights to equal respect and consideration regardless of their nationality, citizenship, or differences (ibid.). Global citizens assume a responsibility for addressing problems of international governance, environmental sustainability, equitable resource distribution, and the maintenance of peace (Isin 2012).

Contrast cosmopolitanism to nationalism, where national interests can override universal humanitarian standards or global concerns. A cosmopolitan belief in the need and value of more open borders, more freedom of movement, and intermixing of groups tramples on the principle of sovereign state rights to control borders and membership (Zapata-Barrero and Pécoud 2012). The distinction between multiculturalism and cosmopolitanism is often articulated as well. The former is routinely (if incorrectly) seen as particularistic, exclusionary, and backward looking. The latter is thought of as universalistic, inclusive, and forward/future looking (Nussbaum 2006; Brett and Moran 2010). Citizenship under a multiculturalism umbrella is bounded by space and specific commitments, whereas a cosmopolitan citizenship is unbounded by either national borders or a sense of a national identity (Trepanier and Habib 2011). Much of what passes for multiculturalism (and people's perceptions of it) is thought to reflect a commitment to preserving differences (at least in the European theatre), but cosmopolitanism is more concerned with bridging differences to accommodate commonalities.

Not surprisingly, cosmopolitanism is touted as an antidote to the excesses of multiculturalism and nationalism (Shinn 2006). However well intentioned this may be, the objective should not be to discard multiculturalism, despite inherent weaknesses of a place-based governance in a transmigrant global village. Rather, the goal is to build on it by incorporating the principles of a post-multicultural multiversalism as a basis for immigrant governance and customized citizenship.

Differences between transnationalism and cosmopolitanism exist as well. Transnationalism recognizes the primacy of people's multiple attachments, whereas cosmopolitanism transcends such attachments in advancing the principle of universal rights and global citizenship. Admittedly, neither cosmopolitanism nor trans-nationalism as modes of governance necessarily entail the displace-ment of the state or state policies. To the contrary, the centrality of the state is reinforced by way of overarching institutions that provide guidelines and sanctions for a complex co-existence (see also Latham 2007-08).

Finally, a cosmopolitanism open to everything yet nothing may be theoretically sound, but implementation is much more elusive. All humans may be of equal moral worth as befitting a cosmopol-itan frame of reference. Yet no less salient is a sensitivity to the im-portance of local relations and obligations, both within and across borders. A "rooted cosmopolitanism" (Calhoun 2007; Kymlicka and Walker 2012; also Brett and Moran 2010) consists of a frame-work in which individuals are situated in a specific national con-text but engage in activities across borders or along transnational lines (think Doctors Without Borders/Médeçins Sans Frontières) (Tarrow 2005; Isin 2012). The resulting creative tension between the local and the global (the glocal), between local attachments and cosmopolitan values, serves to remind us of the slogan "Think globally, act locally."

RETHINKING IDENTITY AND BELONGING IN A POSTNATIONAL CANADA

Debates over citizenship are inextricably linked to the challenges of Canada building. The core theme concentrates on establishing a framework for living together with differences, equitably and in dignity, primarily by making Canada safe for differences, yet safe from them. For those who are inclined toward a nationalist model of immigrant integration, only singular citizenship can protect both Canada's national interests and the fundamental rights of immigrant Canadians. Equality and progress reflect the renunciation of substantive differences to ensure that everyone is equal before the law, with the same rights, entitlements, and obligations. A splintered citizenship cannot function. A dearth of shared values risks the danger of society shattering into a series of fractured communities. Moreover, a customized citizenship is deemed un-Canadian since (a) some individuals are treated more equally than others, (b) special group rights are elevated over individual rights, and (c) the legitimacy of the political community at large is compromised. Admittedly, a common citizenship may acknowledge the need to invoke special treatment for the historically disadvantaged, but such measures are acceptable only if they are temporary, specific to the problem, and justified on the basis of needs rather than racial grounds.

A customized citizenship is consistent with the transnational principles of postnational Canada. A one-size-fits-all singular citizenship no longer resonates in Canada's multiversally divided and transmigrant-based society (Hebert and Wilkinson 2002; Redhead 2003). Entitlements under a singular citizenship often shortchange certain marginalized minorities, especially when formal equality rights (equal treatment) are privileged over substantive equity rights (treatment as equals). Ranking all individuals as similar for political or economic purposes may seem to convey equality but may prove otherwise in practice or outcome (Schouls 1997). Moreover, aside from a respect for political institutions and the rule of law (Transatlantic Trends 2010), Canada can no longer be defined in terms of one nation, one identity, one culture, or one belonging. The fact that nation-states promote dual or multiple citizenships (Macklin and Crépeau 2010; Simmons 2010; Papillon 2012) speaks volumes regarding the distance travelled.[2] Identities today are openly and politically plural, with individuals

49

Managing Citizenship: Conventional Model versus New Model

	Conventional (singular) model	New (customized) model
Nature of society	National society	Postnational society
Ideological orientation	Modern	Postmodern/cosmopolitan
Pattern of governance	Inclusive governance (integration)	Inclusivity governance (accommodation)
Managing diversity models	Multiculturalism	Multiversality
Immigration model	National (European)	Transnational
Model of citizenship	Common	Customized

belonging to many different groups (Karim 2007; Mawani 2008). Box 49 captures the distinction.

Nowhere are the politics of citizenship more sharply contested than in mounting pressure to rethink citizenship as immigrant governance in a postnational Canada. To one side of the debate is the notion of a contested citizenship: An analytical framework is proposed that conceptualizes citizenship as multifaceted and constantly negotiated, both within and between state borders (Stasiulis and Bakan 2005; Hsiung and Nichol 2010). To the other side is a disciplinary model: The politics of citizenship is evolving into a proxy for disciplining migrants and their mobility without undermining the open borders necessary for trade and commerce. For example, many see as misguided the federal government decision to ban face coverings such as niqabs for the citizenship swearing-in ceremony, ostensibly on the somewhat dubious grounds that full veiling is both un-Canadian and

oppressive (Payton 2011; see also Bell 2012). The politics of dual citizenship continues to rankle or provoke as well. Yes, Canada may see
itself as an immigration magnet, although nearly 9 percent (or 2.8 million) Canadians live abroad, second only to Britain among developed
countries. Yet Canadians display an ambivalence bordering on apoplexy toward these transnationals by stigmatizing them as failed immigrants or citizens of convenience, unlike Australians and the Irish,
who actively court their diaspora as a potential asset (Devoretz and
Woo 2014; Friesen 2011b).

Admittedly, questions will prevail in a disputed domain that needs
more sophisticated analysis (Ehata and Mieres 2010). Consider the following questions in search of responses: Is it possible to create a meaningful citizenship in a global world of transnational communities and
diasporic migrants (see also Harty and Murphy 2005; Kernerman
2005)? Can Canadians take advantage of such crossings and connections to embrace specific affiliations without compromising a commitment to commonalities and community? Or is Canada destined to
become a locale of travelling cultures and people with varying degrees
of attachment and commitment (Sandercock 2003)? Finally, how will
debates over globalized migration and citizenship play out in the post-
9/11 era, where anxieties over security and failed immigration exert
political and public pressure to control and securitize residency requirements (Baubock 2008a; Weinstock 2008; Rechitsky 2010)?

Answers to these questions are no less beguiling. Does attainment
of a singular or customized citizenship improve – or detract from – a
sense of belonging and identity? Some argue that children of racialized immigrants are less likely than children of white immigrants to
experience strong feelings of belonging to Canada (Reitz and Banerjee
2007). Others contend that identification with Canada among first-
and second-generation immigrants corresponds favourably with that of
the Canadian-born (Kymlicka 2012). But regardless of who is right or
wrong (keeping in mind that responses reflect differing terms of reference and the phrasing of questions), Canada must acknowledge the
reality of comings and connections if it wants to attract the brightest
and the best. In the era of transmigration, how can it be otherwise
(Fleras 2014b; Satzewich and Wong 2006)? A one-size-fits-all citizenship is unlikely to gain much traction in a deeply divided and multilayered Canada, where some are banging on the door to get in and
others are banging down the door to get out. Yes, it will take time to

convince Canadians that citizens can be alike in different ways yet different in similar ways, while contesting the rules that define what differences count and what counts as differences. Because Canada is better than most in recalibrating citizenship along customized lines, its status as one of the world's foremost immigration societies is unlikely to be tarnished. Nevertheless, the postnational goal of belonging differently together without drifting apart is contingent on divining this seeming conundrum. A genuine and meaningful citizenship in a postnational Canada will materialize only when it is reframed along innovative lines of entitlement, belonging, and identity.

12

rethinking immigration, reframing immigrants

EVOLVING REALITIES, EMERGING CHALLENGES, SHIFTING DISCOURSES

NEW RULES, NEW PLAYERS, NEW GAME

THE POLITICS OF immigration and immigrants are hotly contested, both abroad and (to a lesser extent) in Canada. This is hardly surprising. The need to rethink immigration and reframe immigrants against the backdrop of evolving realities, emergent challenges, and shifting discourses is pressing and overdue. The domain of immigration and immigrants is proving a highly visible indicator of growing global interconnectedness. It also constitutes a foremost expression of the social transformations generated by cross-border flows, transmigrant linkages, and transnational belongings (Cramme and Motte 2010; Duncan, Nieuwhehuysen, and Neerup 2012). O'Reilly (2012, 1) draws attention to the centrality and multi-dimensionalities of global migration:

> International migration affects millions of people across the globe everyday, as migrants and non-migrants. It can arise as a result of rupture in people's lives, it can cause upheavals within communities, and it can reunite families. It can provide much-needed resources for sending and receiving countries, or it can put great strain on destinations or shatter the economies and daily lives when migrants leave. It can lead to emotional, individual, media,

and policy responses. It can be framed with the rhetoric of floods, tides, and influxes or it can be warmly welcomed. Migration cuts to the very heart of who "we" and "they" are, and to notions of identity, home, and belonging.

The challenges of global migration are compounded by worrying gaps between professed ideals and ongoing realities. Canadians may embrace an idealistic image of immigrants and immigration that is unlikely to correspond with the real; news media coverage tends to sensationalize discrepancies between mainstream ideals and immigration realities; and government programs and initiatives capitalize on a commitment to advancing this ideal without rupturing a national consensus. Immigrants themselves are changing as well, in origins, destinations, expectations, and experiences. The growing diversification of immigrant diversity (multiversality) complicates an already evolving reality gap.

A fundamental paradox informs the dynamics of immigration in Canada and abroad. Historically, the world political order was organized around the principle of discrete sovereign nation-states as the final authority in defining membership (Triadafilopoulos 2012; Anthony Smith 2013). But the (trans)migration of newcomers across borders disrupts the political firmament upon which global polity is ordered, relations are organized, and membership is defined. Nation-states must also secure a sense of community, commitment, and belonging in an era when the distinction between the "here" and the "there" is fuzzy and fluid. The changing dynamics of contemporary immigration (whether invited or self-selected, permanent or temporary or circular) put pressure on societies to assert their authority over immigrant status, rights, and responsibilities. Another paradox looms as well: Admission of newcomers is often trumpeted as pivotal in securing economic, political, or ideological interests. Yet in a classic case of needing immigration but not wanting immigrants – or that Canada needs immigrants more than they need Canada – their presence, demands, and interests may provoke fierce rebuke from those with conflicting material interests or different normative priorities (Triadafilopoulos 2012).

The conclusion is obvious: The world of immigration and immigrants is in the throes of a gathering paradigm shift with regard to what is happening, how, and why (Nieuwenhuysen, Duncan, and Neerup

2012). A new lens for thinking about the subject is in the offing, one that situates newcomers as integral to Canada's twenty-first-century realities and prosperity (see also Jurado and Bruzzone 2008); acknowledges migration as a global phenomenon that implicates Canada in the broader scheme of things; and incorporates new narratives and discourses that capture these evolving realities and emergent challenges. Conceptual frameworks for understanding immigration (including policies, assumptions, and programs) and immigrants/refugees (from settlement to citizenship) must be expanded and rethought along lines that often contest or invert what many believe (also Ehrkamp and Leitner 2006). Such an imperative provides a fitting finale to this book.

EVOLVING REALITIES

In recent years, the domain of immigration and immigrants has undergone a transformation. Immigration itself has evolved into a formidable dynamic on the world stage, thanks to the interplay of globalization and ideological shifts that constitute yet are constitutive of mass(ive) migration and transmigrant linkages. The governance of this upheaval in people movements can no longer be framed exclusively along national lines. The reality of a global-national nexus as a primary frame of reference has put an end to that. Notions of identity, belonging, and commitment have evolved in a postnational/transnational era, as the following points reveal (also Fleras 2012c):

> *It's Not Your Grandparents' Immigration.* Since the 1960s, European emigration has slowed considerably, whereas emigration from Africa, Asia, and Latin America has grown exponentially. The choice of destination has changed as well. In addition to immigrant-receiving countries in Oceania, South America, and North America, both Western Europe, Saudi Arabia, the United Arab Emirates, and Qatar have attracted significant numbers (Massey 2003). For example, what were once defined as mass exodus (or emigrant) societies, such as those in Europe, are now destination sites for the destitute and desperate as well as the educated and skilled. European countries increasingly see themselves as immigrant-seeking societies, trolling the world for skilled workers to offset an ageing population, plummeting birth rates, and skilled labour shortages. Patterns are beginning to emerge: Outmigration is most active in the developing countries where economies

are booming, development and structural adjustments create inequality and displacement, and fertility rates are dropping because of greater financial security. Not surprisingly, there is increased evidence that the status of many countries in the global migration order could change, with current emigration countries potentially becoming major destinations in reaction to the shifting demands of the global capitalist economy (de Haas, Vargas-Silva, and Vezzoli 2010).

> *More Movement = More Restrictions = More "Irregular" Movement.* The global economy unleashes powerful forces that incite larger and more diverse flows of migrants from developing countries. This dynamic reflects a combination of structural adjustments, neoliberal governance philosophies, and a growing reliance on commodity export for wealth creation. A contradiction follows: The developed countries of the global North may generate the very conditions that foster the movement of people in the first place. Yet they are just as likely to restrict the movement of the unwanted (unskilled), in the process contributing to the influx of migrants who have few options but to circumvent the restrictions (Brown 2014). A two-tier system, based on a bimodal skills distribution, has evolved in the new global economy of neoliberal globalization. Paul Scheffer (2010, 26) explains this bimodality between the mobile and the immobile:

> The fundamental dilemma in our times is the growing divide between social elites, able to move around at will in a world that has fewer and fewer borders, and an increasing proportion of the population that feels threatened by globalization and is turning its back on the outside world. A vague and unrealistic concept of world citizenship has encouraged a return to parochialism.

In short, highly qualified workers are in demand everywhere and are treated accordingly. Their lower-skilled counterparts are abundant, which allows rich countries to formulate admission rules to suit their own interests. Undocumented workers are not illegal or criminal but subject to policies of exclusion (or demonization) by the rich and powerful. The consequences of more open borders (for some) yet more restrictive controls (for many) elicit controversy, as de Haas, Vargas-Silva, and Vezzoli (2010, 5) note:

While states tend to welcome highly-skilled immigrants, most low-skilled are excluded through legal obstacles that are at odds with policies promoting the "globalisation" of trade and capital. However, the continuous demand for unskilled migrant labour ... defies restrictive immigration policies, leading not to a reduction in migration, but rather to unintended and undesired outcomes, notably increases in people smuggling, trafficking, and undocumented migration.

Central authorities are looking for ways to bypass this double standard of "needed, not wanted," while conveying the impression that they are taking steps to combat immigrant abuses. They have introduced a series of symbolic measures to curb migrant flows by militarizing borders or securitizing admissions (Massey 2003). The once disgraced notion of "guest workers" has resurfaced as a palatable alternative for maximizing benefits without incurring costs.

> *Immigrant Identity in a Transmigrant World.* A new type of immigrant and immigrant experience is arising, one that neither severs ties with the home country nor passively absorbs into the host country. Immigrants increasingly and simultaneously participate in both, while embracing multiple identities across national borders (Bitran and Tan 2013). They no longer automatically rally around one national collectivity, but identify with and participate across multiple communities. That they are able to do so, and to do so without necessarily weakening a sense of belonging, speaks volumes of the challenges in store (Ehrkamp and Leitner 2006). The decoupling of immigrant identities from geographical location, and their relinkage across cultures and regions in transnational and hybrid forms, has proven transformative in contesting the issue of "what society is for."

> *Transnational Citizenship in Postnational Societies.* An expanded notion of citizenship is developing that transcends an exclusive focus on nationality, with a corresponding bundle of rights and entitlements conferred by a singular nation-state. The concept of a nationally bounded citizenship that linked individuals to one nation-state may have flourished in the past, but a notion of postnational citizenship is evolving that acknowledges immigrant claims for rights in both the host and

home county as part of a broader human rights discourse pertaining to social citizenship rights (ibid.).

EMERGENT CHALLENGES

Governments and nation-states confront significant challenges in forging an integrative immigration governance that incorporates evolving realities without spiralling out of control or inciting a public backlash. The challenge of needing immigration yet not wanting immigrants, especially if they entail costs or inconveniences, is compounded by wanting immigrants but bristling at the prospect of needing them. Public opinion may be driving governments to curb the admission of self-selecting asylum seekers, yet economic pressures dictate a recalibrating of the selection system to attract the right kind of immigrants (Somerville 2009). The following challenges to the politics of governance reflect the growing complexities associated with the diversified diversities of transmigrants and transnationalism:

> *National borders in a borderless world?* The relevance of national borders, the authority of the nation-state, and a unitary conception of the nation are at once vigorously asserted and highly contested in this era of globalization and neoliberalism. The "mobility turn" (Sheller and Urry 2006; Marotta 2011; also Bauman 2000) points to a world on the move (literally and figuratively) through virtual travel and instantaneous communication. The upside consists of diverse movements of people, the complex interdependencies between the here and the there, and the social consequences of such diverse mobilities (Urry 2000). On the downside, illegal activities such as human smuggling and trafficking have taken advantage of the mobility turn, given the movement of people in a world of significant disparities, regional conflicts, and the inexhaustible demand for cheap labour, goods, and services (Shelley 2010). Moreover, as nation-states implement extensive deterrence measures, from militarized border controls to carrier sanctions to block illegal activity and deter low-priority migration, they indirectly push migrants into the hands of smugglers and traffickers who promise to circumvent these barriers (Hansen and Papademetriou 2014). A political price comes into play as well. The dramatic increase in flows of money, information, and people creates networks of complex and contested connections of people and relations across space

and through time (Urry 2000). Society as bounded, self-reproducing, internally integrated, and sovereign within its borders can no longer claim exclusive jurisdiction. Yet the bounded nation-state remains a powerful organizing principle of international order, especially as peoples (nations) around the world strive for national recognition, together with the legitimacy/power such a designation bestows (Conference Notes 2013). The paradoxes are unmistakable. Since the fall of the Berlin Wall, wall-building has increased not just in the physical sense, such as the US-Mexico border fence, but also in the possibly futile desire for enclosure and security behind national borders to keep out transnational forces and the dynamics of globalization – both of which imagine a world without boundaries (Brown 2014).

> *Immigration dialectics: needed not wanted.* Globalization has proven conducive to apparent contradictions (McNevin 2012). States are willing to open their borders to global dynamics and wanted immigrants as the basis for economic growth and development. But doing so ups the ante over migration and citizenship in nation-states, which are grounded in the principle of a sovereign territorial political community. Such states are under pressure to close their borders, not only to staunch the flow of unwanted migrants, but also to demonstrate their control of territories and borders (Sharma 2006). A certain selectivity is at play: Borders may be relatively permeable for the privileged but impermeable for the unskilled and those who cross without permission (Bauder 2012-13; Brown 2014). Unwanted migrants are often criminalized or dehumanized, they may lose their political and socio-economic rights, and many frequently experience exploitation and abuse in responding to the demands of a transnational labour market. They inspire so much fear that they become victimized by aggressive and highly militarized border controls, which make a mockery of sometimes exaggerated claims about borderless states in a cosmopolitan world (Hage 2003; Ang 2011).

For example, since 2001 Australia has held ship-bound asylum seekers in remote detention centres or processed them offshore in jurisdictions where they can be declared illegals and dismissed as sources of insecurity and threats to sovereignty (McNevin 2012). In 2013, both Papua New Guinea and the tiny Pacific island of Nauru (21 square kilometres) agreed to process *and* settle asylum seekers whom the Australian authorities intercepted on the high seas. Canada too has imposed a series of restrictions (rights-restrictive policies) to control its borders and secure territorial sovereignty, from legislation such as the 2002 Immigration and Refugee Protection Act to increasing federal powers of detention and deportation (Christopher Anderson 2013). Finally, the United States has launched one of the most ambitious expansions of government regulatory power in contemporary history, in contrast to its tradition of limited government intervention. Why? To secure its borders against undocumented migrants without blocking admission of the legally permitted (Alden 2012; Meissner et al. 2013). Edward Alden (2012, 107) demonstrates how the American government constructed a system in which it alone decides and enforces who is welcome:

> Congress and successive administrations – both Democratic and Republican – have increased the size of the Border Control from fewer than 3,000 agents to more than 21,000, built nearly 700 miles of fencing along the southern border with Mexico, and deployed pilotless drones, sensor cameras and other expensive technologies aimed at preventing illegal crossings at the land borders. The government has overhauled the visa system to require interviews for all new visa applicants and instituted extensive background checks for many of those wishing to come to the United States to study, travel, visit family, or do business. It now requires secure documents – a passport or the equivalent – for all travel to and from the United States by citizens and noncitizens. All border officers take fingerprints and run other screening measures on all travelers coming to this country by air in order to identify criminals, terrorists, or others deemed to pose a threat to the United States.

In short, a networked world creates a paradoxical tension between the national and the transnational (Ang 2010). The global and the national may be irrevocably enmeshed. Yet nationalizing forces are attempting to disentangle the national from the international by enforcing more vigorous forms of border control, outsourcing both the processing and settlement of would-be refugees, imposing civic integration tests, and demanding explicit commitments to a values-based citizenship.

> *State sovereignty versus human rights.* It's commonly assumed that nation-states have the sovereign right to control their borders in specifying who gets in and who qualifies for membership in the body politic (Brock 2013; Fine 2013). But many believe that governments no longer have the resources or the resourcefulness – or even the legitimacy – to do so. The constitutional order of liberal-democratic societies exerts additional pressure to respect universal protocols for protecting the rights of those who want to enter (Ruhs 2012).[1] This conflict of interest is compounded by a growing commitment to cosmopolitanism, with its privileging of human rights that transcends nationality or citizenship. Yet talk of a borderless world of unfettered human rights related to mobility may be a bit premature. National governments still set the rules when it comes to labour migration, and despite repeated references to global migration movements as an uncontrollable side effect of globalization, they still determine who gets in, how, and why (Vogel 2011).

> *Internationalizing immigration: thinking outside the national box.* Policy makers can no longer present immigration as a national issue. A broader frame of reference has evolved for seeing immigration as an international dynamic in a globalized context (for example, globalization creates a demand for immigrant workers). But few international organizations acknowledge the obstacles associated with managing global migration. This omission stands in glaring contrast to the regulated movement of goods/trade and money/finance that follow global norms governed by international institutions (i.e., the World Trade Organization or International Monetary Fund). This dearth of international migration bodies emboldens nation-states to formulate rules (and break them) as they see fit (Deparle 2010). The creation of a global migration governance could well facilitate international cooperation on migration, including better human rights protections for migrant and temporary workers (Cameron and Goldin 2012).

> *Rethinking the immigration agenda: the bigger picture.* The economic gains associated with immigration and migrants are widely anticipated. Governments can no longer passively wait for the arrival of the brightest and the finest. Nor can a country simply tinker with existing immigration policies if it aspires to become a preferred destination for

thinkers, innovators, and doers. Governments must pay attention to a broader spectrum of policy issues to harness the benefits of greater global mobility (ibid.). True, the globalization of policy making poses a challenge because of contradictory demands imposed by outside forces beyond national control. Yet dangers await those who formulate their migration policies and programs without sufficient consideration for the wider global contexts and the uncertainties that influence migration patterns in the long run (de Haas, Vargas-Silva, and Vezzoli 2010). In the words of de Haas, Vargas-Silva, and Vezzoli (ibid., 9, emphasis in original), a holistic approach is pivotal:

> This requires the elaboration of *comprehensive* migration approaches which analyse the evolution of migration systems across space and time – integrating sending, transit, and receiving contexts and linking the multiple ways in which development and change affect, and are affected by, migration. A deeper understanding of past and present migration dynamics and their interaction with broader global transformations will provide the basis for the scenarios.

> *Toward a global/national/local nexus.* Traditional immigration entailed a permanent move and an exclusive commitment to the new country. Attainment of citizenship was the definitive marker that immigrants had transferred their allegiance to the host country (Spoonley 2009). But the transnational character of migrant lives and identities challenges conventional thinking and responses in a world where (a) migrants simultaneously commit to two or more societies (de Haas, Vargas-Silva, and Vezzoli 2010); (b) migration itself is often circular, intermittent, or repetitive; (c) attachment and identity are no longer exclusively territorial; and (d) borders are perceived as increasingly porous. But although borders may have lost their privileged status in securitizing society, nation-states remain ruthlessly pivotal in militarizing enforcement and control (Brown and Cardinal 2007; Kurz 2012; Maas 2013).

> *Achieving integration in a transmigratory and multiversal world of complex diversity.* A sense of dismay inheres in a transmigratory world of fractured belongings, splintered identities, and differentiated differences.

The challenge rests in forging a sense of cohesion and identity in contexts that are increasingly immune to conventional strategies for constructing a citizenry of community, conviction, and consensus (Fleras 2012c). Not unexpectedly, few issues are as pressing, provocative, or profound, and yet more elusive and enigmatic, than national unity, citizenship, and newcomer integration. The governance challenge can be captured in a single question: Does it still make sense to talk about any place-based immigrant governance model such as multiculturalism or citizenship in a world where migration is increasingly temporary, intermittent, circular, or repeated, and where notions of migrant identity and belonging are increasingly disconnected from place (Carruthers 2013)?

> *Re-imagining immigrant identity, belonging, and experiences.* Immigrants themselves are changing in ways that subvert conventional governance models for living together. A world of transmigration and diaspora politics reminds us that they often move in circular and intermittent patterns, thus blurring the lines between here and there. Immigrant identities are not always in competition with each other but mutually constitutive and reinforcing. The end result? There is no inherent contradiction in identifying as Somalian, Muslim, and Canadian, while professing a belonging to Canada as an adoptive home and diasporic space (Berns-McGown 2013). The challenges are all too obvious in constructing unity from diversity, community from strangers, and commitment from expediency. The politics of immigrant governance must also contemplate the possibility of integrating multiple identities and fragmented belongings at a time when immigrants themselves are increasingly uncoupled from place, both physically and psychologically.

> *Citizenship challenges: deconstructing/reconstructing.* At a time when immigrants were expected to identify with a single national community, multiple allegiances were discouraged. This concept of citizenship cannot cope with the realities of a transmigratory world. Nonetheless, a commitment to recalibrate citizenship along inclusionary lines will encounter an equally stubborn force in the nationalism of nation-states. The state in its hegemonic form (both controlling and conformity demanding) is likely to resist any citizenship governance that weakens an undivided loyalty and an unalloyed identity (Baron 2009).

> *Balancing the ambivalences.* Canadians are generally supportive of immigration. Canada itself has no explicitly anti-immigration party or policy, and polls routinely commend it as a welcoming country (Bloemraad 2012; Reitz 2012b). Yet Canadian support is less than it seems. Consensus is mounting that the government is doing a poor job in managing immigration issues (Selley 2011). More worrying still is the public support that is conditional. For example, consider the media-inspired hysteria regarding the arrival of Tamil asylum seekers on the BC coast in 2009 and 2010. Or ponder the possibility of a backlash, especially when migrant unemployment is high and public opinion is disconnected from an elite consensus. What about the frosty reaction to a proposed doubling of annual immigration totals (from 250,000 to 400,000 or 500,000), in hopes of addressing skill shortages while securing more global clout for Canada (Jason Kenney, cited in Friesen 2012b; *Globe and Mail* 2012)? Canadians may endorse immigration in theory but not necessarily in practice, and government programs must be formulated and legitimized in this context of ambivalence. Tradeoffs are inescapable, of course, although the possibility of a backlash raises the question of where to locate the middle without alienating the peripheries.

> *The politics of uncertainty.* A perusal of the reference list at the end of this book should allay any doubt that knowledge is growing regarding the politics of uncertainty. Yet consensus is limited over how social, economic, cultural, and political factors influence the volume, direction, and nature of migration in the constantly changing global context (de Haas, Vargas-Silva, and Vezzoli 2010). There is little agreement over why people leave, how they negotiate the transition, what factors improve their integration in the host country, what the consequences are of militarizing borders, and how (comm)unity is constructed in a world of fluidity and flow. For example, immigrant-receiving societies may want to deter immigration by militarizing borders and detention controls in the name of security. Yet they are unwilling to jettison the potential benefits of more open borders for advancing national and vested interests. The lack of consensus is not to be trifled with: Sending and receiving countries whose policies underestimate or misunderstand the politics and dynamics that drive a global migration order will experience negative consequences.

SHIFTING DISCOURSES

New and shifting discourses are accompanying a world of evolving realities and challenges. How people think and talk about immigration and immigrants differs from the discursive frameworks of the past. Emphasis is increasingly directed at portraying immigration as a field of flows within shifting contexts and across multiple domains (Simmons 2010). There is less inclination to portray immigrants in simplistic and essentialized ways, which results in a debunking of certain misconceptions:

> *Global migration: a new conceptual lens.* How global migration is conceptualized and studied is changing (O'Reilly 2012). Transmigration represents a central dynamic in the process of globalization and a prominent structural feature of the global economy (Grillo 2000), and globalization also constitutes the context for situating contemporary movements of people (de Wenden 2011). In a globalizing world, old migration models based on nationality, linearity, and permanence can no longer handle the complexities and contradictions, especially when migrants increasingly envision themselves as global citizens who are taking advantage of a worldwide marketplace (Schmidtke 2012).

> *The bigger the picture, the better the perspective.* Most migration studies take as their analytic starting point the situation in destination countries of the global North. They focus on costs and benefits, migration control/management, and theories of assimilation or integration. This approach tends to neglect the perspective of origin and transit countries in the global South as well as the realities of migrants themselves. But this myopic outlook is changing in response to new discursive frames that emphasize the global/national/local nexus as a primary departure point for analysis and assessment.

> *Moving beyond binaries: from either/or to both/and.* Migration theories and discourses tend to be driven and dissected by binary oppositions such as international versus internal migration, sending versus receiving countries, forced versus voluntary migration, temporary versus permanent, legal versus irregular, and skilled versus unskilled (King, Skeldon, and Vullnetari 2008). But these categories and dichotomies

reflect bureaucratic inventions and comforting fictions that usually conceal more than they reveal (de Haas, Vargas-Silva, and Vezzoli 2010). In reality, distinctions are increasingly blurred because of geopolitical events such as the changing nature of borders and because migrant journeys are discursively framed as complex and dynamic fields of flows and fluidity. There is much of value in seeing the world as transitional and complex, as contextual rather than categorical. Such a framework demonstrates that relying on binary oppositions (either/or) is prone to simplification or essentialism at the cost of uncovering the nature and drivers of migration processes.

> *Immigration as a verb.* Conventional discourses represented immigration as a thing (noun), with their focus on migration as a one-way movement between two fixed points. But current references increasingly emphasize fluidity, connectedness, and transnationality, involving transmigrant networks of numerous actors, across various domains, and at differing levels. Immigrants are not isolated persons or unreflective robots but negotiate environments ripe with contested contexts, multiple patterns, and intelligent dynamics. This dynamic of immigration is increasing reframed (metaphorically speaking) as a process or activity, a verb rather than a noun.

> *Immigrants as agents.* If immigration can be seen as a verb, immigrants themselves can be perceived as active agents. All too often, the immigration literature portrays them as if they were automatons, especially when employing a structural model of immigration. They are perceived as robots (or victims) who leave, arrive, adapt and adopt, and eventually integrate. By contrast, contemporary discourses that are rooted in transnational narratives present migrants as active agents who make decisions about departures and transitions, their degree of settlement and involvement in the host country, and the level of interaction with their homeland.

> *It takes a community to raise a migrant.* Migrants are often portrayed as ambitious individuals who have the resources to make a choice and emigrate. But the image of the migrant as a rational loner is coming under scrutiny. Family and community members play a key role in supporting a migrant's decision to move. In return, they anticipate

remittances and sponsorships of future migrants. In other words, as Levitt (2007) puts it, immigration is as much about those who stay behind as those who leave.

> *Immigration as (protracted) process.* Immigration and integration are not short-term projects. They constitute long-term processes of varying stages and protracted trajectories. Immigrants may require many years to become truly settled in terms of securing survival and success, involvement and participation in the local community and political domain, and establishing a network of relations (Broadbent 2009b). In short, immigration is not just about entry into the host country – it's a broader transitioning process of getting ready, settling down, fitting in, and moving up.

> *From sedentary bias to normalizing migration.* Conventional discourses tended to frame humans as essentially stationary in nature; as a result, migration was presented as a departure from the norm. But migration is proving more common than originally thought, especially if rural-to-urban, region-to-region, and country-to-country movements are taken into account. As well, the sedentary bias often saw immigration as a dysfunction that needed remedy, through more robust border control or more muscular integration programs. Current theorizing perceives migration as an integral (even routine) component of global transformational processes rather than an anomaly or a problem (de Haas, Vargas-Silva, and Vezzoli 2010). Immigration is no longer couched in terms of being distinct from broader social relationships, intergroup dynamics, or the workings of contemporary society. The focus is now on immigration as a normal aspect of social life related to complexity, contextuality, social change, and diversity.

> *Gendering the discourse.* Once framed along gender-neutral lines, immigration and immigrants are increasingly seen as gendered, since men and women differ in their experiences – from leaving and arriving to settling down and integrating. An engendering of immigration and immigrants exposes uncomfortable truths: Immigrant women and men may possess the same formal rights as the native-born, but, and even more so for women, they must exercise these rights and attain success in a context that neither reflects their realities nor advances their interests.

> *Mediated immigration.* The centrality of the media across all dimensions of immigration cannot be denied. What most Canadians know about immigrants and immigration is rarely based on first-hand experience. Awareness and knowledge are filtered and framed through the media as a primary point of contact and preliminary understanding. Not only does media coverage shape public discourse and influence public opinion – immigrants themselves must live in a community and society defined by media discourses, both positive and negative.

> *A sociological focus.* Reference to the social dimensions of immigration yields insights into the reciprocal relationship between society and immigration. To one side, changes in global immigration and current immigration policy are transforming Canadian society. To the other side, changes in Canadian society and the world at large are transforming immigration patterns and paradoxes, policies and politics.

> *Who needs whom?* Canadians live in a world of intense competition for the talented. Conventional thinking generally assumed that immigrants need and want Canada, which is apparently proved by the backlog of nearly one million people who wish to enter. Not surprisingly, public perceptions and political debates display a strong host society bias. The primacy of national interests related to security, prosperity, and identity is privileged, and little attention is paid to migrants' experiences and struggles except, perhaps, as invited guests who should know their place and ingratiate themselves accordingly (Ehrkamp and Leitner 2006). But as noted elsewhere, a new reality is in place. Just as powerful states once competed for territory and resources in the nineteenth century, they are now competing for brainpower (from scientists to entrepreneurs) to fuel the dynamism of the international economy (Jacoby 2011). A playful inversion may be appropriate. Perhaps it is Canada who needs immigrants more than immigrants need Canada, if only to address labour market shortages and the problems associated with an ageing population and declining birth rates. Discourses must shift accordingly to ensure that Canada capitalizes on the diversity dividend that immigration brings.

Box 50 provides an overview of the evolving realities, emergent challenges, and shifting discourses that underscore a rethinking of immigration and immigrants.

50 OVERVIEW

Rethinking Immigration, Reframing Immigrants: Evolving Realities, Emerging Challenges, and Shifting Discourses

	Rethinking Immigration	Reframing Immigrants
Evolving realities	> From immigration to transmigration > From linearity to multilinearity > From permanent to circular/onward/intermittent > From Canada as unit of immigration to Canada as node in transnational network > Freer movement for First World and highly skilled > Reflect interplay of structure, agency, and ideology (neoliberal) > Toward a just-in-time, demand-driven immigration agenda	> From migrants to transmigrants > Changes in sources, destinations, patterns of movement > Occupying liminal spaces of here, there, and everywhere > From individual focus to migrant networking/community focus > Bimodality: high skilled and unskilled > Settled immigrants + irregular migrants/temporary foreign workers
Emerging challenges	> Challenging exclusive state sovereignty as governance model > Eroding place-based integration models in a transmigrant/transnational, diasporic, and cosmopolitan world > Securitization and militarization of borders in a borderless world > Contesting citizenship: from singular/national/bounded to customized/inclusive/transnational	> Multiple loyalties, fluid identities, splintered attachments > Making a go of it in a competitive environment > Confront devaluation of skills, education, experience

	Rethinking Immigration	Reframing Immigrants
Shifting discourses	> Challenging conventional frames and narratives	> Toward complexity, multiplicity, hybridity
	> From national to transnational	> From national (European) model to transnational model
	> Transnationalism = paradigm shift in framing immigration and immigrants	
	> Beyond binaries: from categorical thinking to contextual to reflect fluidity and multi-dimensionality	> From problem to solution
		> Benefits and costs (not costs or benefits)
	> From noun to verb: from fixed field of location to networked flows of connections and crossings	> A gendered analysis
		> De-essentialize immigrant experiences as static or deterministic
	> From national model to postnational/transnational model (from domestic policy to global/national frame of reference)	> Migrant agency reinserted
		> Immigration needed, immigrants not wanted
	> From sedentary bias to people movement as norm	
	> From common citizenship to customized citizenship	
	> From immigrant integration (multiculturalism) to differential accommodation (multiversal)	

IMMIGRATION IN THE TWENTY-FIRST CENTURY: "BACK TO THE FUTURE"

Perhaps no force in modern life is as omnipresent yet overlooked as global migration, that vehicle of creative destruction that is reordering ever more of the world.

— JASON DEPARLE (2010)

This book began with the simple observation that humans are a species on the move, and thus the story of humanity is a story of migration. Like their modern counterparts, early humans migrated in response to developments in a certain territory, including food scarcity and lack of space, climate and environmental changes, and politics and violence. Such a deeply embedded and ubiquitous dynamic might be rooted in human nature (genes) and intertwined with the social and cultural (Campbell and Crawford 2012). To be sure, no one knows exactly where or when humans actually became humans or how they spread across the world. The most acceptable theory is that prehumans and early humans originated in Africa and dispersed across Asia and Europe. According to most anthropologists, humans *(Homo sapiens)* occupied most of Africa about 150,000 years ago, spread across Eurasia 40,000 years ago, peopled the Americas as far back as 20,000 years ago, and colonized the Pacific Islands around the time of Christ. These migrations brought the species to the position of global dominance and heralded the extinction of competitors (Gugliotta 2008).

The Age of Exploration, coupled with European settlement and colonization, intensified the pace of movement across oceans. During the sixteenth century, thousands of Europeans may have settled the Americas. By the nineteenth century, however, it's estimated that over 50 million people had left Europe for North and South America, in the process displacing or annihilating the indigenous inhabitants (Somerville 2009). Much of the impetus for this movement was economic. The industrial revolution pushed millions of agricultural workers off the land, into cities, and onward to overseas destinations. Industrialization also proved a catalyst for transnational migration, particularly with the increasingly global economy of the nineteenth century. The Europeanization of the Americas and the Antipodes drew to a close following the First World War, only to resume in the aftermath of the Second World War. Post-war European industrial expansion reversed the tide, with the result that most European nations became destinations, especially for temporary foreign workers whose guest status proved more permanent than many expected.

The world appears to be poised for yet another migration transformation. The proportion of immigrants who live in the industrialized countries of the North continues to expand as part of the resurgence in migration and refugees (Manning 2005). Immigrants now account for over 20 percent of the population in Australia, New Zealand, and Canada, 14 percent in Spain, 13 percent in the United States and Germany, and about 11 percent in France, the United Kingdom, and the Netherlands (Perucca 2010; Statistics Canada 2013). The most striking feature of this social transformation is the explosion of cross-border flows of investment, trade, ideas, and (to a lesser extent) people (Castles and Miller 2009). No less evident is a dramatic acceleration of border controls and enforcement (Keung 2013b; Meissner et al. 2013). The impact of this seemingly opposed migration dynamic is subject to the following diverse interpretations:

> For some, a global order anchored in the sovereignty of the nation-state is lapsing into more fluid and contested ways of living together. The term "translocality" captures how nation-states are increasingly displaced as the exclusive space of connectivity, communication, and commitment between and across diasporic communities (Lyons and Mandaville 2008). Also relevant is the concept of cosmopolitanism, with its attendant notion that people can see themselves as global citizens rather than (or in addition to) citizens of nation-states (Kymlicka and Walker 2012; Brock 2013). Even reference to the nation-state may become badly dated as a socially networked global society diminishes the relevance of physical space for a cooperative co-existence (Freeland 2011). Moreover, as Castles and Miller (2009) suggest, migration processes are becoming simultaneously entrenched yet resistant to government control. As a result, new political forms may arise that involve unique patterns of interdependence, transnational organizations, and bilateral and regional cooperation.

> Some are skeptical of any transformative change. The proliferation of transnational networks, with nodes of control in multiple locations, may be one thing, but there is little chance that the nation-state will atrophy because of migration. It remains firmly in control as the fundamental and principled unit of organization in the international

order. It also continues to command the loyalties and passions of most humans so that national boundaries remain as tightly coiled as ever. Even reference to the free movement of people is an exaggeration; more accurately, movement is free for the skilled from the First World but not for the unskilled from the periphery (Tendoh 2009). Besides, critics contend, these so-called newer patterns of international migration (from transmigration to circular migration) are not nearly as new as pundits and polls would have us believe (Kivisto 2001).

> For others, it's not a case of either/or. The nation-state may no longer be the only contestant in the global village, but it's hardly irrelevant because it still determines who gets in, why, and how (Earnest 2008). Indeed, the nation-state continues to play a role in global affairs, albeit as one of many actors that affect people's lives in terms of options or constraints (Barcham 2005).

Ultimately, how should immigration and immigrants be envisaged in the second decade of the twenty-first century? Current international immigration appears to be more complex than in the past, as it connects people over longer distances and across a broader range of countries. That overseas migrants are increasingly returning to their original homelands to take advantage of their opportunities speaks volumes of the complexities involved (Castles, Hugo, and Vasta 2013). Size and characteristics have changed as well. Twenty-first-century immigrants are more numerous, more mobile, more diverse, and increasingly female. They have a wider global reach, stay for shorter periods, and are more inclined to settle outside large cities (also Guardia and Pichelmann 2006; Somerville 2009; Deparle 2010). This transformational dynamic is driven by the globalization of capital and labour, by ideological shifts that place a premium on movement rather than staying put, and by advances in communication technology (de Haas, Vargas-Silva, and Vezzoli 2010). Paradoxically, governments seem confused over how to advance openness without losing control or closure. Trade and tourism remain high on the priority list, yet many feel compelled to seal their borders, hiving off areas as vast as the Arizona Desert or the Mediterranean to protect their territorial sovereignty (Deparle 2010).

The conclusion seems incontestable. Optimism co-exists with gloom in analyzing international migration at the level of policy making and social outcomes. The political and economic contours of an emerging global order remain largely unclear and sharply contested. The old is losing ground yet remains solidly entrenched. The new, in turn, struggles to capture a critical mass for shifting the discourses to accommodate evolving realities and challenges. With respect to Canada, the book has made it abundantly clear that Canada's immigration system is experiencing a significant overhaul that borders on a paradigm shift (Bauder, Lenard, and Straehle 2014). Yet a Canada that once was regarded as a pacesetter in managing migration appears to have abdicated its lofty status as policy innovator and humanitarian leader by turning toward more restrictive immigration schemes (from supply to demand), asylum policies, and citizenship programs, such as those practised in Europe (Soennecken 2014; Winter 2014; Kolb 2014). In light of this turmoil in rethinking immigration and reframing immigrants, Canadians need to engage both critically and compassionately with the broad transformations in managing migration and admission criteria if we want immigrants and immigration to create the kind of Canada that inspires and leads.

NOTES

CHAPTER 1: TWENTY-FIRST-CENTURY MIGRATION

1 Ideal-typical represents a heuristic device for displaying differences and similarities so that one position is largely exclusive of others for analytical purposes rather than as a reflection of reality (Skrentny, Gell-Redman, and Lee 2012).

2 In 1971, according to Statistics Canada (cited in *Globe and Mail* 2012), there was a ratio of 6.6 people of working age for every senior. In 2012, the ratio was 4.2 to 1. By 2036, the ratio is expected to be about 2 to 1.

CHAPTER 2: GLOBAL MIGRATION, INTERNATIONAL MIGRANTS

1 The umbrella term "neoliberalism" refers to the belief in more markets and less government in sorting out who gets what. Neoliberal agendas tend to emphasize aggressive market competitiveness, a flexible labour force for the demands of the global economy, and regulations that work to the advantage of employers (Shields 2003; also Department of Finance 2006). In contrast to a regulatory model that frames immigrants as a destructive form of labour competition, a neoliberal model promotes the competition principle by way of a proactive international labour program to improve Canada's economic competitiveness at home and abroad. The ideology of the market is promoted as the ideal mechanism for matching jobs and immigrants (with flexible skills), while selecting for newcomers who are less likely to require welfare services or who lack access to welfare rights and unemployment benefits (Bauder 2008b). Under the neoliberalism of a market-driven immigration agenda, the commodification of a designer-and-demand-driven labour market has proven polarizing and exclusionary (Zaman 2007, 2010).

2 Globalization as theory comprises two dimensions: (a) worldwide expansion of capitalism and its displacement of pre-capitalist economies/relations; and (b) the internationalization of the production process within an integrated global

market, in contrast to previous patterns that linked nation-states worldwide via commodity exchange. Or as William Robinson (1998) puts it, globalization entails a transition from national societies linked in a world economy to a transnational or global society predicated on a global economy with an international division of labour and countries as sites of convenience in a vast productive loop.

3 The key features of a human rights approach include (a) universality (human rights, which apply to everyone, everywhere, derive from the common humanity and inherent dignity of each person rather than from citizenship in a country); (b) indivisibility (there is no hierarchy of rights); (c) inalienability (rights cannot be denied to anyone or taken away); and (d) equality (all humans are equal and must be free from discrimination) (Ruhs 2012).

CHAPTER 3: WHO GOT IN?

1 Strictly speaking, the overall figures for the federal skilled worker stream are misleading. Totals under the economic class include spouses and dependants who are not processed on a skills basis. Of the 186,881 immigrants from the economic class in 2010, 110,324 were selected due to their relationship (partner or children) with the principal applicant. The remaining 76,557 principal applicants constituted about 25 percent of the total immigrant intake in that year.

CHAPTER 4: RECALIBRATING CANADA'S IMMIGRATION PROGRAM

1 The "mass" in mass migration is rarely defined, although it's typically used in the sense of "many." I prefer to use "mass" in terms *of undifferentiated* (hence the opposite to "customized" or "designer").

2 The term "temporary foreign workers" is problematic. It covers a sprawling range of migrants and activities ranging from workers brought in under NAFTA and other trade agreements; students and researchers; people doing charitable work; professors, postdoctoral fellows, and award recipients; live-in caregivers and seasonal agricultural workers; and both the high and the low skilled (Corcoran 2014). There are growing moves to replace the term with "migrant workers," partly because it more accurately reflects the realities and perspectives of the workers themselves. Reference to migrants as temporary glosses over their long-term structural importance to the Canadian economy, in addition to the decade-long tenure of some migrant workers. Labelling migrants as foreign contributes ideologically to their marginalization as exploitable and expendable in a racialized labour market and hierarchy (Preibisch 2012; Faraday 2012; Hussan and Prier 2012; also Taylor and Foster 2014). In short, the value of language (words and definitions) cannot be underestimated in influencing frames of reference and corresponding ranges of possible actions (Bauder 2013).

3 Technically, the LIC Program is not new because variations of it have existed since the 1950s.

4 Others disagree and argue that 446,847 temporary foreign workers, including agricultural labourers, entered Canada in 2011 (Grant, Curry, and Chase 2013).

5 Those who lose their jobs can stay until their two-year work permit expires. But they are generally ineligible for employment insurance and can take a job only

from an employer who has convinced the government of a specific labour short-age for which there is no qualified Canadian (Clark 2009).

6 Both the International Labour Organization and the UN (via the Migrant Work-ers Convention) have established a series of protocols and standards to protect workers and their families. The UN Convention, which came into force in 2003, makes it illegal to (a) expel workers on a collective basis, (b) destroy or confis-cate their work permits or passports, (c) offer pay, benefits, and health care that differ from those of nationals, and (d) refuse the right to registration of birth and nationality to children born of migrant parents. Canada has yet to ratify the convention (Samers 2010).

7 Twenty agricultural migrant workers died in 2012. Since 2006, migrant workers in Ontario have been able to refuse to perform dangerous work, but none have done so, since no one wants to create problems or run the risk of never being rehired (Jeff Mackey 2013).

8 "Commodification" is used in the Marxist sense of workers who are treated as objects that can be bought and sold; the workers themselves must rely on the sale of their labour power for subsistence and survival. Thus, lower-skilled TFW are seen as disposable, whereas skilled workers are perceived as potential future citizens (Nakache and Kinoshita 2010). Commodification can also be defined in the sense of relying on the market and private sector (rather than the state) to do things faster and more cheaply (Zaman 2006).

CHAPTER 5: CANADA'S REFUGEE STATUS DETERMINATION PROCESS

1 It should be noted that rates can depend on various factors such as the source of refugees. For example, European countries are proximate to asylum seekers from Afghanistan and Iran, whereas Canada's largest source of refugee claim-ants consists of European Roma. Moreover, countries such as Australia block the entry of claimants at the border, whereas Canada provides a right to a hear-ing for everyone who claims refugee status (D'Amato 2013; Koning 2013).

2 Samers (2010) reminds us that the concept of an "illegal refugee" is a contra-diction in terms. Everyone has a right to seek asylum (refuge) by claiming refu-gee status. If an asylum seeker's claim is rejected and he or she remains in Canada without the knowledge of the authorities, only then can that person be considered illegal, but he or she ceases to be an asylum seeker or a refugee.

3 International law stipulates that a refugee should not be subject to refoulement: that is, individuals must not be returned to countries where their lives are endan-gered (Samers 2010).

4 As noted, Japan recognizes 27 refugee claims in a typical year, including 1 per year from 1994 to 1997 (Lamey 2011b). Germany historically had a low accept-ance rate because of its tight citizenship model, which envisioned the country as the homeland of last resort for those of German descent (Lamey 2011b). France and the United Kingdom admit migrants and refugees but do not view their admission or integration as a feature of national identity. Israel is an interesting case. According to the Israel Ministry of Foreign Affairs, the Law of Return entitles all those with Jewish ancestry the right to immigrate and attain perma-nent residency in Israel. Non-Jews seeking residency are generally accorded a

temporary visa. Israel as a rule does not process asylum seekers (Hebrew Sheltering and Immigration Society [HIAS] 2013).

5 Should outcomes in life-and-death applications turn on their merits, or should they hinge on which judge is assigned to decide the application? The fairness of Canada's refugee determination system has come under additional fire for its vast discrepancies in disallowing failed claimants to appeal. Claimants who want the Federal Court to overturn an IRB decision must first apply for leave. After a single Federal Court judge grants them leave, they can argue the merits of their case in court. Overall, Federal Court judges grant leave to 14.4 percent of applicants. However, the grant rate of individual judges ranges from 1.36 percent to 78 percent. In addition, 36 percent of judges who issued grant leaves departed from the average by 50 percent or more (Rehaag 2012).

6 The Office of the United Nations High Commissioner for Refugees (UNHCR) was established in 1950, with the express purpose of protecting refugees and resolving refugee problems around the world. Its main functions include protection for basic human rights by ensuring that refugees are not involuntarily returned to places where they fear persecution.

7 By 2013, the global refugee situation had changed somewhat. The UNHCR's *Asylum Trends 2013* pointed out that 612,700 people had applied for asylum in North America, Europe, East Asia, and the Pacific – the highest total for any year since 2001. Germany was the largest single recipient, with 109,600 claims, followed by the United States (88,400), France (60,000), and Sweden (54,000). Canada received 10,400 claims, fewer than half the number seen in 2012 (20,500). Syria and the Russian Federation have replaced Afghanistan as the world's principal countries of origin for asylum seekers.

8 Efforts to reduce the number of claimants from safe countries appear to be working. Between January and March of 2013, the number of Roma from Hungary who claimed asylum declined to just 33, compared with 724 for the same period in 2012 (Jovanovski 2013).

9 The federal government has been openly criticized for its decision to discontinue covering the costs of drugs and medical care for all refugee claimants until they are eligible for provincial coverage or their claims are rejected. Lawyers for Canadian Doctors for Refugee Care and the Canadian Association for Refugee Lawyers accuse the government of violating Charter rights to life and security of person based on the country of origin (Lorriggio 2013). The *Canadian Medical Association Journal* calls the cuts to refugee health coverage both "economically irresponsible" and "medically irrational" since they do little to protect either the public or the patient (Tobi Cohen 2014). These cuts are particularly punitive for refugees with poorer health because of their experiences of displacement and difficulties in the resettlement process (Marwah 2014; Keung 2014c). Six provinces have opposed federal changes to the Interim Federal Health Program by reinstating access to essential and emergency health care for claimants.

CHAPTER 6: AMERICAN EXCEPTIONALISM

1 Words matter, and care must be exercised in how they are used. For example, "illegal" is not a neutral expression but freighted with normative assumptions

that negatively impact on individual readers and migrant communities by way of inaccurate stereotypes that criminalize or marginalize (Adam Goodman 2012). Harald Bauder (2013) suggests using the term "illegalized migrants" to draw attention to those bureaucratic processes that render people "illegal" rather than blaming migrants for the situation in which they find themselves.

CHAPTER 7: ASSESSING IMMIGRATION

1 For a hard-hitting critique of Canada's immigration program, consult the Canadian Centre for Immigration Policy Reform website at www.immigration reform.ca. Those who prefer a more positive assessment can consult works by Irene Bloemraad, Will Kymlicka, and Jeffrey Reitz.

2 The Fraser Institute states that immigrants pay about half the income tax of other Canadians but absorb about the same amount of services (Carlson 2011). Between 1987 and 2004, every immigrant paid an average of $10,340 in income tax, compared to the Canadian-born average of $16,501. Newcomers received $110 less in government benefits, resulting in a net fiscal transfer benefit per immigrant of $6,051.

3 According to a Policy Brief by the OECD (2014b), immigrants appear to have exerted a largely neutral impact on the public purse of OECD countries over the past 50 years. That is, the cost of state benefits consumed by newcomers was broadly covered by the taxes they paid. In cases where they did have an impact, it rarely exceeded plus or minus 0.5 percent of the GDP. In short, the OECD concludes, migrants are neither a major burden on state spending nor a quick-fix panacea for improving public finances.

4 The interactive voice response method allows respondents to submit their replies anonymously by punching the key pads on their phones or mobiles. Their answers can differ significantly when a live interviewer is used.

5 The question read, "Should Canada accept all qualified immigrants who want to enter the country or should we limit the number of immigrants allowed in each year?" Eliciting a single response to two questions is methodologically unacceptable, and the omission of "qualified" in the second question further undermines the validity of comparing responses to the two questions.

CHAPTER 8: IMMIGRANT EXPERIENCES

1 Skills and competence in an official language profoundly shape immigrants' experiences in Canada and their integration into communities and workplaces (Derwing and Waugh 2012).

2 Readers are encouraged to view the DVD *Where Strangers Become Neighbours,* directed by Giovanni Attili (2007), on the largely positive experiences of newcomers in adjusting to a Vancouver neighbourhood.

CHAPTER 9: INTEGRATING IMMIGRANTS

1 Textual analysis by Fries and Gingrich (2009) of the 1988 Multiculturalism Act yielded five themes: diversity, harmony, equality, barrier removal, and resource.

CHAPTER 10: RETHINKING IMMIGRANT GOVERNANCE

1 "Transnationalism" can be used in the broad sense of communication and inter-actions between people and institutions across the borders of nation-states around the world. More narrowly, it refers to beliefs and practices that are extended from and sustained with reference to a specific homeland (Leonard 2009).

2 Cosmopolitanism is a belief in the need and value of more open borders, more freedom of movement, and intermixing of groups of individuals. It stands in contrast to the authority of states' sovereign rights to control borders and membership (Zapata-Barrero and Pécoud 2012). Cosmopolitanism may also denote notions of global governance and people who see themselves as citizens of the world with an openness to others and willingness to engage with them (Skey 2013).

3 According to Amy Catanzano (2009), the term "multiversal" originated in science fiction but is now accepted as a principle of physics – that reality com-prises multiple dimensions of time and place. York University professor Robert Latham has been instrumental in transporting the concept to the social sciences.

4 Settlement refers to initial and short-term transitional challenges confronting newcomers, whereas integration refers to the ongoing process of incorporation through mutual accommodation between immigrants and society.

CHAPTER 11: CUSTOMIZING CITIZENSHIP

1 Canada is not immune to the principle of citizenship by right of blood. Anyone born outside Canada to at least one parent who is a Canadian citizen is entitled to citizenship. A 2009 act amended these citizenship claims to the first genera-tion born outside Canada (AMSSA 2014; CIC 2014a).

2 Canadians seem relatively indifferent to the possibility of multiple affiliations, except for isolated expressions of outrage, as was prompted by the 2006 emer-gency evacuation of fifteen to thirty thousand Lebanese Canadians who were trapped in Lebanon due to its conflict with Israel (Kenny Zhang 2007). A belief that many evacuees returned to Lebanon upon cessation of hostilities elicited sometimes angry tirades about citizens of convenience who had no sense of alle-giance to Canada (Satzewich 2007-08).

CHAPTER 12: RETHINKING IMMIGRATION, REFRAMING IMMIGRANTS

1 Countries are bound by international law to provide protection for asylum seek-ers and to facilitate the reunification of family members (Vogel 2011).

REFERENCES

AAISA (Alberta Association of Immigrant Serving Agencies). 2013. *Expression of Interest: An In-Depth Review of a New Immigation Model.* Research Brief, December.

Abbott, Michael G., and Charles M. Beach. 2011. *Do Admission Criteria and Economic Recessions Affect Immigrant Earnings?* IRPP Study No. 22. Montreal: Institute for Research on Public Policy.

Abella, Irving, and Harold Troper. 1983. *None Is Too Many: Canada and the Jews of Europe, 1933-1948.* New York: Random House.

Abella, Manolo. 2006. "Policies and Best Practices for Management of Temporary Migrant Workers." Paper presented at the International Symposium on International Migration and Development, United Nations Secretariat, Turin, 28-30 June.

–. 2012. "The United States' and Japan's Immigration Dilemmas in Comparative Perspective." *American Behavioral Scientist* 56, 8: 1139-56.

Abji, Salina. 2013. "Post-Nationalism Re-Considered: A Case Study of the 'No One Is Illegal' Movement in Canada." *Citizenship Studies* 17, 3-4: 322-38.

Abma, Derek. 2013. "Immigration Minister Slams David Suzuki." *Postmedia News.* Reprinted in *Calgary Herald,* 12 July.

Abraham, Carolyn. 2005. "Race." *Globe and Mail,* 18 June.

Abrams, Laura S., and Jené A. Moio. 2009. "Critical Race Theory and the Cultural Competence Dilemma in Social Work Education." *Journal of Social Work Education* 45, 2: 245-61.

Abu-Laban, Yasmeen. 1999. "The Politics of Race, Ethnicity, and Immigration." In *Canadian Politics,* ed. J. Bickerton and A-G. Gagnon. Peterborough, ON: Broadview Press.

–. 2014. "Reform by Stealth: The Harper Conservatives and Canadian Multiculturalism." In *The Multiculturalism Question: Debating Identity in 21st-Century Canada,* ed. Jack Jedwab, 149-72. Queen's University Policy Studies Series. Montreal/Kingston: McGill-Queen's University Press.

Abu-Laban, Yasmeen, and Christina Gabriel. 2002. *Selling Diversity: Immigration, Multiculturalism, Employment Equity, and Globalization.* Peterborough, ON: Broadview Press.

Adams, Billy. 2013. "Boat People Are the Victims of All This Political Expediency." *New Zealand Herald,* 20 July.

Adams, James. 2013. "Leaving Stereotypes in the Dust." *Globe and Mail,* 10 September.

Adams, Michael. 2007. *Unlikely Utopia: The Surprising Triumph of Canadian Pluralism.* Toronto: Viking.

Adams, Michael, Audrey Macklin, and Ratna Omidvar. 2014. "Citizenship Act Will Create Two Classes of Canadians." *Globe and Mail,* 21 May.

Adams, Michael, and Ratna Omidvar. 2010. "Let's Talk about Canadian Citizenship." Maytree Foundation. http://maytree.com.

Adelman, Howard. 2004. "Introduction." *Canadian Issues* (March): 3-4.

Adeyanju, Charles. 2011. *Deadly Fever: Racism, Disease, and a Media Panic.* Halifax: Fernwood.

Agnew, Vijay. 2009. *Racialized Migrant Women in Canada: Essays on Health, Violence, and Equity.* Toronto: University of Toronto Press.

Akdenizli, Banu, E.J. Dionne, and Robert Suro. 2008. *Democracy in the Age of New Media: A Report on the Media and the Immigration Debate.* Los Angeles: Brookings Institute, University of Southern California Norman Lear Center.

Akesson, Lisa. 2010. "Multicultural Ideology and Transnational Family Ties among Descendents of Cape Verdeans in Sweden." *Journal of Ethnic and Migration Studies* 37, 2: 217-35.

Akter, Nasima, Sevgul Topkara-Sarsu, and Diane Dyson. 2013. "Shadow Economies: Economic Survival Strategies of Toronto Immigrant Communities." Toronto East Local Immigration Partnership Workgroup. Toronto: Wellesley Institute.

Alarcon, Krystle. 2013. "The Invisibles: Migrant Workers in Canada." *The Tyee,* 7 January. http://www.thetyee.ca.

Alarcon, Krystle, and Stephanie Law. 2011. "Immigrants Feel Betrayed by Conservative Decision to Make Family Reunion Harder." *The Tyee,* 9 April. http://www.thetyee.ca.

Alberta Federation of Labour. 2010. *Entrenching Exploitation: The Second Report of the Alberta Federation of Labour.* Edmonton: Alberta Federation of Labour.

Alboim, Naomi. 2009. "Adjusting the Balance: Fixing Canada's Economic Immigration Policies." Maytree Foundation. http://maytree.com.

–. 2011a. "From International Student to Permanent Resident: Policy Considerations." *Canadian Diversity* 8, 5: 15-19.

–. 2011b. "A Reflection on Immigration Policy: Two Years after Adjusting the Balance." Maytree Foundation. http://maytree.com.

Alboim, Naomi, and Karen Cohl. 2012. "Shaping the Future: Canada's Rapidly Changing Immigration Policies." Maytree Foundation. http://maytree.com.

Alboim, Naomi, Ross Finnie, and Ronald Meng. 2005. "The Discounting of Immigrants' Skills in Canada: Evidence and Policy Recommendations." *IRPP Choices* 11, 2. http://archive.irpp.org/choices/archive/vol11no2.pdf.

Alboim, Naomi, and Elizabeth McIsaac. 2007. "Making the Connections: Ottawa's Role in Immigrant Employment." *IRPP Choices* 13, 3. http://www. irpp.org/choices/archive/vol13no3.pdf.

Alden, Edward. 2012. "Immigration and Border Control." *Cato Journal* 32, 1: 107-24.

Ali, Mehrunnisa A. 2008. "Second Generation Youths' Belief in the Myth of Canadian Multiculturalism." *Canadian Ethnic Studies* 40, 2: 89-107.

Aliweiwi, Jehad. 2006. "Ottawa Please Take Note: Minorities Want In." *Toronto Star,* 5 January.

Allegritti, Inta. 2010. "Multiculturalism and Cultural Citizenship: Exploring the Contradiction." In *Cultural Citizenship and the Challenge of Globalization,* ed. W. Ommundsen, B. Leach, and A. Vandenberg. New York: Hampton Press.

Allport, Gordon. 1954. *The Nature of Prejudice.* New York: Basic Books.

Alvi, Saljida, Homa Hoodfar, and Sheila McDonough, eds. 2003. *The Muslim Veil in North America: Issues and Debates.* Toronto: Women's Press.

Amnesty International. 2009. "Refugees in Canada: History of Refugees." http:// www.amnesty.ca.

AMSSA (Affiliation of Multicultural Societies and Service Agencies BC). 2014. *Citizenship: Information and Research* 14, 31 March.

Anderson, Bridget. 2013. *Us and Them? The Dangerous Politics of Immigration Control.* New York: Oxford University Press.

Anderson, Christopher G. 2013. *Canadian Liberalism and the Politics of Border Control, 1867-1967.* Vancouver: UBC Press.

Anderson, Stuart. 2012. "America's Incoherent Immigration System." *Cato Journal* 32, 1: 71-89.

Anderssen, Erin. 2009. "Salma's Prom Night." *Globe and Mail,* 6 June.

–. 2012. "Pitch Heard around the World." *Globe and Mail,* 12 May.

Andrew, Caroline. 2009. *Gender, Substantive Citizenship, and Multiculturalism in Canada.* Ottawa: Centre on Governance, University of Ottawa.

Andrew, Caroline, John Biles, Meyer Burstein, Vicki Esses, and Erin Tolley, eds. 2013. *Immigration, Integration, and Inclusion in Ontario Cities.* Montreal/ Kingston: McGill-Queen's University Press.

Ang, Ien. 2010. *Between Nationalism and Transnationalism: Multiculturalism in a Globalising World.* Institute for Culture and Society Occasional Paper No 1. Sydney: Institute for Culture and Society, University of Western Sydney.

–. 2011. "Ethnicities and Our Precarious Future." *Ethnicities* 11: 27-31.

Angus, Ian. 2002. "Cultural Plurality and Democracy." *International Journal of Canadian Studies* 25: 69-85.

Angus-Reid. 2010a. "Canadians Endorse Multiculturalism But Pick Melting Pot over Mosaic." Poll published 8 November.

–. 2010b. "Poll: More Canadians Are Questioning the Benefits of Immigration." 14 September.

Anisef, Paul, and Kenise Murphy Kilbride, eds. 2003. *Managing Two Worlds: The Experiences and Concerns of Immigrant Youth in Ontario.* Toronto: Canadian Scholars' Press.

Anton, Christine, and Frank Pilipp. 2010. *Beyond Political Correctness: Remapping German Sensibilities in the 21st Century.* Amsterdam: Rodopi.

Arbel, Efrat, and Alleta Brenner. 2013. "Bordering on Failure: Canada-US Border Policy and the Politics of Refugee Exclusion." Harvard Immigration and Refugee Law Clinical Program, Harvard Law School.

Arnold, Guy. 2011. *Migration: Changing the World.* London: Pluto Press.

Arnold, Kathleen R. 2011. *American Immigration after 1996: The Shifting Ground of Political Inclusion.* University Park: Pennsylvania State University.

Arshad-Ayaz, Adeela. 2011. "Making Multicultural Education Work: A Proposal for Trans-national Multicultural Education." *Canadian Issues* (Spring): 71-74.

Aspinall, Peter, and Charles Watters. 2010. *Refugees and Asylum Seekers: A Review from an Equality and Human Rights Perspective.* Equality and Human Rights Commission Research Report No. 52. Manchester, UK: Equality and Human Rights Commission.

Atanackovic, Jelena, and Ivy Lynn Bourgeault. 2013. "The Economic and Social Integration of Immigrant Live-in Caregivers in Canada." Paper presented at Metropolis Conference, Ottawa, 14 March.

–. 2014. "Economic and Social Integration of Immigrant Live-In Caregivers in Canada." Institute for Research on Public Policy No. 46.

Attili, Giovanni, dir. 2007. *Where Strangers Become Neighbours.* Vancouver: Vancouver Cosmopolis Laboratory.

Aulakh, Raveena. 2010. "Understanding Canada's Refugee Process." *Toronto Star,* 12 August.

Austin, Carly, and Harald Bauder. 2012. "Jus Domicile: A Pathway to Citizenship for Temporary Foreign Workers." In *Immigration and Settlement,* ed. Harald Bauder, 21-36. Toronto: Canadian Scholars' Press.

Austin, E.G. 2011. "The United States v. Canada." *The Economist,* 20 May.

Austin, Michael J. 2009. "Introduction." *Journal of Human Behavior in the Social Environment* 19, 6: 661-62.

Avery, Donald H. 1979. *"Dangerous Foreigners": European Immigrant Workers and Labour Radicalism in Canada 1896-1932.* Toronto: McClelland and Stewart.

–. 1995. *Reluctant Hosts: Canada's Response to Immigrant Workers, 1896-1994.* Toronto: McClelland and Stewart.

Aydemir, Abdurrahman, and Chris Robinson. 2006. "Global Labour Markets, Return and Onward Migration." CIBC Working Paper. *CIBC Centre for Human Capital and Productivity.* http://ir.lib.uwo.ca.

Bach, Amandine. 2009. "Reframing Immigration, Integration and Asylum Policies from a Gender Perspective: Ensuring Gender-Fair Policies." European Social Watch Report 2009. http://www.socialwatch.eu/.

Backhouse, Constance. 1999. *Colour-Coded: A Legal History of Racism in Canada, 1900-1950.* Toronto: University of Toronto Press.

Baglay, Sasha. 2011. "Provincial Nominee Programs: A Note on Policy Implications and Future Research Needs." *International Migration and Integration* 13: 121-41.

Bakewell, Oliver. 2007. *Keeping Them in Their Place: The Ambivalent Relationship between Development and Migration in Africa.* International Migration Institute

Working Paper 8. Oxford: International Migration Institute, University of Oxford.

Bakewell, Oliver, Hein de Haas, and Agnieszka Kubal. 2011. *Migration Systems, Pioneers and the Role of Agency*. International Migration Institute Working Paper 48. Oxford: International Migration Institute, University of Oxford.

Baldwin, Andrew, Laura Cameron, and Audrey Kobayashi, eds. 2011. *Rethinking the Great White North: Race, Nature, and the Historical Geographies of Whiteness in Canada*. Vancouver: UBC Press.

Banting, Keith. 2010. "Is There a Progressive's Dilemma in Canada? Immigration, Multiculturalism, and the Welfare State." Presidential address at the Canadian Political Science Association, Montreal, 2 June. Printed in the *Canadian Journal of Political Science* 43, 4: 797-820.

–. 2012. "Transatlantic Convergence? Immigrant Integration in Canada and Europe." In *Pluralism Forum, April 2012, Reframing Europe's "Multiculturalism" Debates*. Ottawa: Global Centre for Pluralism.

Banting, Keith, Thomas J. Courchene, and Leslie Seidle, eds. 2007. *Belonging? Diversity, Recognition, and Shared Citizenship in Canada*. Montreal: Institute for Research on Public Policy (IRPP).

Banting, Keith, and Will Kymlicka. 2010. "Canadian Multiculturalism: Global Anxieties and Local Debates." *British Journal of Canadian Studies* 23, 1: 43-72.

–. 2012-13. *Is There Really a Backlash against Multiculturalism Policies? New Evidence from the Multiculturalism Policy Index*. GRITIM Working Paper Series 14. Barcelona: Universitat Pompeu Fabra. Subsequently published in *Comparative European Politics* 11: 577-98.

Barber, Pauline Gardner, and Winne Lem, eds. 2012. *Migration in the 21st Century: Political Economy and Ethnography*. New York: Routledge.

Barcham, Manuhuia. 2005. "Post-National Development: The Case of the New Polynesian Triangle." Electronic text published by Centre for Indigenous Governance and Development, Massey University, Palmerston North, New Zealand.

Baron, Ilan Zvi. 2009. "The Problem of Dual Loyalty." *Canadian Journal of Political Science* 42, 4: 1025-44.

Basok, Tanya, and Marshal Bastable. 2009. "'Knock, Knock, Knockin' on Heaven's Door': Immigrants and the Guardians of Privilege in Canada." *Labour/Le travail* 63: 207-19.

Basok, Tanya, Daniele Belanger, and Eloy Rivas. 2013. "Reproducing Deportability: Migrant Agricultural Workers in South-Western Ontario." *Journal of Ethnic and Migration Studies* [online], 5 November: 1-20.

Basok, Tanya, and Suzan Ilcan. 2013. *Issues in Social Justice: Citizenship and Transnational Struggles*. Toronto: Oxford University Press.

Batalova, Jeanne, and Alicia Lee. 2012. "Frequently Requested Statistics on Immigrants and Immigration in the United States." *Migration Information Source*, March.

Baubock, Rainer. 2008a. "Citizens on the Move: Democratic Standards for Migrants' Membership." *Canadian Diversity* 6, 4: 7-12.

–. 2008b. "Review Symposium: What Went Wrong with Liberal Multiculturalism?" *Ethnicities* 8: 271-88.

Bauder, Harald. 2003. "Equality, Justice, and the Problem of International Borders: The Case of Canadian Immigration Regulation." *ACME: An International E-Journal for Critical Geographies* 2, 2: 167-82. http://www.acme -journal.org/vol2/Bauder1.pdf.

–. 2008a. "Dialectics of Humanitarian Immigration and National Identity in Canadian Public Discourse." *Refuge* 25, 1: 84-94.

–. 2008b. "The Economic Case for Immigration: Neoliberal and Regulatory Paradigms in Canada's Press." *Studies in Political Economy* 82: 131-53.

–. 2008c. "Immigration Debate in Canada: How Newspapers Reported, 1996-2004." *International Migration and Integration* 9: 289-310.

–. 2009. "Neoliberalism and the Economic Utility of Immigration: Media Perspectives of Germany's Immigration Law." *Antipode: A Radical Journal of Geography*, 14 February. http://onlinelibrary.wiley.com.

–. 2011. *Immigration Dialectic: Imagining Community, Economy, Nation.* Toronto: University of Toronto Press.

–. 2012. "Introduction." In *Immigration and Settlement: Challenges, Experiences, and Opportunities*, ed. Harald Bauder, 1-6. Toronto: Canadian Scholars' Press.

–. 2012-13. "Open Borders: A Utopia?" *Spatial Justice* 5. http://www.jssj.org.

–. 2013. "Why We Should Use the Term 'Illegalized Immigrant.'" Ryerson Centre for Immigration and Settlement, Research Brief No. 2013/1.

Bauder, Harald, Patti Tamara Lenard, and Christine Straehle. 2014. "Lessons from Germany and Canada: Immigration and Integration Experiences Compared." *Comparative Migration Studies* 2, 1: 1-7.

Bauer, William. 2009. "Saving Canada's Dysfunctional Refugee System." *National Post,* 12 May.

Bauman, Zygmunt. 2000. *Liquid Modernity.* Cambridge: Polity Press.

Baureiss, Gunter. 1985. "Discrimination and Response: The Chinese in Canada." In *Ethnicity and Ethnic Relations in Canada*, ed. Rita M. Bienvenue and Jay E. Goldstein. Toronto: Butterworths.

Beach, Charles, Alan G. Green, and Jeffrey G. Reitz, eds. 2003. *Canadian Immigration Policy for the 21st Century.* Kingston/Montreal: Queen's University, in conjunction with McGill-Queen's University Press.

Becklumb, Penny. 2013. "Climate Change and Forced Migration: Canada's Role." Library of Parliament Research Publications, Current Publications: Social Affairs and Population.

Beiner, Ronald. 2003. *Liberalism, Nationalism, Citizenship: Essays on the Problem of Political Community.* Vancouver: UBC Press.

Beiser, Morton, and Harald Bauder. 2014. "The Quiet, Ugly Upheaval of Canada's Once-Great Immigration System." *Toronto Star,* 13 May.

Belkhodja, Chedly. 2011. "Introduction." *Canadian Diversity* 8, 5: 7-9.

Bell, Michael. 2004. "Tripping Up on the Dual Citizenship." *Globe and Mail,* 29 July.

Bell, Stewart. 2012. "Widespread Support for Burka Ban, Kenney Says." *National Post,* 23 January.

–. 2013a. "'Birth Tourists' Believed to Be Using Canada's Citizenship Laws as Back Door into the West." *National Post,* 9 August.

–. 2013b. "Migrant Ships Raised CSIS Security." *National Post,* 2 October.

Bellissimo, Mario D. 2012. "Immigration Reform: Fast and Furious, Not Cohesive." *Embassy: Canada's Foreign Policy Magazine*, 15 February. http://www. embassymag.ca.

Ben-David, Esther. 2009. "Europe's Shifting Immigration Dynamic." *Middle Eastern Quarterly* (Spring): 15-24.

Ben-Eliezer, Uri. 2008. "Multicultural Society and Everyday Cultural Racism: Second Generation of Ethiopian Jews in Israel's 'Crisis of Modernization.'" *Ethnic and Racial Studies* 31, 5: 935-61.

Benhabib, Seyla, and Judith Resnik, eds. 2009. *Migrations and Mobilities: Citizenship, Borders, and Gender*. New York: New York University Press.

Benson, Michaela, and Karen O'Reilly. 2009. *Lifestyle Migration: Expectations, Aspirations, and Experiences*. Farnham, UK: Ashgate.

Benson, Rodney. 2010. "What Is News Diversity and How Do We Get It? Lessons from Comparing French and American Immigration Coverage." Paper presented at the News and Inclusion Symposium, Stanford University, Stanford, 4 March.

Benton, Meghan. 2013. "The Changing Face of International Migration Flows [Is] Increasingly Fluid, Diverse, and Unconventional." *Migration Information Source*, December.

Berkeley, Rob. 2011. "True Multiculturalism Acts as a Bulwark against Further Extremism." Left Foot Forward. http://www.leftfootforward.org/.

Berns-McGown, Rima. 2007-08. "Redefining 'Diaspora': The Challenge of Connection and Inclusion." *International Journal* 63, 1: 3-21.

–. 2013. "'I Am Canadian': Challenging Stereotypes about Young Somali-Canadians." IRPP (Institute for Research on Public Policy), 15 January.

Bernstein, Nina. 2011. "Governments Use Privatized Detention, at Hefty Price." *New York Times*, 16 October.

Berry, John. 2006. "Mutual Attitudes among Immigrants and Ethnocultural Groups in Canada." *International Journal of Intercultural Relations* 30: 719-34.

–. 2011. "Integration and Multiculturalism: Ways toward Social Solidarity." *Papers on Social Representations* 20: 1-21.

–. 2014. "Multiculturalism: Psychological Perspectives." In *The Multiculturalism Question: Debating Identity in 21st-Century Canada*, ed. Jack Jedwab, 225-40. Queen's University Policy Studies Series. Montreal/Kingston: McGill-Queen's University Press.

Bertossi, Christophe, and Jan Willem Duyvendak. 2012. "National Models: The Costs for Comparative Research." *Comparative European Politics* 10: 237-47.

Betts, Alexander, and Gil Loescher, eds. 2011. *Refugees in International Relations*. Toronto: Oxford University Press.

Bevelander, Pieter, and Ravi Pendakur. 2012. "Introduction: Implications of Citizenship Acquisition." *International Migration and Integration* 13: 143-46.

Beyer, Peter, and Rubina Ramji, eds. 2013. *Growing Up Canadian: Muslims, Hindus, Buddhists*. Montreal/Kingston: McGill-Queen's University Press.

Bhabha, Faisal. 2009. "Between Exclusion and Assimilation: Experimentalizing Multiculturalism." *McGill Law Journal* 45: 46-90.

Biles, John. 2014. "The Government of Canada's Multiculturalism Program: Key to Canada's Inclusion Reflex." In *The Multiculturalism Question: Debating*

Identity in 21st-Century Canada, ed. Jack Jedwab, 11-52. Queen's University Policy Studies Series. Kingston, ON: McGill-Queen's University Press.

Biles, John, and Meyer Burstein. 2003. "Immigration: Economics and More." *Canadian Issues* (April): 13–15.

Biles, John, Meyer Burstein, and James Frideres, eds. 2008. *Immigration and Integration in Canada in the Twenty-First Century.* Queen's Policy Studies Series. Kingston: School of Policy Studies, Queen's University.

Biles, John, A. Carroll, R. Pavlova, and M. Sokol. 2012. "Canada: Fostering an Integrated Society?" In *International Perspectives: Integration and Inclusion,* ed. James Frideres and John Biles, 79-110. Montreal/Kingston: McGill-Queen's University Press.

Biles, John, and James Frideres. 2012. "Introduction." In *International Perspectives: Integration and Inclusion,* ed. James Frideres and John Biles, 1-16. Montreal/Kingston: McGill-Queen's University Press.

Biles, John, Humera Ibrahim, and Erin Tolley. 2005. "Does Canada Have a Multicultural Future?" http://canada.metropolis.net/pdfs.

Bilodeau, Antoine, Luc Turgeon, and Ekrem Karakoc. 2012. "Small Worlds of Diversity: Views toward Immigration and Racial Minorities in Canada." *Canadian Journal of Political Science* 45, 3: 579-605.

Birt, Yahya. 2007. "Multiculturalism and the Discontents of Globalisation." 25 May. http://www.opendemocracy.net.

Bissett, James. 2008. "Canada: The Truth about Immigration Is That Costs Exceed Benefits." *Vancouver Sun,* 29 September.

–. 2009a. "The Current State of Canadian Immigration Policy." In *The Effects of Mass Immigration on Canadian Living Standards and Society,* ed. Herbert Grubel, 3-38. Vancouver: Fraser Institute.

–. 2009b. "Why Our Refugee System Is Broken." *National Post,* 26 August.

–. 2010. *Abusing Canada's Generosity and Ignoring Genuine Refugees.* Policy Series No. 96. Winnipeg: Frontier Centre for Public Policy.

–. 2013. "Immigration: A Policy Gone Wrong?" *Diplomat Magazine,* 30 September. http://diplomatonline.com.

Bissoondath, Neil. 1994. *Selling Illusions: The Cult of Multiculturalism.* Toronto: Stoddart.

Biswas, Sharmila. 2003. "Immigrant Youth in Canada: Foreword: The GAP." Cultural Diversity: A CCSD Research Program. http://www.ccsd.ca/.

Bitran, Maurice, and Serene Tan. 2013. *Diaspora Nation: An Inquiry into the Economic Potential of Diaspora Networks in Canada.* Toronto: Mowat Centre, School of Public Policy and Governance, University of Toronto.

Black, Debra. 2011. "Immigrants Still Face Wage Discrepancy: StatsCan." *Toronto Star,* 4 March.

–. 2012. "Refugee Trend Called 'Disturbing.'" *Toronto Star,* 2 November.

–. 2013. "Has Immigration Policy Lost Its Compassion?" *Toronto Star,* 30 June.

Black, Debra, and Nicholas Keung. 2012. "Changing the Rules." *Toronto Star,* 29 December.

Black, Jerome, and Bruce Hicks. 2008. "Electoral Politics and Immigration in Canada: How Does Immigration Matter?" *International Migration and Integration* 9: 241-67.

Blackburn, Carole. 2009. "Searching for Guarantees in the Midst of Uncertainty: Negotiating Aboriginal Title and Rights in British Columbia." *American Anthropologist* 107, 4: 586-96.

Blackwell, Tom. 2011. "Despite Long Wait Times, Doctors Can't Find Work." *National Post,* 19 September.

–. 2013a. "The Syrians Are Coming." *National Post,* 22 May.

–. 2013b. "Syrians Grappling with the Persistent Crime Problem in Refugee Camp in Jordan after Fleeing Vicious Civil War." *National Post,* 13 May.

Blanchfield, Mike. 2014. "Kenney Defends Temporary Foreign Workers Program in Business Speech." *Globe and Mail,* 14 May.

Bleich, Erik. 2006. Review of *Shaping Race Policies: The United States in Comparative Perspective,* by Robert Lieberman. *Ethics and International Affairs* 20, 1: 133.

Blinder, Scott. 2013. "Imagined Immigration: The Impact of Different Meanings of 'Immigrants' in Public Opinion and Policy Debates in Britain." *Political Studies,* 17 June. Online version prior to publication. http://onlinelibrary.wiley.com.

Bloch, Alice, and Milena Chimienti. 2011. "Irregular Migration in a Globalizing World." *Ethnic and Racial Studies* 34, 8: 1271-85.

Bloemraad, Irene. 2006. *Becoming a Citizen: Incorporating Immigrants and Refugees in the United States and Canada.* Berkeley: University of California Press.

–. 2007. "Citizenship and Pluralism: Multiculturalism in a World of Global Migration." In *Citizenship and Immigrant Incorporation,* ed. G. Yurdakul and M. Bodemann, 57-74. New York: Palgrave Macmillan.

–. 2011. "'Two Peas in a Pod,' 'Apples and Oranges,' and Other Food Metaphors: Comparing Canada and the United States." *American Behavioral Scientist* 55, 9: 1131-59.

–. 2012. *Understanding "Canadian Exceptionalism" in Immigration and Pluralism Policy.* Washington, DC: Migration Policy Institute.

Bloemraad, Irene, and Els de Graauw. 2012. "Diversity and Laissez-Faire Integration in the United States." In *Diverse Nations, Diverse Responses: Approaches to Social Cohesion in Immigrant Societies,* ed. E. Tolley and P. Spoonley, 35-58. Queen's Policy Studies Series. Kingston: School of Policy Studies, Queen's University.

–. 2013. "Patchwork Policies: Immigrant Integration in the United States." *Canadian Issues* (Spring): 67-72.

Blommaert, Jan, and Ben Rampton. 2011. "Language and Superdiversities." *Diversity* 13, 2. http://unesdoc.unesco.org/images/0021/002147/214772e.pdf.

Blond, Phillip, and Adrian Pabst. 2008. "Integrating Islam into the West." *International Herald Tribune,* 14 February.

Bodvarsson, Orn B., and Hendrik Van den Berg. 2009. *The Economics of Immigration.* Berlin/Heidelberg: Springer-Verlag.

Böhmer, Maria. 2010. "The National Integration Plan: A Contribution of Germany towards Shaping a European Integration Policy." Council of Europe. http://www.coe.int/t/dg4/youth/Source/Resources/Forum21/Issue_No10/N10_National_integration_plan_en.pdf.

Bolaria, B. Singh, and Peter S. Li. 1988. *Racial Oppression in Canada.* 2nd ed. Toronto: Garamond Press.

Bollman, Ray. 2013. "Immigrants: Employment Rates by Level of Education. FactSheet." *Pathways to Prosperity,* March. http://p2p.canada.ca/ebulletin/.

Bonikowska, Aneta, Feng Hou, and Garnet Picot. 2011. *Do Highly Educated Immigrants Perform Differently in the Canadian and US Labour Markets?* Analytical Studies Branch Research Paper Series. Ottawa: Statistics Canada.

Bosniak, Linda. 2000. "Citizenship Denationalized." *Indiana Journal of Global Legal Studies* 7, 2: 447-509.

Boswell, Randy. 2011. "Western, Muslim Societies 'Irreconcilable': Poll." *National Post,* 12 September.

Bouchard, Gerard, and Charles Taylor. 2008. "Building the Future: A Time for Reconciliation." Abridged Report of the Commission for Reasonable Accommodation of Religious and Cultural Minorities.

Boulet, Maude, and Brahim Boudarbat. 2010. *Un diplôme postsecondaire Canadien: un tremplin vers des emplois de qualité pour les immigrants?* Montreal: Institute for Research on Public Policy.

Bourbeau, Philippe. 2011. *The Securitization of Migration: A Study of Movement and Order.* New York: Routledge.

Bowness, Suzanne. 2013. "Training Teachers at the World's Largest Refugee Camp." *University Affairs,* 6 November. http://www.universityaffairs.ca.

Boyd, Monica. 2006. "Gender Aspects of International Migration to Canada and the United States." Paper presented at the International Symposium on International Migration and Development, Turin, Italy, 28-30 June.

–. 2009. "Immigration Trends, Language Skills, and the Labour Market Integration of Recent Immigrants." Paper presented at the Language in the Workplace session at the Metropolis "Language Matters" Symposium, Ottawa, 22 October.

–. 2013. "Changing Migration Management." *Diplomat Magazine,* 30 September. http://diplomatonline.com.

Boyd, Monica, and Naomi Alboim. 2012. "Managing International Migration: The Canadian Case." In *Managing Immigration and Diversity in Canada,* ed. Dan Rodríguez-García, 123-50. Montreal/Kingston: McGill-Queen's University Press.

Boyd, Monica, and Elizabeth Grieco. 2003. "Women and Migration: Incorporating Gender into International Migration." *Migration Information Source,* March.

Boyd, Monica, and Deanna Pikkov. 2008. "Finding a Place in Stratified Structures: Migrant Women in North America." In *New Perspectives on Gender and Migration,* ed. N. Piper, 19-58. New York: Routledge.

Boyd, Monica, and Michael Vickers. 2000. "100 Years of Immigration in Canada." *Canadian Social Trends* (Autumn): 2-12.

Bradbury, Danny. 2013. "Can We Keep Valley Recruits?" *National Post,* 17 June.

Bradimore, Ashley, and Harald Bauder. 2011. *Mystery Ships and Risky Boat People: Tamil Refugee Migration in the Newsprint Media.* Metropolis British Columbia Working Paper No. 11-02. Vancouver: Centre of Excellence for Research on Immigration and Diversity.

Breton, Raymond. 2012. *Different Gods: Integrating Non-Christian Minorities into a Primarily Christian Country.* Montreal/Kingston: McGill-Queen's University Press.

Brett, Judith, and Anthony Moran. 2010. "Cosmopolitan Nationalism: Ordinary People Making Sense of Diversity?" *Nations and Nationalism* 17, 1: 188-206.

Bricker, Darrell, and John Ibbitson. 2013. *The Big Shift.* Toronto: HarperCollins.

Briefing Notes. 2010. "UNHCR Provisional Statistics Show Asylum Numbers Stable in 2009." UNHCR: UN Refugee Agency. 23 March. http://www.unhcr.org/.

Brinkerhoff, Jennifer. 2009. *Digital Diasporas.* Cambridge: Cambridge University Press.

Britz, Emma, and Jeanne Batalova. 2013. "Frequently Requested Statistics on Immigration and Immigrants in the United States." *Migration Information Source,* January.

Broadbent, Alan. 2009a. Keynote speech at the 2009 ALLIES Learning Exchange, Vancouver, 12 June.

–. 2009b. "Now Is the Time." *Maytree Opinion* 10 (July). http://maytree.com/.

–. 2012. "Five Myths about Canada's Immigration System." Maytree Foundation. November. http://maytree.com/.

Broadbent, Alan, and Ratna Omidvar. 2008. "An Open Letter to the Prime Minister from Maytree." Maytree Foundation. http://maytree.com/PDF_Files/Maytree-Letter-to-Prime-Minister-2008.pdf.

Brock, Gillian. 2013. "Contemporary Cosmopolitanism: Some Current Issues." *Philosophical Compass* 8, 8: 689-98.

Brolan, Claire E., Peter S. Hill, and Correa-Velez Ignacio. 2012. "Refugees: The Millennium Development Goals' Overlooked Priority Group." *Journal of Immigrant and Refugee Studies* 10: 426-30.

Brown, Louise. 2011. "Foreign Doctors Drive 'Brain Gain.'" *Toronto Star,* 10 May.

Brown, Wendy. 2014. *Walled States, Waning Sovereignty.* Cambridge, MA: MIT Press.

Brown, Nicholas, and Linda Cardinal, eds. 2007. *Managing Diversity: Practices of Citizenship.* Ottawa: Ottawa University Press.

Brown, Susan K., and Frank D. Bean. 2006. "Assimilation Models, Old and New: Explaining a Long Term Process." *Migration Information Source,* October.

Browne, Anthony. 2003. "The Folly of Mass Migration." 30 April. http://www.opendemocracy.net.

Brownell, Peter B. 2010. "Wage Differences between Temporary and Permanent Immigrants." *International Immigration Review* 44, 3: 593-614.

Brubaker, Rogers. 2005. "The 'Diaspora.'" *Diaspora: Ethnic and Racial Studies* 28, 1: 1-19.

Buckland, Benjamin S. 2008. "More Than Just Victims: The Truth about Human Trafficking." *Public Policy Research* 15, 1: 42-47.

Buckley, David T. 2013. "Citizenship, Multiculturalism and Cross-National Muslim Minority Public Opinion." *West European Politics* 36, 1: 150-75.

Bull, Hedley. 2011. "Foreword." In *Refugees in International Relations,* ed. A. Betts and G. Loescher, i-iv. Toronto: Oxford University Press.

Bunting, Madeleine. 2007. "Immigration Is Bad for Society, But Only Until a New Solidarity Is Forged." *The Guardian,* 18 June.

Burton, Peter, and Shelley Phipps. 2010. *The Well-Being of Immigrant Children and Parents in Canada.* Working Paper No. 2010-09. Halifax: Department of Economics, Dalhousie University.

Busby, Colin, and Miles Corak. 2014. "Don't Forget the Kids: How Immigration Policy Can Help Immigrants' Children." E-brief. C.D. Howe Institute, Toronto, 14 May.

Bush, Jeb, and Thomas F. McLarty III. 2009. *US Immigration Policy: Independent Task Force Report No. 63.* New York: Council on Foreign Relations.

Bygnes, Susanne. 2012. "Ambivalent Multiculturalism." *Sociology* 47, 1: 126-41.

Cairns, Alan. 2000. *Citizens Plus: Aboriginal Peoples and the Canadian State.* Vancouver: UBC Press.

Caldwell, Christopher. 2009. *Reflections on the Revolution in Europe: Immigration, Islam, and the West.* New York: Doubleday.

Calhoun, Craig. 2007. *Nations Matter: Culture, History, and the Cosmopolitan Dreams.* London: Routledge.

Cameron, G., and I. Goldin. 2012. "Harnessing Immigrant Mobility Means Prosperity for All." *Globe and Mail,* 15 May.

Campana, Marco. 2012. "Bottom Line Immigration?" Maytree Conversations. 20 April. http://maytree.com.

Campbell, Benjamin C., and Michael H. Crawford. 2012. "Perspectives on Human Migration: An Introduction." In *Causes and Consequences of Human Migration,* ed. M.H. Crawford and B.C. Campbell, 1-8. New York: Cambridge University Press.

Campbell, David. 2012. "Canada's Pattern of Immigration Spreads East and West." *Globe and Mail,* 24 February.

Campion-Smith, Bruce. 2012. "PM Hints at Profound Immigration Changes." *Toronto Star,* 22 December.

Canada. 2012. "A Fast and Flexible Economic Immigration System: Economic Action Plan 2012." http://www.cic.gc.ca/english/pdf/pub/eco-action-plan-eng.pdf.

Canada News Centre. 2014. "Attracting Skilled Newcomers to Canada." Government of Canada, 18 March. http://news.gc.ca.

Canadian Centre for Immigration Policy Reform. 2010. "Policy Statement." http://www.immigrationreform.ca/.

–. 2011. "Immigration Overview." http://www.immigrationreform.ca/.

–. 2014. "Major Shortcomings Overshadow Progress Made in Canada's 2013 Immigration and Refugee Policy Performance." 6 January. http://www.immigrationreform.ca/.

Canadian Council for Refugees. 2000. "Report on Systemic Racism and Discrimination in Canadian Refugee and Immigration Policies." In preparation for the UN World Conference against Racism, Racial Discrimination, Xenophobia and Related Intolerance. http://ccrweb.ca/arreport.PDF.

–. 2007. "Refugee Claimants in Canada: Some Facts." https://ccrweb.ca/.

–. 2009a. "40th Anniversary of Canada's Signing of the Refugee Convention." http://ccrweb.ca.

–. 2009b. "Open Letter: Principles of Refugee Protection." 19 October. http://ccrweb.ca.

–. 2009c. "Refugees Need Protection, without Discrimination." http://ccrweb.ca.

–. 2009d. "The Year in Review: Erosion of Government Commitment to Refugee Rights." http://ccrweb.ca.

–. 2010a. "Immigration Policy Shifts: From Nation Building to Temporary Migration." *Canadian Issues* (Spring): 90-93.

–. 2010b. "State of Refugees." http://ccreb.ca.

–. 2013. "Overview of C-31 Refugee Determination Process." 21 February. https://ccrweb.ca/en/refugee-reform.

–. 2014. "2013 in Review: Refugees and Immigrants in Canada." January. https://ccrweb.ca/en/2013_review.

–. N.d. "Facing Facts: Myths and Misconceptions about Refugees and Immigrants in Canada." http://www.ccrweb.ca.

Canadian Immigrant. 2014. "Express Entry: New Immigration Model to Launch Next Year." 9 April. http://canadianimmigrant.ca.

Canadian Immigration News. 2007. "Canadians Tops in Tolerance, According to Survey." February. http://www.cicnews.com.

Canadian Press. 2013a. "Canada's Immigration Backlog Down 40 Percent from Last Year." *CBC News,* 26 March. http://www.cbc.ca.

–. 2013b. "'Canadians Should Have First Crack at Jobs': Ottawa to Charge $275 Fee for Temporary Foreign Worker Applications." Reprinted in *National Post,* 7 August.

–. 2014. "Expect More Young Foreign Workers." Reprinted in the *Waterloo Region Record,* 30 April.

Canwest News Service. 2008. "Immigrants Show Sense of Belonging in Canada: Poll." 30 June.

CAPIC (Canadian Association of Professional Immigration Consultants). 2013. *CAPIC Submission Paper on Expression of Interest to Parliamentary Standing Committee on Citizenship and Immigration.* November.

Carey, Elaine. 2004. "Red Tape Deters Needed MDs." *Toronto Star,* 12 July.

Caritas Internationalis. 2010. "The Female Face of Migration." www.vidimus dominum.org.

Carletti, Fabiola, and Janet Davison. 2012. "Who's Looking Out for Tim Hortons' Temporary Foreign Workers?" *CBC News,* 12 December.

Carlson, Kathryn Blaze. 2011. "Immigrants Cost $23B a Year: Fraser." *National Post,* 17 May.

Carpay, John. 2011. "Put Real Refugees First." *National Post,* 16 May.

Carr, Matthew. 2010. "A War against Immigrants." *New York Times,* 7 November.

–. 2012a. *Fortress Europe: Dispatches from a Gated Continent.* New York: New Press.

–. 2012b. "The Trouble with Fortress Europe." Open Democracy. 21 November. http://www.opendemocracy.net/.

Carruthers, Ashley. 2013. "National Multiculturalism, Transnational Identities." *Journal of Intercultural Studies* 34, 2: 214-28.

Carter, Tom, Manish Pandey, and James Townsend. 2010. *The Manitoba Provincial Nominee Program.* IRPP Study No. 10. Montreal: Institute for Research on Public Policy.

Castles, Stephen. 2006. "Guest Workers in Europe: A Resurrection?" *International Migration Review* 40, 4: 741-66.

–. 2007. "Twenty-First Century Migration as a Challenge to Sociology." *Journal of Ethnic and Migration Studies* 33, 3: 351-71.

–. 2010. "Understanding Global Migration: A Social Transformational Perspective." *Journal of Ethnic and Migration Studies* 36, 10: 1565-86.

–. 2013. "The Forces Driving Global Migration." *Journal of Intercultural Research* 34, 2: 122-40.

Castles, Stephen, Graeme Hugo, and Ellie Vasta. 2013. "Rethinking Migration and Diversity in Australia: Introduction." *Journal of Intercultural Studies* 34, 2: 115-21.

Castles, Stephen, and Mark J. Miller. 2009. *The Age of Migration: International Population Movements in the Modern World*. 4th ed. New York: Guilford Press.

Castles, Stephen, and Simona Vezzoli. 2009. "The Global Economic Crisis and Migration: Temporary Interruption or Structural Change?" *Paradigms* 2: 65-75.

Catanzano, Amy. 2009. *Multiversal*. New York: Fordham University Press.

Cavanagh, Matt. 2011a. "The American Immigration Debate: A Chance for Liberal Reform, But Not Yet." Institute for Public Policy Research. 14 May. http://www.ippr.org/.

–. 2011b. "Right to Reply: Why Do So Many 'New Jobs' Go to Foreigners?" Institute for Public Policy Research. 31 August.

Cavanagh, Matt, and Sarah Mulley. 2013. "Fair and Democratic Migration Policy: A Principled Framework for the UK." Institute for Public Policy Research. 17 January. http://www.ippr.org/.

CBC News. 2013. "Toronto Reaffirms Commitment to Services for Undocumented Workers." 21 February.

CCMARD (Canadian Coalition of Municipalities against Racism and Discrimination). 2012. *Toolkit for Municipalities, Organizations and Citizens*. Ottawa: Canadian Commission for UNESCO.

Center for Immigration Studies. 2007. "Backgrounder: Immigrants in the United States." November. www.cis.org.

Centre for Israel and Jewish Affairs. 2013. "Backgrounder: Changes to Canada's Immigration and Refugee System." 15 July. http://www.cija.ca.

Ceobanu, Alin M., and Xavier Escandell. 2010. "Comparative Analysis of Public Attitudes toward Immigrants and Immigration Using Multinational Survey Data: A Review of Theory and Results." *Annual Review of Sociology* 36: 15.1-15.20.

Chacon, Justin Akers. 2006. "War on Immigrants." *International Socialist Review* 47: 1-9.

Chan, Wendy. 2014. "News Media Representations of Immigrants in the Canadian Criminal Justice System." Working Paper Series, Metropolis British Columbia, Vancouver.

Chappell, Laura, and Alex Glennie. 2009. "Maximising the Development Outcomes of Migration Policy: A Policy Perspective." Human Development Research Paper 2009/11. http://hdr.undp.org/sites/default/files/hdrp_2009_11.pdf.

Chappell, Laura, and Sarah Mulley. 2010. *Development: Do Points Mean Prizes? How the UK's Migration Policies Could Benefit the World's Poor*. Development on the Move Working Paper No. 5. London: Global Development Network and Institute for Public Policy Research.

Chase, Steven. 2011. "Wanted: Not-So-New Canadians." *Globe and Mail,* 3 November.

–. 2012. "Ottawa Creates New Fast Track for Skilled Trades Immigrants." *Globe and Mail,* 10 December.

–. 2013. "Palestinian Deported 'to Send a Message.'" *Globe and Mail,* 14 May.

Chomsky, Aviva. 2007. *"They Take Our Jobs!" And 20 Other Myths about Immigration.* Boston: Beacon Press.

Christian Science Monitor. 2010. "Should Illegal Immigrants Be Offered Legal Status?" 25 October.

Chung, Andrew. 2009. "A Crash Course in 'Values.'" *Toronto Star,* 30 December.

CIC (Citizenship and Immigration Canada). 2003. *Annual Report to Parliament on Immigration, 2003.* Ottawa: CIC. http://www.cic.gc.ca.

–. 2006. *Forging Our Legacy: Canadian Citizenship and Immigration, 1900-1977.* Ottawa: Public Works and Government Services Canada.

–. 2008. *Annual Report to Parliament on Immigration, 2008.* Ottawa: CIC. http://www.cic.gc.ca.

–. 2009a. *Annual Report on the Operation of the Canadian Multiculturalism Act, 2007-2008.* Ottawa: CIC. http://www.cic.gc.ca.

–. 2009b. *Annual Report to Parliament on Immigration, 2009.* Ottawa: CIC. http://www.cic.gc.ca.

–. 2009c. "Report on the Review of the Designation of the United States as a Safe Third Country." http://www.cic.gc.ca.

–. 2010a. *Annual Report on the Operation of the Canadian Multiculturalism Act, 2008-2009.* Ottawa: CIC. http://www.cic.gc.ca.

–. 2010b. "The Current State of Multiculturalism in Canada and Research Themes on Canadian Multiculturalism, 2008-2010." http://www.cic.gc.ca.

–. 2010c. "Federal, Provincial and Territorial Governments Agree to Improve Canadian Immigration." News release, 15 June.

–. 2010d. Federal-Provincial/Territorial Agreement. http://www.cic.gc.ca.

–. 2010e. "Supporting Canada's Economy, Government Maintains Historically High Rate of Immigration in 2009." News release, 13 May.

–. 2011a. *Annual Report on the Operation of Canadian Multiculturalism Act, 2010-2011.* Ottawa: CIC. http://www.cic.gc.ca.

–. 2011b. "Backgrounder: Stakeholder Consultations on Immigration Levels and Mix." http://www.cic.gc.ca/.

–. 2011c. *Facts and Figures 2010 – Immigration Overview: Permanent and Temporary Residents.* Ottawa: Public Works and Government Services Canada. http://www.cic.gc.ca.

–. 2011d. "Message from the Minister of Citizenship, Immigration and Multiculturalism." In *Annual Report to Parliament on Immigration, 2011.* Ottawa: CIC. http://www.cic.gc.ca/.

–. 2011e. "Statement: Minister Kenney Celebrates Canadian Multiculturalism Day." 27 June.

–. 2011f. "Canadian Citizenship." http://www.cic.gc.ac.

–. 2012a. *Annual Report to Parliament on Immigration, 2012.* Ottawa: CIC.

–. 2012b. "Backgrounder: An Overview of Reforms to Canada's Refugee System." Ottawa. 16 February.

–. 2012c. "News Release: An Immigration System That Works for Canada." Ottawa. 19 December.

⌐. 2012d. *Canadian Multiculturalism: An Inclusive Citizenship*. Ottawa: Government of Canada.

–. 2013a. *Annual Report on the Operation of the Canadian Multiculturalism Act, 2011-2012*. Ottawa: CIC. http://www.cic.gc.ca.

–. 2013b. *Facts and Figures 2012 – Immigration Overview: Permanent and Temporary Residents*. Ottawa: Public Works and Government Services Canada.

–. 2013c. *Preliminary Tables: Permanent and Temporary Residents, 2012*. http://www.cic.gc.ca.

–. 2013d. *Backgrounder: Expression of Interest (EOI): Preparing for Success in 2015*. http://www.cic.gc.ca.

–. 2014a. *Strengthening Canadian Citizenship Act: A Comparative View*. Ottawa: Government of Canada. http://www.cic.gc.ca.

–. 2014b. *Welcoming More New Canadians*. Ottawa: Government of Canada. http://www.cic.gc.ca.

Citrin, Jack, Richard Johnston, and Matthew Wright. 2012. "Do Patriotism and Multiculturalism Collide? Competing Perspectives from Canada and the United States." *Canadian Journal of Political Science* 45, 3: 531-52.

Clark, Campbell. 2009. "Skilled Immigrants Squeezed Out for Temporary Workers." *Globe and Mail*, 23 July.

Clarke, Andrew, and Mikal Skuterud. 2012. "Why Do Immigrant Workers in Australia Perform Better Than in Canada? Is It the Immigrants or Their Labour Markets?" http://arts.uwaterloo.ca/~skuterud/Mikal_Skuterud/Research_files/clarke_skuterud_census.pdf.

Clarke, Katarina. 2014a. "Florida Sex-Offender Who Had Relations with a 16-Year-Old Granted Refugee Status in Canada." *National Post*, 16 May.

–. 2014b. "UN Watch Presents Jason Kenney with Moral Courage Award." *National Post*, 23 May.

Clarkson, Adrienne. 2011. *Room for All of Us*. Toronto: Allen Lane Canada/Penguin.

Clemens, Michael A. 2013. *What Do We Know about Skilled Migration and Development?* Policy Brief No. 3. Washington, DC: Migration Policy Institute.

CMIP 21 (Canadian Museum of Immigration at Pier 21). 2013. Railway Agreement, 1925. http://www.pier21.ca.

–. 2014. Canadian Citizenship Act, 1947. http://www.pier21.ca.

Coderre, Denis. 2003. Notes for Address to a Forum on Biometrics: Applications and Implications for Citizenship and Immigration. National Arts Centre, Ottawa, 8 October. http://www.cic.gc.ca.

Codrescu, Andrei. 1995. "Faux Chicken and Phony Furniture." *Utne Reader* (May-June): 47–48. Originally published in *The Nation*, 12 December 1984.

Cohen, David. 2011. "Canadian Immigration and the Politics of Fear." Canada Immigration Blog. 28 February. http://www.canadavisa.com.

–. 2013. "What's in a Name?" Canada Immigration Blog. 27 February. http://www.canadavisa.com.

Cohen, Jeffrey. 2011. *Cultures of Migration: The Global Nature of Contemporary Mobility*. Austin: University of Texas Press.

Cohen, Tobi. 2009. "Deportations Surge 50 Percent in a Decade." *Globe and Mail*, 12 October.

–. 2012a. "Hungarian, Latvian Refugee Claims among Those to Be Fast Tracked as Canada Unveils 'Safe Country' List." *National Post,* 14 December.

–. 2012b. "Skilled Migrant Program Returns." *National Post,* 20 December.

–. 2013. "Number of Asylum Claims Drop Dramatically after Ottawa Releases List of 'Safe' Countries." *National Post,* 13 August.

–. 2014. "Medical Journal Calls Refugee Health Cuts 'Medically Irrational.'" *Postmedia News,* 28 January. Reprinted in the *Gazette* [Montreal], 4 February.

Cohn, Martin Regg. 2010. "The Refugee Scandal That Wasn't." *Toronto Star,* 13 April.

Cole, Richard, and John Kincaid. 2013. "Attachments to Multiple Communities and Public Ambivalence toward Immigration in the United States." *Canadian Issues* (Spring): 73-77.

Coleman, Daniel. 2011. "Imposing SubCitizenship." In *Narratives of Citizenship: Indigenous and Diasporic Peoples Unsettle the Nation-State,* ed. Aldys Fleischmann, Nancy van Styvendale, and Cody Maccaroll, 177-88. Edmonton: University of Alberta Press.

Coleman, Daniel, E. Glanville, W. Hasan, and A. Kramer-Hamstra, eds. 2012. *Countering Displacements: The Creativity and Resilience of Indigenous and Refugee-ed Peoples.* Edmonton: University of Alberta Press.

Collacott, Martin. 2006. "Don't Rush to Fix a Temporary Labour Fix." *Ottawa Citizen,* 18 November.

–. 2009. "Too Open-Door Policy." *National Post,* 16 July.

–. 2010a. "A Good First Effort at Refugee Reform." *National Post,* 26 October.

–. 2010b. "Reforming the Canadian Refugee Determination System." *Refuge* 27, 1: 110-18.

–. 2010c. "Reining in Refugee Crisis." *National Post,* 6 April.

–. 2013. "The Citizenship Fire Sale." *National Post,* 20 August.

Collett, Elizabeth. 2010. "Europe: A New Continent of Immigration." In *Rethinking Immigration and Integration: A New Centre-Left Agenda,* 19-36. London: Policy Network.

–. 2012. *Immigrant Integration in Europe in a Time of Austerity.* Washington, DC: Migration Policy Institute.

–. 2013. "Questions of Immigration Control Preoccupy Policymakers Worldwide as Mixed Flows of New Arrivals Continue, and in Some Cases, Surge." *Migration Information Source,* Issue No. 8.

Collier, Paul. 2013. *Exodus: How Migration Is Changing Our World.* Toronto: Oxford University Press.

Coloma, Roland Sintos. 2013. "'Too Asian'? On Racism, Paradox, and Ethno-Nationalism." *Discourse: Studies in the Cultural Politics of Education* 34, 4: 579-98.

Commission for Racial Equality. 2007. *United Kingdom's Second Report to the Council of Europe under the Framework Convention for the Protection of National Minorities.* http://www.kernowtgg.co.uk/shadowreport.pdf.

Conference Board of Canada. 2004. *The Voices of Visible Minorities: Speaking Out on Breaking Down Barriers.* September. www.conferenceboard.ca.

–. 2008a. *Immigration Reforms Put Canada on the Right Track.* 24 October. www.conferenceboard.ca.

–. 2008b. *Renewing Immigration: Towards a Convergence and Consolidation of Canada's Immigration Policies and Systems.* Ottawa: Conference Board of Canada.

Conference Notes. 2011. "The Making of Citizens: Beyond the Canadian Consensus on Immigration," eighth annual Pierre Elliott Trudeau Foundation Conference, Halifax, 17-19 November.

–. 2013. "Contested National Identities: An Interdisciplinary Symposium," Huron University College, University of Western Ontario, London, 16-18 October.

Connelly, Catherine. 2013. "Temporary Foreign Workers Are a Temporary Fix." *Globe and Mail,* 10 April.

Constant, A.F., M. Kahanec, and K.F. Zimmerman. 2009. "Attitudes toward Immigrants, and Other Integration Barriers, and Their Veracity." *International Journal of Manpower* 30, 1-2: 5-14.

Consterdine, Erica. 2013. *One Step Forward, Two Steps Back: Evaluating the Institutions of British Immigration Policymaking.* London: Institute for Public Policy Research.

Cooke, Martin, et al. 2007. "Indigenous Well-Being in Four Countries: An Application of the UNDP's Human Development Index to Indigenous Peoples in Australia, Canada, New Zealand and the United States." *BMC International Health and Human Rights* 7, 9. www.biomedcentral.com/1472 -698X/7/9.

Cooper, James, and Yvette Lopez. 2011. "The Third Rail of US Politics: The Current Immigration Debate in the United States." *Perspective* (Friedrich Ebert Stiftung Institute), June.

Corcoran, Terence. 2014a. "The Myth of the Temporary Foreign Worker as 'Job Stealer.'" *National Post,* 6 May.

–. 2014b. "Ten Reasons to Save TFWP." *National Post,* 22 May.

Cottle, Simon, ed. 2005. *Ethnic Minorities and the Media: Changing Cultural Boundaries.* Philadelphia: Open University Press.

Council of Europe. 2008. *Living Together as Equals in Dignity: White Paper on Intercultural Dialogue.* Strasbourg: Council of Europe.

Counterpoint. 2010. "Rethinking 'The Refugee': An Interview with Peter Gatrell." http://www.counterpoint-online.org.

Couton, Philippe, and Stephanie Gaudet. 2008. "Rethinking Social Participation: The Case of Immigrants in Canada." *International Migration and Integration* 9: 21-44.

Cowan, Richard, and Thomas Ferraro. 2013. "Landmark Immigration Legislation Passed in US." Reuters. Reprinted in *Toronto Sun,* 27 June.

Coyne, Andrew. 2009. "Our Feudal Immigration Policy." *Literary Review of Canada,* 1 July.

Cramme, Olaf, and Constance Motte. 2010. "Introduction." In *Rethinking Immigration and Integration: A New Centre-Left Agenda,* 10-18. London: Policy Network.

Creese, Gillian. 2011. *The New African Diaspora in Vancouver: Migration, Exclusion, and Belonging.* Toronto: University of Toronto Press.

Crépeau, François, and Kinga Janik. 2008. "Submission to the United Nations Human Rights Council in Relation to the Universal Periodic Review of Canada." http://www.cerium.ca.

Crépeau, François, and Delphine Nakache. 2008. "Critical Spaces in the Canadian Refugee Determination System: 1989-2002." *International Journal of Refugee Law* 20, 1: 50-122.

CRIAW (Canadian Research Institute for Advancement of Women). 2003. *Women's Experience of Racism: How Race and Gender Intersect.* Ottawa: CRIAW.

Crook, Clive. 2007. "The Baffling Politics of Immigration." *The Atlantic,* 15 May.

Crush, Jonathan, Abel Chikanda, Wade Pendleton, Mary Caesar, Sujata Ramachandran, Cassandra Eberhardt, and Ashley Hill. 2013. *Divided Diasporas: Southern Africans in Canada.* Waterloo, ON: Centre for International Governance Innovation; Capetown, SA: Southern African Migration Programme.

Cryderman, Brian, Chris O'Toole, and Augie Fleras, eds. 1998. *Policing, Race, and Ethnicity: A Guidebook for the Policing Services.* 3rd ed. Toronto: Butterworths.

Cuccioletta, Donald. 2001-02. "Multiculturalism or Transculturalism: Towards a Cosmopolitan Citizenship." *London Journal of Canadian Studies* 17: 1-14.

Curry, Bill. 2014. "Everything You Need to Know about Temporary Foreign Workers." *Globe and Mail,* 2 May.

D'Amato, Luisa. 2013. "How Welcoming Is Canada, Really?" *Waterloo Region Record,* 20 June.

Dauvergne, Catherine. 2005. "Why Judy Sgro Is Just Plain Wrong – No One Is Illegal." *Globe and Mail,* 2 August.

–. 2009. "In Fear They Flee: Why Ottawa's Visa Decision Is a Step Backwards." *Globe and Mail,* 20 July.

–. 2013. "Refugee Rules the End of Canada's Humanitarian Tradition." *Globe and Mail,* 29 January.

Day, Richard J.F. 2014. "(Never) Coming Out to Be Met? Liberal Multiculturalism and Its Radical Others." In *The Multiculturalism Question: Debating Identity in 21st-Century Canada,* ed. Jack Jedwab, 127-48. Queen's University Policy Studies Series. Kingston, ON: McGill-Queen's University Press.

De Haas, Hein, Carlos Vargas-Silva, and Simona Vezzoli. 2010. "Global Migration Futures: A Conceptual and Methodological Framework for Research and Analysis." International Migration Institute, University of Oxford. July. http://www.imi.ox.ac.uk/pdfs/research-projects-pdfs/gmf-pdfs/global -migration-futures-conceptual-paper/.

De Soto, Hernando. 2000. *The Mystery of Capital.* New York: Basic Books.

De Wenden, Catherine Wihtol. 2011. "Globalization and International Migration Governance." In *The Politics of International Migration Management: Migration Management and Its Discontents.* Proceedings of a Conference at the University of Osnabrück, Institute for Migration Research and Intercultural Studies, November. New York: Palgrave Macmillan.

Dei, George J. Sefa. 2007. "Speaking Race: Silence, Salience, and the Politics of Anti-Racist Scholarship." In *Race and Racism in 21st Century Canada,* ed. S.P. Hier and B.S. Bolaria, 53–66. Peterborough, ON: Broadview Press.

Delgado-Wise, R., and L.E. Guarnizo. 2007. "Migration and Development: Lessons from the Mexican Experience." *Migration Information Source,* February.

Deloitte. 2011. *Welcome to Canada. Now What? Unlocking the Potential of Immigrants for Business Growth and Innovation.* White paper summary of Deloitte's 2011 Dialogue on Diversity. November. http://www.deloitte.com/assets/Dcom

-Canada/Local%20Assets/Documents/About%20us/Diversity/ca_en_
diversity_dialogue_102711.pdf.

Dench, Janet. 2006. "Ending the Nightmare." *Canadian Issues* (Spring): 53-56.

–. 2009. "Getting Tough Won't Help Real Refugees." *Toronto Star,* 24 July.

Deparle, Jason. 2010. "Global Migration: A World Ever More on the Move." *New York Times,* 26 June.

Department of Finance. 2006. *Advantage Canada: Building a Strong Economy for Canadians.* Ottawa: Department of Finance.

Department of Justice. 2012. *Protecting Canada's Immigration System Act,* S.C. 2012, c. 17. Ottawa: Government of Canada.

Der Spiegel Staff. 2013. "The New Guest Workers: A German Dream for Crisis Refugees." Der *Spiegel Online International,* 28 February. http://www.spiegel. de/international/.

Derwing, Tracey, and Erin Waugh. 2012. *Language Skills and the Social Integration of Canada's Adult Immigrants.* IRPP Study No. 31. Montreal: Institute for Research on Public Policy.

Desai, Sabra, and Sangeeta Subramanian. 2003. "Colour, Culture, and Dual Consciousness: Issues Identified by South Asian Immigrant Youth in the Greater Toronto Area." In *Managing Two Worlds: The Experiences and Concerns of Immigrant Youth in Ontario,* ed. Paul Anisef and Kenise Murphy Kilbride, 118-61. Toronto: Canadian Scholars' Press.

Deveau, Denise. 2013. "The Case for Foreign Workers in Canada." *Financial Post,* 13 April.

Devoretz, Don, and Yuen Pau Woo. 2014. "New Citizenship Rules Wrongly Devalue Standing of Canadians Abroad." *Toronto Star,* 19 February.

D'Haenens, Leen, and Tristan Mattelart. 2011. "Media and Ethnic Minorities." In *Media in Europe Today,* ed. Josef Trappel and Euromedia Research Group. Chicago: University of Chicago Press.

Diocson, Cecilia. 2005. "Filipino Women in Canada's Live-In Caregiver Program." *Philippine Reporter* (March): 16–31.

DiversiPro. 2007. "Research on Settlement Programming through the Media." http://atwork.settlement.org.

Donaldson, Ian. 2004. "Identity, Intersections of Diversity, and the Multicultural Program." *Canadian Diversity* 3, 1: 14–16.

Donaldson, Jesse. 2013. "Remembering Vancouver's First Race Riot." *The Tyee,* 1 March.

Dromey, Jack, Don Flynn, Matthew Goodwin, Frank Sharry, and Baroness Falkner of Margravine. 2011. "Global Migration: The Challenges for Western Political Leaders." Chatham House, London. 15 November.

Du, Yang, Robert Gregory, and Xin Meng. 2006. "Impact of the Guest Worker System on Poverty and Wellbeing of Migrant Workers in Urban China." Unpublished manuscript. http://people.anu.edu.au/xin.meng/poverty-migration -paper-new.pdf.

Dujisin, Zoltán. 2011. "Europe: Media Complicit in Rise of Xenophobia." Inter Press Service News Agency. 18 May. http://www.ipsnews.net.

Duncan, Howard. 2005. "Multiculturalism: Still a Viable Concept for Integration?" *Canadian Diversity* 4, 1: 12–14.

Duncan, Howard, John Nieuwhehuysen, and Stine Neerup. 2012. "Introduction." In *International Migration in Uncertain Times,* ed. John Nieuwhehuysen, Howard Duncan, and Stine Neerup, 1-6. Queen's Policy Study Series. Montreal/ Kingston: McGill-Queen's University Press.

Dungan, Peter, Tony Fang, and Morley Gunderson. 2010. "Macroeconomic Impacts of Canadian Immigration: An Empirical Analysis Using the FOCUS Model." Metropolis Project. December. http://canada.metropolis.net/pdfs/fow _21dec10_fang_immi_impact_e.pdf.

Dunn, Kevin. 2005. "A Paradigm of Transnationalism for Migration Studies." *NZ Population Review* 31, 2: 15-31.

Dupont, Louis, and Nathalie Lemarchand. 2001. "Official Multiculturalism in Canada: Between Virtue and Politics." In *Global Multiculturalism: Comparative Perspectives in Race, Ethnicity, and Nation,* ed. G.H. Cornwell and E.V. Stoddard. Lanham, MD: Rowman and Littlefield.

Dustin, Donna. 2007. *The McDonaldization of Social Work.* Aldershot, UK: Ashgate.

Earnest, David C. 2008. *Old Nations, New Voters: Nationalism, Transnationalism, and Democracy in the Era of Global Migration.* Albany: State University of New York.

Economist. 2010a. "Multikulturell Wir?" 13 November.

–. 2010b. "A Smaller Welcome Mat." 16 December.

–. 2011. "The Magic of Diasporas." 19 November.

–. 2013a. "Drowning in the Flood." 2 February.

–. 2013b. "The Jobs Machine." 13 April.

Editorial, *New York Times.* 2011a. "America's Cruelest Immigration Law." 4 September.

–. 2011b. "A Broken, Dangerous System." 11 December.

–. 2012. "Immigrants and Small Business." 8 July.

Editorial, *Globe and Mail.* 2010. "Rethinking Refugees." 23 March.

–. 2011a. "Brain-Drain Relief." 30 November.

–. 2011b. "Canadians Show Ambiguity toward Multiculturalism." 7 October.

–. 2011c. "Raging Grannies, Willing Nannies." 7 November.

–. 2012. "It's Right to Pause for the Overhaul." 2 July.

–. 2013. "The Century's Worst Refugee Crisis." 5 October.

–. 2014a. "Supply, Demand, and Citizens." 16 April.

–. 2014b. "Canada Can Take More Refugees." 28 May.

Editorial, *National Post.* 2013. "Jason Kenney's Canada." 4 March.

Editorial, *Toronto Star.* 2010. "A Good Start on Refugee Reforms." 1 April.

–. 2011. "Canada Poaches from the Poor." 19 December.

–. 2014a. "Canadians Shoved Aside." 28 April.

–. 2014b. "Fewer Guests, More Citizens." 17 May.

Edmunds, June. 2006. "Migration Studies: New Directions?" *Ethnicities* 6, 4: 555-64.

Ehata, Rebecca, and Fabiola Mieres. 2010. "Rethinking Migration and Belonging in the 21st Century: An Introduction." *Political Perspective* 4, 2: 1-5.

Ehrkamp, Patricia, and Helga Leitner. 2006. "Rethinking Immigration and Citizenship: New Spaces of Migrant Transnationalism and Belonging." *Environment and Planning A* 38, 9: 1591-97.

EKOS Politics. 2013a. "Attitudes to Immigration and Visible Minorities: A Historical Perspective." 26 February. http://www.ekospolitics.ca.

–. 2013b. "Immigration, Diversity, and the Political Landscape." 19 April. http://www.ekospolitics.ca.

Elliott, Jean Leonard, and Augie Fleras. 1991. *Unequal Relations: An Introduction to Race, Ethnic, and Aboriginal Dynamics.* Toronto: Pearson.

ENAR Report. 2012. *How EU Policies Support or Hinder the Hiring of Migrants in Europe.* Brussels: European Network against Racism.

Environics Institute (in partnership with Institute for Canadian Citizenship, Maytree Foundation, the CBC, and RBC). 2012. "Canadians on Citizenship: Summary Report." http://maytree.com/wp-content/uploads/2012/02/Canadians-on-Citizenship-Summary-Report.pdf.

Environics Research Group. 2011. Survey prepared for "The Making of Citizens: Beyond the Canadian Consensus on Immigration," eighth annual Pierre Elliott Trudeau Foundation Conference, Halifax, 17-19 November.

Epp, Marlene, Franca Iacovetta, and Frances Swyripa. 2004. *Sisters or Strangers? Immigrant, Ethnic, and Racialized Women in Canadian History.* Toronto: University of Toronto Press.

Esses, Victoria, Kay Deaux, Richard Lalonde, and Rupert Brown. 2010. "Psychological Perspectives on Immigration." *Journal of Social Issues* 66, 4: 635-47.

Esses, Victoria, John F. Dovidio, and Gordon Hudson. 2002. "Public Attitudes toward Immigration in the United States and Canada in Response to the September 11, 2001 'Attack on America.'" *Analyses of Social Issues and Public Policy* 2, 1: 69-85.

Esses, Victoria M., Scott Veenvliet, Gordon Hodson, and Ljiljana Mihic. 2008. "Justice, Morality, and the Dehumanization of Refugees." *Social Justice Research* 21: 4-25.

Faist, Thomas, ed. 2008. *Dual Citizenship in Global Perspective.* Basingstoke, UK: Palgrave Macmillan.

–. 2010. "Towards Transnational Studies: World Theories, Transnationalism, and Changing Institutions." *Journal of Ethnic and Migration Studies* 36, 10: 1665-87.

Fang, Tony, Morley Gunderson, and Peter Dungan. 2011. "Immigration Jump Would Be Good for the Economy." Paper presented at the Metropolis Conference, Vancouver, 28 March.

Faraday, Fay. 2012. "Made in Canada: How the Law Constructs Migrant Workers' Insecurity." Summary Report for the Metcalfe Foundation. September. http://metcalffoundation.com/wp-content/uploads/2012/09/Made-in-Canada-Summary-Report.pdf.

Fatima, R., A.J. Wadud, and S. Coelho. 2014. "Human Rights, Climate Change, Environmental Degradation and Migration: A New Paradigm." Brief No. 8. Washington, DC: Migration Policy Institute.

Federation of Canadian Municipalities. 2011. "Starting on Solid Ground: The Municipal Role in Immigrant Settlement." Ottawa. http://www.fcm.ca/Documents/reports/Starting_on_Solid_Ground_Municipalities_and_Immigration_EN.pdf.

Fekete, Liz. 2012a. "A Critical Introduction to Immigration and Asylum." International State Crime Initiative. 10 September. http://statecrime.org/.

–. 2012b. "From Despair Comes Resistance." Institute of Race Relations. 19 December. http://www.irr.org.uk/.

Ferguson, Barry, Simon Langlois, and Lance W. Roberts. 2009. "Social Cohesion in Canada." *Toqueville Review* 30, 2: 69-101.

Ferguson Yale, H., and Richard W. Mansbach. 2012. *Globalization: The Return of Borders to a Borderless World?* New York: Routledge.

Fernando, Viresh, and Tim Leahy. 2014. "Ontario Needs Immigration Program." *Toronto Star,* 19 May.

Ferrer, Ann, Garnett Picot, and W. Craig Riddell. 2012. "New Directions in Immigration Policy: Canada's Evolving Approach to Immigration Selection." Canadian Labour Market and Skills Research Network Working Paper No. 107, November.

Finch, Tim, and Myriam Cherti. 2011. *No Easy Options: Irregular Immigration in the UK.* London: Institute for Public Policy Research. http://www.ippr.org/images/media/files/publication/2011/05/No%20Easy%20Options%20Apr2011_1837.pdf.

Finch, Tim, and Sarah Mulley. 2009. "Navigating the Migration Debate Out of a Dangerous Cul-de-Sac." *Public Policy Research* 16, 2: 120-26.

Findlay, Stephanie, and Nicholas Kohler. 2010. "'Too Asian'?" *Maclean's,* 10 November.

Fine, Sarah. 2013. "The Ethics of Immigration: Self Determination and the Right to Exclude." *Philosophical Compass* 8, 3: 254-68.

Finney, Nissa, and Ludi Simpson. 2009. *"Sleepwalking to Segregation"? Challenging Myths about Race and Migration.* Bristol, UK: Policy Press.

Finnie, Ross. 2014. "The Skills We Need." *Policy Options* (January). http://www.irpp.org.

Finotelli, Claudia, and Ines Michalowski. 2012. "The Heuristic Potential of Models of Citizenship and Immigrant Integration Reviewed." *Immigrant and Refugee Studies* 10, 3: 231-40.

Firby, Doug. 2014. "Why Canadians Are Willing to Exploit Foreign Workers." *Waterloo Region Record,* 2 May.

Fish, Stanley. 1997. "Boutique Multiculturalism, or Why Liberals Are Incapable of Thinking about Hate Speech." *Critical Inquiry* (Winter): 378-95.

Fisher, Matthew. 2013. "It's a Lot Better Than in Syria." *National Post,* 15 February.

Fitzgerald, David Scott, and David Cook-Martin. 2014. *Culling the Masses: The Democratic Origins of Racist Immigration Policy in the Americas.* Boston: Harvard University Press.

Fitzpatrick, Meagan. 2013. "Don't Bring Parents Here for Welfare, Kenney Says." *CBC News,* 10 May.

Flecker, Karl. 2013. "The Truth about Canada's Temporary Foreign Worker Program." Manitoba Federation of Labour. Originally published in rabble.ca, 17 January.

Fleischmann, Aldys, Nancy van Styvendale, and Cody Maccaroll, eds. 2011. *Narratives of Citizenship: Indigenous and Diasporic Peoples Unsettle the Nation-State.* Edmonton: University of Alberta Press.

Fleras, Augie. 2003. *Mass Media Communication in Canada.* Toronto: Nelson.

–. 2006. "Towards a Cultural Empowerment Model for Mental Health Services." Paper presented at the Mental Health Conference by the Centre for Research on Health and Education Services, Wilfrid Laurier University, December.

–. 2007a. "Aboriginal and Ethnic Media." Paper presented at the Media, Migration, Integration Conference, Dortmund, Germany, 21-22 June.

–. 2007b. "Mis(news)casting Minorities: Biased Coverage or Coverage That Is Biasing? Towards a Systemic Propaganda Model." Paper presented at the Media and Propaganda Conference, University of Windsor, 16 May.

–. 2007c. "Multiculturalisms in Collision: Transatlantic Divides, Intercontinental Discourse." Paper presented at the Universities of Augsburg and Nuremburg (Erlangen), Germany, 6 June.

–. 2007d. *Unequal Relations.* 5th ed. Toronto: Pearson.

–. 2009a. *The Politics of Multiculturalism: Cross National Perspectives in Multicultural Governance.* New York: Palgrave Macmillan.

–. 2009b. "The Politics of Precariousness: Reframing Canada's Immigration Program." Paper presented at the 20th Anniversary of Canada Studies Conference, Augsburg, Germany, 8 December.

–. 2010. "Framing the Other Within: Newsmedia Coverage of Immigration and Immigrants/Refugees." Paper presented at the Conference on NZ-Canada Relations, Victoria University of Wellington, 1 February.

–. 2011a. "Forty Years of Multiculturalism." Paper presented at the 40 Years of Multiculturalism Conference, Ottawa, 25 September.

–. 2011b. "From Mosaic to Multiversality: Repriming Multicultural Governance in a Postnational Canada." *Canadian Ethnic Studies* 43, 1-2: 17-39.

–. 2011c. *The Media Gaze: Representations of Diversity in Canada.* Vancouver: UBC Press.

–. 2012a. "Differently the Same: Multi/Inter/Culturalism as Immigration Governance Models." *Canadian Diversity* 9, 2: 46-51.

–. 2012b. "It's about the Us: Living Together in/with/through Diversities." Paper presented at the Conference on Living Together in Diversity, Budapest, 23 May.

–. 2012c. "Multicultural Governance in a Globalizing World of Transmigration and Multiversalism: A Case for Multiversal Multiculturalism in Canada." *Canadian Journal for Social Research* 2, 1: 117-27.

–. 2012d. "Policing the Kaleidoscope." Keynote address at the annual conference for the Association of New Canadians, St. John's, 21 March.

–. 2012e. *Unequal Relations: The Politics of Race, Ethnic, and Aboriginal Relations in Canada.* 7th ed. Toronto: Pearson.

–. 2014a. *Racisms in a Multicultural Canada: Paradoxes, Politics, and Resistance.* Waterloo, ON: Wilfrid Laurier University Press.

–. 2014b. "Beyond Multiculturalism: The New Politics of Migration in Canada." Paper presented at the Institute for Canadian Studies, University of Augsburg, 14 April.

Fleras, Augie, and Jean Leonard Elliott. 1992. *The Nations Within.* Toronto: Oxford University Press.

Fleras, Augie, and Jean Lock Kunz. 2001. *Media and Minorities: Representing Diversity in a Multicultural Canada.* Toronto: Thompson.

Fleras, Augie, and Roger Maaka. 2009. "Indigenous Grounded Policymaking Framework." *International Indigenous Policy Journal* 1 [online]: 1-17.

Fleras, Augie, and Paul Spoonley. 1999. *Recalling Aotearoa: Indigenous Politics and Ethnic Relations in New Zealand.* Auckland: Oxford University Press.

Fleury, Jean-Guy. 2004. "Canadian Values at Work: The Immigration and Refugee Board." *Canadian Issues* (March): 41-42.

Florby, Gunilla, Mark Shackleton, and Katri Suhonen, eds. 2009. *Canada: Images of a Post/National Society.* New York: Peter Lang.

Folson, Rose Baaba. 2005. *Calculated Kindness: Global Restructuring, Immigration, and Settlement in Canada.* Halifax: Fernwood.

Foner, Nancy, and Christophe Bertossi. 2011. "Immigration, Incorporation, and Diversity in Western Europe and the United States: A Comparative Perspective." *American Behavioral Scientist* 55, 12: 1535-40.

Fong, Eric, and Elic Chan. 2008. "An Account of Immigration Studies in the United States and Canada." *Sociological Quarterly* 49, 3: 483-502.

Fong, Eric, Lan-Hung Nora Chiang, and Nancy Denton. 2013. "Introduction." In *Immigrant Adaptations in Multi-Ethnic Societies: Canada, Taiwan and the United States,* ed. Eric Fong, Lan-Hung Nora Chiang, and Nancy Denton, 3-14. New York: Routledge.

Forrest, James, and Kevin Dunn. 2010. "Attitudes to Multicultural Values in Diverse Spaces in Australia's Immigrant Cities, Sydney and Melbourne." *Space and Polity* 14, 1: 81-102.

Forum Research. 2013. "Racism Alive and Well in Canada." News release, Toronto, 18 September.

Fossum, Erik, J. Poirier, and P. Magnette. 2009. *The Ties That Bind: Accommodating Diversity in Canada and the European Union.* Brussels: Peter Lang.

Foster, Jason. 2012. "Making Temporary Permanent: The Silent Transformation of the Temporary Foreign Worker Program." *Just Labour: A Canadian Journal of Work and Society* 19 (Autumn): 22-33.

Foster, Jason, and Alison Taylor. 2013. "In the Shadows: Exploring the Notion of 'Community' for Temporary Foreign Workers in a Boomtown." *Canadian Journal of Sociology* 38, 2: 167-87.

Foster, Lorne. 1998. *Turnstile Immigration: Multiculturalism, Social Order, and Social Justice in Canada.* Toronto: Thompson Books.

–. 2012. "The Foreign Credentials Gap in Canada: The Case of Targetted Universalism." *Directions* (Canadian Race Relations Foundation) 6, 2: 23-36.

Fox, Nick J., and Katie J. Ward. 2008. "What Governs Governance, and How Does It Evolve? The Sociology of Governance-in-Action." *British Journal of Sociology* 59, 3: 519-38.

Francis, Diane. 2002. *Immigration: The Economic Case.* Toronto: Key Porter.

–. 2009. "Immigration Cutbacks Essential." *National Post,* 3 July.

Franck, Thomas. 2006. "A Canadian Is ..." In *What Is a Canadian?* ed. I. Studin, 37-40. Toronto: McClelland and Stewart.

Frank, Kristyn. 2013. "Immigrant Employment Success in Canada: Examining the Rate of Obtaining a Job Match." *International Migration Review* 47, 1: 76-105.

Fraser, John. 1989. "Refugee Riddles, Dark Mirrors, and the National Honour." *Saturday Night,* 7-8 March.

Freedman, Jane. 2012. "Taking Gender Seriously in Asylum and Refugee Policies." In *Global Migration,* ed. K. Khory, 17-44. New York: Palgrave.

Freeland, Chrystia. 2011. "Immigration Undergoes a Sea Change." *Globe and Mail,* 7 October.

Freeze, Colin. 2008. "Heritage Department Takes Aim at Religious Radicals." *Globe and Mail,* 1 September.

Freitas, Any, Antonina Levatino, and Antoine Pécoud. 2012. "Introduction: New Perspectives on Skilled Migration." *Diversities* 14, 1: 1-7.

Frideres, J.S. 2006. "Cities and Immigrant Integration: The Future of Second- and Third- Tier Centres." *Our Diverse Cities.* http://www.metropolis.net/pdfs/ODC_2_Frideres_e.pdf.

Frideres, James, and John Biles, eds. 2012. *International Perspectives: Integration and Inclusion.* Montreal/Kingston: McGill-Queen's University Press.

Fries, Christopher, and Paul Gingrich. 2009. "A 'Great' Large Family: Understanding of Multiculturalism among Newcomers to Canada." *Refuge* 27, 1: 36-45.

Friesen, Joe. 2010. "The World Would Love to Be Canadian." *Globe and Mail,* 22 June.

–. 2011a. "Kenney Seeks Leeway for Immigrant's Language Skills." *Globe and Mail,* 18 February.

–. 2011b. "A Land of Immigrants, Canada Must Now Deal with Its Emigrants." *Globe and Mail,* 27 June.

–. 2012a. "Breaking Down the Numbers." *Globe and Mail,* 10 May.

–. 2012b. "Canada Ready to Open Doors to More Immigrants, Kenney Says." *Globe and Mail,* 14 May.

–. 2012c. "Canadian Immigrants at Rising Disadvantage." *Globe and Mail,* 3 December.

–. 2012d. "It's Only the Weather That's a Problem." *Globe and Mail,* 6 February.

Friesen, Joe, and Bill Curry. 2012. "Harper's Grand Plan." *Globe and Mail,* 27 January.

Friesen, Joe, and Sandra Martin. 2010. "Part 3: Canada's Changing Faith." *Globe and Mail,* 25 October.

Fry, Hedy. 1997. "Multiculturalism: A Framework for Canadian Unity." *Newsletter of the Royal Society of Canada* 5, 1: 1-2.

Fryberg, Stephanie A., Nicole M. Stephens, Rebecca Covarrubias, Hazel Rose Markus, Erin D. Carter, Giselle A. Laiduc, and Ana J. Salido. 2012. "How the Media Frames the Immigration Debate: The Critical Role of Location and Politics." *Analyses of Social Issues and Public Policy* 12, 1: 96-112.

Fudge, Judy. 2011. *The Precarious Migrant Status and Precarious Employment: The Paradox of International Rights for Migrant Workers.* Metropolis British Columbia Working Paper No. 11-15. Vancouver: Centre of Excellence for Research on Immigration and Diversity.

Fudge, Judy, and Fiona McPhail. 2009. "The Temporary Foreign Worker Program in Canada: Low Skilled Workers as an Extreme Form of Flexible Labour." *Comparative Labour Law and Policy Journal* 31: 101-39.

Fulford, Robert. 2003. "From Russia, with Stories: David Bezmozgis Captures the Essence of Immigrant Life in His New Fiction." *National Post,* 27 May.

Gabaccia, Donna R. 2006. "Huddled Masses Yearning to Breathe Free?" CLA: Contemporary Perspectives on Immigration: A Blog for the Immigration History Research Center, University of Minnesota. http://blog.lib.umn.edu/.

Gaetano, Arianne M., and Brenda S.A. Yeoh. 2010. "Introduction." In *Women and Migration in Globalizing Asia: Gendered Experiences, Agency, and Activism,* special issue of *International Migration* 48, 6: 1-12.

Gagnon, Alain-G., and Raffaele Iacovino. 2007. *Federalism, Citizenship, and Quebec: Debating Multinationalism*. Toronto: University of Toronto Press.

Gagnon, Lysiane. 2008. "Quebec's Own Two Solitudes." *Globe and Mail*, 26 January.

Galabuzi, Grace-Edward. 2006. *Canada's Economic Apartheid: The Social Exclusion of Racialized Groups in the New Century*. Toronto: Canadian Scholars' Press.

–. 2010. Cited in Uzma Shakir, *Canada's Immigration Fall from Grace*. Atkinson Charitable Foundation, 12 May.

Gallagher, Stephen. 2003. *Canada's Dysfunctional Refugee Determination System*. Occasional Paper No. 78. Vancouver: Fraser Institute.

–. 2008a. "Canada and Mass Immigration: The Creation of a Global Suburb and Its Impact on National Unity." Immigration Watch Canada. 4 June. http://www.immigrationwatchcanada.org.

–. 2008b. "Canada's Broken Refugee Policy System." In *Immigration Policy and the Terrorist Threat in Canada and the United States*, ed. A. Moens and M. Collacott, 53-74. Vancouver: Fraser Institute.

Galloway, Gloria. 2010a. "Jason Kenney Trumpets Hard-Fought Immigration Reform." *Globe and Mail*, 1 July.

–. 2010b. "List of 'Safe Countries' among Refugee Proposals." *Globe and Mail*, 31 March.

Gans, Judith, Elaine Replogle, and Daniel Tichenor. 2012. *Debates on US Immigration*. Thousand Oaks, CA: Sage.

Garcea, Joseph, Anna Kirova, and Lloyd Wong. 2008. "Introduction: Multiculturalism Discourses in Canada." *Canadian Ethnic Studies* 40, 1: 1-10.

Garroutte, Eva Marie. 2003. *Real Indians: Identity and the Survival of Native Americans*. Berkeley: University of California Press.

Gaye, Nicole. 2011. "Super Diversity in Canada." Policy Horizons Canada. June. http://www.horizons.gc.ca/sites/default/files/Publication-alt-format/0072_pag_superdiversity_e.pdf.

Geiger, Martin, and Antoine Pécoud, eds. 2011. *The New Politics of International Mobility: Migration Management and Its Discontents*. Osnabrück, Germany: Institute for Migration Research and Intercultural Studies.

Geislerova, Marketa. 2007. "The Role of Diasporas in Foreign Policy: The Case of Canada." *Central European Journal of International and Security Studies* 1, 2: 90-108.

Geissler, Rainer, and Horst Pottker, eds. 2005. *Mass Media-Integration: Media and Migration, a Comparative Perspective*. Berlin: Transcript.

Gelernter, Lior, and Motti Regev. 2010. "Internet and Globalization." In *The Routledge International Handbook of Globalization Studies*, ed. B.S. Turner. New York: Routledge.

George, Usha, Ferzana Chaze, Sarah Brennenstuhl, and Esme Fuller-Thompson. 2012. "'Looking for Work But Nothing Seems to Work': The Job Search Strategies of Internationally Trained Engineers in Canada." *International Migration and Integration* 13: 303-23.

Georgi, Fabian, and Susanne Schatral. 2011. "Towards a Critical Theory of Migration Control: The Case of the International Organization for Migration (IOM)." In *The New Politics of International Mobility: Migration Management and*

Its Discontents, ed. Martin Geiger and Antoine Pécoud, 193-222. Osnabrück, Germany: Institute for Migration Research and Intercultural Studies.

Georgiou, Myria. 2012. "Introduction: Gender, Migration, and the Media." *Ethnic and Racial Studies* 35, 5: 791-99.

Ghuman, Sharon J. 2003. "Women's Autonomy and Child Survival." *Demography* 40, 3: 419-36.

Gibb, Heather. 2010. "Missing from Temporary Foreign Worker Programs: Gender Sensitive Approaches." *Canadian Issues* (Spring): 94-98.

Gibson, Gordon. 2009. "The Politics of Canadian Immigration Policies." In *The Effects of Mass Immigration on Canadian Living Standards and Society,* ed. Herbert Grubel, 213-31. Vancouver: Fraser Institute.

Gilbertson, Greta. 2006. "Citizenship in a Globalized World." *Migration Information Source,* January.

Gilkinson, Tara, and Genevieve Sauve. 2010. *Recent Immigrants, Earlier Immigrants, and the Canadian-Born: Association with Collective Identities.* Research and Evaluation Branch of Citizenship and Immigration Canada, September.

Gillis, Charlie. 2010. "Who Doesn't Get into Canada?" *Maclean's,* 17 June.

Gilmour, R.J., Davina Bhandar, Jeet Sing, and Michael C.K. Ma. 2012. *"Too Asian"? Racism, Privilege, and Post-Secondary Education.* Toronto: Between the Lines.

Glasser, Theodore L., Isabel Awad, and John W. Kim. 2009. "The Claims of Multiculturalism and the Journalists' Promise of Diversity." *Journal of Communication* 59: 57-78.

Glennie, Alex. 2011. "Migration and Climate Change: Old Assumptions and New Ideas." Institute for Public Policy Research. 21 October. http://www.ippr.org/.

Glennie, Alex, et al. 2014. "A Fair Deal on Migration for the UK." March. http://www.ippr.org/publications.

Glick Schiller, Nina, Linda Basch, and Cristina Blanc-Szanton. 1992. "Transnationalism: A New Analytic Framework for Understanding Migration." In *Towards a Transnational Perspective on Migration: Race, Class, Ethnicity, and Nationalism Reconsidered,* ed. Nina Glick Schiller, Linda Basch, and Cristina Blanc-Szanton. New York: New York Academy of Sciences.

Globe and Mail. 2011a. "Canada, a Model of Success." Report co-produced by Randall Anthony Commission. 12 March.

–. 2011b. "Canada's Immigration Policy: Who Is on the Guest List?" 19 February.

–. 2012. "Rethinking Immigration: The Case for the 400,000 Solution." 4 May.

Glover, Robert W. 2011. "Radically Rethinking Citizenship: Disaggregation, Agonistic Pluralism, and the Politics of Immigration in the United States." *Political Studies* 59: 209-29.

Goar, Carol. 2010. "Time to Rethink Guest Worker Program." *Toronto Star,* 20 September.

–. 2013a. "Canada Needs a Better Way to Select Immigrants." *Toronto Star,* 11 February.

–. 2013b. "Influx of Low-Cost Foreign Labour Still Swelling." *Toronto Star,* 6 November.

–. 2014. "How the Myth of Canada's Skills Gaps Was Shattered." *Toronto Star,* 14 May.

Gogia, Napur, and Bonnie Slade. 2011. *About Canada: Immigration*. Halifax: Fernwood.

Goldin, Ian, Geoffrey Cameron, and Meera Balarajan. 2011. *Exceptional People: How Migration Shaped Our World and Will Define Our Future*. Princeton: Princeton University Press.

Goldring, Luin, Carolina Berinstein, and Judith Bernhard. 2007. *Institutionalizing Precarious Immigration Status in Canada*. CERIS Working Paper No. 61. Toronto: Ontario Metropolis Centre.

Goldring, Luin, Jenna Hennebry, and Kerry Preibisch. 2009. "Temporary Worker Programs: North America's Second Class Citizens." http://s3.amazonaws.com.

Goldring, Luin, and Patricia Landolt. 2012. *Producing and Negotiating Non-Citizenship: Precarious Legal Status in Canada*. Toronto: University of Toronto Press.

Goodman, Adam. 2012. "Who Gets to Define Immigrants as 'Illegal?'" *Dissent*, 3 October.

Goodman, Lee-Anne. 2014. "Group Slams Outrage over Temporary Foreign Workers." *Toronto Star*, 2 May.

Goodman, Sara Wallace. 2012. "Fortifying Citizenship: Policy Strategies for Civic Integration in Western Europe." *World Politics* 64, 4: 659-98.

Goodwin, Debi. 2010. *Citizens of Nowhere*. Toronto: Doubleday.

Goutor, David, and Chris Ramsaroop. 2010. "No Thanksgiving for Migrant Workers." *Toronto Star*, 8 October.

–. 2012. "Surge in Migrant Labour Makes Reform Imperative." *Toronto Star*, 10 February.

Grady, Patrick. 2009. "Is Canadian Immigration Too High?" In *The Effects of Mass Immigration on Canadian Living Standards and Society*, ed. Herbert Grubel, 73-85. Vancouver: Fraser Institute.

–. 2011. "A Critique of 'Macroeconomic Impacts of Canadian Immigration ... Using the Focus Model' (Dungan, Fang, and Gunderson, 2010)." 16 May. http://www.global-economics.ca/focus_macro_impact_immigration.pdf.

Granatstein, Jack. 2007. *Whose War Is It? How Canada Can Survive in the Post-9/11 World*. Toronto: HarperCollins.

Grant, Tavia. 2009. "Where the Jobs Are: Skilled Profession." *Globe and Mail*, 28 May.

–. 2011. "Promised Lands." *Globe and Mail*, 31 December.

Grant, Tavia, Bill Curry, and Steven Chase. 2013. "Employers Fume as Ottawa Tightens Rules." *Globe and Mail*, 30 April.

Grant, Tavia, and Jennifer Yang. 2009. "Immigrants Take Brunt of Recession, Recover Less Quickly." *Globe and Mail*, 25 July.

Graves, Frank. 2013. "The 'Big Shift' May Be Moving into Reverse." iPolitics. 1 May. http://www.ipolitics.ca.

Greenspon, Edward. 2001. "Building the New Canadian Identity." *Globe and Mail*, 10 November.

Gregory, David. 2012. Interview with Barack Obama. *Meet the Press*. NBC, 29 December.

Grewcock, Michael. 2013. "Australia's Ongoing Border Wars." *Race and Class* 54, 3: 10-32.

Grez, Evelyn Encalada. 2008. "Migrant Workers Reap Bitter Harvest in Ontario." *Toronto Star,* 28 October.

Griffith, Andrew. 2013. *Policy Arrogance or Innocent Bias? Resetting Citizenship and Multiculturalism.* Toronto: Anar Press.

Griffith, Phoebe. 2013. "Meaningful Integration Must Focus on People, Not Numbers." Institute for Public Policy Research. 20 September. http://www.migrantsrights.org.uk/.

Grillo, R.D. 2000. "Transmigration and Cultural Diversity in the Construction of Europe." Revised version of a paper presented at the "Symposium on Cultural Diversity and Construction of Europe: Complementarity or Incompatibility?" University of Oberta de Catalunya, Barcelona, December.

Griswald, Daniel T. 2012. "Introduction: Is Immigration Good for America?" *Cato Journal* 32, 1: 1-4.

Gross, Dominique M. 2014. *Temporary Foreign Workers in Canada: Are They Really Filling Labour Shortages?* Commentary No. 407. Toronto: C.D. Howe Institute.

Grubel, Herbert, ed. 2009. *The Effects of Mass Immigration on Canadian Living Standards and Society.* Vancouver: Fraser Institute.

–. 2012. "Let the Job Market Choose Our Immigrants." *Globe and Mail,* 11 May.

–. 2013. *Canada's Immigration Selection Policies: Recent Record, Marginal Changes and Needed Reforms.* Studies in Immigration Policy. Vancouver: Fraser Institute.

Grubel, Herbert, and Patrick Grady. 2012. *Fiscal Transfers to Immigrants in Canada: Responding to Critics and a Revised Estimate.* Studies in Immigration and Refugee Policy. Vancouver: Fraser Institute.

Grugel, Jean, and Nicola Piper. 2007. *Critical Perspectives on Global Governance.* New York: Routledge.

Gu, Chien-Juh. 2012. "Women's Status in the Context of International Migration." *Sociology Compass* 6, 6: 458-71.

Guardia, N. Diez, and K. Pichelmann. 2006. *Labour Migration Patterns in Europe: Recent Trends, Future Challenges.* Economic Papers No. 256. Brussels: European Economy.

Gugliotta, Guy. 2008. "The Great Human Migration." *Smithsonian Magazine,* July.

Guibernau, Monserrat. 2007. *The Identity of Nations.* Malden, MA: Polity Press.

Guild, Elspeth. 2009. *Security and Migration in the 21st Century.* Cambridge, UK: Polity Press.

Guskin, Jane, and David Wilson. 2007. *The Politics of Immigration.* New York: Monthly Review Press.

Guterres, António. 2007. "People on the Move: Ideally Out of Choice." *Globe and Mail,* 3 December.

Haas, Eric. 2007. "Losing Our Minds over Immigration." Cognitive Policy Works. 30 November. http://www.cognitivepolicyworks.com.

–. 2008. "To Respect and Protect: Expanding Our Discourse on Immigration: Rockridge Institute Report." 14 April. http://www.cognitivepolicyworks.com/wp-content/uploads/2009/06/Expand-Discourse-Immigration.pdf.

Habacon, Alden E. 2007. "Beyond the Mosaic: Canada's Multiculturalism 2.0." Paper presented at "Putting Diverse Talents to Work," sponsored by the Couchiching Institute on Public Affairs, Orillia, ON, 9-12 August.

Haddad, Emma. 2008. *The Refugee in International Society: Between Sovereigns.* Cambridge: Cambridge University Press.

Hage, Ghassan. 2003. *Against Paranoid Nationalism.* Sydney: Pluto Press.

–. 2006. "The Doubts Down Under." *Catalyst Magazine,* 17 May.

–. 2014. "Globalization and Its Borders." *Allegra: A Virtual Lab of Legal Anthropology,* 26 March. http://allegralaboratory.net.

Hai, Yasmin. 2003. "Sex Is Part of Our Culture Now." *Guardian Weekly,* 13-19 November.

Hall, Alexandra. 2012. *Border Watch: Cultures of Immigration, Detention, and Control.* London: Pluto Press.

Halm, Dirk, ed. 2012. *Migration and Organized Civil Society: Rethinking National Policy.* New York: Routledge.

Hamilton, Graeme. 2008. "Quebec Still Faces Cultural Challenges." *National Post,* 24 May.

Hamlin, Rebecca. 2008. "'Illegal Refugees' and the Rise of Restrictive Asylum Policies in Canada, Australia, and the United States." Paper presented at the ISA's 49th annual convention, San Francisco, 26 March. http://www.allacademic.com.

Hammer, Kate, and Joe Friesen. 2011. "The Myth of the Brainy Immigrant." *Globe and Mail,* 22 January.

Handa, Amita. 2003. *Of Silk Saris and Mini-Skirts: South Asian Girls Walk the Tightrope of Culture.* Toronto: Women's Press.

Handlin, Oscar. 1951. *The Uprooted: From the Old World to the New.* New York: Watts.

Hansen, Randall. 2009. "Immigration and Immigration Reform in the United States: An Outsider's View." *The Forum* 7, 3: 1-13.

–. 2010. "Opening Address." Presented at the International Conference on Migration – Regionalization – Citizenship: Canada and Europe in Comparative Perspective, University of Augsburg, Germany, 8-11 December.

–. 2014. "Assimilation by Stealth: Why Canada's Multicultural Policy Is Really a Repackaged Integration Policy." In *The Multiculturalism Question: Debating Identity in 21st-Century Canada,* ed. Jack Jedwab, 73-88. Queen's University Policy Studies Series. Montreal/Kingston: McGill-Queen's University Press.

Hansen, Randall, and Demetrios G. Papademetriou. 2014. "Securing Borders: The Intended, Unintended, and Perverse Consequences." Migration Policy Institute/Transatlantic Council on Migration, January.

Haque, Eve. 2012. *Multiculturalism within a Bilingual Framework: Language, Race, and Belonging in Canada.* Toronto: University of Toronto Press.

Harding, Jeremy. 2012. *Border Vigils: Keeping Migrants Out of the Rich World.* New York: Verso.

Harell, Allison, Stuart Soroka, and Blake Andrew. 2011. "Canadians' Attitudes toward Immigration: Preliminary Results from an Online Experiment on the Impact of Economic and Cultural Cues." Paper prepared for the Canadian Political Science Association Annual Meeting, Waterloo, ON, 16-18 May. http://www.cpsa-acsp.ca/papers-2011/harell-soroka-andrew.pdf.

Harell, Allison, Stuart Soroka, Shanto Iyengar, and Nicholas Valentino. 2012. "The Impact of Economic and Cultural Cues on Support for Immigration in

Canada and the United States." *Canadian Journal of Political Science* 45, 3: 499-530.

Harell, Allison, and Dietlind Stolle. 2010. "Diversity and Democratic Politics: An Introduction." *Canadian Journal of Political Science* 43, 3: 235-56.

Hari, Amrita, Susan McGrath, and Valerie Preston. 2013. *Temporariness in Canada: Establishing a Research Agenda.* CERIS Working Paper No. 99. Toronto: Ontario Metropolis Centre.

Harmon, Bryan. N.d. "Inclusion/Integration? Is There a Difference?" http://www.cdss.ca.

Harney, R., and H. Troper. 1975. *Immigrants: A Portrait of the Urban Experience 1890-1930.* Toronto: Van Nostrand Reinhold.

Harpaz, Yossi. 2013. "Rooted Cosmopolitans: Israelis with a European Passport – History, Property, Identity." *International Migration Review* 47, 1: 166-206.

Harty, Siobhan, and Michael Murphy. 2005. *In Defence of Multinational Citizenship.* Vancouver: UBC Press.

Hawkins, Freda. 1974. *Canada and Immigration.* Kingston/Montreal: McGill-Queen's University Press.

Hawley, Charlie, and Charly Wilder. 2013. "Rage and Refuge: Germany's Asylum System Hits Breaking Point." *Der Spiegel Online International,* 30 August.

Hawthorne, Lesleyanne. 2007. "Foreign Credential Recognition and Assessment: An Introduction." *Canadian Issues* (Spring): 3-13.

–. 2008. "The Impact of Economic Selection Policy on Labour Market Outcomes for Degree-Qualified Migrants in Canada and Australia." *IRPP Choices* 14, 5 (May): 2-47.

Health Canada. 2000. "Health Canada's Gender-Based Policy Analysis." http://www.hc-sc.gc.ca/women.

Hear, Nicholas van. 2010. "Theories of Migration and Social Change." *Journal of Ethnic and Migration Studies* 36, 10: 1531-36.

Hebert, Yvonne M., and Lori Wilkinson. 2002. "The Citizenship Debates: Conceptual, Policy, Experiential, and Educational Issues." In *Citizenship in Transformation in Canada,* ed. Yvonne Hebert, 3-36. Toronto: University of Toronto Press.

Hebrew Sheltering and Immigration Society (HIAS). 2013. "HIAS Convenes Briefing on Asylum Seekers in Israel." http://www.hias.org/.

Heer, J. 2012. "Introduction." In *"Too Asian"? Racism, Privilege, and Post-Secondary Education,* ed. R.J. Gilmour et al., 1-16. Toronto: Between the Lines.

Heiskanen, Benita. 2009. "A Day without Immigrants." In special issue, *European Journal of American Studies* Document 3. http://ejas.revues.org/7717.

Hennebry, Jenna. 2010. "Not Just a Few Bad Apples: Vulnerability, Health, and Temporary Migration in Canada." *Canadian Issues* (Spring): 73-77.

–. 2012. *Permanently Temporary? Agricultural Migrant Workers and Their Integration in Canada.* IRPP Study No. 26. Montreal: Institute for Research on Public Policy.

Hennebry, Jenna, and Janet McLaughlin. 2011. "Key Issues and Recommendations for Canada's Temporary Foreign Worker Program: Reducing Vulnerabilities and Protecting Rights." *IMRC Policy Points* 11 (1 January).

Hennebry, Jenna, and Bessma Momani. 2013. "Introduction: Arab Canadians as Targeted Transnationals." In *Targeted Transnationals: The State, the Media, and*

Arab Canadians, ed. Jenna Hennebry and Bessma Momani, 1-14. Vancouver: UBC Press.

Hennebry, Jenna, and Kerry Preibisch. 2010. "A Model for Managed Migration? Re-Examining Best Practices in Canada's Seasonal Agricultural Worker Program." *International Migration* 50: 19-40.

Henry, Frances, and Carol Tator. 2002. *Discourses of Domination: Racial Bias in the Canadian English-Language Press.* Toronto: University of Toronto Press.

–. 2008. "A Critical Discourse Analysis of the *Globe and Mail* Editorials on Employment Equity." In *Situating Race and Racisms in Space, Time, and Theory,* ed. J. Lee and J. Lutz. Montreal/Kingston: McGill-Queen's University Press.

–. 2009. *The Colour of Democracy.* 3rd ed. Toronto: Nelson/Thompson.

Hepburn, Bob. 2014. "Local NGO Has Made Great Strides in Matching Jobs with Immigrants." *Toronto Star,* 15 May.

Hernandez, Krystle. 2009. "Paradigms of Racial Stratification." *Helium,* 21 January.

Hiebert, Dan. 2006. "'Winning, Losing, and Still Playing the Game': The Political Economy of Immigration in Canada." *Royal Dutch Geographical Society* 97, 1: 38-48.

Hiebert, Dan, and David Ley. 2003. *Characteristics of Immigrant Transnationalism in Vancouver.* Working Paper Series No. 03-15. Vancouver: Centre of Excellence for Research on Immigration and Diversity.

Hier, Sean, and Joshua Greenberg. 2002. "News Discourse and the Problematization of Chinese Migration to Canada." In *Discourses of Domination: Racial Bias in the Canadian English-Language Press,* ed. Frances Henry and Carol Tator, 138-62. Toronto: University of Toronto Press.

Higgins, Peter W. 2013. *Immigration Justice.* Edinburgh: Edinburgh University Press.

Higley, John, and John Nieuwenhuysen, eds. 2010. *Nations of Immigrants: Australia and the USA Compared.* Melbourne: Monash Studies in Global Movements.

Ho, Loretta, and Harbi Natt. 2012. "Who Succeeds in Integrating Muslim Canadians: France, Quebec, or Canada? A New Study by Jeffrey Reitz." Ethnic, Immigration, and Pluralism Studies, Munk School of Global Affairs, University of Toronto. 12 December.

Hodge, Jarrah. 2006. "'Unskilled Labour': Canada's Live-in Caregiver Program." *Undercurrent* 3, 2: 61-67.

Hodge, Jonathan. 2006. "Let Them Stay." *Socialist Worker,* 15 April.

Hollifield, James. 2012. "Governing Migration." In *Global Migration,* ed. Kavita Khory, 183-97. New York: Palgrave.

Hondagneu-Sotelo, Pierrette, ed. 2003. *Gender and US Immigration: Contemporary Trends.* Berkeley: University of California Press.

Howe, Paul. 2007. "The Political Engagement of New Canadians: A Comparative Perspective." In *Belonging? Diversity, Recognition, and Shared Citizenship in Canada,* ed. Keith Banting, Thomas J. Courchene, and F. Leslie Seidle, 611-46. Montreal: Institute for Research on Public Policy.

Hsiung, Ping-Chun, and Katherine Nichol. 2010. "Policies on and Experiences of Foreign Domestic Workers in Canada." *Sociology Compass* 4, 9: 766-78.

Hugo, Graeme. 2003. "A New Paradigm of International Migration between the European Union and Australia: Patterns and Implications." National European Centre Paper No. 62. Paper presented at a conference at University of Sydney, February.

–. 2004. "Temporary Migration: A New Paradigm of International Migration." *Research Note* (Parliament of Australia) 55 (24 May): 1-2.

–. 2013. *What We Know about Circular Migration and Enhanced Mobility*. Policy Brief No. 7. Washington, DC: Migration Policy Institute.

Humpage, Louise. 2011. "How Have our Expectations of Society Changed?" Marsden Fund Report. Royal Society of New Zealand. 14 April. http://www.royalsociety.org.nz.

Humphreys, Adrian. 2014. "Fate of Refugee Claimants Can Depend on 'Luck of the Draw': Analysis." *National Post,* 16 April.

Hussan, Syed, Mary-Elizabeth Dill, and Abeer Majeed. 2012. "May Day: Immigrant Rights Are Workers' Rights." rabble.ca. 30 April.

Hussan, Syed, and Nate Prier. 2012. "Constructed Categories." *Briarpatch Magazine,* 4 November. http://briarpatchmagazine.com.

Hyman, Ilene, Agnes Meinhard, and John Shields. 2011. "The Role of Multiculturalism Policy in Addressing Social Inclusion Processes in Canada." Paper prepared for the Canadian Multicultural Education Foundation, 1 June.

Hyndman, Jennifer. 1999. "Gender and Canadian Immigration Policy: A Current Snapshot." *Canadian Woman Studies* 19, 3: 6-10.

–. 2008. "Waiting for What? The Humanitarian Dilemma of Protracted Refugee Situations at Home and Abroad." *Metropolis World Bulletin* 8: 24-29.

Iacovino, Raffaele. 2013. "Collective Identity and Federalism: Some Reflections on Belonging in Quebec." *Canadian Issues* (Spring): 31-35.

Ibbitson, John. 2005. *The Polite Revolution: Perfecting the Canadian Dream*. Toronto: McClelland and Stewart.

–. 2010. "'Distorted' Multiculturalism to Blame for Rise in Sikh Extremism, Dosanjh Says." *Globe and Mail,* 21 April.

–. 2011. "How to Stop Demographic Suicide." *Globe and Mail,* 19 August.

–. 2013. "Workers: Ottawa to Address Wage Discrepancies." *Globe and Mail,* 29 April.

Ignatieff, Michael. 1994. *Blood and Belonging: Journeys into the New Nationalism*. Toronto: Viking.

–. 2011. "My Name Is Michael and I Am Canadian." *Globe and Mail,* 29 June.

ILO (International Labour Organization). 2014. *Poverty and Profits: The Economics of Forced Labour*. Geneva: ILO.

Immigration Policy Center. 2009. "Breaking Down the Problems: What's Wrong with Our Immigration System?" Special Report. October. http://immigrationpolicy.org/.

Inglis, Christine. 2007. "Transnationalism in an Uncertain Environment: Relationship between Migration, Policy, and Theory." *International Journal on Multicultural Societies* 9, 2: 185-204.

Inouye, Kimiko. 2012. "Conditional Love: Representations of Migrant Work in Canadian Newsprint Media." *Social Identities* 18, 5: 573-92.

International Migration Institute. 2006. "Towards a New Agenda for International Migration Research." University of Oxford. May. http://www.imi.ox.ac.uk/projects/pdfs/a4-imi-research-agenda.pdf.

International Organization for Migration. 2013. *World Migration Report, 2013.* http://www.iom.int/cms/wmr2013.

Ip, M. 1998. "Gender, Racism, and the Politics of Chinese Immigration." In *Feminist Thought in Aotearoa/New Zealand,* ed. R. Du Plessis and L. Alice. Auckland: Oxford University Press.

Ipsos MORI Poll. 2012. "Global @dvisor Survey Reveals Negative Attitudes to Immigration." 1 June.

Isin, Engin. 2012. "Citizens without Frontiers." 15 October. http://www.open democracy.net.

Ivison, John. 2014. "Despite Mulcair Criticism, Case Shows Conservative Reforms to Refugee System Are Working." *National Post,* 4 April.

Iyer, Pico. 2001. *The Global Society: Jet Lag, Shopping Malls, and the Search for Home.* New York: Vintage.

Jabir, Humera. 2013. "Refugees Are Canada's New Bogeyman." *Toronto Star,* 24 December.

–. 2014. "Family Reunification Out of Reach for Many Newcomers." *Toronto Star,* 17 January.

Jackson, Andrew. 2011. "Recent Immigrants and the Crisis." 17 October. http://www.behindthenumbers.ca.

Jackson, Joanne, and Jari Osborne, co-dirs. 2012. *The Big Wait.* Omni Television and Big Red Media.

Jacobs, Keith. 2010. *Experience and Representation: Contemporary Perspectives on Migration in Australia.* Farnham, UK: Ashgate.

Jacoby, Tamar. 2011. "Germany's Immigration Dilemma." *Foreign Affairs* (March-April): 1-7.

Jakubowicz, Andrew. 2007. "Political Islam and the Future of Australian Multiculturalism." *National Identities* 9, 3: 265-80.

Jakubowski, Lisa Marie. 1997. *Immigration and the Legalization of Racism.* Halifax: Fernwood.

James, Carl, ed. 2005. *Possibilities and Limitations: Multicultural Policies and Programs in Canada.* Halifax: Fernwood.

Janoski, Thomas. 2010. *The Ironies of Citizenship: Naturalization and Integration in Industrialized Countries.* New York: Cambridge University Press.

Jantzen, Rich, Margaret Walton Roberts, and Joanna Ochocka. 2013. "Waterloo Region." In *Immigration, Integration, and Inclusion in Ontario Cities,* ed. Caroline Andrew, John Biles, Meyer Burstein, Vicki Esses, and Erin Tolley, 131-58. Montreal/Kingston: McGill-Queen's University Press.

Javdani, Mohsen, David Jacks, and Krishna Pendakur. 2012. "What Have We Learned about Immigrants, Diversity, and Economy? 16 Years of Metropolis." PowerPoint slides.

Javdani, Mohsen, and Krishna Pendakur. 2011. *Fiscal Transfers to Immigrants in Canada.* Metropolis British Columbia Working Paper No. 11-08. Vancouver: Centre of Excellence for Research on Immigration and Diversity.

–. 2013. "Fiscal Effects of Immigrants in Canada." *Journal of International Migration and Integration,* 8 December. http://link.springer.com.

Jayapal, Pramila. 2011. "Root Causes of Immigration – NAFTA." Paper presented at the Urban Poverty Forum, Seattle, 13 February. http://www.weareoneamerica.org.

Jedwab, Jack. 2007-08. "Dually Divided? The Risks of Linking Debates over Citizenship to Attachment to Canada." *International Journal* 63, 1: 65-78.

–. 2012. "The Economic Integration of Immigrants in Canada and the Quebec Difference." In *Managing Immigration and Diversity in Canada,* ed. Dan Rodríguez-García, 203-22. Montreal/Kingston: McGill-Queen's University Press.

–. 2014. "Introduction." In *The Multiculturalism Question: Debating Identity in 21st-Century Canada,* ed. Jack Jedwab, 1-10. Queen's University Policy Studies Series. Montreal/Kingston: McGill-Queen's University Press.

Jenicek, A., A.D. Wong, and E.O.J. Lee. 2009. "Dangerous Shortcuts: Representations of Sexual Minority Refugees in the Post-9-11 Canadian Press." *Canadian Journal of Communication* 34, 4: 635-58.

Jennissen, R. 2007. "Causality Chains in the International Migration Systems Approach." *Population Research and Policy Review* 26, 4: 411-36.

Jentsch, Birgit. 2007. "Migration Settlement in Rural and Urban Areas of New Settlement Countries: Thematic Introduction." *International Journal of Multicultural Societies* 9, 1: 1-12.

Jhappan, Radha. 2009. "No Barbarians Please, We're Canadian." rabble.ca, 3 December. http://rabble.ca.

Jimenez, Marina. 2007. "How Canadian Are You?" *Globe and Mail,* 12 January.

–. 2012. "Canada's Ethnic Mix a Success." *Globe and Mail,* 23 August.

Jiménez, Tomás R. 2011. *Immigrants in the United States: How Well Are They Integrating into Society?* Washington, DC: Migration Policy Institute.

Jiwani, Yasmin. 2006. *Discourses of Denial: Mediations on Race, Gender, and Violence.* Vancouver: UBC Press.

–. 2012a. "Colluding Hegemonies: Constructing the Muslim Other Post 9/11." In *Islam in the Hinterlands,* ed. J. Zine, 115-36. Vancouver: UBC Press.

–. 2012b. "Racism and the Media." Stop Racism and Hate Collective. http://www.stopracism.ca.

Johal, Rav. 2003. "The Internal Battle of Cultures." *Toronto Star,* 11 November.

Johnson, Genevieve Fuji, and Randy Enomoto. 2007. "Preface." In *Race, Racialization, and Anti-Racism in Canada and Beyond,* ed. G.F. Johnson and R. Enomoto. Toronto: University of Toronto Press.

Johnson, Kevin. 2003. *The "Huddled Masses" Myth: Immigration and Civil Rights.* Philadelphia: Temple University Press.

Jolly, David. 2013. "Immigration Costs to Countries Is Overstated, Study Finds." *New York Times,* 13 June.

Jonas, George. 2011. "Trudeau's Experiment with Multiculturalism Has Been a Failure." *National Post,* 14 September.

Jones, Martin, and France Houle. 2008. "Building a Better Refugee Status Determination System." *Refuge* 25, 2: 3-8.

Jones, Mary. 2010. "New Survey Reveals Attitudes of Canadians towards Immigration." 15 November. http://www.canadaupdates.com.

Jones, Reece. 2013. "Why Build a Border Wall?" *UTNE Reader,* May-June.

Joppke, Christian. 2010. *Citizenship and Immigration.* Malden, MA: Polity Press.

Joppke, Christian, and F. Leslie Seidle. 2012. "Introduction." In *Immigrant Integration in Federal Countries,* ed. Christian Joppke and F. Leslie Seidle, 3-22. Montreal/Kingston: McGill-Queen's University Press.

Jovanovski, Valentina. 2013. "Roma Refugee Numbers Plummet." *Globe and Mail,* 7 August.

Jupp, James. 2011. "Preface: A New Era in Australian Multiculturalism?" *Journal of Intercultural Studies* 32, 6: 577-78.

Jupp, James, and Michael Clyne. 2011. *Multiculturalism and Integration: A Harmonious Relationship.* Canberra: Australian National University Press.

Jurado, Elena, Grete Brochmann, and Jon Erik Dolvik. 2013. "Introduction: Immigration, Work, and Welfare: Towards an Integrated Approach." In *Europe's Immigration Challenge: Reconciling Work, Welfare, and Mobility,* ed. Elena Jurado and Grete Brochmann, 1-15. New York: I.B. Tauris.

Jurado, Elena, and Annie Bruzzone. 2008. "Rethinking Immigration: Work and Welfare in a Mobile Economy." Policy Network Paper. December. http://www.policy-network.net.

Kapur, Devesh. 2005. *Give Us Your Best and Brightest.* Washington, DC: Center for Global Development.

Karim, Karim. 2007. "Nations and Diaspora: Rethinking Multiculturalism in a Transnational Context." *International Journal of Media and Cultural Politics* 2, 3: 267-82.

–. 2009a. "Changing Perceptions of Islamic Authority among Muslims in Canada, the United States, and the United Kingdom." *IRPP Choices* 15, 2: 2-9.

–. 2009b. "Commentary: Pundits, Pachyderms, and Pluralism: A Never-Ending Debate on Multiculturalism." *Canadian Journal of Communication* 34: 701-10.

Kaushal, Asha, and Catherine Dauvergne. 2011. *The Growing Culture of Exclusion: Trends in Canadian Refugee Exclusions.* Metropolis British Columbia Working Paper No. 11-06. Vancouver: Centre of Excellence for Research on Immigration and Diversity.

Kazemipur, A., and S. Halli. 2003. "Poverty Experiences of Immigrants: Some Reflections." *Canadian Issues* (April): 18-20.

Kelley, Ninette, and Michael Trebilcock. 2010. *The Making of the Mosaic: A History of Canadian Immigration Policy.* 2nd ed. Toronto: University of Toronto Press.

Kelly, Philip. 2014. "Understanding Intergenerational Social Mobility: Filipino Youth in Canada." IRPP Study No. 45. www.irpp.org.

Kenney, Jason. 2010. "The Future of Immigration in Canada." Speech to the Economic Club of Canada, Toronto, 9 June.

–. 2012a. "Canada's Immigration System and Our Economic Future." Speaking notes, Economic Club of Canada, Chateau Laurier, Ottawa, 7 March.

–. 2012b. "Conversations from the Frontier." Frontier Centre for Public Policy, 8 June.

–. 2012c. "In His Own Words." *National Post,* 19 April.

–. 2012d. "Speaking Notes." Minister Kenney news conference at Victoria Hospital, London Health Sciences Centre, London, Ontario, 17 April.

Kernerman, Gerald. 2005. *Multicultural Nationalism: Civilizing Differences, Constituting Community.* Vancouver: UBC Press.

Keung, Nicholas. 2009. "A Strange Country, a Desperate Feeling." *Toronto Star,* 19 May.

–. 2010a. "Foreign Workers Increasingly Less Skilled." *Toronto Star*, 15 May.

–. 2010b. "Immigrant Professionals Face Daunting Job Hurdles." *Toronto Star/ Waterloo Region Record*, 30 March.

–. 2010c. "When Their Home Is No Safe Haven." *Toronto Star*, 7 March.

–. 2010d. "Will a New Bill Solve the Refugee Mess?" *Toronto Star*, 4 April.

–. 2011a. "Canada Third Best at Making Newcomers Feel Welcome." *Toronto Star*, 28 February.

–. 2011b. "Immigration Plan Helps Job Research." *Toronto Star*, 20 August.

–. 2011c. "Nannies Must Work Longer to Earn Status." *Toronto Star*, 25 November.

–. 2011d. "Ottawa Helps Gays Fleeing Persecution." *Toronto Star*, 25 March.

–. 2011e. "Quality of Refugee Decisions Criticized." *Toronto Star*, 22 June.

–. 2011f. "Refugee Detention Climbing in Canada, UN Report Says." *Toronto Star*, 12 November.

–. 2011g. "Refugee Judges Fail Tests to Get Revamped Jobs." *Toronto Star*, 24 November.

–. 2012a. "Ottawa to Halt New Immigration Applications." *Toronto Star*, 29 June.

–. 2012b. "Policy Change 'Not in Keeping with Canadian Values.'" *Toronto Star*, 11 December.

–. 2013a. "Canada Immigration: How a Decade of Policy Change Has Transformed the Immigration Landscape." *Toronto Star*, 15 February.

–. 2013b. "Immigration Program Hails First Plumber and Electrician." *Toronto Star*, 17 August.

–. 2013c. "The Undocumented." *Toronto Star*, 14 July.

–. 2013d. "Asylum Claims Plummet after Reforms to System." *Toronto Star*, 14 December.

–. 2013e. "Ottawa Could Have Repealed All Refugee Care, Hearing Told." *Toronto Star*, 19 December.

–. 2013f. "Changes to Refugee Program Ripped by Critics." *Toronto Star*, 28 November.

–. 2014a. "Quick Approval of Skilled Immigrants Needed." *Toronto Star*, 7 January.

–. 2014b. "Couples Frustrated by Prolonged Separation." *Toronto Star*, 20 January.

–. 2014c. "Refugee Kids' Hospital Admissions Doubled After Ottawa's Health Cuts." *Toronto Star*, 15 May.

–. 2014d. "Canadian Newcomers Dread Changes to Citizenship Rules." *Toronto Star*, 3 March.

Khan, Adnan. 2013. "Helping Themselves." *Maclean's*, 13 May.

Khoo, S-E., G. Hugo, and P. McDonald. 2008. "Which Skilled Migrants Become Permanent Residents and Why." *International Migration Review* 42, 1: 193-226.

Khory, Kavita. 2012. "Introduction." In *Global Migration: Challenges in the Twenty-First Century*, ed. Kavita Khory, 1-16. New York: Palgrave Macmillan.

Kil, Sang Hea. 2012. "Fearing Yellow, Imagining White: Media Analysis of the Chinese Exclusion Act of 1882." *Social Identities* 18, 6: 663-77.

King, Russell, Ronald Skeldon, and Julie Vullnetari. 2008. "Internal and International Migration: Bridging the Theoretical Divide." Paper presented at the IMISCOE "Theories of Migration and Social Change Conference," St. Anne's College, Oxford, 1-3 July.

King, William Lyon Mackenzie. 1947. *House of Commons Debates,* 1 May.

Kirby, Jason, John Geddes, and Jamie J. Weinman. 2011. "Is Randy Quaid Abusing Canada's Refugee System?" *MacLean's,* 29 October.

Kirkpatrick, David D. 2013. "Lack of Aid in Rebel Areas Angers Syrians." *New York Times,* 17 March.

Kiss, Simon. 2013. "How Generous Is Canada's Refugee Asylum Process?" *Opinion-Policy Nexus,* 24 January.

Kivisto, Peter. 2001. "Theorizing Transnational Immigration: A Critical Review of Current Efforts." *Ethnic and Racial Studies* 24, 4: 549-77.

Kivisto, Peter, and Wendy Ng. 2005. *Americans All: Race and Ethnic Relations in Historical, Structural and Comparative Perspectives.* 2nd ed. New York: Oxford University Press.

Kleiss, Karen. 2011. "Up to 10,000 Additional Skilled Workers Coming." *Calgary Herald,* 4 November.

Knowles, Valerie. 2007. *Strangers at Our Gates: Canadian Immigration and Immigration Policy, 1540-2006.* Toronto: Dunham Press.

Kobayashi, Audrey, Wei Li, and Carlos Teixeira. 2012. "Immigrant Geographies: Issues and Debates." In *Immigrant Geographies of North America,* ed. Carlos Teixeira, Wei Li, and Audrey Kobayashi, xiv-xxxv. Toronto: Oxford University Press.

Kobayashi, Audrey, and Valerie Preston. 2014. "Being CBC: The Ambivalent Identities and Belonging of Canadian-Born Children of Immigrants." *Annals of the Association of American Geographers* 104, 2: 234-42.

Koenig, Matthias, and Paul F.A. de Guchteneire, eds. 2007. *Democracy and Human Rights in Multicultural Societies.* Burlington VT: Ashgate.

Kohler, Nicholas. 2009. "A Crackdown on Queue-Jumpers." *Maclean's,* 3 August.

Kolb, Holger. 2014. "When Extremes Converge: German and Canadian Labour Migration Policy Compared." *Comparative Migration Studies* 2, 1: 57-75.

Koning, Edward. 2013. "How Generous Is Canada's Asylum Process?" *Opinion-Policy Nexus,* 24 January.

Koning, Edward, and Keith Banting. 2011. "The Canadian Model of Immigration and Welfare." http://www.regjeringen.no.

Kruhlak, Orest. 2003. "Multiculturalism Means Inclusiveness, Social Justice, Empowerment." 37th Annual Shevchenko Lecture, University of Alberta, 14 March.

Kunz, Jean Lock. 2005. "Applying a Life Course Lens to Immigration." *Canadian Issues* (Spring): 41-43.

Kunz, Jean, and Stuart Sykes. 2008. *From Mosaic to Harmony: Multiculturalism Canada in the 21st Century.* Ottawa: Policy Research Institute.

Kunz, Jean Lock, Anne Milan, and Sylvain Schetagne. 2001. *Unequal Access: A Canadian Profile of Racial Differences in Education, Employment, and Income.* A Report Prepared for the Canadian Race Relations Foundation by the Canadian Council of Social Development, Ottawa.

Kunz, Rahel, Sandra Lavenex, and Marion Panizzon. 2011. *Multilayered Migration Governance: The Promise of Partnership.* New York: Routledge.

Kurien, Prema. 2013. "Race, Religion, and the US Today: The Political Integration of Indian Americans." Talk presented at the University of Waterloo, Waterloo, ON, 31 January.

Kurz, Joshua J. 2012. "Transmigration and Precarity: The New Politics of Human Migration." Paper presented at the annual meeting of the Association of American Geographers, New York, 28 February.

Kymlicka, Will. 1995. *Multicultural Citizenship.* London: Oxford University Press.

–. 1998. *Finding Our Way: Rethinking Ethnocultural Relations in Canada.* Toronto: Oxford University Press.

–. 2003. "Multicultural States and Intercultural Citizens." *Theory and Research in Education* 19, 2: 147-69.

–. 2005. "The Uncertain Futures of Multiculturalism." *Canadian Diversity* 4, 1: 82-85.

–. 2007a. "The Canadian Model of Diversity in Comparative Perspective." In *Multiculturalism and the Canadian Constitution,* ed. Stephen Tierney, 61-90. Vancouver: UBC Press.

–. 2007b. "The Global Diffusion of Multiculturalism: Trends, Causes, and Consequences." In *Accommodating Cultural Diversity,* ed. Stephen Tierney, 17-34. Aldershot, UK: Ashgate.

–. 2007c. *Multicultural Odysseys.* Toronto: Oxford University Press.

–. 2008. "The Current State of Multiculturalism in Canada." Report commissioned by the Multiculturalism and Human Rights Branch, Government of Canada. http://www.cic.gc.ca/english/pdf/pub/multi-state.pdf.

–. 2010a. "The Rise and Fall of Multiculturalism? New Debates on Inclusion and Accommodation in Diverse Societies." *International Social Science Journal* 61, 199: 97-122.

–. 2010b. "Testing the Liberal Multiculturalist Hypothesis: Normative Theories and Social Science Evidence." *Canadian Journal of Political Science* 43: 257-71.

–. 2011a. "Invited Symposium: New Directions and Issues for the Study of Ethnicity, Nationalism, and Multiculturalism: Multiculturalism in Normative Theory and in Social Science." *Ethnicities* 11, 1: 5-31.

–. 2011b. "Multicultural Citizenship within Multinational States." *Ethnicities* 11, 3: 281-302.

–. 2012. "Multiculturalism: Success, Failure, and the Future." Transatlantic Council on Migration. February. http://www.migrationpolicy.org/pubs/multiculturalism.pdf.

Kymlicka, Will, and Kathryn Walker, eds. 2012. *Rooted Cosmopolitanism.* Vancouver: UBC Press.

Laegaard, Sune. 2010. "Immigration, Social Cohesion and Naturalization." *Ethnicities* 10, 4: 452-69.

Lafleur, Steve. 2011. "Make Immigration Break Even." *National Post,* 19 December.

Lakoff, George, and Sam Ferguson. 2006. "The Framing of Immigration." Rockridge Institute. 22 May. http://www.buzzflash.com.

Lamey, Andy. 2011a. "Canada's Refugee System Is a Dead End for Terrorists." *Globe and Mail,* 24 May.

–. 2011b. *Frontier Justice: The Global Refugee Crisis and What to Do about It.* Toronto: Doubleday.

Landay, Jonathan. 2013. "Delay in Military Action Mystifies Refugees." *Toronto Star,* 2 September.

Landolt, Patricia. 2007. "Nation State Building Projects and the Politics of Transnational Migration: Locating Salvadoreans in Canada, the United

States, and El Salvador." In *Citizenship and Immigrant Incorporation,* ed. G. Yurdakul and M. Bodemann, 141-62. New York: Palgrave Macmillan.

Landolt, Patricia, Luin Goldring, and Judith K. Bernhard. 2011. "Agenda Setting and Immigration Politics: The Case of Latin Americans in Toronto." *American Behavioral Scientist* 55, 9: 1235-66.

Lang, Georgialee. 2011. "Immigration Should Be about Policy, Not Politics." 20 June. http://www.canada.com/news.

Langille, Justin. 2012. "To Help Migrants, There's Work to Be Done." *The Tyee,* 17 February.

Latham, Robert. 2007-08. "What Are We? From a Multicultural to a Multiversal Canada." *International Journal* 63, 1: 23-42.

–. 2008. "Canadian Society Is Not Just Multicultural; It Is Multiversal." Research Snapshot. York University, Toronto. http://researchimpact.ca/_app/impact/files/tables/files.path.110.pdf.

–. 2009. "After Multiculturalism: Canada and Its Multiversal Future." *Canada Watch* (Fall): 28-30.

Laucius, Joanne. 2009. "Chinese Immigrants Canada's Brain Gain." *National Post,* 5 October.

Lawlor, Andrea. 2012. "Having Your Mind Made Up for You: Framing Immigration in the Canadian News Media." Paper presented at the Canadian Political Science annual meeting, Edmonton, 15-17 June.

Leblanc, Daniel. 2012. "Ottawa Targets Romanian Refugees." *Globe and Mail,* 7 November.

Lee, Edward. 1997. "Canada's Chinese Still Stereotyped." *Toronto Star,* 15 December.

Legrain, Philippe. 2006. *Immigrants: Your Country Needs Them.* London: Little Brown.

Lenard, Patti Tamara. 2012. *Trust, Democracy, and Multicultural Challenges.* University Park: Pennsylvania State University Press.

–. 2013. "Indecent Proposals: Why the Fraser Institute Is Wrong on Immigration." Broadbent Institute blog. 3 September. https://www.broadbentinstitute.ca/.

Lenard, Patti Tamara, and Christine Straehle. 2012. *Legislated Inequality: Temporary Labour Migration in Canada.* Montreal/Kingston: McGill-Queen's University Press.

Lentin, Alana, and Gavan Titley. 2011a. "The Crisis in Multiculturalism." http://www.opendemocracy.net.

–. 2011b. *The Crisis in Multiculturalism: Racism in a Neoliberal Age.* London: Zed Books.

Leonard, Karen. 2009. "Transnationalism and Cosmopolitan Forms of Islam in the West." *Harvard Middle Eastern and Islamic Review* 8: 176-99.

Letourneau, Jocelyn. 2013. "Reconstructing the Canadian Identity." *Globe and Mail,* 1 July.

Leuprecht, Christian, and Conrad Winn. 2011. "What Do Muslim Canadians Want? The Clash of Interpretations and Opinion Research." True North Study Papers. Macdonald-Laurier Institute. http://www.macdonaldlaurier.ca/files/pdf/What-Do-Muslim-Canadians-Want-November-1-2011.pdf.

Levinson, Robin. 2013. "Welcoming a New Breed of Immigrant." *Toronto Star,* 11 August.

Levitt, Peggy. 2004. "Transnational Migrants: When 'Home' Means More Than One Country." *Migration Information Source,* October.

–, ed. 2007. *The Transmigration Studies Reader.* New York: Routledge.

Levitz, Stephanie. 2012a. "Canadians' Hearts Are Hardening Toward Immigrants." *Waterloo Region Record,* 31 October.

–. 2012b. "Federal Immigration Points System Changed." *Toronto Star,* 19 December.

Lewin, J., C. Meares, T. Cain, P. Spoonley, R. Peace, and E. Ho. 2011. *Namasté New Zealand: Indian Employers and Employees in Auckland.* Research Report No. 5: Integration of Immigrants Programme. North Shore City, NZ: Massey University.

Ley, David. 2005. *Post-Multiculturalism?* Working Paper No. 05-17. Vancouver: Centre of Excellence for Research on Immigration and Diversity.

–. 2007. *Multiculturalism: A Canadian Defence.* Working Paper No. 07-04. Vancouver: Centre of Excellence for Research on Immigration and Diversity.

Ley, David, and Dan Hiebert. 2001. "Immigration Policy as Population Policy." *Canadian Geographer* 45, 1: 120-25.

Li, Peter S. 1998. *The Chinese in Canada.* 2nd ed. Toronto: Oxford University Press.

–. 2003. *Destination Canada: Immigration Debates and Issues.* Toronto: Oxford University Press.

Lieberman, Amy. 2011. "Is Domestic Abuse Cause for Asylum?" *Christian Science Monitor,* 7 February.

Ligaya, Armina. 2013. "Most Canadians in Favour of Limits on Immigration: Poll." *National Post,* 11 March.

Lister, Ruth. 2003. *Citizenship: Feminist Perspectives.* Basingstoke: Macmillan.

Liston, Mary, and Joseph Carens. 2008. "Immigration and Integration in Canada." In *Migration and Globalisation: Comparing Immigration Policy in Developed Countries,* ed. A. Kondo, 207-27. Tokyo: Akashi Shoten.

Little, Matthew. 2010. "Fake Refugees a Threat to Immigration: Kenney." *Epoch Times,* 28 October-3 November.

Liu, James, and Duncan Mills. 2006. "Modern Racism and Neo-Liberal Globalization: The Discourses of Plausible Deniability and Their Multiple Functions." *Journal of Community and Applied Social Psychology* 16: 83-99.

Local Immigrant Partnership Council, Waterloo Region. 2010. *Final Report – April 2010.*

Loewan, Royden, and Gerald Friesen. 2009. *Immigrants in Prairie Cities: Ethnic Diversity in Twentieth-Century Canada.* Toronto: University of Toronto Press.

Lopez, William D., Louis F. Graham, Mark Padilla, and Angela Reyes. 2013. "Boundaries in the Lives of Undocumented Immigrants." *Anthropology News,* January-February.

Lorriggio, Paola. 2013. "Federal Cuts to Refugee Health Aren't Legally Valid, Doctors Urge Court." *Globe and Mail,* 17 December.

Lowe, Sophia. 2008. "'Designer Immigrants': Eliminating Barriers." Toronto Region Immigrant Employment Council. 24 September. http://www.triec.ca.

–. 2010. "Rearranging the Deck Chairs? A Critical Examination of Canada's Shifting (Im)migration Policies." *Canadian Issues* (Spring): 25-28.

–. 2011. "Welcome to Canada? Immigration Incentives May Not Be Enough for International Students to Stay." *Canadian Diversity* 8, 5: 20-24.

Lutz, Helma. 2010. "Gender in the Migratory Process." *Journal of Ethnic and Migration Studies* 36, 10: 1647-63.

Lyons, Terrance, and Peter Mandaville. 2008. *Global Migration and Transnational Politics: A Conceptual Framework.* Working Paper No. 1. Fairfax, VA: Center for Global Studies, George Mason University.

Maaka, Roger, and Augie Fleras. 2005. *The Politics of Indigeneity.* Dunedin: Otago University Press.

Maas, Willem. 2013. "Free Movement and Discrimination: Evidence from Europe, the United States, and Canada." *European Journal of Migration* 15, 1: 91-110.

MacDonald, John, and Robert J. Sampson. 2012. "The World in a City: Immigration and America's Changing Social Fabric." *Annals of the American Academy of Political and Social Science* 641 (May): 6-15.

Mackey, Eva. 1998. *The House of Difference: Cultural Politics and National Identity in Canada.* London: Routledge.

Mackey, Jeff. 2013. "Migrant Worker Advocates Call for Changes." *Waterloo Region Record,* 29 June.

MacKinnon, Mark. 2012. "Why Some Chinese Immigrants Feel They Can't Make Money in Canada." *Globe and Mail,* 12 May.

MacLaren, Barbara, and Luc Lapointe. 2010. "Employment Insurance: How Canada Can Remain Competitive and Be Fair to Migrant Workers." *Policy Options,* February.

Macklin, Audrey. 1999. "Women as Migrants in National and Global Communities." *Canadian Woman Studies* 19, 3: 24-32.

Macklin, Audrey, and François Crépeau. 2010. *Multiple Citizenship, Identity, and Entitlement in Canada.* IRPP Study No. 6. Montreal: Institute for Research on Public Policy.

Madokoro, Laura. 2010. "We Need to Extend Pier 21 across Canada." *Globe and Mail,* 19 March.

Maharaj, Rabindranath. 2010. *The Amazing Absorbing Boy.* Toronto: Knopf Canada.

Mahoney, Jill. 2007. "Licences for Foreign Trained MDs on Increase." *Globe and Mail,* 31 March.

Mahtani, Minelle. 2002. "Representing Minorities: Canadian Media and Minority Identities." *Canadian Ethnic Studies* 33, 3: 99-131.

–. 2008. "How Are Immigrants Seen and What Do They Want to See? Contemporary Research on the Representation of Immigrants in the Canadian Language Media." In *Immigration and Integration in Canada in the Twenty-First Century,* ed. John Biles, Meyer Burstein, and James Frideres, 231-52. Montreal/Kingston: McGill-Queen's University Press.

Mahtani, Minelle, Frances Henry, and Carol Tator. 2008. "Discourse, Ideology, and Constructions of Racial Inequality." In *Communication in Question,* ed. Joshua Greenberg and Charlene D. Elliot, 120-30. Toronto: Thomson Nelson.

Mainwaring, Cetta. 2012. "Constructing a Crisis: The Role of Immigration Detention in Malta." *Population, Space, and Place* 18, 6: 687-700.

–. 2013. "People, States, Borders: (Ir)Regular Migrants and Migration." Paper presented at the Sociology Department, University of Waterloo, Waterloo, ON, 23 April.

Malik, Kenan. 2013. "In Defence of Diversity." *New Humanist,* 18 December. http://www.eurozine.com.

Malloch-Brown, Mark. 2011. *The Unfinished Global Revolution.* Toronto: Viking Canada.

Maloney, Joseph. 2013. "In Defence of Temporary Foreign Workers." *National Post,* 17 May.

Mamann, Guidy. 2010. "Open for Discussion." Canadian Immigrant. http://canadianimmigrant.ca.

Manicom, David. 2013. "Temporary Foreign Workers: Recent Research and Current Policy Issues." Paper prepared for Metropolis Conference, Ottawa, 14 March. http://archive.irpp.org/events/archive/20130314/manicom.pdf.

Manning, Patrick. 2005. *Migration in World History.* New York: Routledge.

Mansur, Salim. 2011. *The Muddle of Multiculturalism: A Liberal Critique.* Halifax: Atlantic Institute for Market Studies.

Marchi, Sergio. 1994. Speaking Notes. Tabling of the Strategy and the Immigration and Citizenship Plan. House of Commons, 1 November. Ottawa: Government of Canada.

–. 2014. "Ending the Immigrant Investor Program Was a Missed Opportunity." *Globe and Mail,* 28 February.

Marger, Martin. 2000. *Race and Ethnic Relations: American and Global Perspectives.* Belmont, CA: Wadsworth.

Marketwired. 2009. "Government of Canada Tables 2010 Immigration Plan." News release, Citizenship and Immigration. http://www.marketwired.com.

Markus, Andrew, and Moshe Semyonov, eds. 2011. *Immigration and Nation Building: Australia and Israel Compared.* Melbourne: Monash Studies in Global Movements.

Marotta, Vince. 2011. "New Online Ethnicities and the Politics of Representation." *Journal of Intercultural Studies* 32, 5: 539-53.

Martin, Alan. 2004. "For the Worse." *Maclean's,* 1 March.

Martin, Don. 2010a. "Tamil Ships Bring What the Tories Need." *National Post,* 13 August.

–. 2010b. "Welcome Mat Put Out, Pulled Away." *National Post,* 30 March.

Martin, Philip. 2008. "Temporary Worker Programs: US and Global Experiences." http://canada.metropolis.net/policypriority/migration_seminar/Philip MartinsPaper_e.pdf.

Martin, Philip, Manolo Abella, and Christiane Kuptsch. 2005. *Managing Labor Migration in the Twenty-First Century.* Princeton: Yale University Press.

Martin, Philip, and Gottfried Zurcher. 2008. "Managing Migration: The Global Challenge." *Population Bulletin* 63, 1: 1-24.

Martin, Susan. 2011. *A Nation of Immigrants.* New York: Cambridge University Press.

–. 2013. *Environmental Change and Migration: What We Know.* Policy Brief, No. 2. Washington, DC: Migration Policy Institute.

Martinez, Samuel. 2009. "Introduction." In *International Migration and Human Rights: The Global Repercussions of US Policy,* ed. Samuel Martinez, 1-11. Berkeley: University of California Press.

Martiniello, Marco, and Jan Rath, eds. 2010. *Selected Studies in International Migration and Immigrant Incorporation.* Amsterdam: Amsterdam University Press.

Marwah, Sonal. 2014. *Refugee Health Care Cuts in Canada: System Level Costs, Risks, and Responses.* Toronto: Wellesley Institute.

Mas, Susana. 2014. "Skilled Immigrants to Be Matched with Vacant Jobs in 2015." *CBC News*, 29 January.

Masood, Ehsan. 2007. "Muslims and Multiculturalism: Lesson from Canada." Open Democracy. http://www.opendemocracy.net.

Massey, Douglas S. 2003. "Patterns and Processes of International Migration in the 21st Century." Paper presented at the Conference on African Migration in Comparative Perspective, Johannesburg, 4-7 June.

–. 2009. "The Political Economy of Migration in an Era of Globalization." In *International Migration and Human Rights: The Global Repercussions of US Policy,* ed. Samuel Martinez, 25-41. Berkeley: University of California Press.

Massey, Douglas S., Joaquin Arango, Graeme Hugo, Ali Kouciou, Adela Pellegrino, and J. Edward Taylor. 1998. *Worlds in Motion: International Migration at the End of the Millennium.* New York: Oxford University Press.

Mawani, Aysha. 2008. "Transnationalism: A Modern Day Challenge to Canadian Multiculturalism." Paper presented at the annual meeting of the International Communication Association, Montreal, 22 May. http://www.allacademic.com.

Mawani, Nurjehan. 1997. "Is Refugee Determination Fair?" *Globe and Mail,* 13 December.

Maxwell, Bruce, David I. Waddington, Kevin McDonough, Andrée-Anne Cormier, and Marina Schwimmer. 2012. "Interculturalism, Multiculturalism, and the State Funding and Regulation of Conservative Religious Schools." *Educational Theory* 62, 4: 427-38.

Maytree Foundation. 2011. "Good Ideas from Toronto: An Exchange of Immigrant Integration Practices." 28 November-2 December. http://maytree.com/.

McCabe, Kristen, and Doris Meissner. 2010. "Immigration and the United States: Recession Affects Flows, Prospects for Reform." *Migration Information Source,* January.

McCullough, J.J. 2013. "Jason Kenney vs. David Suzuki: The Great Canadian Slap Fight." *Huffington Post,* 15 July. http://www.huffingtonpost.ca.

McDonald, Ted, Elizabeth Ruddick, Arthur Sweetman, and Christopher Worswick. 2010. *Canadian Immigration: Economic Evidence for a Dynamic Policy Environment.* Montreal/Kingston: McGill-Queen's University Press.

McDonald, Ted, and Christopher Worswick. 2010. "Visible Minority Status, Immigrant Status, Gender, and Earnings in Canada." In *Canadian Immigration: Economic Evidence for a Dynamic Policy Environment,* ed. Ted McDonald, Elizabeth Ruddick, Arthur Sweetman, and Christopher Worswick, 111-32. Montreal/Kingston: McGill-Queen's University Press.

McDowell, Adam. 2010. "New Regime." *National Post,* 31 March.

McGauran, Peter. 2005. "The Australian Government Minister for Immigration and Multiculturalism." *Canadian Diversity* 4, 1: 6-8.

McGovern, Patrick. 2012. "Inequalities in the (De-)Commodification of Labour: Immigration, the Nation State and Labour Market Stratification." *Sociology Compass* 6, 6: 485-98.

McKenna, Barrie. 2012. "Why Training Workers in Canada Beats Importing Them from Abroad." *Globe and Mail,* 16 December.

McLaughlin, J., J.L. Hennebry, D.C. Cole, and G. Williams. 2014. "The Migrant Farmworker Health Journey: Identifying Issues and Considering Change across Borders." *Policy Points* 6. http://imrc.ca/wp-content/uploads/2013/10/IMRC-Policy-Points-VI.pdf.

McMahon, Tamsin. 2011. "Immigrant-Investor Program in Maritimes Collapses in Scandal, Lawsuits." *National Post*, 17 December.

McMurtry, Alyssa. 2013. "Modern Day Slavery." *Canadian Dimension*, 3 April.

McNally, David 2006. *Another World Is Possible: Globalization and Anti-Capitalism.* Winnipeg: Arbeiter Ring.

McNevin, Anne. 2012. *Contesting Citizenship: Irregular Migrants and New Frontiers of the Political.* New York: Columbia University Press.

McPartland, Kelly. 2012. "Jason Kenney's Immigration Revolution Chalks Up Another Success." *National Post*, 22 June.

McQuillan, Kevin. 2013. "All the Workers We Need: Debunking Canada's Labour Shortage Fallacy." School of Public Policy, University of Calgary, Research Paper No. 6.

Medrano, Lourdes. 2010. "Test Bed for Immigration Fight." *Christian Science Monitor*, 18 October.

Meissner, Doris, Donald M. Kerwin, Muzaffar Chishti, and Claire Bergeron. 2013. *Immigration Enforcement in the United States.* Washington, DC: Migration Policy Institute.

Mendelsohn, Matthew. 2013. "Introduction." In *Diaspora Nation: An Inquiry into the Economic Potential of Diaspora Networks in Canada,* ed. M. Bitran and S. Tan. Toronto: Mowat Centre, School of Public Policy and Governance, University of Toronto.

Metropolis Presents. 2004. "Conference Notes on Media, Immigration and Diversity: Informing Public Discourse or Fanning the Flames of Intolerance?" 30 March. National Library, Ottawa.

Mickleburgh, Rod. 2006. "Harper Defends Canadian Diversity." *Globe and Mail*, 20 June.

Migration Integration Policy Index. 2007. "Canada." http://www.mipex.eu/Canada.

–. 2010. "Canada." http://www.mipex.eu/Canada.

Migration Observatory. 2013. "Migration in the News: Portrayals of Immigrants, Migrants, Asylum Seekers and Refugees in National British Newspapers, 2010-2012." 8 August. http://www.migrationobservatory.ox.ac.uk/.

Millman, Joel. 1997. *The Other Americans: How Immigrants Renew Our Country, Our Economy, and Our Values.* New York: Penguin.

Mills, Edward J., et al. 2011. "The Financial Cost of Doctors Emigrating from Sub-Saharan Africa: Human Capital Analysis." *British Medical Journal* 343: 1-13.

Miner, Rick. 2010. "People without Jobs, Jobs without People: Ontario's Labour Market Future." 10 February. http://www.collegesontario.org/policy-positions/MinerReport.pdf.

Modood, Tariq. 2011. "Post-Immigration 'Difference' and Integration: The Case of Muslims in Western Europe." Report prepared for the British Academy, London.

Moens, Alexander, and Martin Collacott. 2008. "Introduction." In *Immigration Policy and the Terrorist Threat in Canada and the United States,* ed. Alexander Moens and Martin Collacott, ix-xv. Vancouver: Fraser Institute.

Monohan, John, Rima Berns-McGown, and Michael Morden. 2014. *The Perception and Reality of "Imported Conflict" in Canada.* Toronto: Mosaic Institute.

Monsebraaten, Laurie. 2009. "They Want Some Certainty ... and So Do We." *Toronto Star,* 22 November.

Montreuil, Annie, and Richard Y. Bourhis. 2004. "Acculturation Orientations of Competing Host Communities toward Valued and Devalued Immigrants." *International Journal of Intercultural Relations* 28, 6: 507-32.

Mooers, Colin. 2005. *Multiculturalism and Citizenship: Some Theoretical Reflections.* CERIS Working Paper No. 37. Toronto: Ontario Metropolis Centre.

Moosa, Zohra. 2007. "Minding the Multicultural Gap." *Catalyst,* 16 March.

Morris, Carolyn. 2009. "Your Money or Your Life?" *This Magazine,* March-April.

Moses, Jonathon W. 2009. "The Politics of Immigration: Introduction to a Special Issue on US Immigration." In special issue, *European Journal of American Studies* 4, 3.

Mountz, Alison. 2010. *Seeking Asylum: Human Smuggling and Bureaucracy at the Border.* Minneapolis: University of Minnesota Press.

Mudde, Cas. 2012. "The Relationship between Immigration and Nativism in Europe and North America." Transatlantic Council on Migration. http://www.migrationpolicy.org/pubs/Immigration-Nativism.pdf.

Mulley, Sarah. 2013. "Europe's Immigration Challenge." IPPR (Institute for Public Policy Research), 11 April. http://www.ippr.org/articles.

Munster, Rens van. 2010. *Securitizing Immigration: The Politics of Risk in the EU.* London: Palgrave Macmillan.

Munz, Rainer, and Rainer Ohliger, eds. 2005. *Diasporas and Ethnic Migrants: Germany, Israel, and Post-Soviet Successor States in Comparative Perspective.* Portland: Frank Cass.

Murphy, Michael. 2012. *Multiculturalism: A Critical Introduction.* New York: Routledge.

Murray, Catherine. 2009. "Designing Monitoring to Promote Cultural Diversification in TV." *Canadian Journal of Communication* 34, 4: 675-99.

Mustafa, Naheed. 2007. "Aqsa Parvez's Death Lays Bare Flipside of Immigration." *Toronto Star,* 12 December.

Nagel, Caroline, and Peter Hopkins. 2010. "Introduction: Spaces of Multiculturalism." *Space and Polity* 14, 1: 1-11.

Naji, Lamia. 2012. "Integrating Young Canadians of Minority Backgrounds into Mainstream Canadian Society: The Case of Somali Youth." Metropolis Conversation Series. http://www.metropolis.net/pdfs/Conversation%20Report%20Somali%20Youth%20Final.pdf.

Nakache, Delphine. 2010. "Temporary Workers: Permanent Rights?" *Canadian Issues* (Spring): 45-49.

Nakache, Delphine, and Paula J. Kinoshita. 2010. *The Canadian Temporary Foreign Worker Program.* IRPP Study No. 5. Montreal: Institute for Research on Public Policy.

Nakhaie, M. Reza, and Abdolmohammad Kazemipur. 2013. "Social Capital, Employment, and Occupational Status of the New Immigrants in Canada." *Journal of International Migration and Integration* 14: 419-37.

Nanos, Nik. 2008. "Nation-Building through Immigration: Workforce Skills Comes Out on Top." *Policy Options,* June.

–. 2010. "Canadians Strongly Support Immigration, But Don't Want Current Levels Increased." *Policy Options,* July-August.

Native Women's Association of Canada. 2004. "Background Document on Aboriginal Women's Health." http://www.nwac.ca.

Nawyn, Stephanie J. 2010. "Gender and Migration: Integrating Feminist Theory into Migration Studies." *Sociology Compass* 4, 9: 749-65.

Nazir, Arif. 2004. "Foreign Trained Dentists Treated like Third Class Citizens." *Kingston Whig-Standard,* 6 July.

Nazroo, James Y., and Saffron Karlsen. 2003. "Patterns of Identity among Ethnic Minority People: Diversity and Commonality." *Ethnic and Racial Studies* 26, 5: 902-30.

Nebehay, Stephanie. 2013. "Humanitarian Tragedy Unfolding in Rebel Held North, UN Says." *Globe and Mail,* 21 February.

Neerup, Stine. 2012. "Social Cohesion and Ethnic Diversity in Australia." In *Diverse Nations, Diverse Responses: Approaches to Social Cohesion in Immigrant Societies,* ed. Erin Tolley and Paul Spoonley, 59-80. Queen's Policy Studies Series. Kingston: School of Policy Studies, Queen's University.

Negi, Nalini Junko, and Rich Furman, eds. 2010. *Transnational Social Work Practice.* New York: Columbia University Press.

Neiterman, Elena, and Ivy Lynn Bourgeault. 2012. "Conceptualizing Professional Diaspora: International Medical Graduates in Canada." *International Migration and Integration* 13: 39-57.

New Zealand Herald News. 2013. "Asylum Seekers Cause $55 Million Damage at Nauru." 21 July.

Newland, Kathleen. 2011. *Migration and Development Policy: What Have We Learned?* Washington, DC: Migration Policy Institute.

Newland, Kathleen, and Sonia Plaza. 2013. *What We Know about Diasporas and Economic Development.* Policy Brief No. 5. Washington, DC: Migration Policy Institute.

News Batch. 2010. "Immigration Policy Issues: An Internet Guide to Understanding Policy Issues." http://www.newsbatch.com.

Nicholson, Mike. 2012. "Refugee Resettlement Needs Outpace Growing Number of Resettlement Countries." *Migration Information Source,* November.

Nielson, Greg. 2009. "Framing Dialogue on Immigration in the *New York Times.*" *Aether* 4: 22-42.

Nieswand, Boris. 2011. *Theorising Transnational Migration: The Status Paradox of Migration.* New York: Routledge.

Nieuwenhuysen, John, Howard Duncan, and Stine Neerup, eds. 2012. *International Migration in Uncertain Times.* Queen's Policy Studies Series. Kingston: School of Policy Studies, Queen's University.

No One Is Illegal. 2010. "The City Is a Sweatshop." http://toronto.nooneisillegal.org.

Noble, Greg. 2011. "Experience and Representation: Contemporary Perspectives on Migration in Australia." *Ethnic and Racial Studies* 34, 10: 1778-79.

Noorani, Nick. 2011. "Why Some Immigrants Fail." *National Post,* 10 February.

Nootens, Genevieve. 2014. "Nationalism, Pluralism, and the Democratic Governance of Diversity." In *The Multiculturalism Question: Debating Identity in 21st-Century Canada,* ed. Jack Jedwab, 173-86. Queen's University Policy Studies Series. Montreal/Kingston: McGill-Queen's University Press.

Nussbaum, Martha C. 2006. *Frontiers of Justice.* Boston: Harvard University Press.

–. 2012. *Philosophical Interventions and Reviews, 1986-2011.* New York: Oxford University Press.

OCASI (Ontario Council of Agencies Serving Immigrants). 2012. "Immigrants Say Settlement and Integration Services Are Working – New Report." News release, 12 July.

O'Doherty, Kieran, and Martha Augoustinos. 2008. "Protecting the Nation: Nationalist Rhetoric on Asylum Seekers and the *Tampa*." *Journal of Community and Applied Social Psychology* 18: 576-92.

OECD. 2012. *International Migration Outlook, 2012.* N.p.: OECD.

–. 2013. *International Migration Outlook, 2013.* http://www.oecd.org/els/mig/imo2013.htm.

–. 2014a. "Is Migration Really Increasing?" Migration Policy Debates, May. http://www.oecd.org/migration.

–. 2014b. "The Fiscal and Economic Impact of Migration." Policy Brief, May. http://www.oecd.org/publications/Pol_brief.

Omidvar, Ratna. 2009. "Tough Choices for Migrant Workers." Maytree Foundation. http://maytree.com/opinion/touch-choices-for-migrant-workers-2.html.

–. 2012a. "Choosing the Right Canadian." *Globe and Mail,* 9 March.

–. 2012b. "Shaping the Face of Canada." *Globe and Mail,* 9 May.

–. 2013. "Temporary Immigrants, Temporary Loyalties." *Globe and Mail,* 20 May.

Ommundsen, Wenche, Michael Leach, and Andrew Vandenberg, eds. 2010. *Cultural Citizenship and the Challenge of Globalization.* New York: Hampton Press.

O'Neil, Peter. 2012. "Immigrants Who Don't Speak English or French End Up Working in Ethnic Enclaves: Report." *Postmedia News,* 13 June.

–. 2013. "Ottawa Blasts Quebec for 'Fraud' Program That 'Takes Money' from Rich Immigrants Who Move to Other Provinces." *Postmedia News,* 1 August.

O'Reilly, Karen. 2012. *International Migration and Social Theory.* New York: Palgrave Macmillan.

Oreopoulos, Philip. 2009. *Why Do Skilled Immigrants Struggle in the Labour Field? A Field Experiment with Six Thousand Resumes.* Metropolis British Columbia Working Paper No. 09-03. Vancouver: Centre of Excellence for Research on Immigration and Diversity.

O'Rourke, Alexandra V. 2010. "Embracing Reality: The Guest Worker Program Revisited." *Harvard Latino Law Review* 11. http://heinonline.org/HOL/Page?handle=hein.journals/hllr9&div=8&g_sent=1&collection=journals#183.

Otero, Gerardo. 2011. "Neoliberal Globalization, NAFTA, and Migration: Mexico's Loss of Food and Labor Sovereignty." *Journal of Poverty* 15: 384-402.

Outhit, Jeff. 2013. "Refugees Still Welcome, But Fewer Are Coming." *Waterloo Region Record,* 15 June.

Pagliaro, Jennifer, and Jill Mahoney. 2010. "Ontario Loses as Immigration Funds Shifted." *Globe and Mail,* 24 December.

Palmary, Ingrid, Erica Burman, Khatidja Chantler, and Peace Kiguwa. 2010. "Gender and Migration: Feminist Perspectives." In *Gender and Migration: Feminist Interventions,* ed. Ingrid Palmary, Erica Burman, Khatidja Chantler, and Peace Kiguwa, 1-11. London: Zed Books.

Pannell, Kerry, and Meryl Altman. 2009. "Minding the Gap: Feminist Perspectives on Policies Affecting Immigrant Labor in the Domestic Services Industry in Europe." *Cahiers de l'URMIS* 12 (June). http://urmis.revues.org.

Panossian, R., B. Berman, and A. Linscott. 2007. "The Missing Piece: The Politics of Identity." In *Governing Diversity: Democratic Solutions in Multicultural Societies,* ed. R. Panossian, B. Berman, and A. Linscott, 7-10. Kingston: Ethnicity and Democratic Governance, Queen's University.

Papademetriou, Demetrios G. 2003. *Policy Considerations for Immigrant Integration.* Washington, DC: Migration Policy Institute.

–. 2012. *Rethinking National Identity in the Age of Migration: Council Statement.* Washington, DC: Migration Policy Institute.

Papademetriou, Demetrios G., Doris Meissner, Marc R. Rosenblum, and Madeleine Sumption. 2009. *Harnessing the Advantages of Immigration for a 21st-Century Economy: A Standing Commission on Labor Markets, Economic Competitiveness, and Immigration.* Washington, DC: Migration Policy Institute.

Papademetriou, Demetrios G., and Madeleine Sumption. 2011. *Rethinking Points Systems and Employer-Selected Immigration.* Washington, DC: Migration Policy Institute.

Paperny, Anna Mehler. 2011. "Manitoba Probes Immigrant-Investor Plan." *Globe and Mail,* 26 December.

Papillon, Martin. 2012. "Social Cohesion, Citizenship, and Diversity in Canada." In *Diverse Nations, Diverse Responses: Approaches to Social Cohesion in Immigrant Societies,* ed. Erin Tolley and Paul Spoonley, 15-34. Queen's Policy Studies Series. Kingston: School of Policy Studies, Queen's University.

Papp, Aruna. 2011. *Culturally Driven Violence against Women: A Growing Problem in Canada's Immigrant Communities.* FCPP Policy Series No. 92. Winnipeg: Frontier Centre for Public Policy.

Paquet, Gilles. 2008. *Deep Cultural Diversity: A Governance Challenge.* Ottawa: University of Ottawa Press.

–. 2011. "About Dumbfounding Aspects of Canadian Immigration Policy." Paper presented at the roundtable organized for the 45th annual meeting of the Canadian Economics Association, University of Ottawa, 2-5 June.

Parekh, Bhikhu. 2005. *Rethinking Multiculturalism: Cultural Diversity and Political Theory.* 2nd ed. New York: Palgrave Macmillan.

–. 2007. *A New Politics of Identity: Political Principles for an Interdependent World.* New York: Palgrave Macmillan.

Park, Hijun. 2011. "Being Canada's National Citizen: Difference and the Economics of Multicultural Nationalism." *Social Identities* 17, 5: 643-63.

Parrillo, Vincent. 2009. *Understanding Race and Ethnic Relations.* 4th ed. Upper Saddle River, NJ: Pearson Education.

Pathways to Prosperity. 2014. "Immigrants: Employment Rates as a Function of Educational Level." Factsheet, February. www.p2pcanada.ca.

Payton, Laura. 2011. "Face Veils Banned for Citizenship Oaths." *CBC News,* 12 December.

Pearson, David. 2001. *The Politics of Ethnicity in Settler Societies.* London: Palgrave Macmillan.

Pécoud, Antoine, and Paul de Guchteneire. 2005. *Global Migration Perspectives.* Paper No. 27. N.p.: Global Commission on International Migration.

–. 2009. *Migration without Borders: Essays on the Free Movement of People.* Herndon, VA: Berghahn Books.

Pendakur, Krishna, and Ravi Pendakur. 2011. *Colour by Numbers: Minority Earnings in Canada, 1996-2006.* Metropolis British Columbia Working Paper No. 11-05. Vancouver: Centre of Excellence for Research on Immigration and Diversity.

Perigoe, Ross. 2006. "Muslims and Media." Paper presented at the Congress of Social Sciences, York University, Toronto, 29-31 May.

Perkel, Colin. 2008. "Highly Educated but Poorly Paid." *Globe and Mail,* 1 May.

Perlmutter, David. 2000. *Policing the Media: Street Cops and Public Perception of Law Enforcement.* Thousand Oaks, CA: Sage.

Perrault, Jean. 2009. "President's Message." Theme Report No. 5 – Immigration and Diversity in Canadian Cities and Communities, Quality of Life in Canadian Communities. Federation of Canadian Municipalities, March. http://www.fcm.ca.

Perucca, Brigitte. 2010. "US Still Top Destination for Immigrants." *The Guardian Weekly,* 17 December.

Peter, K. 1978. "Multicultural Politics, Money, and the Conduct of Canadian Ethnic Studies." *Canadian Ethnic Studies Association Bulletin* 5: 2-3.

Pew Research Center. 2013a. "'Borders First' a Dividing Line in Immigration Debate." Pew Research Center for the People and the Press. 23 June.

–. 2013b. "The State of Race in America." Aspen Institute Symposium, Washington, DC, 22 April.

Philo, Greg, Emma Briant, and Pauline Donald. 2013. *Bad News for Refugees.* London: Pluto Press.

Piché, Victor. 2010. "Global Migration Management or the Emergence of a New Restrictive and Repressive Migration World Order." Paper presented at "Disciplining Global Movements: Migration Management and Its Discontents," University of Osnabrück, Germany, 13 November.

–. 2011. "In and Out the Back Door: Canada's Temporary Worker Programs in a Global Perspective." In *The New Politics of International Mobility: Migration Management and Its Discontents,* ed. Martin Geiger and Antoine Pécoud, 113-32. Osnabrück, Germany: Institute for Migration Research and Intercultural Studies.

Pickus, Noah, and Peter Skerry. 2006. "Beyond Legal and Illegal." Office of News and Communications, Duke University. 22 May. http://today.duke.edu/.

Picot, Garnett, and Feng Hou. 2011. *Seeking Success in Canada and the United States: The Determinants of Labour Market Outcomes among the Children of Immigrants.* Statistics Canada Catalogue No. 11F0019MWE2011331. Ottawa: Government of Canada.

Picot, Garnett, and Arthur Sweetman. 2012. *Making It in Canada: Immigration Outcomes and Policies.* IRPP Study No. 29. Montreal: Institute for Research on Public Policy.

Pierce, Susan. 2011. *Immigration and Women: Understanding the American Experience.* New York: New York University Press.

Pieterse, Jan Nederveen. 2006. *Ethnicities and Global Multiculture.* Lanham, MD: Rowman and Littlefield.

Piper, Nicola, ed. 2008. *New Perspectives in Gender and Migration.* New York: Routledge.

–. 2010. "Temporary Economic Migration and Rights Activism: An Organizational Perspective." *Ethnic and Racial Studies* 33: 108-25.

Piper, Nicola, and Amber French. 2011. "Do Women Benefit from Migration? An Editorial Introduction." *Diversities* 13, 1: 1-3.

Plaut, Rabbi W. Gunther. 1989. "Unwanted Intruders or People in Flight." *Perception* 13, 2: 45-46.

Poisson, Yves. 2012. "Integrating Immigrants into the Canadian Labour Market: Findings from *Public Policy Forum* Research and Activities." In *Managing Immigration and Diversity in Canada,* ed. Dan Rodríguez-García, 184-202. Montreal/Kingston: McGill-Queen's University Press.

Pon, Gordon, Kevin Gosine, and Doret Phillips. 2011. "Immediate Response: Addressing Anti-Native and Anti-Black Racism in Child Welfare." *International Journal of Child, Youth, and Family Studies* 3-4: 385-409.

Poros, Maritsa. 2011. "Migration Social Networks: Vehicles for Migration, Integration, and Development." *Migration Information Source,* March.

Poulton, Ronald. 2010. "Wondrous Strange: A Reply to the Myth of the Evil Refugee." *Refuge* 27, 1: 119-22.

Preibisch, Kerry. 2010. "Pick Your Own Labour: Migrant Workers and Flexibility in Canadian Agriculture." *International Migration Review* 44, 2: 404-41.

–. 2012. "Development as Remittance or Development as Freedom: Exploring Canada's Temporary Migration Program from a Rights-Based Approach." In *Constitutional Labour Rights in Canada: From Farm Workers to the Fraser Case,* ed. F. Faraday, J. Fudge, and E. Tucker. Toronto: Irwin Law.

PROMPT. 2004. "In the Public Interest: Immigrant Access to Regulated Professions in Today's Ontario." Toronto: PROMPT.

Proudfoot, Shannon. 2010. "Migrant Worker Program 'Exploitative,' Researchers Warn." *Edmonton Journal,* 27 April.

Pulitano, Elvira. 2013. "In Liberty's Shadow: The Discourse of Refugees and Asylum Seekers in Critical Race Theory and Immigration Law/Politics." *Identities: Global Studies in Culture and Power* 20, 2: 172-89.

Putnam, Robert D. 2007. "*E Pluribus Unum:* Diversity and Community in the Twenty-First Century." *Scandinavian Political Studies* 30, 2: 137-74.

Putz, Ulrike. 2013. "'Don't Forget Your Photo Albums!' The Flight of Syria's Middle Classes." *Der Spiegel Online International,* 29 January. http://www.spiegel.de/.

Qadeer, Mohammad, and Sandeep Kumar. 2006. "Ethnic Enclaves and Social Cohesion." *Canadian Journal of Urban Research* 15, 2: 1-17.

Quan, Douglas. 2011. "Sri Lanka Refugee Claims Treated Favourably: Data." *National Post,* 14 January.

Radia, Andy. 2011. "Immigration in 2011: Exclusive Interview with Minister Jason Kenney." http://www.canadianimmigrant.ca.

–. 2012. "Immigration Minister Jason Kenney Defends Transformation of Canada's Immigration System." 23 September. http://ca.news.yahoo.com.

Rahme, Thalia. 2012. "Arab World: The Plight of Syrian Refugee Girls." *Global Voices,* 12 October. http://globalvoicesonline.org.

Rajagopalan, Sumitra. 2011. "The Dragon's Den Approach to Immigration." *Globe and Mail,* 31 July.

Rajiva, Mythili. 2005. "Bridging the Generation Gap: Exploring the Differences between Immigrant Parents and Their Canadian-Born Children." *Canadian Issues* (Spring): 25-29.

Raleigh, Elizabeth, and Grace Kao. 2010. "Do Immigrant Minority Parents Have More Consistent College Aspirations for Their Children?" *Social Science Quarterly* 91, 4: 1083-102.

Rampell, Catherine. 2013. "Immigrant Doctors Stymied by American Licensing Rules." *New York Times,* 18 August.

Ramsaroop, Chris, and Adrian A. Smith. 2014. "Time to Address Racism Underlying Temporary Foreign Worker Program." *Toronto Star,* 21 May.

Rankin, Jim. 2007. "Series Exposed an Immigration Scam." *Toronto Star,* 30 December.

Rankin, Jim, and Patty Winsa. 2013. "As Criticism Piles Up, So Do Police Cards." *Toronto Star,* 27 September.

Ratha, Dilip. 2013. *The Impact of Remittances on Economic Growth and Poverty Reduction.* Policy Brief No. 8. Washington, DC: Migration Policy Institute.

Rathzel, N. 2003. "Antagonistic Girls, or Why the Foreigners Are the Real Germans." In *The Social Construction of Diversity,* ed. C. Harzig and D. Juteau, 40-61. New York: Berghahn Books.

Ray, Brian. 2003. "The Role of Cities in Immigrant Integration." *Migration Information Source,* October.

Ray, Brian, and Rose Damaris. 2012. "How Gender Matters to Immigration and Settlement in Canada and the United States." In *Immigrant Geographies of North America,* ed. Carlos Teixeira, Wei Li, and Audrey Kobayashi, 138-57. Toronto: Oxford University Press.

RBC. 2011. "RBC Diversity Blueprint, 2009-2011: Priorities and Objectives."

RBC Economics. 2011. "Immigrant Labour Market Outcomes in Canada: The Benefits of Addressing Wage and Employment Gaps." *Current Analysis,* December.

RBC Financial Group. 2005. "'The Diversity Advantage': A Case for Canada's 21st Century Economy." Paper presented at the 10th International Metropolis Conference, Toronto, 20 October.

Rechitsky, Raphi. 2010. "Rethinking Social Exclusion and Belonging in Global Perspective: The Case of Transnational Migrants in Ukraine." *Political Perspectives* 4, 2: 86-104.

Redhead, Mark. 2003. "Charles Taylor's Deeply Diverse Response to Canada's Fragmentation: A Project Often Commented on but Seldom Explored." *Canadian Journal of Political Science* 36, 1: 61-83.

Refugee Council of Australia. 2013. "Australia's Refugee Response Not the Most Generous, but in Top 25." 19 July. http://www.refugeecouncil.org.au.

Rehaag, Sean. 2009. "Troubling Patterns in Canadian Refugee Adjudication." *Ottawa Law Review* 39.

–. 2012. "Judicial Review of Refugee Determinations: The Luck of the Draw? *Queen's Law Journal* 38, 1. http://queensu.ca/lawjournal/issues/1-Rehaag.pdf.

Reinhart, Anthony. 2007. "A Nation of Newcomers." *Globe and Mail,* 5 December.

Reinhart, Anthony, and James Rusk. 2006. "Immigrants Suffer in Silence within Walls of Suburbs." *Globe and Mail,* 11 March.

Reitz, Jeffrey. 1998. *Warmth of the Welcome: The Social Causes of Economic Success for Canadian Immigration Policy in the Knowledge Economy.* Boulder, CO: Westview Press.

–. 2003. "Canadian Immigration Policy." In *Immigration and Asylum: From 1000 to the Present,* ed. Matthew J. Gibney and Randall Hansen. Santa Barbara: ABC-CLIO.

–. 2005. "Tapping Immigrant Skills: New Directions for Canadian Immigration Policy in the Knowledge Economy." *IRRP Choices* 11, 1. http://www.irpp.org/choices/archive/ vol11no1.pdf.

–. 2006. "Does North American Experience in Immigration Incorporation Have Lessons for Europe?" Keynote address at the third annual conference of IMISCOE (International Migration, Integration, and Social Cohesion), Vienna, 5 September.

–. 2009. "Introduction." In *Multiculturalism and Social Cohesion: Potentials and Challenges of Diversity,* ed. J.G. Reitz, R. Breton, K.K. Dion, and K.L. Dion. London: Springer.

–. 2010a. "Getting Past 'Yes' or 'No.'" *Literary Review of Canada,* July-August.

–. 2010b. "Selecting Immigrants for the Short Term: Is It Smart in the Long Run?" *Policy Options,* July-August.

–. 2011a. *Pro-Immigration Canada: Social and Economic Roots of Popular Views.* IRPP Study No. 20. Montreal: Institute for Research on Public Policy.

–. 2011b. "Taxi Driver Syndrome." *Literary Review of Canada,* March.

–. 2012a. "The Distinctiveness of Canadian Immigration Experience." *Patterns of Prejudice* 46, 5: 518-40.

–. 2012b. "Managing Immigration and Diversity in Canada and Quebec: Lessons for Spain?" In *Managing Immigration and Diversity in Canada,* ed. Dan Rodríguez-García, 61-86. Montreal/Kingston: McGill-Queen's University Press.

–. 2013. "Closing the Gaps between Skilled Immigration and Canadian Labour Markets: Emerging Policy Issues and Priorities." In *Wanted and Welcome? Policies for Highly Skilled Immigrants in Comparative Perspective,* ed. T. Triadafilopoulos, 147-62. New York: Springer Science and Business.

Reitz, Jeffrey, and Rupa Banerjee. 2007. "Racial Inequality, Social Cohesion, and Policy Issues." In *Belonging? Diversity, Recognition, and Shared Citizenship in Canada,* ed. Keith Banting, Thomas J. Courchene, and F. Leslie Seidle, 611-46. Montreal: Institute for Research on Public Policy.

Reitz, Jeffrey, Josh Curtis, and Jennifer Elrick. 2014. "Immigration Skill Utilization: Trends and Policy Issues." *Journal of International Migration and Integration* 15: 1-26.

Rekai, Peter. 2002. *US and Canadian Immigration Programs: Marching Together to Different Tunes.* C.D. Howe Institute Commentary No. 171. Toronto: C.D. Howe Institute.

Renshon, Stanley. 2010. "Paradigm Shift: Updating Immigration Policy's 'Conventional Wisdom.'" Centre for Immigration Studies. 26 August. http://www.cis.org.

Reuters. 2012. "Australia Eases Labor Restrictions on Foreigners." *International Herald Tribune,* 26-27 May.

Reyes, Fernando, J., M. Walton-Roberts, and J.L. Hennebry. 2013. "Inventory of Services Provided to Immigrants and Refugees in the Waterloo Region." *Policy Points* 4. http://imrc.ca/wp-content/uploads/2013/10/Policy-Points-Issue-IV.pdf.

Riddell, Chris. 2013. "Immigration Incentive." *National Post,* 17 June.

Ritzer, George. 2008. *The McDonaldization of Society.* 5th ed. Los Angeles: Pine Forge Press.

Rizzo, Alessandra. 2011. "UN Refugee Chief Wants Borders to Be Kept Open." *Waterloo Region Record,* 21 June.

Robinson, William. 1998. "Beyond Nation-State Paradigms: Globalization, Sociology, and the Challenge of Transnational Studies." *Sociology Forum* 13, 4: 561-72.

–. 2007. "Globalization and the Struggle for Immigrant Rights in the United States." ZNet, 10 March. http://www.zcommunications.org/.

Rodríguez-García, Dan. 2010. "Beyond Assimilation and Multiculturalism: A Critical Review of the Debate on Managing Diversity." *Journal of International Migration and Integration* 11, 3: 251-71.

–. 2012. "Managing Immigration and Diversity in the New Age of Migration: A Transatlantic Dialogue." In *Managing Immigration and Diversity in Canada,* ed. Dan Rodríguez-García, 1-60. Montreal/Kingston: McGill-Queen's University Press.

Roman, Ediberto. 2013. *Those Damned Immigrants: America's Hysteria over Undocumented Immigration.* New York: New York Press.

Roy, Patricia E. 1989. *A White Man's Province: British Columbia Politicians and Chinese and Japanese Immigrants, 1858-1914.* Vancouver: UBC Press.

Royal Geographical Society. 2009. "UK Migration Controversies: A Simple Guide." London. http://www.rgs.org/.

Ruddick, Elizabeth. 2010. "Earnings of Skilled Immigrants: Recent Research Findings." Paper presented at the "Canada's Immigration Policy Conference," Ottawa, 25-26 May.

Rudoren, Jodi. 2013. "A Generation of Syrians Lost to Refugee Struggles." *New York Times,* 19 May.

Ruhs, Martin. 2012. "The Human Rights of Migrant Workers: Why Do So Few Countries Care?" *American Behavioral Scientist* 20, 10: 1-17.

Ruhs, Martin, and Bridget Anderson. 2010. *Who Needs Migrant Workers? Labour Shortages, Immigration, and Public Policy.* New York: Oxford University Press.

Rutter, Jill. 2013. "The Principles of Migration Policy." Left Foot Forward. 18 January. http://www.leftfootforward.org/.

Ryan, Phil. 2010. *Multicultiphobia.* Toronto: University of Toronto Press.

Rygiel, Kim. 2010. *Globalizing Citizenship*. Vancouver: UBC Press.

Safian, Robert. 2012. "The Secrets of Generation Flux." *Fast Company,* February. http://www.fastcompany.com/.

Saggar, Shamit, and Will Somerville. 2012. "Building a British Model of Integration in an Era of Immigration: Policy Lessons for Government." Transatlantic Council on Migration. http://www.migrationpolicy.org/pubs/uk-countrystudy.pdf.

Sakamoto, Izumi, Daphne Jeyapal, Rupaleem Bhuyan, Jane Ku, Lin Fang, Heidi Zhang, and Flavia Genovese. 2013. *An Overview of Discourses of Skilled Immigrants and "Canadian Experience": An English-Language Print Media Analysis*. CERIS Working Paper No. 98. Toronto: Ontario Metropolis Centre.

Samers, Michael. 2010. *Migration*. London: Routledge.

Samuel, John. 2004. "Barriers to Attracting and Retaining Immigrants to Atlantic Canada." *National Post*.

Samuel, J., and D. Schachhuber. 2000. "Perspectives on Canadian Diversity." In *21st-Century Canadian Diversity,* ed. S. Nancoo, 14-35. Mississauga: Canadian Educators' Press.

Sandercock, Leonie. 2003. *Cosmopolis 11: Mongrel Cities in the 21st Century*. London: Continuum.

–. 2006. *Rethinking Multiculturalism for the 21st Century*. Working Paper No. 03-14. Vancouver: Centre of Excellence for Research on Immigration and Diversity.

Sandhu, Ravinder. 2003. "Minorities within Minorities." *Toronto Star,* 26 August.

Sassen, Saskia. 2003. "Strategic Instantiations of Gendering in the Global Economy." In *Gender and US Immigration: Contemporary Trends,* ed. Pierrette Hondagneu-Sotelo, 43-60. Berkeley: University of California Press.

Satzewich, Vic. 2000. "Whiteness Limited: Racialization and the Social Construction of 'Peripheral Europeans.'" *Histoire sociale/Social History* 23: 271-90.

–. 2007-08. "Multiculturalism, Transnationalism, and the Hijacking of Canadian Foreign Policy: A Pseudo Problem?" *International Journal,* Winter.

Satzewich, Vic, and Nikolaos Liodakis. 2010. *"Race" and Ethnicity in Canada: A Critical Introduction*. Toronto: Oxford University Press.

–. 2013. *"Race" and Ethnicity in Canada: A Critical Introduction*. 3rd ed. Toronto: Oxford University Press.

Satzewich, Vic, and Lloyd Wong, eds. 2006. *Transnational Identities and Practices in Canada*. Vancouver: UBC Press.

Saunders, Doug. 2011a. "Obama's Wide Investment Making Life Easier for 'Illegals.'" *Globe and Mail,* 14 May.

–. 2011b. "The Rights of Refugees." *Literary Review of Canada,* July-August.

–. 2011c. "Swedes Look to Canada as a Model for Immigration." *Globe and Mail,* 14 October.

–. 2012a. *The Myth of the Muslim Tide*. Toronto: Alfred A. Knopf.

–. 2012b. "What Would a Canada of 100 Million Feel Like? More Comfortable, Better Served, Better Defended." *Globe and Mail,* 18 May.

–. 2014. "They Won't Be Temporary if We Make Them Permanent." *Globe and Mail,* 26 April.

Schaeffer, Peter. 2009. "Refugees: On the Economics of Political Migration." *International Migration* 48, 1.

Scheffer, Paul. 2010. *Immigrant Nations*. Cambridge: Polity Press.

Schellenberg, Grant, and Feng Hou. 2005. "The Economic Well-Being of Recent Immigrants to Canada." *Canadian Issues* (Spring): 49-52.

Schellenberg, Grant, and Helene Maheux. 2007. "Immigrants' Perspectives on Their First Four Years in Canada." *Canadian Social Trends,* Catalogue No. 11-008, 2-22.

Schlesinger, Arthur M., Jr. 1992. *The Disuniting of America: Reflections on a Multicultural Society.* New York: W.W. Norton.

Schmid-Druner, Marion. 2006. "Germany's New Immigration Law: A Paradigm Shift?" *European Journal of Migration and Law* 8: 191-214.

Schmidtke, Oliver. 2012. *Citizenship and Multiculturalism in the 21st Century: The Changing Face of Social, Cultural, and Civic Inclusion.* Metropolis British Columbia Working Paper No. 12-06. Vancouver: Centre of Excellence for Research on Immigration and Diversity.

Schouls, Tim. 1997. "Aboriginal Peoples and Electoral Reform in Canada: Differentiated Representation versus Voter Equality." *Canadian Journal of Political Science* 24, 4: 729–49.

Scoffield, Heather. 2010a. "Canada Boosting Intake from UN Refugee Camps." *Waterloo Region Record,* 30 March.

–. 2010b. "Moving Target: Migrants and the Law." *Globe and Mail,* 15 October.

–. 2011. "Tories Propose New Immigration Point System to Favour Youth." *Waterloo Region Record,* 18 February.

Sears, Robin V. 2008. "Canada: If You Build It, People Will Come." *Policy Options* (June): 38-44.

Seattle Post Intelligencer. 2010. "Rethinking Immigration." 23 November.

Segal, Uma A., Doreen Elliott, and Nazneen S. Mayadas. 2009. *Immigration Worldwide: Policies, Practices, and Trends.* New York: Oxford University Press.

Segal, Uma A., Nazneen S. Mayadas, and Doreen Elliott. 2006. "A Framework for Immigration." *Journal of Immigrant and Refugee Studies* 4, 1: 3-24.

Seidle, Leslie. 2012. "Canada's Provincial Nominee Programs." Institute for Research on Public Policy, 12 December.

–. 2013. "Immigrant Integration in Federal Countries: Language Skills, Civic Knowledge, and Identity." *Canadian Issues* (Spring): 61-66.

Selley, Chris. 2011. "Canada's Broken Immigration System." *National Post,* 4 November.

–. 2013. "In Defence of Jason Kenney." *National Post,* 2 August.

Semple, Kirk. 2014. "Influx of Immigrants Revitalizes New York." *New York Times International Weekly,* 22-23 March.

Shakir, Uzma. 2010. "Canada's Immigration Fall from Grace." Report published by the Atkinson Charitable Foundation, 12 May. http://atkinson foundation.ca.

Shane, Kirsten. 2012. "Canada Could Face Lawsuits if It Legislates Away Immigration Backlog." http://embassymag.ca.

Shariff, Farha. 2008. "The Liminality of Culture: Second Generation South Asian Canadian Identity and the Potential for Postcolonial Texts." *Journal of Teaching and Learning* 5, 2: 67-80.

Sharma, Nandita. 2006. *Home Economics: Nationalism and the Making of "Migrant Workers" in Canada*. Toronto: University of Toronto Press.

–. 2007. "Freedom to Discriminate: A National State Sovereignty and Temporary Migrant Workers in Canada." In *Citizenship and Immigrant Incorporation*, ed. G. Yurdakul and M. Bodemann, 163-83. New York: Palgrave Macmillan.

Sheller, Mimi, and John Urry. 2006. "The New Mobilities Paradigm." *Environment and Planning A* 38: 207-26.

Shelley, Louise. 2010. *Human Trafficking: A Global Perspective*. New York: Cambridge University Press.

Sherwood, Harriet. 2012. "Syrians at Refugee Camps Struggle with Choking Sand and Wretched Conditions." *Guardian*, 3 September.

Shields, John. 2003. *No Safe Haven: Markets, Welfare, and Migrants*. CERIS Working Paper No. 22. Toronto: Ontario Metropolis Centre.

Shinn, Christopher A. 2006. "Multicultural Books and the Culture Wars in the 21st Century." Paper presented at the Fourth Annual Conference on the Book, Emerson College, Boston, 20-22 October. http://b06.cgpublishers.com.

Shome, Raka. 2012. "Mapping the Limits of Multiculturalism in the Context of Globalization." *International Journal of Communication* 6: 144-65.

Showler, Peter. 2006. *Refugee Sandwich: Stories of Exile and Asylum*. Montreal/Kingston: McGill-Queen's University Press.

Showler, Peter, and Maytree Foundation. N.d. "Fast, Fair, and Final: Reforming Canada's Refugee System: Questions and Answers for Media." http://maytree.com.

Siddiqui, Haroon. 2013a. "Canada Needs a National Debate on Immigration." *Toronto Star*, 23 May.

–. 2013b. "Memo to Chris Alexander, New Immigration Minister." *Toronto Star*, 25 July.

Siemiatycki, Myer. 2005. "Introduction." *Canadian Issues* (Spring): 3-4.

–. 2010. "Marginalizing Migrants: Canada's Rising Reliance on Temporary Foreign Workers." *Canadian Issues* (Spring): 60-63.

–. 2012. "The Place of Immigrants: Citizenship, Settlement, and Socio-Cultural Integration in Canada." In *Managing Immigration and Diversity in Canada*, ed. Dan Rodríguez-García, 223-48. Montreal/Kingston: McGill-Queen's University Press.

Silk, Mark. 2008. "Islam and the American News Media Post September 11." In *Mediating Religion*, ed. Jolyon P. Mitchell and Sophia Marriage, 73-88. New York: T. and T. Clark, a Continuum Imprint.

Silnicki, Adrienne. 2014. "Standing Up for Refugee Rights: Refugee Health Care in Federal Court." Council of Canadians blog, 28 January. http://rabble.ca.

Simmons, Alan. 2010. *Immigration and Canada: Global and Transnational Perspectives*. Toronto: Canadian Scholars' Press.

Simon-Kumar, Rachel. 2012. "Difference and Diversity in Aotearoa/New Zealand: Post-Neoliberal Constructions of the Ideal Ethnic Citizen." Subsequently published in *Ethnicities* 14, 1 (2014): 136-59.

Simpson, Jeffrey. 2009. "Unwieldy Refugee System, IRB Vacancies – Our Canada at Work." *Globe and Mail*, 7 February.

–. 2013. "Has Kenney Found the Right Balance?" *Globe and Mail,* 23 January.

Singh, Kulbir. 2000. "When Two Cultures Collide." *Visions: BC's Mental Health Journal* 9: 25-26.

Sirojudin, Siroj. 2009. "Economic Theories of Emigration." *Journal of Human Behavior in the Social Environment* 19, 6: 702-12.

Skeldon, Ronald. 2009. *The Global Economic Crisis and Migration: Policies and Practice in Origin and Destination.* Working Paper T-32. Brighton, UK: Development Research Centre on Migration, Globalisation and Poverty.

Skey, Michael. 2013. "What Does It Mean to Be Cosmopolitan? An Examination of the Varying Meaningfulness and Commensurability of Everyday 'Cosmopolitan' Practices." *Identities: Global Studies in Culture and Power* 20, 3: 235-52.

Skrentny, John D., Micah Gell-Redman, and Jack Jin Gary Lee. 2012. "Japan, the United States and the Philosophical Bases of Immigration Policy." *American Behavioral Scientist* 56, 8: 995-1007.

Smith, Anthony. 2013. "'The Land and Its People': Reflections on an Artistic Identification in an Age of Nations and Nationalism." *Nations and Nationalism* 19, 1: 87-106.

Smith, Patricia. 2010. "The Great Immigration Debate." *New York Times Upfront Magazine.* http://www.upfrontmagazine.com.

Smolkin, Sheryl. 2013. "Denny's Settles Foreign Worker's Suit." *Toronto Star,* 22 July.

Sodhi, Pavna. 2008. "Bicultural Identity Formation of Second-Generation Indo-Canadians." *Canadian Ethnic Studies* 40, 2: 187-99.

Soennecken, Dagmar. 2014. "Shifting Up and Back: The European Turn in Canadian Refugee Policy." *Comparative Migration Studies* 2, 1: 101-22.

Sofos, S.A., and R. Tsagarousianou. 2012. "Introduction: Back to the Drawing Board: Rethinking Multiculturalism." *Journal of Contemporary European Studies* 20, 3: 262-71.

Solberg, Monte. 2006. "Interview." *Canadian Issues* (Spring): 7-8.

Solomon, Lawrence. 2014. "Discrimination in Immigration." *National Post,* 13 February.

Somerville, Kara, and Scott Walsworth. 2010. "Admission and Employment Criteria Discrepancies: Experiences of Skilled Immigrants in Toronto." *International Migration and Integration* 11: 341-52.

Somerville, Will. 2009. "Future Immigration Patterns and Policies in the United Kingdom." Transatlantic Council on Migration. http://www.migrationpolicy.org/pubs/TCM-UKPatterns.pdf.

Sotloff, Steven. 2013. "Refugees Stuck in Syrian Purgatory." *Toronto Star,* 3 February.

Soto, Lilia. 2012. "On Becoming Mexican in Napa: Mexican Immigrant Girls Negotiating Challenges to Transnational Identities." *Social Identities* 18, 1: 19-37.

Soutphommasane, Tim. 2012. *Don't Go Back To Where You Came From.* Coogee, NSW: NewSouth Books.

Spoonley, Paul. 2009. "Rethinking Immigration." Asia New Zealand Foundation. http://www.asianz.nz.

Spoonley, Paul, and Richard Bedford. 2012. *Welcome to Our World? Immigration and the Reshaping of New Zealand.* Auckland: Dunmore.

Spoonley, Paul, and Andrew Butcher. 2009. "Reporting Superdiversity: The Mass Media and Immigration in New Zealand." *Journal of Intercultural Studies* 30, 4: 355-72.

Spoonley, Paul, and Erin Tolley, eds. 2012. *Diverse Nations, Diverse Responses: Approaches to Social Cohesion in Immigrant Societies.* Queen's Policy Studies Series. Kingston: School of Policy Studies, Queen's University.

Squires, Judith. 2007. "Negotiating Equality and Diversity in Britain: Towards a Differentiated Citizenship." *Critical Review of International Social and Political Philosophy* 10, 4: 531-59.

Stadelmann-Elder, Markus. 2011. "A Fast and Fair Refugee System: A Slogan or a Reality?" Maytree Conversations. 1 May. http://maytree.com/.

Stalker, Peter. 2009. *The No-Nonsense Guide to International Migration.* Oxford: New Internationalist.

Stanford, Jim. 2014. "TWFs Threatened the Conservative Coalition." *Globe and Mail,* 30 April.

Stasiulis, Daiva K., and Abigail B. Bakan. 1997. "Negotiating Citizenship: The Case of Foreign Domestic Workers in Canada." *Feminist Review* 57: 112-39.

–. 2005. *Negotiating Citizenship: Migrant Women in Canada and the Global System.* Toronto: University of Toronto Press.

Statistics Canada. 2008a. "Earnings and Incomes of Canadians over the Past Quarter Century: 2006 Census." No. 97-563-XIE2006001. http://www12.statcan.gc.ca/.

–. 2008b. "Meeting Immigrants' Expectations." http://www41.statcan.gc.ca/.

–. 2011. "Obtaining Canadian Citizenship: National Household Survey (NHS), 2011." Catalogue No. 99-010-X2011003. http://www12.statcan.gc.ca/nhs-enm/2011/as-sa/99-010-x/99-010-x2011003_1-eng.pdf.

–. 2012. "Study: Canada's Immigrant Labour Market, 2008-2011." *The Daily,* 14 December.

–. 2013. "Immigration and Ethnocultural Diversity in Canada: National Household Survey, 2011." Catalogue No. 99-010-X2011001. http://www12.statcan.gc.ca/nhs-enm/2011/as-sa/99-010-x/99-010-x2011001-eng.pdf.

Steiner, Niklaus. 2009. *International Migration and Citizenship Today.* New York: Routledge.

Stoffman, Daniel. 2002. *Who Gets In: What's Wrong with Canada's Immigration Program and How to Fix It.* Toronto: Macfarlane, Walter and Ross.

–. 2008. "Truths and Myths about Immigration." In *Immigration Policy and the Terrorist Threat in Canada and the United States,* ed. A. Moens and M. Collacott, 3-20. Vancouver: Fraser Institute.

–. 2009a. "Are We Safe Yet?" *The Walrus,* May.

–. 2009b. "Immigration." A joint venture between the Dominion Institute and the *Globe and Mail.* http://www.theglobeandmail.com.

Strategic Workshop on Immigrant Women Making Place in Canadian Cities. 2002. *Policy-Relevant Research on Immigration and Settlement – Relevant for Whom? A Working Document.* Montreal: Urbanisation, Culture et Société, Institut national de la recherche scientifique, and Immigration et Métropoles.

Suarez-Orozco, Marcelo M. 2001. "Globalization, Immigration, and Education: The Research Agenda." *Harvard Educational Review* 71, 3: 345-65.

Suhasini, Gloria. 2012. "New Policies Could Change the Demographics of Canada." *Canadian Immigrant,* 9 July. http://canadianimmigrant.ca.

Sumption, Madeleine, and Claire Bergeron. 2013. "Remaking the US Green Card System." Migration Policy Institute Issue Brief No. 6. http://www.migrationpolicy.org/pubs/CIRbrief-LegalFlows.pdf.

Sun, Wanning, Audrey Yue, John Sinclair, and Jia Gao. 2011. "Diasporic Chinese Media in Australia: A Post-2008 Overview." *Continuum: Journal of Media and Cultural Studies* 25, 4: 515-27.

Surette, Ray. 2007. *Media Crimes and Criminal Justice: Images and Realities.* 2nd ed. Toronto: Wadsworth.

Suro, Roberto. 2008. "The Triumph of No: How the Media Influence the Immigration Debate." In *A Report on the Media and the Immigration Debate,* 1-45. Washington, DC: Governance Studies at Brookings.

—. 2009. "Promoting Misconceptions: News Media Coverage of Immigration." Center for the Study of Immigrant Integration. http://csii.usc.edu/documents/suro1_v2.pdf.

Swain, Carole, ed. 2007. *Debating Immigration.* Cambridge: Cambridge University Press.

Sweetman, Arthur. 2011. "Age, Language Are Key to Better Outcomes for Immigrants." *Globe and Mail,* 3 August.

Sweetman, Arthur, and Casey Warman. 2010. "Canada's Temporary Foreign Workers Program." *Canadian Issues* (Spring): 19-24.

Sykes, Stuart. 2008. "A Story of Reefs and Oceans: A Framework for the Analysis of the 'New' Second Generation in Canada." Discussion Paper. Ottawa: Policy Research Initiative.

Tal, Benjamin. 2012. "Long Term Immigration Approach Needed to Maximize Newcomers' Employability." *National Post,* 24 July.

Tannock, Stuart. 2011. "Points of Prejudice: Education-Based Discrimination in Canada's Immigration System." *Antipode* 43, 4: 1330-56.

Taras, Raymond. 2012. *Xenophobia and Islamophobia in Europe.* Edinburgh: Edinburgh University Press.

Tarrow, Sidney. 2005. *The New Transnational Activism.* Cambridge: Cambridge University Press.

Tastsoglou, Evangelia. 2008. "Introduction: The Experiences of Second Generation Canadian Youth." *Canadian Ethnic Studies* 40, 2: 1-3.

—. 2011. "Women, Gender, and Immigration: Focus on Atlantic Canada." In *Immigrant Women in Atlantic Canada: Challenges, Negotiations, Re-Constructions,* ed. Evangelia Tastsoglou and Peruvemba S. Jaya, 1-52. Toronto: Canadian Scholars' Press/Women's Press.

Tastsoglou, Evangelia, Brian Ray, and Valerie Preston. 2005. "Gender and Migration Intersections in a Canadian Context." *Canadian Issues* (Spring): 91-93.

Taylor, Alison, and Jason Foster. 2014. "Migrant Workers and the Problem of Social Cohesion." *International Journal of Migration and Integration,* 15 March. DOI: 10.1007/s12134-014-0323-y.

Taylor, Lesley Ciarula. 2009a. "Best Immigrants Not a Priority." *Toronto Star,* 22 July.

–. 2009b. "Immigration System Hurts More Than Helps, Study Finds." *Toronto Star,* 18 June.

–. 2009c. "Is Mix of Integration Programs Delivering?" *Toronto Star,* 15 January.

Taylor, Peter Shawn. 2005. "Help Wanted." *Canadian Business,* 14-27 March, 29-34.

Tchen, John Kuo Wei, and Dylan Yeats. 2014. *Yellow Peril! An Archive of Anti-Asian Fear.* Brooklyn: Verso.

TD Economics. 2012. "Knocking Down Barriers Faced by New Immigrants to Canada." http://www.td.com/document/PDF/economics/special/ff0212_immigration.pdf.

Teixeira, Carlos, Wei Li, and Audrey Kobayashi, eds. 2012. *Immigrant Geographies of North American Cities.* Toronto: Oxford University Press.

Tendoh, Constance Inju. 2009. "Immigrants' Perspectives about Home and the Politics of Return." 4 August. http://www.articlesbase.com.

ter Wal, Jessika, Leen d'Haenens, and Joyce Koeman. 2005. "(Re)presentation of Ethnicity in EU and Dutch Domestic News: A Quantitative Analysis." *Media, Culture, and Society* 27, 6: 937-50.

Thobani, Sunera. 2000. "Closing Ranks: Racism and Sexism in Canadian Immigration Policy." *Race and Class* 42, 1: 35-55.

–. 2007. *Exalted Subjects: Studies in the Making of Race and Nation in Canada.* Toronto: University of Toronto Press.

Thomas, Derrick. 2010. "Foreign Nationals Working Temporarily in Canada." *Canadian Social Trends.* Statistics Canada Catalogue No. 11-008-X. 8 June. http://www.statcan.gc.ca/.

Thompson, Allan. 2010. "Refugee System Overhaul Has a Split Personality." *Toronto Star,* 10 April.

–. 2011a. "Human Smuggling Bill Lacks Logic and Justice." *Toronto Star,* 25 June.

–. 2011b. "Sponsoring Parents in Canada." *Toronto Star,* 19 November.

Thompson, Ginger, and Sarah Cohen. 2014. "More Deportations Follow Minor Crimes, Records Show." *New York Times,* 7 April.

Thoreau, Cécile, and Thomas Liebig. 2012. "Settling In: OECD Indicators of Immigrant Integration." OECD. 3 December. http://www.oecd.org/els/mig/Secretariat_Press_3Dec2012_Final%20REV.pdf.

Tichenor, Daniel J. 2009. "Navigating an American Minefield: The Politics of Illegal Immigration." *The Forum: The Politics of Immigration Reform* 7, 3.

–. 2012. "The Great Divide: The Politics of Illegal Immigration in America." In *Global Migration,* ed. Kavita Khory, 155-82. New York: Palgrave.

Timberlake, J.M., and R.H. Williams. 2012. "Stereotypes of US Immigrants from Four Global Regions." *Social Science Quarterly* 93: 867-90.

Todd, Douglas. 2013. "Rising Poverty among Immigrants a 'Tinderbox,' Study Warns." *Vancouver Sun,* 28 June.

Tolley, Erin, John Biles, Caroline Andrew, Victoria M. Esses, and Meyer Burstein. 2013. "Introduction: From Metropolis to Welcoming Communities." In *Immigration, Integration, and Inclusion in Ontario Cities,* ed. Caroline Andrew, John Biles, Meyer Burstein, Vicki Esses, and Erin Tolley, 1-20. Montreal/Kingston: McGill-Queen's University Press.

Tolley, Erin, and Paul Spoonley. 2012. "Introduction." In *Diverse Nations, Diverse Responses: Approaches to Social Cohesion in Immigrant Societies,* ed. Erin Tolley and Paul Spoonley, 1-14. Queen's Policy Studies Series. Kingston: School of Policy Studies, Queen's University.

Toronto Star. 2010. "Text of Throne Speech." 3 March.

Tossutti, Livianna S. 2012. "Municipal Roles in Immigrant Settlement, Integration, and Cultural Diversity." *Canadian Journal of Political Science* 45, 3: 607-33.

Toten, Teresa. 2011. *Piece by Piece: Stories about Fitting into Canada.* Toronto: Penguin.

Tran, Kelly, Stan Kustec, and Tina Chui. 2005. "Becoming Canadian: Intent, Process, and Outcome." *Canadian Social Trends* (Spring): 8-10.

Transatlantic Trends. 2009. "Immigration." The German Marshall Fund of the United States. http://trends.gmfus.org.

–. 2010. "Immigration 2010: Key Findings." http://trends.gmfus.org/files/archived/immigration/doc/TTI2010_English_Key.pdf.

Trepanier, Lee, and Khalil M. Habib. 2011. "Introduction." In *Cosmopolitanism in the Age of Globalization,* ed. Lee Trepanier and K.M. Habib. Lexington: University of Kentucky Press.

Triadafilopoulos, Triadafilos. 2006. "Family Immigration Policy in Comparative Perspective." *Canadian Issues* (Spring): 30-33.

–. 2010. "Global Norms, Domestic Institutions, and the Transformation of Immigration Policy in Canada and the US." *Review of International Studies* 36: 169-93.

–. 2011. "Illiberal Means to Liberal Ends? Understanding Recent Immigrant Integration Policies in Europe." *Journal of Ethnic and Migration Studies* 37, 6: 861-80.

–. 2012. *Becoming Multicultural: Immigration and the Politics of Membership in Canada and Germany.* Vancouver: UBC Press.

–. 2013. "Dismantling White Canada: Race, Rights, and the Origins of the Points System." In *Wanted and Welcome? Immigrants and Minorities, Politics and Policy,* ed. Triadafilos Triadafilopoulos. New York: Springer Science and Business.

–. N.d. "A Model for Europe? An Appraisal of Canadian Integration Policies." http://triadafilopoulos.files.wordpress.com.

Triadafilopoulos, Triadafilos, and Shaun P. Young. 2011. "Multiculturalism as a Deliberative Ethic." Paper presented at the Canadian Political Science Association meeting, Wilfrid Laurier University, Waterloo, ON, 16-18 May.

Triandafyllidou, Anna. 2011. *Addressing Cultural, Ethnic, and Religious Diversity Challenges in Europe.* Accept Pluralism Working Paper 2/2011. San Domenico di Fiesole, Italy: European University Institute.

Trumper, Ricardo, and Lloyd L. Wong. 2010. "Temporary Workers in Canada: A National Perspective." *Canadian Issues* (Spring): 83-89.

Tully, James. 1995. *Strange Multiplicity: Constitutionalism in an Age of Diversity.* Cambridge: Cambridge University Press.

Turton, Anthony R., Hanlie J. Hattingh, Gillian A. Maree, Dirk J. Roux, Marius Claassen, and Wilma F. Strydom, eds. 2007. *Governance as a Trialogue: Government-Society-Science in Transition.* New York: Springer.

Ucarer, Emek. 1997. "Introduction: The Coming of an Era of Human Uprootedness: A Global Challenge." In *Immigration into Western Societies: Problems and Policies,* ed. Emek Ucarer and D. Puchala, 1-16. London: Cassells.

UNDP. 2009. *Overcoming Barriers: Human Mobility and Development.* Human Development Report. New York: UNDP.

UNHCR. 2009. "UN Refugee Chief Cites Pressing Needs as Those Uprooted Tops 42 Million." 16 June. http://www.unhcr.org/.

–. 2011. "Addressing Security Concerns without Undermining Refugee Protection: UNHCR's Perspective." http://www.un.org.

–. 2012. "Global Trends 2012." http://unhcr.org/globaltrendsjune2013/UNHCR%20GLOBAL%20TRENDS%202012_V05.pdf.

–. 2014. "Asylum Trends 2013." http://www.unhcr.org/532afe986.html

Urbanski, M. 2004. "What Doctor Shortage?" *Toronto Star,* 19 August.

Urry, John. 2000. *Sociology beyond Societies: Mobilities for the Twenty-First Century.* New York: Routledge.

Valverde, Mariana. 2012. *Everyday Law on the Street: City Governance in an Age of Diversity.* Chicago: University of Chicago Press.

van Dijk, Teun. 1991. *Racism and the Press.* New York: Routledge.

–. 2011. "Text, Talk, Elites and Racism." http://www.discourses.org/OldArticles/Text,%20talk,%20elites%20and%20racism.pdf.

Van Hear, Nicholas. 2010. "Theories of Migration and Social Change." *Journal of Ethnic and Migration Studies* 36, 10. http://www.tandfonline.com/doi/pdf/10.1080/1369183X.2010.489359.

Vanderplaat, Madine. 2006. "Immigration and Families: An Introduction." *Canadian Issues* (Spring): 3-5.

Vasta, Ellie. 2010. "The Controllability of Difference: Social Cohesion and the New Politics of Solidarity." *Ethnicities* 10, 4: 503-21.

Vengroff, Richard. 2013. "Implementing Immigration Policy: States and Provinces in Comparative Perspective." Paper presented at the Johnson-Shoyama Graduate School of Public Policy, Universities of Regina and Saskatoon, 6 March.

Vertovec, Steven. 2005. "The Political Importance of Diasporas." *Migration Information Source,* June.

–. 2010. "Toward Post-Multiculturalism? Changing Communities, Conditions, and Contexts of Diversity." *International Social Science Journal* 61, 199: 83-95.

Vertovec, Steven, and Susanne Wessendorf. 2004. "Migration and Cultural, Religious and Linguistic Diversity in Europe: An Overview of Issues and Trends." COMPAS Working Paper No. 18. http://www.compas.ox.ac.uk/fileadmin/files/Publications/working_papers/WP_2005/Vertovec%20Wessendorf%20WP0518.pdf.

–. 2009. "Assessing the Backlash against Multiculturalism in Europe." MMG Working Paper 09-04. http://www.mmg.mpg.de/fileadmin/user_upload/documents/wp/WP_09-04_Vertovec-Wessendorf_backlash.pdf.

Vickers, Jill, and Micheline de Sève. 2000. "Introduction – Women and Nationalisms: Canadian Experiences/Les femmes et les nationalismes: les expériences canadiennes." *Journal of Canadian Studies* 35, 2: 5-34.

Vineberg, Robert. 2012. *Responding to Immigrants' Settlement Needs: The Canadian Experience.* New York: Springer.

–. 2014. "After 40 Years, Immigrant Settlement Program Needs an Overhaul." *Globe and Mail,* 21 April.

Vogel, Toby. 2011. "Migration Paradoxes." 31 March. http://www.europeanvoices. com.

Vrbanovic, Berry. 2011. "Letter from the President." In *Starting on Solid Ground: The Municipal Role in Immigrant Settlement,* 3. Ottawa: Federation of Canadian Municipalities.

Waldman, Lorne. 2010. "Kenney's Reforms a Step toward Fair Refugee System." *Toronto Star,* 2 April.

Walia, Harsha. 2010. "Race and Imperialism: Migration and Border Control in a Canadian State." In *Racism and Borders,* ed. Jeff Shantz, 73-94. New York: Algora.

Walker, James W. St. G. 1998. *"Race," Rights and the Law in the Supreme Court of Canada.* Waterloo, ON: Wilfrid Laurier University Press.

Walkom, Thomas. 2010. "Refugee Reforms Give Cabinet Too Much Power." *Toronto Star,* 30 March.

Wallis, Maria, and Augie Fleras, eds. 2008. *The Politics of Race in Canada.* Toronto: Oxford University Press.

Walton-Roberts, Margaret. 2011. "Multiculturalism Already Unbound." In *Home and Native Land: Unsettling Multiculturalism in Canada,* ed. M. Chazan, L. Helps, A. Stanley, and S. Thakkar, 102-22. Toronto: Between the Lines.

Wanner, Richard. 2011. *Immigration Policy and the Economic Integration of Immigrants: A Cross-National Comparison.* Working Paper Series WP 11-01. Edmonton: Prairie Metropolis Centre.

Ward, Olivia. 2011. "More Refugees, But Fewer Shelters." *Toronto Star,* 21 June.

Ward, Peter W. 1990. *White Canada Forever: Popular Attitudes and Public Policy toward Orientals in British Columbia.* 2nd ed. Montreal/Kingston: McGill-Queen's University Press.

Waters, Johanna. 2003. "Flexible Citizens? Transnationalism and Citizenship amongst Economic Immigrants in Vancouver." *Canadian Geographer* 47, 3: 219-34.

Wayland, Sarah. 2006. "Unsettled: Legal and Policy Barriers for Newcomers to Canada." Law Commission of Canada/Community Foundations of Canada. http://www.cfc-fcc.ca/doc/LegalPolicyBarriers.pdf.

Webb, Chris. 2010. "Barbarian Invasions: Canadian Migration and the Dynamics of Global Migration." *Canadian Dimension* 43, 5: 24.

Weber, Leanne. 2014. "'No One Can Be Left without Hope': Breathing Life into Global Action for Asylum Seekers." Institute of Race Relations, 20 March. http://www.irr.org.

Weinstock, Daniel. 2008. "Introduction: The Theory and Practice of Citizenship in the 21st Century: A Few International Trends." *Canadian Diversity* 6, 4: 3-6.

–. 2014. "What Is Really at Stake in the Multiculturalism/Interculturalism Debate." In *The Multiculturalism Question: Debating Identity in 21st-Century Canada,* ed. Jack Jedwab, 187-202. Queen's University Policy Studies Series. Montreal/Kingston: McGill-Queen's University Press.

Weld, Madeline. 2009. "Canada's Policy of Mass Immigration: Hoary Myths and Unasked Questions." Population Institute of Canada. http://candobetter. org.

Wells, Paul. 2012. "Our Policy on Roma Refugees Hits a Flat Note." *Maclean's,* 5 November.

Wente, Margaret. 2010. "A Few Frank Words about Immigration." *Globe and Mail,* 7 October.

West, Darrell M. 2010. *Brain Gain: Rethinking US Immigration Policy.* Washington, DC: Brookings Institution Press.

West, Larry. 2010. "Climate Change Creating More Refugees Than War." http://environmentabout.com.

Weston, Mary Ann. 2003. "Journalists and Indians: The Clash of Cultures." Keynote speech at the Symposium on American Indian Issues in the California Press, Los Angeles, 21 February. http://www.bluecorncomics.com/weston.htm.

Whitaker, Reg. 1987. *Double Standard: The Secret History of Canadian Immigration.* Toronto: Lester and Orpen Dennys.

White, N.J. 1999. "Beyond 2000: Home to the World." *Toronto Star,* 23 April.

Whittington, Les. 1998. "Canada Hailed as a Model for the 21st Century." *Toronto Star,* 10 August.

–. 2009. "Ottawa Leaves Workers 'Vulnerable.'" *Toronto Star,* 4 November.

Wilkes, Rima, and Catherine Corrigall-Brown. 2011. "Explaining Time Trends in Public Opinion: Attitudes toward Immigration and Immigrants." *International Journal of Comparative Sociology* 52, 1-2: 79-99.

Wilkes, Rima, Catherine Corrigall-Brown, and Danielle Ricard. 2010. "Nationalism and Media Coverage of Indigenous People's Collective Action in Canada." *American Indian Culture and Research Journal* 34, 4: 41-59.

Wilkes, Rima, Neil Guppy, and Lily Farris. 2007. *Canadian Attitudes towards Immigration: Individual and Contextual Influences.* Metropolis British Columbia Working Paper No. 07-08. Vancouver: Centre of Excellence for Research on Immigration and Diversity.

Willis, Katie, and Brenda Yeoh, eds. 2000. *Gender and Migration.* Northampton, MA: Edward Elgar.

Wilton, Shauna. 2009. "Immigration Policy and Literature: Contradictions of a 'Post-National' State." In *Canada: Images of a Post/National Society,* ed. G. Florby, M. Shackleton, and K. Suhonen, 25-37. New York: Peter Lang.

Wingrove, Josh. 2014a. "Refugee Claims Reach 'Historic Low.'" *Globe and Mail,* 23 January.

–. 2014b. "Five Key Facets of Canada's Shakeup in Immigration Policy." *Globe and Mail,* 27 January.

Winter, Elke. 2011. *Us, Them, and Others: Pluralism and National Identity in Diverse Societies.* Toronto: University of Toronto Press.

–. 2012. "(Im)Possible Citizens: Canada's 'Citizenship Bonanza' and Its Boundaries." *Citizenship Studies,* ifirst article, 1-17.

–. 2014. "Becoming Canadian: Making Sense of Recent Changes to Citizenship Rules." Institute for Research on Public Policy, 16 January.

Wise, Amanda, and Selvaraj Velaytham. 2009. *Everyday Multiculturalism.* New York: Palgrave Macmillan.

Wong, Lloyd L. 1984. "Canada's Guestworkers: Some Comparisons of Temporary Workers in Europe and North America." *International Migration Review* 18, 1: 85-98.

–. 2007-08. "Transnationalism, Active Citizenship, and Belonging in Canada." *International Journal* 63, 1: 79-100.

Wong, Lloyd L., and Roland R. Simon. 2010. "Citizenship and Belonging to Canada: Religious and Generational Differentiation." *Canadian Journal for Social Research* (Winter). http://www.acs-aec.ca/pdf/pubs/CanadianJournal forSocialResearch.

Wong, Milton. 2007. "Introduction: Origins of Multiculturalism in Canada." Paper presented at "Putting Diverse Talents to Work," sponsored by the Couchiching Institute on Public Affairs, Orillia, ON, 9-12 August.

Wood, Ben. 2009. "Workplace Raids: Canada's New Immigration Policy?" *Canadian Dimension* 43, 5: 24-26.

Wood, Patricia, and Liette Gilbert. 2005. "Multiculturalism in Canada: Accidental Discourse, Alternative Vision, Urban Practice." *International Journal of Urban and Regional Research* 29, 3: 679–91.

Woolley, Frances. 2012. "Should Canada's Immigrants Play by Australian Rules?" *Globe and Mail,* 7 February.

World Migration Report 2013. 2013. *Migrant Well-Being and Development: An Overview*. Geneva: International Organization for Migration. www.iom.int.

Worswick, Christopher. 2010. "Temporary Foreign Workers: An Introduction." *Canadian Issues* (Spring): 3-5.

–. 2013. "Economic Implications of Recent Changes to the Temporary Foreign Worker Program." Insight No. 4, Institute for Research on Public Policy, October.

Wortley, Scot. 2009. "Introduction: The Immigration Crime Connection: Competing Theoretical Perspectives." *International Migration and Integration* 10: 349-58.

Wright, Matthew, and Irene Bloemraad. 2012. "Is There a Trade-Off between Multiculturalism and Socio-Political Integration? Policy Regimes and Immigrant Incorporation in Comparative Perspective." *Perspectives in Politics* 10: 75-95.

Wu, Z., C.M. Schimmele, and F. Hou. 2012. "Self-Perceived Integration of Immigrants and Their Children." *Canadian Journal of Sociology* 37, 4: 381-92.

Xiao-Feng, L., and G. Norcliffe. 1996. "Closed Windows, Open Doors: Geo-Politics and the Post 1949 Mainland Chinese Immigration." *Canadian Geographer* 40, 4: 306-19.

Yakabuski, Konrad. 2012. "Ruling on Arizona Crackdown Rouses US Immigration Debate." *Globe and Mail,* 26 June.

Yalnizyan, Armine. 2012. "Changes to Immigration Policy Could Transform Society." *Globe and Mail,* 3 May.

Yang, Jennifer. 2011. "Refugee Board Defends Adjudicators." *Toronto Star,* 22 March.

Young, Audrey. 2013. "New Zealand to Take Boat People." *New Zealand Herald,* 9 February.

Yu, Henry. 2009. "Global Migrants and the New Pacific Canada." *International Journal* (Autumn): 1011-23.

Yuval-Davis, Nira. 2007. "Intersectionality, Citizenship and Contemporary Politics of Belonging." *Critical Review of International Social and Political Philosophy* 10, 4: 561–74.

Zaman, Habiba. 2006. *Breaking the Iron Wall: Decommodification and Immigrant Women's Labor in Canada*. Lanham, MD: Lexington Books.

–. 2007. "Neo-Liberal Policies and Immigrant Women in Canada." *Neo-Liberalism, State Power, and Global Governance* 3: 145-53.

–. 2010. "Asian Immigrants' Vision of an Alternative Society in Australia and Canada: Impossibly Utopian or Simply Social Justice?" *Journal of Identity and Migration Studies* 4, 1: 2-22.

–. 2012. *Asian Immigrants in "Two" Canadas: Racialization, Marginalization and Deregulated Work*. Winnipeg: Fernwood.

Zapata-Barrero, Richard, and Antoine Pécoud. 2012. "Introduction: New Perspectives on the Ethics of International Migration." *American Behavioral Scientist* 20, 10: 1-6.

Zhang, Haimin. 2012. *Centralized vs. Decentralized Immigrant Selection: An Assessment of the BC Experience*. Metropolis British Columbia Working Paper No. 12-04. Vancouver: Centre of Excellence for Research on Immigration and Diversity.

Zhang, Kenny. 2007. "'Mission Invisible': Rethinking the Canadian Diaspora." *Canada-Asia Commentary* 46 (September): 1-15.

Zick, A., T.F. Pettigrew, and U. Wagner. 2008. "Ethnic Prejudice and Discrimination in Europe." *Journal of Social Issues* 64, 2: 233-51.

Zilber, Neri. 2013. "Jordan's 'Five-Star Refugee Camp.'" *Toronto Star,* 15 June.

Zilio, Michelle. 2013. "Canada Experiencing 'Unprecedented' Changes to Immigration Policy, Experts." iPolitics. 16 March. http://www.ipolitics.ca.

Zimmerman, Susan E. 2011. "Reconsidering the Problem of 'Bogus' Refugees with 'Socio-Economic Motivations' for Seeking Asylum." *Mobilities* 6, 3: 335-52.

Zine, Jasmine. 2008. *Canadian Islamic Schools: Unravelling the Politics of Faith, Gender, Knowledge, and Identity*. Toronto: University of Toronto Press.

–. 2009. "Unsettling the Nation: Gender, Race, and Muslim Cultural Politics in Canada." *Studies in Ethnicity and Nationalism* 9, 1: 146-57.

–. 2012. "Introduction: Muslim Cultural Politics in the Canadian Hinterlands." In *Islam in the Hinterlands,* ed. Jasmine Zine, 1-38. Vancouver: UBC Press.

INDEX

Printed and bound in Canada by Friesens

Set in Eames Century Modern, Sero, and Baskerville 10
by Artegraphica Design Co. Ltd.

Text design: Jessica Sullivan

Copy editor: Deborah Kerr

Proofreader: Jacqueline Larson